Klaus Lindemann

HAILSTORM OVER TRUK LAGOON

**OPERATIONS AGAINST TRUK
BY CARRIER TASK FORCE 58, 17 AND 18 FEBRUARY 1944,
AND THE SHIPWRECKS OF WORLD WAR II.**

Wipf & Stock
PUBLISHERS
Eugene, Oregon

Title Page
The Title Page shows the Forth Fleet Anchorage, with ships under attack and smoking. The Aikoku Maru in the foreground. This ship violently exploded later.

Resource Publications
A division of Wipf and Stock Publishers
199 W 8th Ave, Suite 3
Eugene, OR 97401

Hailstorm Over Truk Lagoon, Second Edition
Operations Against Truk by Carrier Task Force 58, 17 and 18 February 1944, and the Shipwrecks of World War II
By Lindemann, Klaus
Copyright©1989 by Lindemann, Klaus
ISBN: 1-59752-347-X
Publication date 9/1/2005
Previously published by Pacific Press Publications, 1989

Foreword

During the past twenty years it has been my good fortune to log more than two million air miles in pursuit of that magic, often elusive, undersea Nirvana.

Some of the underwater hallmarks of my career include the Tuamoto Archipelago near Tahiti, the crystalline waters of the North Pole, the stunning inland waterways of Palau, and the mind-boggling warm water vents of the Galapagos Rift Valley, some 8,000 feet deep. Yet the adventures to be experienced in the exploration of the mysterious shipwrecks of Truk beneath the limpid waters of that magnificent Lagoon remain unparalleled.

My first trip to that unique Lagoon of lost ships in 1973 was like the opening of Pandora's box. Just a year later, I returned to expand on the film work initiated the previous summer. My third visit produced a forty-page color feature in the *National Geographic*. This feature turned out to be among the top five in popularity carried by that publication in 1976.

In 1982, I returned to the Lagoon for the sixth time. What more can I say?

Truk Lagoon remains for me one of the great undersea wonders of the world. During the most recent visit, I had the distinct pleasure of meeting and diving with Klaus Lindemann, the author of this most definitive volume. With help from the legendary Truk Lagoon guide, Kimiuo Aisek, Lindemann has documented the shipwrecks of Truk with an accurate and most imaginative approach.

Lindemann has discovered by himself seven additional shipwrecks during his past three years of work. I have dived with Klaus on two of his latest discoveries: the Nippo Maru and the Momokawa Maru. These deeper wrecks represent two of the most well-preserved ships in the Lagoon.

I heartily applaud his most thorough treatment and am flattered to include my comments in this foreword.

Al Giddings
Ocean Films Ltd.
Berkeley, California

Hailstorm - *Historic Documentation*

FOREWORD
FOR THE SECOND EDITION

Pantha Rhei - Everything changes.

"Hailstorm over Truk Lagoon" remains the authoritative reference book about the US Navy carrier raid of 17/18 February 1944 on the Japanese naval and supply base Truk, in the East Caroline Islands. This edition presented here adds later information and pictures to the book, and corrects errors. After publication of "Hailstorm", research has continued for these two significant days in the Pacific War. Correspondence with sources in the US, but even more with Japanese researchers, elucidated many aspects which were shrouded in obscurity and others which were not known before.

Forty-seven years later, eyewitnesses are difficult to locate. The few which I was fortunate enough to correspond with contributed fascinating details. In many instances the questions I had where way over their head. One has to realize that from the vintage point of a soldier, more complicated matters of tactic or strategy were of no concern. The Japanese soldiers were very poorly informed about military matters.

For the people ashore, the Aikoku Maru, but even more the warships, were almost mystical things, invulnerable and invincible. The sight of the two super-battleships Yamato and Musashi moored between Moen, Dublon and Fefan must have had an undeniable psychological effect.

After the publication of the first edition of "Hailstorm", the Yubae Maru has been discovered, as well as the destroyer Fumizuki. Their detailed descriptions are included in this revised edition. Interesting finds inside the Aikoku, San Francisco, Hoki, Nagano, Heian and Fujisan were recorded and the existing text edited. Errors, where known, have been corrected. And finally, there are persistent reports that the destroyer Oite has been found. That would be not surprising, as the location of the sinking can be easily inferred by the attack photo showing the major islands nearby. The wreck liberates still fuel oil to this day. Now all ships, which sank in depth reachable for sport divers, are accounted for. Not all material from American and US veterans has been included yet, and there remains the task to report about the second carrier raid in detail.

The material of the wrecks weakens. A fisherman from Eten was scared senseless when suddenly a dark low rumble emanated from the sea and the forward mast of the Fujikawa was gone.

Masts fall, funnels sag, parts of the railing just keel over and fall onto the main deck. It is a fact of life: We have to live with the slow disintegration of the wrecks. A hundred years after the ship sank they will resemble nothing more then a crumbled heap of steel.

The number of visitors have greatly increased during the last ten years. It is great that so many people can see this unique collection of wrecks. The visitors also contribute in no small measure to the economy of the State of Chuuk. When I was diving extensively in Truk between 1978 and 1984, the wrecks were in magnificent condition, in fact they were so beautiful and untouched that we wondered why they could not be lifted and returned to duty. But during the intervening years, the wrecks in Truck have changed appreciably. To understand the reason for that we would have to look at the effect of sea water on steel. It literally dissolved steel. The actual process is much more complicated, but the net effect is the same: The once strong steel plates atrophy, they become thin, the rolled steel flakes off in large and small patches, and their welding lines break. The wreck looses strength. Structures, like stacks, masts and the midship superstructures are effected first. The effect is more pronounced on shallow wrecks as the water close to the surface is better oxygenated, which hastens the corrosion process of steel. When a wreck remains undisturbed, a fragile layer of ferric hydroxide forms on the metal, and soon marine organisms settle and grow on the plates. They form a fairly thick cover of about an inch thickness. Both of these layers prevent circulation of seawater, and the process of corrosion is greatly retarded. Ironically, it is the diver who contributes to the acceleration of decay. First, by touching bulkheads and structures, marine organisms are destroyed and the metal bared for faster corrosion. One diver will not do it alone, it is the thousands of small unintentinal actions by the visitors. Then there are the exhalation bubbles. They impact with quite significant force on the steel structures and destroy marine growth fairly quickly. The bubbles then remove the layer of protective rust and set a vertical current in motion during their ascent. With their mechanical action the exhaust bubbles contribute to the faster corrosion. The effects can best be observed at the most popular wreck in Truk, the Fujikawa Maru. The once sturdy superstructure is now a rusted through, flimsy house of cards, with the top upperworks gone and the steel plates so thin one could punch holes through it with the fist. It is a sad sight for anyone who has seen the Fujikawa Maru years ago. But there is little we can do, except refraining from touching and deliberate destroying. The decay is inevitable.

In many instances, the continued use of anchors contributes to the destruction of the upperworks of the Truk wrecks. A heavy piece of steel used by the local dive boats - or worse yet, anchors from cruise boats -

tear up the paper thin and fragile steel structures. They accelerate the process of integration. Damages to stacks and masts, but also to the coral growths, are widespread and deplorable. The Trukese operators still have not been able to get together and buoy the wrecks. This of course would prevent further damages. Insular politics are intricate. If the wrecks are buoyed, it is feared that local divers would take even more of the still abundant ammo, for dynamite fishing, and artifacts off the wrecks. The problem is that since the mid-seventies, when a energetic police officer was in charge and patrolling the wrecks, no such efforts have been undertaken in earnest and continuously, although a levy is imposed on every diver, which would finance such policing.

So, enjoy the sights as long as they are there.

Outright pilferage by former dive operators and "harmless" souvenir hunting have reduced the once numerous artifacts. Particularly beautiful items like large serving platters, ship bells and others have made their appearance in the grey souvenir market, particularly in the West Coast. Fortunately, once again common sense has prevailed and the self policing of todays operators have dammed the damages now. Another well-meant activity contributes greatly to the disintegration of artifacts. There were two or even three places where well meaning divers have brought up artifacts, such as running lights, phono records, guns, pistols, fountain pens and ink wells, and all kinds of neat stuff up. They displayed them nicely, then left them unattended. The problem here was that the artifacts have not been preserved and conserved prior to their display. Salt, deeply penetrated in all meterial, including metal, continued to get to the surface and continued the insidious process of corrosion: Within several years, the beautiful running lights crumbled to copper dust, and the guns resembled popcorn. So, now they are lost forever.

Yet, Truk Lagoon will continue to surprise the serious researcher. We could still run with the sonar between Dublon and Moen and find pieces of wreckage, find, as we did, pieces of the Hellcat shot down, the pilot having bailed out a few moments before the plane crashed.

Taking a clue from a small droplet of oil on the water's surface, I discovered a beautifully preserved trawler right between the Hino Maru 2 and the subchaser. And there is more.

In Eten there is still a hangar buried by a landslide, in Fefan a radar position and unknown gun emplacements may be found, and the Kasuragisan Maru and Motor Torpedo Boat Gyotei 10 are reported sunk but not found. All of this is still there, and maybe will be explored some day.

The new discoveries and other changes, as well as new information made it necessary to issue a revised edition of "Hailstorm over Truk Lagoon". The text of this edition has been generally updated to 1990. New finds, observations or conditions seen at the popular wrecks during my diving visit in Spring 1991 have been incorporated. All this is part of the ongoing research about Truk.

Klaus Lindemann
Jakarta, May 1991

Table of Contents

Forewords

PART ONE :   THE HISTORIC DOCUMENTATION

Operation Hailstone Revisited	5
Chronology	7
The Road To Truk	9
Truk's Defenses	14
The Official Japanese Report	18
Responsibility and Blame	23
Truk Reconnaissance	25

The American Battle Reports

The Battle Reports	27
Organisation of TF 58	28
Task Force 58	29
Operation Schedule	30
The Battle Order	31
Task Group 58.3: The Operation Plan	34
Battle Report Task Group 58.1	41
Aircraft Action Reports: Enterprise and Yorktown	43
Battle Report Task Group 58.2	54
Aircraft Action Reports: Cabot, Essex, Intrepid	55
Battle Report Task Group 58.3	65
Aircraft Action Reports Bunker Hill, Monterey and Cowpens	66
Battle Report Task Group 50.9	79

The Interrogations	83

PART TWO :   WALKS AND TALKS

Walks

Geology, People and Vegetation	97
The Lighthouse and the Xavier High School	98
Two Guns in Dublon	98
... and calmly walked out of the turret	100

Talks

Kimiuo's Visit to the Hotel	102
Storytime on the Boat	110
A Visit to the Blue Lagoon Dive Shop	120
A Day at the Combined Fleet Anchorage	129

Hailstorm - *Historic Documentation*

PART THREE: THE WRECKS

Aikoku Maru	137
Amagisan Maru	146
Betty Bomber	149
Daikichi Maru	150
Dumping Ground	151
Emily Flying Boat	152
The Fleet Tug	154
Fujikawa Maru	155
Fujisan Maru	161
Fumizuki	165
Gosei Maru	170
Hanakawa Maru	172
The Harbor Tug	175
Heian Maru	176
Hikawa Maru 2	181
Hino 2 Maru	182
Hoki Maru	183
Hukoyo Maru	189
Hoyo Maru	192
I-169 Submarine	195
Inter Island Supply Vessel	197
Kansho Maru	198
Kikukawa Maru	203
Kiyozumi Maru	205
Momokawa Maru	208
Nagano Maru	212
Nippo Maru	215
Fighter and Junkyard at Param	223
Oite	224
Reiyo Maru	227
Rio de Janeiro Maru	229
San Francisco Maru	233
Sankisan Maru	238
Seiko Maru	242
Shinkoku Maru	243
Shotan Maru	248
Special Subchaser 38	251
Susuki / Patrol Boat 34	252
Taiho Maru	254
Tonan Maru 3	256
Tony, Val and Zero	258
Unkai Maru 6	259
Ojima, Landing Craft and other Wreckage	262
Yamagiri Maru	263
Yubae Maru	266

APPENDIX

The American Participating Ships	271
The US Planes involved in the Truk Operation	280
The Japanese Ships	284
Japanese Planes involved in the Defense of Truk	287
Ship Recognition and Terminology	295
Glossary of Nautical Terms	298
Notes on Damages	301
The Position of the Wrecks in Truk	303
Bibliography	312
Epilogue	314
Acknowledgements and Equipment	319
Index	320

Hailstorm - *Historic Documentation*

PART ONE
THE HISTORICAL DOCUMENTATION

OPERATION HAILSTORM REVISITED

The big American carriers sailed west. Tabletop models of Truk had been constructed and placed in the briefing rooms. The pilots were apprehensive when told that these islands were their next target. Now they could familiarize themselves with the terrain.

On the Truk islands things had become quiet after almost two days of false alarms. There was time now for the Japanese soldiers to have a big party, for the pilots time with the girls and sake in Dublon, and sleep. It was a rude wake-up call when the alarm sounded. This time it was for real.

The American planes swooped down with the first light of the day, and the pilots strafed, bombed, torpedoed and shot at everything of military importance. After a day and a half everything was over. Only the oiltanks kept on blazing.

The Truk defenders lost almost all planes, all major ships had sunk, the fuel tanks were burning for days and the strategic worth of Truk had dropped close to zero, literally over night.

The road to Saipan, the Marianas, was free for the American forces. And from Saipan, the dreaded Superfortresses flew to lay to waste the Japanese motherland. Finally, Japan succumbed.

The urgency with which the heavy defense guns had been put into their positions was no match to the desire to remove them: They stayed. Nature began its slow process to crack, dissolve and overgrow the remnants of Truk's military past.

On the bottom of the lagoon the ships rested. A few could be seen from the surface, a few with their masts protruding above the water surface, but the majority had just slid to the bottom, never to be seen again. It was not until the aqualung, Cousteau's invention of scuba diving that men started to visit some of the ships.

It was in the 1960's that a particular starfish, acanthaster plancii, occurred in large quantities and threatened to destroy the reefs in the Pacific. In Truk, the Fisheries Department embarked on a program to check the explosive growth of this animal. Men from the islands were trained in scuba diving and eradicated large numbers of the Crown-of-Thorns starfish. This was how Kimiuo Aisek learned to dive.

With the bred-in instinct of a Micronesian, he noticed a small discoloration of the lagoon bed one day when coming back from fighting the starfish population, had the boat stopped and dove . . . on the Yamagiri Maru. Word of this find spread, and the Truk islands were suddenly "discovered" by an ever increasing number of professional and amateur scuba divers. Improvements in scheduled jet traffic allowed more and more people to reach Truk. Accommodations were available and pleasing.

A visit of leading figures in the diving world, like Paul Tzimoulis, Al Giddings, Stan Beerman, Jack Kenney and others was crowned with the sensational find of the submarine I-169, early in the 1970's. Al Giddings produced a film about this discovery and supplied photographs for articles in "National Geographic" on Dr. Sylvia Earle's interesting research on coral growth that she conducted in Truk. Many enthusiastic articles in dive magazines also increased the popularity of the ship graves, and a visit to Truk was either the highlight or the wish of many scuba divers. Still however, comparatively little was known about the wrecks other than those popularly visited, and even less was written about the events during the American attack.

A solitary figure, Sam Redford, based in Kwajalein at the time, tried to put the record straight by searching for the unknown wrecks. Using recently declassified pictorial and written material from the US National Archives, he embarked, in 1972, on a long search. His success was outstanding. Ships like the Shinkoku, Heian, Kiyozumi, Rio de Janeiro, Gosei, Sankisan and a few others were known at the time. They could either be seen from or at the surface or they liberated fuel oil, which gave their positions away. But Sam Redford found many more, deeper wrecks. Among his most outstanding finds were the Aikoku Maru, San Francisco, Seiko, Hokuyo and Amagisan. He was the Father of the Truk wreck finders. At some other times other wrecks were found. Two Air Micronesia pilots, Keith Jaeger and Ed O'Quinn, once saw an enormous oil slick off the south east coast of Moen. They made a mental note of it, and returned a few weeks later with a borrowed depth sounder. They began a search at that general area. Kimiuo Aisek pointed out to this duo the location of the Fujisan where he had seen the ship go down after heavy bombing and a brief fire. The pilots promptly found the ship.

After a lot of prodding and help from Al Giddings, Kimiuo Aisek opened the first dive shop in Truk. His uncanny ability to locate wrecks in the open water of the lagoon made him the eminent figure of diving in Truk. A few years later, former Peace Corps volunteer Clark Graham followed suit and opened Micronesia Aquatics in Moen. Everything pointed to a smooth increase in the numbers of divers arriving in

Hailstorm - *Historic Documentation*

Truk. However, the first dent occurred during the oil crisis in 1973, and when recovery was well under way the tourist trade was again hit by an unstable economic situation, later in the 1970 and 1980's. Due to the lack of popular demand much of the early work done by Redford fell into obscurity.

The Truk legislature passed a law declaring the ships on the bottom a sanctuary. It was forbidden to take any artifacts from the ships, and to this day this provision is rigidly enforced. It works well for the tourists, but less well for natives, who clandestinely recover ordnances from the ships and use them to dynamite for fish. Fortunately, most of the artifacts remain, providing divers year after year with a rewarding diving experience.

Like so many other divers the world over, I always wished to be able to dive in Truk. The opportunity came when I was living in Singapore and took "the other way 'round" to go back after a vacation in Europe and the States. My wife Mary, an avid diver as well, was just as excited to visit Truk. The two weeks stay was indeed thrilling. Diving was at its very best, and we wondered when we could come back. There was just a minute detail about which I was not too happy. Notoriously curious, I wanted to read up on the history of this place but did not find anything of substance. And then we began to repeat dives, after about a week. It seemed as if the dive guides had run out of wrecks to show us.

That was surprising as we had read that more than 30 ships sunk. We returned the next year to try to see more, and looked for Kimiuo Aisek, who was the undeclared custodian of the Japanese Marus. Diving with him was an experience of a lifetime, and after I found the first grave site inside the Aikoku Maru, our enthusiasm was boundless. Fate intervened in the form of a tropical storm. We laid idle for a few days; diving was impossible in the high seas and foul weather. After the first day, I braved the torrential rain and went to Kimiuo's dive shop. In the relaxed atmosphere of people who have a lot of time, he began to talk about the times when he was a youngster. It soon drifted to the time of the American attack on Truk and what he saw and felt at that time. Not only was I fascinated but I also thought that all this would be irretrievably lost once he was gone. I started to make notes. Carrying this a step further, I began to take stock of the wrecks and meticulously jotted down my observations. By the time we had to go back, we had visited all known wrecks, and arrived home with more than a thousand photographs and copious notes. An idea began to take shape.

When Mary went to the States, she was charged with the assignment of going to the Naval Operational Archives in Washington, D.C. Together with the most helpful staff, she was able to locate the first battle reports of "Operation Hailstone". Pictures, dive notes and the files from Washington were the base for embarking on an ambitious project of writing about the events in Truk. Much of my spare time was devoted, from that time onward for the next three and a half years, to collecting information, communicating with numerous people all over the world, and finally composing an expose. After checking the available material very carefully, it became evident that a number of ships were reported sunk, but had not been found up to that date. Subsequently, I wrote to Kimiuo asking him whether he would be interested to do a search with me. He replied affirmatively.

The searches in mid-1980 stretched over a period of five weeks. They were very successful. Not only did we find all ships not accounted for, but we also discovered one vessel, which had been destroyed in a marine disaster half a year before the American carrier raid. We counted no less than 16 new wrecks, but had to admit that a few had been discovered before, however they had been completely lost or forgotten in the intervening years. To give justice to truth, it should be said that we thought we discovered all unknown wrecks, but in fact, there were two which eluded us. We did not know this at the time, but further visits to the Archives uncovered fresh material. The conclusion was inescapable, we had to go back to Truk.

Half a year later we returned. This time the results of the searches were meager, but to make up for it the observations in sito were much more detailed than ever before. We did not succeed in finding the two wrecks. On the other hand, positive identification of the ships found during the previous expedition became easy. The credit went to Dr. Sanae Yamada, in Japan, who was able to supply pictures of almost all ships, as they appeared before the war. During an extended correspondence, he painstakingly answered the many detailed questions I put to him.

There was more than a year's intermission in our activities in Truk. Meanwhile, I was pouring over the records, and began the work of writing the book in earnest. To wind things up, and to tie up a few loose ends, the last trip to Truk was scheduled for spring 1982. Again, we dove with Kimiuo. The dives provided additional data. We found the last of the missing wrecks. The second, we concluded, must have been salvaged. In many hazardous dives we explored the deep recesses inside the Aikoku Maru, where I found many more mortal remains of the hapless soldiers trapped inside this ship. Al Giddings went along and also documented the grave sites. The stay in Truk proved to be the most happy of times. There were long hours when Kimiuo would just sit and talk. Getting on in years, he was particularly delighted to speak about the past. He still had the admirable gift of a born navigator, and never missed a dive. We took Clark Graham and his dive guides to all the new wrecks, to share the knowledge and enthusiasm.

On the subsequent trip to Washington we were able to locate, with the help of Dr. Dean Allard and Mr. Mike Walker, some supplementary material. Shortly afterwards the manuscript was finished. The gap in information about the wrecks and the events of attack has been closed. The history of Operation Hailstone - the raid on Truk Lagoon, Kimiuo's story and all wrecks have been recorded. They shall not be forgotten.

Hailstorm - *Historic Documentation*

CHRONOLOGY
CHRONOLOGICAL OVERVIEW OF SELECTED EVENTS IN THE PACIFIC AND ASIA DURING WORLD WAR II

1941

7 December
Japan launches air attacks on US bases in Hawaii, with extensive damage to the US Fleet at Pearl Harbor. Manila, Shanghai, Hongkong, and places in Malaya and Thailand are attacked almost simultaneously.

7-8 December
Japanese air raid on Singapore. Landings in Thailand and N.E. Malaya

9 December
First Japanese landings in the Philippines, in Luzon

10 December
Japanese aircraft sink the British battleship "Prince of Wales" and the battle cruiser "Repulse" off Malaya (Kuantan). Guam falls to the Japanese.

17 December
Japanese forces land in North Borneo (British Borneo).

24 December
Wake Island falls to the Japanese.

25 December
Hongkong surrenders.

1942

January and February
Rapid Japanese advances through Malaya, Burma and the Philippines.

10-11 January
Japanese begin invasion of the Dutch East Indies, with landings in Dutch Borneo and Celebes.

22 January
Japanese land in Rabaul (Bismarck Archipelago).

30 January
British withdrawal from Malaya.

15 February
Singapore falls.

28 February
Japanese land in Java.

7 March
Japanese land in Rangoon.

17 March
General Douglas MacArthur becomes Supreme Allied Commander, South West Pacific.

9 April
US forces in Bataan surrender, remnants escape to Corregidor.

18 April
Tokyo, Yokohama, Kobe and Nagoya are raided by US carrier borne bombers (Doolittle Raid).

4-9 May
Battle of the Coral Sea, losses on American and Japanese side roughly equal, but set-back for further Japanese expansion.

6 May
American forces surrender in Corregidor.

June and July
Japanese forces capture islands in the Aleutians (Kiska and Attu)

4-7 June
Battle of Midway: Major naval engagement of Japanese and US carrier borne aircraft, for the control of the mid-Pacific. Severe losses of the Japanese in carriers and aircraft. American tactical and far-reaching strategic success.

7 August
US forces land in Guadalcanal, Solomons, and Japanese forces suffer heavy losses in the long drawn-out engagements.

September to November
Australian forces reconquer most of Papua, and remove threat of advances to Australia.

1943

April, May and June
Intense and repeated US air attacks on New Guinea and the Solomons. Japanese Commander-in Chief, Admiral Yamamoto, strips about 200 planes from the carriers to augment land based air forces; heavy losses. Demise of Japanese naval air power.

18 April
Admiral Yamamoto shot down on an inspection flight. Admiral Koga assumed command.

23 May
US forces reoccupy the Aleutians. (May 11 assault on Attu, August 15 Kiska retaken)

30 May
New US carriers coming into fleet service.

Hailstorm - *Historic Documentation*

July
US forces land on New Georgia group in the Solomons.

1 September
Raid on Marcus Island.

4-5 September
US landings at Lae and Salamaua in New Guinea, with powerful air support.

18-19 September
Raid on Gilberts.

5-6 October
Raid on Wake Island.

October- November
Rabaul, the Solomons, and New Guinea are heavily attacked by US air forces. Severe Japanese losses in the air.
US troops land in Bougainville and Kolombangara Island in the Solomons. Solomons in US hands.

1 November
Invasion of Bougainville.

2 November
Battle of Empress Augusta Bay.

5 and 11 November
Repeated carrier strikes on Rabaul.

20 November
US land, and capture with heavy losses, Tarawa, Gilbert Islands.

December
US landings in New Britain, preceded by heavy air attacks.

1944

January and February
US landings in Majuro, Roi Nomoir and Kwajalein in the Marshall Islands. The islands are taken and the remaining Japanese forces in that area are isolated and neutralized.

1 February
Assault on Marshalls.

17-18 February
US naval task force attack Truk, Caroline Island, and inflict heavy losses on Japanese shipping and air power. Eniwetok captured.

22 February
Raid on the Marianas.

31 March
US naval task force assault Palau with heavy shipping losses to the Japanese.

31 March
Admiral Koga lost in a tropical storm enroute from Palau to Davao.

April 22
US forces land in Hollandia, Netherlands New Guinea.

30 April and 1 May
Second US naval task force raid on Truk.

11 June
Begin of assaults on the Marianas.

19-20 June
Battle of the Philippine Sea ("Marianas Turkey Shoot"), stripping away Japanese naval air power.

July- August
US forces capture Saipan, Guam and Tinian in the Marianas.

15 September
US forces land on Peleliu (Palau Islands) and Morotai.

20 October
US forces land on Leyte, Philippines.

24-25 October
The battles for Leyte Gulf. Annihilation of Japanese Navy.

15 December
US forces land on Mindoro, Philippines.

1945

9 January
US forces land on Luzon.

16 February
Begin operations to capture Iwo-Jima, officially secured 16 March.

23 March
Begin operations at Okinawa, secured June 21.

22 June
Emperor Hirohito states that the war had to be ended, during a meeting of his Supreme War Council.

6 August and 8 August
Nuclear explosion over Hiroshima.
Russia declares war on Japan.

14 August
Japan accepts Potsdam Declaration, cease fire.

2 September
Document of Surrender signed on battleship Missouri, at Tokyo Bay.

Hailstorm - *Historic Documentation*

THE ROAD TO TRUK

The Japanese forces invaded Papua - New Guinea and intended to take Port Moresby, to prevent an Allied built-up of forces in Australia, and to secure their southern flank. The terrain of the Owen Stanley Range in Papua made crossing next to impossible. When the Japanese Army finally succeeded they were exhausted and beaten back. It had therefore been planned to take Port Moresby by an amphibious assault. The carrier and surface forces were met by an American carrier group. The result of the Battle of the Coral Sea was the retreat of the Japanese Fleet and the abandonment of the amphibious operation. Despite heavier losses it was a strategic victory for the Americans. Of great importance was the damage the Japanese carrier Shokaku sustained, and the heavy losses by Air Groups of the Zuikaku. It kept both carriers out of the Japanese battle order for their Midway operation, and this turned out to be a decisive disadvantage.

The large volume of radio traffic during the operations in the Coral Sea resulted in the recovery of many code words, and it became easier for American intelligence to piece together planned naval operations transmitted by encoded radio messages. On 05 May 1943 Imperial Japanese General Headquarters issued Order No. 18, directing Admiral Yamamoto, Commander-in-Chief of the Japanese Combined Fleet, to take certain islands in the Aleutians, and to occupy a place coded AF. Japanese-occupied Wake Island radioed weather reports to Tokyo, and made references to AF, this being a submarine and air base. Although not ruling out bases in the Aleutians, American intelligence were fast to guess that Midway was meant. Final proof was obtained when Midway was directed to radio in clear language the planted message that the fresh water distillation plant had broken down. This American transmission was duly intercepted in Wake, coded and sent to Tokyo. The location designator showed up as AF. All doubts were removed. On 20 May Yamamoto issued a long battle order, which was not only intercepted but also deciphered by the Americans. Commander-in-Chief, Pacific Fleet, Admiral Nimitz, was committed to fight for Midway. Early May, Admiral Halsey, in command of a carrier task force, operated in the southern part of the mid Pacific. Just one day before he was recalled by Nimitz to return to Pearl Harbor, on 16 May 1943, his ships were spotted by the Japanese. The Japanese were under the impression that they had sunk the carriers Yorktown and Lexington. With Halsey's Enterprise and Hornet assumed in southern waters, Yamamoto did not expect much resistance from the air.

The objective of the Japanese Battle Order was to force the American ships out of Pearl Harbor, lure them as far westward as possible, strike them with the Mobile Force, i. e. carrier based aircraft, cut off their retreat by interposing the own carriers from the northwest, obliterate the US force with the Main Body of fast battleships, take Midway and some islands in the Aleutians by assault forces and finally evaluate the possibility of the occupation of Hawaii at some later time. This fixed pattern of naval strategic thinking resembled the commitment of forces during the New Guinea-Coral Sea operation. A dual objective, a dislocation of forces, their inability to lend mutual support and to be concentrated at short notice, the assumption of the element of surprise, which was neither necessary nor actually achieved doomed the Japanese plans. It is inconceivable that three US carriers turned back an armada of 8 carriers, 11 battleships and a large number of support and transport vessels if these forces would have been tactically concentrated. As it turned out, the American ships avoided the scouting Japanese submarines because those arrived too late on station, the element of surprise was entirely on the Japanese, the Japanese carriers of the Mobile Fleet were sunk, the American ships did not fall into the trap to get engaged with the Main Body, and from that moment on Japan lost the capability to win the war.

The engagement began with the first contacts on 03 June. American flying boats sighted the Occupation Force, and planes from the air base at Midway flew an unsuccessful attack. In the morning Admiral Nagumo, commanding the Mobile Fleet, was striking at Midway and caused heavy damage. The air counterattack from Midway was ineffective. Yorktown with Admiral Fletcher, in tactical command of the two carrier groups, followed Admiral Spruance's carriers Enterprise and Hornet. Spruance decided to close in on the suspected position of the Japanese carriers. Nagumo, not realizing that the American ships were approaching, followed suggestion by the flight leader to follow up with a second raid on Midway, and had his planes re-armed with bombs. Repeatedly, waves of torpedo bombers attacked the Japanese carriers, but were unsuccessful. The majority of these planes were shot down, but they drew the defending Japanese fighters to low altitude, enabling the dive bombers from Enterprise to drop bombs on the cluttered flight decks of the carriers Kaga and Akagi. Both immediately went up in flames as they had refuelled their planes, and were lost. Yorktown planes attacked Soryu and the ship burst into flames as well. Hiryu, the fourth of the carriers in the Mobile Fleet, escaped attacks and damages, launched a counter attack, which damaged the Yorktown heavily. Tactical command passed to Spruance when that carrier had to be abandoned. In the evening of 04 June Enterprise planes attacked and put out of action the last of the Japanese carriers. During the night Admiral Yamamoto tried a

Hailstorm - *Historic Documentation*

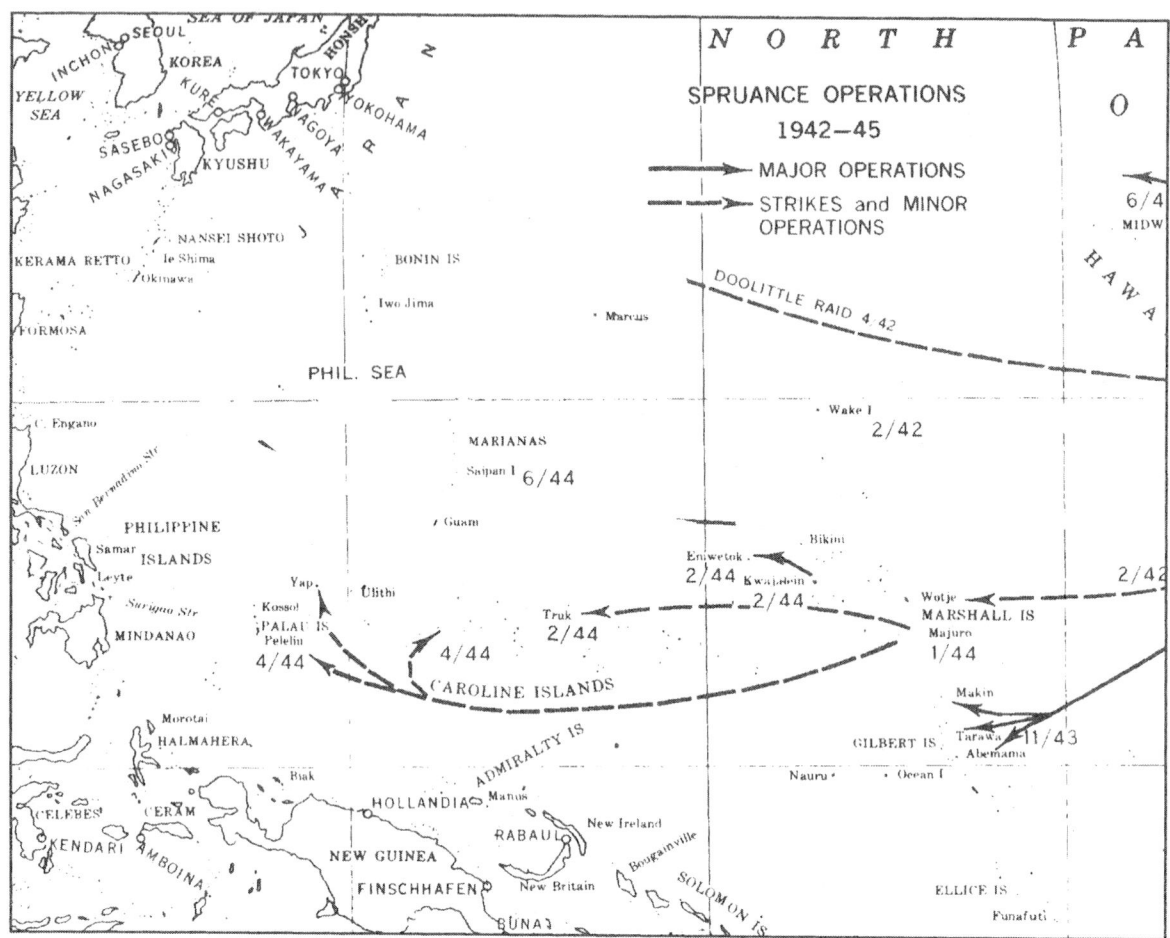

Operations in the Pacific under Admiral Spruance 1942 to 1944

During the night Admiral Yamamoto tried a concentration of his forces, but they were too far apart; the Midway operation was cancelled on 05 May, at 0255 h. The retreat of the main body was harassed by air attacks. Spruance cautious pursuit avoided contact with the Main Body, and dire consequences.

Four fleet carriers, one heavy cruiser were the losses on the Japanese side; the Americans lost the Yorktown. More important was the loss of first-line pilots and the entire complement of carrier based planes, by the Japanese. The engagement cost the Japanese forces the margin of superiority, which had enabled them to maintain the offensive.

After the Battle of Midway, Admiral Nimitz and General MacArthur agreed that the Japanese forces should be kept off balance by a vigorous counter offensive. Both leaders disagreed on how to conduct it. Nimitz was for a step-by-step advance from the Solomons to Palau, while MacArthur proposed a grand slam into Rabaul. Nimitz had no intentions of exposing his few remaining carriers and amphibious troops, which were just in the formation stage at this early time. In Washington, the Joint Chiefs of Staff placed the Eastern Solomons under Nimitz' command. There had been long discussions in late 1942 and well into 1943 about a Central Pacific Force which was to be the instrument for a step by step annihilation of Japanese Pacific garrisons. These operations were supported by a rapidly growing carrier, battleship and amphibious force. Very important was the formation of the long range, fast striking carrier task groups. General MacArthur and Admiral Ghormley (Commander South Pacific) advocated the direct route; the admiral was abruptly recalled shortly afterwards, during the Guadalcanal campaign. The Central Pacific route made full use of mutual supportive naval potential, and the carrier forces could strike fast and unexpected, deep into the territories held by the Japanese. The South Pacific route, of great importance, was predictable to the enemy by the pattern of advance, and would not use the naval forces to best advantage.

To the north, the best suited islands and atolls could be assaulted, taken and used for air strips and fleet anchorages. The Japanese forces would be kept guessing, as they could not expect the location of the next target. Some of the islands held by the Japanese were so small that they could not contain or sustain a great number of defenders. On the other hand, with the help of the newly formed Sea-Beas (Construction Battalions) new fighter strips could be made available

Better defended atolls or those where heavy casualties had to be expected, could be neutralized by air strikes and made useless for the Japanese. Those were Nauru, and a few lesser atolls, but ultimately, the same fate would befall Truk.

This was in no way revolutionary thinking. In

USNA/USNOA

Admiral Raymond A. Spruance

fact, the two flag officers, Admiral Nimitz and his Chief of Staff in early 1943, Admiral Spruance, were very well versed with the studies of the Naval War College in the late 'thirties, of how to liberate the Philippines, should they fall in the event of a war with Japan. These advances were planned in great detail along the Central Pacific route. They found a strong proponent for this concept in Admiral King, Chief of Naval Operations. He in turn persuaded the Joint Chiefs of Staff to adopt this advance, under the assumption of concurrent progress by MacArthur's New Guinea - Philippines axis. None of the two, Nimitz or MacArthur, was given over-all command. It was retained by the Joint Chiefs of Staff. MacArthur's intervention against this decision is one of the livelier episodes of his colorful life.

As early as 09 February 1943, Admiral King asked Admiral Nimitz for comments regarding when and how to secure the Gilberts. At that time Nimitz and Spruance were opposed to to an operation right then because there were not enough ships and trained amphibious forces available. However, current planning indicated a turn of these circumstances in the fall. Subsequently, Admiral King asked Nimitz to submit a plan to capture the Marshalls by November 1943. Various alternatives were proposed and discussed, but the lone voice of Admiral Spruance prevailed with his approach from the south east, via the Gilberts to the Marshalls. The Joint Chiefs of Staff directed that Tarawa and Abemama in the Gilberts be taken by November, together with Nauru, and the Marshalls in early 1944. No other than Admiral Spruance was chosen to command the new Central Pacific Force.

The first operation was scheduled against Tarawa and Makin, in the Gilberts. Nauru was not to be invaded. It was too close to Truk, which harbored the Combined Fleet, and this double operation would just split the American forces without allowing them mutual support. Once the Gilberts and the Solomons had been taken, Nauru would be useless for the Japanese, and could be bypassed. Spruance prevailed here as well, and Makin was targeted instead of Nauru.

The operation on the Gilberts, code-named "Galvanic", made contingency plans for a possible sortie from Truk, by the Combined Fleet, still considered a serious threat. All the time, the Truk base, about which very little was known, exerted a heavy pull on American tactical thinking. Truk had been closed to all outsiders shortly after the end of World War I. It was known that Truk was a large air base with three air fields. Intelligence sources reported up to 300 planes stationed there. Further, the waters of the lagoon had been busy with major warships coming and going. Although three American submarines were stationed to detect any sortie of the Japanese during "Galvanic", the Combined Fleet still reeled under the extremely heavy aircraft losses at Rabaul, where they were engaged in four attack waves by two Task Forces on 01 and 05 November.

The ill-fated commitment of carrier based aircraft in the defense of Rabaul was the cornerstone to Truk's demise, as will be seen. Those aircraft were not available to defend or even repulse, the American offensive which encroached on Truk. The next major set-back was the inferiority of Japanese material, their many green pilots, and their limited resources, which had to be shipped along extended supply lines. Finally, the complicated command structure, particularly in Truk, prevented coordinated defenses, and laid forces bare to the attack.

The Southern Attack Force sailed on 16 November 1943 for Tarawa. One of the Task Groups pounded Mili and laid it to waste, the other Task Force supported the invasion. The Task Forces 50. 3 and 50. 4 now raced to Tarawa, and Admiral Frederic C. Sherman, later to command TG 58.3 during the Truk raid, carried out neutralization strikes on Nauru, on 19 November. Tarawa and Makin were hit on 20 November. Tarawa proved a difficult target, mainly because the defenders were well entrenched and environmental conditions were not in favor of the Americans. Only after heavy casualties, the famous words "Issue in doubt" were finally decided for the attacker.

Admiral Nimitz was directed to take the Marshalls in January 1944. By mid-August the Commander-in Chief Pacific, Admiral Nimitz, had issued a tentative plan to take Kwajalein, Wotje and Maloelab simultaneously by the first of January. The Commander of the amphibious forces and Admiral Spruance objected strenuously against Kwajalein, and advocated that the other two atolls should be taken first. The discussions took place in the Hawaii headquarters, with almost all general and flag officers of the Pacific Fleet present. The participants voted to take the outer islands before Kwajalein. A historic

Admiral Isoroku Yamamoto, a formal portrait.

decision was made when Admiral Nimitz overrode everyone with his calm voice: "Well, gentlemen, our next objective is Kwajalein."

Spruance had his will by taking Majuro first, almost by default, invading on 31 January 1944. The atoll became a most valuable anchorage and fleet base. The coordination of the attack on Kwajalein proved difficult, and was postponed from the first to the seventeenth, and finally to the thirty-first of January 1944. Code-named "Flintlock", it involved even more forces than "Galvanic". However, the landing forces had seen combat before and were better prepared. Ship borne artillery and carrier aircraft gave the low lying atoll island a "Spruance Haircut", which left no stone unturned. After bitter fighting, but comparatively few casualties, the Marshalls were secured.

It may be interesting to digress and see the situation from the Japanese point of view.

The strategic thinking of the Japanese Imperial Navy was heavily influenced by the decisive victory over the Czarist Russian Fleet at Tsushima in 1905. The Russian fleet had, under tremendous sufferings and difficulties, laboriously worked their way from the Baltic ports to the strait dividing Korea and Japan. Here, Admiral Tojo laid in wait, and after a brilliantly fought battle crushed the demoralized Russian fleet.

Taking this as a basic example of applied strategy, the concepts of "One Decisive Battle", winner-take-all, was developed and refined. All along, this strategy can be seen underlying major Japanese naval operations, be it Pearl Harbor, Midway or Leyte Gulf. It never came to the all-out sea battle. The range of the guns had been extended by the use of carrier based aircraft. The American strategy of attrition and acceleration proved successful.

The intellectual Admiral Yamamoto had been right: If America could not be beaten quickly or brought to the conference table, any extension of the hostilities would be to Japan's disadvantage. Despite many convincing victories in South-East Asia, he was a troubled man when American fighters intercepted his plane and shot it down. Admiral Koga, his successor, was a cautious, perhaps even hesitant commander. He had under him a formidable fleet, probably ton for ton as good as the American, with the notable exception of the carriers. But as time progressed, Japan fell behind, and he knew it. Although the pride of the Japanese carriers had been lost, there were still fleet carriers available. Heavy losses in pilots and planes made them ineffective. There was no alternative for the Combined Fleet but to retreat to the relative safety of Truk Lagoon.

All the time the trickling stream of war supplies was yet further diverted - to the bottom of the sea, primarily by the relentless efforts of submarines. Admiral Koga could not launch an effective strike, he knew it. He also had to avoid a major American surprise assault from the air. The pattern of the war had shifted in two major aspects: The Japanese were clearly pushed into a defensive role. This was a situation they had never earnestly planned. Their perimeter was pierced, then crushed. The small garrisons on the outer Pacific islands, at best designed to harass American supply lines and to gather intelligence, were obliterated. Then, the war had shifted from the guns of the warships to the much longer range weapon of carrier airplanes, which were mobile and could deliver devastating strikes deep into Japanese held territory. In the early phase of the war the Japanese had used this weapon successfully. The two expensive and elaborate battleships Yamato and Musashi were almost defenseless without support aircraft - and finally both succumbed to attacks from the air. The Imperial Japanese Fleet had too many ships which were only effective, at this stage of the war, with air superiority. That had been lost.

Looking at the geography of the Mid-Pacific it is obvious that any concentration of ships in Truk is vulnerable to a surprise carrier attack. Admiral Koga was keenly cognizant of the exposed strategic position of Truk, particularly after the Marshalls had fallen. His last doubts were removed when, on 04 February 1944, a high flying B-24 photo plane was seen to pass over Truk. He ordered the combatant ships of the Combined Fleet immediately removed to safer waters, Japan, Palau, the Philippines and Singapore. The Fleet sailed, unknown to the Americans, on 10 February 1944, never to return to Truk. Only supply vessels and minor combatant ships remained, but latter were under orders to depart as well.

Admiral Koga had the foresight to expect a long range, shattering blow from the American fast carrier groups. He envisaged an American thrusts far to the west, to the Marianas, specifically Saipan and Guam, and even Palau. His order for preparations for these anticipated American raids were either ignored, allegedly not received or not believed. However, just when his worst fear came to pass he died in a plane crash, in

Hailstorm - *Historic Documentation*

an Emily flying boat, during a vicious storm enroute from Palau to Davao, Philippines. His successor was Admiral Toyoda, a very energetic admiral, whose adherence to the doctrine of "One Decisive Battle" - the Truk raid, were coordinated attacks. While Task Group 58. 4 softened up Eniwetok, Task Groups 58. 1, 58. 2, and 58. 3 raided Truk. Admiral Spruance expected a major naval engagement with Japanese capital

Commanders-in-Chief of the Combined Fleet. Admiral Koga (right) took over from Yamamato. After Koga's plane crashed in a vicious tropical storm, Toyoda assumed command

paradoxically lost Japan's fleet piecemeal.

After 10 February 1944, the day the Combined Fleet steamed out of Truk, supply vessels were still coming in, and in particular, elements of the 52nd Division were transported into Truk, with few supplies. An invasion was feared. And indeed, there were divided opinions in the American staff whether to take Truk or not. The "nays" had the overwhelming majority. Truk's geography is very much in favor of the defender, and the plan not to take it was reinforced by Admiral King. Instead, the next American target was to be Eniwetok. This atoll lies within the striking radius of planes stationed in Truk. Therefore, operations "Catchpole" - the Eniwetok invasion - and "Hailstone"

ships, and shifted his flag to the New Jersey, but the Japanese fleet had left. The aircraft of the Task Groups sank almost all ships inside and outside the lagoon, and destroyed valuable supplies.

Admiral Koga had been right. The Truk raid had come to pass, and the first strikes on Saipan, Guam and Tinian unfolded on the 23 February 1944. On 30 March, Spruance's fast carriers sortied 1200 miles west of Truk and struck at Palau. But Koga had ordered his ships out a few days earlier.

Vice Admiral Raymond A. Spruance was promoted to full Admiral, back dated to 04 February 1944, and the Central Pacific Force renamed Fifth Fleet.

TRUK'S DEFENSES

In the initial phase of the war, the Japanese forces conquered a vast expanse of the Pacific. The major islands in the west Pacific were garrisoned and used to gather military intelligence and harass the American supply lines. These shipping routes had to be diverted deep to the south for safety from long range bombing and submarines.

When this expansion had halted after the setback at the battle of the Coral Sea, the defeat at Midway and the US landing in Guadalcanal, the possessions had to be consolidated in a basically defensive organization. Four large areas were carved out of the large territory of the west Pacific and an Area Fleet assigned to each: Northeast, Southeast, Central and Southwest Area Fleets. They were to provide static defences and keep approaches and sea lanes open to the wide flung island garrisons.

The Central Pacific Area Fleet was principally responsible for the Marianas, Carolines and Marshall Islands. Under its command were the 4th (Truk), 5th (Saipan), 6th (Kwajalein) and 30th Base Force, the Fourth Fleet (Truk) and the 14th Air Fleet. These forces under Central Pacific Command were not expected to repel or counter an attack. It was very well realized that they would be too weak to accomplish that. They were holding forces, and were in charge of the defenses, to hold out until reinforcements could be thrown against the attacker. This concept was well proven in history, with static defenses to absorb the first shock of an assault and separate forces to strike back energetically.

It is the perennial problem of any defender to be condemned to an initially passive role. Although all his defense lines must be strong enough to withstand a concentrated attack, it is frequently the leadtime the attacker has and the quantity and quality of the reinforcements for the defender which tip the scale of the battle. The advantage the attacker has is timing, surprise and the concentration of his forces. Due to lack of precise intelligence on the Japanese side, the exact time of the American assaults were not known, although the general thrust was anticipated.

The static defense system was not really planned by the Japanese. It was costly and lead, as a consequence, to spread thin their precious resources. Operationally, the war had been expected to be swift, offensive and crushing. However, the events between May and August 42 forced the headquarters to rethink their strategy.

Improvisation is probably not at all to Japanese military liking, and a clearly delineated command structure with set responsibilities are preferred. It is therefore only natural that a complex command structure developed which consistently was thrown off balance by the pressure the advance of the US forces exerted on it. The organization which evolved was highly complicated and required frictionless cooperation of many individual components. It has been reported, though officially denied of course, that the cooperation between Army and Navy was far from perfect, and that even within these forces petty feuds flourished. Sources in Truk mentioned quarrels between Navy and Army units, and among each other.

Although there were many changes in the command structure brought by frequent reorganization and reassignments, it will be attempted to freeze this motion at around the time of "Operation Hailstone". It is important to visualize the dualism of the system, holding and striking dictated by the numerical availability of planes and ships, and the area to be covered. It left the holding forces too weak and the striking forces too far away. That the Striking Force, in particular carriers, had been withdrawn from potential battle grounds was a consequence of daring American assaults on Rabaul in November 1943 and a time-delay consequence of the Battle of Midway. During both episodes, the Japanese aircraft from the carrier division suffered very heavy losses in men and material. The forces designed to counter an American attack vigorously, were condemned to withdraw always one step ahead of the advancing enemy. The intention was to save the ships for the "one fateful encounter" and to replenish the carrier planes. Precious time was thus lost, and the Americans were able to build up their forces considerably faster, and better, than the Japanese.

When the American force began their dual drive, and assaulted Tarawa and later Kwajalein (Roi-Namur) along the projected Central Pacific axis, the defenders put up an exemplary heroic effort. They were doomed as no help could come forth.

The Striking Forces and Area Fleets will be described in more detail, their status being as follows, early 1944:

The Combined Fleet Headquarters, quite consequently, commanded both holding and striking forces. The Striking Forces were fleet and air units intended for an elastic defense and counter attack. They consisted of the

- First Air Fleet
- First Mobile Fleet and
- Sixth (Submarine) Fleet.

The First Air Fleet was (in March 1944) subdivided into unusually large Air Flotillas. Air Flotilla 61 and 62 both comprised of 10 Air Groups each. This concentration of naval aircraft and its organization will be dealt with later.

The First Mobile Fleet consisted of two

subordinated fleets. The Second Fleet was the surface striking force of battleships and heavy cruisers, augmented by destroyers and some other vessels. The Third Fleet was the carrier striking force with surface escort and defense vessels, organized in itself in carrier division, containing about five air groups.

It was the First Air Fleet, the First Mobile Fleet and the Sixth (Submarine) Fleet which the Japanese intended to throw against an American assault in the Pacific, while the Area Fleet was holding off the attack. Major components of the First Mobile Fleet were anchored in Truk and departed on 10 February 1944, one week prior to the assault.

The Holding Forces in the case of Truk were the Central Pacific Forces. Subordinate and under the command of Vice Admiral Hitoshi Kobayashi (from 19 February 1944 onwards Vice Admiral Chuichi Hara) were the Fourth Fleet and Air Fleet 14.

The Fourth Fleet had under its direct command light naval craft, a few light cruisers, a handful of destroyers, submarines and several small surface vessels. Through the Fourth Fleet, the Commander-in-Chief, Central Pacific Area Fleet, controlled originally four Base Forces. They were the 4th (Truk), 5th (Saipan), 6th (Kwajalein) until its destruction in January and February 1944, and the 30th (Palau) Base Force. Each Base Force under the command of a Rear Admiral, were charged with manning and defending the base, harbor and airspace. Additionally, they were to carry out routine patrol and escort duties. For reconnaissance duties, a unit of float planes were attached to the command and did not report to the air groups under Air Fleet command. They were probably stationed at the Dublon seaplane base. A Guard Force, subordinated to the Base Force, was responsible for the coastal defenses and anti-aircraft batteries dealing with surface and air assaults.

After the loss of Kwajalein (Marshalls), a reorganization took place. The Central Pacific Area Fleet now commanded the 4th, 5th and 30th Base Force, and Air Fleet 14. The 4th Base Force was merged with the Fourth Fleet. Operation, supply, harbor transport, construction, repair, maintenance, personnel, civil administration, intelligence, paymaster, medical and meteorological departments came under the direct command of the Commander, Fourth Fleet.

Air Fleet 14 consisted of Air Flotilla 21 (disbanded end 1943), 22 (detached from Air Fleet 11 and moved to Truk in October 1943) and 26 (also detached from Air Fleet 11).

In order to understand the activities of the Japanese planes, the grouping of the naval air forces in and around Truk will be explained in more detail. It has to be realized that the Japanese did not have an independent Air Force, but Army and Navy commanded their own planes. It appears that certain Japanese Army Air Units, or parts of them, were located in Truk. Normally they were not under local command. Also, not in all cases was an Air Group complete. Truk seemed to have become the home of a few units which had suffered severe losses and existed in name or numbers only. A few unit numbers do not appear on the organization chart as it was known then. It could well be that components of Air Groups have been regrouped to form a new one. In as much as it is attempted to provide a "frozen" picture of the organization, it must be realized that everything was in the state of flux.

Until Summer 1943, an Air Fleet generally consisted of two Air Flotillas, but since then their make up may have become very mixed. A few Air Fleets, exposed to the onslaught of American assaults, had been left with only fragmentary forces, whereas other Air Fleets consisted of up to four Air Flotillas. Air Fleet 14 was formed at the end of 1943. The flying units of its command formed the land-based 4th Base Air Force. The Air Fleet consisted of Air Flotilla 22 and 26 and probably remnants of Air Flotilla 21. While the 4th Base Air Force was headquartered in Saipan, the 26th Air Flotilla was headquartered in Palau and the 22nd in Truk.

American intelligence sources put together the following organization:

Air Flotilla 22
consisted of the following numbered Air Groups:
- 202, 301, 503, 755* and 802
(but originally included 252 and 552*).

Air Flotilla 26,
headquarters in Truk, Eten, comprised Air Groups
- 201*, 204*, 501* and 751.

Additionally, the Air Flotilla 21, which was said to have been disbanded at the end of 1943, contained elements of Air Groups:
- 151, 253 and 751.

It was originally headquartered in Tinian, but relocated to Truk prior dissolving; it used to be under the command of the 11th Air Flotilla.

In September 1943, Air Flotilla 25 was headquartered in Rabaul and probably comprised Air groups 251*, 501*, 702 and 751, originally under the 11th Air Fleet command. Although Air Group 582* and 151 have been mentioned, this Air Fleet lost most of its flying units in the fierce fighting in the Bismarck Area.

The official Japanese documentation is slightly different, and is shown below, whereby the level of command is denoted with :

****   Commander of Combined Fleet (Admiral)
***   Commander of Area Fleet or Air Fleet
        (Vice Admiral)
**   Commander of Base Force or Air Flotilla
        (Rear Admiral)

Under command of **** Combined Fleet in the Central Pacific:

1)*** **Fourth Fleet** (Truk, Dublon), commanding:
    ** 4th Base Force (Dublon) with
  - Air Group 902* (Saipan), comprising of
      10 rec. sea plane fighters in Meridon,
      4 rec. float planes in Palau,

Hailstorm - *Historic Documentation*

      4 rec. float planes in Saipan,
      6 rec. float planes in Truk,
      11 rec. float planes in Dublon,
      8 rec. float planes in Moen.

** 5th Base Force (Saipan) comprising of a detachment of Air group 902*, comprising of
    4 rec. float planes in Saipan.

** 22nd Air Flotilla (Tinian) with
- Air Group 755*, comprising of
    10 land based attack planes in Tinian
    10 land based attack planes in Moen.
- Air Group 252, Truk,
    disbanded, no planes, crew went to Japan.
- Air Group 552*, Moen, comprising of
    10 carrier based bombers.
- Air Group 802, Saipan, comprising of
    6 flying boats.
- Air Group 753*, Tinian, comprising of
    3 land based attack planes.

2)*** **11 Air Fleet** (Rabaul), commanding:

** Air Flotilla 26, Truk, Eten, with
- Air Group 201*, Saipan;
    with 20 + 8 carrier borne fighters,
- Air Group 204*, Eten;
    with 31 carrier borne fighters,
- Air Group 501*, Eten;
    with 27 carrier borne bombers,
- Air Group 251*, Truk, Param;
    with 9 night fighters
  and a detachment of Air Group 938*, rec. float planes.

** Air Flotilla 25, Rabaul, with
- Air Group 582 (528* ?), Moen,
  with 5 + 2 carrier based attack bombers.

3)*** **13 Air Fleet** (Surabaya), commanding:
** Air Flotilla 23, Kandary, Celebes (Sulawesi), comprising of
- Air Group 753*, Moen,
    with 10 land based attack planes;

** Air Flotilla 28, Singapore, commanding:
- Air Group 551*, Param,
    with 26 rec. float planes.

4)
*** **Sixth Fleet** (Submarines)
  with a detachment in Truk of rec. float planes.

(Air Groups with an *asterisk are mentioned in the official Japanese account of the attack.)

    The numbers given the Air Groups are of significance because they indicate the kind of aircraft flown, the function of the Group and other details. For example, the 100-digit will indicate information as per the following table on the next page.

    If the unit number of the Air Group is even, the unit has always been numbered. Uneven number signify that it had carried a name before it left the homeland for redeployment abroad. For example, Air Group 202 is attached to Air Flotilla 22, subordinated to Air Fleet 14, under the command of the Central Pacific Area Fleet, equipped with "Ko"-fighter aircraft, supplied, according to plan with 36 operational and 12 reserve planes, originally based in the Yokosuka Naval Station. The Group was originally numbered.

    An interesting point, which in the event proved disastrous, was that the Air Groups were equipped with 1/3 reserve planes of the original contingent but there were no reserve pilots allocated. The Americans undertook every effort to rescue their pilot and never left an engagement area until after a thorough search. During the assault on Truk, there were submarines stationed as lifeguards around the atoll, and destroyers and the small floatplanes of battleships and cruisers were dispatched to pick up downed aviators.. Of the majority of American planes shot down, the pilots were able to waterland their aircraft. Standard equipment for the pilots included rubber rafts, life vests and other emergency gear. The majority of the air crew was subsequently saved. The Japanese planes generally burst into flames and literally fell from the sky. The pilots were frequently trapped in the flaming wreckage. Also, comparatively rarely did Japanese surface vessels have a chance to return to the battle scene to search for survivors.

    In general the Air Groups were equipped with aircraft of one principal kind. Their organization was subdivided into three major divisions.

- Hikotai, flying division; two units (Hikobutai), larger groups had frequently 2 Hikotai.
- Hikokai, flight department, aircraft and equipment repair and maintenance
- and administrative sections.

    Some Air Groups had one principal base and one or more secondary fields, but the problem of group-dedicated ground personnel was that it was just sufficient for one base and could not be split up without sacrifice to the work or relying on the services of other groups flying the same aircraft. Truk was an exception, as the number of ground personnel was much over the standard. There were two reasons. Firstly it had been the staging area for the Bismarcks, and Navy and Army planes were flown, ferried or staged through its facilities, requiring an unusual amount of specialists and secondly, Truk absorbed a large number of ground personnel from disbanded and defeated air unit. Its ground personnel formed the first of a handful to-be organized Air Base Units (Air Base Unit 101) "Koku Kichi Tai" and serviced planes based in Tinian, Moen, Param, Eten and possibly Saipan and Palau.

    The fairly straight command structure - Area Fleet - Air Fleet - Air Flotilla - Air Group - became modified as striking forces were created within the Air Fleet itself. Striking Forces were the flying units of Flotillas and Groups. They received their operational orders directly from the Commander-in-Chief of Air

Digit Function	Allied Code	Japanese Code	Flying Unit/ Hikotai/Class	Remarks
100 recon.	Irving	Naka. J1N1-s	"Gekko"	
	Judy	Aichi D4Y1-4	"Suisei"	
200 Fighter intercept	Zeke Hamp	Mitsubishi A6M1-4	Sentoki Hikotai/S FA	Ko-fighter "Zero"
300 Bomber intercept Night fighter	Jack George Irving Zeke	Mits. J2M.. Kawa. N1K1-J Naka. J1S1-J Mitsubishi	Sentoki Hikotai/S FA	Otsu or "Raiden" "Shiden" Hei-fighter
400 Recon.	Jake	Aichi E13A1		floatplane
500 Bombers, carrier Bombers, land based	Judy Jill Francis Betty Nell	Aichi D4Y1-4 Naka. B6N1-2 Naka. P1Y1 Mits. G4M1-3 Mits. G3M1-3	Kokegi Hikotai	"Tenzan" "Ginga"
600 Mixed units				
700 Attack land bsd.	Betty	Mits. G4M1-3	Kokegi Hikotai/K FA	
800 Flying boats	Emily Mavis	Kawa. H8K1-2 Kawa. H6K1-5	Taisatsu Hikotai/T FA	
900 Float planes	Jake	Aichi E13A1 -"-		
1000 Transport Planes			Unso Hikotai	

(Abbreviations: Naka.= Nakajima, Mits.= Mitsubishi, Kawa.=Kawanishi.)

Also, the 10-digit had significance, representing the home base of the Air Group.
0, 1, 2 - Yokosuka Naval Station
3, 4 - Kure Naval Station
5, 6, 7 - Sasebo Naval Station
8, 9 - Maizuro Naval Station.

Fleet 14, via the Base Force command, and Flotilla and Group commanders were executing them. The separation of flying and ground personnel on Group and Flotilla level had made it possible to create ad-hoc Air Attack Forces for a particular emergency with a unified command. They were disbanded when the emergency ceased to exist. The Attack Force under 4th Base command were called 6th and 2nd Air Attack Force, derived by dropping the ten's digit "2" from both Flotillas.

At the end of 1943, the organization of the flying units into striking forces became prominent with the emergence of the First Air Fleet. This large unit was designed to be thrown into battle to turn back an air assault, and its forces were large and impressive, at least on the chart. First Air Fleet consisted of the 61 Air Flotilla with 10 Air Groups located on the fields of Guam and Saipan, with Air Groups 121, 261, 263, 341 (343*) (521), 523 and 761 (321 and 1021 were reported to have been included as well.)

In Tinian, the headquarters of the 1st Air Fleet, the Air Flotilla 62 was also located with the Air Groups 141, 221, 265, 322, 361, 521, 522, 524, 541, and 762. However, it appears that not all of these Groups had been relocated south from the Empire.

In summary then, the defenses in and around Truk consisted of the static defenses of the Fourth Fleet with a handful of small combatant surface vessels, the escort and patrol vessels of the 4th Base Force, major elements of Air Flotillas 22 and 26 with about 300 aircraft - evidently not all of them operational, and a large contingent of aircraft in the Marianas. Guard Units were manning the anti-aircraft and harbor defenses. In anticipation of an amphibious assault, large components of the 52 Army division had been landed on Tol and other Islands in the atoll, but a large quantity of their weapons and equipment never reached Truk. It was sunk in part during the Operation Hailstone or while enroute, by American submarines, which maintained a stranglehold on the approaches.

Hailstorm - *Historic Documentation*

THE OFFICIAL JAPANESE REPORT

After the outer defense lines of the Gilberts and Marshalls are breached late 1943 and early 1944, Truk itself became vulnerable to an American assault. Truk has been anchorage and supply point of the Combined Fleet since August, and serves as air base for the middle and southeast Pacific.

On 31 January 1944, "Operation T" is initiated, to guard Truk against surprise attacks. The airspaces to the north and northeast are reconnoitered by 8 to 9 aircraft. "Operation T" is broken off on 10 February 1944, and further reconnaissance flights are made by Air Group 755, and later, on 12 February, continues with 10 scout planes stationed in Tinian.

On 13 February, 5 planes from Air Group 755 fly searches towards the East, and 3 from Tinian towards the west. No contact with enemy forces is reported. On the day after next, 15 February, planes are flown into the same areas with the same negative result. From the 5 planes started only 3 come back, but again, no contact is made.

Air Groups 552 and 902 have made air and sea searches, but no enemy forces are found. At this time the Americans begin preparations for the occupation of Green Island. The tension mounts. On 15 February, 4th Communication Unit picks up radio transmissions from the US carrier Essex. An American attack is suspected. Therefore the commander of Fourth Base Forces (Truk) orders highest alarm, at 0230 h on 16 February. At 0500 h, five planes take off from Moen for searches, but again they fail to locate any American forces. The alarm is being reduced to regular alarm at 0900 h, and further reduced to normal preparedness at 1130 h. The status of normal preparedness is continuing until the American attack begins the next day.

It is observed that an American plane makes aerial photographs during an high altitude overflight of Truk on 4 February. According to some report the plane started at Mono and flew on to Tarokina. Subsequent to the overflight search activities are reinforced. 4th Communication Unit lays a direct cable from Eten to Dublon. On the same day a plan is drawn up for contingency supplies for a full year, to be assembled until 15 March. Public buildings are evacuated on 15 February. From 4 February onwards air control is centrally concentrated and is made the responsibility of Fourth Base Force, which now controls all departing and arriving aircraft. Changes in flight patterns are only issued from this unit.

After the American plane has been sighted it is considered unwise to leave the Combined Fleet in Truk. It is ordered by the Commander-in-Chief, Combined Fleet, to move the major fleet units to Yokosuka. The ships depart Truk on 10 February, and arrive in Japan on 15 February. The capital ships involved in the move are, among others, Musashi, Zuikako, Shokaku and Hosho. Smaller units are ordered to Palau. Further, it is considered to establish bunker oil supplies in southerly direction.

After the departure of the fleet a secret order (No. 68, Operation T) is issued by the Commander-in-Chief, which deals with measures of defense, and repulsing fast American carrier formations should they attack Truk. This order already foresees the possibility of an early assault into the eastern seas, in particular Palau, and to the northeast, the Marianas. Air forces under the command of the Inner South Pacific region are put under the command of the Fourth Base Force.

It is claimed later that this order was never received by the commanders in the region, and subsequently uncertainty prevailed about the disposition of forces and their command structure. On 16 February the commander of the Inner South Pacific Forces issues an operation plan for the eventuality of an American assault on Truk and the Marianas.

Immediately after the departure of the Combined Fleet from Truk the role of Commander, Inner South Pacific Forces falls to Vice Admiral Kobayashi. The command structure is highly complicated, as Army and Navy operate with own commanders and forces, and none has distinct superiority over the other. In addition, forces in Truk are found to be under the South West Pacific Command, aircraft under the Combined Fleet, training units of the South east Pacific Command, as well as, the 52nd Division, under Army command.

Air Group 938 is ordered, by Commander, South East Pacific, to train zero-visibility fighting, night attacks and plane recognition. The pilots are expected to fly all types of aircraft. Twelve pilots are relocated from Rabaul to Truk, Param, and are incorporated into Air Group 251. Five Zero fighters are made available for training purposes.

Sunrise on 17 February is 0609 h, sunset 1804 h, and the Moon rises at 2340 h.

On 17 February 1944, at 0520 to 0530 h, radar located in Truk detects the approach of a large plane formation. The Commander, Inner South Pacific Forces (Vice Admiral Kobayashi) initiates highest alarm, up from normal preparedness. It is assumed by the forces, while analyzing the radar reflections that a large bomber formation is approaching. It is thought not plausible that this formation could be carrier based planes.

At about 0600 h the first air attack begins, and it is estimated that more than 100 planes participate. Altogether 9 waves of planes are seen to approach, with about 450 American planes in the air.

Damages on sea and land targets are significant. Altogether 77 airplanes start from the airfields

Hailstorm - *Historic Documentation*

in Truk. No less than 35 Zero fighters take off from Eten, of which 27 belong to Air Group 204FG and 8 to 201FG. Additionally, 25 bombers are launched from Eten, belonging to 501FG, bringing the total number of planes from this island to 60. From Dublon start 8 planes from 902FG, and 4 Rufes. Moen contributes 5 planes from 902FG.

The Japanese planes are subjected to attacks while they are still climbing after take-off. The American pilots have the advantage of altitude and attack in diving runs. It is assumed that about 37 Japanese planes are shot down in the take-off phase, without even entering aerial combat. This leaves only about 40 planes in the air to defend Truk.

Param airfield sees the start of 8 torpedo planes (Jill-12) at 0545 h, from Air Group 551, which are ordered to search for the American fleet. It is intended to locate and attack these ships. At 0645 h one of the fast carrier forces is found at specific quadrants, 45 degrees and 90 miles (150 km) away from Truk. At 0810 h the second fast carrier force is located in the vicinity of the first, about 160 ms (255 km) distant from the lagoon. (Actual position of the American Task groups was only 160 km off Truk.) The same Air Group (551) launches two more aircraft for an attack, but both planes fail to return.

In Moen, Air Group 552 receives a warning about approaching planes just prior to 0530 h, but assumes that the radar echoes indicate large planes. Therefore, it is thought that large-type bombers are approaching. Only when the smaller carrier planes are seen overhead the error is noted.

At 0530 h, 3 bombers start on a search from Moen, but one never returns. Two other planes, started at 0910, also looking for the American ships, do not return either. At 1115 h, a single plane takes off, sights a task force of 2 battleships, 2 heavy cruisers, 4 destroyers, east of Truk, is chased by American planes but succeeds in coming back, and so does another plane which had started at 1100 h. Both estimates the American forces to be 280 ms (450 km) away from Truk. Also, both planes share the same experience being jumped by American planes. The American fighters are suddenly showing from behind and shoot, but the Japanese pilots outmaneuver them. Finally, at 1530 h, two bombers are scrambled in an attempt to attack the American planes, but both are shot down.

On Eten great confusion reigns, and the chain of events can only be surmised. Due to a direct bomb hit in the very early moments of the raid into the headquarters building of Air Flotilla 26 all communications and the command structure are totally disrupted. Organized opposition seems to have been impossible. There are heavy casualties on the staff and plane ground handling crews due to repeated bombing and strafing attacks. Large craters in the runway prevent planes from starting, and most of those parked on the apron are damaged by American fighter board weapons or bombs.

Combined Fleet Command

The news of the large scale attack on Truk is picked up by the staff of the Combined Fleet, and at 1325 h, Order No. 947 is issued. It deals with the general order to reinforce the air forces in Truk with all land and carrier based fighters available to First Base Forces, and to subjugate them to the Commander, Inner South Pacific. This order is followed up with No. 948, at 1622 h, which orders units of the 11 and 13 Air Fleet detached for reinforcement, and clears the command structure.

Air Forces under Base Command

An attack on the American fast carrier formation is planned at dusk, with torpedo planes. This order is conveyed to 26 Air Flotilla, Air Groups 551 and 528, at 1215 h, via radio. However, 6 operational planes from 551 have already flown out of action and retreated to Tinian. On Param all planes have either been burned or are damaged to the extend of being non-operational. From Moen 6 aircraft take off; 4 from Air Group 518 and 2 Rufe float planes, at 1815 h. Two of the planes drop their weapons and return, while 2 have to waterland due to lack of fuel. The crews are picked up by the Tenko Maru. The fate of the remaining two planes remained unknown.

At Tinian, the commander of Air Flotilla 26 orders at 0735 h that the planes of Air Groups 753 and 755 are to be flown to Truk. However, from 753 only 2 land based planes take off at 1526 h. They do not find the American ships. Air Group 755 launches 3 planes at 1516 h. One of them finds the ships and drops a torpedo. It hits a carrier, which is reported sunk. (In reality, the torpedo hit the Intrepid, which had to be withdrawn from the engagement, was repaired stateside and rejoined the battle line later). One of these planes fails to return.

Reinforcements For the Southern Forces

The first day of the carrier borne air raid on Truk sees 32 American planes shot down in air combat and 17 brought down by anti aircraft fire. However, 67 (70) of the Japanese planes do not return. 96 planes are burned or destroyed on the ground.

Type of plane	shot down	destroyed on the ground
carrier based fighters	48	48
bombers	6	0
attack bombers	5	0
sea plane fighters	6	5
night fighters	5	16
reconnaissance planes	0	7
flying boats	0	2
recon. float planes	0	18
Total	70	96
Grand Total		166

The commander of 1st Base Air Force (in Rabaul, with 11th Air Fleet) orders land based fighters and carrier based attack bombers of the 5th Air Attack Force to fly to Truk immediately. The commander of this unit (5th Air Attack Force) reports that these

Hailstorm - *Historic Documentation*

planes are scheduled to leave Bunakanau on 18 February. Central Pacific Area Force sends one unit each of land based attack planes and carrier based attack bombers to Tinian and Moen respectively. These reinforcements are put under the control of the commander of 2nd Air Attack Force, and 1st Training Base Air Force, respectively.

The following forces are reported to have been transferred from Bunakanau to Truk on 18 February: 14 land based attack planes of Air Group 751, at 0430 h (0630 h Truk time), and 6 carrier based attack bombers of the 2nd Air Flotilla, at 0330 h (0530 h).

On 17 February, at 2125 h (2325 h) the commander of 11th Air Fleet reports further transferrable forces as 12 land based fighters from Air Group 751, 6 carrier based attack bombers and 14 carrier based bombers from 22nd Air Flotilla.

An order is issued by the Commander, Central Pacific Area Force at 2200 h (2400 h) on 17 February, to transfer the reinforcement air forces, 22nd Air Flotilla and 1st Training Base Air Force, to be under the command of the 1st Air Fleet. The land based attack planes and the reconnaissance units are to fly to Tinian. Air Groups 705 and 331 are sent off to Meleyon; they and the all other land based fighters remaining in Truk are to be under the command of 26th Air Flotilla.

Further, 11 land based fighters of Air Group 751 leave Bunakanau for Tinian on 18 February. 6 carrier based attack bombers, which leave Bunakanau on 18 February for Truk returned, and make it to Truk finally on 19 February.

Attacks of the Second Day

In the very early hours of the second day the anchorages of Truk are subjected to an attack by specially equipped American torpedo planes. Twelve of these planes bomb the ships for about an hour. They are launched about 100 miles (165 km) east of Truk. It is not possible to determine the exact nature and extend of damages of this night attack.

At 0520 h in the morning a large formation of approaching planes is found on the radar scopes. From 0600 to 1030 h, on 18 February, three large waves of attack planes inflict further major damage on land and sea targets.

Following the raids of the previous day no planes could take off anymore, either because none remained undamaged or because the runways are pock-scarred with bomb craters. Only the anti aircraft guns can be brought to bear against the attackers. Air Group 201 is ordered to fly 24 Zeros to Truk on 17 February, but not until details of fuel supply and command are sorted out do the planes start on the following day. From the airfield in Saipan 15 planes are launched at 1130 h. They search unsuccessfully until 1320 h. 14 planes take off at 1400 h, and a further flight of 15 at 1640 h. None of the planes make contact with the American forces.

In Truk the last American plane departs at 1030 h, and the alarm is rescinded at 1140 h.

Damages

During the two-day air raid 41 ships sink as the result of hits of bombs, torpedoes and gunfire. The Navy looses 10 vessels. 31 transports go to the sea bottom. The Navy reports 9 ships damaged. 270 aircraft are destroyed, of which 70 are shot down and 200 are destroyed on the ground. Damage is reported to workshops, headquarters buildings and runways. Three large oil tanks with 17, 000 t capacity are destroyed, together with 2000 t provisions. Without fatalities on board ships, casualties on land amount to 600 dead or injured.

Convoy 4215

On 11 February 1944, Combined Fleet issued orders to the light cruiser Katori, auxiliary cruiser

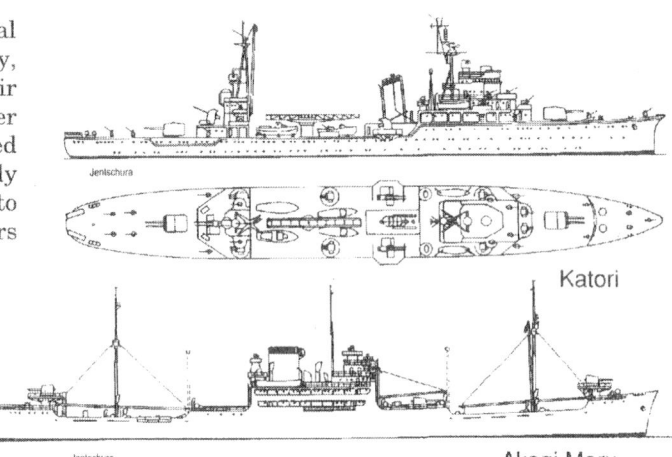

Katori

Akagi Maru

Maikaze and Nowake

Akagi Maru and Destroyer Group 4, comprising of Nowake and Maikaze, to depart Truk on 16 February, to rendezvous with Asaka Maru. However, since loading Akagi Maru is not completed in time, the convoy, under the command of the captain of the Katori, leaves Truk only on 17 February, at 0530 h. When this formation clears the North Pass at 0600 h it is attacked by American fighters and bombers. The Akagi Maru receives bomb hits and sinks already at 1142 h. Katori and Maikaze are subjected to gunfire by two American cruisers, beginning at 1320 h. They sink at 1524 h. Nowake rendezvous with the destroyer Yamagumo on 20 February, and arrives in Yokosuka, together with the Asaka Maru, on 24 February.

Light Cruiser Naka

On 16 February the light cruiser Agano is torpedoed north of Truk. Heavily damaged, the crew of the ship radios for assistance. Naka is detached from Truk and sails towards the stricken cruiser, which sinks, however, before Naka reaches her. The cruiser passes the North Pass and stands off to sea when the air raid on Truk unfolds. She steams back to Truk but is discovered by planes quite a distance away from the pass. At about 0800 h, 20 American planes make a

Hailstorm - *Historic Documentation*

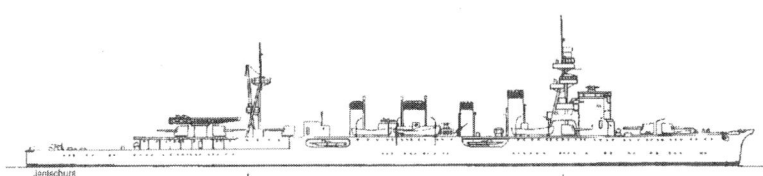

level bombing attack. At 1000 h over 10 bombers dive bomb the ship and at 1300 h another 10 bombers and 4 torpedo bombers attack. Despite hectic damage control and provisional repairs the cruiser succumbs to the repeated attacks and sinks.

Destroyer Group 27

Two destroyers remain in Truk: Shigure and Harusame. Both make up steam immediately and leave the anchorage, going through the North Pass at 0715 to 0755 h. Between 0630 and 0900 h they are attacked by about 45 aircraft. Shigure receives several

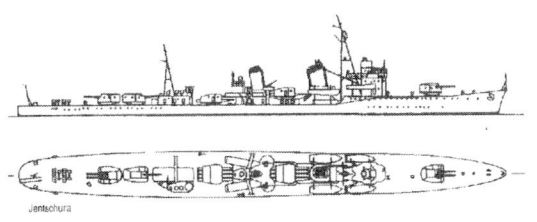

hits. One damages the second gun turret, another detonates on the torpedo tubes and explodes the torpedo storage above the waterline, and the third hits number two boiler room. Heavily damaged, with 21 of her crew dead and 45 injured, the ship remains under control.

Harusame receives comparatively minor damage by bomb close misses, and two sailors are killed. Despite damage to both ships they rendezvous with the seaplane tender Akitsushima, which had left Truk, and escort her to Palau.

Destroyer Tachikaze

On 2 February 1944, Tachikaze departs from Rabaul to sail to Truk with troops and material on board. Two days later the ship runs aground on Kuop Atoll, 5 miles (8 km) and 160 degrees from Otta. The 4th Harbor Division in Truk tries to pull the destroyer off with the aid of a tug boat, but all attempts are unsuccessful. While still grounded firmly the ship's crew counts 30 planes, including F6F fighters, at 1200 h, at 1500 h 34 F6F and TBF on the first day. From

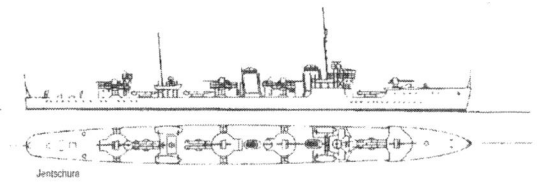

0830 onwards, on the 18 February, an attack is launched against the ship, with 7 TBF and 4 F6F, resulting in a damaging close miss and a direct hit into the engine room. At 0900 h the Tachikaze sinks.

52nd Division

Beginning in early January 1944, 52nd Division is brought to Truk. Most of the troops are stationed in Pata (Tol), but when the air raid begins it is feared that amphibious landing operations would commence soon. Therefore, reinforcements are hurried to Dublon and some to Fefan. On 18 February, at about 1600 h, a great number of troops are rescued by the destroyer Fujinami, from Transport Group 2, sank at Enderby. They are put ashore at Dublon, but muster the next day on Moen.

Statement of the Imperial Headquarters on the Attack on Truk.

On 21 February, Imperial Headquarters issued a statement:

"On 17 and 18 February 1944 Truk was attacked by an American task force operating in the area. The Imperial Army and Navy have fought excellently and repulsed successfully the attacks. The enemy lost two cruisers, and possibly a battleship. One large carrier was sunk and an army ship destroyed. During the operation 54 aircraft were shot down. The own losses are 2 cruisers, 3 destroyers, 13 transport ships and 120 aircraft. Small damage was sustained on the islands."

(Notes in brackets are by the author)

SHIPS SUNK OR DAMAGED

Navy ships sunk:

Katori	light cruiser	5800 t	outside North Pass
Naka	light cruiser	5195 t	southwest of Truk
Maikaze	destroyer	2000 t	outside North Pass
Tachikaze	destroyer	1215 t	Kuop Atoll
Oite	destroyer	1270 t	outside Truk Atoll (error:North lagoon)
Fumizuki	destroyer	1320 t	inside lagoon
Ku No 29	subchaser	440 t	west of Truk
Ku No 24	subchaser	440 t	northwest of Truk
Gyotei No. 10	MTB	85 t	west of Truk
Shonan Maru No 15	(steam whaler	355 t)	near North Pass

Hailstorm - *Historic Documentation*

Damaged Navy Vessels:

Akitsushima	float plane tender	midships bomb
Harusame	destroyer	small damage, bombs
Ro 42 sen	submarine	small damage
Akashi	fleet repair ship	very little damage
Namikachi	destroyer	small damage
Hagoromo M.	mine sweeper	medium damage, beached
Matsukaze	destroyer	medium damage
Soya	aux. ammunit. ship	very little damage, beached
Shigure	destroyer	little damage
Ku toku 20	asc	little damage
I 10 sen	submarine	very little damage

Fleet Repair Ship AKASHI did not get away unscathed. A hit midships severely damaged the No. 2 engine. The ship could not be repaired before it sank in Palau six weeks later.

Flying Boat Tender AKITSUSHIMA was hit midships and aft. The damages aft proved cumbersome. The ship retired to an atoll on the way to Palau to repair her steering.

Auxiliaries Damaged:

Hakuho M,	weather ship	} both ships stranded on reefs.
Hakune M,	transport	}

Transports and Fleet Auxiliaries sunk:

(Note: All ships bear the surfix "Maru")

Shinwa	5,784 t	80 miles (130 km) west of Truk
Gosei	1,931 t	Uman, 50 deg, 1600 m
Heian	11,614 t	Dublon, north, 265 deg, 1850 m
Aikoku	10,437 t	No.6 light, 90 deg, 1400 m
Reiyo	5,445 t	No.6 light, 100 deg, 1060 m
Seiko	5,385 t	No.8 light, 143 deg, 970 m
Kiyozumi	8,613 t	Dublon, north mount, 23 deg, 3150 m
San Francisco	5,831 t	No.8 light, 114 deg, 1330 m
Amagisan	7,620 t	Uman, 23 deg (230 deg?), 1850 m
Tonan No. 3	19,209 t	lagoon
Fujisan	9,524 t	Yanagi 63 deg, 2400 m
Hanakawa	4,739 t	Fala-Beguets 223 deg, 3400 m
Yubae	3,217 t	Uman 298 deg, 1430 m
Sankisan	4,776 t	
Shinkoku	10,020 t	"western highland" 73 deg, 5900 m
Fujikawa	6,938 t	No.8 light, 203 deg, 2300 m
Zuikai	2,700 t	outside North Pass
Akagi	7,389 t	outside North Pass
Hoki	7,112 t	captured ship
Shotan	1,999 t	131 deg, 350 m from Nagano
Hokuyo	4,216 t	No.8 light, 131 deg, 1315 m
Hoyo	8,691 t	
Daikichi	1,891 t	unknown
Nagano	3,824 t	No.8 Light, 96 deg, 2050 m
Rio de Janeiro	9,626 t	Uman, 73 deg, 2500 m
Yamagiri	6,438 t	
Unkai No.6	3,220 t	Uman, 225 deg, 2500 m
Momokawa	3,829 t	No.6 light, 60 deg, 980 m
Taiho	2,827 t	Uman, 5 deg, 2700 m (270 deg)
Kansho	4,861 t	unknown
Nippo	3,763 t	No.6 light, 28 deg, 1500 m

Hailstorm - *Historic Documentation*

RESPONSIBILITIES AND BLAME

The overflight of the Liberator photo plane on February 4, 1944 had significant consequences for the Japanese forces in Truk, apart from supplying intelligence to the US Pacific Fleet.

The Japanese Combined Fleet under their commander-in-chief, Admiral Koga, ordered the withdrawal of the fleet units, and this was accomplished on 10 February 1944.

With the departure of the C-i-C of the Combined Fleet, Vice Admiral Kobayashi Jin automatically became supreme commander of the Truk naval base. The admiral was commander of the Forth Fleet, concurrently with being the Commander of the Inner South Sea Force. Between these three commands, Truk Base, Forth Fleet and Inner South Sea, the chain of command of the available air forces was *"not very clear"*, in other words, extremely confused.

Apart from aircraft assigned to the Forth Fleet, there also were numerous planes assigned to the South East Area Fleet, as well as to the South West Area Fleet. In the words of the Japanese after the war: *"When he was placed in command, Vice Admiral Kobayashi Jin, commander of the Forth Fleet, should have issued orders concerning the new disposition and chain of command of all units in this area. Instead, he heedlessly did nothing, and the American task force carried out an air raid on Truk on 17 (and 18) February. Consequently, extreme confusion resulted in defense operations while trying to cope with this enemy air raid."*

The chain of command during the time of the attack was as follows:

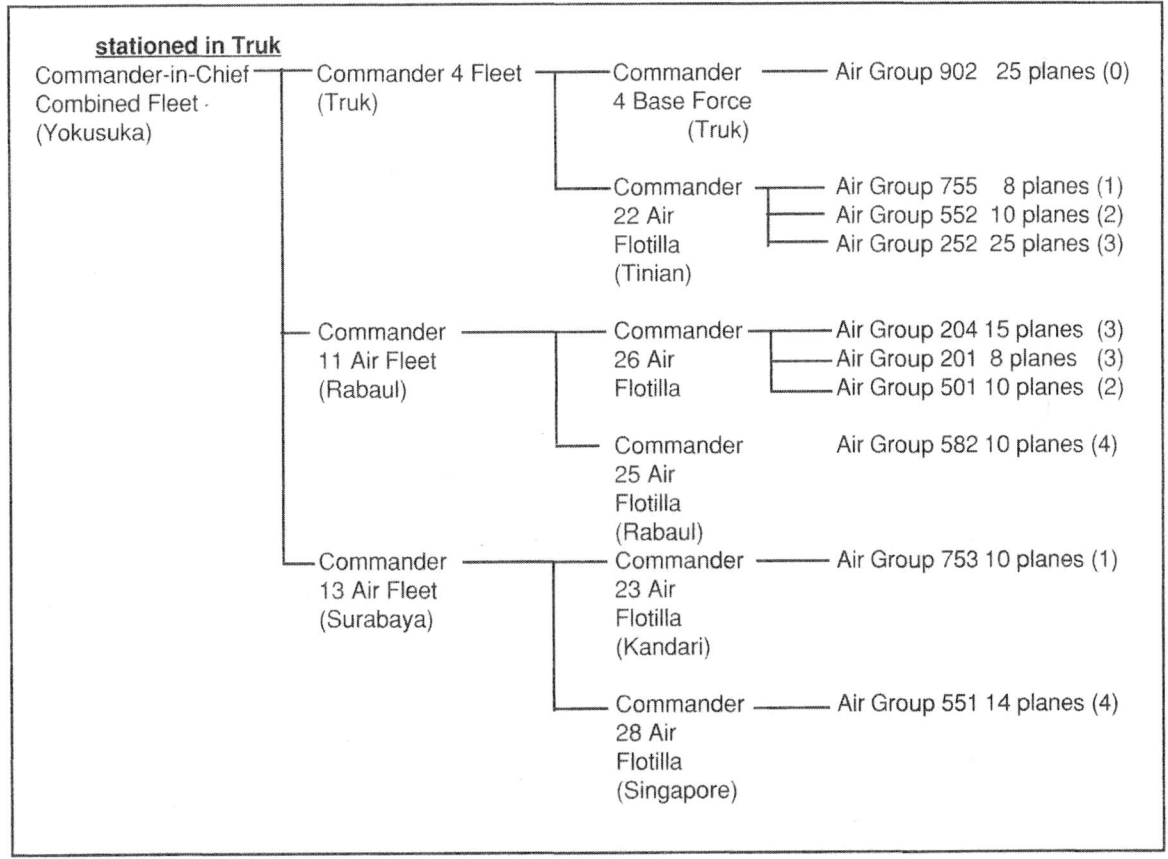

Compare this information with the organisation given in the Chapter The Defenses Of Truk.

(0) seaplanes   (1) land attack planes   (2) carrier bombers   (3) fighters
(4) carrier attack planes

Hailstorm - *Historic Documentation*

The commander of the 26 Air Flotilla had been ordered to engage in training and reorganization of the forces in the Truk area. Only in case of emergency, i.e. during an enemy attack, was he under the command of the Commander, Forth Fleet.

Units of the 13 Air Flotilla had been sent to the Inner South Sea area, following the Gilberts operations. They were placed under the Commander of the Inner South Sea Forces after they arrived in Truk. The commander of the Inner South Sea used the planes under his command in Truk mainly for patrolling and did, as a matter of routine, not get involved in the operations of other attached forces.

The lesson learned from this command structure, in the eyes of the Japanese was: *"In such case as above, when there is a unified force with a complicated chain of command, it is vitally import that the supreme commander in this area distribute (sic) the forces appropriately and expedite (sic) the unity of control of the forces in view of the pressing situation existing. However, it must be noted that no consideration had been given whatsoever in this matter."*

In the morning of 15 February 1944, the routine of sending six land attack planes (Betty bombers) and three carrier attack planes (Zeros, Hamp) on a patrol to the seas east of Truk was maintained. Two Bettys failed to return. Moreover, the 4 Fleet Monitoring Unit reported the interception of a radio voice broadcast emanating from an US carrier (Essex) plane. The interception, probably due to some freak atmospheric conditions, was made in the morning of the 15 February, but it took until 2100 h for the message to reach Admiral Kobayashi. This again points a finger to a grave deficiency in the Japanese communications.

Kobayashi ordered the highest state of alarm for the following day, the 16 February, because correctly he had assumed that an attack was eminent. The alarm began at 0300 h and surveillance was increased.

Air patrols were sent out in the same pattern as the previous day, but two of the Bettys were given the additional task of looking for the missing Bettys and their crews. This may have created a hole in the search pattern, but nevertheless it is incredible that the searches were not carried out more vigorously.

The expected attack did not take place, and by afternoon, Kobayashi rescinded the alarm and allowed military personnel to take leave and to go into town in the afternoon.

The following chronology is revealing:

The US carrier planes attacked at 0455 h and the 7 Tenzan (Jill) planes that had left early for patrols spotted the task force at 0700 h. By that time the attack had already moved into its second phase. Also radar detected approaching US planes *"thirty minutes prior to the raid, but preparations to meet the attack were greatly hampered as many of the air crew had not yet returned to their units."*

However, as the Japanese account will have it, by 0500 h, that is only 5 minutes after the fighters arrived over Truk, according to the Japanese time table, the defenders managed to get 40 fighters airborne, in order to intercept the US fighters. *"Thirty planes were downed, but our losses, too, were heavy. On that day, a total of approximately 450 planes attacked Truk with nine waves between 0455 h and 1700 h. By 1300 h the number of first line planes on our side was reduced to twenty fighter planes and four other planes, a total of 24 planes. By 1800 h the number was further reduced to one fighter plane and five carrier attack planes."*

The Japanese counted between 70 and 80 planes in first class condition out of the 135 available on the island, and stated that the carrier raid continued on the 18 February, *"causing great damages and losses to the ships in Truk harbor and land installations at Truk".*

In summary, the blame for the surprise raid was squarely laid on Vice Admiral Kobayashi's doorstep. It is inconceivable that the high state of alertness was not maintained and air crews were physically away from their planes. The terrain and location of the airfield in Truk does not allow a quick response if the pilots are not on the same island as their planes. Furthermore, it would have been prudent to reinforce the patrols - even without the benefit of hindsight.

The US losses of aircraft were exaggerated.

Hailstorm - *Historic Documentation*

TRUK RECONNAISSANCE

It is commonly believed that the overflight by Marines planes on 04 February 1944 was the first and only reconnaissance flight over Truk. However, the Australians did a yeoman's job of keeping tabs on Truk and even bombing it very early in the war.

However, the tides of war were heavily running in favor of the Japanese at that time. The Australians quickly lost the bases from which they staged their missions, Rabaul and Kavieng. Activities against Truk came to a halt. Only the US submarines played a deadly game with the shipping, as the American intelligence had broken the minor code with which the harbor master of Truk dutifully reported all ship movements to his seniors in Tokyo.

Flight Lt. R. Yeowart casts a tall, slim figure and has a face undescribable British. He wrote an article in the Australian magazine FLYING in May 1944, well after the first, and at the same time of the second, raid on Truk. He was the only survivor of this reconnaissance flight; all others met their death in the fierce fighting in New Britain and New Guinea. None of these men were decorated, but certainly, their accomplishments were outstanding.

It has been widely assumed that the February 1944 overflight of the B-24 reconnaissance was the first one. In fact, it was the third. The first and the second were carried out in January 1942, by Australians with American built planes.

When the Japanese push southward became a definite menace to Australia, the Australian forces took desperate measures to slow the advance. Japanese bombers, reported to be based on Truk, had given Rabaul a repeated work-over. Consequently, the Australians decided to pay the Japanese in Truk a visit. Catalinas were ready for a bombing job, but it was decided to make a reconnaissance flight first to establish what the bombers were up against. Two new Mark IV Hudsons just had arrived from the US. These were the aircraft Yeowart said they were waiting for.

The whole squadron volunteered for the reconnaissance work. The flight crews spent a few days for getting used to the new craft and finally, with R.R. McDonnell as co-pilot, Bill Ellis as radio man and Frank Marriner as tail gunner, the pilot Yeowart and his plane, called Titwillow, set out on the Mikado Run, together with Flight Lt. Greens plane Yum-Yum. They set off for Rabaul, at that time still in Australia's hand, on 06 January 1942. At Rabaul the carburetors in Green's plane cracked. He was left behind, cursing his luck.

The plane piloted by Yeowart proceeded to Kavieng, which was the jumping-off point for the 1220 miles flight. Of course, nobody knew exactly what was going on at Truk, as nobody else than Japanese were allowed to visit the islands of Truk. The Australian suspected that there would be strong resistance and fortifications, despite the fact that the Japanese were not supposed to build the place up for military purposes.

Yeowart got into Kavieng flying at 14000 ft and evading a flight of Japanese bombers hell-bent to Rabaul, which fell to the Japanese on 23 January 1942. At dinner time, Yeowart received orders to carry out the reconnaissance flight on Truk and took off from Kavieng on 09 January 1942 at 0544h.

McDonnell informed that the plane was supposed to be over the target while they were flying at 13000 ft. The time was 1010h. Yeowart let the plane down, went into a heavy squall and when he emerged he was right above Truk Harbor. The crew counted 12 warships of destroyer and cruiser sizes, an aircraft carrier, 3 large cargo ships, a hospital ship and 8 four-engined flying boats at anchor. On the runway of a small island (probably Eten), bombers were packed wing tip to wing tip.

They pulled the plane up and began the photographic run. They were already halfway through when the Japanese began to open fire with their anti-aircraft guns.

From below they saw that fighters were taking off and prepared their defenses. The plane went in for a second run to obtain detailed pictures and not to come back empty handed. The run was very low, and there was plenty of multiple calibre anti aircraft fire.

By this time there were many planes in the air and the Japanese were chasing the plane, which was amply and deftly defended. It was the luck for the Australians that the weather was so squally. The water-based fighter planes closed in from both sides and scored a few hits, none of them bad. The tail controls went out momentarily, but there was no problem to keep the airplane under control. Yeowart was diving through a large electrical storm during his retreat and lost his pursuers. The plane made a landing in Kavieng, with just enough time for a snack and refuelling the plane. From there they went to Townsville, and turned the film over to Intelligence.

The pictures came out perfect and three weeks later a flight of Catalinas dropped the first bombs on Truk.

Truk was one of the least known atolls to the Americans. When the political climate heated up in 1939, considerations were given to reconnoiter some of the Marshalls and Caroline Islands. Nothing of substance was actually done but just about two days before the infamous Pearl Harbor Day, a B 24 Mitchel landed in Hawaii. This was the first of two specially fitted reconnaissance aircraft. It was designed to undertake a mission approved by the War Department on 26 November 1941. One of the special missions

Hailstorm - *Historic Documentation*

was indeed the taking of aerial photographs of Truk. The fate of this particular aircraft is not known, but it was certain that the higher echelons were attaching a great deal of importance to Truk and wanted its picture taken real badly.

The war was not running in the Americans favor, initially, and there were a number of higher

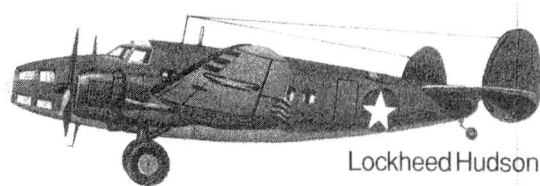
Lockheed Hudson

priorities for other operations, but when the Japanese expansion had ground to a halt it became obvious that Truk was the staging area for supplies into the eastern and south Pacific. Truk supplied Rabaul, and from Rabaul, Japanese reinforcements were thrown against the Americans in Guadalcanal and on their way up the Slot.

Time passed by, and the murderous advances in the Solomons were breaking the strength of the Japanese forces in the air and depleted their shipping. Yet Truk remained an unknown quantity in the equation. What and how strong were the facilities? How could Truk be taken? The amphibious landing was still under consideration.

Seizure of Tarawa, the daring carrier raid into Rabaul and finally the assault of Kwajalein was an indication for the Japanese High Command that their base in Truk was not secure anymore against a concentrated carrier raid. When two PB4Ys, the photo version of the B 24, appeared over the skies of Truk, on 4 Februaryn 1944, and even made it back to their base, it was the writing on the wall. The Japanese Combined Fleet sortied from Truk and never returned.

The two pilots which were commanding the 10-men PB4Ys were Major James R. Christensen and Captain James Q. Yawn. Their mission flushed the Imperial Navy out, but the results of the pictures were interesting.

The two planes departed Sterling Island in the night of 03 February 1944, and flew about 1600 km northwest to Truk. They arrived there in the morning of the next day, at an altitude of 20, 000 ft undetected. There was a partial cloud cover, so not all of the atoll could be photographed. But what could be seen was certainly enough to confirm the fears of the naval planers. The Second Fleet with flagship Musashi could be made out. Although the coverage was incomplete, the evaluators counted at least one carrier, either nine or ten cruisers, about 20 destroyers and 12 submarines. There were also many cargo ships anchored inside the lagoon. Five airfields were counted, one each on Eten, Param and northwest Moen, with seaplane facilities in Moen and Dublon. The waters of Truk were covered with ships.

It must have been an eternity for the crew of these airplanes, but in actuality only about 20 to 30 minutes were spend over the clouds. They came in undetected and made their first runs unmolested. But then suddenly, there were puffs of smoke from a battleship and the shooting began. The planes ducked from cloud to cloud but when they saw fighters taking off, they dived for the clouds in earnest and flew to the Solomons. There were only one or two Zekes and a few float planes which the Japanese managed to scramble. None of them damaged the photo planes, which landed in Piva after a total flight time of 12 hours.

This was certainly a very daring raid. But it alerted the Japanese. The Second Fleet took off shortly thereafter, which units departing the atoll on the 9 and 10 February, while ships from other fleets were spaced out, partly going to Japan and partly to Singapore. Suppliers were to establish a base in Palau. Units of the Fourth Fleet and the Second Submarine Squadron of the Sixth Fleet (submarines) delayed their depar-

Consolidated PB4Y was a modification of the B24 bomber

ture and were promptly caught on their way out during the raid of the 17 and 18 February 1944.

There is little doubt that the arrival overhead of photo planes alerted the Japanese in Truk, and that the combatant ships left the lagoon as a direct consequence. The value of the photo mission is therefore doubtful and difficult to assess. We do not know how much was known about Truk before the overflight. Considering the detailed information passed out for the briefing for the attack raises the question whether all of that had been gleaned from aerial photography. Perhaps there were other sources, such as POWs. At any rate, the information available for the raid of 17/18 February was surprisingly complete. The point is that what might have happened if the Combined Fleet had not pulled out of Truk. Clearly, the US Navy did not run any chances and had taken their main battle line with the fast battleships along, together with the brand new battleships Iowa and New Jersey cum the commander of the Fifth Fleet. But there was no naval engagement, and the commander took a pleasure cruise with their battlewagons around the atoll, sinking a few cripples in the process.

Hailstorm - *Historic Documentation*

THE AMERICAN BATTLE REPORTS

The dates given by the Americans for the first carrier based air raid on Truk, Operation Hailstone, are the 16 and 17 February 1944. The days are Wednesday and Thursday, operationally called "Dog-minus-one-Day" and "Dog-Day", respectively. The dates in the Japanese and local Trukese records are 17 and 18 February 1944. This discrepancy is explained by the fact that the Americans did not change their dates when they crossed the International Dateline. The reason was ease of communication with their headquarters in Hawaii and with the continental US, as this Line was passed often. However, Truk is located well within the Eastern Dating, and therefore, technically, the American dates are not correct. The Japanese dating is accurate, and has been used throughout the text.

All times shown in the original battle and action reports have been adjusted to reflect local Truk time. For operational reasons the Americans evidently did not correct their time pieces to local time. This avoided confusing changes as they passed frequently from one time zone into the next. The "Ship's Time" was consistently 2 hours ahead of the local Truk time. In trying to reconstruct and determine the chain of events during the two days of operation it appeared more logical to use the local time. For example, the planes of the Initial Fighter Sweep over Truk were launched when it was still dark, and the fighters crossed the reef shortly before and during dawn. They were over the target at about sunrise, and not well into the morning, as the Ship's Time would indicate. Sunrise in Truk is about at 0610 h, sunset at 1830 h, preceded, respectively followed, by a short time of twilight. The 24-hour-designation has been used. The Japanese time given in their reports are one hour behind local Truk time. They also have consistently been changed to reflect the local Truk time.

The carriers were operating approximately 100 miles (165 km) northeast of Truk, when the first strike was launched. They stayed in this general area. Whenever planes were launched or recovered the formations pointed their bows into the wind, to northeast. During a lull in flight operations the Task Groups maneuvered independently on fairly short-legged zigzag courses, often with the fleet axis pointing downwind. There were two reasons for this. It prevented the ships to open the distance too far to Truk and was employed as a basic anti-submarine stratagem. During the night zigzagging was continued, but the individual Groups performed a number of radical emergency turns when "bogeys", i.e. Japanese planes approached them. TG 58.1 steamed into the wind when the night fighter was launched and recovered and Enterprise launched the Minimum Altitude Radar Night Attack.

Task Group 58.2 ceased to exist temporarily as an independent formation when the remaining ships were amalgamated with TG 58.1, after the departure of the damaged Intrepid and her escorts.

The times of launching and recovery of the individual strikes has been incorporated in the text, to enable reconstruction of events during the raid. It may be assumed that it took the planes roughly an hour to reach the targets. Consideration must be given that they did not fly at maximum speed, and had to climb with their load. They then rendezvoused at the general area of the North Pass and skirted the outer perimeter of the lagoon before they broke off for their attack. On the way back they rendezvoused over the northern part of the lagoon or outside it, and flew back in individual divisions. The strike planes were airborne for an average of three hours. If another hour is calculated for the flight back to the carrier, preparations to land, the average time over the targets could be taken as about 60 minutes. During this time the planes executed their first run, strafed, climbed back for the second dive and attacked again. On several instances secondary strafing was done as well.

In summary, the naval engagement was minor. The sinking of a few old destroyers, the destruction of the training-cruiser Katori, being a flagship of a submarine flotilla, the breaking up of an old, almost useless cruiser, the Naka, did not materially weaken they fighting ability of the Imperial Japanese Navy. The loss of the Maikaze was more severe. The Japanese stated that the loss of shipping was not serious, because these ships were employed in the service for the Marshalls and Carolines which were already lost. This is a sour-grape statement. There were certainly a number of ships which were extremely useful, modern liner. And to shrug off an instant loss of a quarter million tons shipping space is not the right reaction. With the ships, desparately needed supplies were destroyed. And the American planes and submarines raised havoc with the materiel for the 52nd Division. The destruction of so much shipping space, in form of the Marus, dealt a sharp blow to Japan's ability to supply the Motherland and to bring in reinforcement to the defenders in the Pacific. Also the other parts of the Greater Co-Prosperity Zone, suffered less prosperity and more deprivation. And this was the kind of attrition which had to lead to Japan's downfall - and which had been foreseen by Admiral Yamamoto.

Hailstorm - *Historic Documentation*

ORGANIZATION OF TASK FORCE 58

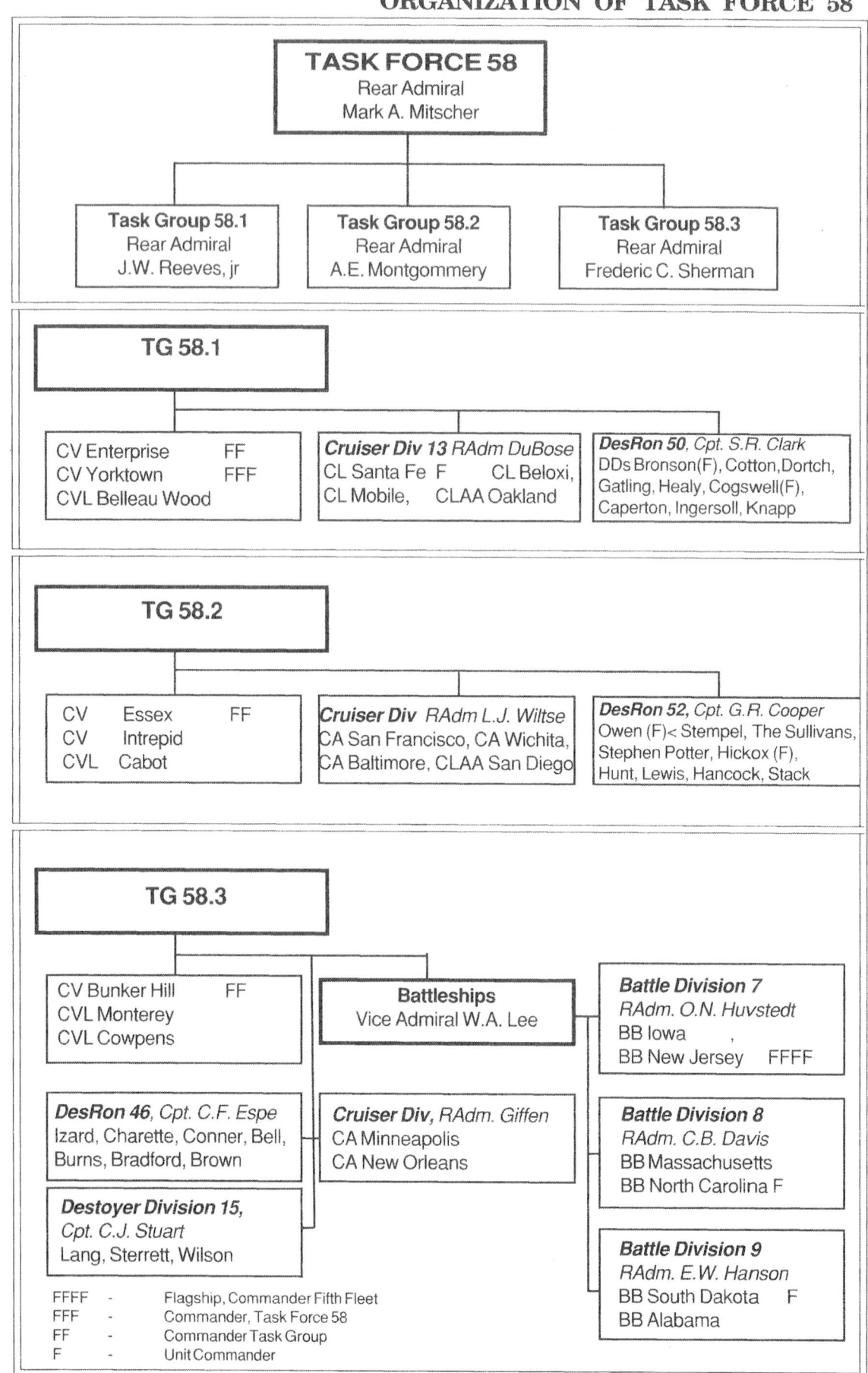

TASK FORCE 58
Rear Admiral Mark A. Mitscher

- **Task Group 58.1** — Rear Admiral J.W. Reeves, jr
- **Task Group 58.2** — Rear Admiral A.E. Montgommery
- **Task Group 58.3** — Rear Admiral Frederic C. Sherman

TG 58.1

CV Enterprise	FF
CV Yorktown	FFF
CVL Belleau Wood	

Cruiser Div 13 RAdm DuBose
CL Santa Fe F, CL Beloxi, CL Mobile, CLAA Oakland

DesRon 50, Cpt. S.R. Clark
DDs Bronson(F), Cotton, Dortch, Gatling, Healy, Cogswell(F), Caperton, Ingersoll, Knapp

TG 58.2

CV	Essex	FF
CV	Intrepid	
CVL	Cabot	

Cruiser Div RAdm L.J. Wiltse
CA San Francisco, CA Wichita, CA Baltimore, CLAA San Diego

DesRon 52, Cpt. G.R. Cooper
Owen (F)< Stempel, The Sullivans, Stephen Potter, Hickox (F), Hunt, Lewis, Hancock, Stack

TG 58.3

CV Bunker Hill	FF
CVL Monterey	
CVL Cowpens	

Battleships
Vice Admiral W.A. Lee

Battle Division 7
RAdm. O.N. Huvstedt
BB Iowa,
BB New Jersey   FFFF

DesRon 46, Cpt. C.F. Espe
Izard, Charette, Conner, Bell, Burns, Bradford, Brown

Cruiser Div, RAdm. Giffen
CA Minneapolis
CA New Orleans

Battle Division 8
RAdm. C.B. Davis
BB Massachusetts
BB North Carolina F

Destoyer Division 15,
Cpt. C.J. Stuart
Lang, Sterrett, Wilson

Battle Division 9
RAdm. E.W. Hanson
BB South Dakota   F
BB Alabama

FFFF - Flagship, Commander Fifth Fleet
FFF - Commander, Task Force 58
FF   - Commander Task Group
F   - Unit Commander

Hailstorm - *Historic Documentation*

TASK FORCE 58

Task Force 58 was part of the forces under the Commander Central Pacific Forces, Vice Admiral (backdated promotion to Admiral) Raymond A. Spruance. He participated in the operation against Truk, flying his flag in the battleship New Jersey.

The Officer in Tactical Command (OTC) of Task Force 58 was Rear Admiral Marc A. Mitscher, in USS Yorktown. The Task Force was subdivided operationally into three Task Groups for the strike on Truk. The fourth group participated in the occupation of Enewitok, at the same time.

Task Group 58.1 was commanded by Rear Admiral J. W. Reeves, Jr. in Enterprise. It consisted of the fast attack carriers Enterprise and Yorktown and the light carrier Belleau Wood. Cruiser Division 13 under Rear Admiral L. T. DuBose, was subordinated to the Group and comprised of the three light cruisers Santa Fe (flagship), Biloxi and Mobile, as well as the new light anti-aircraft cruiser, Oakland. The screen was made up of nine destroyers under Captain S. R. Clark (DesRon 50): C.K. Bronson (flag), Cotton, Dortch, Gatling, Healy, Cogswell (flag), Caperton, Ingersoll and Knapp.

Task Group 58.2, under Rear Admiral A. E. Montgomery in Essex, was made up similarly to the other group. Two fast attack aircraft carriers, Essex and Intrepid, were reinforced with the light carrier Cabot. Three heavy cruisers, San Fransisco, Wichita and Baltimore, and the anti-aircraft cruiser San Diego were commanded by Rear Admiral L. J. Wiltse in San Diego. Captain G.R. Cooper was in charge of 8 destroyers (Des Ron 52, Temporary): Owen (flag), Stempel, The Sullivans, Stephen Potter, Hickox (flag), Hunt, Lewis Hancock and Stack. After withdrawal from the Truk operation and dismissal of Task Unit 58.2.4, Task Group 58.2 reported to Task Group 58.1 at 1301h on 18 February.

Task Group 58.3 was formidable by comparison. Commanded by Rear Admiral Frederic C. Sherman in Bunker Hill, the Group consisted of the following units and subdivisions:

Bunker Hill was the only fast attack carrier, Monterey and Cowpens were light carriers. The battleships were subordinated and under the command of Vice Admiral W. A. Lee, Jr., in North Carolina. Battle Division 7, commanded by Rear Admiral O. N. Hustvedt, consisted of the brand new fast battleships Iowa and New Jersey, the largest the Americans ever built. In case of a naval engagement, Vice Admiral Lee was supposed to pull out of TG 58.3, all battleships, and he would be Officer in Tactical Command of the battle line. Admiral Spruance set his flag on New Jersey, which experienced her very first battle engagement. Battle Division 8, under Rear Admiral C. B. Davis, included Massachusetts and North Carolina. Battle Division 9, Rear Admiral E. W. Hanson in command, contained the battleships South Dakota (flag) and Alabama, and under Rear Admiral Giffen, the heavy cruisers Minneapolis and New Orleans. Captain C. F. Espe with Izard, Charette, Conner, Bell, Burns, Bradford, Brown and Cowell made up Des Ron 46 as screen, together with Destroyer Division 15 under Captain C. J. Stuart with the destroyers Lang, Sterrett and Wilson.

Task Group 50.9 - On 17 February at 1127 h (0927 h, local Truk time) a task group consisting of the battleships New Jersey and Iowa, the heavy cruisers Minneapolis and New Orleans and the destroyers Burns, Bradford, Izard and Charette was detached from Task Group 58.3 under personal command of Vice Admiral Spruance. It proceeded to make a counter-clockwise sweep around the lagoon in order to destroy crippled vessels leaving the lagoon. Rendezvous with Task Group 58.3 was accomplished at 0750 h (0550 h) on the next day.

Task Unit 58.2.4 - After the torpedo hit on the Intrepid, the carrier was withdrawn from the operation. Under the command of Captain H. E. Overesch in San Francisco, the crippled carrier was escorted to Majuro by the light carrier Cabot, the cruisers San Francisco and Wichita and four destroyers. The unit was formed and detached at 0100 h (2300 h) on 18 February (17 February, resp.).

This powerful fleet was assembled to strike a crippling blow to what was thought to be Japan's largest base outside the homeland. It reflects clearly American strategic thinking that Truk as a base had to be neutralized to prevent future intervention to the operations planned in the Central Pacific area, in particular Saipan and Guam. On the tactical level, the air strike against Truk was to prevent interference to the simultaneous operation Catchpole, the occupation of Enewitok. Due to limited intelligence, no chances were taken, should the Imperial Japanese Combined Fleet operate in or around Truk.

An important part of the operation was the execution of air activities. The Commander approved specifically the following Master Air Plan, governing the operations of all carrier groups. This is the central part of the air raid against Truk of 17 and 18 February 1944. Under the heading "hours" the local Truk time is given when the planes were supposed to be over their targets.

OPERATION SCHEDULE

Valid for 17 and 18 February 1944 Sunrise - approx. 0610 h Sunset - approx. 1803 h			
Time at Target	Task Group 58.1 ENTERPRISE YORKTOWN 1 light a/c Belleau Wood	Task Group 58.2 ESSEX INTREPID 1 light a/c Cabot	Task Group 58.3 BUNKER HILL 2 light a/c Cowpens Monterey
hours	Strike	Strike	Strike
0600	Fighter Sweep Low Attack 24 fighters	Fighter Sweep Interm. Attack 10-15 000 ft 24 fighters	Fighter Sweep High Cover 25 000 ft 24 fighters
0615-0630	1 A		
0630-0645		2 A	
0645-0700			3 A
0815-0830	1 B		
0830-0845		2 B	
0845-0900			3 B
1015-1030	1 C		
1030-1045		2 C	
1045-1100			3 C
1215-1230	1 D		
1230-1245		2 D	
1245-1300			3 D
1415-1430	1 E		
1430-1445		2 E	
1445-1500			3 E
1615-1630	1 F		
1630-1645		2 F	
1645-1700			3 F

Hailstorm - *Historic Documentation*

THE BATTLE ORDER

The orders to go into battle are called Operation Plan. Code named "Hailstone", the carrier raid against Truk on 17 and 18 February 1944 was called "Cen 5-44", issued by Vice Admiral Spruance, Commander Central Pacific Forces. They were directed to Task Force 58, Rear Admiral Mitscher. He issued Operation Plan 2-44 to the three Task Groups under his command.

The Operation Plan 2-44 spelled out the disposition of the American forces, the assumptions of what may be expected during approach and attack, the objectives of the strikes and their duration, the chronological sequence, rescue, night fighter and gun fire procedures and a number of other details.

As a general remark, orders must be drawn up to coordinate the forces efficiently to reach the objectives. On the other hand, they have to provide the individual combatants, from commander to gunner, with enough flexibility and initiative to respond to the fast pace of the action.

ASSUMPTIONS

A - Air

During the approach and strikes, the Task Force was within range of land based Japanese planes from Truk, Nomoi, the Marianas and Wake. Sea planes from Truk, Ponape and Wake could sortie the fleet.

The total air strength in Truk, based on the search flight of 4 February 1944, was thought to be 75 fighters, 28 reconnaissance bombers, 12 torpedo bombers, 12 medium bombers, 5 flying boats and 54 float planes: a total of about 186 aircraft. It was well recognized that this number would fluctuate, because Truk was used as an intermediate stop for ferried aircraft being channeled from Japan to the Bismarck area. Opinions were all in agreement, that even more planes would be in Truk at the projected time of the strike. Further reinforcements could be flown in from Japan via Iwo Jima and Tinian.

Tinian and Saipan could be potential sources of air reinforcements. The total of 48 fighters and 45 medium bombers (augmented by an assortment of other planes) were available on these islands. As a matter of fact, the majority of planes participating in the night attack on the carrier force of 17 February were thought to be staged from Saipan, located about 950 km (595 miles) to the northwest of Truk.

Other air fields and sea plane bases were considered too poorly equipped or too heavily involved in fighting to bring any help to Truk.

The discernible pattern of anti-submarine patrols flown by the Japanese was disrupted by the American invasion of Kwajalein. Subsequently, the commander of the Task Force had received no fresh information from his intelligence sources about Japanese scout plane activities. Apparently they were kept up, but the search net was too loosely knit and too large to detect the approach of the American carrier force. The loss of the Betty search plane on 14 February was taken by the Japanese in Truk without any much comment nor subsequent vigorous action to find the reason for its disappearance.

B - Shipping

Photographic interpretation of the pictures brought back by the 4 February overflight, indicated the presence of the battleship Musashi, 2 carriers, 8 heavy cruisers, 4 light cruisers, 20 destroyers and 12 submarines - indeed a large fleet. As always at important bases, a substantial number of oilers, tenders, and transports were at their anchorages in Truk.

It was reasoned that fewer and fewer combat ships would remain in the lagoon as the danger of an American air attack would become obvious, due to their success in the Marshalls. Instead of being moored inside the lagoon, the ships were thought to operate in the seas to the West of Truk. This assumption proved to be partly correct. Admiral Koga actually withdrew the Combined Fleet and their service ships to Singapore and the Philippines, on 10 February. Only units of the Fourth and Sixth Fleet (2 cruisers and 6 or 7 destroyers) were left in or around Truk.

A large number of transports and oilers remained anchored in the lagoon, however. Even the day before the attack, the Aikoku Maru came in from Ponape, roughly on the same course the American ships were sailing, but remained undetected.

C - Defences

The shore based flat trajectory guns were of no interest to the American forces because the ships were not scheduled to go near them. Anti-aircraft guns were thought to be concentrated at Moen, although photo coverage was not complete. There was no anti-aircraft battery reported to be in Dublon, but there were at least two 5 inch twin barreled guns placed on the mountains. In contrast, Param was thought to be well defended.

The information available was very sketchy. It made no references to the sharp shooting gunners at Fefan or any batteries in Uman. Of course, from the great height the observation plane was flying when

Hailstorm - *Historic Documentation*

the pictures were taken, the position of automatic weapons could not be made out. There is a reference in the Operation Plan to the intense ship borne fire at Rabaul at a previous strike, a few months before this operation.

D - Weather

Prevailing North-East Trades and partial cloud cover was expected.

E - General

The North Pass was considered the favorite escape route if any ships would attempt to leave the lagoon. None of the ships using it got very far, except the destroyer Nowake. By contrast, Akitsushima and Akashi went out of the South Pass almost umolested.

OBJECTIVES

Local air superiority had to be achieved fast. This lesson could be recited by every air cadet after his first lesson in Tactics. Consequently, the air activity on both days of the raid were devoted to shooting down the planes opposing the attack, and to prevent others from being scrambled. The main objectives were strikes against Japanese shipping and aircraft installations at and around Truk. Ships outside the lagoon were to be immobilized by aircraft, and, if necessary, destroyed by surface action. The three Task Groups were ordered to supply their own Combat Air Patrol and Anti Submarine Patrol.

The primary objective of the initial fighter sweep was to attain control of the air. The prime targets were therefore planes airborne and on the ground.

Primary targets for the combined strikes of fighters, torpedo bombers, and light bombers were ships in the following order of priority:

- combat carriers, battleships, cruisers and submarines,
- fleet oilers, transports, auxiliary ships and destroyers.

There were no carriers, battleships and probably no submarines in Truk during the attack, so the emphasis shifted to the two cruisers, the merchant vessels and the few destroyers. Secondary targets were aircraft and fleet service facilities.

Admiral Mitscher stressed that air searches, observation and scouting had to be conducted at his direction. Battleships and cruisers were to have float planes in readiness to pick up downed aviators.

ASSIGNMENTS

The assignments were laid down in broad terms. Excessive duplication of attacks should be avoided and target assignments shifted to accommodate changing conditions during the battle.

The Task groups were assigned:

58.1 - Combined Fleet Anchorage,
58.2 - South of Eten and Sixth Fleet Anchorage,
58.3 - Fourth Fleet Anchorage.

As the strikes unfolded, it could be noted that these assignments were frequently shifted around.

The first strike of each day called for the bombers to be loaded with fragmentation clusters and incendiary bombs, to be dropped on the airfields according to the following assignments: 58.1 - Eten airfield, 58.2 - Dublon sea plane base, and 58.3 - Moen bomber strip and sea plane base.

For the last strike of the first day, the planes were to be armed with bombs with delay fuses, activated between 1 and 12 hours, to be dropped on the airfields. The fuses were set to go off at irregular intervals to prevent aircraft from getting off the ground at night, and to hinder repair work. The assignments were thus: 58.1 - Moen Island bomber strip, 58.2 - Param, and 58.3 - Eten airport.

The last strike on the second day was supposed to be an attack on ground facilities, particularly fuel depots and buildings: 58.1 - East Dublon, 58.2 - West Dublon, 58.3 - Eten Island.

For the first two days after the departure from Majuro, all groups were to launch a 4 - fighter Combat Air Patrol. The launch was to begin 30 minutes before local sunrise. The time of each individual patrol was one fourth of the total time, so that every patrol shouldered the same burden. The last patrol was to be recovered by the carrier at dusk. The patrols were to be relieved at station with a 15 minute overlap. Additionally, 4 planes were to be ready for launch with warmed up engine, spotted for take-off, and pilots in the ready room. From 14 to 18 February, the Combat Air Patrol was to be increased to 8 fighters in the air and 8 fighters in readiness.

The same procedure was to be applied for the Anti-Submarine Patrols. However, the decision of composition and how many of which type of planes to be used, was left to the discretion of the three individual Task Group Commanders.

Submarine sanctuaries were established for the American submarines detailed to rescue downed plane crews.

GENERAL

The Task Groups had to endeavor to remain tactically concentrated to permit visual communication with the Officer in Tactical Command. The OTC, as he was called for short, was Vice Admiral Spruance, until he ordered Task Group 50.9 formed, and delegated the OTC function to the Commander of Task Force 58, Rear Admiral Mitscher. The endeavor to remain concentrated required judgement on the part of the individual Task Force commanders, because they also had to consider necessary mutual support and room to maneuver their ships when under attack.

It was left to the discretion of the Task Group commanders to use bombs and/or torpedoes for the attack on shipping. In fact, the torpedoes were considered somewhat ineffective because of the many shallow spots inside the lagoon. During an attack on Japanese shipping in Rabaul a few months earlier, torpedoes dropped by the Avengers proved to be a great disappointment. Apparently, the depth setting of the torpedoes was too low and the majority of the weapons passed underneath the ships without doing harm. Furthermore, the pilots were used to dropping bombs on land targets. They had not polished up, or did not feel too comfortable, with torpedoes - or if the plane crew did, their commanders had only a limited confidence in this weapon. It was, according to the records, only Bunker Hill, Monterey and Cowpens, i.e. the carriers of TG 58.3, whose planes were using torpedoes inside the lagoon. Other carriers did load torpedoes into the Avengers, but dropped them only on ships outside the atoll. Nevertheless, it was the bold decision by Torpedo Squadron 17 on Bunker Hill, which scored the most ships sunk.

As moonlight was expected after midnight, a night torpedo attack was considered a great danger. Should the carrier have to defend itself, the 5 inch anti aircraft guns were to be employed at ranges above 4000 yards - or meters, on high trajectory. On low flying planes these guns were not to be used, except by permission of the Task Group commander. If planes penetrated the protective screen, automatic weapons should be fired. The best defence against night torpedo attacks was still thought to be radical turns of the ship formations.

Another option left for the Task Group commanders was whether and when to launch night fighters. Obviously, the formation had to turn into the wind for launch and recovery, putting restraint on their use. A special order concerning gun fire was to be issued when a night fighter was in the air. This order followed established doctrines and was issued by the Groups.

In order to avoid the ever present menace of a surface attack, the Task Group commanders were advised to station radar pickets and to report their station. They were charged with the responsibility of employing defensive measures and to immediately report contacts.

Finally, the commanders had to make provisions for the escort, protection and withdrawal of damaged ships.

THE OPERATION PLAN - TASK GROUP 58.3

The Operation Plan of this Task Group was an expanded version of the orders received from the Commander Task Force 58, tailored to the specific needs of this large group of ships. Of course, it repeats basic operational objectives of the original plan, and adds instructions for the individual Task Units of the groups. It is a fascinating glimpse behind the planning of the operation.

The other two Groups issued similar orders. The Operation Plan 2-44 of Task Group 58.3 was chosen to represent the other plans because it is more detailed. It includes orders for the surface combatant ships. Also, Bunker Hill, the flagship, was certainly the most successful individual carrier, and the leadership of this Group was masterly executed. This remark should not distract in any way from the able handling by the commanders of the other Groups.

Rear Admiral Frederick C. Sherman used his option more widely to load the Avenger torpedo bombers with torpedoes and his planes chalked up more ships sunk than any one of the other carriers. There was a certain reluctance to attack with torpedoes but the results of this carrier raid confirmed the rule, that bombs essentially cripple ships, but torpedo hits were killing.

I - TASK ORGANIZATION

Task Group 58.3:

Carriers   Task Unit 58.3.5 (under direct command)

CV Bunker Hill	(FF)	Air Group 17
CVL Cowpens		Air Group 25
CVL Monterey		Air Group 30

Battleships   Task Unit 58.3.1
Rear Admiral Lee

Battle Division 7
Rear Admiral Hustvedt

* BB Iowa	(F)
* BB New Jersey	(FFF)

Battle Division 8 (temp.)
Rear Admiral Davis

BB Massachusetts	(F)
BB North Carolina	(FF)

Battle Division 9
N.N.

BB South Dakota	(F)
BB Alabama	

Cruisers   Task Unit 58.3.2
Rear Admiral Giffen

* CA Minneapolis
* CA New Orleans

Screen (Destroyers)   Task Unit 58.3.4
Captain Espe

* DD Izard	(F) Des.Ron. 46
* DD Charette	
Conner	
Bell	
* DD Bradford	Com.Des.Div. 92
* DD Burns	
DD Brown	
DD Cowell	
DD Lang	Des.Div. 15
DD Sterett	(F)
DD Wilson	

Note:
(F)   denotes flagship Unit Commander,
(FF)   flagship, Commander Task Group,
(FFF) flagship, Commander Task Force
(FFFF) flagship, Commander Fifth Fleet

---

*   Ship was detached from 58.3, formed TG 50.9 and taken around Truk Lagoon in search for a naval surface engagement.

The main objective of Task Group 58.3 is to destroy enemy shipping, aircraft and aircraft installations at Truk and in the adjacent seas. It will be accomplished by air strikes and, if desired, by the Officer in Tactical Command, by surface action. The operation is in support of the seizure and occupation of Eniwetok and to advance future offensive operations against Japanese forces. Vice Admiral Spruance elected to take over command of the surface group (TG 50.9).

The carriers will conduct air strikes, combat air patrols, anti-submarine patrols and photographic flights. The planes of the carriers will conduct air patrols prior and subsequent of the strikes, as directed by Commander Task Group 58.3. Air searches will be prepared, aerial observation provided and reconnaissance flown as ordered. Ponape is designated as future target, depending on the direction of the commander. Bunker Hill will take over fighter director control of Task Group 58.1 and 58.2 when directed by Admiral Mitscher, as well as to be ready to launch night fighters.

The battleships are to defend the carriers day and night against air and surface attacks. From dawn onwards they will maintain two seaplanes during daylight for rescue of downed carrier aviators. When weather conditions will make seaplane operations unsafe, they will inform the commander, who will be informed conversely when operations can be resumed. The planes from the heavy cruisers will be included in the operation.

The cruisers will primarily defend carriers against day and night attack from the air and the surface. Rescue services are scheduled in conjunction with the battleships.

Destroyers will screen the heavy ships against submarines and all other attacks. They are to maintain readiness to provide rescue service for downed aviators and to direct Combat Air Patrols. They are to provide the visual link between the Officer in Tactical Command in New Jersey, when ordered. They must be prepared to tow or to be towed on minimum notice. If being towed, the gear is to be rigged so that it can be cast off immediately in case of an air attack, and recovered and re-rigged afterwards. Screening destroyers will be assigned to the towing group as necessary. Damaged vessels will proceed to Eniwetok, unless otherwise directed.

All ships will conform to the movement of the senior carrier. The major ship axis will be turned into the wind. During continuing air operations, 4 destroyers will stand up-wind and maintain those stations until flight operations are over for the day. One destroyer will be positioned downwind and act as plane guard. All other destroyers will maintain their screening positions.

II - AIR PLAN

Striking groups must adhere as closely as possible to the Master Air Plan in order to reduce interference between groups and to keep the raid rolling. No time should be wasted by the planes when returning to the carrier after the attack. As the schedule is crowded, the planes should go at a few extra knots after rendezvous if they have enough gas.

General rendezvous areas have been assigned as follows:

58.1 - 15 miles North of North Pass
58.2 - 15 miles Northeast of North Pass
58.3 - 15 miles East of North Pass.

If the Japanese were to get on to this system, the areas may be shifted as desired.

The primary objective of the initial air strike is to gain control of the air by destruction of Japanese aircraft. The primary target for the combined strikes is enemy shipping in the order of priority:
Combat carriers, battleships, cruisers, submarines, oilers, other auxiliaries and destroyers.

Secondary targets are aircraft installations and fleet servicing facilities. Eten Island is assigned to Task Group 58.3 in case primary targets are destroyed or if the shift to secondary targets becomes desirable.

Photographic reconnaissance is especially valuable. On the first day of the attack, Cowpens will endeavor to take photographs of Udot and Ulalu Islands. Bunker Hill will endeavor to take pictures of Tol and Fala-Beguets and the atoll fringe. Carrier planes should obtain photographs of the results of the strikes as far as it is practicable and without detriment to the major mission to destroy enemy aircraft and shipping, without appreciably increasing the hazard to the planes.

Sufficient belly tanks to supply fighters with additional fuel are not available for all flights. The first fighter sweep and Strike 3 A should have belly tanks only. After this, except for the last strike on the second day, they should not be required.

Strict radio discipline must be maintained. Hundreds of friendly planes using the same frequencies are in the area. Flight leaders are responsible that this is carried out.

The Target Observer is charged with the responsibility of keeping the commanders constantly advised as to the situation at the target. He shall also give the Flight Leader of an incoming flight, information regarding valuable targets, as he may have available.

Planes kept on the hangar deck which will not be launched until sunrise the next day must be degassed. This must be completed prior to sunset. It is expected, that the initial launching will take place 100 miles (160 km) from the target.

Torpedoes are to be set at 6 ft (1.8 m) running depth.

III - NIGHT FIGHTER AND GUN FIRE DOCTRINE

If a night air attack is imminent or probable, night fighters (F6F-3N) may be launched on orders of the commander. All ships will be informed. No more than two night fighters will be in the air at any one time. They will be controlled by the fighter director of Bunker Hill or another designated ship. At all times the fighters will be kept sufficiently separated so that contact between them is impossible, unless they are ordered to return to the carrier. The fighter controller must keep them clear of the other Task Groups.

When night fighters are launched after dark the order "Hold Fire" will be given over radio. No ship will open fire when this order is given, except when the order is revoked by "Batteries Released" in case of a positively identified Japanese aircraft. The last order will indicate that the fighters are clear of the firing range.

The fighter director will keep the planes outside of a circle 12 miles in radius from the controlling ship. At no time will the night fighters come inside this circle, unless Commander Task Group 58.3 specifically allows it. When the planes are ordered within the 12 miles radius, the orders to hold fire will be given over radio. Correspondingly, the orders to release batteries will be given once they are out of the radius. All night fighters will have IFF (Identification Friend/Foe) turned on. In case radio communication with the fighters fails and it becomes necessary to return to the carrier or close the formation for any other reason, the night fighter will fire the standard two star recognition cartridge to indicate his friendly status. All gun crews should be able to recognize and identify this signal.

IV TARGET INFORMATION.

General - Location

Eten Island is located at
Latitude : 07 degrees, 21 minutes, 25 second North,
Longitude : 151 degrees, 53 minutes, 20 second East.

Importance

The major Japanese base of Truk provides the only fleet anchorage in the Mandated Islands, which is both unlimited and well protected. Occupying a central and strategic position in the Carolines, and situated midway between Saipan and Rabaul, Truk has served as an advanced base in support of most major Japanese naval operation to date. It has also assumed an important role in the Japanese land based air force system, serving as staging and reserve base for army fighters and bombers.

There are at least two known major air fields and two or more supplementary air fields. Recently, Truk has been developed as a supply center. Fuel oil storage capacities have been increased, while food stores are being maintained not only for the Mandated Islands but also, to a certain extent, for the Rabaul area. Truk is the naval and defence headquarter of the Carolines area.

As a naval base, Truk has excellent natural defences and is strongly fortified; it is not, however, believed to be well adapted for the repair or maintenance of large vessels. Terminal facilities are of minor scale. No wharfs at which a ship larger than a destroyer can tie up have been reported.

Distances (in miles)

Nomoi	175	Kwajalein	955
Ponape	370	Port Moresby	1050
Guam	565	Henderson Field	1120
Saipan	590	Tarawa	1305
Rabaul	695	Espiritu Santo	1650
Nauru	1005	Fanafuti	1875
Palau	1035	Midway	2170
Wake	1095	Nandi (Viti L)	2180
Yokohama	1835	Pearl Harbor	3075

Physical Geography

Truk Atoll consists of a group of about 84 coral and basaltic islands. A barrier reef, roughly circular in shape, encloses the larger islands in a lagoon about 30 miles in diameter. Six major islands lie within the lagoon. Dublon is the center of the Japanese settlement, Tol, Moen, Fefan, Udot, and Uman. Tol, the largest island is about five miles in diameter. Uman, the smallest, is only two miles in length. These islands have, in general, conspicuous summits and are covered with tropical trees. Mount Tolomen, near the southwest shore of Dublon, which is near the east side of the atoll, is 1168 ft high. Moen is always sighted first by ships entering the North Pass. Its highest point is Mt. Teroken, 1233 ft high.

There are almost 50 small islands and islets on the surrounding reef, but they are so small and widely separated that the reef is almost devoid of a proper land rim. Within the lagoon there are about 14 volcanic, basaltic and 25 small coral islands.

Kuop Atoll lies across the one and a half mile wide channel opposite the southeast corner of Truk, where Otta Pass, formerly the main southern entrance into Truk Lagoon- but now probably seldom used- is situated. Four other main entrances into the lagoon, all navigable by vessels of the largest size, are North Pass, Northeast Pass (now probably heavily mined), Piaanu Pass on the West, and South Pass, the main southern entrance. The Kuop Atoll consists of four low islets of coral sand, covered with coconut palms. This atoll is eleven miles long and three miles wide.

It is reported that Truk is incorrectly charted, being five to ten miles too far East by North.

Weather

The Northeast Trade prevails throughout the greater part of the year. According to observations made in December 1942, the Northeast Trade was prominent during clear weather, while the overcast days were calm. There were, however, a few days when the wind came from the South. As a general rule, it fell off during the night, but started up early in the morning. The wind rarely exceeded force four. In early March 1943 the seas were frequently calm. Cloud cover is estimated to be about four-tenths on the average, but should be expected at any time of the day. In December 1942, only 25% of the days were overcast, but the visibility was excellent. The average annual rainfall in Truk is about 120 inches (3050 mm), which is less than for other Pacific islands. Rainfall does not vary very much between Winter and Summer, although there is more rain in the Summer. December to March is generally the dry season.

Airfields

According to the latest information, there are four, possibly five airfields in Truk. Of these two are major fields: one on Eten and the other on Moen. Another fighter strip may be located in the north-central part of Dublon. There is a field on Param, and a second field on the southeast part of Moen.

The best known airfield is on Eten. It measures about 4100 ft by 570 ft (about 1250 m by 175 m), and it is large enough to accommodate bombers. It extends the entire length of the island on the northwest side facing Doublon. A substantial landfill extended it northeastward. At its southwestern side, the runway curves around southward into the hillside, where two hangars are believed to be located. Numerous planes have been seen at this end. A taxiway runs along the south side of the island, connecting both ends of the field. Construction of these facilities appears to have been a major undertaking as the island is formed mainly by a hill rising to a height of about 197 ft (60 m). Levelling operations were began in 1936, but the field has only recently been brought up to its present state of completion. Underground stores and fuel tanks, in addition to the underground hangars, are reported to have been constructed in the hillside. Homing beacons are present. There are buildings at the northeast corner of the field.

Two airfields are located on Moen. One is on the northwest section, the other on the southeast. Army aircraft repair facilities have been installed at the former, although they are probably only capable of handling minor repairs.

There is a new field on Param, still under construction on 4 February 1944, which has, nonetheless, a serviceable runway of 4300 by 365 ft (about 1300 m by 110 m).

There are reports, dubious at best, about two airfields on Dublon. The most definite indication is a fighter strip situated in the north-central part of the island. This information could not be verified by the photographic reconnaissance of 4 February.

An airfield on Tol has been reported on the isthmus separating Lenotol Bay and Tol Harbor, but its existence is also not confirmed.

Air Activity

Land and seaplanes of all types have been observed at Truk. There are large and important air transport, plane ferrying, assembly, repair and air depot facilities. Since December 1942, the Japanese Army Air Force has made increasing use of Truk as a staging and reserve base for fighters and bombers enroute to Rabaul and New Guinea.

Routine patrols, particularly for submarines, are run from Truk. Single engined float planes appear to be most used for this purpose. Flying boats have been reported as well. A large number of aircraft, particularly seaplanes and carrier planes must be expected to be based at Truk during normal operations.

Truk, as an aircraft reserve base, appears to serve primarily short range planes, such as fighters, seaplanes and carrier-type dive and torpedo bombers. Reserves of medium bombers appear to be based in the Empire with some advance training facilities at Saipan and Tinian.

Seaplane Base

Almost unlimited room for seaplane anchorage is found throughout the lagoon, although the waters often become choppy. Two seaplane bases exist at Dublon, one at the southwest corner and another just west of Dublon Town. Four-engined flying boats have been noted between these jetties. There may be slipway facilities. A ramp, a concrete apron and two or three large hangars have been observed at the seaplane base west of Dublon Town. They have been used by commercial seaplanes before the war. On the overflight on 4 February, at least 55 planes have been observed, most of them probably fighters and 3 Marvis.

Seaplane facilities also exist on Moen. A base is

Hailstorm - *Historic Documentation*

located at the southern tip. Another seaplane anchorage is reported inside the reef, opposite Ollan Island, which is south of Tol.

Anchorage and Naval Base

The well-sheltered, virtually unlimited and excellent defended anchorage space of Truk is continually used by Japanese capital ships as well as merchant vessels and auxiliaries. Aircraft carriers make frequent use of this base, because they can use the local facilities. Cruiser, destroyer and submarine divisions are based in Truk.

The entire lagoon has an area of about 500 square miles (almost 1300 square kilometers) and forms an unlimited anchorage, although there are many reefs, shallows and concealed coral heads. While the surf on the outside of the barrier reef is generally very heavy, the water inside is comparatively smooth, with only a few white caps showing.

This barrier reef provides almost perfect protection against approaches by sea. The four main passages into the lagoon are dominated by fortified heights and are probably mined. Most of the anchorages are at a considerable distance from the fringing reef. Eten anchorage (south of Dublon and east of Eten) is about 6 miles (10 km), Moen and Dublon anchorages are about 10 miles (16 km) west, and the east Moen anchorage is about 5 miles (8 km) from the reef, being protected by the heights of the islands. There are also minor anchorages east of Udot, west of Tsis and at Tol.

The use of the anchorages in Truk has assumed a roughly discernible wartime pattern. Eten is primarily serving merchant vessels, but carriers, cruisers and destroyers have been seen here as well. An anchorage or berthing for submarines is reported north of Eten, while submarine tenders anchor south of this island. Destroyers anchor between Eten and Fefan. A new dry dock for destroyers has been seen recently on the northeast shore of Fefan.

Japanese capital ships, cruisers, destroyers and submarines anchor regularly in the well protected area west of Moen and Dublon, north of Fefan. Battleships and large carriers have been reported in the vicinity of the floating dry dock west of Dublon. Several carriers have anchored west of Moen, battleships have used the waters just south of Moen on occasion.

Wharfs

There is no definite information available that large docks exist in Truk. As has been previously said, there are only two wharfs to which ships up to 2000 ts may tie up. Major unloading facilities are apparently not present. No large cranes have been reported and a reliable report from 1943 indicated that it was not possible to unload objects heavier than 10 ts. However, more recently a crane of about 30 ts weight lifting capacity has been installed. This apparent lack of terminal facilities may be in part due to the fact that reefs surround the individual islands. Shore based facilities exist as follows:

Dublon

At the northwest corner is a 160 ft (50 m) long jetty, and about 1000 yards south is an equally long jetty. Immediately adjoining these jetties is an artificial basin. About 650 yards south a 300 ft (100 m) long jetty is located with terminates in a small square extension. A submarine base may be located just south of it. The floating dry dock already referred to has been observed about 400 yard off the west shore on a line just south of Mt. Tolomen. At the southwest corner, at the suspected seaplane base there are two jetties, one about 300 ft (90 m) and the other 550 ft (165 m) long. Two piers have been reported west of the inlet at Dublon Town. These are equipped with narrow gauge tracks. A long pier, about 600 ft (180 m) long with a square extension at the seaside may be capable of accommodating larger ships of up to 2000 ts. Three small piers, close together and uniform in size have been noted on the east side of the inlet.

Fefan

There is a jetty with a wharf extension on the northeast shore facing the southwest corner of Dublon. Another jetty is located about midpoint of the west shore with several buildings at the shore end. A new wharf has been reported to be under construction at the northwest corner of Fefan.

Tol

A 800 ft (240 m) jetty is located at the south side of the entrance of Tol harbor. This jetty carries a pipeline leading back to a large building 200 yards inshore. This is probably an oil dock. A small jetty with a rectangular slipway extension seems to be located at Illick harbor. A third one was seen with buildings nearby at the head of the bight north of Tol harbor.

Moen

There are three jetties to be seen at the west shore of Moen, which may be serving the seaplane base.

Communications
Radio

At least 5 radio stations are believed to be located in Truk. A major link in the Japanese network is on the south side of Dublon, just above the Town. The two 275 ft (85 m) high towers are said to be clearly visible from the town. The station has been operated on 72, 123, 438, 500 7300 and 14320 kHz. Its call letters were JRT. Power is received from generators which are positioned 50 yards away from the station. Another important radio station is suspected to be on the west side of the hill on the northeast peninsular of the island. In Dublon, it was reported, is another major station located at the southwestern part of the island, consisting of a number of radio masts in a compound together with a large building. A radio station is reported in the central area of Moen, possibly located at the western slope of an 880 ft (260 m) hill, about a mile east of Mt. Teroken. On Tol is a radio station at least capable for inter-island transmissions.

There is a telephone system in Dublon. Cable

communications to the other island of the atoll are existing. Skirting the road on the south shore of Dublon a submarine cable is installed extending the full length of the shoreline, but its entry and exit points could not be established. Telegraph station and a post office augment the communication facilities. Telegrams have been reported to be radioed to Yap.

Radar

Reports indicate that there are as many as 7 radar stations operable in Truk. Observations show that these are located in Uman, Fefan, Moen, Tol and Pis - at the northern part of the barrier reef - with possibly ones on Ollan and Dublon.

In view of the general disposition of the terrain, these radar stations are probably located as follows: Two installations on Uman are on the south slope of Mt. Uroras, searching mainly the southern area. On the west slope of a hill on Polle, the southwestern part of the peninsular of Tol, two radar sets are placed to cover the western approaches. Two more installations are on the slopes of a mountain near the east central part of Moen island. On the northwest slope of Mt. Iron, located at the northwest section of Fefan island, is a single radar installation which searches an area north-northwest. This station in conjunction with the other sets covers the complete circle.

Roads

Communication between the north and south side of Dublon is over a hard-surfaced three-lane highway. This highway goes past the headquarters and the officers' recreation center. Several roads on Dublon are suitable for movement of artillery units. One of the roads leads from the town to an abandoned signal station near the summit of Mt. Tolomen.

V DEFENSES

It has been reported that the atoll is fortified with guns from 6 to 16 inch calibre, although the existence of guns above 7.9 inch is not verified. There are guns on the heights of Moen, which control the North and Northeast Pass, while guns on Uman, Tol and Ulalu dominate the other passes.

In view of the fact that Truk is used as an advance fleet and air base, heavy anti-aircraft gun concentrations may be expected. The airfields are probably fortified with light, medium and heavy anti-aircraft guns. Six heavy and four light of these weapons are known to be located, at the Param airfield. There are two possible guns on Tol.

The following list summarizes the fragmentary information available on gun positions:

Dublon
Possibly 5 inch guns on the south coast of the island, west of the harbor at the area of the seaplane base. Heavy guns are reported but not located.

Udot
Three heavy guns are reported but their location is uncertain. An unconfirmed report indicated a 6 inch gun on the south-central shore line.

Ulalu
Unconfirmed report of a 16 inch gun.

Eten
Two anti-aircraft guns on the hill south-east of the air field, possibly of 4.7 inch calibre.

Tol
Three, probably 6 inch guns, are located on a hill about half a mile east of the southwest corner of the island. There are buildings nearby. An unconfirmed report speaks about a 16 inch gun east of Mt. Tumuital. A 6 inch gun is reported to be situated on the west side of the North Point.

Moen
A report of a 16 inch gun on the north side of Mt. Teroken is unconfirmed. Two 6 inch guns are reported to be at the southeast shore. Five inch anti-aircraft guns are near the west central shore line. Other anti-aircraft guns are reported, but they are not located.

Uman
Two or three 6 inch guns are said to be on the southeast side of the island. Other heavy guns, among them 7.9 inch artillery are reported, but they are also not located.

Fefan
Possibly two 6 inch guns are situated near the northeast tip of this island. Anti-aircraft guns are located at the north end.

Other Islands
A 6 inch gun installation exists just north of the Northeast Pass on Mor. A clearing has been observed here. Gun positions exist also on Northeast Island, 5 miles north of Mor, and on Polle, Salat, Otta and Faleu.

Naval Defences

Both air and surface patrol craft operate continually in the Truk area. Patrol cutter, and small boats of the trawler type have been frequently observed around Truk. A new type of patrol craft has been seen often. Small patrol craft have been seen as far as 60 miles out, while a report dating from 1943 relates that anti-submarine patrols have been run as far as 160 miles out of Truk. Patrol vessels have not been reported to use echo ranging, but the use of surface detection radar has been noted. Destroyers have been reported, but in most cases they were engaged in escort duties. Active anti-submarine aerial patrols were maintained in moonlit nights.

Hailstorm - *Historic Documentation*

Aircraft do patrol the Truk area, and their activity has become increasingly intensive. Small fleet-type observation planes have been seen. One particular plane was reported to have dropped depth charges about 200 miles from Truk. Navy flying boats and large bombers have been reported, but it was not evident that they were on patrol duty. According to a report submitted in March 1943, plane coverage of the area around Truk is sufficiently thorough to make undetected surface action by submarines difficult.

There are at least 11 search lights which have been observed to sweep the horizon at dusk or dawn. They are located on Moen, Eten, Dublon and Tol. Other searchlight are located at the gun positions.

Underwater sound detecting devices have been established to cover the approaches of the North and South Pass. These detectors are believed to take the form of so-called underwater sound loops. Searchlights are accurately guided on the bearings of submarines in these areas.

The purpose of lighted and marked buoys noted southwest of Truk is not certain, but the possibility exists that they support indicator nets or small mines set at depth to catch submarines. Torpedo nets were observed only around battleships in October 1942. On 4 February nets were reported in the lagoon, but none of the warships actually had nets around them. Net protection may be anticipated as a possibility for battleships, carriers and cruisers.

Mines

There are unconfirmed reports that all passes in the reef are mined, and some are probably closed to shipping. Few, if any, ships have used Northeast Pass during the war, nor have patrol craft been active there.

Ships leaving through the North Pass have been reported to steer northeast for a short distance before cutting back on a north or northwest course. This practice suggests that a minefield extends for some distance outside this pass. According to one report, a sweeping formation preceded a sortie of combatant ships destined for Guadalcanal. Minefields are believed to exist inside the lagoon, as ships have been seen to steer zig-zag courses. Mines and cables are available in Truk.

Air and Naval Strength

The Operation plan quotes the paragraphs from the Battle Order.

VI SUPPLIES AND STORES

Until recently, Truk was not a major supply base, but current reports indicate that the facilities are rapidly developed. Fuel storage for about 60 000 tons are planned for Truk and Saipan. The main oil storage of Truk is located on the eastern shore of Tol. Large quantities of food, including refrigerated provisions are stored on Dublon.

At the south side of the entrance to Tol Harbor, the 800 ft jetty carrying a pipeline, probably serves the main oil storage and indicates a vital target, possibly a fuel reservoir. Extensive camouflage of all buildings in this vicinity reinforces this impression.

Four large oil tanks have been noted in a cut on the hillside above and to the west of the seaplane hangars near Dublon Town. These tanks are estimated to be 30 ft in diameter and 10 ft high. A pumping station is possibly located below the tanks. Earlier reports have already referred to the existence of a rock walled underground storage chamber about 100 ft square, which may be used either for fuel or ammunition.

Underground aviation fuel and supply stores are said to be concealed in the hillside south of the airfield on Eten, in connection with the hangars at that location.

Munitions, rations and clothing storehouses, together with a large lumber yard have been reported on the west side of the inlet near Dublon Town. There may be an ammunition dump near the southeastern shore of Moen.

BATTLE REPORT TG 58.1

The Task Group departed Majuro at 0500 h on 13 February 1944, proceeding towards Truk. Two days later, during refuelling operations on the 15 February 1944 at 1304 h, when Belleau Wood, the light carrier, was flying Air Combat Patrol over the formation, radar picked up an aircraft. The patrol was vectored to intercept. A single Betty Bomber approached the ships from due west at a distance of 40 miles. The Hellcats had an easy task and surprised the Betty, which was shot down so fast that the crew could not even transmit a radio message, and before they had a chance to sight the carrier formation.

There is no doubt that this was the plane reported missing by the Japanese officers when they were interrogated after the war. A flight of four Bettys was launched, but one of them failed to return. This baffled the Japanese. Shortly thereafter, the formation was approached by an American search plane, which reported its finding. Whether the Japanese assumed that the Betty was shot down by this plane, as they possibly intercepted the radio transmission, or thought that the Betty was downed by a mechanical malfunction, is not clear. They did not follow up vigorously on the search, although an attempt seemed to have made during the afternoon of that day to locate the missing plane with a scout aircraft. At any rate, the Task Group continued their approach undetected.

The first day's operation began with a fighter sweep. As was standard practice during the time of the attack on Truk, only the large carriers sent their planes over the target area. The aircraft were confined to the primary targets, i.e. aircraft, shipping and air installations. The last strike on 18 February selected the prominent oil storage facilities on Dublon. The restraint to hit them as a Parthian Shot proved to be good judgment, because the gigantic smoke columns from the fires drifted southwest, obscuring the Sixth Fleet Anchorage, which, by that time, was almost wiped clean of ships. Combat Air Patrols of 8 Hellcats each were flown from the light carrier Belleau Wood on both days.

During the night of 17/18 February, Yorktown sent up a night fighter, and Enterprise launched a minimum altitude radar attack, which was very effective.

Commander Task Force 58 was Rear Admiral Mark A. Mitscher, and he was also Officer in Tactical Command (OTC). His flag was in the Yorktown. The skipper of this carrier was Captain R.E. Jennings. The commander of Task Group 58.1 was Rear Admiral J.W. Reeves, Jr., in Enterprise; the Enterprise was commanded by Captain M.B. Gardner.

Task Group 58.1 suffered 8 personnel missing, believed dead, with a loss of 4 fighters, 1 bomber and 2 Avengers due to combat action. Operationally, no planes were lost.

Hailstorm - *Historic Documentation*

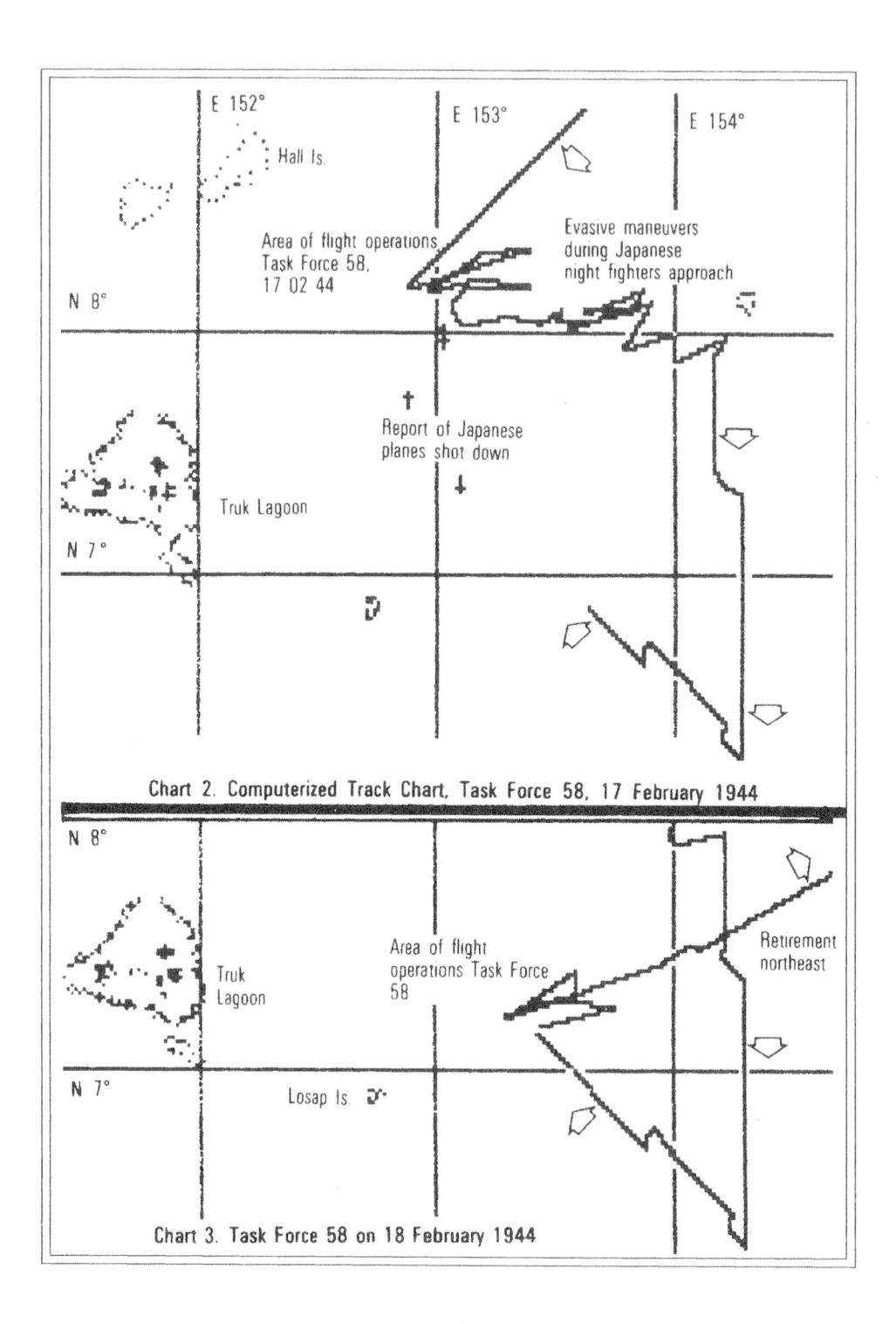

Chart 2. Computerized Track Chart, Task Force 58, 17 February 1944

Chart 3. Task Force 58 on 18 February 1944

AIRCRAFT ACTION REPORTS

ENTERPRISE

Summary

"Big E", as the Enterprise was called affectionately, remained the only pre-war aircraft carrier in service then. She was battle-proven and combat operations went smoothly. For the Truk air raid, her fighter planes were selected to form the lowest of the three layer high fighter offensive during the initial fighter sweep. These planes had to expect the heaviest air opposition.

There was no element of surprise as far as the Fighter Squadron VF 10 was concerned. The dogfights which ensued were vicious, and the Enterprise fighters proved that they were very well up to this tough assignment. The confidence in their fighting capabilities was fully justified. In all, 74 sorties were flown on the first day.

During the initial fighter sweep, the squadron counted 47 Japanese fighters airborne, and shot down 16, with the loss of a single Hellcat. The commander of VF 10, Lt.Cmdr. Kane, and two of his pilots, each scored 3 planes shot down. During the operation, they downed 29 Japanese planes and damaged 10 in the air. The Aircraft Action Report submitted at the time makes most interesting reading, indicating a high degree of skill on part of the pilots, and a superb performance of the planes. Although this squadron did not sink any ships outright, it damaged the light cruiser Katori, two destroyers and two oilers by strafing. Ground action reported 38 Betty bombers destroyed, and bombs with delay fuses dropped on Moen airfield. Compared to these achievements, the toll was small. Only 3 planes were lost in combat, none operational. Two of the pilots were rescued, the third was missing in action.

The Bomber Squadron VB 10 flew 64 sorties and destroyed a tanker. They damaged the seaplane tender Akitsushima and made runs on the Katori, a destroyer, and inflicted damage to one tanker and two merchant vessels. Although they encountered 15 Japanese planes airborne, only a few attacks were made on the Dauntless. These were repulsed with the loss of one Japanese aircraft. Without losses to themselves, they destroyed 10 to 20 twin engined planes on the ground.

No planes were lost by the Avengers which, as Torpedo Squadron VT 10, made 38 sorties and damaged 7 ships. They dropped bombs on Eten and Moen, but did not encounter airborne fighters. No planes were lost during the first day of the strike.

Retaliatory action by Japanese planes began at 1904 h (2104 h ship's time). An aircraft approached but was chased off by fire from screening ships.

A few hours before dawn, "Big E" launched a minimum altitude night radar attack under the leadership of Lt.Cmdr. Martin, in which 12 Avengers participated. It was highly successful. The crews of the planes had received special training and subsequently, no less than 8 ships were claimed to have been destroyed. During this action one plane was shot down by anti-aircraft fire, unobserved by any of the others. Plane and crew were lost.

On the next day, the fighters flew 41 sorties, including a repeat of the initial fighter sweep, and escorted the strikes 1A to 1C. It is interesting to note that they did not encounter any Japanese planes at all in the air. As the sky was all theirs, they resorted to

Hailstorm - *Historic Documentation*

strafe merchant vessels and barracks, with no losses to themselves. No ship was seen to sink as a direct result of their strafing attacks, but one freighter, an oiler and a patrol boat were damaged.

Regarding ships sunk, the bombers were more successful. During their 31 sorties they claimed one tanker, one cargo ship and a small auxiliary sunk. A second oiler and two more freighters were damaged. An ammunition dump was blown up, oil tanks set ablaze and dock facilities were damaged. However, one plane was lost with its crew.

It was a bit quieter for the Torpedo Squadron VT 10. They had been involved in the night action, and subsequent to that only 9 sorties were flown. They broke up a destroyer, Tachikaze, and that was about all on the second day.

Altogether, 59 sorties were flown by the Avengers. They dropped 55 tons of bombs, scored hits on 4 warships, 3 freighters and 2 oilers. There was not a single plane which escaped damage by anti-aircraft fire. One of them was shot up so badly that the carrier crew threw it overboard, or in official terminology, jettisoned it.

Pre-Dawn Fighter Sweep   17 02 44

About an hour before dawn, between 0444 to 0454 h, 12 F6F Hellcat fighters were launched from the Enterprise. The other carriers also launched 12 fighters each. It was noticed that an alarm for incoming hostile planes had originated from Moen. The fighters located at the base, at the northwest corner of this island, were scrambled. Subsequently, there appeared to be a total breakdown in the Japanese communication network. Some other factors, connected with the cumbersome command structure in Truk, contributed to the fact that Eten airfield was not put into the same degree of readiness as Moen. A few planes took off from the Param strip. At any rate, the fighters of the Enterprise engaged in furious and vicious dogfights with the Zekes, Rufes and Hamps from the Moen and Param airfield and the seaplane bases.

The commander, Lt. Cmdr. Kane, tangled with two Tojos (Nakajima Ki-44 Shoki) and a Zeke (Mitsubishi A6M). These planes were the best Truk defences could muster, and the Tojo was the Japanese interceptor. In wild acrobatics, the American ace shot them down, by aiming, as much as he could, at the gas tank and the cockpit. He realized that those were the weak points in the Japanese machines. The Japanese had not yet employed the wide use of self-sealing tanks, armour for the pilots, and bullet-proof glass for the cockpit. Hits into the gas tank and the engine transformed the Japanese planes into flaming torches. The pilots of his squadron were engaged with the Zekes and Hamps - another variant of the Zero-fighter-, and one of them equalled the score of his commander with three Japanese planes shot down.

In the air battle, a total of 17 Japanese planes were shot down and 5 damaged. When the Japanese aircraft were piloted with experienced men, the Hellcats could generally not quite match the maneuverability of the Zekes, Hamps and Rufes, and could keep up only for a short time. To make up for it, their firepower was superior. For a floatplane, the Rufe showed a remarkable performance. It was only slightly slower than its sisterplane, the Zeke. Some American pilots were astonished to find that the Zeke and the Rufe could outclimb and outturn the F6F, but again, once hit, the Rufe would burn fast and fiercely.

Eten airfield, on which very little activity was seen, was strafed on repeated runs. Here, the American pilots found 5 fighters, 3 Bettys, 9 Zekes and 4 Tojos parked wingtip to wingtip. The nature of the fire started by strafing of the airfields indicated that the planes were gassed up. One Zeke was shot down immediately after take-off at Param airfield. This wreck can be seen today, broken into three parts, about 500 yards off the western edge of the former airstrip of that island.

The American forces suffered the loss of one plane and its pilot. It was last seen over the target on a strafing run, but was hit by anti-aircraft fire. Three fighters were damaged, but could be repaired on board the carrier. The section leader received a bad hit into the wingroot, which sprayed fragments into the cockpit, injuring him slightly.

Strike 1 A   17 02 44

The planes were launched at 0500 - 0516 h and recovered between 0714 and 0755 h. Eight Hellcats made up the cover for 10 Dauntless and 7 Avengers. The Dauntless observed 15 ships at the Moen anchorage and an equal number at Eten. They encountered intensive but inaccurate anti-aircraft fire, mainly from the warships. Their most conspicuous target was the seaplane tender Akitsushima. They thought to have hit it twice with their 1000 lbs bombs. One hit was recorded midships, the other on the stern. The ship did not sink. They dropped two near misses on what they thought was a light cruiser, but turned out to be a modern destroyer, probably east of Moen, but completely missed an oiler. A formation of one cruiser with destroyers was observed heading towards the North Pass. This was the light cruiser Katori, and the two destroyers Maikaze and Nowake. Fires and explosions were seen on the Moen and Eten airfields. Many of the ships inside the lagoon fired small calibre weapons at the planes.

The Avengers were armed with fragmentation and incendiary clusters. Their intention was to knock out as many Japanese planes on the ground as possible before they had a chance to get airborne. After dropping their clusters on Moen airfield, they followed up with strafing. It was estimated that about 100 planes were on that field. The pilots of the fighters collaborated the observations made earlier, i.e. that the small arms fire was intensive and that several warships, as well as merchant ships, were seen to be underway, heading for the North and the Northeast Pass. Anti-aircraft fire from these ships was intense. This was the armed Convoy 4215, with Destroyer Group 4.

There were still Japanese planes in the air. The 8 Hellcats had all hands full to shoot down 9 of the 18 planes seen. These were mainly Rufes and Zekes. At the end, Katori was strafed by the fighters, but there were no visible effects on the cruiser.

Hailstorm - *Historic Documentation*

Strike 1 B   17 02 44

Seven Avengers were launched, together with 12 Dauntless and 10 Hellcats, between 0658 and 0711 h, returning at between 0917 and 1023 h, together with a Combat Air Patrol and Anti Submarine Patrol.

About 20 to 30 miles (about 35 to 40 km) northwest from the North Pass, bearing 295 degrees, the Avengers found their target and dropped 1000 lbs bombs on the Katori, which fired anti-aircraft weapons in response. Two hits were obtained. One bomb exploded midships, aft of the stack, starting a fire, and the other hit at the bow. After a missed regrouping the planes flew over the Katori again, where they saw a destroyer nearby which seemed to have been damaged as well.

About 25 miles (40 km) west of Piaanu Pass, a cruiser was reported steaming away from the lagoon at high speed, estimated to be about 25 knots. It was the light cruiser Naka, which had not been damaged yet. The observation regarding her course may have been correct, however, shortly afterwards the ship was reported to have run back towards Truk. A group of ships was observed about 10 miles (16 km) northwest of the North Pass. This formation, Convoy 4215, was formed by one large cargo ship, another one aft of it, and several smaller ones, probably including destroyers. This group certainly consisted of the Akagi Maru, 7,389 ts, the heavily armed auxiliary cruiser, possibly the Zuikai Maru, 2,700 ts, as well as a few destroyers, including the Maikaze and Nowake. These ships were strafed but not bombed, by Hellcats from Yorktown and Enterprise. There was no air opposition for the Avengers. They returned to the carrier with holes in the wings from anti-aircraft fire from the ships.

The Dauntless had their share of holes as well. They encountered 8 Japanese planes. One was shot down and a second was left with a smoking engine. The Japanese pilots were now somewhat timid. Had they coordinated their attack, they could have probably brought down the next to last American plane, which just managed to escape into the clouds after a wild chase. The Dauntless were detached from the Avengers and entered the lagoon from the northeast. One division made a run on a tanker north of Fefan, but all bombs missed. However, the second division was vectored in to attack this large ship, as well, which was the Tonan Maru 3. They scored two hits on the stern, which blew out the sides and some of the superstructure. The pilots reported that part of the starboard quarter was missing, and that debris was flying high through the air. The ship immediately began to settle by the stern. In fact, there are parts of the superstructure and one of the two funnels on the sea bed, where this ship sunk. The Tonan Maru 3 was later salvaged, but the pieces of wreckage remained where the force of the explosion had flung them. Then, the Akitsushima was attacked again. A single bomb exploded midships, causing a fire. The ship did not sink, despite the damage inflicted earlier and now.

The next to the last plane of that division was jumped by 4 Zekes and a Rufe. The American pilot managed to shoot down one Zeke, which crashed spectacularly into the sea, but then he really scrambled into the clouds at maximum speed of 190 knots, to escape the combined attack. He managed to reach the carrier with his badly shot up plane.

In the meantime, the Hellcats, launched as escort, had a rough time with 6 Zekes, but it proved an easy task to intercept a single Sally (Mitsubishi Ki 21). The crew of this twin engined Army plane probably never knew what hit them when a Hellcat fired a long burst with her automatic weapons on the wave hugging aircraft. Immediately, the bomber caught fire and crashed. The Zekes again showed their maneuverability, but 4 were shot down, however, not before they had scored several hits on the American planes. The Aircraft Action Report comments on this occasion: "Three of our F6F were shot up, but all returned to base, testifying to the ruggedness of our planes, as compared to the flimsy construction of the Japanese aircraft."

Strike 1 C   17 02 44

The 8 Avengers, loaded with 4 bombs of 500 lbs each, 10 Dauntless with one 1000 lbs bomb each, and 11 Hellcats were launched at 0903 - 0914 h. The last plane returned at 1211 h.

The planes began their attack from the southeast end of the lagoon and skirted the rim of the reef on the east, towards the North Pass. They saw a freighter heading south. At this time a pilot of one of the Avengers lost the formation, and before he could join up with his own group - he failed to connect with planes from other carriers - he got jumped by a Zeke. The Avengers opened fire, but the Zeke was faster. Repeated hits into the wing and the cockpit caused a big hole at the wingroot, out of which large flames shot. A black smoke column trailed the plane. The fire burned fiercely, and the pilot got close to the water to be able to make a waterlanding. He was not seriously injured and just managed to keep the wobbly plane under control. The fuel tank sealed itself, and the flames subsided. The plane just made it back to the carrier, but being badly damaged by bullets and the fuel fire, was considered beyond repair. Upon return to the carrier it was jettisoned.

A large cargo ship of about 10,000 ts was just steaming west out of the channel between Moen and Dublon, when it was attacked and straddled with 2 bombs. The ship immediately reversed its course and sought shelter between the anti-aircraft batteries of the two islands. It is not quite clear which ship this could have been. The only ships sunk while not at anchor, inside the lagoon, were the Nagano Maru and the Fujisan Maru. This late, most ships underway were either damaged or had left the lagoon. On the other hand, on several occasions pilots reported ships to be underway. Those ships which had steam up, ran and a few escaped sinking and major damages.

The attacking planes saw how some Rufes were taxiing at the Moen seaplane base, and those of the American planes which had dropped their bombs already, went in for strafing. The remaining Avengers climbed back into the clouds to begin their second run. The target was a freighter, somewhat smaller than the one previously attacked, positioned at the southwest

Hailstorm - *Historic Documentation*

side of Moen. The ship was underway and heading west. One bomb hit midships, at the bridge; fire and smoke were observed. As the anti-aircraft fire was intense, the planes retired into the clouds, then broke out again at 4000 ft (1220 m), saw a Zeke, pursued it, but after a short chase, the Japanese plane escaped into the cover of the shore line.

Upon retirement to the rendezvous point, one Avengers was pursued by a Zeke. After being shot at, this plane broke the engagement off and disappeared. While in the process of joining up, one Avengers saw a Zeke positioned above and behind. It made a solid running attack on the American plane, which escaped after being hit at the tail by suddenly diving steeply, making the Japanese plane overshoot and ruining its run. The Avengers made it back to the carrier, a little worse for wear.

The Dauntless had been given a different assignment. Their mission was to destroy the warships outside the lagoon. The group of ships included the Katori, a cargo ship, the auxiliary cruiser Akagi Maru, both burning and stopped dead in the water, and two destroyers. One of these received a close miss, which temporarily stopped it. However, it was soon making headway again. The pilots identified the destroyer as belonging to the Fubuki-Class. These ships were rather similar to the Kagero-Class, and it is almost certain, that the Maikaze was damaged. The second destroyer got away from this attack unharmed.

Although the Hellcats observed two Hamps, they made no contact and suffered no losses or damages. A large freighter at the Dublon anchorage returned fire when strafed, but this episode was inconclusive for both sides. On the way back to the carrier they strafed the Katori. They estimated the position to be about 4 miles (6 km) off the North Pass.

In the meantime, Combat Air Patrol shot down a Mitsubishi Zero Mark 2, 30 miles (50 km) to the south of the carrier. 18 minutes later a second Japanese plane crashed into the water after been hit by planes of the Combat Air Patrol, vectored after it, 31 miles, bearing 258 degrees. Four other planes were reported by the Command Center, but were out of reach.

Strike 1 D   17 02 44

Seven Hellcats and 11 Dauntless, loaded with one 1000 lbs bomb each, and 4 Avengers with four 500 lbs bombs each, were launched from 1059 to 1107h.

The mission of the torpedo bombers was to destroy the ships leaving the lagoon. Again, the Katori was sighted, this time zigzagging. Her position was estimated to be 10 miles (17 km) east of the North Pass. Most of the bombs, dropped from 3500 ft, were misses. The bombs of one of the planes did not release and the pilot opted for a second round. Hits were seen on the bow and the port beam of the cruiser. A Val made its appearance, and an unsuccessful attack. It was driven off and hugged the waves all the way back to the North Pass.

The Dauntless went in after the Avengers had completed their run. They scored near misses on the port bow which tossed the foreship out of the water. Two very near misses were so close that they must have inflicted some damage. The Katori was now lying dead in the water, a wreck with smoke billowing up and obscuring the bridge and the aftship.

Quite a distance further out, the pilots estimated more than 25 miles (40 km), a destroyer was seen to rescue survivors from an unidentified ship. The pilots then went on an excursion towards Namonuito Atoll, returned, spotted the Katori again and dropped the rest of the bombs on the ship, which, incredibly enough, had just begun to make some headway again. In the distance they saw the ships of Task Group 50.9 approaching.

The Hellcats went over to Truk, while the other planes were involved with the cruiser. The Hellcats did not encounter any Japanese planes in the air, and began strafing runs on Param and Moen airfields. Three Bettys were destroyed. A small personnel carrier was shot at as well.

Recovery of the planes was a bit drawn out as the strike returned in sections. The bombers and the fighters came back at 1354 h. Avengers were recovered between 1434 and 1444 h, together with 2 Hellcats.

Strike 1 E   17 02 44

At 1300 h, the next strike was launched. It consisted of 13 fighters, 8 Avengers and 10 Dauntless. One Hellcat was flying on a special mission. Recovery was finished by 1546 h.

The fighters had it easy now as the sky was all theirs. The Hellcats observed a Tony, but the plane was too far away and was not engaged in combat action. The pilots observed an oiler underway, course south, to the west of Moen. This ship was without doubt the Fujisan Maru. The Heian Maru was reported to be ablaze at the North Dublon Anchorage, the Combined Fleet Anchorage. An oiler, the Hoyo Maru, was seen to burn at that anchorage as well. Two destroyers were observed. The smaller one was beached at Uman and was on fire; the second anchored at Eten. While strafing Param airfield, the Hellcats ignited two bombers and 3 Hamps. After a repeated strafing run on Eten the planes returned to their carrier.

Originally, the Avengers were ordered to Dublon, but they were vectored to Eten instead. They dropped no fewer than 24 bombs on a single freighter, all of them missed. Another merchant vessel received a similar treatment - 4 misses. There was only one plane which had bombs left, because they had not released earlier. Subsequently, this pilot tried his luck on a destroyer which was running for the North Pass, being about 5 miles (8km) inside the lagoon. The pilot reported two definite and one probable hit. It left the destroyer dead in the water and smoking. One of the planes attempted to take some pictures of Moen with the board camera, but encountered stiff anti-aircraft fire. He broke off and left it at that, having obtained 12 exposures taken of Moen airfield.

The targets of the Dauntless were the ships at the Moen or Combined Fleet Anchorage. A tanker was hit at the stern, immediately it was set ablaze. It was the Hoyo Maru, anchored at the Repair Anchorage. The fuel bunkers were set afire, and continued to burn. Two hits were recorded on a 10,000 ts freighter, probably the Kansho Maru, at the stern and midships. The ship began to list and burned. A second freighter was attacked. The pilots believed they saw two hits midships. Both ships were fairly close to each other. The larger of the two ships was the Kiyozumi Maru, the other the Kansho Maru. There is evidence of a bomb explosion midships at the Kiyozumi, and at least two bombs were very close misses, which severely damaged the shell plating. The damage on the Kansho Maru is also apparent. The dented funnel, the disarrayed anchor way forward, the broken back, the damage on the stern, and the compression mark on the hull bear evidence of the violence.

It is very difficult for pilots and crew to observe correctly the location of a bomb hit. Many times the pilots of all carriers reported a definite hit, where evidence from the wreck shows that it was a miss. The water and smoke column hurled into the air from the explosion does not allow to pinpoint the center of an explosion to such a high degree of exactness. Also, the smoke and water were quickly driven aft by the fresh winds. Only torpedo hits were reported without fail.

There was an interesting observation. An oiler was seen to be under attack by Avengers from another carrier, resulting in the sudden and dramatic disintegration of this ship. The planes were from the carrier Bunker Hill, TG 58.3. The pilots reported a bomb hit midships on a 4,000 ts ship, believed to be a tanker. A huge explosion followed. It was probably the Daikichi Maru, which totally disintegrated, and of which only large pieces of the hull remain on the sea floor.

A single Avengers was recovered at 1620 h.

Strike 1 F   17 02 44

This was the last strike of the first day. It was intended to bomb the Moen airfield to prevent any Japanese planes taking off for a night raid. The strike was launched between 1510 and 1527 h and the planes were recovered from 1755 to 1809 h. Avengers were armed again with 100 lbs fragmentation and incendiary clusters. On the way into Moen they had to jink to avoid the anti-aircraft fire, which was mainly shot from the 5 inch batteries. It was not particularly accurate. The guns seemed to search for range and were shooting a barrage, also reported by other planes. This kind of fire was not particularly effective against dive bombing attacks. The bombing was, therefore, quite successful. Many fires were started on the ground and nearly all planes seemed to be hit. The runway suffered damage as well.

The Dauntless dropped their bombs into the revetments and counted nine hits on Betty bombers. A building was destroyed by an explosion. The results of the bombing was interesting. The planes reached by the explosion of the bombs erupted into huge palls of flames and smoke, indicating that they were all gassed up. Anti-aircraft fire seemed to come from the planes on the ground, suggesting that they had been manned, and that they were exactly ready to do what the Americans tried to prevent: Taking off for a night attack. On the way back the bombers saw a submarine, apparently under attack by fighters.

The 12 Hellcats had a bit more trouble and observed 4 Zekes, 1 Hamp and 1 Rufe. Except for the Rufe, all other planes were shot down, not without losses to the American planes, however. Two F6F were shot up really badly by the Zekes, and crashed outside the lagoon. The pilots managed to escape from their sinking planes and were picked up a little later by American destroyers. One of the fighters was pursued by a Zeke, trying for a kill. Already being damaged, the pilot turned off the IFF on the way to the carrier, in order to attract the attention of the Combat Air Patrol. Before they arrived, the plane had to be ditched. The pilot was rescued by the destroyer Lang.

The mission to drop long delay fused bombs on Moen airfield was successful. Waterlogged bomb craters were seen the next day on the runway. One of the planes made a strafing run on the second island east of the North Pass, where the pilot saw a large coastal defence gun.

The planes returned to the carrier. Later in the night, the Minimum Altitude Night Radar Attack was launched with Lt. Cmdr. Martin directing the raid. This officer had been a pioneer in applying the new technique of a radar night attack. He had the foresight to train his squadron at every opportunity in this new style of combat. When the time came to prove that it was effective he was grounded and could not lead his men. Unfortunately for him he slipped and fell while doing his daily exercises on the forecastle deck on 31 January, breaking his elbow. However, he briefed his pilots and instilled in them the will to perform. His distinguished career ended with his retirement, as an admiral, long after the war.

The Night Raid From USS Enterprise

In the night of 17 to 18 February, Enterprise executed a minimum level radar night attack. Twelve Avengers were launched between 0208 and 0232 h from the catapults. Launching was intended to begin at 0200 h sharp, but Lt Cmdr. Martin took time out for a pep talk. Preparations and checks by the deck crew were particularly careful and thorough, to add to the confidence of the plan crews. The planes were loaded with bombs. At this time, the Group was steaming into the wind, about 100 miles (165 km) from the northeast side of Truk. All Avengers were equipped with radar. It took only about an hour to brief the crews on their mission. At the time of the launch, there was a quarter moon and about 40 % cloud cover. The planes proceeded at 500 ft (152 m) altitude, and Truk Atoll was detected on the screens when they were still 20 miles (32 km) away.

The planes split into two groups; their rendezvous points were just outside the North and Northeast Pass, respectively. From these points, the planes took off individually at one minute intervals. The targets were the ships at the Combined Fleet and Fourth Fleet Anchorages. The Avengers were immediately detected when they crossed the reef. The hospital ship, Hikawa Maru, showed all her lights, to forestall an attack, and her Red Crosses were prominently displayed. A warning flare was shot from Moen. Soon after this, anti-aircraft guns opened up fire. It was of medium intensity, but considering the night-

Hailstorm - *Historic Documentation*

time conditions, fairly accurate. One plane was shot down, unnoticed by the others. Plane and crew were lost. Seven others sustained damages.

The planes were detected so early because their new model exhaust fire dampeners were not very effective. As soon as any plane flew over and past a gun installation, they were fired upon. Their ineffectively dampened exhaust flames were a dead give-away. The torpedo bombers remained 30 minutes inside the lagoon, in search for suitable targets. Search and homing was accomplished by radar. There are several small islands in the lagoon. Attacks had to be abandoned when the target, showing an identical echo to a ship, turned out to be an islet. Another problem for the crew was the proximity of some ships to large islands. The echoes of the ship and the island merged, and the run had to be repeated from another direction.

The approaches were generally made at a speed of 180 knots and an altitude of 250 ft (76 m). In most cases, the actual bomb drop was made on visual contact, but the "Mark!" of the radar operator increased the confidence of the bomber. Most of the pilots dropped two bombs in the shortest possible interval as a salvo on each target. The squadron recorded 13 direct hits, which destroyed or sank 8 and damaged 5 ships. Seven bombs detonated within a beam's width of the target. The percentage of hits and close misses was considerably higher than during day attacks.

A searchlight was switched on at the Moen air base. These lights are hated by the pilots, because they destroy their night vision. After a short while a large explosion was seen in the vicinity of the light, and it was promptly switched off. The Japanese probably had thought that the planes had attacked it, but certainly it had been a bomb with a long delay fuse, dropped by the last strike, which went off.

The planes retired from the atoll at irregular intervals as soon as they had expended their bombs. As they cleared the reef they saw the planes of the first fighter sweep approaching. This meant that the last of the planes arrived at the carrier, guided by beacons and radar, shortly before sunrise, at 0555 h.

It was a night of personal satisfaction for the commander of the squadron. His suggestion to set a carrier aside exclusively for night attack operations was not heeded at that time, however. Higher authority did not concur because carriers were scarce and could not be spared for exclusive use on a specialized mission. The flag officers were unanimous in their praise for the achievements of the squadron.

This attack was considered the first of its kind in the war, and proved to be very successful. However, the ship's count of vessels sunk and damaged has not been included in the official tally. It is therefore listed here, realizing that location and status of the ships when left could not be determined.

A- Direct Hits   B- Ships damaged   Apparent Size

Pre-Dawn Fighter Sweep 18 02 44

The 12 fighters launched, at 0445 h, just before the full first strike of this second day of the attack on Truk, did not encounter any airborne opposition. The planes available to the Japanese had been either reduced to wrecks or could not start because the runways were heavily damaged. The activities of the fighters during the second day are summarized:

(claimed destroyed)	(hits claimed)	
1 Tanker, medium 2 Cargo, medium 4 Cargo, large 1 Tanker, large	3 Cargo, med. 2 Cargo, small	small <300 ft medium about 400 ft large > 500 ft
8 ships destroyed	5 ships damaged	

All three major airfields, Moen, Eten and Param were strafed, and planes on the ground seemed to burn. There were several merchant ships in the lagoon which were strafed with the board weapons of the fighters. One freighter burned in the lagoon. One cargo ship was observed to run east of Moen and later Dublon; it was probably Shotan Maru. Later it got hit by a bomb and sank. One merchant ship each was reported north of Fefan, at the Dublon anchorage, smoking, and one at the Otta Pass. A small vessel was attacked outside the lagoon, southwest of the Kuop Atoll. A larger cargo vessel was seen in the vicinity, or near the beached Tachikaze. These ships were strafed. A tug boat or a vessel of similar size was shot at, close to the North Pass. Several buildings and barracks were taken under fire on various islands, and finally, on the last run of the day, bombs were dropped on the oil tanks in Dublon.

Strike 1 A   18 02 44

Twelve bombers were launched with their fighter escort of 8 Hellcats, between 0456 and 0506 h, and recovered from 0730 to 0745 h. This flight arrived at the lagoon before it was light enough to commence the attacks. The planes circled for about 10 minutes. The first division dove on an oiler underway between Moen and Dublon. Of the three bombs dropped, one each was a near miss on port, a hit on the stern and another near miss on starboard. The ship lost all headway, drifted before the wind, burned at the damaged area at the aft engine room, and began to sink. This ship was the Fujisan Maru. A freighter, the Shotan Maru, was underway at the Fourth Fleet Anchorage, and was hit just aft of midships. These two vessels were the only remaining ones in that area.

One of the Avengers went on an attacking dive, but failed to pull up. It crashed into the water. Pilot and plane were lost. A small vessel on the way to the seaplane base at Moen was taken under attack. When the planes retired to the north they saw a small picket boat of the "40-44"-Class coming in from the North Pass. It fired machine weapons at the planes. The strafing attack resulted in a fire with a subsequent explosion, and the ship sank. The hospital ship Hikawa Maru was proceeding towards the North Pass. It was observed that the small calibre anti-aircraft batteries had been moved during the cover of the night and placed on those shores where they could best intercept the American attacks, which had evolved in a discernible pattern, basically attacking into the wind.

Strike 1 B   18 02 44

Flight operations were resumed after the flag was flown half-mast, for the burial at sea of the two deceased airmen, in Yorktown, at 0645 h, with the launch of 8 Hellcats, 8 Dauntless and 7 Avengers, which were armed with one 1000 lbs bomb each. Their target was the Tachikaze, still firmly grounded by the bow on the reef on Kuop Atoll.

Forty miles (about 70 km) south of Truk, at the edge of the submarine sanctuary, a sub was detected but not attacked. The flight then turned towards Truk to destroy the Tachikaze. The destroyer remained afloat, apparently undamaged, its bow still firmly beached on the reef. Three hits were scored, the ship was destroyed and sunk. However, one of the pilots, thinking that he had delay fused bombs, got caught in the blast of his own bombs as they exploded on impact. Fragments were sent flying high into the air and damaged the plane severely. It was just barely able to make it back to the carrier. Another bomb exploded just next to the bow, within 15 feet off the hull. The pressure wave blew the shell plating inward. About 2 miles (4km) south of the Tachikaze, a freighter of about 5 to 6, 000 ts was steaming on a southwesterly course, at 12 knots. The bombing attack left this ship badly burning and dead in the water.

Five Avengers made a dive bombing run on a large, about 600 ft (183 m) long vessel, which seemed to be the only undamaged ship at the anchorage at Dublon. A near miss caused debris to fly off the starboard bow. The other 3 planes attacked ships already smoking. 5 ships were seen damaged and smoking inside the lagoon. The main anti-aircraft fire seemed to come from Dublon and Param. At the Moen seaplane base, three 4-engined flying boats, Emilys or Mavis, were seen to be undamaged.

The strike was recovered between 0923 and 0957 h.

Strike 1 C   18 02 44

The strike consisted of 13 fighters, 10 bombers and 2 torpedo bombers. They were flown off the deck between 0845 and 0857 h.

Although the main objective was to destroy shore installations at Dublon, a large cargo ship underway between Eten and Dublon town was bombed, resulting in 2 close misses. The other hits were scored on the oil tanks in Dublon. They went up in flames and blanketed part of the lagoon with thick black smoke. An ammunition dump exploded with great force.

Anti-aircraft fire seemed to be intense, coming also from the ship attacked. At Eten, several Bettys were observed, apparently still intact. The planes were recovered, without losses, from 1119 to 1139 h.

This concluded the raid, and after the planes were recovered, the Task Group retired at high speed to the east.

YORKTOWN

Summary

The Yorktown was in the launching position in the early morning hours of 17 February, with 36 F6F Hellcats, 18 TBF (Avengers), 28 SBD (Dauntless), and 4 F6F(N) night fighters in commission. On this day the ship's log reports that the generally fine weather was marred by numerous showers and squalls until noon. The seas were moderate. Rain before dawn on the second day gave way to generally sunny and partly cloudy skies. The Trade Wind was blowing between 13 and 18 knots from east-northeast, 70 degrees. Visibility, when not diminished by rain, was up to 12 miles (19km). The carrier was positioned with the guide, Enterprise, at her port quarter.

The planes of the Yorktown were under the command of Air Group 5. For the individual strikes of the first day, 12 to 15 Dauntless and 4 to 9 Avengers were committed, escorted by 6 to 16 Hellcats. The Air Group Commander, escorted by three fighters, acted as Target Observer. On the first day, planes of Yorktown were flying 220 sorties over the target. They carried 81.5 tons of 500 lbs and 1000 lbs general purpose bombs to the targets.

Losses to the American planes were light. One fighter was shot up by Japanese planes; the pilot parachuted into the water northeast-north of the barrier reef. His wingman radioed the position and circled at low altitude until his plane got low on fuel. Although he managed to climb into the life raft, the downed pilot appeared to have drifted onto the reef, possibly at the vicinity of the North Pass, where he was later captured and killed. Another plane, an Avenger, was badly shot up by intercepting Tonys. It more or less stumbled back to the carrier and made a crash landing, but the radioman succumbed to the wounds received from the bullets of the attacking planes. The gunner was severely wounded but the pilot escaped almost unhurt. The American plane was in such bad shape that it was thrown overboard. All other planes returned safely on the first day.

During the night, Yorktown launched a night fighter, at 2123 h, which pursued a few of the contacts of Japanese night fighters. It was the first combat mission of this kind for the carrier. Due to incorrect vectoring, this plane apparently remained in shooting range of Task Group 58.2 and permitted the launch of a torpedo by the Japanese plane on the Intrepid. The intruding plane escaped unscathed. The night fighter was recovered at 0031 h. While on inspection, the Commanding Officer of Air Group 5, Commander Patten, fell down the elevator pit and was injured.

On the second day of the attack (18 February), Yorktown began the day's operation by again launching a pre-dawn fighter sweep. However, since airborne opposition was almost nonexistent, the planes continued to strafe and bomb the airfields. Four Bettys were destroyed together with nine single engine planes. Three more fighter planes were destroyed by explosions. One Avenger was shot down outside the lagoon. The crew was rescued by the US submarine Searaven. A pilot of a bomber was injured by anti-aircraft fire.

Yorktown did not have a SM radar (for detecting low flying aircraft) and this proved to be a great disadvantage. The commander had to rely on plots received by the carriers Enterprise and Bunker Hill.

The type of armament the planes would carry into the target area was left to the discretion of the Commander Task Groups. Despite reports received, probably from Bunker Hill, that torpedoes had been used very successfully against targets in and out of the lagoon, Yorktown's planes continued to be loaded with bombs only. Therefore the Action Reports make critical references to the rigid bomb loading doctrine. This was rebuffed by the Task Force Commander, and it appears that everybody concerned was somewhat unhappy about the accuracy of the bombing. It was mentioned that there was a total of 55 ships in the lagoon, of which about ten were left floating. Bombs were crippling ships, and of course could result in sinking, but the torpedoes were the real killers.

The loss of the fighter pilot downed outside the lagoon gave rise to severe criticism of the rescue procedures. Despite the circling of his wingman over the raft and frequent broadcast over shortwave and VHF, no rescue attempt was made immediately. When the covering plane had to leave because of low fuel, the pilot endeavored to have a plane from another carrier take over the cover. He could not get his message through. Three hours later, the same plane returned, but the raft was gone. A thorough search was made in the area of the North Pass, but no trace of the pilot was found. In contrast, the fighter pilot parachuting northeast-north of the North Pass the next day was, however, kept under constant observation and the submarine could be guided to pick him up. Although a sea anchor was set by this pilot, the raft had been blown almost six miles (10 km) in six hours towards the reef. It was then only two miles (3 km) away from the atoll rim when it was reached by the sub. The pilot was rescued.

Initial Fighter Sweep - 17 02 44

Yorktown and Enterprise, the two large carriers, launched a pre-dawn fighter sweep. The aircraft of Yorktown were launched at 0445 h. As planes of both carriers were assigned the lower altitude fighting, they had to overcome the fiercest Japanese airborne resistance. Yorktown planes, in wild and turbulent dogfights, shot down eleven planes. On arrival over the target eight Hellcats proceeded to strafe the seaplane base in Dublon. The remaining four planes stayed at 8000 ft (2500 m) to fly cover. Many Zeros and Rufes were airborne and soon a general melee began. The fighters stayed together and managed to shoot down 3 Rufes, 4 Hamps and 1 Hamp and Pete each.

The Japanese planes seemed to be scattered and did not follow any tactical organization. They were flying between 10, 000 ft (3000 m) and sea level. A few attempted aggressive overhead or head-on attacks but were not successful. The Hellcats performed well, and outclimbed, outturned and outdove the Japanese planes which only seemed to have an edge at slower speeds.

Strike 1 AY - 17 02 44

The flight was launched at 0500h, and all planes were airborne 18 minutes later. They were back on board after two hours and 18 minutes.

After rendezvous one 4-plane division of Hellcats covered the Dauntless on their dives, giving protection against Japanese airborne fighters. After the bomb drop the planes assembled but met two Zekes, which were shot down. Four more Zekes showed up; three were set aflame and crashed. The fourth escaped. The fighter division went on a strafing run on a freighter which was left smoking. The ship was reported to steam inside the lagoon. The other division of Hellcats covered the Avengers on their attack. The Hellcats pulled up and strafed a destroyer at the Eten anchorage. The small calibre anti-aircraft guns of this ship were silenced.

Altogether 15 Dauntless were launched and attacked ships anchored north east of Fefan at the Combined Fleet Anchorage, and south west of Dublon, at the Sixth Fleet Anchorage. A 4000 to 6000 ts freighter was subjected to a number of misses off the bow and port beam; the ship did not seemed damaged. The second cargo vessel received two observed hits. One was seen at port bow, the other at the stern on starboard. Another bomb missed the ship off the bow. A small merchant ship was rocked by a bomb miss off the bow and one on each beam. Also, two bombs dropped on a 2-4000 ts ship missed and threw water geysers over the decks.

The Avengers were hampered by a thick cloud cover over their target and had to circle for a while before the sun went up. The planes selected their own targets. A ship at the south west shore of Dublon got away from the first attack fairly unscathed, as the bombs splashed forward off the bow. A transport was located to the west of Fefan. Four bombs exploded in a salvo 50 to 100 ft at the starboard quarter. One of the pilots believed that a cargo ship was underway north of Eten, on a course of 275 degrees, but the bombs intended for the ship missed. A cruiser, more likely a destroyer, was sailing east, north of Uman. Misses on the port quarter and the bow showered this ship. Another freighter was anchored just north of Fanamu, but the bombs missed. The pilots who made the attack on this vessel reported that it was about to get under way. The last target was located between Dublon and Fefan, and the bombs missed on the port bow.

The pilots attributed these rather modest success of their bombing to strong cross winds, and modified their approaches to the target on the following strikes.

The planes were recovered between 0713h and 0751h, together with planes from the fighter sweep. The Air Observer was launched at 0630 h. The four Hellcats were in the air by 0632 h. Three minutes later, the destroyer Cogswell reported an unidentified submarine contact, which was quickly lost.

Strike 1 BY - 17 02 44

Launching began 0659h and ended 0711 h. It consisted of 8 Avengers and 13 Dauntless, escorted by 12 Hellcats.

The Hellcats escorted the other planes on their attack on ships outside the lagoon. A single Japanese plane with two engines was shot down just outside the rim. At the end of their mission they strafed the Katori with unobserved results. The pilots saw two distinctively different groups of ships in the target area.

The Dauntless did not lose much time to attack a modern type destroyer off the North Pass, but the bombs missed the ship. The Katori received a hit, which showed as fire and black smoke near the stack. It did not slow the ship down. The next target was the Naka, steaming at about 25 knots west of the Piaanu Pass. Also this ship managed to evade the bombs intended for it. With no losses to themselves, the Dauntless returned to the carrier.

The Avengers were slightly more successful. They first dive bombed what they thought was a three-stack cruiser, but it was most certainly a destroyer. A bomb was observed to explode midships, carrying away two of their stacks, and made it now look as it was supposed to do if it was the Maikaze. This ship was heavily damaged, and the smoke from the explosion reached up 500 ft (150 m) into the air. The Maikaze slowed down and trailed black smoke. The Katori fared slightly better. The many bombs dropped on her were all misses.

Strike 1 CY - 17 02 82

There was now quite an accumulation of ships northwest of the North Pass; the Katori, two destroyers and the Akagi Maru. The flight, which was launched between 0903 and 0915 h, was vectored into this area.

The fighters, finding no airborne opposition commenced with two strafing runs on the Katori. The two destroyers sailing with her endured six runs. Another destroyer, definitely not part of this formation, was located about 2 miles (3 km) north of the North Pass, while the Katori was estimated to be about 15 miles (24 km) north of the Pass.

A bit of confusion was evident regarding the identity of the ships outside the North Pass. The large freighter was thought of as a cruiser, and the freighter was indeed the Katori. Only the photos taken during this sortie confirmed the identity. A salvo of three bombs exploded off the starboard beam of the freighter, and two more hit the water at the port bow, apparently without doing damage. One destroyer was running through churned up water, which indicated that the bombs missed, as did the bombs dropped on the second destroyer. Katori received one observed hit on starboard quarter. The pilot reported that the ships had formed a cruising formation. The freighter was leading. The Katori followed immediately astern, flanked by the destroyers. The speed was estimated to be 12 knots.

On this third strike, 12 fighters, 8 torpedo bombers and 12 bombers participated. They were a little over two hours in the air, and commenced landing at 1128 h, interrupted by a change of course by the carrier for 18 minutes, and completed by 1204 h. Altogether, this strike was not particularly successful, and the plane were recovered, together with the Air Observer, between 1007 and 1032 h. One Avenger returned early and landed at 0822 h.

Strike 1 DY - 17 02 44

Launching began at 1110 h, ending at 1122 h. This attack was described as the masthead attack, because the planes flew their sorties very low.

There were 16 Hellcats flown off the deck of the Yorktown for this strike. One division, after flying escort for the Avengers, began a strafing run on the Eten airfield, starting a fire. Then they climbed to cover the Avengers, which gained altitude after their bombing attacks, in preparation of the second run. Several encounters with Zekes, which came from above were inconclusive for the Hellcats. Another division of Hellcats assumed the covering role after the other pursued the Zekes. The covering planes were suddenly attacked by 10 to 15 Zekes, which came out of the sun at about 20, 000 ft (6000 m). Numerous passes were made by these fighters with a noticeable lack of coordination and poor recovery technique. While the American planes stayed together they were able to shoot down six Zekes and damaged two, thus effectively braking up the attack. Two planes of a third division of Hellcats got involved in the aerial shoot-out and brought down two Zekes. The other two planes of this particular division had already commenced their strafing run against Eten. After they pulled out they participated in the battle and were credited with three Zekes shot down. One Japanese plane was heavily damaged and attempted an emergency landing on Eten airfield. It only succeeded in crashing into a group of four Kates. All five planes were consumed in a big fire. Only two Hellcats received minor damage.

The first attack of the low flying Avengers on two freighters, one at anchor east, the other west of Eten, produced no observed results. One pilot saw a submarine just in the process of submerging. He pressed home his attack, although his plane was jumped by Japanese fighters. His bombs dropped on the submarine. Their 4 to 5 seconds delay fuses, necessary because of the low altitude the plane was flying at, had a similar effect to depth charges. The bombs exploded above and below the submarine. A large water fountain was seen, and an oil slick formed on the water.

Indeed, there is a reference to a submarine, Ro 42, in the Japanese records. The boat was slightly damaged during the raid, but further references are missing. This submarine was sunk later off Kwajalein, in the Marshalls. A further American reference is the report by planes from another carrier, Enterprise, on Strike 1F of the first, and 1B on the second day, when a sub was sighted. The submarine wreck found between Dublon and Moen (I-169) is not connected with these events, as it sunk during the second carrier raid.

The Avengers continued their mast-head attack. West of Eten a freighter was damaged by a hit on the stern, but the effects could not be observed. The length of this ship was given as 300 ft (91 m). South of Eten a ship was the target. Of the two bombs dropped one was seen to explode on the deck, the other off the starboard quarter. A medium sized transport was thought to be underway between Eten and Fefan. The bomb seemed to have hit the stern and an explosion followed. Two bombs dropped on a small freighter anchored at the southwest side of Uman. Only the explosion in the water were observed.

The medium long delay fuses of the bombs produced a peculiar effect on a freighter anchored southeast of Eten. As the plane flew low, the angle at which the bomb hit allowed it to enter the port quarter, exit on starboard and explode immediately upon emerging from the hull. Splinters were observed to fly and the vessel began to burn. A near miss on the starboard beam of a transport reported at anchor just south of Fanamu blew the bow around so that it faced north instead of north east. It was last seen on this strike to settle by the stern. Although a pilot identified an island as Onna, the location of a freighter anchored north of it was not confirmed. It was seen, however, that the mast of the ship was carried away from the blast of the bomb which exploded very close to the ship. A second ship was anchored west of the same island. The attack resulted in near misses on starboard beam, which started a fire.

Two of the Avengers were attacked by a Tony and a Tojo fighter plane. The Tojo was shot down, but the one Avenger was so badly shot up that it just barely made it back to the carrier with the radioman killed and the gunner injured on the head, over the eyes. Despite his injury, and without his gun sight, which was shot off, the gunner fought off and destroyed the Tojo and extinguished left-handed the fire, which had started in the radioman's compartment.

This strike was recovered between 1353 and 1413h.

Strike 1 EY - 17 02 44

Four Hellcats for the Air Observer and Command Group were launched at 1237h. Then preparations were concluded and launching began for Strike E at 1302h, and took 11 minutes, for 12 Hellcats, 6 Avengers and 13 Dauntless.

The Hellcats escorted the Dauntless and Avengers. They were soon engaged in a short air combat. Three Japanese fighter planes were shot down, and afterwards the Hellcats swooped down to make strafing runs on Eten airfield, an oiler, two freighters and a small sized destroyer which exploded midships.

The Avengers set a vessel west of Eten on fire with one or two hits. Near the north shore of Fefan, one hit and one near miss severely damaged a freighter, possibly the Kiyozumi Maru. No hit was obtained despite the two bombs dropped on an anchored vessel on the northern shore of Uman. The same probably happened to the Yamagiri Maru, identified by lying northwest of Fefan. The Dauntless selected the same target, and one bomb was seen to explode on the ship, whereas the other missed. One transport, described being at anchor east of Eten, was reported damaged by a bomb, while a second exploded in the water. Fragments were hurled through the air. Northwest of Fefan a bomb damaged a tanker. From the location this could only be the Shinkoku Maru, but there is no apparent bomb damage visible on the wreck. A single bomb was seen to explode on a freighter north of Fefan.

Hellcats are been launched from the Lexington. A battleship of the North Carolina-Class ploughs through the water, while the Yorktown and another carrier of the Essex-Class are steaming in the far background [USNA]

At the Combined Fleet Anchorage, northwest of Fefan, a freighter was believed to have been hit on the bow. Two barges, which were tied together at the Repair Anchorage, were sunk by a hit. It was probably the Kansho Maru, which received a shower from a miss. The ship was reported to have anchored between Dublon and Fefan. Recovery was effected by 1544 h. The Air Observer was landed as well.

Prior of the recovery of this strike, a single Avenger made an emergency landing with an injured crew member - at 1322 h. Exactly one hour later the same occurred, but this time there were two injured crew members on the three-seater plane. One of the air crew succumbed to his wounds upon arrival.

One of the Hellcats of the Target Observer team was shot down. The other three scored each one Japanese fighter downed.

Strike 1 FY - 17 02 44

The intention of this strike was to destroy service facilities at the air fields. Launching was begun at 1514 h and finished at 1525 h; recovery took place between 1751 and 1812 h. Eight tons of long-delay fused bombs were dropped on the Param air field rendering it temporarily unserviceable, and denying it to the Japanese as a base for night fighter operations. Bombs with short-delay fuses were dropped on parked planes and service facilities. Large fires were started.

On this strike 33 planes participated: 17 fighters, 4 Avengers and 12 Dauntless.

Night Fighter Activity - 17 02 44

At 2123 h, Yorktown launched a nightfighter to intercept and shoot down Japanese attack planes. The first Japanese plane was contacted by ship's radar and the Hellcat vectored after it. Contact was not established and the Japanese plane soon faded out of range. Afterwards the Hellcat pilot was directed to intercept an extremely low flying plane. Contact was briefly made but quickly lost when the pilot's attention was focussed on retuning his radio set, which drifted out of the assigned frequency. The plane was landed without incident.

Summary of Air Activities - 18 02 44

During the second day of the attack, Hellcats were launched for the Fighter Sweep. On the first strike, 7 Avengers and 15 Dauntless sortied over Truk. 8 Dauntless and 3 Avengers went in on the second strike. These planes were escorted by 8 resp. 6 Hellcats. 59 sorties were flown, including the Air Target Observer, the Group Commander. A total of 20,5 tons of bombs were released over the targets.

Initial Fighter Sweep - 18 02 44

Before dawn on the second day of the attack, the Yorktown launched 12 fighters. The sky belonged almost exclusively to the Americans, with no airborne opposition. The sweep was launched between 0445 and 0455 h and recovered from 0730 to 0751 h. All planes landed safely after their strafing runs.

Strike 1 AY - 18 02 44

The first full strike of the second day consisted of 8 Hellcats, 7 Avengers and 15 Dauntless. North of Moen, the Avengers attacked their first target after the launch at 0455 to 0513 h.

A hangar at the southwest corner of Eten was destroyed with a two bomb hit, and the Moen sea plane base was damaged by two 500 lbs bombs. A freighter escaped serious damage from an attack because the bomb release delayed dropping of the bomb. The location was given as west of Eten, were this and two more ships seemed to have survived the attacks of the previous day. There was evidently a small transport under way to the west of Small Island, but bombs intended for it missed.

Ensign O'Sullivan was shot down with his crew. A hit into their plane destroyed the oil line, and the plane trailed black smoke. The pilot managed to bring his Avenger down in the water. It floated for a few minutes before it nosed down. The crew had ample time to get into the rafts and were finally picked up by a submarine on life guard duty. At the time of rescue the raft had drifted about a mile per hour despite the sea anchor, and was now almost two miles east of the rim reef. All the time the crew was in the water, there was at least one Avenger circling over the men.

The Dauntless sortied against ships in the Uman/Fefan/Dublon area. An apparently large transporter of about 10,000 ts gross was covered with three bombs; the pilots reported two hits and one splash. A freighter between Uman and Fefan was missed with three bombs. An oiler, located at the Repair Anchorage, probably the Hoyo Maru, received a hit midships, but the results were not observed. Near Eten a transport was the target, and was rocked by two close misses. The aircraft were recovered together with the Hellcats from the fighter sweep, between 0730 and 0750 h. One Avenger was shot down; the pilot was rescued.

An Air Observer, the Commander of Air Group 5, was launched with escorting planes at 0710 h, together with the following strike.

Strike 1 BY - 18 02 44

From 0650 to 0703 h, this flight was launched. It consisted of 2 Hellcats, 2 Avengers and 8 Dauntless. At the same time, 4 fighters were started, as Command Group 2, and one photo plane took off as well. In addition, 12 Hellcats were started for Combat Air Patrol, and 8 Avengers for Anti submarine Patrol, bringing the total of this launch to 37 planes. The events were anticlimactic. Neither CAP or ASP saw any action. The planes over Truk did not fare much better. Only the photographic plane brought home a few interesting pictures, which can be found in the Theodore Spawn Collection in the US National Archives. Only one hit was recorded, resulting from this strike. The bombers dropped one bomb onto the bow of a freighter.

This was the last strike of Yorktown on the second day of the first carrier raid on Truk.

Hailstorm - *Historic Documentation*

BATTLE REPORT TG 58.2

On 13 and 14 February 1944, the Task Group sortied from Majuro. They refuelled all ships, except the two large carriers, enroute on 15 and 16 February. The Task Group continued their approach undetected, and made the run to the initial launching point during the night of 16 February. Planes were launched according to the Air Master Plan on 17 and 18 February.

Yorktown launched a night fighter, which was directed from Enterprise. At 2226 h on 17 February, the group was approached by a Japanese fighter plane. The order to open fire was given, and ships having a good radar fix on the intruder began shooting. The plane withdrew without being hit. About one and a half hours after the initial contact, a second Japanese plane approached. It was pursued by the night fighter. The contact was code named George. Due to a probable malfunction of the radar set of this night fighter, the attacking plane could not be intercepted, although the range closed to about half a mile. The American plane was ordered to break off the pursuit to enable the anti-aircraft batteries of TG 58.2 to open fire. No proper vectoring was given for the plane, so that as a consequence, it stumbled in and out of the effective range of the American ship borne anti-aircraft guns. Batteries were not released therefore, as the night fighter was still in range. The Task Group was speeding at 25 knots through the water and maneuvered to keep the Japanese plane astern of the formation.

At about midnight, this low powered monoplane, the pursuing American pilot had identified it as a Betty, made a sharp turn to the left, dived to 50 ft (15 m), and released a torpedo when 300 yards abeam of the Intrepid. In the moonlight the splash could be seen from the ship, but not the wake. The torpedo struck the carrier as it made a high speed left turn, at starboard quarter. The explosion occurred at 0011 h, centered at the rudder post, and resulted in a jammed rudder, accompanied by flooding of the steering engine room. Shell plating was ripped open from the keel to the fourth deck over 18 1/2 frames on starboard. The largest hole measured 20 by 30 ft (6 by 9 m). The Intrepid could be steered fairly well with the propellers at speeds above 18 knots. Personnel casualties were 5 killed, 6 missing (believed killed) and 10 injured.

The Intrepid was immediately withdrawn and detached from the formation.

At 0100 h, 18 February 1944, Task Group 58.2.4 was set up to bring the Intrepid to Majuro. The light carrier Cabot provided aircraft escort and San Francisco, Wichita and four destroyers were detached as well. Upon reaching Majuro, the Intrepid was sent

The extent of the torpedo damage to the stern of the Intrepid (CV 11) was revealed when the ship went into drydock in Pearl Harbor on 26 February 1944. The starboar side and the rudder machine suffered significant damages.

to Pearl Harbor and subsequently to San Francisco for repairs. The remaining units were held over in Majuro for further deployment.

The two air attacks were the only contacts Task Group 58.2 had with Japanese forces. After the strikes on Truk, Essex and the remaining ships of TG 58.2 were amalgamated with Task Group 58.1 to effect a better concentration of forces.

From the 129 planes claimed to have been shot down by the Americans in air combat, 48 were credited to TG 58.2. Out of this total, 31 were fighters, 30 Zeros and 1 Oscar. 61 planes were reported to have been destroyed on the ground or on the water by fire and 20 were said to be severely damaged. In turn, 9 planes were lost by the Group in combat and 3 operational, with 14 losses of personnel. These light losses have to be compared with 556 sorties flown during the 2 day operation. They resulted in 4 ships confirmed sunk, 2 left sinking, and 24 estimated to have been damaged.

AIRCRAFT ACTION REPORTS

CABOT

Summary

Cabot, the light carrier of Task Group 58.2, with Air Group 31 aboard, furnished Combat Air and Anti Submarine Patrols during the both days of the raid. However, twice Avengers (TBM-1C) were flown off the deck to participate on direct combat missions with planes from the attack carriers.

The first was a sortie to bomb shipping outside the lagoon. Launch of 3 Avengers was completed at 0925 h, on the first day, and all planes were back by 1158 h. Each plane carried 4 - 500 lbs general purpose bombs with short delay fuses. During approach to the target, a Japanese plane was seen in the distance, close to the carrier formation, maneuvering radically to avoid American ship-borne anti aircraft fire.

The targets were found 15 miles (25 km) outside of the North Pass, on bearing 292 degrees, and attacked between 1040 and 1045 h. There were two ships. One was thought to be a light cruiser of the Yubari-Class - the Katori bears a superficial resemblence - , and a large freighter of the Amagisan-Class, actually the Akagi Maru of that class.

Both ships were in the process to complete a tight circle to starboard; the Katori being in the lead, at about 10 to 15 knots. Originally, all planes, which included 3 TBF Dauntless from VT 9, Essex, attacked the ship, but all bombs dropped on her missed, while 4 did not release. The flight leader lost the cruiser out of his sight while going through a cloud, so he corkscrewed and got on to the freighter. He dropped 4 bombs on it in a salvo. The first bomb was a close miss to starboard, the second and third exploded on the aft welldeck, and the fourth was a close miss to port. A violent explosion followed. The Akagi Maru settled rapidly by the stern and began to sink. When the planes departed the decks of the aft ship were already awash. Shortly afterwards other planes reported the freighter sunk.

During the attack, the Katori fired heavy anti-aircraft guns, which were close in altitude but off in deflection, at the planes. Until hit, the Akagi hammered with twin machine weapons at the American planes, but her fire ceased after the explosion. The Katori emerged aft of the Akagi Maru, having passed through the smoke, when she completed her turn.

On the second mission, 3 TBM were loaded with fragmentation clusters, instantaneously fused, to be dropped on Moen Island. The flight section was joined by planes from Air Group 9 (Essex), and Air Group 6 (Intrepid).

The lead plane laddered down to avoid anti-aircraft fire, which was particularly intensive in that area, and broke through the cloud cover almost entirely overhead of several dispersed Betty's on the northeast, northwest and south side of the field. Bombs dropped on the northwest side did not show any damages. The load of the next plane ignited 4 or may be 5 Betty bombers. Finally, the third plane was not content with a just half-well executed run, but climbed out of it and came in from a different angle. Although his second approach had been expected, and his plane met with a hail of machine weapons fire, the pilot dropped his clusters on 7 Bettys, which all exploded and burned to wrecks on the ground. It confirmed earlier observations that the Japanese kept their planes gassed up and manned, a technique for which they suffered the highest possible casualties.

Heavy anti-aircraft fire was reported from Moen, but Dublon's defenses were considered even more intense.

Cabot — USNA

ESSEX

Summary

The initial launching point, 90 miles (145 km) northeast at bearing 60 degrees from Dublon, was reached before dawn on 17 February 1944. During aircraft launching and recovery the ship steamed into the wind on a northeasterly course. While her strikes were airborne she zig-zagged on various courses until flight operations resumed. The basically northeasterly course was followed by a southerly tack in the night of the 17th to 18th February. The Essex ran on a parallel course to the Intrepid, which was 2000 yards off her starboard beam, when the latter carrier was hit by the torpedo. The second day's operation was begun from a point about 80 miles (129 km) east of Dublon. The carrier steamed on bearing 70 degrees during the flight operation, and followed the same pattern as on the previous day. Retirement was commenced about noon on 18 February on an easterly course, at 25 knots.

During the raid, 277 sorties were flown altogether, with 260 sorties over targets in Truk, 14 sorties for Combat Air and Anti-Submarine Patrols, and the remainder Air Target Observer. A total of 415 bombs (91.75 tons) and 6 torpedoes were dropped. The majority of the 36 confirmed Japanese planes shot down (20 were Zeros), were downed during the initial fighter sweep for which Essex supplied intermediate cover. 37 planes, 12 of them float planes, were estimated to be destroyed on the ground. Two hostile planes were shot up so badly that they were believed to have crashed. Almost 79,000 rounds were shot from the board weapons during aerial combat and strafing attacks on shipping, hangars and service installations on the Truk Islands. Although five ships were reported sunk in the Action Report, Task Group 58.2 only took credit for 4 actual sinkings. 28 ships were reported to have been damaged.

Carrier Air Group 9 was based on the Essex. There were 85 planes on board (36 Hellcats, 18 Avengers and 31 Dauntless). Three Dauntless were out of commission. During the first day of the operation, one Hellcat was shot down while on the Initial Fighter Sweep, one Avenger was downed on Strike 2B, one Hellcat made a waterlanding, the pilot was rescued by the destroyer Bell. On Strike 2E, one Avenger was lost operationally. It crashed over the starboard bow of the ship during the launch, and the crew was lost. The pilot of a Hellcat, lost operationally on Strike 2D, was recovered. During the second day, a Hellcat was downed inside the lagoon. The pilot bailed out and was recovered by a float plane. This happened during the Initial Fighter Sweep of the second day. A total of 79 planes remained on board the carrier, of which 6 underwent extensive overhauls.

Initial Fighter Sweep - 17 02 44

Launched at 0441 h, eleven Hellcats were over the target at 0555 h. The pilots were charged with two objectives: Strafing of the airfields and wrestling down airborne resistance. Five strafing runs were made on the Moen sea plane base, where about 25 planes were parked on the ramp and in the shallow waters. The pilots reported 10 to 12 Rufes destroyed by their board weapons before they could take off. The planes then attacked Param airfield and strafed repeatedly. Japanese planes on the runway and apron were identified as Kates and Bettys. Again, 12 planes were seen to go up in smoke.

Although they flew high at 14,000 ft (4270 m) the last division of Hellcats were attacked from above by several Japanese fighters. This came as a complete surprise to the Americans, as the Japanese pilots expertly came out of the sun and from behind. The American planes had to resort to independent evasive actions, mainly steep dives, to draw the Zekes down to their level and to turn the tables on the attacker. In wild fights these three Hellcats accounted for 5 Zekes and 3 Rufes confirmed shot down. Also the second division of this flight, consisting of 3 Hellcats, was continuously engaged in air combat. During almost 45 minutes of turbulent dogfights, until they headed back to the carrier, they were credited with the destruction of three Zekes, and one Rufe and Oscar each.

The first division made two circles around the target area to see whether they would be required to render assistance. It was difficult to make heads and tails out of the general confusion, and the Hellcats seemed to have the upper hand. The section leader therefore began the strafing runs. While the strafing was in progress, the American pilots observed Japanese planes in the process of taking off. Four Kates and an equal number of Petes were shot down in the air. It was estimated that at least 50 Japanese planes were in the air, some of which had just become airborne. It was also observed that one Hellcat shot a long burst into another Hellcat, which went down trailing smoke. Neither plane was from the Essex.

It was recommended that in future a Combat Air Patrol should be maintained over the target area. Firstly these planes could keep down airborne resistance and prevent a built-up during incoming waves of American planes. Secondly, they should be able to prevent dangerous interception by defending planes of slow and more vulnerable bombers and torpedo bombers.

The Avengers were recovered at 0725 h.

Strike 2 A - 17 02 44

Ten Hellcats, nine Avengers and 17 Dauntless were launched at 0514 h. It took only 23 minutes to get all 35 planes airborne. Bombers and torpedo bombers were loaded with 500 lbs general purpose and 1000 lbs armour piercing bombs. Two Avengers returned with engine trouble before reaching the lagoon. The targets were ships at the Fourth Fleet Anchorage. Secondary attacks were planned on Dublon shore installations.

The Hellcats had an easy time, as airborne

Hailstorm - *Historic Documentation*

opposition was virtually wiped out in the sector the planes were covering. The bombers made gliding attacks on what they thought was a cruiser, anchored southeast of Eten, and plastered bombs around the stern. A hit was reported, black smoke engulfing the ship. It is interesting to note that Yorktown, on Strike 1B, also attacked what the pilots took as a cruiser. The ship was reported to have been in the same area. The attacking planes of Yorktown claimed to have hit the ship as well. Frequently, fleet destroyers have been mistakenly identified as cruisers. Enterprise pilots reported a destroyer south of Eten on Strike 1E. Earlier, the same pilots reported the presence of the seaplane tender Akitsushima in the general area, during the first two strikes of the first day. Intrepid reported the Akitsushima on the first strike of the first day, and the planes from Bunker Hill made an attack. It appears, therefore, that the cruiser south of Eten was indeed a destroyer, while the Akitsushima was located at the Fourth Fleet Anchorage, in the vicinity of the Aikoku Maru, but farther east.

A cargo ship, located 3 miles (5 km) northeast of Eten, on bearing 60 degrees, was observed receiving a direct hit on the stern. When the smoke cleared away the stern appeared to be missing. This ship may have been the Hokuyo Maru. About 3 miles (5 km) east-northeast of Eten a cargo ship was attacked and the pilots believed they saw two hits. One was midships, the other just aft of the bridge. Two large secondary explosions were reported and the ship was burning. All evidence points to the Reiyo Maru. This ship is damaged midships and aft, and signs of a severe fire are eminent. The location is also in basic agreement with the report. The third ship's position is given as just southwest of Eten. A bomb dropped near the bow, and black smoke was seen enveloping the vessel. From its position it could have been either the Fujikawa or the Rio de Janeiro Maru. The Rio shows some damage on her bow.

The first target of the Avengers was a 300 ft (91 m) long ship, tentatively identified as an oiler. The decks were painted red. It was anchored about two miles (3 km) east of Dublon. One bomb was seen to explode at the bow, and the ship seemed to burn when the planes left. A salvo of four to six bombs straddled and finally hit a cargo ship at anchor in the middle of the Fourth Fleet Anchorage. After the black smoke from the bomb explosion had cleared the ship smoked from hits midships. A third cargo ship of large size was the next target. It was at anchor two miles east of the north part of Dublon. The four 500 lbs general purpose bombs hit on or around the stern. The size of the next target was given as about 10,000 ts. The freighter or oiler, painted grey, was anchored about 1200 yards from the south tip of Eten, on a bearing of 150 degrees. The bombs were dropped near or on the midship area and slightly aft. Also this vessel was left burning and heavily smoking. A destroyer, originally identified as a light cruiser, was subjected to the last attack and began to smoke as well. The position was reported to be 1.5 miles (2,5 km) east of the northeast point of Dublon. The bombs detonated near the stern. The ship was painted in two tones of green.

The planes were recovered at 0725 h to 0814, together with the Hellcats returning from the Initial Fighter Sweep. One Avenger was lost in combat, one fighter for operational reasons. One Hellcat from the Cabot was landed on Essex.

Strike 2 B - 17 02 44

At 0711 this strike was launched with 14 (the ship's log indicates 12) Hellcats, 9 Avengers, and 12 Dauntless. Targets for the bombs were ships south and west of Dublon. In the meantime, the Japanese scrambled quite a number of fighter planes. Upon arrival at the target area the Hellcats broke off in divisions of three and six, respectively. One division covered the Dauntless when they were on their bombing dives, while other divisions were engaged in heavy air fighting. One of the Hellcats strafed Param airfield. Although many Japanese planes were discovered on this field, the other Hellcats did not have a chance to go down and strafe; they had all hands full to fight airborne resistance.

How important it was to fly escort for the Dauntless became evident when one Hellcat pilot saw three Zekes off his port beam. The American pilot made a sharp turn and managed to get his gun to bear against the second Zeke. Being hit, the Japanese plane fell smoking. The third of the Zeke was taken head on, and the shells could be seen hitting the Japanese plane. It spun out of control and hit the water. A Hamp was doing a slow turn to port and the same pilot fired at it. Immediately, the Japanese plane trailed smoke and the pilot bailed out. A second Hellcat demolished an attacking Hamp, which also burst into flame after being hit. Two American fighters had the opportunity to meet two Zekes head on. Both Japanese exploded, and the American pilots recognized that the Japanese planes, once hit, generally burst into flames. A single Zero made an approach from starboard and above on a Hellcat, then at 3,500 ft (1070 m), just recovering from a strafing run. The pilot and his wingman chased the Zero into a cloud. When it emerged again they were above and behind it. The Japanese pilot commenced a vertical climb, to a loop, but when he reached the highest point the American bullets hit the plane. The Japanese pilot attempted to fall off and turn behind the Hellcats, but they managed to turn inside and commenced shooting. Also this Zero went down in flames. These American pilots continued to climb, and encountered another Zeke, which they shot down. The total on this flight was 14 Japanese fighters destroyed in the air. One Hellcat made a water landing as it had run out of gas. The pilot was rescued by a destroyer. Another Hellcat landed on the Intrepid.

The first target of the Dauntless was what was thought to be a light cruiser but probably was a destroyer at anchor west of Dublon. An explosion was observed at the bow. A transporter of about 7000 ts was tied alongside this warship and received a bomb hit amidships, which started a fire. Both ships were reported west of the southwest tip of Dublon, 270 degrees and 1200 yards from the shore. The report about a warship west of Dublon, and a freighter tied alongside it is very interesting.

Hailstorm - *Historic Documentation*

Northeast of Fefan a tanker was located, but the bombs destined for it missed the ship. The last target of the Avengers was a cargo ship at anchor about 1 mile (1,6) west of Dublon. Its size was given with 5000 ts. Of the three bombs one was seen to explode on the stern.

Japanese planes repeatedly attacked Avengers. They were repulsed, with one Zero confirmed, and another believed, to be shot down. The Avengers then attacked a prize bounty. A 10-12000 ts ship was anchored approximately two miles (about 3 km) east of the eastern point of Dublon. It looked very much like a large ocean liner, with a large midship superstructure and a big, single stack. Two hits were observed. The ship was seen to explode with terrific force and sank immediately thereafter. No other planes were seen between the time of the attack and the explosion. There is no doubt that this was the Aikoku Maru, which met her violent end around 0825 h. However, the pilots evidently did not see that planes from the Intrepid were on their tail, which began their drop immediately after the Essex planes had recovered. While the pilots from the Essex Avengers felt that there was a few minutes between bomb hit and explosion, and the bombs had hit midships, Intrepid's pilots had a different version, and Japanese survivors of Truk still another yet.

The next ship was the second one from the east at the anchorage. The pilots reported two hits at the aft holds or the stern. They started a fire, and the ship was left burning. Also left burning was a third vessel anchored about a mile east of the northern tip of Eten. The bombs exploded near the midship section. Close by, a fourth transporter was at anchor. The location was given as being one mile off the northern tip of Eten, and the size of the ship about 10,000 ts gross. Identification is not certain, but it could have been the San Francisco Maru, Hokuyo Maru or the Seiko Maru, which were attacked. Three bombs resulted in smoke coming from the aftership. The ship being farthest north in the Fourth Fleet Anchorage was selected as next target. The diving attack resulted in one bomb exploding near midship port, the other starboard beam or quarter. This freighter, estimate to be 10,000 ts large, began to burn and roll over to starboard. Evidence of the damage sustained by the Nippo Maru suggests that this ship was attacked. When it sank it had developed a list to port.

The last victim was located about two miles (about 3 km) southwest of Eten. Two bombs exploded in the water on port midships and port quarter. This ship was slightly smaller than the previous four. It began to list to starboard. The tonnage was estimated to be 8,000 ts.

Meanwhile, at 0842 h, four fighters were launched as Air Observer, proceeding to the lagoon, and the fighter from Cabot was returned. At 0908h, Combat Air Patrol reported a rapidly submerging submarine on bearing 277 degrees, at a distance of 18 miles.

During a glide bombing run an Avenger was seen not to pull out of the dive and crashed into the water. The crew of three and the plane were lost. The other planes were recovered from 0942 h to 1020 h. The ship's log reports the recovery from 1003 h to 1025 h.

The ship received the report that Yorktown's Combat Air Patrol had shot down a Val torpedo plane at a bearing of 268 degrees and 27 miles distant. At 1026 h a report of another Val shot down was intercepted. It was credited to Monterey's Combat Air Patrol. The event occurred 18 miles to the north.

Strike 2 C - 17 02 44

Together with the planes for this flight, 3 Avengers were launched as Anti Submarine Patrol. They were armed with 325 lbs depth charges. The primary targets of Strike 2C were the combat ships northwest of the North Pass. The strike was launched at 0924 h and consisted of 14 fighters, 3 torpedo bombers, and 15 bombers. They were joined by 3 planes from Cabot. They strafed the Maikaze, about 15 miles (24 km) northwest of the North Pass. The ship seeped oil and an explosion was observed midships. The bombers were not successful, scoring only near misses on the destroyer. However, the Avengers attacked the Katori nearby, while she was circling at about ten knots, bearing 330 degrees, and 15 miles (24 km) off the Pass. Three hits midships and on the stern stopped the cruiser dead in the water.

Those Avengers which carried a torpedo in the bomb bay attacked the ships of the formation. Due to incorrect vectoring and a misidentification the majority converged on the fast moving and radically maneuvering destroyer, and promptly, all torpedoes failed to hit the ship. The Katori was not so lucky when the two remaining planes attacked her. One torpedo hit midships port, sending a huge plume of smoke and water skyward. One of the torpedoes could not be dropped. A merchant ship of about 6-7000 ts, circling with the cruiser, was hit with three bombs on the stern. It settled fast by the stern while smoking, and had sunk when the next flight arrived.

The planes were recovered from 1148 h to 1228 h. They were launched and recovered without losses at the same time as Strike 2C.

Four Hellcats were launched in addition to the planes of this strike. They were designated observers, and circled the ship formation at 13,000 ft (4000m), without being engaged by hostile planes. They saw that two destroyers, one cruiser and one large cargo ship were located about 15 miles, bearing 345 degrees from the North Pass. Several attacks were made in waves by all three types of planes. The freighter received two hits and was burning, while the cruiser suffered one direct hit and several close misses. It smoked for a short time. One of the destroyers was left dead in the water while the other appeared to be undamaged. Another destroyer, not part of this formation of ships, cleverly used cloud cover for hiding. It was attacked by Dauntless, but the bombs missed. A flight of Hellcats strafed the destroyer, which was last seen re-entering the lagoon.

Strike 2 D - 17 02 44

The planes returned to the already crippled cruiser and the destroyer outside the lagoon, off the North Pass. Ten Hellcats were joined by 8 Avengers, 6 of which had been armed with torpedoes and 2 with two 500 lbs bombs each, and 12 (10, according to the log) Dauntless. Launching began at 1122 h, and was completed at 1144 h.

Again, the bombers did not score full hits, but churned up the water close to the destroyer. The Avengers were slightly more successful. A single torpedo hit the Katori at the foreship, on the port bow. It ripped a large hole into the shell plating, which was later observed from the battleship Missouri when the Katori finally succumbed to the gunfire. While capsizing, the damage inflicted by the torpedo was exposed. An explosion followed the torpedo hit. Hellcats swooped down to make strafing runs on the ship. The planes were recovered at 1354 h, with the operational loss of one Hellcat. The landing hook had been shot to pieces by anti-aircraft fire, and landing was not possible. The pilot ditched his plane off the starboard bow and was rescued at 1425 h.

Strike 2 E - 17 02 44

In eleven minutes, from 1330 h to 1341 h, 31 planes were launched. Param airfield was the target for this strike and the six Avengers were loaded with fragmentation clusters. These bombs have a devastating effect on soft land targets and parked aircraft, as the many fragments produced on explosion pierce the fuselage and may render the parked plane unserviceable. Even today, the aircraft damaged by this bombing can be seen at Param. The Japanese just threw the irreparable planes over the runway into the water. The jagged holes in the thin metal speak for the effects of fragmentation bombs. Fires were started on the airstrip. The pilots reported that none of the grounded Japanese planes escaped damage. 5 planes were destroyed.

The 11 Hellcats went in low and shot long bursts of their board cannon into the destroyer Tachikaze, which was grounded at Kuop Atoll, just southeast of the South Pass. The damage was considerable. The anti-aircraft fire of this ship was much reduced and was not quite the menace it had been for planes passing overhead. On the western side of Kuop, not far from the Tachikaze, a small picket boat was strafed. It exploded and sank. Strafing continued on a small transporter in the vicinity of the two other ships. Damage could not be determined. The planes were recovered at 1604 h, with the exception of an Avenger, which crashed on take off and was lost, together with the crew. However, only 5 Hellcats were counted on he flight deck, and 6 were missing. They came in exactly one hour later.

Strike 2 F - 17 02 44

At the same time as this strike was launched, 7 fighters went into the air for Combat Air Patrol. 28 planes, comprised of 8 Hellcats, 7 Avengers, and 13 Dauntless, armed with a varied load of 100, 250 and 500 lbs bombs, continued to bomb Param airfield. They were launched at 1516 h and returned at 1746 h, without losses. The last plane was recovered together with the Combat Air Patrol, at 1815 h. A submerging submarine was reported just after launching 10 miles away at 320 degrees.

The sky unchallenged, the fighters made strafing runs on a small destroyer, starting a fire midships. The ship was seen about three miles (5 km) south of Udot. At the outer rim of the lagoon, near Quoi Island, an impressive looking yacht was anchored. The ship was damaged by strafing, but did not burn. On Quoi a network of trenches and pillboxes were seen.

The other planes added to the mayhem on Param airfield. About 20 planes on the ground were subjected to strafing. The Avengers and Dauntless dropped their incendiary and fragmentation clusters on the facilities and Japanese planes parked alongside the runway. Many fires were started.

Summary of Air Activities - 18 02 44

The fighters went in at dawn, and finding no airborne opposition, strafed airfields and shipping. On the two strikes, the planes reported the sinking of three ships, and damaged 4 more. However, some of the targets had been attacked before. The second strike ended the operation for that day.

Initial Fighter Sweep - 18 02 44

As on the first day of the raid, the fighter sweep of the second day was launched before dawn, from 0449 h to 0500 h, with 10 Hellcats. They skirted the rim of the lagoon, finding no airborne opposition.

The Hellcats made strafing runs on the shipping in the lagoon. Anti-aircraft fire was intense and scored a hit on Lt. (jg) Blair's plane. It made a forced water landing due south and about 15 miles south of Mt. Toloman, almost exactly halfway between the south tip of Uman and the atoll rim. The Hellcats of the flight were rendezvoused over the spot by the flight leader by voice call, and all kept the pilot in sight. There were 9 Hellcats in the sky, a Japanese destroyer in the vicinity and one downed pilot in the water. The planes went low on gas. The destroyer made up steam and nosed into the area to investigate. The nine planes formed a circle and continuously strafed the ship. It turned around and left the scene. Four of the fighters had to return to the carrier, which had received information about the incident already. The destroyer made another run. Again, the planes ganged up and prevented the ship from getting near the pilot. It heaved around and turned away, only to turn around and to wait for the next opportunity. The five planes circled for another 30 minutes. Then, 3 had to leave as their gas got dangerously low. Promptly the destroyer turned around and made a high speed approach. The two remaining planes skimmed the water and keep one set of fingers at the gun triggers and the others crossed. After a hair-raising moment the crew in the destroyer evidently thought that enough is enough, and abandoned the scene to the west. The ship continued its retreat, while the planes had to fly back to the carrier. The pilot was left alone in the water and slowly drifted towards some islands at the southwest end.

Rescue operations were put into motion at TG 58.2. Two of the fighter planes of Strike 2B-2 were ordered to stand by and escort the rescue plane, a Kingfisher, from the cruiser Baltimore to the scene. A

Hailstorm - *Historic Documentation*

long search was averted when the location was corrected. The tiny Kingfisher made a hazardous landing, executed with admirable courage and skill, on the choppy water of the lagoon. The rear seat man had been taken along in case the downed pilot was injured and needed assistance. For weight considerations the plane could not be gassed up completely, but just enough fuel was taken along as was needed. After a very bumpy start, with the dripping Blair on the lap of the rear seat man, the Kingfisher made it back to the cruiser. When the plane was hoisted up and de-gassed, there was less than a pint of gasoline in the tank.

Except for the one Hellcat lost, the other planes landed on the Essex by 0751 h unscathed, except for 2 Hellcats, which stayed over the downed pilot, for more than half an hour, and were relieved by a special rescue mission.

Strike 2 A - 18 02 44

Between 0523 and 0741 h, 4 Avengers for Anti Submarine Patrol and the planes for this strike were launched. The first flight consisted of 8 Hellcats, 6 Avengers and 10 Dauntless, loaded with 500 and 1000 lbs bombs. Shipping at the Eten Anchorage was the main target.

The Avenger zeroed in on a freighter believed to be under way, making about 4 knots, on a bearing of 60 degrees, about 1000 yds from the Eten runway. The attack was executed by three planes, and the ship received hits aft and misses midships and forward. It listed to port, burned furiously and sank. There is little doubt that this was the Shotan Maru. It is one of the two ships which were underway and had her anchor retracted. From her present position it looks as if the crew tried to beach her at Fanamu. They did not quite make it. The Shotan Maru must have sunk quickly because she did not even heave into the wind. The second target was a freighter of about the same size, bearing 85 degrees from Dublon Town. Large flames were seen to emanate from this ship.

Three ships were the subject of attacks by the Dauntless. One of them was anchored southeast of Eten, and was showered by bomb misses. The second freighter was just as lucky at that time, but the third ship really got hit. Bomb hits midships and on port bow caused an explosion and the ship sank quickly. The location suggests the Momokawa Maru.

All planes were back on the carrier by 0741h.

Anti-Submarine Patrol - 18 02 44

Four Dauntless were launched at 0523 h and recovered without incident at 0937 h. Their load of depth charges was not released.

Strike 2 B - 18 02 44

Launched at 0715 h, the 7 fighters, 4 Avengers and 10 bombers (the ship's log deviates from the Aircraft Action Report), again filled with bombs, were to attack the shipping at Fourth Fleet Anchorage. The Hellcats immediately went to the Eten Airfield, finding no airborne opposition, and strafed five Japanese planes on the southeast apron. Fire resulted and the planes were considered destroyed. The fighters then joined the bombers and Avengers on strafing runs on ships at anchor.

Dauntless bombed two transports. The first was hit by a bomb on port quarter, with three other bombs being close misses. The ship burned aft. The location was given as 1000 yards due south (180 degrees) of Eten, but the identity of the ship is not clear. The second vessel was anchored about two miles (3 km) southwest of Eten, on a bearing of 220 degrees. Two bombs were seen exploding at the bow, three other bombs were straddling the ship. The explosions were so forceful that they lifted the bow out of the water, but the actual damage could not be ascertained. The location points to a ship at the Sixth Fleet Anchorage.

In the meantime, the Avengers dropped two bombs on a freighter anchored about one mile east-southeast of Dublon. One bomb hit at port quarter, the other closer than 80 ft (24 m) off the stern. The ship was sinking then, and only a small part of the bow showed above water. It could have been the San Francisco Maru. The last ship attacked by the planes of Essex was a slightly smaller vessel, which was beached on a reef, 1 1/2 miles (2,5 km) east of Dublon. Damage was sustained on the midships superstructure by two bombs, and it immediately began to settle by the stern. A medium sized freighter can be seen in one of the photographs taken by Yorktown planes, which is grounded with the bow on the reef due east of the south-easterly peninsular of Dublon. Evidently, this ship was salvaged and may have been the Hakune Maru. Without further incident all planes were recovered by the carrier at 0937 h.

Special Rescue Mission

Two fighters were launched at 0900 h, to escort the float plane from the heavy cruiser Baltimore. The rescue was successful, as reported. The fighters returned to the Essex at 1043 h. These were the last planes out, and following their successful recovery, flight operations ceased.

INTREPID

The Intrepid was the second large carrier of Task Group 58.2. The raid against Truk was the second battle engagement, and the operation earned this ship - as well as the other carriers - a Battle Star.

However, the Intrepid was probably not the luckiest of ships. It had a certain affinity to accidents, which ranged from grounding inside the Panama Canal to being repeatedly hit by Kamikaze bombers, thus

Hailstorm - *Historic Documentation*

earning the carrier the nickname "The Evil I". Shortly after midnight ship's time, on 18 February 1944, a Japanese plane dropped a torpedo, when the formation made an emergency turn, which hit the carrier in the vicinity of the rudder post. The rudder jammed. The ship could barely maintain steering way with the undamaged propellers, and was detached a few minutes later with a selected group of surface ships. They retired to Majuro. It was decided there, that the hazards of getting into the lagoon would be too great. Course was set to Pearl Harbor, where she arrived on 24 February. A jury rigged sail had to be used to stabilize the movements of the ship which was severely weather-rocked by the strong winds. The inspection in Pearl Harbor revealed extensive damage. The ship was ordered to Hunters Point, San Francisco. Almost three days into the voyage to the mainland, the Intrepid had to give up, as her limited ability to steer was more than matched by the prevailing winds and swells. She had a tendency to point her bow towards Tokyo. The skipper was convinced that this course was premature, and the escorting destroyers towed her back to Pearl Harbor. She left, this time under tow, and finally arrived in San Francisco on 22 March 1944.

Summary of Air Activities:

The planes were organized in Air Group 6. During her one day operation against Truk, planes of the Intrepid flew 193 sorties and lost 7 aircraft. 11 planes were damaged. The planes were involved in quite a bit of action and shot down 17 Zekes and other types of Japanese aircraft. On the ground they claimed to have destroyed 43 Japanese planes. The light cruiser Katori was immobilized; the seaplane tender Akitsushima, 2 destroyers and 9 other ships were damaged. One freighter was definitely sunk, and the Aikoku Maru was taken as sunk by the Intrepid in the reports. A total of 224 bombs were dropped, and 12 torpedoes launched against targets outside the lagoon.

Initial Fighter Sweep - 17 02 44

The Hellcats were flown off the flight deck at 0440 h. They were over the target area at 0605 h, just at sunrise. Planes could be seen and Betty bombers took off. Anti-aircraft fire was intense while the strafing runs were executed. The last Hellcats were attacked by a group of six or seven Zeros. It was two against seven. The Japanese had altitude advantage and showed no reluctance to attack so early in the hostilities. In wild acrobatics the Hellcats avoided most of the shots directed against them and maneuvered successfully to get the Japanese planes down to their altitude. Once this was accomplished the Hellcats counterattacked. Following the Zeros down in steep dives from 8000 ft they managed to shoot down three of their adversaries. The fourth escaped into a cloud, but the pilot of the Hellcat outfoxed him by starting to climb into the sun. The Japanese pilot emerged and was totally surprised by the American plane coming from above. The American pilot aimed at the wing tank of the Japanese plane and set the plane ablaze. Seconds later it exploded in mid-air. The American pilots were convinced that the Japanese pilots were inexperienced and failed to press home their advantage.

In the meantime the ten other fighters arrived and began strafing runs on Moen airfield. The Commanding Officer of Fighter Squadron 6 raced like an avenging angel up and down the Moen fighter strip, strafing continuously on all 12 runs. 15 Betty bombers were set afire and 8 Zekes and one unidentified plane destroyed. The planes made forty runs on Moen, continued to rake Param, and on their pull-out continued to strafe the sea plane base at the southwest tip of Moen. The burning planes on these runways smoked heavily. At 0710 h the Commanding Officer saw a lone Zeke which he attacked. The evasive reaction of the pilot were slow and it was hit burning with a red glow inside the cockpit. It crashed into the water southwest of Param. Another Zeke was encountered at about 3500 ft (1000 m) altitude, flying in the same direction as the American plane. One Hellcat chased after it and fired a short burst from the distance. The American pilot was convinced that the distance for the shooting was much too long, but to his surprise the Zeke flared up at the wingroot and exploded. Many more Japanese planes were met in aerial combat, and altogether 11 were shot down. It was believed that 24 were burned on the ground. Enroute to the rendezvous point for retirement, the Katori was spotted heading north between North and Northeast Pass. Apparently, the cruiser was steaming to a point to the east, as there were two or three destroyers waiting slightly west of the North Pass. Again, the squadron commander led his planes on a strafing run, but his luck had run out. He was shot down by anti-aircraft fire. He made a waterlanding right outside the lagoon, west of the North Pass and drifted towards the atoll rim. His wingman orbited around his position while he saw the Katori-group pass through the North Pass, sailing northwest. This only Hellcat strafed the Akagi Maru, which passed closest by the downed pilot, and started a fire on the ship. Heavy anti-aircraft fire came from the ships and the Hellcat was hit repeatedly. One round sprayed fragments through the bullet-proof canopy glass, injuring the pilot in the face. He nevertheless dropped his dye marker, float and water rations to the water-treating pilot, who had the somewhat dubious pleasure to see all four ships pass by him closely. Eventually he managed to get to Alanenkobwe Island. He was seen twice thereafter, having written his name with rocks on the beach and waving to passing planes. Arrangements had been made to rescue him the next day by the Commander Task Group 58.2, but the Intrepid was not informed whether he was indeed picked up. They had enough problems themselves then.

Strike 2 A - 17 02 44

34 planes were launched at 0520 h. The mission of the 13 fighters was to fly escort and maintain air superiority. The 12 Dauntless were armed with 1000 lbs bombs to be used against shipping, and the 9 Avengers carried a load of incendiary and fragmentation clusters to be dropped on the seaplane

Hailstorm - *Historic Documentation*

base at the southwest corner of Moen. It was reported that they destroyed 1 Mavis and 10 to 15 Rufes. The enterprising snorkler may still find some pieces of plane wreckage - mainly radial engines - quite a distance from the hotel dock. The record is a count of 13 individual engines on one long snorkel excursion.

During their mission to protect the other planes, the Hellcats shot down one Oscar and a Val.

The flight leader directed his planes to attack a fast moving ship which was thought to be a light cruiser. The ship was steaming north and was located slightly west of the East Pass. The bomb dropped close to port beam but the ship continued with a sharp turn, firing medium and light anti-aircraft guns.

One division of planes did not join into the chase but attacked ships located to the east of Eten. One plane obtained a hit on a sea plane tender. It had a heavy platform aft of the stack and was thought to be the largest ship in the anchorage. The bomb exploded midships, blew the sides out and started a large fire. It was the Akitsushima, which was used as a cargo ship at that time. It had just taken on board large amounts of war supplies from the Aikoku Maru, and was scheduled to have soldiers transferred from the same ship on that day. The Akitsushima was seen during the next strike, burning and low in the water. This ship received a number of hits and near misses, but was only partly damaged. It remained in service and was sunk later in the war.

The Executive Officer of Bomber Squadron 6 was shot down and killed.

Strike 2 B   17 02 44

The planes were launched at 0715 h. The flight consisted of 12 Dauntless, armed with 1000 lbs bombs, 8 Avengers with a load of 2000 and four 500 lbs bombs respectively, and 12 Hellcats acting as escort. One torpedo bomber lost altitude during take-off and plunged into the sea. The crew was rescued.

On the approach to the target area the planes saw two warships attempting to clear the North Pass. They reported them as cruisers, but there is no doubt that it was the destroyer Shigure and Harusame. The Avengers loaded with 2000 lbs bombs were directed to drop them on the Eten airfield. Only two bombs released and hit the target.

The remaining torpedo bombers dropped their load on the merchant vessels between Eten and Dublon, obtaining one certain hit. At 0825 h, one of the Avengers, piloted by Lt. Bridges, was last seen when it made a dive bombing attack on a very large vessel to the east of Dublon. Just when it was over the target, the ship, being under simultaneous attack by planes from Essex, exploded with terrific force. The explosion threw up a mushroom cloud higher than 1000 ft (300 m). The Intrepid plane was caught in the shock wave and disintegrated in mid-air. The pilot, the two crew and the plane were lost. It was the Aikoku Maru which went up in a huge fireball and sank immediately. A Japanese eye witness account remembered that the plane was hit by anti-aircraft fire and crashed into the foreship of the Aikoku Maru. At this time the cargo of explosives had not been unloaded.

The Avengers came under attack from Zekes, during their pull-out. These Japanese planes had taken off from Eten airfield, using only about two thirds of the runway. Although the Zekes were able to outmaneuver the American planes their fire power was inferior. These Japanese flyers were judged to be poor shooters and pilots by their American counterparts. One Avengers was damaged by anti-aircraft fire and made a water landing outside the lagoon. The crew was picked up by the destroyer Bradford.

Although the target for the bombers was the Dublon seaplane base, 3 of them dropped bombs at 0900 h on a large freighter south of Eten and reported a hit. The remaining 9 Dauntless attacked their assigned target, destroying 4 planes and a number of buildings. Also, these planes encountered several Zekes, which pressed home their attack. One plane, piloted by Lt. Philips, was hit and seen to cross the lagoon in an easterly direction, losing altitude. He reported that the plane could not be held in the air and that he was too low to jettison his bombs. As his wingman was busy to shoot Zekes off his tail he failed to see Lt. Philips go down. It is probable that his plane waterlanded on a reef at the north east side of Dublon, and that it was him who was observed by natives and Japanese lying injured in the shallow water off the Fourth Fleet headquarters buildings. He was later pulled out by the Japanese.

The fighters saw some action. They shot down 2 Zekes in aerial combat.

Strike 2 C - 17 02 44

This strike was launched between 0915 h and 0930 h, and was probably the least successful. There were 32 planes in the air: 12 Dauntless were armed with 1000 lbs bombs, 5 of the 8 Avengers were loaded with torpedoes and the rest with four 500 lbs bombs each. Twelve fighters escorted the planes.

On arrival at Truk three Avengers, loaded with torpedoes and six Dauntless were directed to attack a destroyer. It was described as "old type with two stacks, one gun mount forward and a turtle back". It was the Shigure, which was steaming back to the North Pass. The speed was estimated to be 20 knots, and a large oil slick indicated that the ship had come out of the North Pass, engaged in several violent maneuvers and had just completed a full circle. One bomb hit the aft edge of the stern. The destroyer maintained his sharp turn, indicating that the rudder was jammed. The location of the ship was given as being about 5 to 10 miles (8 to 16 km) northwest of the Pass. All torpedoes missed the target. A bomb from a Dauntless was seen to hit midships, but the destroyer continued with the same speed and direction. When the planes commenced their retirement they saw an Oscar on the tail of a lone Avenger. The American plane was shot down. The Oscar then turned into the flight leader of the Intrepid Avengers, but was driven off with his engine smoking.

The second division of Dauntless with the remaining six planes attacked a fast and maneuverable "old type" destroyer. This ship headed north in the direction of the North Pass and stood about four miles

Hailstorm - *Historic Documentation*

(6 km) west of the northwest corner of Moen. The bomb dropped were all close misses. During their rendezvous for the flight back to the carrier they saw a friendly plane making a forced water landing.

The Commanding Officer of the Intrepid Fighter Squadron, Lt. Cmdr Philips, and his wingman were Target Observer and went directly to Truk. Nobody ever heard anything again of these two pilots. The Strike lost 2 aircraft due to anti-aircraft fire. Among the pilots killed was the third officer of senior rank lost in this operation so far.

Strike 2 D - 17 02 44

The planes of the Intrepid were vectored to the group of warships under heavy attack northwest of the North Pass. It was this strike, which spelled the end for the Katori and the destroyer Maikaze. The aircraft were launched at 1132 h and comprised of 7 Avengers with one torpedo each, and 11 Dauntless with one 1000 lbs bomb each, escorted by 16 fighters. The ships were found 15 to 20 miles (about 30 km) from the North Pass. The initial run on the cruiser was made by a few Dauntless which delivered a bomb midships, rocking the ship. The torpedo bombers moved in at 1315 h. The first torpedo hit the Katori just aft of midships, the second exploded on the starboard bow. The cruiser developed a heavy list and stopped dead in the water. The bombers had taken the Maikaze to task, which was slightly northeast of the Katori. A bomb detonated on the bow and stopped the forward movement of the destroyer. Another ship was sighted close by. It was tentatively identified as a destroyer, but may have been the Nowake, which continued a high speed retirement to the north west. Significantly, the pilots observed floating wreckage, life boats and a large oil slick about two miles west of the Katori. It had been the site of the disaster which befell the Akagi Maru.

The American battleships of Task Group 50.9 were seen to approach; they were about 15 miles (about 25 km) distant to the east, closing the range.

The planes observed another destroyer, Nowake, making radical turns about 5 miles (8 km) north of the Katori.

Strike 2 E - 17 02 44

At 1330 h, 12 fighters and 12 bombers were launched. The Avengers did not participate in this strike as they were detached for patrol duty. The planes were taken out of the hot spots and directed to attack a group of ships seen 80 to 90 miles (about 150 km) west of Truk. The Dauntless were loaded with one 1000 lbs bomb each.

The group of ships consisted of one freighter which was estimated to be 10 to 12,000 ts, a second one of about 4,000 ts, and an oiler of 5,000 ts, being escorted by what appeared to the American pilots a sea going tug. The three transports were sailing in a column. The first ship looked like a tanker, the next was a medium sized transport and the third ship, flanked by the tug was the largest ship the pilots and gunners had seen so far. There were well decks at the fore and aft ship, a single, high stack and a low-profile midships superstructure. The well decks fore and aft of the midships superstructure were piled up high with crated, almost as high as the bridge. This ship had little cargo storage facilities, because it was an old fashioned tanker, the Zuiho Maru, of 7,360 ts, built in 1917. The speed was a slow 5 knots, on a course of 280 degrees. It appeared as if the convoy was informed about the attack on Truk and had turned around.

This large ship was attacked first. Four amor-piercing 1000 lbs bombs were dropped. One hit very near the stack. The ship immediately belched bright red flames, which were followed by a terrific explosion. The Zuiho Maru sank within five minutes. The leading oiler was subjected to the second bombing attack and sustained a hit aft of the superstructure. An explosion followed. It was the Shinwa Maru. The ship sank later. The smaller vessel escaped damage; the bombs intended for it missed.

A destroyer was observed 15 miles (24 km) east of this group on the way to Truk. It definitely was the escorting vessel, which had made up steam to run to Truk, perhaps under the assumption that it could be of some help there. A second destroyer was spotted 75 miles west of Truk. It steamed away from Truk on a course of 270 degrees at very high speed. It was the Nowake, only surviving ship of the Katori formation.

The flight leader intended to inform Task Group 50.9 about the situation by means of a message drop on the battleship. When his formation passed the ships, he banked and returned for the drop. The orders "Track friendly plane, do not fire" were misunderstood by one 20 mm gun crew on the Iowa, who efficiently demolished the plane in the air. With it the fourth of the ranking officers was killed.

In the meantime, the fighters flew cover for the Avengers from Essex and later wrestled down the anti-aircraft defences of the grounded destroyer Tachikaze, but were not too successful. A small freighter was seen to explode at 1615 h from a bomb hit about 10 miles (17 km) southwest from Eten.

Strike 2 F - 17 02 44

The strike was launched at 1515 h and was the last one taking off from Intrepid on this operation. It consisted of 11 fighters, 8 Avengers and 11 bombers. The bombs hit Moen airfield and the revetments, causing significant damage and burned up one Zeke. The bombers were protected by the Hellcats which downed another Zeke and burned one Betty bomber on the ground. The Avengers went to the area around Eten and attacked a small cargo vessel. On another ship off the east shore of Fefan, three bombs were believed to have hit. Two bombs were observed to have hit the stern and one near the bow. The damage is consistent with the appearance of the Kansho Maru. The second ship was located at the south shore of Dublon, near the south west tip. A direct hit amidships was believed to have been seen, causing an explosion and smoke. The airfield on Eten was damaged by several specially long-delay fused bombs.

Combat Air and Anti Submarine Patrols

For the CAP, 7 fighters, and for the ASP, 6 Avengers were launched. No contacts were made and

Hailstorm - *Historic Documentation*

the planes were recovered without incident.

This ended the daylight operations of the Intrepid against Truk. Several hours later she was the victim of a Japanese torpedo plane attack.

The Intrepid Torpedoed

When Task Group 58.1 and 58.2 were about 120 miles (193 km) east of Truk, they were attacked by Japanese planes. These attacks resulted in a torpedo hit on the carrier Intrepid. The weather was fine, one third of the sky was cloudy. The wind was as usual from east-northeast with a velocity of 18 knots. The moon was not yet visible in the sky.

The first radar contact was a single plane coming from the west at 2104 h, ship's time, 40 miles (64 km) out, and with an estimated speed of 120 mph. Ten minutes later, Yorktown was ordered to launch a night fighter, but the catapulting had to be delayed. The Japanese plane passed about 5 miles (8 km) north of the group. Anti-aircraft fire was held by the destroyer screen. It was believed that the plane had not seen the Group. After it had passed it made a 60 degree turn and disappeared.

When the first plane was closest to Task Group 58.1, a second plane showed in the radar scopes at a distance of 45 miles (72 km), pursuing a northeasterly course. It was at 7,000 ft (2130 m) altitude, flying at 140 mph. The Group made a turn to starboard at 2135 h, when the plane was 14 miles (23 km) to the south. It passed the ships about 6 miles (10 km) astern, and the Group made another turn to starboard. The plane turned to the right and proceeded to the vicinity of Task Group 58.3. At 2145 h, it made another turn to the right and returned to Truk at the same altitude. The formations continued to zig-zag.

At 2206 h, the third plane was detected 40 miles (64 km) on a westerly course. It was flying at low altitude, but began to orbit and climb to 3,000 ft (914 m). A flare was seen being dropped from the plane, and the ships made a turn. At 2211 h, the Commander Task Force 58 indicated that a radio message had been intercepted, directing the Japanese planes to join up and attack. Ten minutes later, Yorktown was ordered to launch a night fighter, but this launch was again postponed. The Japanese plane on the radar screen made a spiral approach. As the formation changed course repeatedly, there was a danger of disrupting the formation and the plot on the plane, so that further turns became hazardous. The plane made a gliding torpedo approach to the flank of the ships, reducing the altitude to 200 ft (61 m). Torpedo splashes were not seen, and Santa Fe fired with her 12,7 cm anti-aircraft guns without obtaining a hit. The plane soon faded to the northwest of Task Group 58.2.

Ten minutes after this particular plane had disappeared, a fourth showed up, 25 miles (40 km) to the northeast on a southwesterly course. Flying at 2 500 ft (762 m) altitude, it disappeared at 2233 h without closing in.

The fifth and sixth contacts were probably the same plane as the last one. It succeeded at the end to torpedo the Intrepid. At 2300 h, the plane came out of the south, heading north. Yorktown launched her night fighter at 2320 h. The Japanese plane made a 30 degree turn to the right and disappeared 20 miles (32 km) to the north. The night fighter had no target, but another ten minutes later this plane showed up again, 35 miles (56 km) to the north on a westerly course. Although the night fighter was vectored after it, the contact faded again before it came closer.

At 2347 another contact was made and the fighter vectored after it. It caught up to within half a mile, but could not make contact, apparently because of a faulty radar set. The Japanese plane made a spiral approach, and at,0007, it turned towards Task Group 58.2. The night fighter was withdrawn from the vicinity of the formation in order not to be jeopardized by gun fire. In the meantime, the Japanese plane made a 90 degree turn and commenced a low level attack on the Intrepid. It was now coming from astern on a slightly converging course with the ship. The formation was making an emergency starboard turn at 25 knots.

A splash, but no wake was observed. The torpedo struck the Intrepid at 0011 h, close to the rudder post. The explosion jammed the rudder, the steering engine room flooded and the hull was opened. A substantial quantity of water poured inside the ship. Two Dauntless were blown over the fantail, 9 others were damaged.

The Intrepid was detached from the formation and proceeded with escorts first to Majuro, then to Pearl Harbor and finally to San Francisco, were the complicated repairs were made.

BATTLE REPORT TASK GROUP 58.3

The air attacks on Truk were carried out, with minor variations, according to the Operation Plan 2-44. The weather throughout the period was generally favorable for flight operations. There was good visibility, broken clouds, and steady East North East Trade Winds of 15 to 22 knots, from 70 degrees.

After departing Majuro on 13 February 1944 at 1400 h, local Truk time and date, the Group refuelled all ships, with the exception of the battleships and carriers, on 15 February at 0700 h from the fleet oilers Platte and Cimarron. This operation was finished by 1300 h. Task Group 58.1 refuelled to the north, and 58.2 to the south, at the same time. Admiral Spruance then assumed the duties of the Officer in Tactical Command. His flag was flying in New Jersey.

The Group proceeded without further incident to the area designated for the strikes, 94 miles (151 km) northeast of Dublon. The general disposition of the Task Force had not changed. TG 58.1 remained to the north, and TG 58.2 to the south of TG 58.3. The flight operations and attacks on the first day proceeded as scheduled. The Japanese forces in Truk were taken by surprise. There was no organized opposition encountered in the air. A number of other contacts were made on the first day:

- A submarine was sighted to crash-dive by the Combat Air Patrol at 0905 h, about 4 miles (6 km) to the southwest of Task Group 58.3. A sound search was initiated by the destroyers Lang and Cowell, but nothing was found.

- Fighters from Monterey Combat Air Patrol shot down a Val at 0954 h, 33 miles (53 km) away on bearing 245 degrees.

- A second Val was downed by Monterey fighters, about 42 miles (68 km) off the Group, on bearing 215 degrees, at 1036 h.

- Fighters from Bunker Hill shot down a Hamp 25 miles (40 km) from the formation.

Vice Admiral Spruance detached Task Group 50.9 from TG 58.3, at 0926 h, assuming command of TG 50.9. He ordered Commander Task Force 58, Rear Admiral Mitscher, to be Officer in Tactical Command of the three carrier groups, excluding TG 50.9. This formation consisted of the battleships New Jersey and Iowa, the heavy cruisers Minneapolis and New Orleans, and the destroyers Izard, Charette, Bradford and Burns. Fighter cover for the group was furnished in rotation by all Task Groups. At 1640 h a report was received that a fighter from Cowpens had water-landed, 70 miles (113 km) to the southwest of the formation. Seaplanes from the Massachusetts were ordered into the air, and were launched at 1600 h to recover the pilot. The last planes flying patrol over Task Group 50.9 did not return to the Cowpens after sunset; the 8 fighters were recovered without incident, however. This was accomplished by 1858 h. Immediately afterwards, the course was changed to the southwest, as Minton Reef was uncomfortably close - directly upwind. This low lying reef was marked by the wreck of a Japanese freighter which showed up clearly on the radar scopes.

After nightfall, Japanese planes began to make their appearances. The first contact was picked up at 1914 h, 39 miles (63 km) west of the group. The previously tight formation of the three groups was now opened to allow radical defensive turns. Probably as a result of these turns, Task Group 58.2 was soon about 25 miles (40 km) further south. For the next hour and a half, 4 or 5 single Japanese aircraft were combing the area, but only one got within a radius of 20 miles (32 km) of TG 58.3. The plane continued on its course, which led it to pass about 6 miles (10 km) astern of the formation. Although orders had been given to open fire when a good resolution of the heavy anti-aircraft guns could be obtained, the South Dakota held fire. This seemed to be a wise decision, as obviously the ships were not detected.

At 2104 h, Task Group 58.1 was firing, and at 2125 h a night fighter from Yorktown was in the air. For Bunker Hill all screens appeared to be clear. A course due south was steered until 0030 h, when a change was made to bring the carriers to the launching point, about 100 miles almost due east of Truk, and to the projected rendezvous with Task Group 50.9. Burial ceremonies were held at sunrise for two dead plane crew members.

Also called "The Cripple Hunters", Task Group 50.9 was about 30 minutes late, and joined the Task Group 58.3 at 0630 h.

The air attacks on Truk continued on the second day according to plan as well. It was ordered that the raid should be terminated with the second strike of the day, i.e. Strike 3 B. This order was given at 0950 h, ship's time, 0750 h local Truk time, respectively, but not received by Bunker Hill until 1000 h, local time. Therefore, the third strike was already over the targets, but was immediately recalled. The planes jettisoned their bombs and returned to the carrier at high speed. Vice Admiral Spruance resumed command of all ships and began the retirement at 25 knots to their next refuelling rendezvous.

BUNKER HILL

AIRCRAFT ACTION REPORTS

Summary

The activities are described on a strike-by-strike basis. There were 6 strikes on the first, and 3 on the second day. All strikes consisted of planes from Bomber Squadron VB 17, using Helldivers; Torpedo Squadron VT 17, with Avengers; and Fighter Squadron VF 18, flying Hellcats. No strike left Bunker Hill without an escort of Hellcats. Additionally, fighters were launched on other missions, such as the Initial Fighter Sweep at the beginning of the first and second day, and Combat Air and Anti Submarine Patrols.

Initial Fighter Sweep Over Truk - 17 02 44

At 0450 h, until 0500 h, local Truk time, 23 Hellcats were launched. It was before dawn. The planes arrived over Truk but did not engage in combat right away. The majority of action took place at a lower level. The fighters of Bunker Hill had been given the highest layer for cover, 20 to 25,000 ft (6 to 7,000 m). This high altitude cover proved to be necessary because of the tactics the Japanese fighters had developed. If they were engaged at lower levels, they would run out of the combat zone, beginning to climb out of sight of the fighting planes, until they reached a high altitude. From there, they would begin a renewed attack, this time in an advantageous tactical position: from the sun, diving down. To prevent them from doing so, Bunker Hill's fighters watched the tops. Sure enough, one lonely Zeke was coming from behind, diving from the sun. The Hellcats dropped their belly tanks, turned sharply to meet the other plane head on. Despite some long range, high deflection shooting, the Zeke saw what was coming to him, commenced an extremely tight turn which the Hellcats could not follow, rolled over and dove away. It escaped.

A few minutes later, a single Hamp was flying at 12,000 ft (3,660 m) over Tol towards Eten, when it was totally surprised by 4 Hellcats jumping it. Evasive actions were to no avail, bullets from the .5" automatics hit the Hamp, setting it aflame, and it tumbled down, crashing into the sea.

The division led by the Air Commander encountered 6 Zekes, crossing the reef in the direction of Uman. They were climbing, obviously following the pattern expected from them. The two lead Zekes were attacked, when the rearmost Hellcats made turns to meet them. They took immediate evasive actions and disappeared. The third Zeke pulled up into a steep climb, but was peppered by the American planes which stayed with him. The Japanese plane burned and performed a "falling leaf". The fourth Zeke beat off the attack of the Hellcats, but then scrambled. The commander, who had delegated his duty to his wingman because of radio failure, was not able to hear the warning as he pulled away, into the guns of an approaching Zeke. This wingman positioned himself between the planes, got hit, but managed to fight the hostile plane off. He was hit repeatedly by the 7.7 mm board fire of the Japanese plane, but the damage was minor. No more planes were engaged, but some ships were strafed. The flight landed safely at 0707h.

Combat Air Patrol and Spotter for TG 50.9

Three Hellcats, including the Commander, saw the two crippled Japanese warships, and reported the result of the gunfire. The Katori was now dead in the water and had developed a list. The destroyer had also lost all headway. Some miles to the northwest, another destroyer was circling to avoid attacks, but when the surface action began, it stood off at high speed to the northwest. By the time the Katori and the Maikaze had been sunk, the Nowake had half an hour's advantage. Although New Jersey and Iowa began shooting with their 16" forward turrets and increased the speed to 31 knots, the Nowake continued to draw away. The spotters noted the salvoes straddling the destroyer, but no direct hits were observed. Anti-aircraft fire from that ship had been heavy and accurate, and the spotters made no serious attempt to strafe the fleeing Nowake. The planes were close to three hours in the air, from 1114 h to 1400h.

The second patrol over the Task Group 50.9 was launched at 1513 h and recovered uneventful at 1730 h. Enroute to their battle stations it encountered 3 Val dive bombers in a tight formation. When attacked, the leading two Vals made a sharp right turn, but one of the Hellcats got the first into his sight. His tracers set this plane ablaze with the first burst. The same Hellcat then made another turn, which got him onto the tail of the second Val. His weapon blew up that plane, the pilot bailed out as a live torch. The third Val was just too slow to escape the pursuing plane, and its evasive actions were to no avail. It went down, burning. After this combat, the flight had lost the battleships and could not find them. As darkness was approaching, they were ordered back to their carrier.

Strike 3A - 17 02 44

The first strike took off between 0515 and 0527 h. It consisted of 17 Helldivers of Bomber Squadron VB 17, 8 Avengers of Torpedo Squadron VT 17 and 4 Hellcats of Fighter Squadron VF 18.

Helldivers and Avengers were equipped with a mixed load of 500 lbs, 1000 lbs and 1600 lbs bombs. Their target was the shipping in Truk. The planes rendezvoused and climbed to 13,000 ft (4,000 m). Although the cloud cover was heavy, the pilots were able to see targets west of Dublon and Moen Island (Combined Fleet Anchorage). Two bombing attacks from Task Group 58.1 and 58.2 had proceeded them and were in their final stages. When the Helldivers arrived over Param, they began their dive in a general easterly direction. Their major target was what was thought to be the escort carrier Zuiho. This ship was located off the southwest point of Moen. 11 Helldivers attacked, the pilots and several plane crews of the Avengers confirmed two direct hits, one of which was located in the center of the flight deck. Low clouds prevented further observation. The ship was not seen later, and it was believed that it was sunk. This report of an attack on a carrier, specifically the Zuiho, is a complete mystery. According to Japanese records the carrier was not in the lagoon. The Zuiho was actually sunk in the Battle of Leyte Gulf on October 25, 1944.

One Helldiver attacked a 4,000 ts oiler and scored a direct hit. A fire broke out and the ship, west-northwest of Dublon, was considered heavily damaged. Two Helldivers went after a cargo ship, the Kansho Maru, one mile northwest of Dublon, but the three bombs released missed the target.

Anti-aircraft fire was not particularly intensive or accurate. It came from the south shore of Moen, from Dublon east and from a battery on top of the hill of Eten Island.

Upon completion of the dive bombing attack on a ship, one of the Helldivers made a turn east between Moen and Dublon. It was hit by anti-aircraft fire, evidently from the ship it had bombed. The plane crashed and exploded. Plane and crew were lost.

The pilots of the Helldivers noted that about 20 cargo ships were at anchor east of Eten, a large ship was exploding immediately east of Uman (the Rio de Janeiro Maru) - not the result of their strike - one or two destroyers were running for the North Pass, and there were probably two light cruisers east of Moen. Although thought to be cruisers, these ships were destroyers. Also, a few freighters and a hospital ship, were steaming towards the North Pass.

The Avengers took a little longer than the Hellcats, but when they reached the North East Pass they saw a cruiser about 5 miles (8 km) north of Moen, making for the North Pass at high speed. Two more warships, the size of destroyers, followed some distance aft. All 8 Avengers made a bomb attack on the cruiser from southeast to northwest and released 19 bombs. The cruiser undertook violent evasive action and none of the bombs hit her. The pilots thought it was a ship of the Agano Class, but in fact it was certainly the Katori. Both classes of light cruisers look deceptively similar. A following destroyer was attacked, but not hit.

Close examination of the records reveal a coherent picture: On 11 February 1944 orders were given for the Katori, Destroyer Group 4, consisting of Nowake and Maikaze, and the auxiliary cruisers Akagi Maru to sail on 16 February to Yokosuka, Japan. The departure was delayed because the Akagi Maru had not finished loading. Therefore, all ships waited, and weighed anchors at 0530 h on 17 February. The leading Katori had reached the open sea, the destroyers were just outside the pass, while the Akagi Maru was just passing through the mine fields off the North Pass. They were detected by the American planes. In the end, the Nowake escaped, and all others were sunk by a combination of bombs, torpedoes and gunfire. About one and a half hours later after Convoy 4215 passed through the North Pass, two destroyers, the Shigure and Harusame run through the northern part of the lagoon and entered the North Pass when they where attacked. Although both vessels remained afloat, the Shigure was severely damaged by two bomb hits, and the Harusame sustained lighter damage. Both rendezvoused with the repair ship Akashi, which had received a bomb hit, impairing her speed, and escorted her to Palau.

The fighter planes did not engage in much action. They covered Strike 3A and 2A, did not meet air opposition, and did not strafe. On their way back to the carrier, they were vectored out to investigate an unidentified radar contact. It turned out to be an American plane.

Four 500 lbs bombs did not release, all others were spent. In addition, the Helldivers fired about 4500 rounds of .30 and .50 ammunition. Except for one of the planes lost in combat, only minor damage to the starboard wing of one Helldiver was sustained, requiring repair. Another plane damaged its propeller on landing. At 0812 h, plane recovery was finished.

Strike 3A was not overly successful. In summary, one Helldiver attacked a 4000 ts oiler and scored a direct hit. Two Helldivers went after a cargo ship, one mile northwest of Dublon, but the three bombs released missed this target.

The riddle of the carrier Zuiho, allegedly hit, has never been solved completely, but there are a few conjectures which would make sense. The pilots reported that the suspected carrier had just made up steam and began to move, making a slow turn to the south. This points to the fleet repair ship Akashi, anchored at the Repair Anchorage, but weighed anchor and began to sail already at the early morning hours of the first day of the strike. This ship has a general configuration resembling a small carrier when seen from above. Wide open spaces are located aft, while forward she carries a small superstructure. Significantly, no planes were observed on the flight deck. The damage reported by the pilots, a hit midships, is consistent with Japanese records, showing damage at the middle of the ship. Fate caught up with her in Palau, when almost the same American forces raided this base. Another candidate for the Zuiho was the converted whaler Tonan Maru 3. It also has wide deck spaces and was a very large ship. However, this ship was severely damaged by sub torpedoes, and did not move at all. Finally, there was a floating dock.

Strike 3B - 17 02 44

At 0705 h, the second strike against shipping in Truk was launched. The operation was suspended for a few minutes at 0724 h, because a plane crashed into the water. The carrier changed course in order not to pass over the crash site, and resumed course and operations immediately afterwards, completing them at 0730 h. Immediately after launching, a torpedo bomber from the Intrepid crashed into the water only 100 yards off starboard quarter, at 0735 h. Half an

Hailstorm - *Historic Documentation*

hour later the crew was picked up by Bradford.

On this strike, 17 Helldivers and 9 Avengers participated. As on the previous strike, the planes carried a mixed bomb load of 500 lbs, 1000 lbs and 1600 lbs bombs with short delay fuses. They were escorted by 4 fighters from Bunker Hill and 17 Hellcats from Cowpens. Torpedo and dive bombers as well as fighters of the other two Task Forces joined in this strike.

After assembling, the formation approached the northern part of the lagoon from the East. They saw the cruiser Katori, which had been previously unsuccessfully attacked. It had now cleared the North Pass and was standing off in a northwest direction at high speed. The Avengers all swung to the North and attacked her, together with 2 Helldivers. The Avengers took a 50 degree dive from 12.000 ft (3 660 m) altitude, released 27 bombs at 1800-1200 ft (365 to 550 m), of which three or four were hits. Two were definitely confirmed to have hit the ship directly, one on the stern and one on the bow. The Helldivers claimed also two hits, one confirmed and the other a possibility or a close miss. These 1000 lbs bombs exploded midships. Large fires and explosions crippled the cruiser, slowing it down to a crawl. Anti-aircraft fire was weak and almost completely ceased as a result of the hits and the strafing of the fighter planes. Almost 2000 rounds from the board weapons were spent strafing the cruiser.

A nearby destroyer put up a significant amount of anti-aircraft fire. A few rounds from a 3 inch gun were observed coming from an island east of the North Pass. However, it was also reported that a large merchant vessel just inside the lagoon was putting up heavy anti-aircraft fire. This may be a reference to the Akagi Maru. The second target attacked by the Helldivers which had not yet dropped their bombs, was a tanker, estimated to be 13,000 ts gross and 550 ft long, steaming just through the North Pass towards the sea. Out of the 7 bombs dropped, one hit the ship, causing a large explosion and fire. There are no Japanese records confirming the presence of a tanker underway and they do not collaborate on the existence or sinking of another tanker in Truk.

The possibility exists that the Fujisan Maru was attacked. It has been mentioned before that a large tanker was seen tied up at the jetty off south Dublon. A photograph taken at the beginning of the operation shows this large ship, evidently empty, south of Dublon, and it is known from reports during the day that a tanker first ran north, then reversed some time at noon and steamed back south. Finally, the ship was sunk, while underway off southeast Moen. It was the Fujisan Maru. The hull shows some damage, apart from the destruction at the stern, where she was hit. There must be some overlapping in time and reporting, because pilots from the Enterprise reported a tanker heading north inside the lagoon on the next strike.

It has to be borne in mind that detailed observation is difficult under battle conditions. The only merchant ship known to have left the lagoon was the auxiliary cruiser, Akagi Maru and possibly another vessel, the Zuikai Maru. Akagi and Zuikai were again attacked shortly thereafter and sunk. At one time, pilots from commercial airline Air Micronesia reported a hull lying outside the North Pass, when they were still taking an approach towards Moen via a large circle over the lagoon. Meanwhile, the 4 Hellcats from Bunker Hill were flying escort for the bombers and torpedo planes at 12,500 ft (3,800 m) and stayed on that altitude during the attack. Two Japanese planes were seen over the north part of the lagoon. One was identified as a Zeke. No contact was made.

Strike 3B lost one Helldiver, which experienced engine failure on take-off. The crew managed to jettison their bombs, and although the plane was lost, the men were rescued unharmed. Two Helldivers were damaged by 7.7 mm anti-aircraft fire, one on the starboard, the other on the port wing. They were repaired on the carrier. A mishap occurred while handling a recovered plane, which resulted in minor damage. Because the attack took place at the extreme north of the atoll, observation of the shipping at the anchorages was very difficult. A destroyer was located in the northern part of the lagoon. A great number of ships were seen east of Dublon and Eten, and a cluster of ships appeared to be located at what was later identified as Repair Anchorage, west of Dublon, north of Fefan. At this time, two ships were already burning at the Fourth Fleet Anchorage. Fires could be seen at the airplane bases on Eten and Dublon.

This strike was successful. The cruiser was put out of action and was easy prey for the guns of Task Force 50.9 which sunk her a few hours later. The Akagi Maru was sinking. These results were achieved with no harm to any of the air crews, and the planes were recovered between 0946 and 1014 h. Two minutes later the carrier deck crew witnessed a plane crashing off the starboard bow; the pilot was rescued by the destroyer Bell. At the same time a Helldiver returned from Strike 3C, with a faulty engine.

Strike 3C - 17 02 44

The third strike on the first day was launched between 0935 and 0946 h. 12 Helldivers were loaded with 1000 lbs bombs set with fuses of varying delays. All 6 Avengers carried one torpedo each, with a depth setting of 6 ft (1,8 m). Fighter Squadron VF 18 was sent off with 12 Hellcats, their board weapons all well loaded. The weather over Truk was fine. Clouds covered almost half the sky, but the visibility was excellent. The target was a light cruiser, sighted 25 to 30 miles (48 km) southwest of the North Pass.

This was the strike of the Avengers. They first searched for the cruiser and soon found it steaming a fast 25 knots in a northeasterly direction 25 miles (40 km) southwest of the Piannu Pass on the way to Truk. The Helldivers and the Avengers made a coordinated attack. As soon as the attack unfolded - the Avengers diving down from 14,000 ft (4,260 m) to 300 ft (91 m) - the warship began a very tight circle to starboard. The Helldivers released their bombs, but did not score. The Avengers continued their dive, and began their torpedo drop after they had turned onto the stern of the ship. Circling the ship's course in exactly the opposite direction, they released the torpedoes when 800 to 1000 yards away, aiming at the oncoming bow.

One or possibly two torpedoes hit and exploded. Immediately afterwards, 3 large explosions came from within the ship itself, indicating that the magazines had blown up. One of the Avengers made repeated strafing passes over the ship, but at that time, the bow was already awash and the forward gun turret surrounded by water. The fighters went in and continued to rake the cruiser from stem to stern.

One of the Avenger pilots saw a yellow life raft floating outside the lagoon, about 3/4 mile east of the southeast side of the outer rim. He dropped his own life raft, as he saw 3 men in the float. They signalled that they were ok, and he reported the incident. He then saw a rescue water plane, a Kingfisher, approaching and left the area with the rest of the planes. Prior to this incident, the fighter saw a second raft about 3 miles (5 km) north of the sinking cruiser and radioed its position to base. All planes pulled up, but came under anti-aircraft fire from a destroyer, the Tachikaze, grounded with the bow on the reef midway along the southwestern side of Kuop Atoll. The ship was hardly damaged, but definitely immobile. When flying under the clouds over Truk, the bombers observed 10 to 12 cargo ships east of Eten, of which 3 were on fire. 3 merchant vessels were anchored west of Tsis, a large tanker located east of Tol - the Shinkoku Maru, and several vessels on each side of Uman.

On the way to the Task Force, the Hellcats saw a Kate ahead, about 25 miles (40 km) north of Truk. It was flying at an altitude of 3,500 ft (1,770 m) while the fighters were at 2,000 ft (610 m), on opposite course. Two planes turned to intercept, while the Kate dropped to wave height, and turned. The fighters bracketed the Kate and when the port fighter opened fire, the Kate evaded to starboard, just to fly into the guns of the other plane. Hits were seen to enter the cockpit and the wing root of the Kate. It burst into flames and crashed into the water.

All planes were on board by 1243 h. One Helldiver made a forced landing in the water on return, as the engine failed due to a hit by anti-aircraft fire. The pilot and bomber were rescued by Sterett. Another plane sustained minor damage. One wingtip and the tail wheel were torn off. It was repaired immediately on board. The Helldivers and Avengers fired more than 600 rounds, the fighters 2900. This strike severely damaged the light cruiser Naka, a 19 year old 5000 ts, 4 stack veteran. But despite the report of her sinking, she remained afloat and crawled back towards Truk. Avengers from USS Cowpens delivered the coup-de-grace a few hours later.

Strike 3D - 17 02 44

At 1114 to 1143 h, launching of the fourth strike was commenced. 34 planes took part, together with 4 Hellcats of Combat Air Patrol. 12 Helldivers were loaded with 1000 lbs bombs armed with contact and short delay fuses, respectively. The 10 Avengers carried a single torpedo each. Finally, 12 fighters (Hellcats) flew escort and followed an overlapping schedule with the bomber, torpedo bomber and fighter squadrons of Task Groups 58.1 and 58.2. The visibility was excellent. The cloud cover was about 60%, a little more than in the previous raid. The cloud ceiling was from 2,500 to 10,000 ft (3,050 m). The planes were beginning their attack at 1250 h. After assembly, they all climbed to 12,000 ft (3,660 m) and reached Truk close to the North East Pass. The bombers then swung to the north, around the northeast tip of the lagoon, where they were passing the New Jersey and Iowa of TG 50.9 which were steaming 15 miles (24 km) off Truk. They continued to skirt the rim of the atoll to a position northeast of Tol. From there they turned east. The Avengers continued south until they could approach the ships anchored at the South side of the anchorage between Fefan and Uman.

It is interesting to note that the Helldivers and Avengers approached their targets from different directions. A fairly strong wind (15-20 knots) was blowing from the northeast. The ships were at anchor, their bows pointing into the wind. To have the greatest chance of success, a torpedo should ideally be launched perpendicular to the axis of a ship, aiming at the beam. Therefore, the torpedo planes attacked from a general southeast direction. For bombs on the other hand, the best chance for a hit are when the plane flies over the length of the ship. The Helldivers logically preferred a west-east approach.

The Helldivers encountered very little anti-aircraft fire, and none of the ships attacked shot back. However, some rather inaccurate anti-aircraft fire came from Uman and the outlying islands, and some machine gun and rifle shots were aimed at the planes as they strafed targets. One of the planes was harmlessly hit in the wing by a bullet.

The cloud cover afforded protection during the initial dive, from about 12,000 ft (3,660 m) to 1,500-2,000 ft (460 to 610 m), when it was clear for pilots to see their targets. The Helldivers' first target was a large cargo ship, estimated to be 500 ft (152 m) in length and 10,000 ts, off the southwest shore of Uman Island upon which 5 planes descended.

There is little doubt that this was the Amagisan Maru. The ship was hit by one bomb at the stern. Right afterwards, 4 Avengers unleashed a torpedo attack. One torpedo was a certain hit, just slightly forward of the midship superstructure, with the unconfirmed report of two more exploding. While burning heavily and sending up a huge column of smoke, the ship went down by the bow and was gone by the next strike. Today the Amagisan Maru rests on the bottom with a heavy list to starboard. The torpedo hit on starboard can be clearly seen. The nature of the damage at port quarter confirms the observation of a bomb hit.

The next target was a smaller cargo ship with an estimated length of 450 ft (137 m) and 8,000 ts gross, which was located west of Uman. It was hit by a bomb forward. 4 Helldivers participated. This ship was the Sankisan Maru. Despite the report of the hit forward the ship remained undamaged at this attack.

The third ship (about 360 ft, 110 m, and 4,000 ts), at anchor at the northwest side of Uman, was hit midships, causing a fire with heavy smoke. The ship was left severely damaged. It was probably the Taiho Maru, which broke apart later - the foreship disintegrated, while the aftship drifted before the wind for a

Hailstorm - *Historic Documentation*

while longer, aided by the two barges tied to it.

One of the Helldivers, a photo plane, bombed a tanker off the southwest corner of Tol, but missed. This ship remained unscathed until the first strike of the following day. Although reported to be a tanker, it was a freighter, the Hanakawa Maru. As the bombers had dropped their bombs, they resorted to strafing. The Avengers took on their first target, a cargo ship of about 450 ft (137 m) length (8,000 ts), which was attacked by 4 of the planes. One torpedo hit was reported for certain at the stern, and a second torpedo believed to have been seen exploding. The ship burned severely but then sank quickly off the southeast tip of Fefan. When the planes departed the decks of the sinking ship were awash. This was the Yubae Maru.

Just one plane made a sortie on a destroyer, underway and making about 20 knots east of Tsis. The warship got away because it swerved hard to port after the release of the torpedo. The weapon consequently missed, passing 20 ft (6 m) astern.

The last of the Avengers made an attack on a ship off Fefan, but the torpedo failed to release. While this plane retired to the east, the pilot saw a large cargo or passenger ship 2 miles southeast of Eten which put up a great amount of anti-aircraft fire. It was apparently underway, making 5 knots. He made a second run, aiming at this ship. This time the torpedo released and hit the target. His wingman, who had launched his torpedo previously, diverted the anti-aircraft fire and strafed. The ship began to burn very heavily and no more anti-aircraft guns were fired subsequently. From the course of the two planes, the location of the ship and the nature of the damage, as well as its size, it may be deduced that it was the Hoki Maru. However, the ship was not underway. On the last strike of the first day, this ship was seen still burning fiercely.

Except for this defensive anti-aircraft fire, only small arms were shot at the planes. One of the Avengers was hit by a bullet from a rifle which entered the cockpit and killed the radioman instantly. A machine gun bullet lodged inside the craft without doing damage.

The fighters principal role was the escort of the Helldivers and Avengers, as well as the photo plane. But since no interception was attempted by the 3 Zekes, 1 Val, 1 Nell, 1 Mavis and possibly a fourth Zeke seen in the air, they strafed targets. 4 Hellcats repeatedly attacked a small freighter near Fanamu. The ship began to burn, and it is almost certain that this was X 14, an unknown small freighter thus attacked. Altogether, 960 rounds were spent while strafing on dives from 3000 to 5000 ft. Two planes made for a ship already hit by a torpedo and 8 Hellcats poured very heavy fire on 3 patrol boats, southwest of Tarik, leaving one dead in the water and the others burning.

During the strike, the planes saw a lot of activity around Dublon, and reported a cargo ship severely smoking east of Uman, probably the Rio. Two cargo ships were seen east of Eten, one of which was sinking, with only the bow sticking out of the water, and the other being on fire. A tanker between Eten and Fefan exploded, with smoke rising up to 5000 ft (1 500 m). Although this high smoke column was reported by planes from other carriers as well, the ship could not have been a tanker. All oilers sunk were located North of Fefan, with the exception of the Fujisan Maru. However, the Unkai Maru 6 burned fiercely after a hit. This smoke column was reported by other planes as well. An attack photo shows this ship burning, and the location is correct for the Unkai Maru 6.

A large cargo ship was smoking west of Dublon. This was the Heian Maru. After being hit, probably only by rounds of plane automatics and a bomb near miss, the ship began to burn severely and the fire went completely out of control, raging for a full day. It left this large ship a burned out hulk. Anti-aircraft fire was not particularly intense. None of the vessels attacked fired at the planes.

The aircraft returned to the carrier and were recovered between 1321 and 1414 h. During the landing, one of the planes from Torpedo Squadron 12 made an emergency landing on Bunker Hill with a severely injured crew member. He had been hit during an attack on the Katori convoy by anti-aircraft fire, and succumbed before help could be administered.

Strike 3E - 17 02 44

15 Helldivers loaded with 1000 lbs bombs containing various fuses, 6 Avengers armed with torpedoes, and 12 Hellcats were launched between 1310 and 1330 h. The afternoon sun was shining in a partially cloudy sky when the planes approaching the atoll from the east, turned right (north) at the South Pass, and were fired upon by the ill-fated, beached destroyer, Tachikaze, at Kuop Atoll. Further anti-aircraft fire came from small islands in the southwest of the lagoon. Several 5 inch guns were shooting from Fefan and Eten. Heavy batteries fired a barrage at 13,000 ft, which was not directed against these planes, but against the squadrons of the other carriers, which attacked simultaneously. Two destroyers were taking evasive action at the northern part of the lagoon.

The bombers broke off for attacks southwest of Fefan, aiming for ships west of Dublon, north of Fefan (Combined Fleet Anchorage) and the others for Eten and Uman (Sixth Fleet Anchorage). The dives were executed into the wind (west to east). 8 Zeke float planes were seen at the beginning of the dive, but they high-tailed off. About 13 freighters were observed in the area adjacent to Eten and Uman; three of them were burning. At the northwest of Dublon the pilots estimated that 8 ships were anchored, of which 3 were burning badly.

From 2000 ft, 8 Helldivers attacked an oiler (estimated length 400 ft (122 m), 5,500 ts, anchored northwest of Fefan, and scored one hit out of 7 bombs dropped (one did not release). The bomb was observed to explode midships, causing a secondary explosion and a large fire, which severely damaged the ship. There is only one ship not properly identified, X 10, resting, broken up, northwest of Fefan. The Japanese records show one unidentified ship, its final resting place unknown. It is the Daikichi Maru, a 2000 ts coastal vessel. It may have resembled a tanker from above, if it had the engines at the quarter deck. The pieces of wreckage found, part of the superstructure and the funnel attached, suggests a ship of the 2000 ts-class. The discrepancy between reported and actual tonnage is consistent with differences in other reports. Then, 2 planes released their load on a cargo ship with an estimated length of 440 ft (7,500 ts). One bomb hit just aft of midships, increasing a fire with high black smoke. This vessel was located between Eten and Uman. It was left damaged. It was the Unkai Maru 6.

A single Helldiver attacked what the pilot reported to be a slightly smaller vessel (400 ft, about 5,800 ts) from 1000 ft and scored aft with one or two armour piercing 1000 lbs. The ship, anchored just northeast of Uman, was undamaged prior to the attack, but now started to burn. The chronological sequence may have been reversed in the Aircraft Action Reports, because location and size of the ship is a ringer for the Unkai Maru 6.

Four bombers congregated over a 450 ft -137 m-long merchant ship of approximately 6,500 ts east of Uman and obtained one certain, but possibly two hits, which started fires. This ship was damaged in a previous attack. Some of the planes strafed during their dives. The Gosei Maru had been attacked before, but the ship remained afloat, and the observed hits were in fact close misses.

Avengers from Monterey joined this strike. The torpedo planes initially had some problems keeping up with the bombers and fighters because the heavy torpedoes slowed them down. But they managed, and started their attack, again diving from the south. They formed 3 divisions of 2 planes each, and searched the southern part of the lagoon for targets. The southernmost four ships were the Unkai Maru 6, Fujikawa Maru, Seiko Maru and San Francisco Maru. Four ships for three divisions was too much. The Seiko Maru, already damaged, burning at the three quarter deck and sinking by the stern, was therefore spared a renewed attack.

The first cargo ship (estimated to be 350 ft - 107 m - long, 4000 ts) west at the south point of Eten was not hit despite the two torpedoes launched. One ran into a coral reef, about 100 yards short of the target, exploded and took off part of the corals. The other was a dud. It was again the Unkai Maru 6 under attack.

The next group had more success. Although one of the torpedoes could not be observed, the other hit the target located south of the south tip of Eten, and started a fire. This ship was observed to be a large (500 ft, 10,000 ts) cargo liner, the Fujikawa Maru. The hit was observed by 3 pilots and crew, also reported, and credited to the Monterey planes. The ship began to settle by the stern. The hole ripped open by the torpedo can be seen on starboard at hold 4, consistent with damage expected for a weapon drop from the southwest.

The third group of Avengers successfully ruined a stretch of the reef southeast of Eten with one of the two torpedoes launched. The next weapon hit a 450 ft - 137 m -, 7,500 ts ship which subsequently listed. The San Francisco Maru was lucky. Although the torpedo hit just below the aft deckhouse, it did not explode the warhead. The impact of the weapon damaged the shell plating, and close inspection of the damaged area reveals a semi-circular hole of slightly less than 2 ft - 60 cm - diameter in one shell plate. The adjoining, riveted plate is torn and bent inwards. Water rushed into the aft hold of this very heavily laden ship. The fire, as reported by the pilots of the attacking plane, was obviously confined to the bridge; the ship had been burning in this area for a while. At any rate, it did not reach and ignite the heavy ordnances, torpedo heads in the aft and mines in the forward holds.

One small sampan was strafed and left burning by the Hellcats, which wanted to get into the act as they did not meet any airborne opposition. They observed the hits, but also witnessed one of the Hellcats from another Task Group, bursting into flames and crashing during its attack on a target at the south tip of Moen. In that general area, anti-aircraft fire was more intensive. Bunker Hill lost a plane in this area as well, at a later strike.

Six ships were heavily damaged during this strike, with no damage or losses to the planes. A flight of 8 Zekes was reported by the bombers. Recovery was accomplished between 1524 and 1548 h with one Helldiver having damaged its wing on the carrier.

Strike 3F - 17 02 44

In all, 26 planes participated in the last attack of the first day. Avengers and Helldivers were loaded with bombs. The objective of this strike was to damage the airfield on Eten and to render it unserviceable. The aircraft were launched between 1513 and 1521 h, together with 4 planes of the Combat Air Patrol, and returned, with the loss of one crew member, who died due to a hit of anti-aircraft round, at 1730 h, just before dusk.

When the Avengers and Helldivers arrived over Eten, the island was partly obscured by clouds and smoke coming from damaged installations and burning planes previously hit. The planes had to approach from southwest and dropped their bombs in trains of about 150 ft intervals. It was observed that the majority of them fell within the designated area, and large explosions and craters were seen. One pilot lost sight of the runway, but continued his dive to find himself just right for a drop on one of the twin 5 inch antiaircraft guns. He did not think twice, but released his bombs. His radioman confirmed that this battery was hit. It remained silent during the rest of the raid. In fact, an attack photo taken on the second day shows the eastern gun emplacement with the gun intact and a large circular crater where the second gun used to be.

It was only with difficulty that the plane crews could verify the location of their hits, but at least 5 bombs landed on the service apron and 24 on the runways and buildings. Further observations in this area were made difficult because the Japanese brought to bear all available machine weapons against the low flying planes. The 5 inch anti-aircraft guns from Dublon followed the retirement and were aiming fairly accurately. The pilots jinked their planes to avoid hits.

The Hellcats strafed, and while pulling up and out of the run, came to pass a large ship lying southeast of the southeastern prong of Dublon, just lying parallel to the plane's line of flight. They dipped down again and every fighter strafed it from stem to stern. It was

Hailstorm - *Historic Documentation*

the Momokawa Maru being attacked.

During this strike, the Helldivers contributed the following observations about ships east of Eten:

The bow of a ship still showed above water. A medium sized freighter was almost sunk, its decks awash. A third ship was stern down with the foreship burning. Finally, there was a large cargo ship or combined passenger-cargo liner southeast of Dublon apparently undamaged.

Initial Fighter Sweep Over Truk - 18 02 44

The squadron detailed again 24 fighters, 23 according to the ship's log. Launching began at 0450 h, the planes were recovered at 0755 h. 48 planes from the other carriers participated. There was no air opposition encountered at all, and the "hop" was considered uneventful. However, heavy anti-aircraft fire from Dublon burst within 50 ft to the side and 50 ft higher than where the planes were orbiting. The Hellcats resorted to some heavy jinking and no damage was sustained. The commander remained over the target area, as Air Target Observer. He dropped with his flight to 10,000 ft and lead the first strike of the first day. No shots were fired and no damage sustained.

Strike 3A - 18 02 44

The first strike on the second day began before dawn, with launching operations between 0516 and 0528 h. The 13 Helldivers carried a load of either one 1000 lbs bomb (7 planes) or two 500 lbs bombs (6 planes), whereas the 8 Avengers stowed one torpedo each, again set at 6 ft running depth. Four fighters functioned as close escort. Three Helldivers had mechanical defects and were not launched.

The Helldivers reached the North Pass, and followed the western side of the atoll reef to the south until they were turning into the wind, then dived on targets at Uman. A freighter, estimated to be 350 ft long and 4000 ts gross, anchored about 1/2 mile west of Uman, was attacked. One of the seven bombs dropped, one hit midships, setting the ship ablaze. The ship was left heavily damaged. It is possible that the Sankisan Maru was attacked again and exploded later. There has been no other ship sunk of that size and in that location.

The next 5 Helldivers took on a cargo ship, anchored immediately northeast of Uman. Nine bombs were released over the target at an altitude of 1000 ft, with one or two hits. The ship was damaged.

The varying cloud cover prevented one plane from executing the attack on a ship, but the pilot followed through with his dive and placed the 1000 lbs bomb onto the service apron of Eten. The result was not observed. The last of the armed planes made a run on a medium large freighter, but the explosion of his bomb was also not observed. The location of this ship was given as east of Fefan.

The Avengers were originally following the Helldivers, but when the latter turned east, they continued to skirt the outer rim and turned north on the South side of Tol. The flight leader broke off the formation for a two plane attack on what he thought was a large tanker near Tol. These two planes passed the target in a sweeping S-turn which enabled them to deliver a broadside attack from the South. The rest of the flight had ringside seats for observing how the first torpedo struck this big ship which had been reported but not attacked the previous day, and the second torpedo disappeared in the giant explosion which ensued. The ship disintegrated, debris was flying out of the smoke, and the ship was gone except for a few large puddles of burning oil at the sea surface. This strike came just seconds before 4 Avengers from Monterey released their torpedoes. It was too late to stop them, and all these torpedoes were wasted, as the ship was already gone.

All these observations were quite accurate, with one exception: The oiler was the freighter Hanakawa Maru. The damage which can be observed at the ship is consistent with the report of the pilots. A torpedo hole shows on starboard beam forward, at the forward hold. This is the side attacked if the planes made a sweeping S-turn, coming from the south, passing over to the north, back to south and finally attacking from the south towards north. The ship was pointing into the wind, which came from the east-northeast. Therefore, the attacked side is starboard. The cargo of gasoline drums were immediately ignited, and the hatch cover beams were flying high into the air, followed by flaming drums. Hatch cover beams and dented drums can be seen even today up to a few hundred feet off port beam. The ship literally disappeared in the conflagration. While sinking quickly by the bow, the burning gasoline spread rapidly over the water's surface towards the mangrove at the shoreline of Tol. The Japanese had all hands full to prevent spreading of the flames, shooting at the planes and tending their injured. During the interrogations of the Japanese officers after the war, it was confirmed, that it was the Hanakawa, which was mistakenly identified by the Americans as an oiler.

The torpedo bombers found a very hard nut to crack. In fact, the next target, a second tanker, defied the torpedoes. Two sections of 3 planes each attacked it, but none of the 6 torpedoes hit and the ship remained unharmed. The waters appeared to be too shallow and the weapons failed to run, evidently spending themselves pushing the sea bed. The altitude of release was 300 ft. As the location of the ship was reported to be east of Eot, it was the Shinkoku Maru, although its size, as given with 8000 ts, is too small. After the spectacle of the Hanakawa Maru everything else might have looked small.

It was at about this time that the Avengers, on their way to the East side, ran into some anti-aircraft fire which appeared to be generally inaccurate. However, unobserved by any of the others, one plane was hit. It crashed, and the crew was lost.

The planes strafed a few small craft, leaving one dead in the water, and together with the Helldivers, made the following observations:

The large liner, Amagisan Maru, west of Uman had sunk. Southeast of Moen Fujisan Maru was sinking, deck awash, succumbing to bombs of the planes from the Enterprise. Two more ships were smoking east of Eten. A hospital ship was attempting to clear the North Pass. A destroyer, Oite, approached the North Pass from outside the lagoon. The Akashi, the repair ship, was seen heading towards South Pass. Three more large merchant vessels anchored between Uman and Fefan were undamaged. Two large ships were east of Uman, one going down by the stern, and one liner burning near Onna, the latter being without doubt the Hoki Maru, and Onna taken for Fanamu.

The Hellcats had the air unopposed and felt at liberty to severely damage, by strafing, two patrol craft which were five miles southeast of Tol. They observed a destroyer entering the North Pass. It was the Oite, which was attacked on the next strike.

Apart from the downed TBF-1C, one Helldiver crashed on deck and into the barriers when the landing hook failed to extend. The aircraft required major repairs. A similar fate befell a Hellcat, which also crashed on the flight deck. Two planes were hit by anti-aircraft fire, requiring on-board repairs.

In summary, one ship was destroyed, two damaged, with the loss of a plane with an aircrew of three. The planes landed between 0737 and 0821h, to-gether with the Hellcats from the Initial Fighter Sweep.

Strike 3 B - 18 02 44

This was the last effective strike of the raid on Truk. Of the 23 planes launched, 10 were Helldivers (5 of them loaded with 2 x 500 lbs bombs, the others with one 1000 lbs bomb each), 9 Avengers (armed with torpedoes) and 4 were Hellcats. The weather during the launch and over the target was again ideal. With 15 miles visibility, the cloud cover was about 33 %. After the bumpy start of the 3A launch, the second also left 3 planes behind due to mechanical failures. Soon however, the formation arrived at 12,000 ft, respectively 10,000 ft over the southern end of Truk. The Helldivers broke formation first, nosing into the wind, while the Avengers continued a little further south, turning inside the lagoon and sweeping north again.

Two Helldivers attacked a 450 ft long ship of about 8,000 ts, 1/4 mile off the southeast tip of Dublon. This vessel had been damaged before, but was level. After a hit by a 1000 lbs bomb midships, a big explosion occurred. The ship burned and quickly went down stern first, the bow protruding the water for a while.

Another huge explosion was initiated by a 2-bomb hit on a 400 ft, 6,000 ts merchant vessel. The cargo of ordinance must have been set ablaze as the blast was tremendous. The ship was gone after the smoke lifted. This happened in the vicinity of the first victim, off the southeast tip of Dublon. This ship was the Momokawa Maru. Nothing but pieces of debris remains of this vessel.

A third explosion, this time on what appeared to be a 550 ft - 168 m - long freighter estimated to be of 13,000 ts gross, was the result of a double bomb hit. The ship was located west of Fefan. It was the Yamagiri Maru. The black smoke went up to 5000 ft. This ship was extremely heavily damaged, and sank. 4 planes attacked and 7 bombs were expended on this target and the damage is evident on the wreck. The only plane left with bombs was diving towards a large oiler south of Eten. The bombs missed.

In the meantime, the Avengers went to the assistance of the Hellcats which were strafing a destroyer with all they had. This destroyer was the same one previously reported in the vicinity of the North Pass. It was running south now at almost full speed. The board weapons of the fighters started a fire aft of her stacks, but this apparently did not impair her speed or maneuverability. The destroyer started evasive actions, beginning in a S-turn and ending in a full circle. The planes started their coordinated attack. The five Avengers dropped their torpedoes, and the destroyer caught one abeam of the bridge as it was completing its turn. The ship immediately broke in two. Black smoke was seen, and in less than two minutes nothing was left of the ship which was described as being of rust color and old design, the Oite. It has been said that the Oite came in from the outside of the lagoon, after she had rescued almost 450 officers and sailors of the Agano, sunk the previous day way outside Truk.

The remaining armed Avengers aimed for two targets off Dublon. The first ship attacked, and hit by two torpedoes, was reported to be 10,000 ts gross and 500 ft - 152 m - long. Anchored just west of Dublon leaves no other explanation than the Heian Maru. She received her coup-de-grace now. The second ship was smaller. It was located slightly to the west of the former, and suggests the Kansho Maru. Her repairs never finished, she was sunk at the Repair Anchorage.

The planes headed back to the carrier, and retrieval was accomplished by 1002 h. One Helldiver chose the Yorktown as a new home base. This involuntary switch was due to a heavy oil leak of the engine, resulting in loss of power. At 1000 h the lookouts reported a plane splashing 6,000 yards off the starboard beam.

Apart from all bombs and torpedoes, more than 7000 rounds were fired from the board weapons. In summary, this was a very successful attack. Two cargo ships and one destroyer were sunk, two other ships were damaged and sank later.

Strike 3C - 18 02 44

In 12 minutes 12 planes were launched, but they did not make the headlines. A rare glimpse of the tight discipline governing flight operations is afforded by this aborted strike. While the aircraft were over the target area, two radio messages were received that all planes were immediately to return to the ships, which had launched them at 1128h. Despite some interesting targets, all pilots immediately turned back. As no explanation for the recall was given (the message having been delayed by several hours!), bombs were kept initially but jettisoned, after clarification. In a rare case of humor, the Aircraft Action Report of VF 18 reads: "The bombing planes jettisoned bombs on a school of fish suspected of Japanese sympathies, while enroute back to base", at 1321 h.

This concluded the operation against Truk. Combat Air and Anti Submarine Patrols were launched and recovered at regular intervals until dusk, while all ships retired.

MONTEREY

Summary

Fighters of the Monterey made up fighter cover for the individual strikes and Combat Air Patrol, and subsequently are covered under the description of strikes by Bunker Hill. Fighter Squadron 30, assigned to Monterey, flew two Combat Air Patrol, the first one at 0720 h, returning 1010 h on the 17 February 1944. The second Combat Air Patrol was launched at 1930 h and retrieved at 1145 h.

Four planes of the first patrol were vectored about 30 miles south of their carrier to investigate a radar contact. They sighted a Val but did not seem to be sighted themselves. When the Val started an evasive glide, however, one Hellcat was on its tail firing a short burst. The Val continued with an even steeper dive and started to smoke. It crashed into the water still carrying a large bomb.

On the second Combat Air Patrol, 3 Hellcats - one having to return to the carrier because of mechanical trouble - were vectored 45 miles to the southwest and sighted a single Val. The pilot in the Val saw the incoming planes and met them as they were climbing to get above and behind him, firing its board weapon. Two of the Hellcats fired when they overtook it, but to no visible effect. The third plane shooting from the stern into the Val tore parts of the wing away, but the Val made a very steep climb, to the extend of stalling, while still being fired upon. In the meantime one of the other Hellcats was able to get his gun sight on the plane. The Val was falling, spiraling over the right wing, burning fiercely. It crashed into the water almost totally consumed by the fire.

During 3 escort missions, Hellcats found opportunity to strafe 7 cargo ships, 2 destroyers and a few barges. All of them were left burning or smoking. One of the planes dropped his partially filled belly tank on a freighter, hit it, and started a large fire. The planes were also participating in the strafing of the destroyer inside the lagoon, the Oite, and started a fire and later sank it. The other escort missions were routine and the pilots observed hits and strafed targets in the water, but stayed clear of land areas.

The Avengers of VT 30 were launched twice on the 18 February. The first was at 1318 h until 1512 h, the second from 0938 h to 1121 h. They carried torpedoes and were joining planes from the Bunker Hill and Cowpens. One of the planes had to be ditched within the Task Group because of engine failure. On approaching the water, the landing gear came down and the plane turned violently over. The crew was saved, except for the pilot, who went under with his plane.

The main target looked like a big tanker off Tol, which was then sunk by a torpedo hit. It was the freighter Hanakawa Maru. A cargo vessel was attacked; two torpedo were hits.

One the second mission the Avengers dropped two torpedoes on a cargo ship anchored between Uman and Eten, possible the Fujikawa Maru. The first torpedo ran well, then porpoised changed course and hit the runway at Eten, on the south-western end, but did not explode. The second torpedo ran true, but then the pilots observed that the wake stopped and thought the torpedo had sunk. As the planes continued low over the water to avoid anti-aircraft fire, they could still see how suddenly there was a big explosion midships of the attacked freighter and a fire. A few smaller patrol vessels were strafed.

One torpedo started a dry run inside the bay and damaged the bay doors, so it could not be jettisoned. On several other occasions erratic runs of torpedoes were noted. The Avenger pilots were considerably more reserved with their praise of the performance of their torpedoes.

COWPENS

Summary

The light carrier Cowpens had a more offensive tactical role in this operation than its sistership Monterey. An average of 25 fighters and 8 Avengers were available during the raid. The normal complement of this vessel was 24 fighters and 9 bombers. Two additional fighters were carried. On the 17 February 1944, the torpedo bombers made raids on Moen airfield, and in separate attacks, shipping and aircraft installations. The fighter aircraft escorted two of the three torpedo bomber missions, escorted one bomber attack by planes from Bunker Hill, furnished 2 Combat Air Patrol for the surface fleet, to the north and westward of the atoll, made a bombing strike on Moen airfield, flew escort for the second strike, and finally made a photographic flight, furnishing its own escort for this mission. One plane was lost due to anti-aircraft fire. The pilot was rescued.

On the second day, 18 February 1944, planes from the Cowpens furnished 4 Anti-Submarine Patrol and 4 Combat Air Patrol for the Task Group 58.3. There were no incidents recorded on these occasions.

Strike 3 A - Cowpens - 17 02 44

Eight Hellcats were launched from the deck at

0526 h, to escort the Helldivers and Avengers from Bunker Hill, as well as, Avengers from Cowpens. They were supported in their duties by 4 fighters from Bunker Hill. The rendezvous was uneventful. The formation crossed the reef from the South, at Kuop Atoll. They were flying intermediate cover at 1750 ft (530 m), and high cover, 3000 ft (900 m) above the other planes. One division followed the Avengers when they bombed Moen airfield, and observed hits on the targets. No hostile planes were encountered in the air.

The other division followed the Helldivers, which bombed Eten airfield. They stayed above these planes, and saw one Zeke flying high above them. A second was lower and came in from astern. The American pilots were familiar with this tactic of the Japanese fighters, which used the leading plane as decoy, while the other started a run by swinging across to port attempting to attack from the 7 o'clock position. The Hellcats executed a climbing turn to port to meet the intruder head on. The Zeke saw the attack on himself unfold, and pulled up, across the American planes, without shooting. It was in a better tactical position, and although one of the Hellcats began to fire, no hits were seen. The turn for this American plane was too tight, it "mushed out", and the pilot had to recover speed and position. Both Zekes escaped. The rest of the flight was considered routine, and the last plane was recovered at 0745 h.

Immediately before the Hellcats were flown off the carrier, 9 Avengers were launched from the deck. They carried a mixed load of each 12 times 100 lbs bombs. These came in clusters of 6 each, and comprised of incendiary, general purpose and fragmentation bombs. The target was the Moen fighter strip. The planes were joined by 8 other Avengers and 17 Helldivers from Bunker Hill. They continued to follow the eastern rim of the atoll, even after the planes from the larger carrier had broken off and had began their attack. Only after a due South-North approach could be made, Cowpens' Avengers went into their dive. This approach was not advantageous. The airfield lay in the shadow of a steep hill, located along the northwestern coast of Moen. The installation was built at the same location where the present civilian airport is today.

The target was not easy to make out because the mountain cast a shadow in the rising sun. The pilots made careful runs with all bombs falling in the runway area. The bombs from the first plane already started a big fire at the southern end. A Betty bomber, parked at the inland side of the southern part of the runway burst into flames. The following attackers started many more fires to the North. Japanese planes had been parked under camouflage netting. The bombs went through the nets and exploded with devastating effects. At the southeastern part of the runway, 10 Vals and Kates, all painted dark blue, were parked side-by-side. Bombs dropped by an Avenger destroyed most or all of them.

The only anti-aircraft fire came from a platform east of the runway; some machine gun fire from the hill above it. Twelve vehicles were counted, parked near the northern end. The entire airfield was covered with thick smoke when the last plane left.

The pilots reported large fires at the area of the Dublon seaplane base, and at Eten. The anchorages were full of ships. A light cruiser and several destroyers were heading towards the North Pass. When the planes retired between the North and the Northeast Pass, they drew anti-aircraft fire from a destroyer nearby. Extensive radar and communication facilities were seen on Ulalu.

The planes returned to the ship at 0746 h. Except for a few 20 mm bullet holes in two of the Avengers, no damage was received.

Strike 3 B - Cowpens - 17 02 44

Sixteen Hellcats formed close (500 to 1000 ft - 150 to 300 m), intermediate (1500 to 2000 ft - 450 to 600 m), and high cover (3000 ft - 900 m), after launch at 0708 h. The bombers and torpedo planes attacked ships at the North Pass. One of the four divisions attacked a small island off the North Pass, from where anti-aircraft fire was seen to originate. Two hits were observed from bomb drops by Bunker Hill planes, and shortly before retirement, a single Oscar was seen flying over the North Pass in easterly direction. Subsequent to that, two Zekes were observed heading towards Moen. The distance was too far, and an attack was not attempted. The other three division covered the other bomber and torpedo bombers. They reported repeated close misses on the Katori, and strafed a destroyer. The last planes from Bunker Hill attacked a cargo ship just outside and 3 miles East of the North Pass. Bombing and strafing did not have any visible effect on this ship. The performance of bombing let a lot open to be desired, as can be seen in the next strike. Particularly moving targets, such as the ship formation outside the Pass, and the Naka were difficult to hit by bombs. The rest of the flight was considered routine, and the plane were back on board by 1006 h.

Strike 3 C - Cowpens - 17 02 44

The launch was commenced at 0943 h. The mission of the eight Hellcats was to escort 9 Avengers from the Cowpens, while they were flying attacks on the 4-stack light cruiser Naka. They were joining 17 Helldivers and 8 Avengers from Bunker Hill, which also had 12 Hellcats in the air as cover. The Naka was steaming southeast at 25 knots estimated speed, coming from the southwest towards Truk. The planes witnessed a single hit, which slowed the ship down, and departed when the bow was awash. All planes were back at the carrier at 1238 h, after they had drawn vigorous anti-aircraft fire from the Tachikaze, beached on Kuop Atoll.

At 0930, nine Avengers were launched to augment the attack planes from Bunker Hill. The formation approached the Truk Atoll climbing to 12000 ft (3700 m). When they were close to the Otta Pass they were ordered by the Target Observer to go 20 ms (32 km) west of the North Pass, where a fast moving single ship was spotted. It was correctly identified as a light cruiser of the Juitsu (Sendai) - Class. It was the Naka, and she began firing at the planes even when they were still about 10 miles distant. The ship was moving on a course of 120 degrees. The attack was commenced

Hailstorm - *Historic Documentation*

in 3-plane sections, from 11,000 ft (3600 m), at a dive angle of 45 degrees and 300 knots speed. The bombs were released at 3000 ft. They all missed. In fact, they were not even close enough to inflict damage. Planes from Bunker Hill orbited until the Cowpens' planes had finished their attack, and the Helldivers went in next. The cruiser undertook violent evasive actions. All bombs missed again.

The Avengers from Bunker Hill were loaded with torpedoes; they commenced a well coordinated attack. One torpedo hit the cruiser just aft of the bridge structure and hurled an orange fire ball 300 ft - 100 m - into the air. A second torpedo missed the bow only by a few feet. The ship was at a high speed turn, but slowed down, and was barely underway. A large oil slick began to form astern. A lot of light 20 mm anti-aircraft fire and 5 inch shells from a gun forward was directed against the planes.

The pilots were disappointed with the results and modified their approach at their next sortie. The planes were recovered by 1225 h.

First Combat Air Patrol - Cowpens - 17 02 44

Fighter cover for the surface attack force was furnished by the Hellcats, which were launched at 1122 h, but returned only at 1536 h. The first attempt to locate the four big ships was unsuccessful. Only after a second try they were found 70 miles west and 15 miles north of the North Pass. The pilots witnessed the destruction of the trawler, which was quite a spectacle when it exploded. It was the Tonan Maru 15, a whaler. They also saw the Katori and the Maikaze sink while subjected to heavy fire. The fourth ship was seen to flee the scene of the engagement, steaming at high speed 10 miles to the west, and not being under attack. The flight leader reported the position of the destroyer Nowake, but did not get an acknowledgement, and the report is not shown in the transcripts.

The planes were vectored out on several occasions. Two runs were made on a destroyer, which they located 40 miles west-southwest of the North Pass, but the ship did not seem to be affected. The other destroyer, Nowake, continued retirement at high speed to the southwest.

The second division were told to vector 160 degrees. No altitude was given, and as there was a high layer of cumulus clouds, the planes split in search for the hostile aircraft, below, in, and above the clouds. A Val was sighted in a break, carrying a bomb. It was only 5 miles away from the surface force. The Val approached the ships while it was pursued by the much faster Hellcats. Five inch anti-aircraft guns were shooting at the planes, and the leading American pilot began to fire at the Val, in order to indicate his status as friendly plane, to the ships. The measure worked, and the American pilots heard over their headsets the message to the batteries, from the Fighter Director in New Jersey, to cease firing. Two Hellcats had caught up with the Val, in the meantime, and opened fire with their board weapons. They immediately obtained hits, and the plane literally incinerated in mid-air. No further contacts were made.

Strike 3 E - Cowpens - 17 02 44

The fighter escort, originally intended for these planes, was diverted to be the first Combat Air Patrol, for the surface ships.

Therefore, this was probably the only formation ever which went to the attack without fighters. Consequently, they were directed to seek and sink the light cruiser, Naka, which had been previously attacked and sustained a torpedo hit. Airborne opposition was not expected in that area. The formation consisted of 9 Avengers, of which 5 were loaded with a single 2000 lbs general purpose bomb, whereas the rest carried one 1000 lbs armor piercing bomb each. The planes were launched at 1321 h.

After the western rim was followed, the formation left for the South and located the Naka about 5 miles from the place of the first attack. The ship was approaching Otta Pass with a speed estimated to be between 3 and 6 knots, and trailed a 2 miles long oil slick. It was amazing that she was still underway, crawling to the comparative safety of Truk, after the heavy damage midships. A small patrol vessel was hovering nearby, while a smaller vessel was about 5 miles distant. When the planes began to circle the cruiser to take aim, the larger vessel moved off.

The dives were commenced from 11,000 ft again, and most of the bombs were very close to the target. One of them glanced off the hull on starboard quarter, close to the stern, and exploded in the water. Debris was seen to fly high, but the nature of the damage could not be ascertained. The leader of the third section hit the cruiser at the stern, just forward of what appeared to be the catapult. This class of cruisers had their catapult removed from their forward and installed on top of the aftermost 14 cm gun. Fire and fragments were hurled several hundred feet into the air. An armour piercing bomb exploded just aft of the third stack, and engulfed the whole mid and aft section in flames and smoke. The cruiser came to a dead stop, and the fires on board intensified in the next minutes. Although mortally wounded, the antiaircraft fire from this ship never completely stopped. Only for a few moments was silence, after the hit midships. When the smaller vessel was strafed it also answered with machine gun fire.

The pilots witnessed that the crew abandoned the cruiser, going into rafts, and being picked up by the two vessels seen before. Although the cruiser was not seen to sink, three hours later, when planes of the second Combat Air Patrol passed over the area, no trace was left of the Naka. While retiring over the South of the Truk Atoll, the planes got under heavy fire from the grounded destroyer Tachikaze. All planes were back on the deck, undamaged, after dropping all bombs and expending 2500 rounds of board ammunition, at 1625 h.

Second Combat Air Patrol - Cowpens - 17 02 44

At 1329 h, the carrier launched eight Hellcats to patrol the airspace above the Iowa, New Jersey, Minneapolis and New Orleans. At this time, the ships were 55 miles to the west of Truk on a southerly course.

Hailstorm - *Historic Documentation*

Naka
IWM

About 30 miles east of the force, two floatplanes were encountered. Special warning had been given not to confuse the floatplanes with the Kingfisher launched by the surface ships, and used to pick up downed pilots in and around Truk. The flight leader of the port division correctly identified these two planes as Jakes (Aichi E 13 A1), however, and the six planes opened for the attack. The leader, closing in from above and astern, began to fire when he was 400 ft away. Sporadic 7,7 mm fire came from the rear of the Japanese plane, but then the shells of the American weapons reached the plane. The rear gunner seemed to jump up from his seat, but then sprawled dead over the edge of the cockpit. The Jake burst into flames, and crashed into the water. The second Japanese plane did some very crafty acrobatics, but there were just too many hunters around. Hit and burning, the plane went down, after the crew release the bombs and bailed out.

Plane recovery was at 1859h, after sunset.

Photographic Mission - Cowpens - 17 02 44

Four Hellcats, two of which carried cameras, the other two to act as fighter cover, were launched at 1330 h. They took oblique angle pictures from the North Pass, counterclockwise to 240 degrees. The islands of Tol, Fala Beguets, Ulalu and Udot were assigned for coverage by these planes. In addition, photographs were made of Eten, North and Northeast Pass. While making pictures of Udot, the planes came under intensive and accurate 40 mm anti-aircraft fire from batteries on the northernmost peak of Udot, and from a destroyer at anchor, about 2 miles off the Northeast shore. The planes were recovered at 1544 h, undamaged.

Strike 3 F Cowpens - 17 02 44

The target of the 42 planes from Bunker Hill, and the 5 fighters from Cowpens, which were launched at 1517 and recovered at 1712 h, was to bomb airfields. The Hellcats carried bomb racks for a single 1000 lbs bomb. Two of these had a two hour, and the others a six hour delay fuse.

The planes attacked from the south-west, flew over Fefan, and dropped their load. Two of the bombs were hits on the airfield installations on Eten, the others splashed into the water. The planes were subjected to intense and accurate fire from the top of the mountain in Eten and the south shore of Dublon. One of the planes was hit by a 5 inch shrapnel, at the port wing and the engine. The pilot nursed his damaged aircraft to a position about 35 miles west of the carrier group, when he had to waterland. He had used the time constructively to prepare his dye sack, dinghy, Mae West, while his engine gradually lost power, and the propeller fell into full low pitch. The waterlanding was perfect. After 10 seconds, the pilot had climbed out of the cockpit, stepped on the wing, inflated his life vest, and jumped. The Hellcat nosed down, the pilot was caught by a stabilizer and pushed down, but bopped up after swallowing some sea water with green dye. The dingy was then inflated and after an hour or so, a Kingfisher from the battleship Massachusetts arrived and picked him up.

This concluded the action for the first day. On the second day of the raid, planes from Cowpens did not participate on the two very successful and the third, abandoned strike by Bunker Hill. Cowpens' planes flew Combat Air Patrol and Anti-Submarine Patrol for the Task Group 58.3.

Hailstorm - *Historic Documentation*

ASSESSMENT

OWN DAMAGES of TG 58.3
a - **Losses**
In Combat:
    1 Avenger   - missing
    1 Helldiver - missing
    1 Hellcat, damaged by a/a fire,
        waterlanded, pilot rescued.

    2 Pilots missing in action
    3 Aircrewmen missing in action.
    2 Aircrewmen killed by anti-aircraft fire.

In Operation:
    3 Helldivers lost,
    1 Avenger lost.

    1 Pilot missing, believed killed.

b - **Damages:**

5 Avengers, minor damages from a/a fire.
4 Helldivers, minor damages from a/a fire
1 Hellcat, minor damage from a Zeke.

DAMAGES TO JAPANESE SHIPPING

Ships Sunk

1 Tanker	- 12 000 ts -	2 torpedoes
1 Cargo	- 10 000 ts -	1 x 1000 lbs bomb, 1 torpedo,
1 Cargo	- 8 000 ts -	1 x 1000 lbs bomb,
1 Cargo	- 6 000 ts	2 x 1000 lbs bombs,
1 NAKA, cruiser	- 5 595 ts -	1 x 2000, 1 x 1000 lbs, 1 torpedo
1 FUMITSUKI destroyer[1]	1 315 ts -	1 torpedo
1 Cargo	- 4 000 ts -	1 torpedo

Total: 7 ships   - 46 910 ts

Ships heavily damaged and probably sunk:

1 Cargo	- 13 000 ts -	2 bombs
1 Carrier[2]	- 12 000 ts -	2 bombs
1 Cargo	- 10 000 ts -	1 torpedo
1 Cargo	- 8 000 ts -	1 or 2 torpedoes

Total: 4 ships - 43 000 ts

Ships heavily damaged:

1 Tanker	- 13 000 ts -	1 bomb
1 KATORI	- 10 000 ts -	2 bombs
1 Passenger ship	- 10 000 ts -	1 or 2 torpedoes
1 Cargo	- 10 000 ts -	1 torpedo
1 Cargo	- 7 500 ts	1 torpedo
1 Cargo	- 6 500 ts -	1 bomb
1 Cargo	- 5 800 ts -	1 bomb
1 Tanker	- 5 500 ts -	1 bomb
1 Cargo	- 4 000 ts -	1 bomb
1 Cargo	- 4 000 ts -	1 bomb
1 Cargo	- 4 000 ts -	1 bomb
1 Cargo	- 4 000 ts -	1 bomb

Total: 12 ships   - 84 300 ts

Ships damaged:

1 Cargo	- 8 000 ts -	1 bomb
1 Cargo	- 7 500 ts -	1 bomb
1 Cargo	- 4 000 ts -	1 torpedo

Total : 3 ships   - 19 500 ts

---

[1]   Actually OITE

[2]   The aircraft carrier reported here was not in Truk at the time. The planes attacked either the Tonan Maru 3, the floating drydock, or the repairship Akashi.

BATTLE REPORT TASK GROUP 50. 9

At 0918 h (1118 h ship's time), Vice Admiral Spruance directed Task Group 50. 9 formed and detached from Task Group 58.3, at 0926h. He assumed tactical command of the formation, which consisted of battleships New Jersey and Iowa, the two heavy cruisers Minneapolis and New Orleans and the four destroyers Izard, Charette, Burns and Bradford. These ships were to make a counter-clockwise sweep around Truk to destroy any Japanese ships encountered.

Initially, the ships in the formation, New Jersey leading, followed by Iowa, Minneapolis and New Orleans - the destroyers screened them - set on a southwesterly course towards Truk to close the 80 mile range. When they were about 15 miles (24km) or so north of the North Pass, course due west was taken, and the speed of 25 knots maintained. At

Admiral Nimitz, Commander-in-Chief, Pacific Fleet, Admiral Spruance, Commander-in-Chief, Fifth Fleet and Rear Admiral F.C. Sherman, Chief of Staff, on board Spruance's flagship, battleship New Jersey. This picture was taken in Majuro, after the raid on Truk.

Hailstorm - *Historic Documentation*

1215 h, the air observer reported two light cruisers and a destroyer about 30 miles (48km) dead ahead of the ships. A small vessel resembling a tug was seen 20 miles (32km) ahead.

When the formation of American warships was about 13 miles (21km) north of the North Pass, the targets were identified as a Katori-Class light cruiser, an Asahio-Class destroyer, a trawler carrying a substantial quantity of explosives - seemingly unaware of the approach of the hostile ships-, and finally a large fast destroyer. Smoke was observed on the horizon, and when the range closed to 20,000 yards (18 km), it could be seen that the Japanese ships were subjected to an intense air attack which resulted in secondary explosions and fires.

As the formation closed to 15,000 yards (13.5 km) at 1309h, the destroyers opened fire on the trawler. Ten minutes later it was dead in the water, drifting in the wind at the head of the column. Then, the New Jersey opened fire with her port 5 inch battery, at only 800 yards. The trawler blew up violently and disappeared. It was interesting to note that the initial range of 15,000 yards proved excessive for the destroyer guns and hits were only scored when the range was closed. A lot of ammunition seemed to have been wasted.

The next ship receiving the brunt of the artillery was the light cruiser Katori. It was 17,400 yards (15.5km) distant and just managed to crawl through the water at 3 knots, being heavily damaged by the preceding air attacks which left the ship smoking from the bridge on forward. Bradford and Burns opened fire and discharged two torpedoes which were believed to hit. The two heavy American cruisers were ordered to destroy the ship and sheered out of the formation to bring their 8 inch guns to bear. Their initial range closed from 21,000 to 13,700 yards (19 to 12km). The deflection was not consistent, but hits were obtained. The Iowa joined in with her secondary batteries, which were on target. Despite this overwhelming firepower, the light cruiser shot back. Probably the aft batteries were either destroyed or could not be brought to bear through the heavy smoke drifting aft, but the forward twin mount kept on shooting at the American ships. No hits were made, but the splashes were as close as 50 yards from the Minneapolis port beam. It speaks for the manly fighting spirit of the crew and the excellent design of the training cruiser that active and well placed resistance was maintained until the ship sank. The Katori listed to port and capsized, showing large holes in the underwater shell plating when she rolled over. Shortly thereafter, she sank by the stern.

At the same time the Katori was fired upon, the other ships of the Group opened up on the damaged destroyer. It was the Maikaze, a ship of the Kagero-Class, not as earlier identified Asahio. The Maikaze fought back bravely, but could only bring the twin mount aft to bear. Considering that the destroyer was very heavily damaged and in almost sinking condition, the fire thrown against the far superior American ships was both rapid and fairly accurate. Izard, against which the fire was directed, changed course and speed, and "fish-tailed" to throw the aim of the Japanese gunners off. The Air Observer issued an urgent warning that torpedoes had been released by the cruiser or the destroyer, which enabled the American ships to turn and "comb" them. They were considered so accurate that a certain hit would have resulted on the cruisers. Almost 20 minutes after the surface action began, the Maikaze capsized and sank, at 1340 h.

It had been reported earlier by planes of Bunker Hill, that a formation of three warships had weighed anchor and passed with high speed through the North Pass. There is little doubt that these were the Japanese ships attacked by the planes outside the lagoon and sunk by the Task Group 50.9. What, however, happened to the third warship? Initially, it stood by, close to the Katori, and checked whether to render assistance. When the plot thickened and it became obvious that it would be suicidal to remain, the skipper of the Nowake stood off to the west at flank speed. This ship was a sistership of the Maikaze. At the time the Maikaze sank, the range to the Nowake had opened to 34,000 yards (31km) from the Iowa. Both battleships opened fire with their 16 inch main batteries. Straddles were observed, but the destroyer was already behind the horizon. After Iowa fired 40, and New Jersey 18 shells, fire was ceased. One of the triple guns was put out action on the New Jersey by an operational fault. Therefore she fired only with five of the six barrels of her forward turrets. The battleships increased their speed to 31 knots. The Nowake was faster and drew away. She escaped. Nobody had given any thought to attack her with planes.

A group of ships was located about 90 miles (145km) west of Truk by 12 Avengers from Intrepid. They attacked and sunk one freighter, and damaged a tanker. A second freighter and a destroyer remained undamaged. Upon return to the carrier, the planes passed the Task Group. The flight leader decided to drop a message to inform the American ships about these targets. After the flight formation had passed the ships on starboard beam, the leader's plane banked into a turn when abaft of the port beam. Although the plane was recognized as friendly, a misunderstanding in communication resulted in one anti-aircraft battery opening fire. The spray of machine weapons proved to be accurate and the plane was shot down, with the loss of the crew.

The Japanese Submarine Chaser #24 strayed into the radar screens at 1616 h. At 1634 h Burns opened fire and closed the range so that the 40 mm machine weapons could be used as well. The little Japanese vessel had no chance and sank 7 minutes later. Just 6 survivors were rescued and later transferred to the New Jersey.

The rest of the sweep was uneventful and no further targets were sighted. Task Group 50. 9 rejoined the carrier formation at 0630 h the next day. Shortly afterwards, the Task Force was withdrawn from operations against Truk.

Hailstorm - *Historic Documentation*

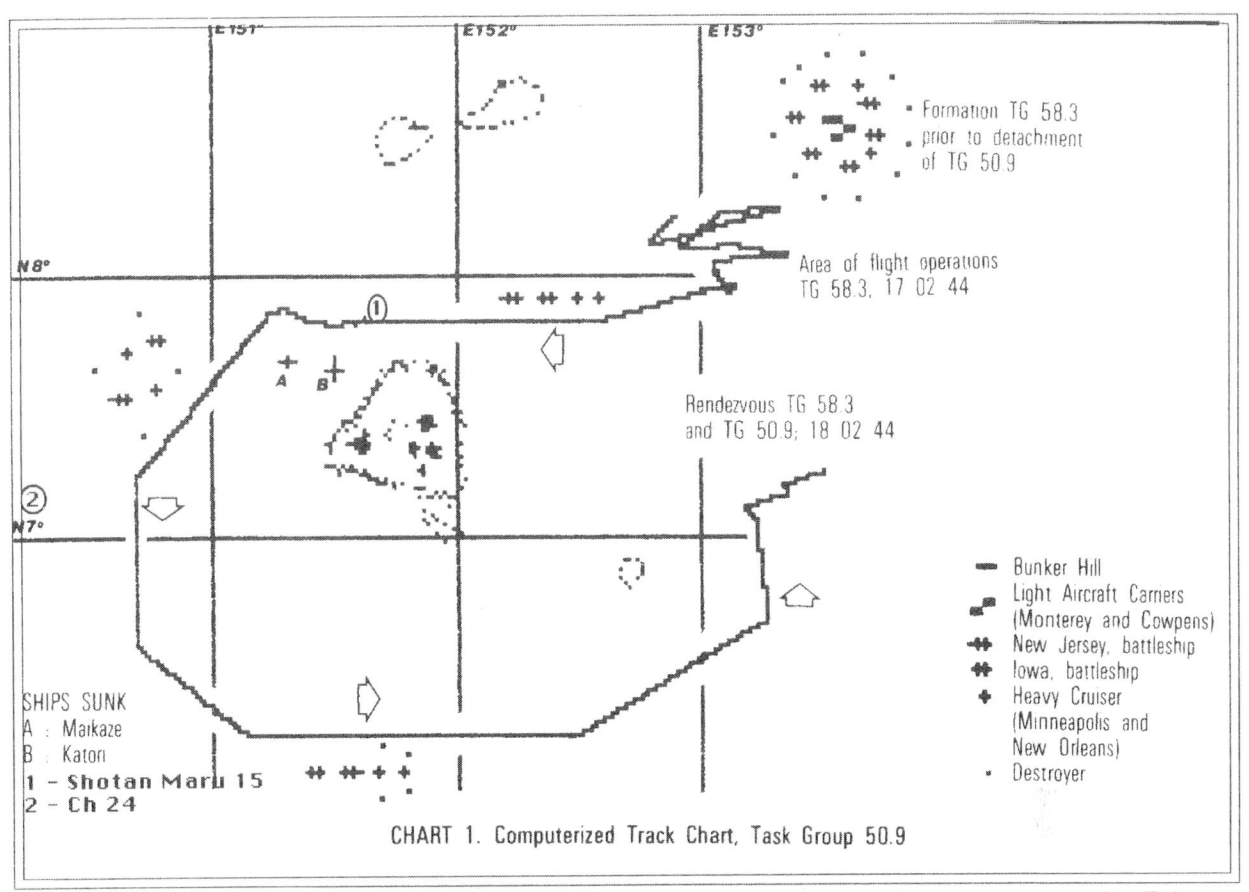

CHART 1. Computerized Track Chart, Task Group 50.9

Legend:
- Bunker Hill
- Light Aircraft Carriers (Monterey and Cowpens)
- New Jersey, battleship
- Iowa, battleship
- Heavy Cruiser (Minneapolis and New Orleans)
- Destroyer

Formation TG 58.3 prior to detachment of TG 50.9

Area of flight operations TG 58.3, 17 02 44

Rendezvous TG 58.3 and TG 50.9; 18 02 44

SHIPS SUNK
A : Maikaze
B : Katori
1 - Shotan Maru 15
2 - Ch 24

Task Group 50.9, commanded by Admiral Spruance, was detached from TG 58.3 and made a sweep around the Truk Atoll. The ships sank one training cruiser, the Katori, and a destroyer, Maikaze. A trawler and Subchaser 24 were sunk by gunfire. Destroyer Nowake escaped.

The Katori, seen burning in this picture, was designed as a training cruiser, and converted to a flagship for a submarine squadron in the war. The ship was slow and too lightly armed to be a frontline combatant ship. The ship lost all headway. The bow wake is painted on the hull. An explosion rocked the ship: The circular waves are moving away from the ship. A large oil slick is forming abeam the ship. The white water midship starboard originates from the rocking and the run off water from the hit, which threw a large water column up. A torpedo wake can be made faintly out at the stern. The Katori is mortally wounded and sinks after gunfire.

Hailstorm - *Historic Documentation*

Shigure, the destroyer, seen here under strafing attack, lived the nine lives of a cat. The ship was severely damaged by a bomb hit into the torpedo storage area, which set off a bad explosion. One of her machines was badly damaged, and there was significant damages from strafing. Yet the Shigure made it of the Lagoon and finally managed to reach Japan for a refit and repair. She was in company with the Harusame, a destroyer of the same class. The wake of the Harusame can clearly be seen port of the Shigure. Tracks of the plane's automatics can be seen in the water off the ship's starboard foreship. Damages and some smoke from a small fire can be seen way aft.

The steam whaler Shonan Maru 15 has been subjected to gunfire by the American destroyers of TG 50.9. Both masts have been damaged, and also their aft deckhouse.. The bridge seems deserted. Moments after this picture had been taken the ship exploded violently after the range was closed to 800 yards (700m) and the secondary guns of the battleships had opened fire.

Hailstorm - *Historic Documentation*

INTERROGATIONS

Reports Of The Japanese Officers in Truk

Foreword

After the surrender of Japan on August 15, 1945, several Japanese Navy and Army officers stationed in Truk were questioned by a team of American officers which arrived a few weeks after the cessation of hostilities. The Americans were interested in details of the work done, and operations planned and executed. At times the questions, however, went beyond this narrow scope. It is only human that the answers by individual Japanese officers sometimes diverge.

Another fact to be considered are the circumstances under which the officers were questioned. They had to attend questioning sessions on the US cruiser Miami and in their headquarters building in September-October 1945, a few weeks after they had received the radio message of the surrender. They themselves had been by-passed and abandoned, yet felt capable of fighting. Food was scarce and malnutrition wide spread. Ammunition was available, albeit not abundant. The large coastal defence guns had been well placed in protective shelters dug into the mountains. The former fleet base was ready for an invasion, and as far as this garrison was concerned the war could almost go forever. True, the weakest soldiers died slowly of malnutrition, but there were still about 35,000 men on the islands.

The spirit in which the interrogations were held varied significantly with the personality of the officers involved. Some Japanese officers either pretended not to understand, or in fact could not understand, the questions put forward to them by a US junior officer, or even the interpreter had problems communicating with the Japanese. The answers frequently reflected their attitude. Sometimes they were sketchy, or of the "I-don't-know, not-my-line"-type, rarely deliberately misleading, and certainly most of the times the Japanese officers made a courageous attempt to answer in word and spirit of the questions, with the exception of the POW issue.

The questions were factual and for the most part related to the nature of work, but sometimes also required value judgements. It appeared difficult for the Americans to avoid a bias in a few instances. Frequently, the Japanese just said their oriental "yes" and were done with that question.

These interrogations fill a substantial amount of files. Information serving as background to understand the significance of the base and the effects of the attacks, have been extracted.

As explained, there are a few contradictions in these statements. No attempt has been made to edit them out of the text. Firstly, it is not known which answer is right. Secondly, they are part of the reply made during the interrogations, and therefore are a matter of record. The written original Japanese records of almost all activities had been destroyed before the end of the war. The Japanese systematically destroyed sensitive files, particularly about POWs. Officially, it was reported that there was an accidental fire at Fourth Fleet Headquarters shortly before the raid, which destroyed the majority of files. Near the end of the war, in June 1945, during the English carrier attack, the Japanese Navy and Army systematically destroyed their files, in anticipation of an amphibious assault.

There were two major carrier based air raids on Truk. The one we are dealing with occurred in February, 1944. However, after the occupation of Hollandia, by the US forces, on 21 - 24 (22 - 25) April 1944, almost the same formations from the February raid sortied against Truk again on 29 and 30 April (30 April and 01 May). There were two significant differences in these two raids. The February air assault was more or less a surprise to the Japanese in Truk. Probably not all radar sets were operable. Early warning was given, but evidently the communications failed somewhere. Subsequently, a great number of fighters taking off were intercepted in their climb and shot down by the Initial Fighter Sweep. The majority of pilots of the Eten airfield seemed to have been on Dublon; when they were shuttled to Eten their headquarters were destroyed. The command structure was complicated, the commander of some units stationed in Eten was in Saipan. And there were many merchant ships at the anchorages. In April, everything was different. Radar was used effectively, early warning of the attack given, many fighter planes opposed the advance already in the air (and were shot down), but there were hardly any ships left in Truk. The second attack was flown mainly against shore installations and air fields. Losses of American planes were also more severe.

From then on, Truk was the target of frequent long range bombing raids, during the daytime, as well as, in the night. Most of these bombings were carried out by B-24 bombers, but later B-29 were used as well, in high altitude attacks. Japanese guns and fighter planes could not reach the B-29. An American fighter plane, a P-58 collided with a Japanese aircraft in January 1945, which suggests that not only bombers were in the skies over Truk.

Finally, there was a small scale, not very effective carrier raid in the closing days of the war by English/Australian forces, and an Australian cruiser, the Canberra, briefly shelled islands of Truk. Although the Japanese in Truk took precautions against an assault, they judged the raid as fairly ineffective.

Particular attention has been paid to the question of why the first carrier strike in February 1944 was a surprise. All evidence points to the fact that radar was installed, but not all sets were in operation in February 1944. The Japanese expected an attack, but for reasons unknown, they expected it to occur around February 21, 1944. Hindsight is always per-

Hailstorm - *Historic Documentation*

fect. Perhaps an attempt should be made to put the reaction to the unfolding attack into perspective. The upper echelons of the hierarchy had said that any attack should not be expected until a week later. Then there was the false alarm, precipitated by a clear voice transmission by one of the approaching carriers (Essex). The radio waves, normally have a reach of line-of-sight, bounced around due to atmospheric conditions and made it obligingly to Truk. Admiral Kobayashi kept Truk on Red Alarm for 24 hours. When the alert was rescinded Truk was hit. So, when the echoes of the approaching carrier planes showed up on the radar screens, they were regarded as a bomber attack. A major carrier raid did not appear to have been in the framework of thinking. This evidently rigid adherence to fixed tactical thinking, found at other times at other places when Japanese forces were on the defence, contributed to the isolation and demise of Truk.

When reading the statements of the Japanese officers about radar, it must be realized that they generally refer to the second attack. As they give an account of the operation of the radar sets, they refer to either the second strike or subsequent bombings.

The last commander of the Fourth Fleet, Vice Admiral Hara, expressed best the problem of accuracy in dating operations and events in Truk, saying that the sun shines every day, flowers blossom all the time, and daily they are bombed: "So, why remember?"

The statements are the recollections of men, who, for about 1 1/2 years, eked out an existence, and whose undoubtedly once vigorous countenance had been sapped by the tropical climate, scarcity of nutritious food and limited medical facilities.

Tactically it Was Sound Not to Take Truk.

Captain Nobuo Higuchi was a senior staff officer under Admiral Hara. He arrived in Truk in October 1941, and stayed there until the end of the war. He relates that Truk was considered to be Japan's second most important base outside the homeland, behind Rabaul. The primary function of Truk was a supply base. It served, but was not in charge of, the Gilberts, the Marshalls, Nauru and Ocean. As an air base, it was used as a stop for aircraft on the way to Rabaul. Army units began to arrive in Truk after December 1943. In case of an assault on Truk, tactical decisions for land operations would be made by the senior officer of the Army forces, General Mugikura, in conference with other high ranking officers.

Captain Higuchi thought that Truk was not adequately defended in any category because of the shortage of material in Japan. Scarce transport facilities prevented a major build-up. It was a strategic error on the part of the Japanese to have the supply lines overextended. The American submarine activities affected Truk substantially. Supplies were cut some time before the carrier attack of February 1944. The counter measures against the submarines were only partially successful. Patrol aircraft searched the area and made several attacks on submarines, but the results were not known to him. The priority targets of the submarines were tankers. It led to a shortage of diesel and fuel oil in Truk.

When the US forces assaulted and took Tarawa in the Gilberts, the Second Fleet moved to Kwajalein. It remained there only a few days and steamed back to Truk because an attack by American carrier based aircraft could not be ruled out. Besides, Kwajalein had no facilities to protect and service a fleet, although it was the Sixth Naval Base under the command of the Fourth Fleet in Truk. A marine garrison, manning coastal guns, was all there was to the base in Kwajalein, as far as the Navy was concerned.

When the B-24 reconnaissance plane photographed Truk, the following ships were inside the lagoon, according to his recollection:

Battleships	-	Musashi, Yamato, Nagato and Fuso,
Aircraft Carriers-		Zuikaku, Shokaku, Zuiho and Hiyo (?),
Cruisers	-	Takao, Atago, Tone, Chikuma, Mogami, Kashima, Kumano, Agano, Naka, Isuzu, Nagara and Katori.

These ships operated between Palau and Truk, returning to Japan for dry docking, fuelling, and replenishing and to exchange crews. Truk had only docking facilities for destroyers and smaller craft. Only small repairs could be made for large fleet units.

When the fleet cleared out on 10 February 1944, it went first to Palau. Then part of it went on to Japan, including Admiral Koga on Musashi. The other ships continued to Singapore and the Philippines. As the US power moved closer to Truk, the defence lines were withdrawn behind Truk. Therefore, Truk lost its importance as a naval base even before the carrier raid. The deciding factor of Admiral Koga's order to take the Combined Fleet away from Truk had been the American search flight on 4 February. The fleet never returned. At that time an invasion was expected. A request for reinforcements was sent to Japan, but an answer never came. It was not clear for Captain Higuchi, whether transports were sent and sunk enroute, or whether the request was ignored.

After the February 1944 air raid, Truk was neutralized as a supply and air base. The B-24 bombing raids in March, the second carrier raid in April (and May) and the June attacks eliminated all strategic value Truk retained at that time. There was not much left structurally, except equipment, which could be protected in caves and bombproof shelters. Consequently, the later B-29 air raids had hardly any strategical value to the US anymore. Truk was kept isolated due to the continued blockade by submarines. The strategic plans were never changed officially, and on paper Truk was regarded as a major supply base. But if the US forces would have attacked Truk on the surface, they would have had to divert enough forces to extend the duration of the war. Indeed, Truk could have been taken by an all-out attack, but it would have been a very costly operation for the attacker in terms of casualties and material. It would have taken a longer time then the success in Saipan, because on the ground, Truk was much better defended and the terrain advantageous for the defender. In retrospect, the captain commented, the American tactics not to take Truk were sound and correct.

On the question, why only 80 to 100 planes opposed the first carrier strike, he said that many of the planes were in from or to Rabaul, for servicing, crew training and repairs. It was true, that some of them, particularly at Eten, were parked nose-to-tail because they were only partially operational. Most of the planes were inferior and too lightly armored for serious aerial combat.

Artificial smoke was to be used as defence against air attacks and in the event of an invasion. It was tried out only once on a raid alert. Smoke generators were lit off Dublon and the island was covered, but the attacking planes only showed up after the smoke was exhausted and had cleared away. In the defence plan, smoke was to be used to conceal the fleet, by running small boats with mounted smoke generators windward of the anchorage, thereby concealing the ships. This method was never used as the fleet had left before the first strike.

In regard to ordnances and weapons, Captain Higuchi mentioned that some magnetic mines were placed in certain channels and passes. Some of them were not controlled, but there were a few magnetic needle-type ground mines. They were laid at the beginning of the war. The US were observed dropping 6 magnetic mines in March 1944 at the North Pass. At Selat Pass, one Japanese mine, and in the West Pass, two mines were anchored. At the North Pass, 4 acoustic mines were laid. They contained underwater microphones and indicated the presence of a ship. An operator on land could detonate these weapons when the propeller pitch was highest. At the end of the war, no mines were considered active. Divers had been sent to locate them, but failed. It was thought that Japanese aircraft, which bombed them later in the war, exploded them. Further, once these mines broke loose, they deactivated, as the firing circuit was broken. The remote chance that marine growth closes the circuit should be considered. The battery used for these mines was not a dry cell and it would not run down. The acoustic and magnetic mines on the other hand, contained dry cells, which were rendered useless, about 8 months after installation.

Detector cables, or loops, were placed at the North Pass, with a listening post at Northeast Island. Other such loops were installed at the South Pass, with Uman as the post. Warnings of unidentified ships were transmitted via an underwater cable and telephone to the headquarters. The detector loops picked up approaching surface vessels and submarines from quite a distance away. These soundings were relayed and continuously monitored. No US submarine was ever detected entering the lagoon.

Submarine service and supply facilities were destroyed during the February carrier raid. The submarines were moved to Saipan in April 1944. The Sixth Submarine Fleet was regrouped in Kure and the Seventh Squadron stationed in Truk. It consisted of 5 or 6 boats. They attacked the invading American ships in Saipan, and watched when Ulithi was built up as a fleet base. The squadron left for Yokosuka because fuel and supplies ran out in Truk. Once a month a submarine would arrive in Truk. These were large boats, which carried about 80 tons of supplies.

There were no shore based torpedo tubes installed in Truk. The shallow reefs surrounding each island made it impossible for torpedoes to be launched. There were, as a substitute, torpedo boat stations placed strategically in the lagoon. Kaiten, one-man suicide torpedoes, were located in shelters and caves on several islands inside the lagoon and on the rim islands. Each one of these bases had two Kaiten available. To launch them, they were wheeled out into the water on tracks where the pilot would man them. Originally, it was planned that the pilot would close the range to 200 m and then abandon the craft. But later, the pilot was supposed to stay with it until it found the target. The range of the Kaiten was about 6000 m at a speed of three knots. It was intended that they should be used only at night against anchored ships. These one-man-one-way torpedoes came in two sizes and were modifications of the standard ship torpedoes. The so-called torpedo boat was a gasoline powered, small landing craft with a maximum speed of 8 knots. They carried two torpedoes, the standard aerial torpedo, lashed to both sides of the ship. Their range was 3000 m with a speed of 35 knots. The warhead contained about 300 kg (660 lbs) of compressed picric acid explosive.

Twelve rocket launchers, with about 30 projectiles per launcher, arrived in Truk in March 1944 from a supply ship. The launching device was a long trough on legs which could be adjusted to change the trajectory. The rocket itself, weighing 60 kg (132 lbs), had a range of 600 to 1000 m and was propelled by a rocket engine. They were accurate. The plan was to set up a barrage-type fire in an area of a known target. Six installations were set up in Dublon to protect the potential landing sites. The other six launchers were placed around Moen airfield. They were placed on mountain slopes, and manned by navy personnel. Additionally, there were 120 Truk-made, muzzle loading bomb launchers placed on the main islands of Dublon, Moen, Uman, Fefan, Udot, Eten and Param. They consisted of a barrel which was fashioned from an oxygen welding tank with the end cut off, and legs attached to it to hold it at a 45 degree angle. The powder charge was rammed into the muzzle, followed by a hardwood plug, with a detonator on top of the powder. The bomb was dropped into the barrel, similar to a mortar shell. It would detonate the powder and expel the bomb. The range could be adjusted, in a way, by changing the powder load. The bomb was fused and would go off on contact.

Some supply ships did manage to get into Truk after the bombings, until May 1944, but none put in after Saipan was taken.

Doctor Degree on Sweet Potato Raising - for a Vice Admiral

On this occasion, Lt. General S. Mugikura, Commanding Officer of the 31st Army and its 52nd Division, and his Chief of Staff Colonel W. Tagima

Hailstorm - *Historic Documentation*

were present. From the Navy, Vice Admiral C. Hara, Commander-in-Chief Fourth Fleet and his Chief of Staff, Rear Admiral M. Sumikawa participated. The American officers, Rear Admiral C. T. Durgun, USN, Commanders Jones and Dew, and Lt. Wyatt Brown conducted this interview on 16 November 1945 in the old Headquarters of the Fourth Fleet in Dublon.

The first echelon of the Army, except for approximately 300 officers and men of the Headquarters Company and Signal Corps which had arrived in November 1943, landed at Truk on 5 January 1944. Before this date only the few hundred troops and Navy components were in Truk. About 14,000 troops were brought in on 05 January. When the first carrier attack was made, troops were located on Tol, Moen and Dublon. The two battalions on Tol were immediately brought to Dublon during the night and one battalion was left on Moen to stem an invasion which seemed possible at that time.

Before the arrival of these troops in January 1944, there were no defenses set up by the Army, only personnel for the naval shore batteries were present. The Army then started fortifying the islands with pillboxes and the Navy completed its coastal defence positions in January 1944. Certain naval batteries arrived at Truk in June 1941 and consisted of 5 and 6 inch guns. These guns were mounted in concrete pillboxes with ammunition rooms below, located on Tol, Moen, and Uman. Four twin mount, dual purpose, 12.7 cm anti-aircraft guns were installed on Dublon and Eten in mid-1941, prior to Pearl Harbor. The coastal defence guns were removed from Truk and taken to Rabaul, immediately after its capture in 1942, because the guns destined for Rabaul had been delayed, and it was thought necessary to protect the new acquisition. The guns initially intended for Rabaul were subsequently sent to Truk. Before the war, fleet servicing facilities, including seaplane bases, and Eten airfield, which was used for accommodating carrier base planes, were established in Truk. According to the Japanese interpretation of the Mandate Agreement, they were not restricted in building fleet facilities, but were kept by the Mandate from building actual defences. Therefore, a fleet base was established to maintain and supply a sizeable fleet and an airplane base for carrier planes. All the defence positions in Tarawa and Kwajalein were started after the war began and were built as outer bastions for Truk. Even Okinawa and Iwo Jima had been lacking in defensive installations before the war, and were prepared defensively after the war started. It was not until after the United States occupied the Gilbert Islands that the Army made plans to reinforce Truk with the 35,000 troops present at the end of the war.

Vice Admiral Hara said, "I heard many broadcasts from the United States describing Truk as a powerful stronghold. We could not help but laugh at this, knowing how weak we really were. I had the South Seas Blues for fear that you would find out the truth. We were especially concerned after your attack on Saipan, where you found out how weak our defenses were. We thought you would draw the conclusion that Truk was not well defended either. But then, of course, there was no point for the US to take Truk anymore."

Shortly after Admiral Hara arrived to take command of the Fourth Fleet at Truk (23 February 1944), he had the guns brought back from the outlying reef islands to the main islands of Dublon and Moen as he thought they would be of little use on the reef. They could not be protected or sheltered on these low lying islands without control of the air and could be easily destroyed by air and ship artillery bombardment. Also, the mine fields were laid after the war began.

The Admiral admitted that the Japanese gave the US reasons for suspicion as to the work they were doing in the Mandated Islands when they did not permit any foreign ships or personnel to visit. He pointed out that the Japanese had never planned to fight a war of defensive tactics, and that budget restrictions did not permit building up the defenses of Truk and at the same time to build up a Navy. The policy was to create a mobile surface fleet which would carry the attack to the enemy.

Upon questioning, Vice Admiral Hara remarked that he believed the terms of the Mandate which had assigned the Marshalls and Carolines to Japan, permitted the establishment of fleet service facilities, recreation, supply and a base for seaplanes at Truk. He said that the Japanese may have transgressed the term of their agreement, but he had not believed so prior to this discussion.

No heavy fortifications had been installed prior to February 1944 other than that in June 1941. Four 6" shipborne guns which had been used in the Sino-Japanese war of 1895 and two medium 6" guns were brought to Truk. For ammunition, the old metal shells and cases with new powder were used. Further, Admiral Hara said, "Definitely, there were no other shore batteries installed here prior to the war."

Lt. General Mugikura was sent to Truk in December 1943 to defend and hold Truk because the Japanese Government knew it was a most important fleet base and knew it had to be held. The government did not, however, provide sufficient Army and Navy facilities to defend it properly. Without superior airplanes to maintain control of the air, all Japanese officers said it would be impossible to hold Truk. After the fall of Saipan, the General said, he knew that Truk was of secondary importance, and that the Americans would probably make no attempt to capture it.

Conversation drifted off to reasons for not remembering dates. Admiral Hara said, "There are no seasons, so everything runs together. You sweat every day, flowers bloom every day, it rains every day, you are bombed every day - so why remember!"

The admiral explained that he grew potatoes for the table of his staff. It was a form of keeping fit. "I have what I call a South Seas Doctor of Potatoes Degree. For discipline purposes I should strut around giving orders, but one cannot act like a glorious Vice Admiral when naked with a potato -hook in his hand, digging potatoes."

Torpedoes In Truk

The following summary of the report of Japanese officers after the war may give an indication of the intentions and strength of the torpedo defences in Truk. They were organized in the 85th Submarine Base Force. In March 1944, a single 12 cm flat trajectory gun was landed by a submarine. In September 1944, 130 torpedoes were available. 16 torpedoes were organized for the Surprise Attack Force. These may have been Kaiten suicide attack torpedoes. Their stations can still be seen at Yanagi, Udot and Fanamu and other islands. Furthermore, 40 torpedoes were available for the Torpedo Raiding Force. In January 1945, the 85th Submarine Base Force was disbanded and amalgamated with the 41st Guard Unit.

Radar Installations

As the Fourth Fleet report indicates, there were several radar sets operable in Truk. However, it appears that only the ones at Uman and Moen were installed before the first carrier raid. It is not clear from the record whether one or both were in working condition then. At any rate, the question of whether any advanced warning was issued, is clear. There was. Some sources indicate that a warning was issued from Moen, but the transmission regarding the imminent attack suddenly broke off before the American planes crossed the outer reef. According to another source, Truk radio went off the air. The messages had been intercepted by the Enterprise. Official records do not exist. Regrettably, Japanese sources are vague about the exact chain of events. It may be assumed that warning was given, but that the Japanese were in a low state of preparedness, and subsequently the warning was too short. By the time the Initial Fighter Sweep arrived over their assigned targets, the Japanese fighters were in their take-off and climbing phase and thus the majority became easy prey.

Uman Island
    2 radar sets type 2, No. 1, Model 1, revision 2
Range 300 KM
Installed August to October 1943
    2 Radar sets Type 3, No. 1 Model (temp.)
Range 300 KM
Installation - first set, July to September 1944
    second set, August to October 1944

Moen Island
    Radar Type 2, No. 1, Model 1, Revision 2
Range 300 KM
Installed September to November 1943
    Radar Type 2, No. 1, Model 2
Range 150 KM
Installed February to March 1944
    Radar Type 3, No. 1, Model 3 (temp.)
Range 300 KM
Installed June to September 1944
Instaled in air raid shelter, probably cave, September 1944.

Tol Island
    1 Radar Type 2, No. 1, Model 1, Revision 2.
Range 300 KM
Installed May 1943 to January 1944
Damaged air raid, 29 April 1944

Located on western tip of southwest Tol.
    2 Radars Type 3, No. 1, Model 3 (temp.)
Range 300 KM
Installation - first radar, April 1944;
    second radar, March to April 1945.

Fortifications

The Japanese 52nd Division reports there were no fortifications on land for the Army at Truk before their arrival in January 1944. Afterwards, the building of field fortifications, particularly beach positions, was given highest priority.

As a result of lessons learned in the Marianas Campaign, it was decided, on August 1944, to put all major weapons and facilities into caves in order to prevent damage by bombardment. It was also decided to construct anti-tank traps and barriers and to plant many land mines on the beaches.

The cave fortifications were generally completed by June 1945. However, a few were not finished, owing to the shortage of dynamite. With the cessation of hostilities, the division stopped the work.

One Float Fighter Almost Caught Up...

Petty Officer Eiichi Okamoto, a pilot, refers in his answers to seaplanes only, not to the land based fighters. He reports that at the time the B-24 photo plane passed over Truk on 4 February 1944, no Japanese fighters were in the air. A battleship in the harbor sighted the US plane, and opened fire. That was how its presence was first discovered. Two or three Zeros, two or three float planes, Rufes, and also one Rufe observation plane took off in pursuit of the photo plane. One float fighter almost caught up, but the B-24 evaded, increased speed, and got away.

In general there was no special condition of readiness ordered. Fighter seaplanes, Rufes, were not regularly in the air, but they were warmed up each morning. Some of them, with machine gun ammunition loaded, were in the state of readiness in order to go out on training flights. About fifteen minutes advanced notice was necessary to get them airborne.

After 4 February 1944, three float fighters were kept at instant readiness at all times. A special alert a day to two before the 16 February 1944 carrier strikes was caused when four Betty bombers were out on a routine search, and one of these planes failed to return. This is a reference to the Betty shot down during the approach of the US Task Force 58, specifically to the Combat Air Patrol of Task Group 58.1 which downed the plane. A special search for the lost Betty was sent out, but there were no precautions taken to prepare against an attack, at least not at the seaplane base. Okamoto was not sure when exactly this special mission was flown, but believes it was in the afternoon of the day the Betty was lost.

No planes took off to attack US fleet on 17 February 1944 to the best of his knowledge. The three other officers present at this session who were stationed at Param, Eten and Moen, insisted that they knew of no planes from Truk attacking the US fleet. They suggested that the attack may have come from Tinian or elsewhere. They all thought that by the

Hailstorm - *Historic Documentation*

evening of the 17th there were no planes remaining which were in good enough condition for an attack.

The following estimate was ventured in regard to the total number of planes airborne during the two day attack.

Dublon Seaplane Base - 10 fighters, 7 reconnaissance, 10 observation

Eten Field - 30 fighters, 6 night fighters

Param Field - 21 torpedo bombers, 2 night fighters

The officers make no reference to the land based fighters from Moen and the other airfields.

In August 1944, two observation seaplanes (Myrts) were received, equipped with radar. When the topic of interrogation shifted to the second carrier attack, 29 and 30 April (30 04 and 01 05) 1944, Okamoto indicated that a radar station gave a warning at 0420 h, Truk time, which was about 20 to 30 minutes before the first wave arrived. Five Param based torpedo planes were out on a routine search at this time. One of these planes tried to make a contact report, but not until after the radar station had warned of the attack. The message was not completed and communication was lost. It is not known whether the plane was trying to report the fleet or had seen enemy planes only. None of the five planes returned.

The routine searches flown from Truk by seaplanes were only short range patrols of two types. The reconnaissance planes vectored out up to 250 km. Six planes were launched at dawn each day. Each plane was assigned a sector by the flight leader. The sector was a triangle with the apex at Truk, the sides 250 km and the base 50 km long. These sectors would be varied each day. The flight lasted about 4 1/2 hours. The second type of patrol involved observation planes flying out only about 150 km. Six planes were launched at dawn and they also covered a 360 degree area. Their flight lasted about 3 hours and was basically an anti-submarine patrol. These early morning sorties were the only daily seaplane flights.

Land based search planes went out farther. Only one submarine was sighted in May or June 1944. It submerged before it could be attacked. A Myrt made a flight to Ulithi. Other reconnaissance flights were made from the end of 1944 onward, until the end of the war. No attacks were flown by these planes. Regarding self-rescue, he said that fighter pilots and the occupants of all small planes wore parachutes, but not the air crews of Betty and other large planes.

Regarding flights made to Guam during the Marianas campaign to evacuate certain people from there, Okamoto only knew that a Betty sortied and brought back four pilots. They had flown to Guam from Truk previously but their planes were destroyed there. Six observation seaplanes and probably 12 land planes remained operational after the Marianas campaign at Dublon seaplane base.

The Truk Weather Station was the control weather station for the Mandated Islands. Before the Marshalls were lost, Kwajalein had a station which received reports from all other stations in that area, consolidated them and sent a report to Truk. Palau did likewise for the Western Carolines Area. Truk then consolidated all reports and broadcasted a weather report for the whole area.

Staff Officers Know Most...

Lt. Colonel Seiichi Yamamoto was staff officer of the 52nd Division, and reports that the Army mission at Truk was purely defensive. There were no plans for any offensive as far as the Army was concerned. The only troops moved through Truk were for islands under jurisdiction of the Truk (Forth Base Force) command; the Eastern Carolines - Ponape, Enderby and Nomoi. These troops were transported by ship. There were only small movements among islands in the Carolines under General Mugikura. He stated that Ponape, Enderby and Nomoi were not under Truk jurisdiction prior to March 1944.

Very little training was done on shore-to-shore combat because only 12 landing craft were available at Truk. The state of training of the troops stationed in Truk was quite varied. Some had been in the Army two or three years, some had previous battle experience. Everyone received some basic training before coming to Truk. The Army did not receive, even not as an emergency measure, untrained troops. They manned peripheral defenses on each island. Anti-tank mines were placed around each of the main islands, about 200-300 m from shore, on reefs.

The Navy controlled all anti-aircraft guns. Originally, 6 anti-aircraft guns on Dublon were under Army command but 3 were turned over to the Navy in April 1944, the other 3 in June 1945. This change of command was made because anti-aircraft defences were considered most essential and should be concentrated under one command. Also, the Navy controlled the early warning systems, as well as the fighter defence. The coastal artillery was under Navy command as well. Coastal artillery was placed on reef islands, but in August 1944, the removal of these guns to the main islands was completed. They were guns of 14, 15, and 20 cm calibre. The reef islands are flat and offered no protection. The guns were moved back by order of Vice Admiral Hara. He believed they could be destroyed too easily on the exposed positions of the reef islands by aircraft and ship bombardment.

Lt. Col. Yamamoto ventured the opinion that he never thought to expect an amphibious assault on Truk because it was unlikely that ships could get past the outer reef. However, when a British carrier force attacked Truk, the Command saw the possibility of a British/Australian landing operation. Contingency measures were set in motion. Apart from readying the defences and putting the troops on alert, almost all records were destroyed. This is one of the principal reasons why many facets of the war years in Truk are so sketchy.

The defence plan against air and amphibious assaults included the following measures:
Coastal artillery, emplaced on the main islands, manned and controlled by the Navy, was charged with engaging ships operating close outside the atoll reef or enter any

of the passages. Naval mines laid in the passes and channels provided additional protection. Anti-submarine and anti-torpedo nets were placed by the Navy in strategic locations around docks and anchorages.

As landing craft would approach within 1000-2000 m of any island, Army artillery would open fire, but the barrage was limited in volume by shortage of ammunition. The Navy had some rockets with a range of 800 m. If the approach continued over the reefs, which averaged two to three hundred meters off shore, locally made mortar, machine guns, anti-boat guns and small arms would open up with a heavy cross fire from well dug-in positions along the beaches of the main islands.

Pre-constructed secondary positions were available to fall back to in case of necessity. Machine guns, light mobile artillery and 37 mm hand drawn anti-tank guns had about five alternate and supplementary positions prepared, and regular shifting of these guns was planned. Ammunition shortage required careful use of the artillery. Most gun positions were inter-connected by tunnels.

Barbed wire was used mostly for protection around the gun emplacements, however tactical wire with lanes of machine gun fire was also employed to some extent. There were no tanks on Truk, although the personnel of a tank unit was here, employed as infantry. Their tanks are probably on the Nippo and San Francisco Maru.

The plan of defence accepted temporary withdrawal to regroup and counter-charge, but the primary plan, in case of lack of orders to the contrary, was dug-in, all-out fighting, such as happened in many places, including Iwo Jima and Okinawa. There was no plan for moving troops from island to island, and lack of boats would have prevented this in any case.

All of the larger caliber guns were emplaced to withstand bombardment, and in many cases could be withdrawn into rear caves and strong bombproof shelters. All of the larger islands had at least one bombardment proof tunnel, about six by six feet, and from 10 to 100 meters in depth. These tunnels were troop shelters against heavy air or naval bombardment. Special protection was available for guns of all sizes and heavy machine guns. Personnel shelters consisted of tunnels. There were three of these tunnels on Dublon, one on Moen, and other islands had one or two each.

The Navy had small landing craft type boats with torpedoes. They also had shore based torpedo launchers. Some of these were on the small reef islands. This is a reference to the Kaiten suicide torpedo stations. Practically no ammunition was brought in during the war. For this reason, very little practice firing could be done. When Vice Admiral Hara was asked why sufficient ammunition was not supplied, he answered, "You should ask your US submarine commanders".

Artillery concentrations were registered on reef openings as much as possible, concurrent with the limited supply of ammunition. Mortars were not registered at all. Artillery placement locations were designed so that they could be fired on adjacent islands if these were captured. Data was predetermined and recorded for most guns on most all important targets and areas. Although the primary consideration for coastal artillery was bomb proof emplacement, as great an arc of fire as possible was planned. Bomb protection was by moving the guns back into bombardment proof emplacements when not being fired.

The command structure in Truk was such that the Army and Navy each operated under their own commander. The Fourth Fleet and the 52nd Army Division were both under the command of the Grand Fleet, but neither was charged with local overall command. However, the Navy's role was primary in repelling attacks, until such time as enemy troops actually landed, when both services assumed charge of their own operations.

All hands did manual labor, this included officers of high rank. Work was done on tunnels and emplacements at night with the result that the men were tired. Poor food did not make the long hours of toiling easier. Guard duty lasted 24 hours with about 6 or 7 men to a post, one hour watch at a time. Guard duty came about once a week for each man. Working parties were recruited from specific units such as special ship unloading units, freight handlers, engineers, etc.

No trucks were available for deploying troops rapidly during an attack. It was interesting to note that the radar system in Truk functioned so well - after the February 1944 raid - that the night and day alarms given were correct and bombing by American planes generally began about 1/2 hour after the first alert. There were hardly instances of false alarms.

What Hurt About Truk...

An interesting interview took place in Tokyo, on 27 November 1945. Captain Genda, Imperial Japanese Navy Staff, was asked a few questions about the strategic and operational aims before and after the attack on Truk. Captain Genda was on the staff of the First Air Fleet until June 1942, became Air Officer of the carrier Zuikaku until September 1942, moved to the staff of the Eleventh Air Fleet up to November 1942, and served in Imperial Headquarters in Tokyo until January 1945. He then became Commander Air Group 343 (Fighters), until the end of the war.

Major fleet units remained at Truk between the Gilbert landing and the Kwajalein landing by the US forces on 31 January 1944. The purpose in holding the main units of the fleet at Truk was to use them with the support of land-based air forces against American forces should they come so far out. He expected an amphibious assault on Truk from the direction of Kusaie and Ponape. A direct thrust was not necessarily expected, rather an island to island advance.

The defence of Truk in 1943 was extremely weak, and Captain Genda believed it could have been easily taken. The strengthening commenced in January 1944. Initially there was no Army force in Truk, and Navy consisted of a land party with not more than 1000 men. The fleet was there of course, but since it was without carrier air force worth mentioning, it would have been either destroyed there or would have had to flee in a major assault. It was noted with deep regret that almost all Japanese carrier airplanes had been sent to Rabaul, and were shot down there. This accounted for the fact, that the Combined Fleet was vulnerable to any air attack.

By the time that the landings around the Marshalls commenced, the Japanese High Command was able to estimate fairly well the strategic situation in that region. There was no change in Admiral Koga's fundamental policy: Seeking one single decisive engagement. The new situation forced the decision to make the Marianas and the Western Carolines the last line of defence.

The Fleet Air Force was practically obliterated, so it was decided that all possible land-based planes, both in Japan and at the various fronts, should be concentrated in the Marianas for a big air battle, with surface units participating to as great an extent as possible. Admiral Koga was determined to lead the Japanese forces in this final engagement himself. In pursuance of this new plan, he came to Tokyo aboard his flagship on the 17th of February 1944 for consultation with Imperial Japanese Headquarters. He had ordered previously the Second Fleet under Admiral Kurita to Palau, and Admiral Ozawa's fleet to Singapore for training.

Captain Genda continued in his narrative, indicating that it was specifically for the purpose of getting the approval of headquarters to this new distribution of forces that he came to Tokyo. The approval was readily given, not only by headquarters, but approved by both the Army and Navy. The Navy in particular was interested in concentrating all their force in this region. It was decided that the regrouping should be completed by June.

By that time the American landing operations in the Marshalls had already commenced so that the new strategic position was quite clear to the general staff. The withdrawal from Truk on 10 February was, therefore, made for two reasons. First, it was felt prudent to make the preparation for the next stage as quickly as possible. Secondly, the Fleet remaining in Truk would be subjected to almost certain destruction when attacked by the US Task Force, since it had virtually no own air support left. The interview then drifted to the events before the carrier raid.

"A photo reconnaissance of Truk was made in early February by Marine Corp planes. Was the fact of that flight known to you, and did it somewhat influence the subsequent movement?"

Captain Genda replied, "Yes, we knew that a Liberator made a reconnaissance flight over the island, and that strengthened our feeling that the Fleet, if allowed to remain there, would be subject to attack from your Task Force in the near future, and consequently, served to speed up our withdrawal from Truk."

"Why then was the sizeable amount of merchant shipping left in Truk?"

"Some of those merchant ships were those which were engaged in sending supplies to Rabaul. All had been subjected to attacks from your planes, and although there were many, there were many of them so badly damaged as not to be operational." This is a reference to the Kiyozumi, Hoyo, Kansho and Tonan Maru, undergoing repairs at the time of the first carrier raid. These ships were locayted at the Repair Anchorage, together with the fleet repair ship Akashi.

"I assume that the conferees received reports of the Task Force strikes on Truk on 16 and 17 February. What was the nature of the reports they received at Headquarters?"

"Generally speaking", the Japanese officer continued, "the feeling was that what they had anticipated, had come to pass. In other words, there was no great surprise. One thing that hurt about that attack on Truk was the fact that an air combat corps, numbering 50 or 60 planes, which could have been sent out to the front with a little more training, was completely wiped out in Truk. Although we lost a considerable number of supply ships in the harbor, that was not particularly seriously felt, because the routes on which they would subsequently have been employed, were virtually cut off anyway. There was one other effect of this Truk attack which might be mentioned, and that is that the strengthening of the line of defence on the island was started in the beginning of 1944 and it was scheduled for completion by June. After this first attack, we went to work in earnest to build up the defence, with the result that it was completed in about one month. Upon completion of the works around the middle of April, the local command informed the Fleet that thereafter, they would take care of themselves. What the outcome would have been if they received such an attack, I do not know."

He added that in addition to a slight increase in the number of naval personnel, one and a half Army divisions, numbering about 30 000, were brought into Truk to defend the atoll. They trickled in, beginning in January and the relocation was completed by the end of March. The main body, he believed, came early in February.

Radio Communications

From the statements made by Major Minoru Kobata it became apparent that the Army had little to do because Truk was a naval base. He was Supply Staff Officer of the 52nd Division, and said that the Navy controlled almost completely the communication facilities on Truk. Army CW-equipment was used mostly for inter and intra island communication. The supply of batteries limited the number of usable radios. Allied jamming of communications from Tokyo was partially successful. Due to dispersal and protection given by caves, neither personnel nor equipment were materially damaged during raids. The Navy had complete control of radar.

The bombing raids did not affect the radio transmissions. The antennae were merely stretched between trees and could be replaced readily. Remote control stations were used in conjunction with the radio transmitters. Underground control cables connected the control station with the transmitter, thus affording protection to the operators. These cables were severed several times by bombs.

The reliable radar sets gave combined 24 hour

coverage. There were never false warnings.

Fortifications

There were no fortifications on land, made by the Army, at Truk before the 52nd Division arrived in January 1944. With the arrival of the 52nd Division, the building of field fortifications, particularly beach positions, were given highest priority. Of course, the Navy had built extensive installations.

As a result of lessons learned in the Marianas Campaign, it was decided, in August 1944, to put all major weapons and facilities into caves, in order to minimize damage by bombardment. It was also decided to erect anti-tank traps and barriers and to plant many mines on the beaches.

The above mentioned cave fortifications were generally completed by June 1945. However, owing to the shortage of dynamite, some were not finished. With the cessation of hostilities the division stopped the work.

Army Troop Accommodations

It was arranged by the Army and Navy headquarters in Tokyo that the Navy should assume the responsibility for the accommodations, and material supplies, for the 52nd Division in Truk. Because of the lack of transport facilities, materials then available in Truk had to be extensively used. For example, civilian houses and native dwellings were utilized for barracks, and bread fruit trees for timber. Therefore, the 52nd Division never had barracks available or had been able to build any. Although there were plenty of houses available, they were actually insufficient for the purpose of quartering troops. After the first attack the buildings were used which were not destroyed, but the troops had to be dispersed in small houses over a wide area. Later, after having been bombed, each man was assigned to his battle station in pill boxes etc. for his living.

Available houses were used mainly from January to February 1944. At first civilian facilities such as primary schools and civilian houses were converted, as well as navy buildings, but a part of the army had to live in tent camps.

In the second period from March 1944 to August 1944, it was tried to disperse the houses, and to make them lower in structure, so that the damage caused by the aerial bombardment in the frequent attacks could be limited. This was done after the raid in February, and especially the one on 29 and 30 April 1944. The houses in that period were half under ground and so small that only 12 to 13 men could live in each. The construction of houses was very simple: The roofing was made with tin plate or woven leaves. The floor had no matting. Blankets were put directly on the floor; the soldiers slept on them. Each person in these huts occupied three square feet, on the average.

The third period was from September 1944 to August 1945. On account of the more frequent bombings, caves were dug which were used as battle stations. Accordingly, the troops lived in camps erected near the respective station. Part of the men could live in these caves. Materials were extremely scarce during this period. Wooden boards were especially short in supply.

After the war the condition of housing was much the same as in the third period. Gradually, however, the soldiers moved out of the dispersed sheltered structures into the open fields.

Dublon Nechap Water Supply System

The construction work on this particular system was begun in November 1942. Originally it was planned that the Nechap Works would have a daily output of 200 tons, but frequent changes were made, and the final plans called for an output of 600 tons daily. Three inlets had been completed and the foundations for the reservoir, the filtering pond, and the distribution pond had been about 80 percent completed. Purified water was not distributed, but since the latter part of 1943, it has been possible to supply the 85th Submarine Base with unpurified water. Construction work was begun in November 1941. The following is an outline of the plan:

Position	:	Lala Valley in Dublon
Output per day	:	1000 tons
Objective	:	To supply water to all land forces.

During The Day Attacks, The Japanese Planes Flew Out Of Range ...

Captain Tamura arrived at Truk in July 1944 after various assignments as an instructor of pilots. He had little knowledge of events prior to that date.

In July 1944, six fighters and six seaplanes were based at Truk, only four of each type were operational. Three of each type were present, at the end of the war. Fifty pilots were stationed at Truk in July 1944, twenty of these were still present, in 1945. There were no aircraft brought into Truk for reinforcement after he arrived. One plane stopped at Truk in July 1944 enroute to Rabaul from Tokyo.

Between November 1944 and March 1945, five monthly mail flights were made from Tokyo to Truk. However there were no flights during the summer of 1944 because of the low priority given Truk compared with other bases.

No supply vessels have visited Truk after the fall of Saipan. However, two submarines succeeded in reaching Truk in April and May 1945 bringing food and supplies. A third submarine in July 1945 brought two Myrts. These planes were never used.

Four Myrts flew to Truk from Japan in January 1945. Two of these refueled at Marcus and two at Iwo Jima. The two that stopped at Iwo reconnoitered Guam on the way to Truk. All six planes were used solely for reconnaissance. Approximately six missions have been flown altogether since July 1944, one to Guam, one to Eniwetok, one to Ulithi, and the remaining three were searches. None of the reconnaissance planes executed Kamikaze attacks.

The bombing attacks by B-29 had detrimental effects. They kept the fields and installations in a constant state of disrepair. Targets were successfully destroyed prior to the B-29 attacks, but the small-scale, accurate bombing kept them out of order. Most

Hailstorm - *Historic Documentation*

damage from these raids was done to airfields. Small bombs scattered over the airstrip were most effective against airfields. Delayed action bombs were particularly troublesome for the defenders.

As no naval or merchant vessels used the harbor facilities, and because Truk was visited by submarines only three times, bombing directed against the airfields was most effective. Frequent small raids kept the base out of commission.

Not after July 1944 was there an overall defense plan to repulse air attacks. There were only 40 anti-aircraft guns on the islands. They were not in good shape and were not radar controlled. The few planes under Navy command on the base were never used for combat. During day attacks they flew out of range, at night they were dispersed on the fields. The aircraft which took off to escape destruction were the ones seen near Truk by the B-29. Ammunition, though not scarce, was used frugally in expectation of yet another carrier attack. Regarding advance warning, radar invariably picked up bombers still 200 miles (320 km) away from the islands.

The fields of defense of the islands were distinctly separate. The Navy had sole control of the anti-aircraft guns although 50 Army personnel were assigned to assist. The Navy was responsible for defense up to the water's edge. From the water's edge the Army assumed responsibility.

Defence against an assault landing attack was the strongest point. Defence plans were very detailed and defensive measures and precautions had been taken. The strategy in repelling an amphibious assault was to attack with aircraft outside the reef, to shell once the invaders had gained entrance into the lagoon; and to resist at the water's edge and in the hills, to death. At least the part of defending Truk with aircraft indicates some unrealistic rigid adherence to outdated defense plans. Assault was expected to come from the North, through either the North or the Northeast Pass.

Captain Tamura insists that the two forces cooperated perfectly, the Navy handled operations and defense while the Army "planted and cultivated potatoes and dug trenches". Taking the general climate between Army and Navy into consideration, these statements are an attempt to white wash. The greatest weakness of the group of islands lay in its inability to ward off aerial attacks.

New pilots at Truk had 200 hours flying time, experienced pilots had 1500 hours. He attributed the disproportionate losses to inferiority in numbers and made no further reference to the inferior Japanese planes. The most important consideration after July 1944 was food. Training came a poor second, as a considerable amount of time had to be expended in planting, cultivating and harvesting crops.

Finally, Captain Tamura related to the English carrier attack of 16 June 1945: Two waves of fifteen aircraft each were sent over, one at 1000 h and the second at 1400 h, attacking Dublon, Eten, and Moen. Four Seafires were lost to flak. (the word "flak" is originally a German abbreviation - Flugzeug Abwehr Kanone - anti-aircraft gun.) The bombing partially destroyed some records. Fearing an amphibious assault when a cruiser bombarded Truk on the second day, the Japanese burned systematically records and statistics. Practically no damage resulted from the attack. Strafing attacks were ineffective, being made from excessive altitudes.

The Japanese officer mentioned that in January 1945 an attacking U.S. P-38 collided with a Japanese plane. The American pilot bailed out, was taken prisoner and later sent to Japan. The date is not consistent with other records about POW's, and the event may have happened in 1944.

North Pass was mined heavily ...

Commander Shigeju Ago was gunnery staff officer of the 6th Naval Base (Truk). His career included duty on the Jingei, submarine mothership of the 7th Flotilla, he was gunnery officer of a destroyer and a light cruiser. He narrated that all Japanese naval vessels could anchor in Truk, but supplies and water were scarce. But despite these shortcomings Truk was used, even before 1941, as a fleet anchorage, on a minor scale. The facilities had been intended only for smaller ships and minor repairs. The shipborne anti-aircraft was very inadequate in quantity and quality.

After the attacks, construction was more or less confined to rehabilitate damaged buildings and to dig underground shelters.

Truk could feed its own forces very meagerly and could support them indefinitely, but its value as a base was lost. Tokyo left Truk to his own devices, giving no orders regarding future missions. Subsequently only reconnaissance and observation missions were carried out on a small scale. There was not enough equipment to cover very much area. Since they had only so limited resources they could gave Tokyo headquarter very little information.

In case of a surface attack, the 40 or more 12 or 13 cm guns placed on the islands inside the lagoon - none on the outlying islands - were expected to hold ships off at a distance. Close range combat was planned to repel invading troops due to the small amount of ammunition available. The large islands were considered most important and most gun emplacements were located there.

Picket boats were not used for patrols because of scarcity of these vessels and poor communication. An invasion was expected before the assault on Saipan and Guam. There were 40.000 troops and that number was considered adequate. An invasion was expected from the North Pass, South Pass and from the East. The North Pass could have been the best entrance point because it was farthest away from the main islands. Therefore it was mined heavily with moored contact mines, 8-10 magnetic mines, 4 or 5 electric mines, which could be set off from the beach. The South channel was mined only with contact mines.

On the question whether any U.S. submarines ever entered Truk Lagoon, the answer was that to everyone's knowledge no submarine ever penetrated the passes. The Japanese 6th Submarine Flotilla moved out of Truk to Saipan and only once in a while supply subs reached Truk. Some midget submarines were stationed in Truk said Commander Ago. They came in before February 1944, but no more after that.

History of the Fourth Fleet Headquarters

The Fourth Fleet was organized on 15 November 1939 and was to guard the "Inner South Sea", which was the term used for the Mandated Island area of the South Pacific. The "Greater East Asia War" broke out, and Guam, Wake, the Gilberts, Nauru and Ocean Islands were occupied. These islands were partly garrisoned. Under the control of Commander-in-Chief, Fourth Fleet, the 4th Base Force, headquarters on Truk, manned the Carolines. 5th Base Force, headquarters on Saipan, garrisoned the Marianas. 6th Base Force, headquarters on Kwajalein, fortified the Marshall Island and 3rd Special Base Force, headquarters on Tarawa Island, garrisoned the Gilberts, Wake and Ocean Island.

With the occupation of the Gilbert Islands (Tarawa) by the American forces at the end of November 1943 and the annihilation of the 3rd Special Base headquarters, Nauru and Ocean were placed under the control of the 6th Base Force, Kwajalein.

With the Americans occupying the main islands in the Marshalls (Kwajalein) at the beginning of February 1944, and with the annihilation of the 6th Base Force headquarters and garrison, the remaining islands which had been under its control were placed under the direct control of the Commander-in-Chief, Fourth Fleet, except Nauru and Ocean Islands, which were placed under the command of the 4th Base Force.

Near the end of January 1944, the 30th Base Force was newly organized with headquarters in Palau, the Western Carolines were placed under its command.

In March 1944, the Central Pacific Fleet was newly organized and the Fourth Fleet came under its command. Also, the Commander-in-Chief, Central Pacific Fleet, had direct control of the 5th and 30th Base Forces. The Commander-in-Chief, Fourth Fleet's defence district was shortened to the 4th Base Force which included East Carolines, Nauru and Ocean, and the 6th Base Force which included a part of the Marshalls and Wake.

On 1 May 1944, the 4th Base headquarters was demobilized, and the Commander-in-Chief, Fourth Fleet took over direct control of the 4th Base Force.

With the American occupation of the major islands in the Marianas and the destruction of the Central Pacific Fleet headquarters in Saipan, the remaining islands under the control of the 5th Base Force came under the control of the Commander-in-Chief Fourth Fleet, except the 30th Base Force, which came under the control of the Southwest Fleet, headquarters in Manila.

Location of the Fourth Fleet Headquarters.

15 November 1939-
Fourth Fleet organized, flagship Kashima.
10 November 1943-
Headquarters transferred from Kashima to Truk, 4th Naval Supply Building. Personnel of the Fourth Fleet Headquarters throughout each period consisted of about 250 persons. The location of the Kashima is undetermined, but the ship was probably in Truk.
01 April 1944-
Headquarters transferred to the air raid shelter at the summit of the Civil Government mountain.
01 May 1944-
With the demobilization of the 4th Base headquarters, when placed directly under the command of the Commander-in-Chief, Fourth Fleet, headquarters were moved to a place on the northeast peninsular on Dublon where the Fourth Fleet headquarters was located until the end of the war.

Commanders-in-Chief of the Fourth Fleet:

15 November 1939 - 15 November 1940,
Vice Admiral Hidekichi Katari
15 November 1940 - 11 August 1941,
Vice Admiral Shiro Takasu
11 August 1941 - 26 October 1942,
Vice Admiral Shigeyoshi Inoue
26 October 1942 - 1 April 1943,
Vice Admiral Baron Tomoshige Sameshima
1 April 1943 - 19 February 1944,
Vice Admiral Hitoshi Kobayashi
19 February 1944 - end of war,
Vice Admiral Chuichi Hara.

Why the Aircraft in Eten Were Parked So Tightly.

Rear Admiral Michio Sumikawa, Chief of Staff of the Fourth Fleet, reports:

"The best our radar could do after the carrier strike was to distinguish between heavy bombers and fighter aircraft. When the B 29s attacked, we had few fighters left and they were not high performance aircraft. At first they carried air-to-air bombs, but our aircraft could not climb to the altitude where the B 29s were flying. Instead we used our 20 mm guns. An experiment of installing 30 mm guns proved unsuccessful. Our aircraft did not maneuver well at high altitude because they were only patched up wrecks; however, we did succeed in damaging one B 29. The B 24s from Eniwetok and the Admiralties which attacked us in 1944 were very skillful. Although the B 29s were only on training missions, their accuracy was excellent. The B 29s effected little damage to personnel or equipment because by the time they attacked, we had our equipment moved underground and had good air raid shelters.

Photo reconnaissance would check the area and then the B 29s would come. It indicated excellent team work between photo reconnaissance and bombers. We had better success in shooting down B 24s than B 29s, but that in itself does not mean anything. In early 1944 when the B 24s attacked, we had more aircraft; also, these aircraft were of higher quality than those we had later.

Our night fighter is a two seater aircraft. It has a fixed machine gun on the topside of the fuselage behind the pilot. This gun is fixed at a 30 degree angle and is fired by a gunner. The pilots fly their aircraft below the bombers and parallel with their course; the gunner judges the proper moment to fire the gun. They had success at first. The B 24s would be picked up by a searchlight and our night fighters would attack. All

Hailstorm - *Historic Documentation*

their victories were of aircraft caught by searchlights. It did not take the B 24s long to develop an evasive technique. When caught, they would dive rapidly and make a sudden turn in one or the other direction. With the advent of this evasive action, the effectiveness of our night fighters dropped considerably.

In May of 1944, by order of Command-in-Chief, First Air Fleet, 71 of our aircraft, 59 of them fighters, were transferred to Yap and Guam. This action was based on a supposition of the General Staff that the weight of the Allied attack would swing south. The air power was reshuffled, leaving 40% in the north and sending 60% to the south. Because of this strategic error, Truk was denuded and unable to protect Guam. When the Marianas Campaign began, all the remaining aircraft were sent to assist the meager air strength based in the Marianas. None of them ever returned. Eight fighters were sent to us from Palau. We began patching together parts of planes damaged from previous raids, managing to bring our total up to eighteen. This explains why the quality of Japanese aircraft based on Truk was inferior after July 1944. We also managed to patch up one night fighter and two carrier torpedo planes. Six three-seater seaplanes and two spotters were never removed from Truk. Later six reconnaissance aircraft were flown down from Japan. This made a grand total of 35 aircraft. There were never more than six to seven fighters operational at one time. Out of the 165 aircraft based on Truk, only 41 (of which only six to eight were fighters), were under Fourth Fleet control. The remainder were 26 Air Squadron aircraft, headquarters Rabaul, Vice Admiral Sukamaki, commanding. The aircraft in transit were brought to Truk by two aircraft ferries.

The aircraft were parked nose to tail on Eten airfield during the first carrier raid, 17-18 February 1944. This happened for three main reasons:
 1) There was insufficient space on the airfield.
 2) Ferry pilots had not yet arrived form Rabaul.
 3) The captains of the aircraft ferry (Fujikawa) felt that a delay in unloading might by too dangerous, and discharged cargo haphazardly."

It may be mentioned here that within a space of one month, three aircraft ferries, among them the Fujikawa Maru with 30 Jills, according to his recollection, brought in more than 120 planes. These were not operational and had to be serviced, being located in Eten. The aircraft in the Air Arsenal (Ferry Depot) were partly armed and ready for combat, and partly in need of modification. Some were packaged in crates. Only a few were armed and ready to fight. The following aircraft were airborne during the two day attack on 17-18 February 1944:
 Eten   10 Zeke,
 Dublon   6 - 8 seaplane fighters, 3 - 4 spotters,
 Param   6 - 7 carrier torpedo planes.

The aircraft from Param attacked the Intrepid. None returned." Again there is no mention of sorties flown from Moen airfield.

"All of these aircraft were lost, and possibly two more from Eten. In addition, the following aircraft were burned or seriously damaged on the ground:
 Operational Wings: 125
 Air Arsenal: 110

This means that out of the 365 aircraft on Truk at the time of the raid, only about 100 escaped unscathed. We were able to rebuild 30 Zekes from the damaged aircraft.

Regarding the British carrier attack, 16 June 1945, it is my opinion that only one carrier took part in the attack. The aircraft attacking were Spitfires, TBFs and SBDs. The Spitfires, acting as top cover for the bombing attacks, strafed at low altitudes after the bombers left. The aircraft acted as if they had imperfect information. Unlike the American aircraft, they did not approach the target rapidly. Rather, they stayed at high altitude for some time surveying the area. When they did attack, they bombed and strafed insignificant targets. They broke formation outside the reef and circled the main islands at 3000 meters, gradually descending to 1000 meters from which altitude they commenced their attack. The TBFs and SBDs bombed from a 30 degree dive, releasing their bombs at 500 meters. The Spitfires strafed very low. The attack was divided into waves, one in late morning and the other in early afternoon.

First wave:
1. 18-24 Spitfires, reconnaissance;
returned to carrier, followed immediately by
2. 15 TBFs and SBDs escorted by 6 - 9 Spitfires.
 Second wave:
1. Same as in 2 above.

No fighters met in the attack because it was a complete surprise. One Spitfire was lost. Its wings came off while it was pulling out of a dive. Practically no damage resulted from this attack.

Between July 1944 and the present, about three submarines came to Truk; before that, very few."

Contradictions on Radar

Commander Kitari Kaneko was a staff officer of the 4th Fleet, commander of the 4. Communications Department and the 4. Meteorological Department. He arrived in Truk after June 1944, about four months after the air raid in February.

After which date radar was operational, he did not know. The time references give no indication that radar had been used before the later bombing raids. The Japanese at Truk used radar only for early warning and not for gun control. They possessed a total of eight sets on three islands and were well placed on the highest points. The information was distributed to the planes and the ground forces. As there was no radar control on the antiquated guns, and the communication system with the planes was poor, very little gain was obtained from radar. Truk did not have adequate modern equipment.

None of the fighter airplanes had radar, but the newest submarines were equipped with it. The radar sets functioned well in Truk and were well maintained. The bombing raids had hardly any effect on their performance. Three sets were located on Moen, three on Uman and two on South West Tol. No air sound detection devices were installed as their value as an early warning device was very controversial. After Kaneko came to Truk in July 1944, there were no picket vessels stationed to detect raids. All Japanese vessels were instructed however, to flash a warning when they observed any Allied planes.

In August 1944, there were quite a few outposts. The ones north and east of Truk were abandoned and the personnel brought back to Truk. Two were maintained until the end of the war, one at Puluwat (Enderby) and one at Nomoi. The radio transmitters used to communicate an approaching air raid were so weak that great reliance was placed in the radar operated in Truk. Each out-post island had only two or three radio operators, and they were insufficiently trained.

One way to detect ships was by radio detection (RDF), and at the South Pass there was a supersonic detection device in working order. Neither Allied ships nor submarines were ever detected by it. This device had a range of ten kilometers.

Raids from the north were usually detected by the radar on Moen. Radar information from the specific radar detecting the raid was sent to a command post. The command post informed first the airfield in Moen, then Fourth Fleet Headquarters, Dublon Island, subsequently all lookout stations on Moen Island and the other radar stations on Moen Island as to range and bearing of the approaching raid The Uman and Tol radar stations operated in a similar manner. When the telephone wires were broken, the radar station used radio transmitters to pass the necessary information on to headquarters. A siren was used as an air raid warning device on Dublon and Moen. The other island used bells and gongs.

Moen No. 1 fighter air strip was the only strip to have voice communications with its fighter planes. When the planes were more than 60 km distant they could no longer hear the radio transmission from Moen which limited their effectiveness. Often the quality of the interceptions were poor. Subsequently, the fighter planes were given only range and bearing of the attack bombers. This communication was in plain language. Probably altitude, speed and number of planes in an attack could not be determined with accuracy. Only a qualitative statement could be made. A broad pip on the radar scope, for example, indicated the presence of many planes.

At night, searchlights were used to spot planes and to place the guns on target. It was difficult to train the lights; probably as difficult as to direct the anti-aircraft guns onto the plane. In addition, ammunition supply was short. The equipment being sent to Truk for radar controlled anti-aircraft guns was lost when the ship carrying it was sunk off Guam.

The great weakness in the defence of the island was mainly the lack of adequate fighter aircraft. Insufficient fire power was due to a relatively small number of guns, the fact that the guns were relatively antiquated, the ammunition supply was low and that they were not radar fire controlled.

The early warning radar in Truk was adequate. They were air search models, but could also pick up surfaced submarines. Sometimes they were used for that purpose. Against air targets, the range was maximum 250 kilometers, reliably up to 150-180 kilometers, with a frequency of 150 MHz.

The radar on the various islands was operated in shifts with the sets taking turns operating. Their combined coverage was 24 hours daily until a target was located, when all of the radars were switched on. This alternating was done to prevent operator fatigue, and damage to the machines due to overheating. The men continuously watched the radar scope for two hours at a stretch. Regular power transmission lines were used between generator and set, supplemented by an auxiliary six kilowatt gasoline generator for emergency use. Only one radar on Tol was damaged slightly in March 1944 by a bombing raid, but was soon placed back in operation. In general, the air raids did little or no damage to the radar. Moisture damaged component parts of the radar; mold was particularly troublesome.

To determine if planes were Japanese or Allied, it was known that Japanese returning came in on a fixed bearing which was occasionally changed.

The interrogators, Lt. (j.g.) Young and Lt. (j.g.) Benson then asked an important question:

"During the carrier attacks of 16/17 February 1944, our aircraft were only opposed by 80 Japanese planes while Japanese planes were grounded outside revetments, parked nose to tail. Why did this occur?"

"I do not know, I think we were surprised."

The American aircraft were too fast for the antiquated anti-aircraft guns. They could not reach the high altitude planes and at low altitude they zigzagged, making them difficult to track. Despite the large amount of flak thrown up, much of it was inaccurate for this reason.

American Prisoners of War

Truk had no facilities to encamp prisoners. According to the statements, all of them were sent to Japan at the earliest possibility. This was normally accomplished by ship transport. Merchant vessels and warships were used. After June 1944 and the American Saipan campaign, shipping came to an almost complete halt, and POWs were flown out by night via float planes. All reports have been destroyed as a bomb hit the house accommodating the files; and after the war, the picture was pieced together by interrogations and written statements of Japanese personnel involved. However, a war criminal trial in Guam held in 1946 convicted a number of Japanese officers because of POW killings.

From the S.W. Pacific, three POWs arrived in Truk in November 1943 and were sent to Japan on the cruiser Takao in the same month. A destroyer brought in 41 POWs, part of the crew of an American submarine which had sunk. It was USS Sculpin, which homed in on a convoy, but was sighted and depth charged. The depth meter failed, and when it was decided to go to a shallower depth because of damage inflicted, the sub broached. Despite her immediate dive, the depth charges damaged the ship severely and she was taken to the surface. She was then fighting with her deckgun the well armed destroyer, and the toll on personnel was severe. The order was given to abandon the sinking ship. The skipper went down with her voluntarily because he was privy to secret information. The rest of the crew was rescued by the

Hailstorm - *Historic Documentation*

destroyer Yamagumo. Two of the crew had to have arm amputations because of severe injuries. It was performed in Truk. 21 of the POWs were sent on board of the Unyo Maru No. 1, a merchant vessel used for mine laying. 20 POWs came on board of the Chuyo, an aircraft carrier. She was sunk on 4 December 1943 by the US sub Sailfish and lost. One of the POWs of this party survived the war.

From the Marshall Islands eight POWs were received early in February 1944. They were to be shipped to Japan aboard the light cruiser Katori. All of them were lost when Iowa and New Jersey and two heavy cruisers blasted it out of existence.

Six US and two Australian prisoners arrived on 20 February 1944 and were held. Deserted islets around and inside the Truk Atoll were searched after the raid, on 21 February 1944. The 41 Japanese Garrison sent two boats on that day to check the south half of the atoll; and then on February 23, these two boats embarked on a search of the north half. A tent made from a parachute was discovered on a nameless islet north of Ran Island. When the boats approached, they found an US aviator, and took him to the headquarters of the garrison the same day. In the beginning of March, this prisoner was said to have been flown to Japan by a seaplane. All other POWs were evacuated in March as well.

From April until November 1944, five POWs were accommodated. Except for one P-38 pilot, they were the air crews of the heavy bombers which attacked Truk. The P-38 pilot had made a forced landing on Hotaru Islet, was captured and later flown out.

Following the carrier raid of 16/17 (17/18) February, one corpse was recovered and buried on 20 February 1944; and three dead aviators from the April raid were washed ashore a few days after the attack and buried. A POW was killed when transported from an outlying island to Uman during the April raid. The fishing boat he was travelling in had been raked by board weapons of attacking planes and sunk. One fighter pilot was rescued from Fala-Beguets on 17 February 1944 and brought to Tol. He died the same day.

At the end of May 1944, two aviators were rescued from their life raft after being at sea for more than 10 days. They were given the same rations as Japanese soldiers in Enderby and transferred to Dublon in July. Subsequently, they were evacuated aboard the Sub I 365 on 16 November 1944. It is unlikely that they survived the war, as this Japanese submarine was torpedoed by the American sub Scabbardfish off Japan on the 29 November 1944.

The Japanese interrogated were at pains to stress that the POW had been given the same rations as they themselves had available, and were not maltreated. However, hospital personnel, doctors and a few individuals were held back in Truk after the general repatriation of the military personnel. At a military trial in Guam in the second half of 1946, several individuals were convicted for war crimes, specifically maltreatment of prisoners, and sentenced to death. They were executed. Their conviction was due in part to statements made by native Trukese, who were flown to Guam for the trial.

PART TWO
WALKS AND TALKS

First Part - WALKS

GEOLOGY, PEOPLE AND VEGETATION

The Truk islands are a near-atoll, and consist of 12 volcanic and many flat coral islands inside a lagoon which measures roughly 50 by 65 km (30 by 40 mi). They are enclosed by a coral reef. The rise of the volcanic islands range from 8 by 3 km (5 by 2 mi), to the smallest which is less than 400 m (quarter mile) in diameter. There are several peaks on the large islands which are higher than 300 m. The highest mountain can be found on Tol. It is 443 m (1453 ft). The sea bottom in the lagoon varies significantly in depth. Whereas parts are fairly uniform (between 50 and 60m in the north, and between 40 and 50 m in the south), significant underwater mountains and rolling underwater hills may be found in the middle. Outside the coral rim, the bottom drops off and a short distance from the reef, depths of 100 m (330 ft) are reached, descending steeply outward to 300 m (1000 ft) and far below.

The mountains, slopes and alluvial plains are covered with fairly dense jungle vegetation. Particularly the alluvial plains, lower slopes and low lying coral islands carry coconut palms, breadfruit and other semi-cultivated growth.

The Truk atoll is the remnant of a large shield volcano. It has weathered down significantly to form valleys and gullies. The whole complex has descended, submerging the majority of the original land mass. The Truk volcano, long extinct, extends almost 5000m (16 000 ft) from the ocean floor to the surface. There is no evidence of a crater wall anymore in present day Truk, but geologic signatures point to three central craters, located northeast of Tol, north of Udot and north of Fefan, approximately in a line from west to east. The partially violent eruptions can be traced from thick beds of unconsolidated breccia. Most of the lava issued from fissure vents. These are represented by dikes and dike swarms. Some lava types are similar to those found in Hawaii, but some types found here are not represented in Hawaii and visa versa. The ejecta from the central craters include several rock types not found otherwise at the surface, and lava and dikes have been altered under pressure and temperature. Limestone found within the ejecta suggests that coral grew on the sides of the original volcano when it had reached sea level, and before the shield volcano was formed. After the growth of the shield volcano, erosion dissected the cone, it then subsided to submerge the shield. The velocity of submergence was slow enough to enable corals to build up a fringing reef, which encloses the unsubmerged remnants of the Truk shield volcano.

The Truk District encompasses 45,4 square miles, or 117,6 square kilometers. The population in 1975 was 31,600 people.

The people of the Carolines are classified as Micronesians. Anthropological evidence suggests the origins of the inhabitants to be Malaya and South East Asia. They are characterized by medium stature, brown skin, straight to wavy black hair and high cheekbones.

Great language difference exists in Micronesia. Every large island or group of islands have developed either their own language or distinctive dialects. There are nine major languages being spoken, of which Trukese is one.

The lush vegetation on the islands is deceiving as an indication of soil fertility. High rainfall erodes or washes out the soil, making it deficient in basic plant nutrients, such as nitrogen, phosphates, potassium, and trace elements. It was estimated that as much as 75 percent of the available plant nutrients are contained in the vegetation and must be recycled by decomposing in order to permit, or sustain, continued plant growth.

The soil is generally made up of decomposed volcanic or coral rocks and small quantities of humus. On steep slopes the soil layer has been eroded. Alluvial plains towards the coast contain soils of moderate fertility. In swamp areas, taro is grown as staple food. Some alluvial plains and gentle slopes, including coral islands, are being used to grow coconut palms, breadfruit trees, bananas, cocoa, yams, dry land taro, sweet potatoes and some vegetables. Mangrove swamps and the rain forest supply a limited amount of timber for the construction of the simple houses.

On the coral islands, with their highest elevation rarely more than a few feet above the water, the soils are very porous. They consist of shell fragments, coral sand and clumps and very little organic matter. They are very well suited for coconut palm growth, but are not very suitable for anything else. Pits, laid out with grass and leaves and so on, are used for taro cultivation. For subsidence farming the soil may be suitable, but soil amendments must be provided to sustain continuous productive yields.

The primary jungle in many places had been cut down and replanted with fruit trees during the Japanese Occupation. These areas reverted mostly back to secondary jungle after the war. Large, surfaced areas, like airfields, have been used later for coconut palm tree growing.

Modern history in Truk probably begins with Spain annexing large parts of Micronesia. The Christian religion was successfully introduced. After the Spanish-American War, Spain decided 1899 to sell their Pacific island possessions to Imperial Germany, who administered them until shortly after the outbreak of World War I. Japan was quick to move into the undefended islands. They were ruled under a mandate of the League of Nations. From 1920 onwards, Japan closed the Mandated Islands to all outside visits. Later, it appeared that they had been built up as military bases. In Truk, which was clearly recognized to have great strategic value due to its sheltered anchorages, military activity evidently did not start until well into the 1930ies. Fleet and aircraft facilities were built, but because of limited resources, fleet facilities remained relatively minor. Nevertheless, Truk remained an important staging and storage point. Large elements of the Japanese Imperial Navy and the Navy Air Force put in repeatedly into Truk. The facilities were heavily damaged in two major carrier borne assaults in early 1944, and the Japanese personnel staying there were left to their own resources. They were effectively by-passed and did not contribute anything to the Pacific War anymore. After the Japanese surrender, the Japanese were repatriated and the islands put under the trusteeship of the United States. Today, Truk is an independent state on the Federation of Micronesia, and has changed its name to read Chook, since about 1990.

THE LIGHTHOUSE IN MOEN AND THE XAVIER HIGH SCHOOL

There is an old Japanese lighthouse on the East end of Moen. It is not shown on the chart anymore.

Following the road past the airport and staying on it, one drives along the coast and past small villages. Over small rivers, over and around bays, the very bumpy road passes a beautifully painted yellow church from the early colonialists. Eventually, the street forks. The right part goes steeply uphill, forks again and finally ends at Xavier High School.

There is something odd about the thick concrete walls, the massive steel blinds, the austere military lines and the sinister look of it all. That's no wonder: The buildings, arranged like a loose "U" were the communications center of the Japanese fleet. Today, they are painted somewhat and converted into a school. The view from here to the lagoon is breathtakingly beautiful. It is here that Jesuits teach the children of the Truk District, and show their impeccable hospitality to the stray visitor.

Going back down to the second fork, and following a hardly recognizable foot path to the right, through thick undergrowth, will lead, with a little luck or better yet, knowledgeable locals, to the light house. But it is not an easy march. Not that it takes overly long, only about an hour or slightly less, but walking through rotten breadfruit, tearing plants with thorns, past native lean-to's, women wearing a sarong and not much else, uphill, downhill at total humidity, takes time and a bit of breath. Then, suddenly, one ascends a few beautiful steps with a stone bannister. A cistern and other remnants of the commandant's house are to the left. Reasonably scratched up, hot and sweaty, the skyward pointing structure of the old lighthouse is reached. (A slightly less strenuous way to reach the lighthouse would be to continue on the coastal road for about a mile, and to cut into the bushes at a conglomeration of the little native huts.)

Many lighthouses have been built with a thick inner core of reinforced concrete, a spiralling staircase on the outside, and the whole enclosed by an outer shell of concrete. This lighthouse is no exception. While climbing the stairs, big holes in the outer wall are passed, and once in a while big pieces have been gouged out of the stairs as well. But the inner core is not severely damaged. Regardless how heavy the hit was on the outside, it remained standing firmly.

Reaching the top, the extent of the damage can be seen quite clearly. The structure is riddled with cannon shots from fighter planes. Huge ragged depressions mark the impact of rockets, but the lighthouse remained standing, albeit scarred. Even the quarter inch thick steel ladder shows a clear circular hole of a canon round. Every plane seems to have used the lighthouse as target practice. Of course all lighting equipment has long gone.

The visit is worth the effort. As from the High School, the vista from the lighthouse is magnificent. The breeze is refreshing. Rarely can the natural, unspoiled beauty of the Truk Islands be more appreciated than from this vantage point. With great reluctance does the visitor tear himself lose from this view.

TWO GUNS IN DUBLON

After a long period of procrastination, we finally decided to hike up to the two guns, up the mountain in Dublon, ready to brave the secondary jungle ... .

We tied the boat to a piece of steel sticking out on the old jetty, which, together with a second, forms a basin. It was used in former years to receive and handle cargo. This was old Dublon Town. The problem is that all this area had been built up during the Japanese rule. Roads, paved and partially blasted out of the mountain, allowed vehicular traffic at one time. They were heavily damaged during the bombing raids, are overgrown and mostly unrecognizable. And nothing remains intact today. Despite the heavy toils of a generation before, everything has been laid to waste.

There were a great number of buildings in this general area, and it must have been a very industrious estate - at one time. Today however, hardly anything but traces remain. There is a machine gun here, a 25 mm a/a there, a steel structure, concrete shells of buildings, stairs, fancy gate posts, a huge sunken gasoline storage tank in the hillside, molten fuel tanks and traces everywhere. A few concrete bases and dilapidated structures are just a hint of what had been here before. There is a lot of growth, and our local guides march us across very slippery stones, bushes with beautiful flowers but small little thorns, and grasses that cut.

It is impossible to see the guns from below. They have disappeared in the green. Therefore it is unavoidable to enlist the services, as a guide, of a local boy or two ... or five. They are happy for a dollar each.

Talking and shouting, the ascent begins. We start off at the area of the old tide house. From there we go through a settlement close to shore. It is a curious combination of corrugated rusty tin sheets, attap roof and walls of any material suitable for this purpose.

The villagers view visitors with a certain amount of friendly detachment. Not necessarily do they smile on their own accord. They observe in dignity. But they never fail to answer a smile with a smile and a friendly greeting with a happy greeting. It is particularly the youngsters who are looking at us and laugh. With a little friendly gesture or a little boyhood trick, their hearts are won over quickly.

We made a bad mistake to begin with. The fact that we did not have anything but rubber sandals, the thongs, on our feet delayed our ascent significantly. We were always in danger of slipping - and did so - and of spraining an ankle, which fortunately we did not. Eventually, we had no choice but to resort to walking barefoot. The net result was that our feet were scraped up and our soles hurt a lot. Thorny branches add a lot of scratches to the legs, and wearing slacks is of great advantage to prevent this. A towel may be carried - it is great to towel off the sweat ...

It is a lot of fun to climb up, over stones, up steep inclines, and through bushes, with our brown friends. Most of us are probably not in such good shape or plainly not used to rough climbing, so the sweat will drip and the breathing will resemble panting. But all in all, it works out to be a lot of fun.

Once in a while the inconspicuous path leads through a little hamlet, and here it is not uncommon to find the folks at their native costume. The women would be wearing a brightly colored skirt and a flower in their towering and beautiful hair.

As we were going barefoot skirting the houses, we had to be a little careful about broken bottles. And sometimes the little community had a massive pig, which was eyeing us. Dogs, on the other hand, were quite differentiated in their behavior. One had to be held back, the other ... well, she was about to take a tentative pull on my jeans, which I discovered just in the very last second. I did not like it, and barked at the dog in no uncertain terms. She put her tail between her legs and ran a few paces, cowered and cautiously barked back. To end the argument I gave her a final growl and moved on, unmolested.

Just when I thought - or hoped - that we had made it, as the path was horizontal rather than vertical, we had to climb again, but then we were finally there. Where exactly the location of the gun is I cannot tell, but the emplacement is very well on top of the mountain on the Eastern part of Dublon.

This gun is in beautiful shape. In ruins and stripped, but yet, massive, threatening and powerful. It is built into a circular concrete emplacement of about 10 ft depth and 30 ft diameter. The walls are slightly slanting. On the base are a few recesses, probably to store ammunition. There is also a 1 1/2 foot by 1 1/2 foot shaft into the ground, housing the ammo lift. Obviously the shaft turns to the right for the storage area.

The gun has two barrels. The calibre is 12 cm, close to 5 inches. It is a dual purpose gun, i.e. it can be used against air and land targets. Its primary purpose was to be used in aircraft defences. The barrels are clean; they do not show the deep gouges of the gun in Eten. Both guns are of the same model and were of fairly modern design. In some ways they are similar to the American dual purpose twin 5 inches, although the length of the barrel may be longer (45 against 38 times calibre of the American counterpart).

The major components of the drive mechanism may still be seen. The barrel was elevated by motors which were coupled via a gear box and clutch onto the drive. Motors, gears and clutch have long disappeared, but the housing is still evident, and part of another component lies on the bottom of the emplacement. The four tubes for the recoil springs are open, and the springs have long said farewell to their housing. Both locks are open. They obscure a well preserved sign from the manufacturer. Since neither lock nor sign can be moved, this sign remains illegible.

On the left of the gun is the command stand for the gun director. From here he trained the gun and triggered it. Although the splinter protection is still more or less complete, the stand inside is totally stripped. But even so, it gives an idea about how it must have once looked. The instrument console and the stand on which the gun sight was mounted remain.

Circling the gun towards the left and viewing it from the command stand, one can only be impressed by this sight. The shield here looks intact, everything is in place, and it appears as if, with a little bit of cleaning and repairs it could be used again.

We had to make our little friends understand that taking pictures of them draped around the barrels is one thing, but we also wanted to shoot documentary photographs without contemporary decoration. Once they caught on, they very considerably and obligingly moved out of the view.

It came the time when we said we wanted to go back. Out of nowhere, another local gentleman appeared with a large machete. He indicated that there was another gun, somewhere in the thicket. We were a bit reluctant. Taking our hesitation as modesty, our new friend moved on, and urged us to follow.

It would have been totally impossible to find this gun. The path was cleared with the machete, which cut through thumb - thick branches like butter in the skilled hand of our new friend. After a few minutes we arrived suddenly at a concrete emplacement.

Vines had grown over, and totally obscured, this emplacement. After a couple of well aimed strokes with the big knife the canopy cleared and the gun could be seen. It was an exact duplicate of the previous one, resting with the dual barrels down in their depressed position, and looked as if it had never been shot. Here we found some pieces which had been taken off and discarded. The recoil springs had been removed, as well. This gun looked in good condition and was hardly attacked by rust.

It was time to begin the descent, which was not comparable to the strenuous ascent. Within half an hour we were back at the village at the pier and boarded our boat. With a last thank you, a last picture and a wave we departed to our next dive site.

... AND CALMLY WALKED OUT OF THE TURRET.

Of course, we had heard about the gun on Eten. We arranged to be taken to see it, to satisfy our curiosity. This one would be different from the one seen on Moen, we were assured. After a dive, when we had to spend some time on the surface anyway, we tied up the boat at the north side of Eten. The embankment tells a story. The waterfront consists of a wall, constructed by putting up stones very orderly. The neat and accurately straight line is broken in a few places where exploding bombs had carved out craters. The site of the bomb hits are shown as scars, which even today indicate the ferocity of the blasts.

In the middle of the mile long sea wall is a ramp leading into the sea. No mean affair this was either. It had been designed and built to take heavy loads. The concrete of the surface is a foot thick. Today, the ramp is in a deplorable state of disrepair. The large concrete blocks have shifted as their foundations were washed away by decades of waves. Losing support from below, the slabs cracked and tilted.

Above the seawall, tall coconut trees stretched their fronds. They were growing too densely and evenly as to be the result of random growth. In fact, they were deliberately planted on the former runway of the airfield. Holes were hacked into the concrete, and seedlings planted in them. It was, in a way, one man's revenge for the abuse of another: Never again should the island be used as the immobile aircraft carrier it resembled so much in the aerial photographs. The long, spacious runway pointed into the trade winds. South was the carrier's bridge in the form of a half mountain. The other half had been cut away and used as a source for building material, and as landfill. On the west was a huge apron, and a series of buildings, containing headquarters, stores, workshops and accommodations.

The attacks from the air blasted many large craters in the runway. Many of the densely parked aircraft were destroyed on the ground - and the few which scrambled, got wiped out. The reinforced concrete walls of the buildings, a foot thick, got shattered by the bombs. Now, all of this was obscured, hidden from view by the palm trees and thick undergrowth. On such an island we set foot at noon time.

Nobody should move at noon at Truk. When the sun shines, it is unbearably hot. The jungle drips with humidity. After the first few steps up the incline, sweat is dripping. The wayside, a small path, is slippery. This is either because the grass is wet and acts like an oil slick, or one steps onto a rotting breadfruit. It does help to wear sneakers. It is anything from dangerous to annoying to don sandals. Anyway, we followed our friend Cheney "Shipwreck" Tipweck, Kimiuo's apprentice, boot handler, diver, guide and tank-over-board-hanger-and-loser.

Right after we jumped over the cracks in the concrete ramp, we passed a grocer's little shop and hut, with the children looking at us, and then passed the tiny church, doubling as community center. In the pleasant shadow of a giant rain tree, utterly twisted railroad tracks were lying around. The ground felt firm here, but soon we got into jungle growth, with a small path winding through. Some very soggy and soft area had to be skirted. Within the next clearing, but well hidden by bushes, was a two storey structure. When we got closer, unfriendly grey walls appeared. It had been quite a substantial building before, but what had happened to it? Some of the supporting posts had shed their concrete, and the steel reinforcements had buckled under a tremendous strain. On one side, the support of the second floor had held, yet the ceiling angled down. It had collapsed on the far side upon the first floor, in its entire length. The extent of the devastation could clearly be seen when we entered. The large and sturdy staircase, now in a dilapidated state, had a touch of class. Some thirty or forty years back, a carpet would have been right to decorate it.

We went on to another building on our way to the gun. It had received a blockbuster hit. Underneath the 10 ft circular hole in the ceiling, the two layers of steel reinforcements were hanging down. It looked like a giant basketball net. It seemed strange, that the room appeared fairly intact. The walls and the floor did not show any sign of damage.

A few men were working on a small field. We passed them on our way. They hacked up the soil for planting, but what they were turning around were small, sharp edged stones, remains of the landfill, crushed stones from the mountain.

We arrived at the hill, and if its face was not exactly vertical, it was very near it. We had to climb up the narrow, little path in true alpine serpentine fashion, like mountain goats. Not only was the way extremely steep, the footholds precarious at best, but we were also exposed to the tropical sun. It was incredibly hot and uncomfortable. I was wondering whether this was the right activity after a dive to rid the body of nitrogen, by boiling it out. Finally, we reached the top. Finding a nice breeze going, we stood still here for a few moments and enjoyed the nice air on top of the mountain, hoping we would stop sweating.

The gun was right in front of us. It is located in a circular emplacement, which is about 3 m or 10 ft deep. The sides are nicely finished with masonry. The gun stands straight in the middle with its rust colored steel barrel and the four recoil springs. The single barrel is located asymmetrically to the right. It is obvious, that the second barrel is missing. There is no doubt, that this was one of the twin barrelled 12 cm anti-aircraft guns. The gun shield and the cover on the right side had been removed. Parts of it could be seen on the bottom of the emplacement. At regular intervals, recesses have been built into the wall. The ammunition lift on the floor is totally obscured by weeds.

The firing and the training mechanisms are gone, and so are the electrical motors, which were used to turn the turret. All what is left of the gun is one of the barrels, its mounting, the recoil tubes, the springs and the gun director's stand. All of them show obvious signs of repeated strafing and hits by board weapons.

Large pieces of metal have been gouged out, particularly on the gun barrel and the tubes, which contain the recoil springs. These tubes have been penetrated in several places, and the springs can be seen inside. Judging from the many hits, the planes must have inflicted heavy casualties on the gun crews.

The second gun barrel had been pulled out from behind, by a scrap company. After the war a concession was granted to salvage scrap. The company involved also began work on this particular gun, but abandoned it. The barrel is now located about 20 ft behind the gun, where it is almost hidden in the grass.

The higher ground behind the gun is crisscrossed with little trenches. They are either totally overgrown or partially filled-in today. The gun crew and the ammunition hauler certainly sought shelter here from strafing. Bomb hits have not been seen in the vicinity. Pictorial evidence suggests, that a second gun of the same model was positioned nearby. A report of one of the carriers supports this assumption. The other gun had been hit by a bomb, more accidentally than by deliberation. The plane had missed the original target, a ship, as it was shrouded suddenly in a cloud, but it continued the dive, when suddenly the gun position showed in his bombing sight. The pilot quickly released the bomb, and obtained a full hit, putting this battery out of commission for good.

Despite the damage to the gun, and certainly the heavy casualties among the crew, it was kept firing to the very last day. The fire direction control was completely mechanical. This model, called Mark 89, was never used with radar fire control, and the design of the gun and fire control was considered obsolete by the time the first air raid began. It was not particularly effective against the small carrier borne aircraft, because they were able to outmaneuver the clumsy control. The gun did not have sufficient reach to be dangerous to the B 29 bombers. They were flying just too high. The B 24 was the most vulnerable.

The gun looks, as if the gunnery officer folded his logbook, checked that the barrel was at its rest position, calmly climbed out of the turret and walked off.

Second Part - TALKS

A - KIMIUO'S VISIT TO THE HOTEL

... IT IS UNHEALTHY TO DISASSEMBLE YOUR GUN!

(About artifacts, secret codes and spies, and how unhealthy it is to disassemble your gun.)

Kimiuo and his wife, Taeko, had taken the boat from the dive shop, and arrived in the pouring rain at the hotel. We had met for dinner, and finally sipping coffee in the chilly dining room, we were ready to "talk story". We rarely would do this in the dining room as it was just too cold there, and adjourned to our room. Walking on the half covered landing passing the lobby, we descended the stairs and faced the rain. Coats firmly wrapped around, we skirted the two large puddles which inevitably formed after each rain, turned right and reached the second block of hotel rooms. Shaking the raindrops off, we entered. With an elaborate ceremony, I offered our guests seats and poured some drinks, diet-soda for Kimiuo and coke for the rest of us. The ladies retreated to the other part of the room and Mary showed Taeko her Malay batik. I pulled out charts and books and we would just sit there for a few moments, doing some small talk. I lit my pipe, and after I got it going I stated, "The other day, Kimiuo, I was talking to this guy in the hotel. He wants to pull out all the guns from the islands."

"There are plenty of guns around," he replied.

"But can he just get them out?" I was surprised.

"You know, they are on private land. All land is owned by Truk people. They got it from their fathers. It's theirs ... also what's on it. They can do what they please."

"Sell it?" The land I meant.

"No..."

"Well, this guy claims, he got a very accurate map of the gun installations, by paying some money in Japan.... Really, I mean, I can't believe that. That's not the right way ... doesn't sound right.... Anyway, he said he'd found all the guns he was looking for."

"What's he going to do with the guns?"

"Says that it is really high grade steel, which is quite high in price ... about $ 5000 a piece ... something like that. Rubbish, that. Those old guns were wire wound and the barrels made out of composite steel. So he pays the landowner a few bucks, says he. You know how it is, most people are glad to have a bit of cash for something they hardly knew was there. So he wants to pull them." I don't think I said this very convincingly, but Kimiuo did not argue the point, and followed with his own thought.

"Most of them are in caves, fairly well hidden. They just left them there. I don't remember anyone taking out a lot of guns after the war. They did collect a lot of scrap right at the end of the war, but that scrap company was after copper cables and bronze, not steel."

"Yes ... but they pulled the barrel on the Eten anti-aircraft gun." I had hiked up to the gun and it had been almost too much.

"Right. But they gave up. Too much work," Kimiuo grunted.

"Well, if the steel price is right...But I can not imagine somebody pulling the guns, and then transporting them as scrap for $ 5000 a piece ...That sounds like a cock-and-bull story really, but he said the Japanese are really hot after the steel."

"Maybe not good for a few, but if he gets enough together. Now they are after copper and brass. Cleaned out the two dumping grounds. You know that one off Fefan, they got all the propeller and a lot of other stuff. Got most of the empty cartridges out of the other dump, off Dublon."

That's exactly what we are needing, somebody cleaning out Truk. So I added, "Well, does he have a contract?"

Kimiuo looked at me. "Sure, what do you think?"

"Well I guess it's got to be lucrative to everybody. Who signed the contract?"

"I don't know. No idea. I suppose this is a matter for the Governor...guess he okays it."

"Sure," I said. "That's a matter of interest. with whom is he working?"

"Some gang from Tol." Kimiuo could not sound less interested.

I knew that response. If he was positively infuriated, he would either throw some verbal punches to make his point, or become disinterested if he could not change it. So I put it to him and wondered whether he would take the bait. "So that's it then, you have some people interested in picking up the brass and get some people who don't care so much what's down there, and champagne flows for everybody."

"What's champagne?", he asked, and almost killed the subject.

"It's the brass cartridges today, and the propellers of the ships tomorrow, with the argument,'Who's looking at propellers?' Then they clean out the ship, because who wants to look at the cargo? What about the ship's bell? That's beautiful brass, take it out and make a quick buck, take the engine telegraph, take the copper lines and there you have it, creeping destruction. Who is going to care about it?", I said, becoming more and more involved.

"I heard they can't take artifacts," Kimiuo said in another attempt to kill the topic, but I wasn't through yet.

"Alright, what's an artifact? Is the propeller only a part of the ship or an artifact? Where does it stop. I'll be frank with you, I am concerned about the future of the ships, the gravesites. I am terribly concerned about all this....disturbing the graves of the fallen Japanese. That's what I'm uptight about. Because some powerful people maybe, sort of get involved.

That's what bothers me, I tell you!" Certainly, I was excited.

"I can see that," he said, and looked at me with a long glance.

There was a long moment of silence, and I tried to contain myself, wondering why he did not comment. Here, there was a matter of unforeseeable consequence and all I got was some noncommittal remarks. I turned around and looked at him exasperated.

Finally I said, "You know Kimiuo, he also said that he was led on the mountain top, by some youngsters, had to use their machetes to clear a path, as everything was overgrown. Uman it was. Came to a large circular platform with a shaft, and went into it with a rope. Looked like accommodations underneath the platform. But then there was a thick steel door, firmly closed."

"Might have been the radar station," Kimiuo stated. "I had a friend, Kato was his name, the commanding officer there."

"He also said, that it was the secret nest of spies, and that the commander flashed signals to overflying American planes." I was doubtful.

"Oh, that's nonsense!", Kimiuo exclaimed.

"The Americans knew a lot about Truk, considering, that nobody ever set foot on the islands."

"Ah ... there were sure other ways to get information about Truk."

"There was this February 4, overflight by that photo plane ..." I let this thought trail off, and he picked it up.

"Yes ... right. I have read that the Americans broke the Japanese code."

"You are right, Kimiuo. It has been written up, and was a fact ... that's how they won Midway."

"If they listened long enough, and with the material from that plane, they probably could get a story about Truk..."

I turned to Kimiuo again, and breathed in deeply, preparing for a long speech. "You know, there is something you probably have not heard before, so I will tell it to you now. There was probably not a single spy who reported all the things about Truk. It was the Japanese who supplied the Americans with most valuable information. That is now being written up in quite interesting detail. I found these books in Hawaii a few days ago. You see it was like this. The Americans had formed a very competent intelligence department, which managed to crack the diplomatic code and decipher almost all military transmissions. The Japanese had major and minor codes. Of course they changed periodically, but from the point of getting the new codes to all the military stations, that was a task almost impossible to do. Imagine you had to deliver the new code books to all radio transmitting stations. Very difficult. So, many times the outlying garrisons were sending their communications in the old code."

"You're kidding", Kimiuo said fascinated, but not so much doubting as in amazement.

"No I don't," I said emphatically. "Then, you see, there was the harbor master in Truk. He was responsible for the orderly ship traffic and had to keep records of the comings and goings of the ships. Of course he had his boss in Japan, and dutifully he reported each and every ship, its arrival and departure. He radioed these reports in a minor code, which the Americans could break and read. Just imagine, they knew all the time which carrier was in, which cargo ship was coming and which units left the lagoon through which part. All this was known, and it played an important part in the war. Much more decisive than just Operation Hailstone. For example, the first major set-back for the Japanese Navy was the battle of the Coral Sea. The Americans knew that the Commander Fourth Fleet had temporarily set up headquarters in Rabaul and had ordered three large carriers out of Truk, to go through the South pass at a specific time. They even knew their names, because the harbor master sent all this information to Tokyo, and the radio waves obligingly made it also to Hawaii. That is how the Americans knew who was coming and when, and you can imagine that this was very important for them."

"So they lost the battle because of that?" Kimiuo was absolutely taken.

"No, not like that, but it was important information to know what they were up to, and who was in the battle, who was commanding it."

"Inoue, Vice-Admiral Inoue?"

"Exactly Kimiuo. But the story goes on. You see, Truk was also informed about arrivals to be expected. And why do you think the Japanese lost so many ships enroute to Truk? Because the submarines lay in wait at the convoy routes. That was no coincidence. That was cool, calculated ambush. That's why it hurt so much. Why do you think some of the ships leaving Truk got torpedoed? Because the subs were waiting and ready. That's another thing, but there is even more. You probably recall that the Americans knew that the Japanese were up to some really major operation, later referred to as the Battle of Midway. You see, the Americans knew that something was coming, but they could not figure out where. A signal to Truk from Yamamoto, for the Second and Fourth Fleet, confirmed the impending operation, because he ordered the ships and carriers to resupply with ammunition and bombs for the planes, to be ready for a forthcoming operation. They thought that the Japanese would attack Midway, but this they could not decipher, they did not know for sure. So they had the commander in Midway report that his water plant had broken down, in clear language. A day or so later, a Japanese radio transmission was intercepted reporting that Midway had no water, and they used the code for Midway. From there on, the Americans could go back to previous transmissions and find that the Japanese had mentioned Midway all along."

"Oh yes, I have heard about that," Kimiuo nodded vigorously.

"Regarding Operation Hailstone, you told me you were surprised that the Japanese search planes did not see the Task Force approaching. See, this was another of the military secrets. One man in Hawaii, Dick Emoroy, had followed the pattern of the search planes, and methodically as the Japanese are, he could reconstruct the search patterns. When it came to approach Truk, the information was given to Rear Admiral Mitscher. He chose a hole in the pattern, and therefore completely surprised the Japanese in Truk."

"Oh boy," Kimiuo sighed.

We reflected. More to close the subject than to elaborate on it I said, "The reason many ships still came in was because the subs could not sink all ships in a convoy. They had a batch of real bad torpedoes. And even success had to be limited, otherwise the Japanese could wise up and think again about their unbreakable code. Come to think of it, you were mentioning the load of American sailors captured from the submarine, and brought to Truk."

"Yes, sure. I remember that", he agreed.

"Well it was the sub Sculpin, and she got sunk by the Japanese destroyer Yamagumo. But the skipper, Cromwell, went down with her voluntarily, because he knew about the impending operations at the Marshalls and knew about the code breaking, because he had been supplied special information. Fearing that he might collapse under torture, he chose to go down with his sub. So you see, there was no spy, it was intelligence work," I concluded.

"Is that true, I mean that is all correct?"

"Certainly." We sat there and I let this news slowly sink in. Only after a long pause did I continue. "Well Kimiuo, about this scrap hunter we were talking about earlier, he heard that a spy got killed by the Japanese."

"Yes. There was such a rumor... people said the general got executed," Kimiuo explained.

"General?" As far as I could remember, the island was occupied by the Navy.

"No, probably an admiral. Took him to another island and chopped him." Kimiuo's choice of words confused me.

"How do you mean?"

"Chopped his head off with a sword."

"Oh, they did that, then?"

"It was like this: When the attack came, all guns in Uman were taken apart, I guess for cleaning and maintenance. Would make sense, as you told me, they did not expect an attack a week later. So, all the major guns were stripped. Only the machine weapons were firing. And a few anti-aircraft guns. What was not ready was the heavy artillery, and that was only the coastal defence guns. They never got ready, but also, they were never needed. So, I guess, Uman was not ready." After this statement we paused, and I tried to visualize the shock the Japanese surely must have felt.

"They needed a scapegoat. Somebody to punish for their own mistake ... is that it ?", I asked.

"Guess so ... Anyway, he was seen leaving the island with the police, and he never returned. Nobody saw him afterwards. But some people saw the party landing on a small island."

"Do you know where?", I asked, wondering whether he knew details. But he had only heard about it and could not confirm its validity.

"No."

"So they made a spy out of him. Sounds more interesting anyway. Same as the submarine, which was supposed to have gotten into Truk and landed a few people at Fefan ..."

He interrupted me, "Param."

"Ok, Param. After sneaking in behind a Japanese vessel."

"Crock-a-bull...", he said full of disdain.

"Hmm ... you know there is something odd. Very faintly odd, but never mind ..."

"What do you mean?"

"Can't tell you for sure, Kimiuo ... You know, the question whether the Japanese ever detected an American submarine getting into Truk was actually asked by American officers after the end of the war, when they interrogated Japanese officers. Of course, the only way such a thing could have happened, was if the sub would sneak in behind another vessel, as they had these detector cables and hydrophones mounted at the South Pass. That preceding ship would just veil nicely the existence of the sub. It's been written up, except, there is positively no information available on such a mission in the literature published up to today." I was puzzled, the story about the sub did not ring true and it was one of those rumors, certainly.

"Somebody else may have read the same stuff you was reading. Thought about it, or mentioned it. Somebody else along the years and the many people talking about it, got it all wrong."

"So you say we chase a shadow," I admitted.

"Maybe..."

"Yes ... Another thing, Haouli said that there is a tunnel carved out of the mountain of Param. Inside are three trucks. They are in beautiful condition, he says. The entrance to the tunnel has collapsed. Do you know anything about that?"

"Never heard about it."

"Well, our friend does not tell weird stories ...", I said defensively.

"I've not said it's not there. I just haven't heard about it. There are plenty of unexplored caves at Mt. Tolomen. Talk to me about Dublon." I would be coming back to this, and made a mental note.

"Ok ... Well, this guy, this man at the hotel, said that there was a large barge at the North Pass. It was full of shell casings."

"A barge full of shell casings? ... A barge ?" He gave me a startled look.

"But somebody unloaded it. Said he had the suspicion it was some Filipino scrap hunter." But I didn't believe that either. Too many wrong stories tonight, I thought, so maybe we should move on to some firmer ground.

"I don't know. A barge? ... There is a ship outside, pretty well broken up, that wreck. When I was going to sea, I could see it sometimes, when we were near the Pass."

"Speaking about broken up ... not far from the Kiyozumi, a bit closer inshore, you know, Hoyo, that area, there are a few funny pieces of wreckage. Looks like boiler, cylinders. Strange." Here we go. I was sure he could relate to those, and he certainly did.

"The Japanese brought them along, when they salvaged Tonan Maru 3 in 1951. Used them as floats. After they got her upright, they did not need them anymore. Cast them lose. They drifted to shore. Some of them are right there, others drifted over and are at the mangrove at Dublon. A lot of them ..."

There was this other question which had always nagged me. "There's got to be the floating dry dock somewhere. From the war, you know. Could take destroyers up to 3 500 tons. Must have sunk between Fefan and Dublon."

"It never sank," Kimiuo stated. So what was it then?

"The Aircraft Action Report of Bunker Hill claims they hit a carrier. They thought it was the Zuiho. But the Zuiho was not in Truk at the time ... anyway, she got sunk someplace else later. So it must have been the dry dock."

"Wasn't, I tell you..." He got slightly impatient.

"What else did they hit, swimming in the water and looking like a carrier?"

"They couldn't tell whether they hit or missed. It may have looked like a carrier, but the dry dock was never damaged."

"Oh ... never?" I was surprised.

"Well, it was taken by the Chinese in 1948, and towed away. What the Japanese did during the attack ... well, see, they always had plenty warning before an attack, except for the first one. They had about half an hour of warning before the planes were coming. They flooded it."

"So, it disappeared from the surface...", I interjected.

"Right."

"Ah, that explains it... They were just lowering it, it was still visible. The pilots thought it was a carrier and bombed, but missed it. When they came in for seconds, it was gone. So they thought they sunk it. But it was just flooded."

"Right." He looked at me slightly amused by my reasoning.

"But this can only be right for the raid after the first one."

"How do you mean?"

"See, Kimiuo, there was no general alarm ahead of the first attack. I read, that after the initial warning was sounded in Moen about planes approaching the reef, the communications system in all Truk broke down completely."

"I have heard about this, as well." It was said slowly, as if doubting. There was the riddle.

"You see, Bunker Hill pilots attacked that ship on the first strike of the first day. Afterwards it was not seen anymore. The location was right for the dry dock. It was the Repair Anchorage. But the dock was small ... too small to be taken as a carrier."

"Yes, I am not sure how long it was, but may be 450 ft."

"Carrier would be larger ... But there was another ship. It was also located at the Repair Anchorage, looked unusual because of the open spaces on deck. It moved off, the same as the pilots reported seeing the ship getting underway, and was seen later passing out of the South Pass, and finally escaped with only minor damages," I explained.

"Which one was that?"

"The fleet repair ship Akashi. It was under orders to follow the Combined Fleet, and was ready to move, in fact, had probably weighed anchor, and was getting underway."

"This is the one then?"

"Quite honestly, maybe or maybe not...Maybe not. There was the sea plane tender, Akitsushima...", I said.

"You mean, maybe ?" He grinned.

"You, my friend Kimiuo, say that," and we both laughed. He took a sip from his drink, and in the ensuing quietness we could hear the rain, and the palm fronds moving almost uniformly with the heavy winds. It was dark outside and a few rain drops reflected the light of the outside spotlight like flashing silver pearls. Maybe it would be a lousy day tomorrow, but then nobody could tell. It may be a good idea to talk about one of Kimiuo's favorite topics.

THE EYEWITNESS

"You were 17 years old when the attack took place, Kimiuo?" I began.

"Yes. Some people say that day was 17 February when the attack came, others say 16."

"That is because of the Date Line. The Americans adhered to their own date to avoid confusion, and that's why in all American documents the attack started on the sixteenth, and the second day was the seventeenth. That's Wednesday and Thursday. For you, it was the 17 and 18 February, Thursday and Friday. That's actually correct..." I did not want to tell the story. The next question brought him back. "You had finished school then?"

"Right. I was working."

"You and your family lived on this other side of Dublon, on the other side of all the installations, where the two or three houses are."

"Right, on the northeast, used to be five houses," he said.

"So every morning you had to go to your work over the hills, through the bushes?"

"They had roads. We could walk on the roads." That little attempt at jest did not go over too well.

"You mentioned before... You were doing loading and unloading of cargo."

"Right. Everything had to go through this. You know, all the things go to Dublon first, because the officer was there. Then they ship to other islands or ship out of Truk." That seemed somewhat cumbersome.

"You were loading barges?"

"Yes, but mainly landing craft."

"On this particular morning you were at work or walking to work?"

"I was at home."

"It was Wednesday or Thursday,...why did you stay at home?"

"I did not go to work." This line of argument doesn't get us anywhere, I thought.

"Yes, I know, you told me that. Why?"

"That attack started very early in the morning. Just when the sun came up. It was too early to go to work. We were shaken out of sleep. So, I did not got to work."

"First you thought they were doing gunnery

practice again."

"Because we had heard that noise before..."

"Until something told you that it was a real attack?"

"Is no much doubt if bombs explode around you and machine guns fire all over." He certainly had a way to make one feel particularly stupid after a stupid question.

"What did you do?"

"Went into the shelter. My uncle ordered everyone into the shelter." Whenever he mentioned his uncle, Kimiuo spoke with a certain finality. It signalled that he was the authority, his word was the law.

"But you ran out?"

"Once in a while you said you had to go out, what can he do? So we ran, seek cover under the coconut palms and ... well this side of Dublon, there was this big tree at the shore, so we go there and watch." That would be typical of the young rascal Kimiuo.

"From there you could see the e eastern part of the 4th Fleet Anchorage. Ships like San Francisco Maru and Seiko Maru you could not see from where you stood?"

"Right."

What was the time?"

"I don't remember exactly, I did not have a watch. Maybe seven or eight, and then during the day, once or twice again I went out."

"Did you recognize any ships, did you know their names, had you been on any?"

"No, except the Aikoku. The Aikoku was big and had a silhouette you could not mistake. The others I did not know by name."

He hesitated for a moment, and then said, "I am not sure it was the Aikoku all the time. We could never tell exactly which ship it was. Yes. I guess it was Aikoku most of the time. But sometimes when Uchita would not come, it may have been one of her sisterships. I really don't know." He paused. A new idea struck him. "Most of the time she would come in with the Yasukuni Maru."

"Oh, that was a beautiful ship," I exclaimed.

"Even bigger than the Aikoku," he added.

"Right. Passenger liner, bit larger than Heian Maru."

"Much bigger superstructure. But they almost always come in together. Or just about a day later."

"Did you know that they were together on the last voyage?" I asked him.

"Yasukuni did not come here like Aikoku, on the day before the attack."

"True. She was sunk on the way from Japan to Truk. But let's get back to Truk, Kimiuo. Can you remember what you saw?"

"You know, right there, on the marker on that bad reef. I never saw her there. Just never knew she was there."

"You mean Nippo Maru, the wreck we found?"

"Right. All the time I have been thinking, how come she's there. Must have gone down very early. Before I got out the first time. But there was no sign, no big explosion.." He had probably been in the shelter.

"She was anchored, she was not running!" I had seen that her anchor was out. But I was puzzled as well. The Nippo did not show up on any attack photo, none of them.

"This big container washed up on the reef. I was thinking what is it doing there? It must have come from some wreckage, and then drifted before the wind," he said.

"Which container?"

"Remember, you were snorkeling on that reef?"

"I see, you mean those pieces of steel, mainly edge reinforcements, was a container...this thing, where I found mercury?"

"Right. That's what's left of it," he confirmed.

I began to reminisce. I had taken the binoculars one day and looked for the containers on the reef. There were two white dots which definitely were not waves. "That's what you have not seen. We have found it. I mean, you had the suspicion, Akao saw oil one day and caught fish there, I blew the whistle when I found her, and when you ran across her. We lost her a few times, but finally we hooked this fantastic wreck. But what about the things you saw?"

"Like on the Aikoku...there were already several ships on fire. The smoke...you could not see too well. Some of the ships were far out on the anchorage. In between them, some bombs made these high water columns. It was all very confusing. But they were attacking the Aikoku. Several times. But up there, on the ship, they were firing like mad...kick up so much...several planes would just go away, you know, not continue to go at her..."

"'Veered off...yes, she certainly had a bit of fire power." It was easy to imagine how the machine weapons on the bridge and boatsdeck hammered away while the big guns fired single bursts of fire and shell.

"Until maybe 7:30. You could see three groups of aircraft attack her, dive bombers and torpedo planes from different directions. All at the same time. Must be difficult to concentrate your fire if they come from three different directions. The torpedo planes come in low, and another group dive from the sky. Then comes this bright white-yellow flash, like the sun. Then I saw one of the planes break up in the air, but my eyes really hurt. Just then something hit me in the chest real bad, like pushing, but harder, so I almost fall back. Then come the noise-it blow my ears off. Hurt my ears. Just then I see all these pieces fall in the water, big ones first, and then it looks like like rain. Same time, this big smoke balloon, red and black on top, rises. Started to go in the sky, but no more noise. Water fall back down. After a minute, I see the sea again, but the ship...no more....no trace....all gone...nothing. All empty, except for the smoke. Only the landing craft...started to change course and no more going to the pier, just go on the beach, go to the next land. In there, all people dead, except three in the bridgehouse. They have bad eyes. All got eye injury. Some other people on that side, all complained about their eyes..."

"Yes...really big explosion. You saw the high intensity flash first, then you saw the pressure wave demolish the plane in mid-air, then it hit you, the pressure and the sound. Took a few seconds to come, because of the distance. Water got thrown up. The explosion also made an underwater crater, the grave of the Aikoku. You know, she is lying in her own crater...on both sides it rises a couple of ten feet...And, actually, the sand slowly fills it in. That's why she is embedded in the sand to about the propeller hub. That's perhaps four to six feet.

"What caused the explosion?"
"I don't know. I could not tell."
"She was heavy in the water..."

"From what people tell me, there weren't any people left from the Aikoku...they have been loading ammunition like mad, all day before. Maybe during the night also, transferred the storm troops, you know, the Japanese Marine Corps...invading troops... to the aft. Suppose she was about ready, one half ammo, one half troops. and then somebody drops a bomb in the ammo. Just before, they were taking the wounded off. So they had this one landing craft running back to Dublon with the sick. The other landing craft was tied to her stern."

"Which wounded?" I asked a bit skeptically. This seemed to be a bit unconfirmed. There was loading activity, but probably only forward.

"Well, they took those troops off, which got injured during the strafing by the planes, before they dropped the stone on the eggs."

"Here's what I have gathered, Kimiuo: The Aikoku ran in a convoy, together with the Yasukuni Maru, which got sunk on that voyage by an American submarine. The Aikoku ran at flank speed, zig-zagging towards Truk. Both ships transported troops. She must have come in late afternoon, a few days before the attack..."

"Right. She did." He turned to me and nodded.

I knew he was back on the Aikoku. He had been on this ship several times and had even eaten in the mess. That's when he was unloading and loading ships, so I continued. "From her being low in the water, I would think that all the war material was still on board. The hit came in the worst possible moment. Good and sturdy design that she did not completely disintegrate, like X-8 and X-10, of which we only found pieces..."

"She was also bigger. Another thing I saw...the Fujisan. she was running full ahead and just came into my view from the fairway between Moen and Yanagi. She was running real fast for that area..."

"Was that the only one you saw running?" I asked curiously. But now it was the Fujisan and the second day.

"Running to round Dublon, and make it through the Pass, maybe. But she had not even turned north, and the planes went for her. She got hit. Seemed like a few bombs. So, she slows down, starts burning and puts her bow to north, then is dead in the water."

"Yes, no power...She would turn abeam, broadside, to the wind. So she faces almost north-south direction. And the explosion probably heaved her over, so she faces north. Probably sank by the stern, did she?" I asked,

"Yes. It took a while. She drifted a while before she went under."

"Yes, tankers have a lot of airtight compartments. If the bulkheads don't get staved in, it takes a tanker a while. All of them got hit aft, into the engine room...Shinkoku, Hoyo, Fujisan, Tonan. Sure way to sink them...If she had drifted a little while longer, she may have wound up on the Yanagi reef. Did you see any more actual sinkings?"

"No. I don't remember. I could see only part of the 4th Fleet Anchorage. And we had to use an excuse, so my uncle would let us out of the shelter."

"How long did the raid last?"

"Seemed like a week...but by late afternoon everything was quiet. They came back the next morning," he replied.

"By that time many ships had been sunk."

"I don't know, but the 4th Fleet Anchorage was empty..."Kimiuo said slowly.

"No more ships?"

"No," he confirmed. "I was asking about some ships running. Well, the Americans tried to sink as many as possible before they could get steam up and run. They would be much harder to hit. Sitting ducks are easy prey."

"There was the Soya..."

"...this special duty ship?" I interrupted.

"Yes."

"You know, they never got her...She was doing duty in the new Japanese Self Defense Forces even in the seventies as a research vessel." I had read about her because she was listed as damaged and beached. I was curious whether Kimiuo could confirm this.

"She really got a smart captain. Come the attack, he was running her between this stretch, Dublon on the east side, up and down," Kimiuo remarked.

"There is hardly any space to maneuver."

"Whenever they went for her, she would start running as fast as she could forward, then full speed astern, forward and back. That's all she could do in that narrow strip." I wondered why no other ship had done that.

"Ah, I see, they could not throw a torpedo, they would bounce it on the land or on the reef. Smart. Must have been a lot of strain on the engine and the gears."

"Yes, but she was an ammunition ship. Better strain than the other way."

We both probably thought about the violent explosions which had ripped so many ships apart. It was interesting to know that a few vessels had been running. It was still not quite clear whether any ships had been abandoned by their crew, after a hit. Some of the boat davits pointed outward, but this was weak evidence.

I got up and got another pipe. Standing at the window I watched the weather outside. we made some small talk, and I sat down again.

THIRTY THOUSAND NEUTRALIZED ... THAT'S SIGNIFICANT

"Almost thirty thousand ... I can't believe it!" I almost jumped from my chair. Kimiuo had casually mentioned that about 30 000 military and civilian personnel had been present in Truk.

"Maybe a few less, but 30,000 was the number,"

Kimiuo said calmly.

"And they all got trapped in Truk? Couldn't they get out?" I still had a hard time believing it.

"No. They stayed. Nothing moved. They were just here, and that was it," he said definitely.

"I suppose at that time Japan already had quite a shortage in transports. I remember, the American submarines ..."

"... and aircraft!", he interjected.

"Yes, right. Truk soon got into range of land based bombers. The B 24 could have reached it and B 29 in the later days ... Actually, did you know that they were using Truk as target practice? After they'd taken the Marshalls and ... I guess it was Saipan, they used Truk for target practice. Real nice ... Dress rehearsal for their bombing raid on Tokyo - real bad, tried Truk first! ... I think it was October 44 ... These soldiers really got trapped here. Didn't the Japanese run at least some provisions into Truk?"

"They couldn't get in. Except for submarine transport ... then there was the odd convoy ... and some single freighters before Saipan fell."

"They had to support lots of fighting troops. Supply lines were long and vulnerable ...but listen, Kimiuo, thirty thousand troops neutralized, that's significant!" But in the powerplay of nations, it always seemed difficult to understand how the Japanese treated men, in a way more expendable than the US. Kimiuo interrupted my train of thought.

"They weren't all Navy. Army had most, you know. I told you about problems in Dublon. First of the troops, they come only in January 44, and the Navy didn't want them in Dublon. So they made them go to Tol. No way they want them on Dublon. Also, no supplies from the Army. They brought weapons, but no food, no clothing, very little of that. They really got a headache to take care of them ...Then come the attack, and now what do they do? Ship all the troops back to Dublon, Moen and the other islands. Even during the attack. Running little barges and a few landing craft ... but you know what the Navy did? They asked the Army to come over please, please, please. Three times."

"Suppose, they got worried the Americans would begin landing operations ...," I speculated.

"Right. So that's how they finally got to Dublon."

"I see. So the Navy was in Dublon with their headquarter, and in Moen and Eten ..."

"... Param and Uman ...", he added.

"... Must have been awfully cramped living on these islands. How many of you Trukese people were living at that time?"

"Oh, at that time, not many. About 20,000 may be 25,000."

"You call that not many?"

I was really surprised. It had never occurred to me that there were that many native Trukese, but then Kimiuo said, "There weren't too many then. We have got more now."

"How many Trukese are living here now, do you think?" Should be more now, I thought.

"May be thirty two thousand," Kimiuo said obligingly.

"One doesn't see so many on Moen. Are there many living in Tol?"

"Yes, there are quite a lot living over there ... they hardly come here ... not often ... keep to Tol, but quite a lot live there." There always was a certain hesitancy to talk about the other islands. Kimiuo was a tribal chief in Dublon, and a man of significant statue - in Dublon. He had been to Guam and Hawaii, even to the US mainland for all I knew. He certainly had seen many of the atolls around Truk, but I seriously doubt that he had ever set foot on Tol.

"Well, Truk is not self-sufficient. Today it depends to a very large extend on aid ... to have the people fed, there is massive aid needed."

"Right ..., true. Difficult to make it work, the aid. But now they have projects. Put the money in some projects. Some are very good - education, you know, vocational training. Everybody wants to be mechanic ... no surprise with the outboards," he muttered. "Always same problem." Then he fell back to the topic of aid. "And other jobs, they prepare them for it. There is very little to make money from. Hardly any natural resources ... No minerals, fruits, just nothing. Maybe, they would do some fishing. Deep sea fishing ... for tuna - not doing that bad. Some time is good, other time not so good. Fishery Department develops new techniques for fishing ... You see what happened to the fishing vessels they gave us? Too much work. Well, these two fishing boats ... you know their rusting hulls ... people come from the airport, think: oh, first wrecks already here ... That's very romantic, but couldn't be further from the truth. These boats were thrown up the reef by a typhoon and abandoned ...", and he laughed.

"I heard that the aid is continuing. I mean, the States will continue to support Truk, but the money will be less every year." I did not know any details about Congressional Approval and Budget, but I had just seen a bunch of accessors, direct from Washington, here to review the expenditure. They were lodging in the hotel, and one of their most outstanding features was that they never talked about diving. Everybody else did. "That's going to be difficult later on ... .Alright, but certainly some money could be made with fishing?"

"Maybe ... That kind of fishing is tedious. Going for tuna. Laying long lines for tuna is plenty of work. Must be processed, the ketch. Then you sell ... where?" He was a bit skeptical.

"Some progress is done, I hear. I don't know whether it will work in the long run. They are looking for some capital."

"That's where the Japanese came back in... .Maybe Japanese help, capital and selling."

"How far is it developed now?" I was curious.

"Fisheries are still experimenting ... this year was good. They are building a new dock at Dublon," he added.

"But they used to have all the facilities in the old days. That cold storage for fish ... processing and even the docks - right at Dublon, facing Fefan ... whatever happened to it?" It was only a day or so ago that I had climbed on the remains of a seawall, a jetty with pipes and remains of a narrow gauge railroad track. I had gone to two or three buildings, solidly constructed, but now damaged beyond repair. There was obvious damage from bombs exploding nearby, and one of the buildings had received a hit. The original refrigeration plant could be seen, the base for the machinery, the pipes and remains of the insulation on the walls and ceiling. The floor was covered with tiles. All this was totally demolished now.

"Some got bombed, some got blasted. Got diesel for the engine running it, but just two machines ok. Ripped the place up and blew it up. Nobody care."

"Neglect, disrepair, cannibalized, that's it." I felt sad about the demise of the once thriving place.

"Yes, all useless," he said fatalistically. I felt like looking into the future.

"Apart from fishing, what else is there to make money?"

"See the many coconut trees?"

"Copra?" I followed his thought.

"Right."

"Does it give good money?"

"It's not that bad. Suppose one can live. But price always change."

"How about tourism?", I said.

"What can I say about this ... Sometimes many, next time very few. Not steady."

"It is a bit dependent on the economic situation," I reflected.

"Many times there are tours and there are plenty people for a few days ... dive like mad on Fujikawa and Shinkoku."

"Well, I've seen it, believe me, Kimiuo, tourism, that's not all roses, either ... got its really ugly sides ..." So I'd stuck myself with this topic, but not for long. "After that attack, didn't they bomb the warehouses as well?"

"Yes, and hit them, too!"

"But what was there to eat, tell me!"

"Everyone became a gardener," he said matter-of-factly.

"What, thirty thousand mini-farmers?"

"Yes! Oh, yes, everyone worked quite hard ... raise vegetables, potatoes ..."

"That may give the people some staple food. Starch mainly, I guess ... I suppose they did not have it so tasty like the breadfruit you toasted for me." I remembered the delightful taste of the toasted breadfruit slices he had offered me when I visited his shop one day.

"Well, no ... we use oil on that one."

"So, what about a bit of protein. I mean, meat or fish? Speaking of a balanced diet."

"The Americans gave."

"How do you mean that? They certainly did not drop their Thanksgiving Turkey, I bet. They were making sure nothing was getting in and nothing getting out of Truk ... So?"

"Well, when they flew another bombing attack, of course, not all the bombs hitting the target, some missing even the island ..." I was quick to catch this one. "... but exploded in the water and killed the fish!"

"Right. They sent us out in our little boats to collect, right after the raid. Bad if the bomber returned for seconds. But the fish may easy sink after a short time. Some did. So we grabbed as many as we could."

"They let you go out and collect the floating fish ... ?"

"Right ... Normally we were never allowed to go on boats, not even our own. Could not go fishing. They had forbidden to us go fishing. I mean, all of us are fishing. But not at that time. We could not get into our little boats ... Never could go fishing ... You got shot when seen to paddle in the lagoon... Just to pick up dead fish."

"Just consider all which got spoiled when they sank..", I remarked, always so concerned about the environment, and for a moment forgetting the mass of desperate, starving men on Truk.

"If you really come down to it, it was not total famine. Starving ... yes. Few, perhaps, died of lack of food alone. Some were so badly run down that the poor rations just finished them off. Some of the wounded died. Just that everybody was on real small rations and nobody got fat."

"And yet you were required to work." I wondered.

"Yes. We had to dig these tunnels."

"I bet. Night and day, I would think." I would like some more information I thought. Later.

"Oh, yes, day and night."

"Did you work in something like shifts?" How long could a man stand it in these atrocious tunnels and work his fingers to the bones?

"There were four shifts and we worked all day and through the night."

"That must have been miserable, I am sure. Did you have to use a hand pick?"

"Yes, most of the times. Sometimes they blasted. The rocks were not as sturdy or solid as they looked, yet they were solid enough to make life miserable."

"Well, the rock is fairly well fractured already. I can just imagine, picking at it and carrying it out by the basketful."

"Yes, we ran the basket from man to man."

"Was it wet?" I meant inside the caves.

"Mostly. It was dripping from the rock ... When it was not dripping from the rock, we did it for the rock."

"When did you really start digging tunnels?"

"After the attack." That was a little misleading because the Japanese had dug shelters for equipment before, but Kimiuo had escaped that work by being drafted to unload ships and doing other work for the Harbor Division.

"Ah, before they felt that nothing could touch Truk, was that it?"

"Yes, the Japanese were absolutely convinced of that! Some tunnels were built before that time. The gun emplacements. And we carved up the mountain of Eten, if you include this kind of thing."

"Did you actually shift from worksite to worksite?, I asked.

"No! We never moved. You could not go from one island to the next without a special pass. That was not easy to get. You had to have a reason. That all was very strict. Actually these passes were only good for a given number of hours or for the most, days."

"They really had a strict regimen, didn't they?" All military rule is tough, I am sure.

"Yes."

"When you finished work - what would you do afterwards?"

"Building our own shelter." Kimiuo said it as if it was nothing.

"What, you just came out of the tunnel and went into the next?", I asked astonished.

"Well, that was not really a tunnel. More like a shelter. Cave-like. You know. For the family."

"Guess, everybody was digging ..."

"... You better believe it. These bombs could go anywhere. And I wasn't waiting for any bomb. And when they used the big bomber they also used big bombs. Tunnels were OK. ... Did you know they used time bombs?", he said, changing the subject and catching me by surprise.

"How do you mean?"

"See, the planes dropped time bombs ... mainly on Param. The Japanese thought, really stupid, these Americans can't even make good bombs. So they started to collect them ... those which did not go off ... Carry them to a place. All of a sudden these quarter ton bomb go off. Plenty got killed. Then a day later another go off. All over the place for one week it was going off. Nobody dared go near it. Boy, was that ever some explosion ... Could feel it in Dublon."

"That was at Param?" The Americans seemed to have a certain preoccupation with Param, I thought.

"Yes."

"They said they had intended to use Param as base for Kamikaze."

"Oh, really?" Now it was Kimiuo who was surprised.

"Couldn't do it, though. The bombs damaged the runway so badly ... the effect of those big bombs was like digging a well. Water got in. They kept bombing it also with these time fuses ... so they could never use it for the Kamikaze." It never occurred to me that they didn't have the planes either. A few, but not many.

"But planes were flying up to the last ..."

"... to run away, would you believe, Kimiuo."

"... How so?" He looked at me unbelieving.

"Most of the planes ... well, they were just put together from damaged planes ... see, they take a few damaged planes of the same type and make one good one out of it. Patched up, make shift, cannibalized, the rest they dumped. You know, all these damaged planes after the attack ..."

"Oh yes." We were obviously back to what he had seen or heard.

"But these patched up planes were not so good. Just not the old Zeros of 41 and 42. Three were old and outmoded. Still flying, but not fighting ..."

"Oh ... that's why ... come the American planes, the Japanese take off before they arrive ... Americans come from the North, Japanese fly off to the South ..."

"... to preserve the planes!" That was right. The Japanese got their radar going and had almost half an hour advance warning. Particularly, as the Americans underestimated the range of the radar and dropped to wave level (to avoid detection) after they had already been spotted by the radar.

"Yes ... Never saw the dogfights again ..."

"For another ... except for the April/May 44 raid and the English raid of September 45, they used bombers ..."

"... Yes, sometimes at night ..."

"... and they just could not reach them ... just fly too high. Zeros just could not get close ... and the anti-aircraft gun not either! So they take off and disperse ... from Moen and Eten ... what was left of it."

"So what happened to the Kamikaze?" Obviously Kimiuo was digesting that information.

"Did not get off the ground ... I was wondering, Kimiuo, whether they had enough fuel."

"Yes, they had. Plenty of drums in the caves ... tunnels. Safe there ... even from the big bombs ... what explosions!"

"Oh, yes. You don't have to tell me. I have been through that. Bombers overhead, earthquakes underneath, and volcanos all around!", I said, very well remembering those dreadful times.

Kimiuo excused himself and got up and went to his room. I looked out. The swimsuit tied to the lanai waved in the gusty wind like a flag. The palm fronds shook the last drops of rain through the beam of the outside spotlight. Every so often, the howling of the wind increased to a crescendo and then died for a few seconds. It seemed to me as if these moments of respite were more frequent than before, and I got up to open the sliding door. The air outside was warm and saturated with humidity. In my limited experience, hot humid wind bade bad news, but I hoped I was wrong.

The outside door opened and Kimiuo came back in, walked to his chair and laboriously sat down. I closed the sliding door, thinking about the Trukese and their martial overlords.

B - TALK STORY ON THE BOAT

Many of our "talk sessions" happened totally impromptu. Most of the time these free wheeling talks began sometime on the little dive boat, which was battling the white caps on the way to the dive site. As we set out on our first assignment for the day, I really had nothing special to do. I was not required to strain my eyes looking for a strange echo to show up on the fast rotating disk of the instrument, and check the subsequent recording on the graph paper, nor was it time yet to suit up.

I have to admit, it was not always the most comfortable place sitting on top of the cabin, feet firmly planted on the foredeck, because every so often the boat was ploughing through a particularly obnoxious wave and showered us. That's really not so much fun; the fun was talking with Kimiuo. After the boat had pulled away from the hotel jetty and the boys managed to get both outboards going, and I had carefully stowed away my huge underwater strobes and the cameras, I was free to join him.

I would carefully crawl up on the cabin deck, tip Kimiuo on the shoulder and ask him whether I could sit with him. That was just part of the ritual. When it was a fine day he would slide over and make space for me. If it was a particularly fine day he would grunt:"Better sit here", so that I got less exposed to the cascading water from the bow.

Naturally, the conversations were a bit disjointed, particularly after a big shower, and we switched subjects often and fast, just as they came to our minds. On this occasion, we were running to the Fourth Fleet Anchorage, the weather was wonderful: a few cumulus clouds in the sky, and the sun pleasantly warm. It was even before nine in the morning, and the heat of the day hadn't arrived yet. The steady trade winds had blown during the night, and continued. They had blown long enough to allow the usual waves to form, and most of them formed white caps. In order to make him understand, and to hear his reply, I leaned over and talked into his ear. There was a subject which interested me, because I had not quite figured out the solution to a riddle which plagued me: When and by what action did the Shinkoku Maru sink, and I started out:

"I was wondering... you mentioned the Shinkoku and that you were talking to survivors of the Shinkoku."

"No, not me," Kimiuo shook his head. "Not me, but Peter Wilson. You know, the director of Fisheries. He also talk to the captain of Mushashi."

That was a switch. I wondered, obviously he wanted to talk about something that was on his mind. "What has he got to do with that?", I asked.

But Kimiuo continued, "He also talk to captain of Mushashi. The captain damaged his eardrum. He explained why that happened, how his ear drum broke, because of the explosion on Musashi. You know they got hurt when they bombed her. Anyway, he survived."

"Very few did," I said a little absentmindedly.

"Then Peter asks this Captain Ikata from the Mushashi, whether he knows about the shells on Yamagiri. The answer was yes." They knew. They needed the shells because something big was planned. So they wanted to load up again, and go to Rabaul or Philippines. Then the American planes trapped the Yamagiri here and she sank with all the shells. "So in the meantime, while talking to Captain Ikata, he also asked about survivors of Shinkoku. No luck here. But later on he runs into a man from the Shinkoku, a survivor. Then they talk about the Shinkoku and he asks when, what time she sunk. This survivor mentioned about 4 o'clock in the morning."

"Strange." It was, the round about way he came back to the Shinkoku via the Musashi and Yamagiri.

"But you know, 4 o'clock in the morning, it's still dark here."

"Yes it is, surely," I confirmed.

"But I wanted to say when it all began." He knew that I was interested. "You see, when there is an explosion, you can hear that very well here. I think you need to remember, when I was half asleep I was almost awake, the guns were shooting. Boom, boom. But I was thinking maybe just...practicing, because they shoot at the target towed by the airplane."

Kimiuo had mentioned this before, and now I interjected, slightly impatient, "Okay, so you were sleeping and heard the guns but didn't think much about it."

"I don't pay any much attention about that. I was just thinking, oh, maybe they are practicing. All of a sudden my uncle came and woke everybody up."

I could imagine the moment of disbelief, maybe even the terror when the elder man shook the kids and they jumped up. But when was it? "Before the sun came up, before it was light?"

"No, it's already light."

"So like 5:30 h."

"Uh huh," he vigorously nodded his head, and I had my next question ready, what were they thinking that dreadful morning?

"And you think you may have heard an explosion? And anti-aircraft fire?"

"That morning, yes. When I ran out from the shelter, I looked back and saw this house, this house for the plane, like garage for the planes."

He wrestled for the right word. I put it to him, "Hangar", I said.

"It's big on fire and a lot of smoke, grey smoke, this hangar. Then in a few more seconds I walk to this tree. I saw this destroyer running with the fire."

The boy must have looked in total amazement, so I asked, "You did? Which way did the destroyer go?"

"Well, she went straight up to the reef, then turns to Herit." Kimiuo was referring to the "bad reef" east of Dublon, and the island between Dublon and Moen, to the east.

"So maybe trying to run to the North Pass?" I remembered that this was the usual route.

"I think North Pass. There were two of them on the first day" he continued. "They come out, that morning I mean."

That triggered my memory. I had seen the report and had written about it, so I asked, "Very early, right?"

"Very early," he confirmed. "I really don't remember what their names were. They go out and turn and go that direction, to the North Pass. When they approach Farida, they pass inside. Then I saw Katori was going out again. Katori was following them. Far apart, come from Uman, and pass at the end of Dublon, heading straight up north."

"Those destroyers were Nowake and Maikaze." He did not react. Most times he could not remember the names of the many destroyers which put up in the lagoon.

"Then after Katori, two more went out, but later. One was on fire, the first one. The first two come up from Fleet Anchorage, this side. They ran out. One catch fire up by the second smoke stack. Still running though. And they still shoot. That's the time I recognize something went wrong."

There was a moment of silence. We were now getting close to Yanagi, but kept nearer to the shores of Dublon because it was more sheltered there. There was another mysterious matter, the big merchant ship which caused all the other ships to get into this mess. "But nobody seems to know anything about the Akagi Maru." I hesitated, then added by way of an explanation, "Same size as Kiyozumi maybe."

"I heard that. Wait a minute." He turned to me and looked at me thoughtfully for a second. "Somebody told me that Akagi Maru loaded up the civilians. She had the civilians on board, was supposed to take them back to Japan. You know, no more place for women and children, they have to go back. So I heard that many civilian families go back on Akagi Maru. One Japanese guy came in 1975 to my shop and asks me if I know where Akagi Maru sunk. I told him I don't know. I try to mention all the ships I know, which I've been diving on. Again he ask me if I really don't know where Akagi Maru was sunk. I told him sorry. If I knew I would have told him, but I don't know where she's sunk."

I had expected that, but I wished he could tell me whether he knew her or had seen her running, so I said, "Outside the North Pass. Akagi Maru was the last ship to leave. It was Katori, then the two destroyers and Akagi Maru. She blew up. A big explosion. She sank in a few minutes. Have you heard anything about the people?"

"No, I don't."

I had, but only indirectly. There is a monument, of recent construction, in Dublon for the Akagi Maru. "No, I don't think there were any survivors. You haven't heard of any destroyer coming back in?" I was trying to jog his memory, but I drew a blank.

"No. I don't hear of any destroyer coming back in."

Somewhere there was a reference in the American reports about a destroyers rescuing survivors of a sinking ship, and a destroyer running back into the lagoon on the second day, which succumbed to the skill of the torpedo bomber pilots from Bunker Hill. But that was beyond Kimiuo's knowledge, so I tried to get back to our original topic. "That's not surprising, because they didn't make it. They got torpedoed in the north part of the lagoon off the North Pass. And I thought what we had been looking for was a destroyer, not a Maru. Anyway, let's turn back to Shinkoku, because this is really quite interesting. Of course she was damaged and sunk slowly, finally going under at 4 o'clock. Because we found the skeletons in the aftship, maybe she was on fire, flash fire perhaps. Where she got hit is very close to the bunkers and where she carries the bunkers, her fuel."

"I don't think there was much fire, because those depth charges in the big hold would blow up."

"Which depth charges, Kimiuo?"

"There are four depth charges in that big hold aft, together with a lot of cable, coils. By the gun," he added and continued. "So that's why I think that she just got hit, then she went down. Maybe she did not even burn, because if there is a fire, those depth charges would go off. And the shells for the stern gun, they're still in the box at the gun."

The dive boat lunged, then the bow crashed into a wave and a sheet of water descended upon us. Kimiuo did not stir. I cursed quietly, took my shirt off, wrung it out, quickly toweled myself off, wrung it out again and continued, without bending towards him, and a little louder, "That's interesting, but we have not figured out why the survivor said that she went down at 0400 h."

"Maybe he was using Tokyo time."

"That would make sense," I agreed.

"Truk was run by Japanese military. No more civilian government with power...already powerless and the governor has nothing to say. You know, even those lieutenants, those second lieutenants are more powerful than the governor." He managed to convey in a few phrases, with an inflection of his voice, the disdain the military had for the civilians, and their total loss of power.

The going on the boat became rougher. We had passed Yanagi now and the waves just kept rolling in. I had a problem maintaining my perch, and it took me a few moments to recover my balance. The area was now exposed to the wind and waves, and the showers became more frequent. It also made conversation more difficult. But I had something to find out. Had he talked to any survivors of the ships? So when I had a chance, having recovered from the latest bout of spray, I stated, "In the 70's, I think most of the Japanese survivors came here. In the early 70's or mid 70's, more survivors came to Truk than today."

"Yes. Not much this year. Last year there were quite a few."

"The Heian must have had many people on board," I remarked.

"Yes she had. Since the ship started burning, I think many people also got away."

"Did you see her burning on the second day? You were going to the other side of Dublon, so you could see Yanagi. You said on the second day you didn't look out into the Fourth Fleet Anchorage, but more towards Moen. See Yanagi, there", and I pointed back to the island we had just passed. Not that I had to, he knew perfectly well where Yanagi was, but just in case he could not hear properly in the wind we were racing through and the loud droning and pounding of the boat.

"Yes, I could see Yanagi."

"Did you see the Heian?"

"No. She is way inside and hard to see from that point where I was on the very end of Dublon."

No luck here either. I paused for a moment. Maybe we could get to the answers if I could get him focussed on the ships present in the Anchorages at the time. "At the time, just before the attack, what work were you doing then?" Sometimes Kimiuo was not very interested to talk about work and I had to prod him a lot.

"I was working on the island. Painting. You know, chipping and painting on the chains and buoys. You know, they got a lot of markers and chains. We clean, paint and replace the buoys again. Very hard work. That's work I really hated. The chains were really big."

I agreed. "Very hard work. When was the last time you saw Combined Fleet Anchorage?"

"That day the reconnaissance plane came, on February 4th. I was off that day, I didn't go to work. I went up that day to the hospital to ask my friend for some medicine for headache. I got the medicine and was just about to leave when I heard the boom of the guns."

Kimiuo had never mentioned that particular event before. "Who was shooting?", I asked.

"The gun you went to visit at the east end of Dublon, on the mountain. Then some of the ships guns, because Fourth Fleet was full of ships too, you know." He said it like I had to know that.

As he began to continue, I could feel how he reached back in time, reconstructing the events. "Okay. We went out to the carrier on the 2nd of February, because she was the massive supply carrier too. So we got the aircrew from that ship and brought them to Moen on a small landing craft. Daihatsu, like the one we saw yesterday."

"Was she anchored off Eten?" I asked.

"Yes, Sixth Fleet Anchorage," he replied.

"Where you pointed out, close to where the Heian was normally anchored?"

"Close to there." And back he went to the pilots he had helped to ferry to the island. "I think there were about 15 of them. We took them straight to Moen. They're fresh you know. Young guys," he said reflectively.

"Very little experience too," I stated.

"Very young guys," he repeated.

"Tell me, on the 4th of February during the overflight of this plane, you heard the gun in Dublon shoot, the battery there," and I pointed to the northeast plateau of Dublon.

"Japanese name, Kanshogu. Kanshogu means weather station. Used to be weather station on the other side of the gun. The weather station was west. I already left the hospital. Then I heard the shooting."

"You thought they did their practice shooting?"

"Yes, I thought the practice shooting started, but they said it was an enemy plane."

"Could you see the plane?", I asked with much interest.

"Yes, I saw it. Very high, but I saw."

This totally surprised me. I had thought, for one reason or another, that the plane was so high as to be always invisible. Now I was keen for some details. "How much clouds were there?"

"Oh, not very much clouds. And all these Zeros got very excited and flew up," he replied matter-of-factly.

"Zeros?" Again I was surprised.

"Yes and seaplanes."

"Before the big guns made this noise, started shooting, did you hear any other guns?" I asked this because in the interrogations it was stated that the plane had been spotted by a battleship which started the shooting, but Kimiuo had his answer ready.

"No, I suppose the battery opened up first."

"You're sure?"

"Yes. When it's shot maybe 3 times, then I heard some other places starting to shoot too. The one on Moen, the ships, Fefan, everywhere the guns were shooting."

"Did any of the soldiers talk about this plane?"

"Too much propaganda at that time."

Well if there was so much propaganda, as he put it, maybe they claimed to have shot the photo plane down. "Did they say they caught it?"

"Yes, they caught it."

Of course they had not downed the US plane, and I got a little sarcastic. "Unfortunately, all the photographs were rescued and went straight to Honolulu to Admiral Nimitz. And then they made big eyes because at least Musashi or Yamato and three big carriers were in Truk."

"Yes. I think 6th Fleet, 2 carriers were there," confirmed Kimiuo.

"That's right," I exclaimed.

"And at the Combined Fleet Anchorage were 3 carriers. 3 or 4. No, 4 carriers because one was smaller. 3 big ones. 5 carriers, 6 carriers all together. That's a big mistake of the United States though."

I tried to understand, but failed to see what he meant. "What?"

"Send the reconnaissance."

"Not quite. Why do you say that?"

"Otherwise they would have found everything here, because they would not have moved out."

This seemed obvious, but it was in no way true, and certainly underestimated the strategic intelligence of Admiral Koga and the Japanese Navy. It was known that they considered Truk to be exposed when Kwajalein fell, and the defence lines had indeed been moved further back beyond Truk. Even at this time Truk had been literally given up strategically, although on a tactical level, it was probably hoped to involve the US forces in a long drawn-out, very costly fight. However, the Americans saw this and declined the fight for Truk. All those decisions had been made long before the overflight, but I did not feel this was the time to tell Kimiuo about it. I side-stepped the issue by saying, "The Americans were a little disappointed that none of the fleet was here."

"Yes. I do believe this, because according to the Navy report, the photograph, the lagoon was full of big ships. That afternoon, about 1 o'clock, they took off."

I wasn't sure what he meant, but he referred to the fleet. "A week later?"

"No," replied Kimiuo. "Just that afternoon."

"Who did?"

"Combined Fleet, all move out. Sixth Fleet, all move out. Not Sixth Fleet, but those carriers on the other side," Kimiuo reported with conviction.

"Afternoon?"

"On that afternoon."

"Did you ever see these carriers move, when they weigh anchor and move out?" I tried to establish whether he saw it himself or just heard about it, to judge the reliability of this information.

"I was there. When I watched them that day, they went straight up, go by Fanamu."

"Go west. Oh, they swung around," I said.

"They go by Fanamu and go out from South Pass. Most of the time they used the South Pass. At the North Pass they had staggered mine fields, so they did not use it. Only when the attack came, all the planes came from the south and from west, so they thought that they better take North Pass. Katori and the destroyers", he added.

"All of the ships that went through the North

Pass, they really had a problem." I hesitated then. We had bee discussing what happened to those ships many times and I wanted to switch the topic. The waves helped. The boat was now pitching badly and we got drenched several times in a row. But we were rounding Dublon on the east, going south, and in a moment we would reach calmer waters behind the "bad reef". When it was a little calmer I continued, "When these carriers went out, did they have airplanes over them, circling around?"

"No," stated Kimiuo.

"Americans always have. Called Combat Air Patrol." That got Kimiuo going again.

"The Japanese didn't have aircraft circling them. Then among us Trukese, we talk. Where's the fleet now? How come empty, no more war ship? They all went out. Maybe they go to fight again."

"But they were gone for good," I remarked.

"Not that good. Some of them, they were destroyed in Palau."

"Yes, but not major ships," I added.

"Akashi was caught over there."

"Akashi was caught over there and a destroyer and many merchant ships too."

Kimiuo then brought the topic back to Dublon. "You know, we live there and then we always see the fleet, Combined Fleet, go in and out, in and out. The anchorage is here, the pass is south, that's the only way they can go. Around here, they go to the anchorage. So when we look out and no more ships, we wonder about this."

"That must have really been some sight when the fleet was in. These big ships."

"I even saw when they brought in this destroyer, you know, which went down at the west side of Dublon, the one with the false bow."

He had never mentioned this before. I felt like a card player when the partner pulls one ace after another, and I exclaimed, "Oh, the destroyer. You see the Susuki come in with false bow?" That's what I had read, that the Japanese welded some plates to the ship in New Guinea as a bow. But again, wrong. Kimiuo had a different account.

"No, not false bow. That false bow they made here. Because there's already two they made here. They just make false bows and send the ships back to Japan."

"Do you remember when this was?"

"I'm sorry. I..." He hesitated, not wanting to give me wrong information and because at the time he had not really paid any attention. Also, since there was more than one ship, he was not sure. "I think this was 43 they brought those half ships in."

"At the same time?"

"No, I think maybe 3 months in between. Because one was already finished and sent back to Japan."

"Why was this never sent back?"

"They were going to send her back, but it was too late. She just got out of the dock about two days before, then they waited to fit her out again. She was stripped before they got her in the dry dock, some guns, machine guns, and other stuff. But it was too late. No more chance."

Kimiuo's definite statement cast doubt on the identity of the ship. Many times this had happened before that I had to go back to the "drawing board", because he had shattered some conclusions I had arrived at earlier. Nothing but the truth, I had insisted. "But when did she sink?"

"During the first attack. She was out of dry dock for about 2 days, as I told you, with the false bow."

"So they put her in the Repair Anchorage. Then come the attack, she got sunk," I stated, and continued. "It is very hard to see where the damage is. She either was on fire very severely or the bombs just blasted her superstructure away. I was thinking this damage may have been caused by big waves, because she's so shallow, waves could have torn off the superstructure. But there is a steering post, a command post with a big steering wheel. And the whole house, the deck house, just got twisted around 90 degrees on its side. I had always assumed it got sunk sometime during the second raid. But you don't remember when they brought her in?"

"I'm sorry. I just don't remember. You know, I don't really pay much attention to those damage, because they were always saying: Oh, not much damage. They never admit losing anything. Really fool themselves, always say they win, all the time. Hey listen, let's suit up."

We had arrived at the spot almost opposite the reef marker, inside the long reef. Chenney had cut the first outboard and gone into shallow water, where he dropped the anchor. The boat was steady now, and I went aft to get into the dive gear. For the next hour there would be little talk, I knew that. Kimiuo was not to be disturbed when he lined up his landmarks. This would be my tenth dive on the Aikoku Maru. He never failed to put the anchor close to the stack of that wreck. This required his full attention and I just remained quiet and watched.

I will never cease to be amazed about the skill with which Kimiuo directs his boys to the right spot, a spot in the middle of an anchorage, a mile away from the nearest island, and for all I knew, in the middle of the ocean. A few years ago I eagerly asked him, whether he was on it. He did not even bother to turn around to look at me. He just said, very tentatively, "Maybe." On that particular day he had missed the funnel by two inches and he'll never hear the end of it. Today he would do the same thing. I have infinite faith in his "nose", his scientific way as he called it. Not everybody has his scientific ways, but he really tries to teach the boys how to use the landmarks properly. These teaching sessions generally wind up with Kimiuo exasperated and the boys choosing a particularly fast moving cloud over "that hill there", or the midnight sun over this wave. He isn't always very pleased about that...or the time when he tried to direct a new boat handler to the Emily flying boat, indicating he should run towards the edge of the High School in Dublon. The boy mumbles something, and Kimiuo turns around very slowly and deliberately, and asks in English: "Now, how many High Schools in Dublon?"

I am sure that I would have been hopeless in

remembering a set of landmarks for one particular wreck, but to remember all of them accurately for all the many ships at this anchorage would be too much for me to learn. The boys too were slow in picking up the skill of this great Micronesian seafarer.

I brought out the bunch of flowers from the cabin. We would lay them down at the gravesite, and remain motionless, reflecting and praying. Then we would enter, as I wished to document the mortal remains for the families in Japan.

Everything on the dive had gone according to plan. We had seen the other two wreaths we had put down before and the candle. Kimiuo had shined his light onto them and grunted. I knew what he meant. The other flowers, although they had been submerged for three days and longer, almost looked as if placed today. My strobe had gone off and the picture taken. I had a chance to take photographs and found a second site, which we hadn't seen before. The water inside the various compartments had remained clear and undisturbed, and we were very careful not to touch anything. Afterwards, we swam through the starboard passageway of the superstructure and were able to find the ship's bell again. Although the 19 minutes decompression were behind us, Kimiuo had the habit of extending it. And after he came up, there was no story telling until we were back on firm land. The trip to the old dock in Dublon was quick. The boat tied up and we were soon relaxing on the old quay. I had mentioned to him the day before, what I thought about the gravesite and wanted to hear his opinion.

Kimiuo began, "What do you think, what I was mentioning about telling all the Japanese, the families of all those people who died on the Aikoku and the other ships? Please leave them alone! Please, they're peaceful. Don't disturb them."

"You were saying that I should mention that there are many living things around their grave."

"Yes, I did. I asked you to put it in the story. There are many living things, polyps, sponges, oysters and soft coral of course. And because it's a grave, that's why we put the flowers there. Some years ago, whenever I go down, I put flowers on the Aikoku and pray to those dead. Now, they may think why I do this, because I'm not part of the Japanese. I'm not of Japanese blood. The reason I'm doing this, is the man whom I'm really friend with. I knew this man on the Aikoku. He was chief petty officer or maybe later he became warrant officer. Works in damage control. I don't know for sure whether he was on that last trip. Uchita ... Uchita was his name. First time I met him was 1942. Asks me for a coconut drink, and I understood what he said, because they teach us Japanese, Kanji, in school. So he asks where I live, and so we go to the, what you call...hut. My uncle, he is there, also speaks Japanese...about the same age as Uchita. My uncle was half Japanese...uncle Shirai. He has some octopus, cooked and served in coconut milk and we all eat. After a while I ask him why he got on the Aikoku. Because he's good at welding, that's why they make him go to damage control. So I ask him why he is in the war. Everything was very quiet. My uncle looks to the ground and the others are all quiet. Then Uchita, he starts saying something and stops. I look at him. I see tears running down. I really pity him. After a while he turns to me and says, 'I have family in Japan, four kids. But come to this time, I have to go.' That's the reason I love that ship Aikoku. Because of the poor man and his family."

I really did not want to say anything, and Kimiuo was back in 1943, his mind with his Japanese friend. For moments we were silent. Finally, I said in a low voice, as tactful as possible, "So you think of the many people who died on the Aikoku, you have one friend, and one is for all of them."

"Yes, one for all of them." He reflected. Then a thought occurred to him. "If anyone from Japan wants to come pay their respects or want to put flowers or whatever, come to me or come to my boys in case I'm not on the island. Ask them to take them out there, then they will take whatever they want put on the Aikoku. They can do that for them. I did this for the chief engineer's brother once. I just took something down for him, some flowers."

"You put them on the Aikoku?"

"Yes. We never had seen the room you discovered, but we went on the port side, by the sink. There are some skeletons in there. It's a long time ago, I never go to there after I put the flowers there."

"They have a very good grave, peaceful," I said.

"Yes. I do believe that. Very quiet."

"So you're not going to take any people, divers, on it, the Aikoku, to the grave. "

"No, I don't think so."

"I don't think you should do that, because if worse comes to worse, they make big fuss."

"Right."

"No point." As if it was a full stop we again halted. We both had the same idea, and were in total agreement. My thoughts went back on the dive we had just completed, and I remarked, "It was quite moving when I went down this time on the Aikoku. Down the stairway, moving the other way around, I saw your flowers in the middle of the grave. It was very good. The families of them will be happy to know that."

"You know the flowers I put there a few days ago, when I shine my light to them today, they still look to be alive. What I did, I moved them and put them in this beautiful round glass bowl, remember I told you about before. Then I set them to those heads."

"Strange that this glass survived, did not break," I said. "So on the port side there are more skeletons."

"I think 3 or 4 persons died there."

"Well, as I said, we both know where the grave is, and it's well taken care of, we respect it and honor the dead. I think that's all that is needed. No more people should go there."

"Right," Kimiuo said with a nod of his head.

This was final. After a moment I excused myself and was grateful to see Chenney approaching with two fresh, open coconuts. I took the two, thanked him and went back to Kimiuo who had stretched out in the shadow of a large bush. I passed the one to him and drank from the other.

"When you sneaked out on the second day of the attack, what did you see?", I asked. His answer surprised me. He was not going to discuss the second day, he was still thinking of the attack on the first day.

"The container was on the reef. Two containers. Then just about when I get to those trees, then I look out. I saw Aikoku. All of a sudden those bombers dove on her."

"Could you see Fanamu?"

"Yes, I saw Fanamu. I think at the time I went out, the Nippo was already gone."

"Must have," I remarked.

"Because what I saw is just those containers."

"They ripped out. They must have been empty, or half empty. They just floated up. A lot of drums floated up from that ship."

"Canned food too, you know."

"Food?"

"Yes, you know the bay, the island Dublon, and the bay goes in."

"Yes. Food washed up in there?"

"Cases of sardines sealed in a barrel, these big wooden barrels. Today, Americans are using paper, cardboard, for casing the sardine or Mackerel. Japanese use wood, thick wood, to make a box for their beer, all their canned food also. That's why it floated and washed up." I had never given it much thought, but there certainly was a lot of flotsam also. Kimiuo's next words were chilling.

"Dead bodies wash up there too, in the bay."

"Many?"

"Oh yes, many. The hospital people came down and took them out. Not only the hospital people, but also soldiers."

I thought only from the Nippo...because of the wind..."And did they make a proper burial? cremate them? Burn them?"

"They don't burn them, they buried them in a large grave. In one grave. No more time. Time is running out."

"It has to be very fast. Here in the tropics the bodies decompose very quickly."

"Some were already bloated, after a day. Ugly. Actually not very much time to pick them up on the 17th and 18th. Then they start carrying the dead on the stretcher. Oh, that heavy! There were about 500 or 600 bodies."

"Most of the people from shore or washed up?"

"Some from shore, some washed up."

"Particularly around Dublon. Dublon south?" I inquired.

"Dublon, Fefan."

"Fefan also?"

"Yes, Fefan. They bury them on Fefan."

"But on Fefan, not so many dead."

"Oh yes, where the gun was. That's where their target is you know, the guns and the machine guns."

It was time to change the subject. The coconut water threatened to turn my stomach. "After the attack, the Japanese were searching the outer islands, the rim islands, for pilots. They went out with a boat, but a few days afterwards. Two days?"

"Two days after."

"They took a little boat and a couple of soldiers and went from one island to another? But I thought many islands had no people living on them."

"They don't bother to go on those where military people are. For an example, like Pis. They don't go to Pis, but the next island they go. And those in Northeast Pass they don't have to go, but outside they go."

"They found a few pilots or a few people there, didn't they?"

"They don't. Not during the raid. Later at the B-24 night attack, when they knocked the bombers out of the sky, they found one pilot on Udot."

"You were mentioning that, yes."

"You know how they spotted him? Remember I told you the first look out station, I pointed to you yesterday and second look out station, you know, the one we look out here, the northeast side of Dublon, looking north."

He pointed up the hill at Dublon and I said, "There was Number 2 here, looking down this way, and Number 1 was looking out to Fourth Fleet Anchorage."

"Yes," Kimiuo nodded. "Even Number 2 can look out to Fourth Fleet too. Except Sixth Fleet, they cannot locate that. But half of Fourth Fleet they can see, or most. You see how wide Seiko is, all that except Sixth Fleet."

"But there is Eten in the way."

"Yes. So that's how the first look out station was, early in the morning about 8 o'clock. That guy was walking on the beach. So they spotted him and then telephoned to the Harbor Division, who went out and caught him."

"But you don't remember that 2 days after the first raid, they went out and came back with other pilots," I insisted.

"No. Actually they did not capture any as I know. The Americans rescued them, except for that colored guy I told you about. He parachuted down, actually on Dublon, right at the shallow reef in front of Fourth Fleet Headquarters." He had shown me the spot.

"Did you see that?"

"I did not see it myself, but the old man told me. He's dead now. And why I also believe this is because the guy, George Player, told me this story. He was shot down too, but in the south of the lagoon. Then he got out and inflated his raft and was drifting. One of the destroyers tried to run him down."

Yes, I remembered that this had happened, had read it in the Aircraft Action Report.

Kimiuo continued. "He said it was a destroyer. Then he got cover from his squadron. They bombed the ship. She got on fire and ground on the reef he said."

That was again one of the little inconsistencies which forced me to take a new look at the reports. If he was by himself, he probably had been a fighter pilot, because they flew alone, which would tally with the report. But in that case, they would not bomb the ship, but strafe it, unless of course, the other crew of a bomber got killed. Well just another piece of research ahead.

"Then the ship's crew tried to machine gun him, but the planes really got wild and strafed that ship. Oh boy, they chopped it up. Then finally the Kingfisher came, landed and pulled him out. When they flew up, they checked the gasoline, half quart. 1 quart. They land on west side of Kuop and the PBY came to give them some gasoline. That's what he told me."

That was again strange, and I said, "No PBY's. Must have also been a kingfisher. Maybe they had some PBY's. Maybe they didn't report it. But there was no place for a PBY. A PBY is not a fleet plane."

Kimiuo picked up where he had left off. "One plane came and gave them the gasoline and they flew up again and went to the Minneapolis and from the Minneapolis, to his carrier."

"Which carrier?"

"I forget. That's my mistake, I don't ask what his carrier was."

"But it says in the report the cruiser was Baltimore."

"Minneapolis," maintained Kimiuo.

Again, this did not make any sense, and there was a possible solution to that. "Let's see. Minneapolis was pretty busy. She was part of that Spruance group of battleships which swept around the atoll. So since it probably was not Minneapolis, but he said it was, maybe we are talking about the second carrier raid. Anyway, Minneapolis probably did not launch the Kingfisher. They sank the Katori."

Kimiuo looked at me, and I knew what he was thinking. Why was I asking all these questions and having doubts when he was told this story by a survivor himself. The answer was very simple. I wanted to have confirmation before I wrote about it, and what he was telling me did not coincide with the information I had previously. Then I had to see what the reason was. Probably we were talking about events at a different time. No doubt he was right, just as right as on his landmarks when he spotted the wrecks. So I left this part of the conversation with a neutral remark, took a good sip from the coconut, then got up, went to the boat and got some sun cream to doctor my nose.

When I returned, Kimiuo was still sitting in the shade. He had not moved. He was looking east onto the water, half turned to Eten. I picked up my coconut and finished the thirst-quenching water. It was hot now, but in the shade, reasonably comfortable. I started, "One of these guys that responded to the newspaper article wrote strange things about the officers of Fourth Fleet having a good time on Dublon, with the girls."

"Not Fourth Fleet, Fourth Base Force. I heard that story too. That's why not many pilots took off. Those guys that flew that morning, the day of the attack, they're not really fliers, they're mechanics. You know, there is maybe 5, 6 or 7 minutes after the first attack of the carrier planes on the airfield before they come around again and machine gun all the planes. One wave comes, turns back. So they have little chance. Some planes were undamaged and who jumped in and flew them, I heard it was the mechanics, because most of the fliers were on Dublon when the first wave came. Some pilots from Moen, some from Param also, everybody went to Dublon. They say that they going to have a big celebration for some guys, coming in from Rabaul, on Dublon. Wrong place," he added with emphasis. "You know, I heard that the attack was conducted by a spy so that all the pilots were in Dublon. Don't forget the gun on Uman was torn down also, the heavy 6" gun on Uman. It was disassembled for overhaul and painting. But the Japanese, they say what's the point of the plane taking off? They just go to the enemy planes and the Americans shoot them down, because they are not really fliers, pilots, but mechanics. This was the sort of word we got here starting on the 18th and 19th. Things became very quiet. They are shaken and keep quiet. Then there was a lot of complaining between the Japanese. They argue with each other, they blame somebody and someone and so on. Blame each other. Some, they blame the fleet, some they blame the pilots in Truk. What were they doing on Dublon? Why did they go here? But why do we stay in our station? And why don't they stay in their station? But this is war. But whose fault? Why do they bring the girls? That's what they say."

"So they found somebody to blame and chopped his head off?"

"So far, I learned that the captain on the gun, the commanding officer of the battery on Uman, was executed. Some other people too. There were many officers executed after the attack. If I'm not mistaken, I think that's why they move Takaeda out, because of the attack and all the damages." Kimiuo proceeded then with the Japanese accusations. "I exactly hear from the Japanese, they blame each other. They blame the fleet saying, What the hell the fleet doing? Why they go? What they do? They're supposed to stop them way out. That's the kind of words they were using. And what the pilots doing on Dublon? I didn't hear this from the Japanese, that all the pilots came to Dublon. This I heard from some of the Trukese, little bit high ranking Trukese. The Japanese didn't mention that to me. Not until later on, then they talk. After that they were just squawking among themselves. Army blames Navy. Navy blames Army. And some blame the Fleet, the navy blame their pilots. I heard that when the first wave was gone and the mechanics took off, all the pilots swam out to Eten. Then they got beat up by their 2nd Commanding Officer."

"They swam over? Must have been a boat there."

"Yes, but they try to excuse themselves, instead of riding a boat. Actually, not very many boats were running at that time."

"Well, plenty of boats brought over, a little bit later though, the army from Tol. But that was probably in the afternoon," I added.

"Yes. They reached Dublon at night."

"Actually, they make a little bit of an indirect reference to the pilots on Dublon, in the Japanese book. They said that most of the pilots were on Dublon."

"They even themselves mention that too?" Kimiuo raised an eyebrow. "Well, it's probably right then."

"Also there were a lot of planes which had just been put on shore. Right? In Eten, for example from the Fujikawa and two other aircraft carriers which had just arrived a couple of days earlier. More than 30 planes I think. 11 or so from the Fujikawa alone, which were already unloaded. If I'm not mistaken, you see there are no hatch cover beams in the aft holds which could mean they have unloaded the aft holds already, and put the planes on Eten runway. So they couldn't use these planes."

Kimiuo nodded, "I heard that those planes weren't put together yet."

"They were disassembled. Just as you see on the Fujikawa, the engines are out."

"Then on that night of the 17th, they went out and tried to put everything together."

"Those which were not yet damaged."

"I heard them say that some were in a cave."

"They had caves for airplanes?" I wondered. That was again something I had not known.

"They did," Kimiuo said affirmatively.

"Really? What a lot of work. An airplane needs a lot of space."

"They weren't put together, they were packed in crates."

"I see.

"They also had some German planes, you know," he stated.

"German planes?!", I asked startled. "Where?"

"On Eten."

This was really interesting. "What kind of planes?"

"Boy were they fast. They sound much different than the Japanese...and fast...they really shot up. We could always tell, even in Dublon, when they where up. With two engines, crew of three, if I remember. "

"Sounds to me like Messerschmidt, the 109. They were faster than the Zero..anytime."

"...Really fast!"

"How many were there?"

"I don't know, but I heard there were six destroyed on the ground. But they had a few more disassembled. So they had some."

"I wonder whatever happened to them?", I asked. What a sensation that would be if we could discover them. A few years later after this talk, the secret was lifted. These airplanes were deceptively similar to the German Messerschmidt 109D and 109G. They were Judys, Yokosuka D4Y Suisei, or Tonys, Kawasaki Ki61 Hien. Indeed, they were flying away from the contemporary Zekes any time, provided their powerplant, a liquid cooled license built Daimler-Benz DB 601A engine, would run reliably. That was a big problem plaguing these aircraft. And there is a Tony located in 50 feet of water off the northwest coast of Eten. It crashed off the runway - the propeller blades are bent - and hit a coral head when it landed on the bottom of the sea. But on the other hand: Two engines, different engine sound and a crew of three ?

"I always wonder whether they shot them down somewhere or lost them or whether they bury them or …. You know those caves they used to have airplanes inside? After the war, or at the end, they used explosives and caused a landslide. All the caves were buried on Eten."

I turned to him in amazement. There were so many things he knew, and slowly he let one fascinating detail follow the other. I pointed towards Eten, which stretched along the south. "On the hill, the half hill? On which side? Dublon side?"

"Facing Dublon", he confirmed. "Then some guys on Eten, long after the war, they dig and got into one of them. Then they get some gasoline out. Maybe that's the gasoline they were using for their outboards. All their outboards burn out."

"That's too good stuff. That's high grade special fuel," I exclaimed.

"They got just the drums out."

"And the planes are maybe still there?"

"I forget. There are some planes in those caves. You know something very important, the Japanese don't keep things. They rather throw them away into the water, in the ocean, or they bury them in a good place."

"There's no good place to bury in Truk. You don't get very far, you hit stones very quickly." I remembered how arduous the planting of taro was, and when the Trukese turned up the soil, they immediately came to stones. But Kimiuo did not think of burying in the soil.

"In a cave."

"You mean they buried them with a rock slide over the entrance?"

He nodded. "They slide rocks or dirt down."

"That's interesting. One should really look into this." I really wished I could, but we would never get it done. Time and resources were much too limited. Then Kimiuo dropped another bomb.

"And there is a big graveyard by the Naval Station."

"The other side of Dublon, not far from the Heian, on land?"

"Yes."

"What do you mean by gravesite?"

"There is a tunnel going inside to the mountain. Going in from that side of the road to the mountainside, I think 120 to 150 people, close to 200 people got buried, trapped in there. It happened during the last bombing. Then a week later, then the surrender is announced."

"And the bomb hit and all the rocks fell down. And what happened? They just left them there?" I was surprised.

"Yes. Oh, they try to dig. Some soldiers come out from different holes in the cave. Then they try to dig at that cave entrance. The commanding officer gave them just 3 hours. Just try the best in 3 hours, whatever we can. They were digging as fast as they could, but they never reached them. After 3 hours they stopped, said they are already dead. Some stupid American wants to go and dig the cave after the war. They want the swords. And they try to get some people to dig. 2 days, 3 days, and then they give up. Cannot reach the tunnel."

Why on earth, I wondered, did they limit themselves to three hours of digging? Did they really think that those soldiers in the tunnel had expired? And so considered the area a gravesite, and did not want to disturb the dead? It seemed different, I suppose most people would try to recover the human remains. But then, maybe the Japanese had other priorities at the time. "So they're still buried there. How many people know about that?"

Hailstorm - *Walks & Talks*

"Plenty people know about that."

"Must have been a really bad landslide. It's buried so deep. Because this rock is all fractured here. You have been digging tunnels so you know the rock has many fractures. Didn't it come down on you sometimes?"

"No. I was just lucky. I just lucky the thing never got me."

"Pretty damn hot in there." I could just imagine the toiling people inside a deep tunnel with no ventilation.

"Yes, and damp too."

"Very hard work. Did you have any electricity? Did they put in electricity in there so you could see?"

"Sometimes we have electricity, sometimes we don't."

"What do you do if you don't have electricity?"

"Kerosene, diesel lamps. Smells, takes away your oxygen. You work. Doesn't matter. You have to work. No choice." Kimiuo said this without any emphasis, just as if he was talking about the weather. Maybe even less so, because he could get very excited about the weather, particularly tropical storms.

"So you really think there may be some planes buried this side of Eten? Because I'm still puzzled about your saying there are these 2-engined planes there."

"The Japanese say they were German."

"Strange. I mean the Germans didn't have any planes to give away, you know." I was thinking about how the German planes got wiped out in Europe. Maybe they delivered a single plane to the Japanese for comparison and for technical assistance, but not for operational duty."

"Well maybe the planes were sent to Japan. The engine is different from Zeros. You know when the German planes were flying, it sounds like...," And here Kimiuo made one of his famous impressions of a high pitched engine noise, like an outboard at high speed. "Of course there is a ...," and a lower pitched sound followed. "But the German plane sounds like a Susuki outboard, yes, they sound like that. Must be very powerful planes, because they are a fairly big plane, much bigger than a Zero. The Zero was a fairly small plane actually. But those German planes are 3 person planes. 3 person, but 2 engine."

"Until when did you hear them? Until the end of the war?"

"Until... 45. Yes until the end of the war."

Kimiuo got up and walked over to the water's edge, motioning me to follow. "See there," and pointed to the two bushes just a stone's throw to the east at the shore line, "That's where they had a repair shop."

"There's a small ship half in the water, or what's left of it, right underneath the green," I said.

"Right. A Daihatsu landing craft."

"I see the engine block in the water, and there are four cylinders, two of them broken off. There in the shallows right next to it, there are the other two. Not much left of the ship."

"Okay, let's go to the shore."

With that he walked down the jetty, but stopped when I remarked, "Look at this! There is a wreck on the other side," I said while pointing east.

"That's one of the water carriers, same as the Inter-Island Supply Vessel you've been diving on."

"Really, that rusting hulk here?" I was surprised.

"Same kind," he confirmed.

"How did it get there?", I asked.

"Used to be the water jetty there. One side oil lines, other side water pipes. It was quite a long jetty. That ship just sank there, maybe was flooded after the war. I don't know ... See that round thing over there?"

"Sure, on the sea wall on the same side, but joining our jetty here, that bollard?"

"It's not a bollard," he replied. "That one used to be a boom. This area we unload all the stuff from the landing crafts and barges coming from the ships. See, as I told you. The ships which come to be unloaded, they bring them up from Fourth Fleet Anchorage and put them there." He pointed to a spot between Dublon and the east end of Eten. "It's closer for unloading. Then we ran the boats between the ships and here. This boom, it was operated by hand. Would turn on that round base and the boom goes over the barge, lifts up the cargo and then you had to turn it over to the quay and set the load down. Up and turn and down, all day."

"So this was the cargo area then."

"Right," he said and moved on.

"I can see the slipway now, here," and I pointed again to the right, east, where the Daihatsu lay hidden underneath the bush. "And now I can see the bow, the forward part is much more intact. Ah, there's the landing ramp. Yes, must be a landing craft."

We continued to go inland and passed a little hutch like object, resembling a large, closed box. "That's for drying copra, isn't it?", I inquired.

"Yes, they store and dry copra there," he confirmed.

We were approaching a very large breadfruit tree with a huge tree trunk and wide branches amidst of coconut trees. Beyond it I could see a big brown object. "Hey, what is that?", I asked in surprise.

"Have a look," he said and carefully picked his way over the many roots of the big tree. Now I could see. It was the hull of a small ship, perhaps the size of a tug. The hull was tilted to the side, there were no decks, and it rested on a slipway, stern toward the water. The counter was beautifully shaped, the cast frame enclosed the hole for the propeller shaft and the rudder post. Some of the shell plates were riveted to the ribs, others were only pinned down with heavy bolts. Obviously, the work was half finished when it was abandoned. The length of the keel was about 70 ft. In several places the shell plates showed holes where the rust had eaten through them. The lines of the bow were straight and of simple design. The ship looked large on land. The many bolts sticking out of the side gave it somewhat crude looks and from forward it looked like what it was supposed to have been, a workboat.

"How did this ever get on land like this?", I asked bewildered.

"That, my friend, is the only ship ever built on Truk," he said and continued sarcastically, "The first one and the last one. Never got wet from below."

"Why didn't they finish it?", I wondered.

"No more time, too much bombing, no more parts coming in from Japan." There it lied, a pathetic sight. Abandoned, sticking out, unreal, strange, displaced in the thriving vegetation, it was a total misfit, symbol of hopelessness and despair, brown and ugly in between lush green. I walked around it, on it's port side. It was much darker there and many coconut husks had been thrown there. Immediately I was attacked by Truk's national bird, the mosquito. Cursing under my breath, I went to the other side. Kimiuo had disappeared and I went back slowly to our dive boat. I found him standing near our old place and he pointed to Eten saying, "There, on the other side of Eten, that's where the Heian was anchored most of the time."

"Where the Fujikawa is now."

"No, not quite, just a little bit to Uman and south. That's Sixth Fleet Anchorage. That's where they had the Katori also."

"Sixth Fleet Anchorage, the submarine fleet ... I see. That's where the Gosei is. No wonder she had torpedoes for the subs, and the Heian - periscopes."

"Supply for subs, right," Kimiuo said.

"Got any tankers that way too?", I asked.

"No. Tankers anchored on the other side, north of Param, where the Shinkoku is. That was the tanker anchorage. From there, west a bit and south, they put the carriers. And between them and the islands, they anchored the battleships. Then almost north of the middle part of Fefan, they had mooring buoys for the Yamato and Musashi. East of that was the anchorage for heavy cruisers, and further east, north of Dublon, you could see the light cruisers and destroyers. So you had a long, thick ribbon of ships from east to west, destroyers and light cruiser, heavy cruisers, Yamato and Musashi, and the other battleships. And to the north of them were the carriers and forward of them, a bit out, the oilers."

"So what about the Heian, where she is now?", I asked.

"That's where the Naval Station was. She was just in the deep waters off the Naval Station. And the subs, just to the south."

"Near the Repair Anchorage."

"Right, just north, and close to Dublon," he said.

"Now that makes sense if you look at the location of the I-169. She must have turned right north from her mooring and began to dive when she flooded."

"Came right from that area, right."

"And the tankers for loading or unloading, they ran around Dublon to the east and tied to the water and oil jetty."

"Exactly," he replied. "But only tankers. Otherwise they would run small supply vessels."

"That one attack photo shows a tanker, empty at the jetty, but we talked about that. Guess it was the Fujisan."

"Maybe," he said consoling, for he knew that this was one of my favorite speculations, and we were quiet for a moment.

We had been "talking story" for a long time now. I wanted to come back to the subject of the first day, but we were so far away from that topic, that it would better rest for a day. And, I thought, maybe he would remember the one or the other detail. It was now time to get our little expedition together and go searching on the Fourth Fleet Anchorage for an hour. We had to spend some more time on the surface anyway, to allow more nitrogen out of our tissue, and any dive before then would carry a heavy penalty on decompression. Kimiuo got up slightly stiff-legged, called Chenney, who was having a chat on his own with friends on Dublon, and we all moved to the boat.

C - A VISIT TO THE BLUE LAGOON DIVE SHOP

COMMAND PROBLEMS IN TRUK

I woke up to a howling wind and driving rain. This was by far the worst I had ever seen. A full sized storm, or as I learned later, the fringes of a typhoon which passed over the ocean a hundred miles northwest of Truk. The waves inside the lagoon were large, coming from the west, and slapped incessantly onto the hotel's sea wall. The small hotel pier was inundated. This I had seen when I braved the storm to take a look after breakfast. No diving today, I thought, and went to the telephone at the reception, calling up Kimiuo at the dive shop. There was no discussion about sitting the bad weather out, but I said that I might come and see him if I could catch a ride to town. The opportunity presented itself later in the morning when a Trukese taxi stopped at the hotel. These taxis are worth mentioning. They are just little Japanese pick-ups, and passengers sit on the back platform. The price was right. It used to cost 25 cents to go from anyplace to wherever one wanted to go. In the age of inflation, the price had now doubled. But the ride was worth it. It made one keenly aware of the many bones in the body, and that the spine is a delicate part of the anatomy, particularly its lower part. The road from the hotel was a series of evil potholes, which the truck negotiated with the highest possible speed, sometimes approaching 30 km/h. My rain jacket kept me fairly dry and after 20 minutes or so, I arrived at the Blue Lagoon Dive Shop, which served Kimiuo, his family and friends as a place of abode. I entered the little ante-room and looked to my right. Kimiuo was standing there, slightly leaning against the counter with both hands firmly planted on the top. I saluted and stepped inside, immediately starting a tirade that all this was his fault, the weather that is, and that he was chicken not to dive just because the going got rough. He motioned me to take a seat. I went out took my yellow rain jacket off, shook the water off and returned. He reached over and passed me a mug of coffee, which I gratefully accepted.

"I guess you and I have a lot to talk," I began. This was followed by short moment of silence. Then he turned to me and looked at me as if to say something about a sassy city boy, but his face lit up suddenly, as if a thought had occurred to him and he began, without any preamble.

"You know what the problem was in Dublon? (Vice Admiral) Hara was Commanding Officer in Truk. And, you know, his problem was the same as Koga had with Nishimura. There is this guy with the name of Mirua. He was commander of ... you know, in the Japanese Navy they had something like special shipping, so all those things had to be handled by the fleet when they ship something, instead of a stevedoring company to handle the cargo ... so this guy Mirua was the Commanding Officer of that. In 37/38 he was the Commanding Officer of the Naval Station in Dublon. Then they transferred him from there to the Navy Shipping Operation as commander. He resigned from the Navy, but come the war, came back. So come 1944, he was nothing but arguing with Hara. Because they both went to the same school and both graduated. Apparently Mirua was better in school. Then Mirua retired from the Navy, but Hara continued. So, when later Mirua came back, he came back with the rank of a captain."

"Lower rank than Hara!", I interrupted.

"Right. So when he was coming back, he was just captain, but he said he was smarter than Hara on everything. He couldn't make up the rank, however, because of his previous retirement from the Navy."

"So, there was always fight between the two."

"On the Fourth Fleet, always fight between the two. And in between Army and Navy also always fight. Lots of problems."

The officer, Kimiuo is referring to was the last commander, from 07.10.1943 onwards, of the Fourth Harbor Department, Rear Admiral Tomosahuro Mirua. I had seen his name mentioned in the interrogations.

"How did you know that they were always fighting?", I asked.

"I know from a man named Kato."

"Oh, Kato ... that's the man from the radar station, the officer in charge there."

"He's the one who told me the story," Kimiuo affirmed.

"How come you were talking to him? Did he come back after the war?"

"Yes. Twice he was here. Some of the travel agents asked him to take people to Truk since he knew much about Truk."

"What else did he tell you about the radar?" I was curious about the radar because I was still puzzled by the obvious failure of the Japanese to be combat ready.

"The radar - he told me ... This guy, he went to school in Los Angeles before the war and returned just before the war started. So, he knew a bit about American machines, but when he left, he did not know anything about radar. When he read something, he put the things together, as he had learnt in school, things would come back to him ... He could understand, for example, some engineering and electrical things ... and could speak American ... boy, he really could speak. That's why they accused him of being a spy." I decided not to follow up on the spy part, but tried to get back to the radar installation.

"What did he say about the radar installation?" I asked.

"First of all, he did not believe it at all. Then he work and work and work, and finally his work was successful. At the far distance they spotted attacking aircraft."

Now Kimiuo had managed to confuse me a bit. "He did not believe what?"

"That this thing was really going to work."

"That the radar would work?" It seemed that the Japanese had some misgivings.

"Yes, but when the radar worked in a perfect way, he told me, no use, anymore, because we are fighting a losing war."

"He thought so at that time already, before the attack, before '44?"

"Well ..." He managed to insert a bit of skepticism with justification, as it was hard to see why anybody would have been so negative before the attack. Probably a case of hindsight, I thought.

"Where did you say the radar installation was?" Kimiuo had mentioned it one of our dives on the Rio, when we were near Uman.

"In Uman, on the high mountain."

"And they could pick up aircraft?" I wondered.

"Yes."

"But how come the people, the defences were not ready when the attack came?"

"Because the installation was not ready until very late '43. Early part of '44 that thing was there, ready." It did not really answer my question, but maybe he meant to say that the other radar sets gave the Japanese a better resolution.

"That's at the time of the attack!"

"Come the attack, not all radar was working. If working, only one set at a time. They got the equipment. They got the machine, but I don't know whether all were working," Kimiuo remarked.

"Oh .... Some sources said they had radar at the time."

"What can I say ..."

"So they nevertheless continued to assemble the other stations?", I asked.

"Yes." He nodded, and turned around to face me. I continued.

"You see, some of the American sources said they had radar, so they were really warned, but they could not get the message through, because the telephones did not work." Kimiuo scowled and I added, "... at the time of the attack."

We were getting on slippery ground, as the circumstances surrounding the raid were not clear. There was a danger that we got into speculating too much, so I said, "OK, but you said that they did not have all radar sets ready, so why call anyway when everything was already started, I mean, when the bombs were already falling?" It was a bit of an academic question, and I was rewarded accordingly.

"Well .. what can I say about this ... . But the first attack was on Moen. Then on Dublon. Same wave. Some come, attack Moen, and then they should have called Dublon or Eten .. and Param, or wherever ... I'll tell you later another reason for the surprise."

"Well, but didn't they attack Dublon, Eten and Param at the same time?"

"Well, not exactly the same time. The same wave. Not the same time." The time lapse between the initial Fighter Sweep and the first strike was probably taken as a staggered approach.

"So the very first attack got on Moen, and then followed the other airfields?" Well, Moen was close enough I thought.

"Right...and as I said," Kimiuo continued, "there was only one radar station. On Uman. That's the one I know about. But there may have been more later ... This is why I ... ah, remember I said that was a complete surprise attack? You know, of course the fighters took off many times from Moen, Eten and Param for training and search missions. So you got used to all that noise and planes in the air. Was almost daily. So, why care? And when the Yamato and Musashi were in Truk they sometimes fired from their moorings. They were at their mooring buoys, here, right between Moen and Dublon for the Yamato and little more to the West and off Fefan for the Musashi ... and then they would fire their big guns."

"Oh, man, those big 46 cm guns of the main artillery? Those shells we have seen still in the Yamagiri ... those monsters?"

"Yes. Well they would shoot blind on a target at the North Pass."

"That must have been some sight ..." These monstrous guns must have shaken the earth and sky when they fired.

"... Even more noise. - So, when I tell you, that noise is nothing to us, we did not quite understand what was happening," Kimiuo stated emphatically.

"You are saying, you got so conditioned to war noises that initially you did not quite catch on that that was the real thing, I mean the real attack," I summarized.

"Right. Yes ... we did not, until we saw that the planes were different, sounded different and dropped bombs, which went off with a big explosion."

"I suppose the guns were shooting as well."

"It seems long before they started shooting." I could imagine how the Japanese defenders frantically scrambled to get the guns into operation. It must have been hectic, to say the least.

"The guns were shooting at sight, even the big guns were shooting ... with plotters ... but not radar controlled?" The Japanese had equipped Truk with some fairly old, and by 1944, outmoded guns. The guns looked menacing. They did so even today, overgrown. But the development of weapons had moved on, and these anti-aircraft weapons were not able to combat aircraft effectively. The attacking aircraft reported that they were shooting a barrage, but this type of defence was not effective at all.

"Right ... no radar control. They had gun plotters. At night they got these search lights, these huge lights. At night they would sometimes catch a plane with these lights, and the gun would knock it down, sometimes."

"They had searchlights here? Where were they?", I asked.

"Not far from the guns, on that mountain of Dublon ..."

"Mount Tolomen?"

"No ... at that mountain to the East. There was one on it. And then there was one on Fefan ... this gun on Fefan ... this guy was a real sharpshooter. Knocks more planes down than all the others. On Moen, was a light as well."

"These huge, circular searchlights!", I exclaimed.

"Yes, yes. Yes," he nodded.

"They showed up at night like giant white fingers into the sky."

"Right," Kimiuo said.

We paused. The silence was filled with the roaring of the storm. I was surprised that the coconuts on the palm tree had not been shaken down. The low clouds were racing toward the east.

PLANES IN TRUK

I rose from the narrow bench and walked out. Kimiuo followed me to the door. It was storming heavily now, but the rain came only in showers. It was very warm and humid. Kimiuo talked to the boys in Trukese. After a short while, one of them came through the storm and gave me a can of orange soda. I thanked him and said to Kimiuo, "I really don't like this. The wind comes from the west, The air is too warm. Something's not right."

"Right," he replied. "Bad storm."

"How long will it last?"

"I don't know. Sometimes it's a day, can be a week."

"That's great," I said. "That sound you just heard by the way, was my stomach hitting knee-caps."

"What's wrong with your knee?" he asked.

"Oh gee, really now ... everyday we are not going out gets my schedule out of tilt." I was a bit upset at the prospect of being forced to lay idle. Well, at least we could "talk story", and that was great.

I pointed to the left. "There is this air plane propeller in front of your shop, Kimiuo. Where does it come from?"

He made a big sweeping movement with his right hand. "This side was all part of the airfield. So they dumped a lot. Later I fished it out of the water."

"You mean the Moen I airfield was so big?", I asked.

"It was very large. The road you see today ... pass that Police Headquarter, the Fire Brigade, and go over to the shop, that was all part of the airfield. The runway was where the airport is now ..."

"On the same spot?"

"Yes, same spot ... and then they had a lot of workshops, hangars, all kind of different buildings, it was large. That road there on the police station was a drive where planes taxied ... part of the apron ... so where my shop is now, it was all part of the airfield."

I had seen it in one of the photographs. It was a very large area. Previously it had been a settlement of the Trukese, but the people had been moved out. I continued, "It was bombed badly, wasn't it."

"From what I heard, yes. I didn't see it. I was in Dublon. After the war, there was plenty of grass."

"There is one picture which shows all the stripes painted on the runway for camouflage." It really looked well camouflaged.

"I don't know about that. It was all restricted area, but the major roads this side of town were all part of the airport," Kimiuo replied.

I came back to the corroded 3-bladed propeller. "How about the propeller?"

"After the attack they just dumped all unusable parts into the water. They cleared all the junked planes ..."

"Was the propeller unusable?" I wondered.

"You have seen the bent tip? The parked plane probably dropped to the knees when the bomb exploded nearby and landed on the blade. It bent then. There is no way one can use it. Besides, probably the alignment got damaged. There were plenty of these around. It's an adjustable propeller ..."

"Tell me, did they dump planes off the Eten field?"

"Quite a number. If you look closely, you can still see Zero and Val parts. You have been snorkeling on them. And then there is my private plane, off Dublon, in 60 ft of water," he added.

"How about Param?"

"Param ... could never use the airstrip. Big bombs put craters to the runway ... they fill up with water. Was difficult to repair. Some people told me they threw parts and damaged aircraft into the water off Param."

"Yes ...," I hesitated for a moment. Then I told him what I had seen there. "I have been there just the other day. There is a real junk yard of damaged aircraft parts. All kinds of pieces from the fuselage, tail assembly ... all kinds of stuff. They are still in pretty good shape. The aluminium is holding up quite well. But on many you see the damage. There are plenty of small, jagged holes, you know, the kind caused by fragmentation bombs. That damage is quite bad. As a matter of fact, there is a Zero fighter plane about 500 yards off to the west of the western edge of the old Param airfield. The plane is broken up, and there are three major parts scattered around a big coral head. That's the only coral head around in that area... Actually, that plane got shot down by Hellcats from Enterprise, just seconds after it took off from Param. It immediately went up in smoke and crashed. They describe it, there is no doubt about it. We have been skin diving on it. Its in about 30 to 40 feet of water. Actually we made some other interesting observations. When we were snorkeling out from the hotel we found 13 airplane engines. We went quite far out, really. Also there is a wing and diverse other parts of planes."

"That was Moen II airfield," Kimiuo stated.

"That was an airfield?"

"The area where the hotel is now - was all an airfield. For fighters, but mainly for sea planes. It was the sea plane base here. You've probably seen the wrecks of the Zero-floatplanes, which got shot up during the attack."

"Then the ramp leading into the water was for sea planes?", I asked.

"Yes ... there is one ramp," he explained. "There is another, at the area farther East, where they are building the ferro cement ships."

"I was wondering ... so this area was all a base?"

"You can still see the cement. They planted coconuts later. They really rained bombs on that one. Next to the hotel pier ... there is one bomb crater left and right ... It almost heaved that pillbox around."

"Yes ..." I thought for a moment, visualizing the area. "There are quite a number of pillboxes, 3 or so right from that sandspit to this side of the pier and one further. Then there is this barge but further up north at the little pier, there is another pillbox, a big barge and part of the fuselage of a PBY waterplane. I have seen a couple of old bomb craters inside the jungle area ... Speaking about old stuff, there is part of a generator close to the beach and a set of propellers."

"Right ... do you want to visit the Zero floatplane in 60 ft, off south Dublon, at the other major seaplane base?", he asked.

"Not right now," i laughed. "If you improve on the weather, yes, I might. But we have a lot of other things to do, remember?"

Kimiuo did not answer, but went back into the house and motioned me to follow. "Here," he said, "take it," and gave me a few slices of what looked like toast, except for the shape.

I took one and ate it. "That's great stuff." It tasted really pleasant, particularly at noon. "What is it?", I asked.

"Breadfruit, toasted."

I loved the way it was prepared and helped myself to another piece, sipping my orange drink in between bites, and sat down again. This time he also took a seat, on a rickety old chair.

THE BUOY AT YANAGI

"What's that thing there by Yanagi, Kimiuo? It looks like a big piece of concrete," I asked.

"That's a buoy," Kimiuo stated.

"What's a buoy doing there?", I said surprised.

"It was a mooring buoy. For the Yamato. It used to be in deep water. But come to the typhoon 72, it broke lose and took off ... and washed up there."

"I see, it go trapped on this reef which curves east and south and looks like a crescent ... Yanagi."

"It was a real bad west wind." Oh dear, I thought. Here we go with the west wind again.

"This is really a huge buoy. Have you looked at that shackle! Do you think it will still float?" I was excited as if I had just made a discovery.

"It pounded on the reef. I guess, it was thin from rust ... You know, when I was working for the Fisheries, in the evening we would take the boat home and tie it to that buoy. Then we go on the buoy and have a few beers ... boy, did we have a good time ... This thing, it never moved. You had waves, this thing never move. Steady as a rock." He was drinking quite a lot then, I guess. But not only had he given up drinking, Truk was dry these days. No more beer.

"Well, if they tied the Yamato to it ... a ship of that size. They Yamato was weighing more than 64.000 tons." I thought I could impress him with that, and I was right.

"How much?"

"See, the Yamato and Musashi were the biggest battleships ever built. Quite a big bigger than what the American built, the Iowa-class. They would weigh about 64.000 tons a piece, fully equipped even almost 72 thousand ... Speaking about the sister ship Musashi, did she also have a mooring buoy?"

"Yes, she had. Also Kaga and the other aircraft carriers," he confirmed.

"Where are these buoys?"

"During the war, during the attack, the planes made target practice. Sunk them all, except for this ... strafed and sunk them." That was stupid, I thought.

"You said, it was located between Moen and Dublon?" There was a buoy symbol on the chart.

"Yes," he said.

"Then it was the buoy marked as "D2" on the chart?"

"Yes."

"Listen, that thing sits right on top of E 151 degrees 50 minutes." As if it would make any difference to him, but I had wondered about it.

"Before the war, when they were stationing the Combined Fleet here and put the buoys up, they had quite a number of men there, who took a week of measurements. With a ..., what you call ... sextant. So they put it there on purpose. It was a big deal."

"That was Flagship Combined Fleet buoy?", I asked.

"Well, I don't know about that, but it was big, real big."

Yes, I thought, it certainly was. But about the mooring buoys ... "When we were diving on the Heian Maru, off the shore of Dublon, I noticed that she was also tied to a mooring buoy."

"Yes, that's right," said Kimiuo.

"I thought she would move out with the submarines?" I had always thought they would use it for replenishment at sea.

"Not the Heian. Not at the end. Her sister ship, the Hiye Maru would go out. Earlier, also the Rio de Janeiro Maru."

"What happened to the Hiye, I don't remember that name ... she did not sink here?"

"She went out with the Fleet one day and never came back."

"They were all submarine tenders. The Rio would go out with ammunition, fuel and an exchange crew and rendezvous with subs of the Sixth Fleet, then come back."

"No, I don't think so. They would go to Kwajalein and come back sometimes for supplies. And the Rio, in she came and out again."

"That's right. She got reclassified as transport and was running troops and supplies."

"Yes, Sixth Fleet, they had the light cruiser Katori," he remembered.

"As flagship ... they battered her to death, real bad, when she was fleeing out of the lagoon ... out of North Pass." I read it in the reports and I had seen the picture.

"I did not know that," he exclaimed.

"But about the Rio de Janeiro: Did she bring in the troops, the Army, to Truk? In January 44, I mean."

"No ... the ships I did not know. There were four or five - difficult to tell with all the comings and goings," Kimiuo answered.

"Were they freighters or troop transport?"

"Both ... You know, the Navy sent them out to Tol right after they arrived in Dublon. Then they were rushed back to Dublon and Moen ... on the double ... real fast, emergency... all during the night, following the first day of the attack, on the 17/18 of February. With everything still afloat, with their weapons and all," Kimiuo stated.

"Did they have any barracks on Tol?"

"Some ... few ... but not so many, not enough ..."

"That's what the Hanakawa Maru had loaded, building supplies for the troops in Tol ... she got sunk at Tol." we had made a dive on that unlucky ship which had a cargo of gasoline drums loaded forward and cement bags aft. Of course ..."

"Maybe ... But when the troops came, may be some 14 thousand, these transports run off again ... in a real hurry ..."

"They always do that ... don't want to be caught in the crossfire ... That reminds me ... something was puzzling me, why was the Heian moored at Combined Fleet anchorage, but belonged to Sixth Fleet?"

"She switched a lot." Kimiuo moved his hand to and fro as explanation. "Took on supplies, move over to Uman, come back here. When her sister Hiye came, the Heian moved from Uman to Dublon. Went many times between these spots," he added.

"There is this cable running out from the bow of the Heian, her mooring buoy, straight East, parallel to the two big chains. What for ... power, communication? Do you know?"

"Well I don't ... know. Telephone, maybe. Not power ...I'd never seen it," he said.

"Did you know that there is a huge anchor right next to the buoy of the Heian ... One of these very large ones, like there is outside Police Headquarter in Moen, ... same as the two close to the destroyer Susuki ... between Dublon and Fefan ... with the shank sticking out ..."

"For mooring ... these are mooring anchors. Normally they put them down in a triangle ... The chains running east, from the Heian, have another anchor maybe forward ... When Ise and Fuso were here they anchored about between Moen and Yanagi." Kimiuo was referring to the two large Japanese ships.

"They were here, too?", I asked in amazement.

"They didn't have mooring buoys. Put down their anchors. They were really big. Sometimes Hyuga and Yamashira would come, too."

"You've seen most of the battleships ... They must have been really gigantic ... Why didn't they have moorings?"

"I don't know ... But they were also shooting sometimes with their big guns." Always these surprises, I thought to myself.

"Why did they do that?"

"Gunnery practice. Yamato and Musashi fired on to the North Pass."

"But they couldn't see!", I burst out.

"Right. They used gun pointers ... observers."

"What did they shoot on?"

"A tug - with a target."

"That must have been fantastic to see that, see these guns go off."

"Shook you up, alright. And didn't I say we almost overslept the attack. See, that's because we thought it was gunnery practice again," he laughed.

I got up and walked over to the shelf, inspecting the copper dive helmet. It is a wonderful piece, very solid. I tried to lift it, but it was really heavy. "That's the one taken up from the junk heap between Dublon and Fefan, isn't it?"

"Yes," said Kimiuo.

"It went to California for restoration and they sent it back to you to display. Isn't this the one?", I asked.

"How do you know?", he asked.

"I've read about it someplace ...", I said absent-mindedly.

The wind had even increased in force, but the rain had petered out. The trees in front of the dive shop were bending and straining. These palm trees really were sturdy plants, i thought. My thoughts drifted back to the last dives we had made, and the excursions in between.

LOGISTICS, GUNS AND PASSES

"Remember that rusting heap of iron, Kimiuo? The one that looks like an old barge. Was it Japanese ... from the war? You know the one I mean, the one right off the destroyed pier on Dublon."

"It had a crane on top. It's the one ... they tried to raise the submarine with."

"That 35 t - crane, they tried to bring up the I 169?" That piece should be persevered, being so famous, I thought.

"Right"

"There is this long jetty at the far end ... At the end of the old shore installations."

"We called it Water Pier."

"What about fuel?", I asked.

"A coastal tanker. Had to do a few trips for Yamato before she was refuelled."

"How many?"

"Depends ... sometimes three, but sometimes five ... They would never go very close. Never tie up alongside ... Heave a line over and put the oil pipe along. Never got very close," Kimiuo remembered.

"How close?"

"I don't know ... few hundred feet, may be", for all he knew.

"Why?" So far away, I thought.

"They did not want anyone close to Yamato. Did not want to have people get too close for inspection. Always they were ready to run. With a ship tied up, there would be a delay. Could be dangerous and messy ..."

"Is that the inter-island tanker off the North shore of Uman, not far from the Sankisan?"

"Maybe it's the water ship ... But I remember that one. It would go alongside the ships and pump the stuff over."

"So this oiler always had to run around Dublon, between Moen Yanagi and Dublon easterly, to get to the Combined Fleet. I mean they never went between Dublon and Fefan?"

"No ... bad reefs ... You have seen that one, between Fefan and west of Dublon."

"Where the waves were breaking?"

"No, at the light blue spot ... The Japanese dynamited that reef so many times, but it's just too shallow. Could never open a passage. It's still deeper than the other ..."

"So, where did these big ships go ... in and out of Truk ... through the North Pass?"

"Always South Pass," Kimiuo stated, then added, "They also put guns on the islands ..."

"On the outer islands, on the reef?", I asked.

"Yes, there were some around the passes."

"I remember, they pulled the guns out after the air raid and put them up in the big islands. Like the one on Moen, up the mountain from the hospital." I had read about this.

"Right. But not all. On this island, west of the North Pass, there are still guns," Kimiuo said.

"What type of gun?"

"Same as on the Fujikawa ... Same kind."

"With the shield ... Well these were old cruiser guns. They had these light cruisers, built around 1900 - some of them even fought in the battle of Tsushima Strait 1905/06, Russian Japanese War, and later, I don't know when, the ships were declared obsolete and taken out of service. But they kept the guns. They were 4.7 and 6 inch guns. They kept the guns in storage and used them to arm secondary ships and shore installations."

"Remember the brass plate on the gun on the Fujikawa?"

"Yes ... the bow gun," I replied.

"What did it say?" He had trapped me on the calibre of the gun now.

"Some English manufacturer, Vickers Armstrong, the year of 1899 and 6 inch calibre ... You are right, that gun on the Fujikawa is one of the old 6 inch guns, as the oldest battle ships had then. So they did not relocate the gun? I mean from the outer island?"

"No, that one is still there." He was firm about that.

"And they never used the North Pass?" I meant for passage of ships.

"Not that I know. The big ships all went ... pass Yanagi, then that bad reef off the East of Dublon, it had a maker on it ..."

"... It's still on the chart ...", I interjected.

"...They pass that on the outside, East, then pass south of Eten and go between Fefan and Uman, right to the Pass."

"Cut right through Sixth Fleet Anchorage."

"Right," affirmed Kimiuo.

"But when the destroyers and Katori fled, they were running through the North Pass ... right into the guns of the American battleships."

"In that situation ... never mind, they just run out of this here, fast."

"Well, one destroyer got away. They shot at it at a range of 22 miles, but it made a run for it and escaped. From the records it looked as if the light cruiser Agano got torpedoed by a submarine the afternoon of the day before the attack, and a destroyer was there to pick up the survivors. The Japanese records say that still another light cruiser, the Naka, ran out that afternoon before the attack. Looks as if in the morning they ran back to Truk. There were quite a number of destroyers in and around Truk at the time of the attack. I only know, that the Maikaze was destroyed by the big guns of the surface ships, the Nowake escaped, the Tachikaze, still grounded on Kuop Atoll, was destroyed by bombs on the second day, and a small destroyer was beached on the shores of Uman, and burned. Might have been the Susuki. And finally, there was the Oite, which got torpedoed by planes from Bunker Hill on the second day, and another, which tried to pick up the American pilot, who crashed inside the atoll, and who was later rescued. The Fumizuki sank off Eot. The Oite was sunk a little bit later. Two more destroyers were taking off for the North Pass. They also were bombed, but both made it to Rabaul with the Akashi. They were the Shigure and Harusame. Then there was the convoy about 80 miles northwest of Truk, which Intrepid planes attacked. They sank one or two ships, but a destroyer was reported picking up survivors and ran to Truk afterwards. Seems to have been the Fujinami. But," I added, "there's a lot of confusion about all these destroyers in Truk.

I went over to the bench and considered how beautiful a place Truk really is, in the sunshine, and how miserable when the weather turned foul. I could not even see Mt. Terokken, as it was obscured by low flying clouds. The sky looked as if it would collapse any moment now. The waves crashing about 30 m west of Kimiuo's dive shop could be heard. Their spray was driven further inland. The best place to be was under the sea, where the wave action could not reach. That reminded me on submarines and their little, deadly off-spring, the Kaiten.

KAITEN IN TRUK

The Kaiten-type submarines were one-man suicide submarines. They are the naval equivalent to the infamous Kamikaze aircraft of the Army and Navy. Kaiten were designed and built at the end of the war, when Japan's military position became untenable. They were intended as a last ditch defence against the Allied forces. It was considered an honor by the Japanese to die in such action, subsequently there was never any lack of volunteers.

The Kaiten, looked like a torpedo, were built around an engine for a torpedo, and had a conning tower. It was just a trifle under 50 ft long. Two counter-rotating propellers were located aft. These mini-subs were intended as coastal defence weapons, because the radius of action was very limited, such as about 50 miles, when the vessel would travel at 12 knots. It dropped to about 15 miles at a speed of 30 miles. The Kaiten could be launched either from surface vessels, such as destroyers, submarines were modified to carry a few, and then they could be put in fixed positions on land.

So I asked Kimiuo,"In the South Pass, Kimiuo, were there a lot of cables? Or was there any ship detection gear? Would you know anything? What was there, what was going on there?"

"No, I really don't know ..."

"Do you know why I asked?", I asked deviously.

"Well ..."

I moved to the wall with the chart mounted on it, and pointed with my finger to the South Pass. "Do you see all these lines around this island on the other side of the South Pass ... they are cables. And see ... they all cross the Pass. They end at this island here ... and here. There are too many for power and communication alone. ...and there is nobody to telephone."

"Oh, there was!"

"Where?"

Kimiuo got up and pointed to and island. "On this island ... here, East of the Pass."

"There was a telephone, a communication station ... an outpost?"

"They put a big gun on it. And they put a gun on that island as well, the one next to it ... they put a gun there, as well," he said, pointing to a few islands on the rim reef.

"I would have never thought of that, but after all, that South Pass was their major thoroughfare. So, they put one on this one, too?"

"Oh yes, but it has already been taken off ... after the attack, and put on one of the major islands," Kimiuo said.

"Ok, but why so many cables?"

"You are right, there are many. They go to Dublon, Moen and so on. May be they were communication cables. One leads to Eten. There was a communication center in Eten."

"But these cables and their arrangement look to me like magnetic detection gear. You know, if some ship tries to get into the South Pass the cable would act as a coil and pick up the magnetic field, and so the people know."

"One this island, called Fanamu, where this cable leads to, nobody stayed there," stated Kimiuo.

"Why?"

"Only thing I know is, they put the human torpedo on Fanamu. One human torpedo."

"You mean, they had Kaiten there?", I exclaimed.

"One ... yes. And they put one on Yanagi."

"Also? How many?"

"One. One on Fanamu and one on Yanagi. You can still see the tracks there and the wall to protect it." Yes I remembered that from our excursions to these islands. I had gone over them with a fine tooth comb and discovered many interesting things.

"There weren't any people on Yanagi?"

"Yanagi was Army. There were about 15 soldiers stationed. They also had a few tunnels and machine gun emplacements. But in Fanamu, nobody was there."

"But the torpedo was there. So, somebody had to go to Fanamu to get inside the torpedo ... so there ought to be people stationed there."

"Three people. Maybe mechanics to get the thing ready and launch it. You saw the tracks, you understand, it needs a bit of a push."

"I mean, that is really strange, the one on Fanamu faces Dublon." I wondered, because the tracks headed out straight in that direction.

"Yes, but the two on Udot face South-west ... but they never got completed."

"Oh, is that what it is ... these two round holes in the rock, right at the shore?" We had seen those on the way to the Hanakawa Maru.

"Yes, that was for human torpedoes as well," Kimiuo confirmed.

Despite the storm, I had to get back to the hotel soon. On the other hand, we had just fallen so nicely into the story telling mood, that I felt that we better continue for at least a little while longer, so I asked him about school and work when he was young.

SCHOOL AND WORK

"Kimiuo, you had to go to school, all of you?"

"Yes. We went from our tenth to our fifteenth year," he replied.

"That's fairly late, wasn't it? How long a school day did you have?"

"Generally from the morning until noon." Seemed like a regular school day.

"Did you have to work after that, were you required to work?"

"No, only after you were older than 15 years." Very human I thought, but maybe this was before the war.

"What did you learn, I mean calculating, reading and writing?"

"Japanese." They taught the kids Japanese, and he still could read and speak Japanese very reasonably.

"So, if you wanted to learn our script, you could not?" I sometimes wondered why he had a little problem writing our script. He painted the letters.

"Well, you could learn it from the missionaries," he said.

"Really, they had missionaries at that time?"

"We had four German missionaries here. One lived in Tol and had a family." He had mentioned that before.

"What happened to them? After the war ...?"

"I don't know. But they were old people. I think they were sent back."

"When did they get to Truk?" Probably they spent all their life there. There was the rumor that some of them were executed after the German surrender.

"I think they were there at my parents time. They had little schools, and you could go there ... in Dublon, Tol, Moen, may be in Uman, I am not sure. Some new came. There are some German missionaries here."

"Is this where you learned to write and read our script?", I asked.

"Right ..."

"... and Japanese in school?"

"Yes. Some still speak Japanese."

"The old folks?"

"Some of the children learned from their parents here. Not very much, but a few words," Kimiuo commented. After a moment of reflection, I took the up the conversation again.

"The other day we were talking about life after the attack. You mentioned that on Moen there was some form of entertainment. There were girls?"

"Some or the officers and some for the men, yes," he said indifferently.

"Wasn't this a bit unusual?"

"No, not a bit. Not if you understand Japanese culture." There was a trace of disdain in his voice, if I heard it right.

"There were also Koreans here. How were they treated?", I asked.

"Real bad. Looks as if the Japanese didn't like them."

"But there were other people here."

"From Nomoi and Resop." From the Marshalls, I thought.

"Why?"

"I don't know. Seems like labour." Probably the Japanese moved them out when they built their military installations.

"Did Japanese soldiers and local girls meet, I mean, go together?" I did not want to have this question follow so directly after my question regarding the Japanese girls.

"No. See the Japanese had girls, and so they were discouraged to go with our girls ... they didn't ...but some business men, they married." There was a good portion of Japanese blood in many of the natives and a few had very distinct Japanese facial features.

"But the Japanese did not really treat you bad?", I asked to get off the subject.

"Was alright. Was not easy, I mean nobody had it easy here ... Plenty work, little food. Guess, was ok ... Don't forget, that Truk had been in Japanese hands since a long time and was their major navy base. They treated it as their land. And probably were a little more tolerant with us, as compared to the people in the occupied countries."

"Yes, I understand," I nodded.

"Also the administrators, with whom we had the most contact, did not change so fast as the soldiers. We did not have much contact with soldiers," Kimiuo explained.

"They probably did not encourage these contacts between civilians and soldiers. Secrecy was the word."

"True." The Japanese were paranoid about secrecy, but they missed the point. The knowledge of the fairly simple minded natives, who, for the most part were on their side anyway, was not the real danger, but the unshakeable belief in their own superiority, and the intelligence of the Americans. That's where the danger was.

"What kind of work did you have to do. I mean, we talked about the tunnels, but what else."

"Earlier a lot were busy constructing Eten airfields. There a lot of construction on the other islands. Building, stores gun emplacements, pillboxes and so on. Actually, these were ok jobs. One did not mind. Otherwise we had to do all these things they would not like to touch."

"Like what?"

"Oh, toilet cleaning ... things like that," Kimiuo said emotionlessly.

"What did you do?"

"Well, I was working on the pier, loading, unloading ... in Dublon. Everything had to go to Dublon. Never could go to another place, but must go through Dublon first. Sometimes we did work on the ship. Ride the landing craft to the ship ... did a lot of work on the ships, but always got food."

"Most of the material was war material?"

"And food. Rice, and beer ..." Judging from the huge amounts of beer bottles on the wrecks, they had allocated quite a lot of space to that beverage.

"What time did you start work?"

"About 6, to half past." That was after dawn.

"How long ?"

"About five-thirty."

"That's a long day ...", I said, almost to myself.

"Nay ... Look what we did yesterday ..." It had been a long day and we had not returned before 5 o'clock. "But you got slapped if you didn't show up for work," he added.

"That means, you were beaten if you didn't show up?"

"Yes,... but pilots also got beaten."

"Pilots?!" How did he ever know that?

"Yes ... if they were late getting into the air. Come to return, they got slapped."

"They did an awful lot of slapping after the attack ...?"

"Funny." It may have been, but not really. It did happen, as he admitted later.

"On the subject of schooling, was there any chance to learn more? Could you go to other schools?"

"Well, you could if they told you. The best students were sent to Palau. They went to more schools and came back as supervisors. At construction sites and so on."

"I see. So there was a chance." There was a carpenter school, maybe also for other vocations.

"Very small. They did not need too many supervisors."

"There was a rumor, that a new anti-aircraft command post with radar and so on was on the way to Truk, but the ship carrying it, got sunk by an American submarine." A thought...It was a fairly solid rumor.

"I have heard about it," he admitted.

"Hmm ... I believe it was said by a Japanese officer after the war ... You know Kimiuo ... I was wondering, because there was always this puzzle in my mind ... I was thinking how come they got so surprised by the attack. One day, they run their fleet out, the other they get surprised. It does not make sense."

"They expected something. But later. Much later ..."

"Yes, that's right ... "

"Plenty of rumors, all the time ..."

"There must have been more anti-aircraft guns than that one on Eten."

"Oh, yes, every island had at least one. Over there, in Dublon, there was one there ... another gun fired from there. Then there was one on Fefan ... Param."

"Did it get knocked out later?"

"I don't think so."

"Would be nice to check it out," I said reflectively.

"Are you kidding? Plain jungle. Nobody's been there in ages."

"OK, OK. We don't seem to have enough time. I am quite partial against your secondary jungle, anyway. Still, would be interesting ..."

We paused. I looked at my watch and as if that was a command, I suddenly felt tired. The air was oppressive and the concentration was taking its tool. I got up, put my raincoat on and said that he better get some better weather up. I would leave him now, so he could work on that. He grinned, I poked him in the ribs, and thanking him, moved out to the street, more pushed than straight walking on account of the wind. A nap in the hotel would be the best thing to do with such rotten weather, I thought and yawned.

SURRENDER - TIME

"There wasn't any resistance against Japanese rule in Truk? I mean, you guys never grumbled or thought it would be nice to be left alone?", I began.

"You are kidding. What do you want? These guys ... they let us go to school." Kimiuo was genuinely surprised. It seemed to be clear that this thought had never occurred to him.

"Treatment wasn't bad?", I asked in attempt to take the sting out.

"Treatment wasn't bad. I mean, you were OK, they were OK. Most of them. Some very nice guys. Of course a few not so good ones..."

"Slapping ...?" According to some write-ups, it appeared to be the favorite Japanese past-time. How distorted could it be?

"They didn't go round slapping everyone. You go work ... you work, you are OK. You get food ... we get rice, some fish. Sometimes had holidays ... When Germany ... you know these guys had a parade, a celebration when France give up ... or the Bismarck."

"Yes, she blew the Hood up. That was something." Despite my elation that news of that feat had even reached Truk, I was astonished.

"Had a real holiday ... Why not under the Japanese? Looked like winners, most of the time ... us independent ...didn't know the word."

"Well, with Spanish, then German, then Japanese ... always somebody on top of you people ... Well, now you're independent."

"Great ... yea! In a way we had it OK. There were still Germans around ..." I could not read that. It seemed sarcastic, but it was not Kimiuo's style to comment on politics. And he moved off quickly.

"The missionaries ?"

"Yes. Nice people. Old ... We respect age ... They bring peace to the islands. It was bad in the old times, as my mother told me. Kill people from the next village, next island, next atoll, always killing... Like I was telling Momo here."

Momo was one of the boys in Dublon who worked for him at the time. He had his house, and a giant box of outboard spares, right across from the Heian, where the old Naval Station used to be. After we found the Momokawa Maru, we were kidding him all the time that we welded the letters of his name on the ship's bow.

"I was wondering... were you telling old stories, like the parents do ?"

"Right ... You know, before the Spanish came, there were these two families in Dublon, here. One at the foot of Mount Tolomen, the other living higher up. My mother used to say ... so, one day, the women from the higher village came down to the water to go fishing, as they always did. These other people were waiting for them and made an ambush. All of these women got their heads chopped off, and they were running around with these heads on poles. That made the chief really mad. Because one of the women was his daughter ... I tell you, lots of killings ... People in Uman don't like people in Dublon. And nobody here likes people in Tol. You can't go to any other island without offending somebody ... and all that."

What a pity, I thought, that I could not partake in the "talk story" Truk style, and hear the many anecdotes. Not to get too upset about this I moved on. "About winning ... this attack - it must have come as a shock."

"I was thinking, how come they can destroy everything? And then so fast. I had no idea. Could not believe it. Always thought nobody can touch us here."

"They were not quite happy over their own defences, thought they were overrated." That was mentioned by the Japanese with perfect hindsight, after the war.

"Well; for us it was great. Why worry? Had been going on for years. With ships like Yamato - who can defeat them?"

"Well, they were never matched from the surface. Planes got them. But tell me, you had rarely seen white men before. Didn't you think the Americans were little devils or monkeys?"

"What are monkeys?"

"All right ... What I mean is, were you not terribly afraid about the Americans coming to Truk?", I continued.

"I don't know. Never thought about it much," he said indifferently.

"So you were not particularly apprehensive ..."

"Did I tell you I didn't know what to expect? When you were young, you are more curious than afraid." I guess he was right. I never had any comprehension of danger when I was a boy confronted with tanks, guns and ammunition. In fact, we could hardly get close enough. War material was fun, and we just didn't know fear.

"When did the Americans come, finally?", I inquired.

"Quite a time after surrender. I mean surrender was in August - not until September... Came with the Portland ..."

I knew this aging attack cruiser. "That old heavy cruiser ... built in 32 and long since decommissioned ..."

"A few destroyers and a big landing ship too," added Kimiuo.

I wondered what he meant with landing ship and what it should do. "What for the landing ship?"

"See, that is ... well, you know, they sign the surrender on the Portland and then what happens ... They got all these landing craft and they bring food."

"Food?" That definitely was news...the first thing the Americans did was to bring food to the island.

"Yes, food. We finally get something to eat."

"Surprise!", I exclaimed.

"I was thinking, these guys cannot be all that bad ... Bring food. So, that was my first encounter ... People bring food cannot be so bad, maybe."

We were quiet for a moment. In the meantime, it had become rather late. I sensed that Kimiuo had talked enough and wanted to go. He shifted to and fro in his chair and I said something about a long day ahead and heavy diving and all that. He agreed and slowly stood up, walking to the door, together with Taeko, and I had wondered where she had been all this time. We had been so engrossed in our talk, that the presence of the ladies had gone unnoticed. I escorted our guests to the door and stepped out with them.

The wind had almost completely abated, but it was raining "shower curtains" as we called it. Kimiuo and his wife did not have to go through the quietly pouring rain. They just walked along the front porch to their room, which adjoined ours. With a final "Goodnight", they closed the door behind them.

D - A DAY AT THE COMBINED FLEET ANCHORAGE

All morning we had been criss-crossing the eastern part of the Combined Fleet Anchorage. Kimiuo had said that he had heard from the old man that another ship had sunk in this area, east of Yanagi. Using this little island, Moen, Dublon and Fefan as reference points, Kimiuo had woven a tight search pattern. The weather, always a major concern when we went on a search, had been good, although the Trades had blown with their usual force. The spray of the white-capped waves had drenched our small crew repeatedly. There was no escape from that. As the ships all basically pointed east when they sank, the best way to find them is running from north to south and the other way round. This is what Kimiuo did again, taking the waves on the beam. It was really hard on me, although I had the best spot in the boat. I was sitting way forward in the cabin and braced myself as well as I could against the rolling and occasional pitching. Jammed tightly against the other side of the boat was the depthfinder, connected to the transducer mounted on the transom, and the batteries forward. I had been watching the instrument intently now all the time, and my head threatened to spin like the indicator disk, which revolved 5 times a second, flashing the depth. At the same time it made a tiny mark on the advancing graph paper. A line resulted, showing the bottom contours.

This part of the lagoon was particularly difficult to follow because the sea floor consisted of a chain of steep underwater mountains, which showed as sharply ascending slopes on the paper. They produced an echo which was very similar to wrecks at first glance, and only after two or three seconds the difference could be seen. I knew how the echo of a wreck looked like. We had been very successful at the Fourth Fleet Anchorage, but at the Combined Fleet Anchorage I had been fooled several times, and blew my whistle vigorously. At that moment the boys had thrown the engine in neutral, Kimiuo scrambled up and cast the anchor forward into the wind. The line unravelled itself for a few moments and then stopped. Kimiuo looked around, memorizing the landmarks. I would look stupefied at the instrument, check for confirmation, and finally crawl out of the cabin, mumbling something unintelligible about hiding a wreck again, apologizing for the inconvenience, and asking why the anchor was not up yet, whether the crew was having a rest or had a late night, what kind of a crew this was anyway I had to work with and similar nonsense, then I disappeared into the cabin again.

I had to give Kimiuo credit. He never complained. A bad throw, we had tacitly agreed, was better than a missed wreck. It did not take me too long to sharpen up, and the false alarms had ceased. When I was sitting in the sticky cabin on bruised parts of my anatomy, watching the instrument, I thought about the comments of my friends to whom I had described the searches we had made and our finds. All of them had listened, and remarked how exciting this must have been. Not in the least. It was tedious, sometimes boring, but nevertheless hard work. Many evenings we had gone home thoroughly disappointed, even disheartened when we had burned more than 30 gallons of Gasoline, and spent one day after another on searches finding not a trace of a wreck.

The excitement was when I had blown my whistle on a double echo, and when we were making the first dive on it, never quite knowing what to expect. On the other anchorages, after a futile day, Kimiuo sometimes had directed the boat over a known wreck. I could not see well from the cabin where the boat was, so when the echo showed up I excitedly blew my whistle. When nothing else happened, and Kimiuo continued to direct the boys with his typical sparse movements of one hand in that or the other direction, I would crawl out from below and let loose a string of appropriate remarks. Not accepting wrecks anymore, had enough, and so on. After that I felt much better and went back down to the instrument.

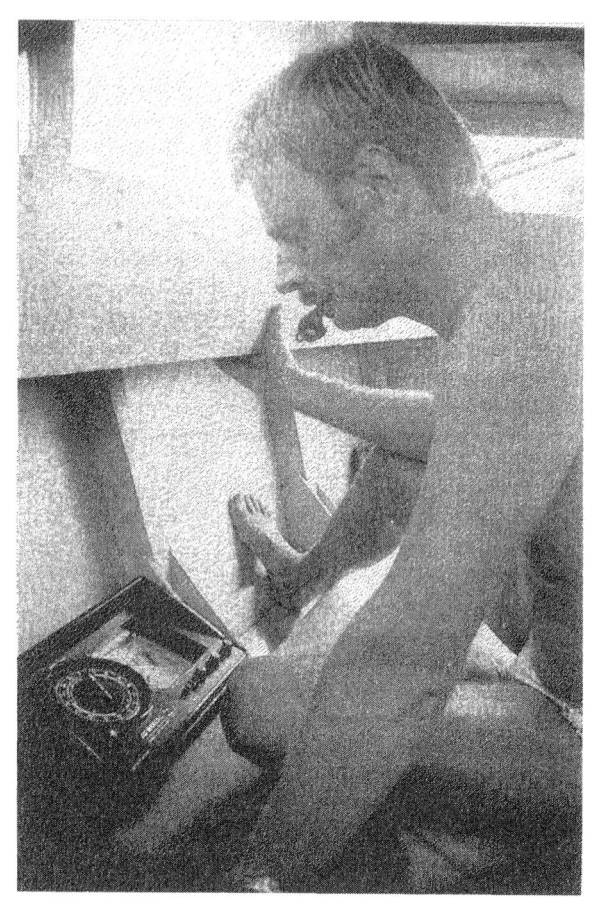

Author, depthfinder and whistle

Just for the record, Kimiuo's antics did not go without revenge. We were criss-crossing a certain area. It was hardly bearable in the semi cabin. Not only was it hot, but also the hard bouncing jarred the spine out of alignment. So, after an hour of nothing, I would suddenly stir, looking intently to the depthfinder. This immediately found the attention of the boothandler. Then I would be pointing my finger to the depthfinder and blow up my cheeks, as if to blow heartily on the whistle. The boathandler, who had anticipate my blowing, threw the engines in neutral and made everybody fall all over the place. "Did you see a wreck here? Or do you want me to blow the whistle first?", I asked, and so on ... .

Today was not a day of tricks, and there were no lighter moments. We had put our noses to the grindstone. It was after one and a half hour that I indeed had blown the whistle. I reported a strange object on the bottom. We had gotten used to the ability of the instrument of picking up small objects in the depths of the lagoon, and I had proven this by test dives on these echoes. This was how we found the wrecks and debris around the Kikukawa Maru. This strange echo, I had now said, was not an underwater mountain, but it looked like a piece of wreckage. It was too small for an intact ship. Dutifully, Kimiuo had thrown the anchor, but it did not catch. As usual, I got stuck with making a decision. The boat had drifted off the site, but bringing it up into the wind got us back on. I said that we would be going to make an exploratory dive. Since the boat was not secure, only Mary and I would be going, while Kimiuo would be trying to keep the boat from drifting too far off, and to pick us up after the dive. I set the bottom time of the dive for max. 20 minutes.

Quickly, Mary and I had suited up and made our entry. The dive was calculated to be a no-decompression dive. We had to assume that there would be no line to ascend and decompress on. We would not find it easy to return to the line if the boat continued to drift.

We descended the anchor line, and saw the anchor dragging over the bottom. The depth was 100 feet, but in a little while the anchor would hang free over a deeper part, as we could see. We followed the trail left by the anchor forward. After several minutes swimming, we saw a shadow forward. When we came closer, it turned out to be a large piece of the superstructure of a ship. Pieces of the shell plating were attached. The wreckage lay on its side. Railguards and portholes could be seen, and in the middle of the uppermost deck, the funnel remained standing. That was surprising, because on both ends the steel plates were ruptured, and part of the ship had been blasted free from the rest of it. Evidently we were on some ship which had exploded violently. Ventilators were laid out orderly on the sea floor, next to the funnel. We had memorized the wreck as well as we could, because for mobility's sake we had left the cameras on the boat.

We continued a bit farther in the same direction and found a second shadow, which turned out to be another piece of wreckage. The size suggested that it was part of the same wreck. Our suspicion about the sinking was confirmed. The ship had been ripped apart by a major explosion. It could have very well been a gasoline or oil explosion, from the looks of the debris. After this find we had no choice but to ascend as our time was up. The boat, which was a fair way off, moved in and picked us up.

I reported what we had seen, took my equipment off, toweled myself dry, and we ran the search for another half hour, but found nothing more. So we abandoned the search on that day, and Chenney started the second engine. The boat shot through the water. Then Chenney turned to the other boy and asked in Trukese whether there was any point in letting the fishing lines out for trawling. Kimiuo, sitting at his usual place on the forward edge of the cabin deck, overheard the question. Slowly and deliberately he turned around and said in English, "You guys gonna catch jet-fish?" The line stayed on board.

We ran to the west side of Dublon, to the old fisheries jetty, where Kimiuo had the boys tie up the boat. It was very calm here. We had a rest now, and Mary and I got rid of the nitrogen build-up from the dive. We wanted to go on a second dive. It was scheduled on the Kansho Maru, where I wanted to check the damage at the forward masthouse. Before we would go out again we would have lunch, and I hoped, another "talk story" session with Kimiuo.

Lunch consisted, as usual, of white rolls and Spam. This time the boys had taken along a can of mackerel as a special treat for me. Spam was nice twice a week, but to have it everyday was too much. I dug into the can of fish and managed in the shortest possible time to make a genuine pig of myself. The others ate the Spam, more or less contented, and somebody had the audacity to ask: "Anyone for some mackerel?", pointing at the tiny pieces of fish floating in the fat. Disgusted, I lowered the can carefully into the water, and said: "Mackerel Maru, see", but it had only a short operational career as a floating can. This wreck I salvaged however.

We all moved to land and were standing under a coconut tree. The discussion started on the Shinkoku Maru again, her survivors and the skeletons on starboard, in the aft superstructure. Sometime ago a memorial service was held, and that was where I picked up the conversation.

"So they had a ceremony".

"They had a ceremony over there by that party house at the hotel. I think it's two months ago this happened." Kimiuo answered.

"Two months ago? In February or when?"

"Yes somewhere around that time, around the anniversary time, just before."

"Do you remember any name at all from those guys?" I was curious, because may be it offered a chance to get in touch with Japanese survivors. My hopes were dashed by Kimiuo's reply.

"No sir. Because I don't even go to them." Evidently he had not known about this in time, and the Japanese had made the mistake not to contact him.

"Do you remember the date exactly? How long were they here? How many days?" If he knew, may be the hotel register could be consulted.

Kimiuo hesitated. "Maybe three days." He was not sure.

"The only ships where people came and dropped flowers were the Aikoku and the Shinkoku?"

"Yes." He nodded.

"Not on other ships?"

"I think they might have a long time ago. Some young kid did on Fujikawa ... and that one from Aikoku. He said his brother was chief engineer on the Aikoku. He came directly to us, so we take him. But few people came to Aikoku, few know."

Yes, I thought, the Japanese do not know exactly where she rests, but I continued with a question: "Why?"

"Nobody dives on her but us. That's why. This boy, he got the information from some Japanese in Guam, also some of the divers from Japan, that I know." He added: "So they came to me."

The word "boy", I thought, is used by Kimiuo for every male who is younger than he.

"That was the only one from the Aikoku?"

"Yes. That is the only one to ask for Aikoku."

Kimiuo Aisek, in 1980

"Strange, so many people died on the Aikoku, that there are not more to hold memorials." I wondered.

"You know, I don't know if they have the records of the Aikoku in Japan, who was on the Aikoku, what troops, the names and so on."

"I'm sure they know who died on the Aikoku." Kimiuo stared for a few moments out to the sea. He was moved. Every time we were talking about the Aikoku Maru it ended on a sombre note. I was sure he was thinking about his friend again. He did not say it, but I felt very strongly that he wished me to find out whether this man was still alive, or had perished with the ship. I made a mental note. It was really stirring, the compassionate love he held for his old friend. After a long while he bent down and took a sip out of the water bottle, and began: "On those commanding officers of the Base Force, they had their names on everything. All the department commanders put their name on equipment belonging to their outfit, but come to 1943, they don't put their name on anymore. You know, on the trucks, front of the entrance of their buildings, they always put the captain's name. Always the captain, commanding officer's name on bicycles, automobile or boat. But after 43, no more name. Number … they just put down the number. Maybe Number 41 is Naval Base, Number 13 - Harbor Division."

"41 was the Guard Unit." I had seen references to this unit before.

"Yes."

"No more names," I reiterated.

"Guard Unit 41 controls all the branches of the Naval Station. The headquarters was there on Dublon, but they got one on Moen, they too got one on Uman, every island they used to have this unit stationed. Even on the small islands. You know the gun emplacement, all people there come from the headquarters and the Naval Base as well. Ok, this Naval Base headquarters was under the Fourth Base headquarters. When they want to change something, they have to let Fourth Base headquarters know first. Actually, during Hara's time, he controls Fourth Base and Fourth Fleet, but no more fleet that time right after the raid. So actually he just control the Fourth Base, Base headquarters. And many of those captains, they got promoted, just before the war was over. I know the commander of the communications station was promoted to Rear Admiral. Of course, Muira was promoted to Rear Admiral, too. I think this guy on the Naval Station was promoted also. But no use anymore." He laughed, and sighed, dropping his shoulder, in a gesture of resignation.

"So many Rear Admirals?" I asked.

"So many. Just so many," he said earnestly.

"When did they get promoted?"

"I think in May, shortly before the war was over," Kimiuo said.

"Who promoted them?"

"Maybe Vice-Admiral Hara."

"Well they had nothing to do anymore. Right?" and I could vividly imagine the newly promoted Rear Admirals, commanding literally nothing; what a farce.

"No more," he confirmed.

If that was the case, I asked myself, how come they were, what appeared to be so grossly incompetent to have a valuable ship stranded on the reef, and not able to pull it off, and I phrased my ideas:

"One thing I don't understand is that they had this destroyer on the reef at Kuop. Grounded on Kuop, they couldn't pull it off. That was early February, before the raid, and they had everything intact then. You remember, the Tachikaze."

"We didn't knew even exactly where she went. Or she went down on the drop-off. You were mentioning about they were shooting at all the planes," Kimiuo said, but it did not really answer my question.

The reef in that area drops off very steeply, and there was a good chance that the stern was in very deep water, despite the fact that the bow was firmly grounded. I seemed natural that the Japanese would not go around broadcasting the stranding and immobilization of a destroyer. Therefore it may very well have been that Kimiuo did not hear about it. To run a ship aground is not considered a credit to the captain. I followed up by what I knew about her fate.

"And the second day it got destroyed. So I guess it just slipped off and…"

"Went down…" he added.

"…over the drop-off. You know, they had this big tug here, the fleet tug. Why the hell didn't they pull it off? It was sitting there so long. More than two weeks. Must have made a mistake navigating at night. If she went to South Pass and came from say Rabaul or Palau."

Unconsciously we both had turned around and faced south.

"Even if she came from Ponape or anyplace else. They still have to go around that way. Between Kuop and the reef of Truk, the tide is very dangerous for navigating at night. So she might go around the south side, then try to come up, but then hit the reef. I don't know. Sometimes we were mistaken too when we ran the same route."

"Funny, eh? Sometimes they make mistake, that's for sure."

A picture exists, an attack photo. It shows the destroyer over the reef, bow obviously in shallow water, and a barge tied to her port side. I was thinking that the Japanese might have tried to lighten the ship by stripping the foreship. At any rate, all efforts were futile. May be she sustained heavy damage to her hull. But there was no more information available from Kimiuo, so I changed the subject:

"The other day I was looking at some pictures. Actually they are also in Clark's little book. I believe they are of Dublon, this side, Naval Station. But there are still a few transports there, you know...end of April, first of May, that raid... They had the second big carrier raid, remember?"

"Yes," he said, but that did not get me anywhere.

"They really go for the ground," I said, meaning that at that time they attacked mainly ground installations.

"I think this was the 30 or 31st."

"31st and 1st. Remember, there is the difference in dates. They really go for the ground and storehouses. But this time the Japanese had a lot of planes in the air. So they built Truk up again after the first attack?" I asked.

"Yes. Same group of carriers?" he meant the attacking ships.

"Yes, almost other."

Kimiuo came back to the second raid.

"Okay, on that time it was very late. The siren went off at 6 o'clock. Everybody move to the shelter. I work for the Army then. On that same place where our family was living... you know where I was standing on the first day of the first attack ... they move the strongest guys there, then they put them there, close to shore, front line." Kimiuo said.

"For digging tunnels or what?"

I was lost. Why the strongest soldiers, and why at that spot, I thought.

"To stay there."

"Stay where?"

"What I told you, where I was during the first raid." Kimiuo meant where his family's house was.

"The strongest guys they put there? Why?" I really failed to see what he meant, and looked at him sheepishly.

"Because they going to defend that line over there. Front line."

"Oh, it became a defense line," I exclaimed.

"Yes. You know, in case of invasion, so they are the one who have to stop the attack."

Now it dawned on me. They selected the best fighters to man the first defenses.

"Right at the southern peninsula of Dublon? Where you stayed the first attack?"

"Northern peninsular and east end. That's where they put the strongest."

"Northeast." I said to be sure.

"Northeast. You know the point coming out facing to the battery. That's where they put those."

That was consistent with the Japanese expecting an invasion at the time.

"During the first attack, during the night?" I asked. But it was evident, that total chaos reigned during the first attack, while the Japanese prepared static defenses in the following weeks.

"No, later raid. The night of the 17th, the troops move out from Tol to Fefan, from Fefan to Dublon. Boy, those guys struggle, I tell you. They travel with wheel and their...what you call that? Just like the one the soldiers are towing in the Western films, with the wooden wheel."

Kimiuo struggled again for the proper word.

"The guns."

"The guns." Kimiuo stated, but I was not quite content. Soldiers do not drag real guns around, they are too heavy.

"Howitzers they're called." I added.

"The guns go on Nippo - those are good because those have tires, rubber tires. But those the troops were hauling are heavy, like the one on the bow of Seiko; they got wooden wheels. They got this piece of steel on the side and they make big scraping noise. You know the road on Dublon, nothing but crushed rock. Very difficult to move on and lousy road for guns. So they go through until night. Then come to this, the 18th, they remain. They stay where they are. Okay, now they call up everybody. Army. All together. Okay. This battalion code they have, the strongest guy they put from this side to the end. Defense, frontline now. Then I work for them. You know, when they came, we still got our house there. They move us. Move! Okay, you guys work for us. But I worked for the Navy I said. Work for us, the Army says. Then they try to come out, take us, take me. No more work for Navy. We need them here with the Army. I tell you, is really hard work for the Army. Hard working guys. Have to dig a hole here, a hole there, over there, up to the highest point. Sometimes I talk story and ask why is this? So they say, first of all we have to fight over there, you know, the first hole. Then move, come to the next one. When they come across, we move to the third one. Then we have to move to the fourth one, the fifth one and then move in. Then I asked them what about if they come from the other side. They go like that, Hara-kiri, that's it. But I tell you the difference between the Army and Navy. Navy, they're soft. Even in the war, they are soft, soft to the people. But not the Army." His eyes glistered.

"You mean soft to the people?" I asked.

"Yes, to the natives of the island. They're not so friendly, the Army. Of course they make friend, but not that friendly as the Navy. I don't know what kind of different rule they use."

Maybe for Kimiuo it was a matter of a book, of a rule. I rather thought it was a matter of attitude.

"So you dug these tunnels for guns or supplies or people or what?" I asked.

"Anything. For supply, for people to fight. We dig and dig, maybe from that coconut tree to here, then a long ... like ditch. I asked them what that was for. The tanks gonna come up and get in there, cannot go out anymore."

"Tank traps." I explained.

"Yes. And they were making the stone wall. Oh I tell you, that's the hardest work I ever done in my life when I was young. If you go on the island of Dublon, on the other side, you see the stone wall we built for defense." He looked at me straight, and in his eyes shone the strength of youth.

"Where is it, the stone wall?"

"In the place, but inland, not by the sea." Kimiuo said vaguely and absent-minded.

"How far inland?"

"Not that far."

"At the northeast peninsula?" I tried to narrow it down.

"Yes. Big, huge stones. Heavy!" He said.

"Built a wall?" I asked again.

"Very small wall, but is very amazing. When I look at it today, I think, 30 years ago I work on that wall. I just couldn't believe that the human man could move those rocks."

Kimiuo sat down, as if the memory of his hard work had exhausted him. I thought, it is always amazing, man's preoccupation with rocks. They built pyramids, places of warship. Cultures, long fallen into obscurity left their mark in stones, with that fulfilling their dream of eternity. And the native Trukese slaving for the military to build tank traps. But Kimiuo did not reflect too much about this topic and brought us back to a much nearer event:

"So let's get back to the talk of the attack. We waited, you know everybody went to the shelter and waited and waited. Maybe they don't come, we thought. Finally, machine guns, the sound of the airplanes. When will you get it? Oh, oh. And we got it again. This time they go for the buildings, they go for the gun emplacement, they go for land now."

"Bombs and board weapons from the planes?"

"Yes. These machine guns and board cannons, they are really strong. Punch holes through steel. Also the lighthouse there on Moen. They punch hoes in it."

Very true. One should go and see these clean gun shots through half inch steel. Or the scars on the gun on Eten. But not only that:

"So they set everything on flame?"

"On flame. You know that time when the Army moved their supply from Tol. What those guys in the planes do is burn the supplies down on that April raid. So much stuff, no caves, no warehouse to put everything, just lay on the side of the roads."

It seemed that once the Army had moved major units to Dublon there was not enough space to store their equipment and supplies safely, and they had left it in the open.

"All got spoiled." I had meant the equipment, but Kimiuo misunderstood me.

"No, not the food. But the ammunition and all the equipment, weapons, all burn down, fly away. Some kind of, I really don't know what to call that stuff, they dropped from the airplane. Is not a bomb, not exploding, but it built a fire. You know they drop it down, that thing make a popping noise and make the fire. That's how all this equipment catch fire. All ammunition and all the things blow up, burn up." Kimiuo remembered.

"Nepalm."

"Is that what they call that?" He had not heard of that dreadful substance.

"Like as if you put gasoline over it?"

"Right, exactly right. And some of them never go off. Then they open them looks like jelly inside, but smell of gasoline."

"It is jellied gasoline," I explained.

"First time I see that though. I never see that from the Japanese. That's the kind of stuff that burned down all the buildings. Burns the gun emplacement. Burns all the ammunition. Can you imagine, so much supply around Dublon because all over Dublon they just put their supplies. From the mountain to the soil, nothing but supply of ammunition and equipment and weapons. All destroyed. You can imagine about one island, this island full of weapon. Just think, that thing was burned down and also Fefan, which they tried to build up for the main supply place, plus those ships went down with many stuff."

"Also burning?"

I was not sure about Kimiuo's reference. There were two or three ships sunk on the second raid, but now we misunderstood each other, so Kimiuo continued.

"No. But those went down in February 17th. Then come to April, everything left over on the land. I think that's why they lose the war, because not very much left of equipment."

"They couldn't put it in shelters? Wheren' the shelters ready yet?" I asked.

"Tons by tons by tons." Kimiuo did not hear the question, so I asked again:

"But in the shelters it was okay."

"The stuff in the cave, that's okay. But under trees...hide them under trees, it was not okay. Of course, they do cover them with the canvas...all gone." He made his hands fly up. The only thing missing in his commentary was the sound 'puff', I thought.

"Did anymore ships sink then?" I asked.

"I don't know, according to some people they say there was some ships sunk that second raid."

"Hino No. 2." I stated.

"Oh yes. I don't see much ships that time. By that time I don't work for the Harbor Division anymore, so I could not see them."

There were a few, which could be seen on the attack photo.

"So much stuff got burned up. But Tol wasn't hit so bad?"

"Not that bad. They don't throw much bomb on those island. Of course they do throw some, but very few. But us, actually the people on Dublon move, they move them and people on Moen, they move them too."

He had never mentioned before that the Japanese moved the natives to other islands. It had been known from other atolls, so I asked:

"To Tol?"

"This one they move them to Udot. Some on Ramanoon. Some on Tol. Dublon they also move some to Tol and Udot. Very few of us remain on Dublon. I tell you, if there was an invasion of Dublon, maybe we all die with the Japanese. Because we mix up with them.

We stay with them, especially me."

"Where did you sleep? Did you have a little hut or what?"

"In the cave sometimes."

"That's lousy, isn't it!"

I wondered how many times they had moved, during the night, from the open into the caves, when a bomber raid appeared over Truk.

"Sort of..."

"I guess there must have been a lot of rats."

"No more. No rats that time. Come to the starving time, they eat anything. They're worse than us. Of course we do eat grass, but we choose what kind of grass we going to eat. Then they check the animal crawling on the trees or on the ground..."

"Lizards?"

"Lizard, yes. They inspect it. They say that's Vitamin B, good for you. They inspected the rat. Vitamin B, that's good for you. So they eat it almost everyday. That's why I say they're more worse than us, because we do eat grass, but we choose the kind of grass we going to eat."

"You knew from your parents which grass?" There must have been a lot of wisdom passed down from generation to generation.

"Oh yes. That time no more taro. Funny thing, not even anymore season for breadfruit that time. The season moving very slow. I don't know why."

"No more breadfruit?"

"Hard to get breadfruit. When the season comes up, sometime it lasts us four or five month. But during the war, just one month time, then no more. One and a half month there, then no more. So many people go for the fruit."

"Pick them when they're not ripe." I stated.

"Yes, exactly. We even pick them when its not the right time to pick." And this brought a disapproving expression in Kimiuo's face.

"Because if you don't pick it, somebody else will". Imagine the race for the small and unripe fruit.

"Yes. Actually turns out that you have to get permission to get fruit from your own tree. No more trees for you, no more soil for you, no more taro patch for you. You own nothing. Military owns everything."

"Who was doing the taro fields? Soldiers?"

"Yes, but after they eat up all the taros, there was nothing. You know taros are very slow to grow, you have to wait for that and it takes a year and a half. Then you can get taro. So they won't plant taro, not even a plant you can see, anymore. Some of the other island like Tol, Pollo, Udot, they do have taro. But not on Dublon or Moen anymore. So what they do, they grow this thing called watercress. That's what the have....You have one coconut, a hard one they bring from Tol or Udot, you know how much cost one coconut? The hard one? 250 yen. If you can see one."

It is bad to pay for a coconut, to begin with, but a hard one, to boot?

"That's a lot of money then." I guessed, not knowing the real value of money in Truk at the time.

"They give us very small pay, but nowhere to spend. So even one coconut, if you can see, 250 or 300 yen, you buy. You know they have one coconut, take the money. Actually, not very much people care for money that time. Most of us only care for food."

"Sure. You cannot eat money."

Kimiuo had experienced classic monetary problems and laws, but that did not interest him.

"So everybody turned to farming, from the high ranking officer to the low ranking man. Everybody turns to farmer. Somehow someone thinking that everybody has to go plant potatoes. You don't plant potatoes, they slap you or ... so everybody go for the potatoes. That's how we survive. First we eat the leaves of the potatoes. Then when we cut the potatoes, we have the roots. Then you know what, come to the end of the war, they still have plenty canned stuff. Plenty rice, but most of the rice grains are empty, all eaten up by the rice insects. So when you put in the water, everything floats up. But you have to wash and cook them. Still good."

"But a lot of damage to the food," I confirmed.

"Then the Americans came and brought the food when the war was over. At that time, the Japanese bring out the canned food, everything. There is still some, but they still hoarding it instead of eating it because they were thinking on the last assault if they invade the island, that's the time they are going to divide the food to everybody, to all the soldiers. At first when the potatoes came, then instead of eating rice, they all go for the potatoes."

"What kind of cans did they have?"

"Can of sardines, salmon and whale and beef. Oh their roast beef was very good. The whale meat can was pretty big. It tasted very good, very delicious. You know how they prepare, with soya and sugar."

"Did you eat octopus?" I asked.

"Yes." He nodded.

"How did you catch them?"

"We go to the reef. We see them in the hole. And then we spear them."

"Never seen any here. How do you eat them?"

"Boil them. Then we flavor them with coconut or we just put soya and lime on it. The best way to cook is to boil them first, then slice thin and cook in coconut milk. That's very tender." Kimiuo replied.

"They never go big style for fish." The Japanese, I meant, during the war.

"They do. Some fishermen do. Every unit go fishing. Of course, the local fishermen still going with their fishing boat, together with Japanese fisher. They come back, they sell it to the supply division."

"They were still fishing, the fishing boats?" I asked.

"Yes, but they don't fish for us, they fish for military only."

"Same time fishing for submarines."

"I think so. Convert the boats. Chase subs. Put a gun on it. Put depth charge on it, and try to get subs. How to win the war this way?"

That salient comment by Kimiuo ended our talk. I went to the ruins of the fishery, and promptly got attacked by millions of mosquitos. Nevertheless, I was standing, thinking of the tremendous waste which had occurred here... .

PART THREE
THE SHIPWRECKS

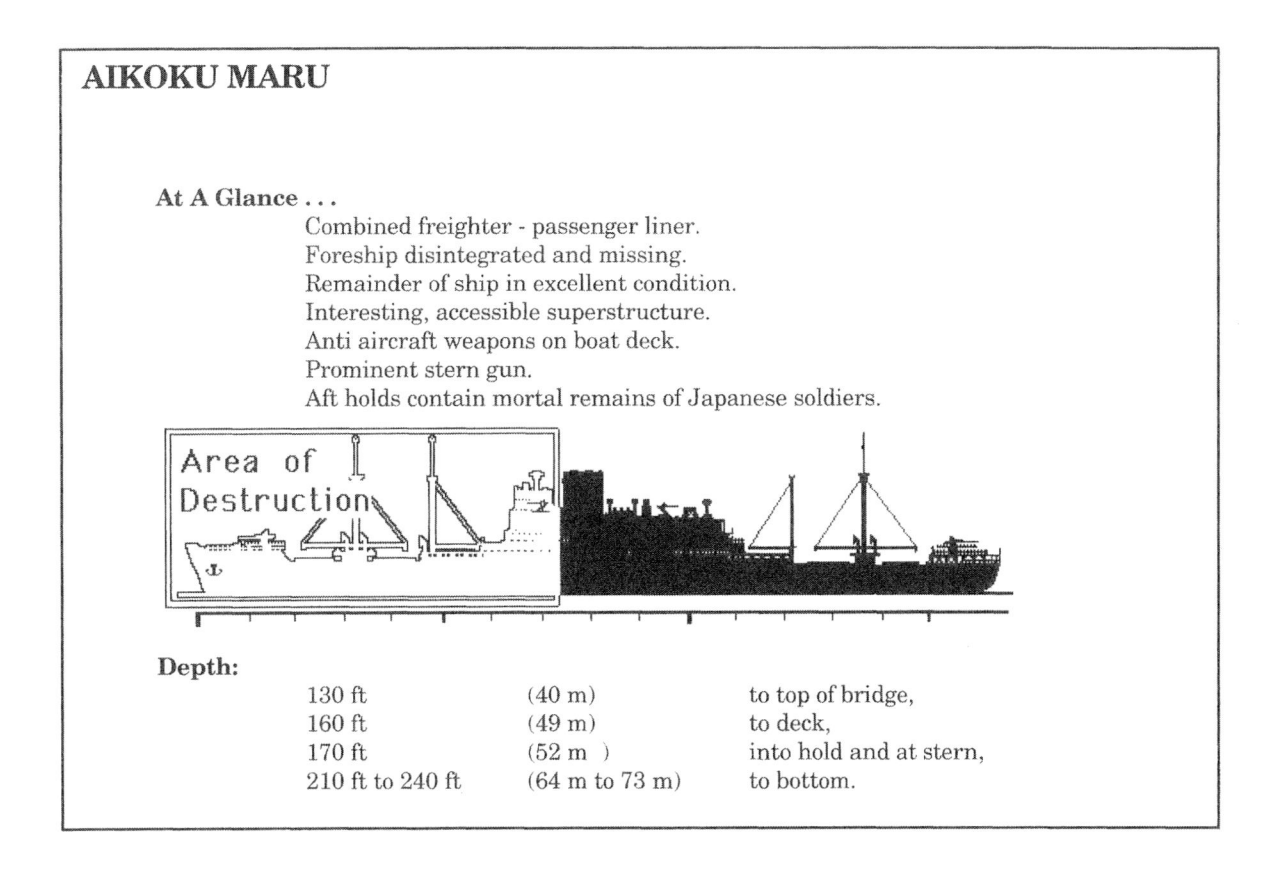

AIKOKU MARU

At A Glance ...
- Combined freighter - passenger liner.
- Foreship disintegrated and missing.
- Remainder of ship in excellent condition.
- Interesting, accessible superstructure.
- Anti aircraft weapons on boat deck.
- Prominent stern gun.
- Aft holds contain mortal remains of Japanese soldiers.

Depth:

130 ft	(40 m)	to top of bridge,
160 ft	(49 m)	to deck,
170 ft	(52 m)	into hold and at stern,
210 ft to 240 ft	(64 m to 73 m)	to bottom.

The Aikoku Maru is the most magnificent wreck in Truk. Despite the fact that the foreship is gone and the forward part of the superstructure is heavily damaged, the lines of this ship have class. The modern OSK - liner never entered civilian service. Shortly before fitting out of the ship was completed, the Navy took her over for an active role in the war. Violence begat violence. The Aikoku Maru captured and sank enemy ships. Finally, she blew up in a spectacular explosion, which reached out and killed the attacker.

Today, the forward part of the superstructure, in front of the stout stack, plunges almost vertically from the navigation bridge to the sea bottom. The hull is severed here. Large pieces of the shell plating remain attached to the starboard beam forward, however, the area conveys the impression of utter destruction. Bulkheads of the superstructure, formerly vertical, are pushed backwards.

It all looks as if a huge hammer has pounded against the remaining part of the bridge. The navigation deck and the decks below are bent down with great force. Their forward facing bulkheads, which lent the elegant appearance to the ship, are obliterated.

The ship rests in a shallow depression of the sea bed, which is deeper in the area where the foreship once was. This is the result of a terrific explosion in the forward holds. The magazines for the gun were located in those holds. In addition, mines, ammunitions, bombs and other high explosives were carried.

There are two different scenarios. Both differ only in some details. They have been related to by crew members of the Akitsushima, which was anchored about two miles away from the Aikoku Maru, and a Japanese soldier, who survived the explosion because he was transferred from the ship to Dublon in the early morning. In both scenarios it may be assumed that a secondary explosion resulted in a catastrophic detonation, totally ripping up the foreship. The debris was hurled high into the air and fell like rain around a mushroom cloud. When the smoke cleared the rest of the ship had disappeared, and only white water and a veil of smoke drifting downwind marked the spot where the Aikoku Maru had anchored. With the ship, everybody aboard perished, without exception.

The explosion was so violent that not even traces of the foreship have been found, although several searches were made, except perhaps for a corner of a hatchway.

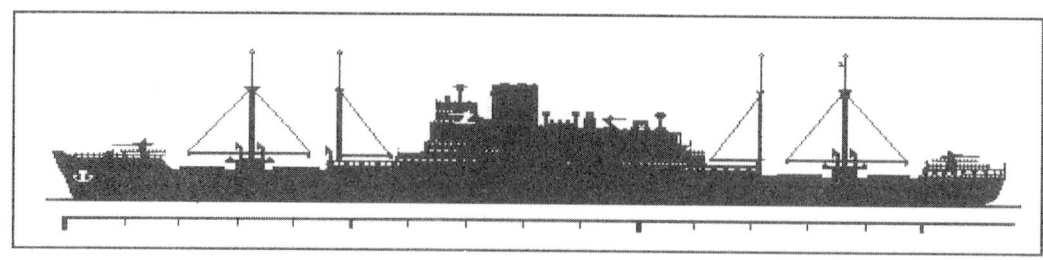

Hailstorm - *The Wrecks*

As mentioned there are other possibilities to explain the disintegration of the large ship. These two other explanations have one thing in common: They involve the disappearance of an attacking airplane. Legend has it that in the air above, an aircraft which made a run on the ship, was hit by the shock wave of the explosion. The plane disintegrated in mid-air, and the plane was lost. A few facts lend some credence to this story, as a plane, an Avenger from the carrier Intrepid, was lost during this flight, and none of the other pilots saw it disappear. There was nobody who could account for the Avenger, piloted by Lt. Briggs, and his crew of two.

The Japanese accounts differ somewhat in the sequence of events. An eyewitness on board the Akitsushima, an Emily seaplane tender, at that time used for general cargo transport from Truk to the outlying garrisons, related that the explosion of the Aikoku occurred later then the attack by Avengers from Essex. He confirmed the attack, but said, that immediately following this attack a single plane spun out of control while on the approach to the Aikoku Maru. This plane, he believed, had been hit by anti aircraft fire from Dublon. This plane crashed into the bridge of the ship and fell as a flaming wreck into the forward hold. Only afterwards did the Aikoku explode violently.

The effects of the explosion do not allow an analysis of the sequence of events. All traces are lost beyond retrieval and we will never find out whether the explosion was caused by a bomb or torpedo hit or whether the hapless Avenger of Lt. Briggs disintegrated in mid air or was hit by anti-aircraft fire and splashed into the ship. The explosion was so forceful that all traces have been obliterated.

Midship

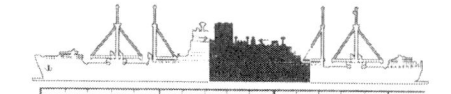

The bridge itself is more or less gone. Only parts of its decks are hanging down. The structure on top of the superstructure, next to the break in the hull, is the smoke stack. It towers unscathed above all. Considering the violence of the explosion and the extensive damages to the foreship and the midship it is just inconceivable that the stack remained standing without apparent damages.

Nothing is left of the life boats abaft of the stack at the edge of the boat deck. Remains of the engine skylights can be seen slightly behind the funnel, and further aft, a twin barrel anti-aircraft automatic weapon is positioned on each side of the sun deck. These guns have been fastened to special reinforcements of the deck plating, and therefore remained in their original position.

These weapons were twin mounted 13.2 mm (.52 inch) Type 93 anti-aircraft guns. They were air cooled and gas operated, originally based on a Hotchkiss design. Maximum range was 6000m (6560 yards) and they had an effective ceiling against aircraft of 3980 m (13 060 ft) when the barrels were elevated 85 degrees. These were not particularly effective weapons due to their small calibre and the light, non-explosive round they fired. In most cases when the American aircraft were hit they shrugged it off and were able to return to base. It was a different matter, of course, if the pilot was hit.

The starboard twin gun clearly shows that it had been in action up to the last second. Ready ammunition is lying next to it on deck. The barrels point up steeply. At the moment of the explosion, the gun had been shooting at planes making a bombing run on the ship.

On the gun on port, both barrels are in the depressed position. One of the two barrels appears to be shorter than the other. This is proof, that the weapon has been fired to the last second. The barrels alternate during shooting. After a round has been fired, the barrel moves back to expel the spent cartridge and to receive the next round. It may be assumed that this gun was in action against a low flying plane, and the firing sequence was interrupted just at the time of the explosion. Computer analysis of an attack photo of the Forth Fleet Anchorage, with Aikoku Maru being prominent, shows that smoke came from the stack and from the location of the two guns.

A large structure has been erected abaft of the anti-aircraft guns, forward of the slightly rounded boat deck amidships. It is about 8 feet (2,20 m) high and is heavily overgrown with sessile marine life. Evidently, this object was a search light platform, but could have been also part of the fire control system.

It is not difficult to enter the various decks below sun deck. Maindeck, shelter deck, promenade deck and the sun deck can be seen. The former three have passageways on both sides, while on sun deck the ship shows an array of ventilators, fan housings, ventilation trunks and the guns with the stack and skylights. Promenade deck shows a fairly wide passageway alongside the superstructure, and the sides are secured with rail guards.

Several doorways can be used to enter the inside of the ship. The walkways on shelter deck are comparatively narrow, and are protected by a high bulwark. There are two doorways leading inboard. The maindeck passageway is inboard and windows are showing in regular intervals. However, it appears that part of the openings on maindeck aft have been plated over during the ship's second refitting in 1943.

Penetration into the superstructure requires cool nerves and a fair acquaintance with the general outlay of a ship of this type. The author, with the benefit of blueprints of the ship, made several penetrations. The doorways leading into the ship are all open now. The doors on the upper decks were made out of wood, and have long since rotted away. Dim light coming from the other side of the ship can be seen when one of these narrow doorways on promenade deck is entered. Strands of electric cable hang from the deckhead, and are in the way, when swimming through one of the doors into the passageway inboard. These cables are remnants of the circuitry. Originally, they were clamped to the deckhead but some of the fasteners corroded away, allowing part of the cables to fall down, and the conduits form large hanging loops.

It is easy to get entangled in them, and therefore a reliable underwater light must be taken along, to see, and to avoid, the traps. Dodging them, a doorway will be reached which faces forward. It terminates into a small bathroom, called head on board. Inside is a sink, which has broken loose from the bulkhead, and tumbled down, taking its pipes down with it. It lies on its edge and is filled with brown sediment. This sediment, indicative of a large quantity of organic material in this area, such a carpets, wood partitions and ceilings, furniture and other things, is quite high and stirs up very quickly.

The spacious main cabin midships will be entered, after the head has been passed, and the passageway followed farther in-board. Size and position of this room suggests that it has been the smoke saloon, any partitions have gone. After the almost total darkness of the passageway, the saloon seems well lit. Light comes in from the windows facing aft. The glass is gone, of course, but the window partition are still in place. The room is wide open. Cables are hanging from the deckhead here as well. They can be easily avoided. The sediment on the deck is very thick.

When exiting through the aft windows, the small promenade deck will be reached. This small extension of the deck has a semi-circular shape. Rail guards and stays are in place at its aft edge. The first hold aft can be seen from here when looking down. The kingpost looms in the hazy blue distance.

When back-tracking outside of the superstructure on port, it can be noticed that the passageways and windows at the second deck are narrower than those one deck higher. The doorways in this passageway are open as well, as the wooden doors have disappeared. Upon entering one of the doorways the first thing that comes into view is a head and a bathroom on the left. It is a little more elaborate than the one a deck above, and contains a tiled bathtub and a sink with a ceramic cistern. Both are still fastened to the bulkhead. The tub and the sink are filled to the brim with fine brown sediment, which has settled here over the decades. A strange looking white sponge grows on the bulkhead.

Continuing to swim inboard, a second doorway comes into view. No light penetrates to this area and it is pitch black in this room. The beam of the underwater light shows a second bathroom with tub and sink. The knee of a large ventilator pipe has fallen on top of the sink and covers it almost completely. Hanging cables present obstacles, also in this room. These wires are menacing traps and can easily entangle in a tank valve. It takes slow and deliberate maneuvering with minimum fin action to get around them. Great care must also be exercised not to move around too much. The brown sediment stirs up with the slightest movement. Particles, in size from fine dust to fist sized pieces, are loosened from the deck head by the exhalation bubbles, and rain down. The originally clear water will soon be muddied, and visibility will become poor. It may lead to the danger of disorientation.

The visit into the compartments midships on shelter and promenade deck is breathtaking. A lot of light shines in from the large aft windows. The immediate attention is focussed on a sink, located right in the middle of the room, standing all by itself, and resting on its drain pipe. Close inspection of the bottom of this room reveals traces of plywood partitions, which have disintegrated long ago. They have divided this room into individual staterooms. The cables, hanging from the ceiling, are reminiscent of garlands decorating a ballroom. Doorways show their black rectangular frames, leading starboard and forward into a maze of other cabins.

An interesting object can be found when diving through the passageway on starboard shelter deck. It is just wide enough for a diver to swim through comfortably. About midships, slightly aft and below the smoke stack, an object can be seen in the dark, hanging from the deckhead. It is the ship's bell. It is firmly attached to the ceiling, almost a foot (30 cm) in diameter, and does not move at all.

The ship's galley is located underneath the promenade deck aft. A huge stove and other utensils for the work of the cook can be found here. A long sink has crashed to the deck when its wooden base disintegrated. The faucets which delivered hot and cold water to the sink remained firmly attached to the bulkhead, together with their pipes. Many bottles can be found at the base of the sink. It takes only little imagination to imagine that there were soy sauce bottles, but it is surprising that they were left intact considering the violence of the explosion. There are certainly many more objects buried in the sediment here. Other debris is scattered around in the cabin forward of the galley.

In a particular spot a lot of frame-like structures can be seen. From their angular shapes it may be deduced that these are the remains of closets or cupboards. Furniture steel reinforcement edges complete this still life. This room has been the mess. Swimming around to the aft part of the superstructure, and continuing forward on port in the passageway above shelter deck, a rather wide steel double door will be reached. Originally it was closed. This door is a bit recessed into the bulkhead, and the corners are well rounded. The pressure of the explosion opened the top of one wing and rolled it open like a sardine can top.

Generally, the passageway is easy to swim through between the bulwark and the superstructure, but it is remarkable that there are many pieces of steel plating lying around on deck. They have been flung here from the foreship when it disintegrated, and are yet another indication of the ferocity of the blast. A large, twisted steel plate rests on the promenade deck right over the first of the aft holds, on port. At shelter

Hailstorm - *The Wrecks*

deck, forward of the first aft hold, three doorways are built into the bulkhead. The middle one leads to a fairly small cabin which does not have another exit. The one on starboard can be entered easily. It leads forward inboard on shelter deck level. Although this inside passageway appears spacious, many cables hang from the ceiling and are running in large loops parallel to the engine casing.

Individual staterooms had been constructed at the outside bulkhead. Their partitions are gone, but each had a window. It is easy to swim alongside the the engine room casing. Two wide doorways lead to the outside passageway. They are flanked by steel partitions which show large, symmetrically arranged lighting holes, to save weight.

There is no way out forward, as the bulkheads are totally destroyed in that area. It is necessary to turn back, and, if the the cables are dodged, the doorway may be used to exit. It is also possible to descend one deck through a companionway. This would be the forward passageway on maindeck. Certainly, part of the wreck is considerably darker, but otherwise very similar to the arrangement on shelter deck. At the forward part, a large panel of steam valves can be seen at the engine casing.

At this level it is possible to exit forward. It is a bit frightening to look at this area of total destruction, right at the torn off forward part of the superstructure. Approaching the area somewhat gingerly where the light comes in in the hope to find an exit and not to have to go back again through the passageway, access to the free water finally is gained by weaving around a number of torn and twisted sheets of steel, devoid of any regular form.

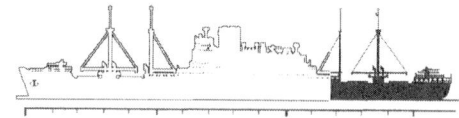

Aftship

The hatchway of the first of the aft holds looks small, compared to other ships similar in size to the Aikoku Maru. It is elevated one deck over main deck. Swimming across it, the winch house will be reached. An open doorway faces forward, towards the approaching diver. Two large electric motors, cargo winches, and blowers take up about all the space inside. The substantial electrical circuits remained in their places.

Instead of the normal arrangements of tween decks inside the hold, bulkheads on all four sides lead straight down. The hatch has the appearance of a shaft. The bulkheads are bent inward on their forward and starboard sides, witness of the forces of destruction which tore the ship apart. Only below, tween decks have been built onto the sides of the hull.

On days with good visibility, a few large objects can be seen on the bottom of the hold. It is too deep however, to take a close look, and they could not be identified. Two levels of hatch cover beams in this hold remained in their place and are heavily overgrown with many forms of sessile sea life. In fact, they are so closely spaced that they are singularly uninviting to swim around and down in the hatch. It is therefore not surprising that the tween deck accommodations were not discovered earlier.

A doorway opening can be seen and is very dangerous to enter. The sediment in the cabin is about 25 cm (10") deep and stirs up with the slightest movement. Together with the brown "rain" from the deckhead, visibility will be immediately reduced and orientation will be quickly lost. Since the cabin has several dark corners and passages leading further away from the entrance into the black, partly obstructed insides of the lower part of the superstructure, penetration is strongly discouraged.

At the entrance, three skulls are resting among the many bones of skeletons. They are partially buried in the thick sediment. Remnants of bunks can be recognized as straight lines, parallel to the bulkheads. On the right, a few lines up the inside bulkhead indicate where the bunks were originally fastened.

A few skulls, bones, but also bottles and bales probably tightly folded blankets protrude above the sediment inside the cabin, near the middle as well as on both lateral bulkheads. The numbers of human remains increase towards forward, where eventually the left bulkhead recesses in a curve and continues at a right angle, athwartship.

Now more and more bones come into view, up to the point where the deck is covered with them. The sediment now becomes much thicker and forms a large mound, from which a few plates protrude. On the side of this mound there are so many mortal remains that they are heaped on top of each other. The area is several yards long and at least 5 yards wide. A 60 cm (2 ft) high open sided box stands on its end. It is surrounded by more skeletons.

Several shoes are scattered at the base of the box, and a white ceramic object is buried here. The box appears to be made of wood which has withstood the immersion in sea water quite well, except on the top where some of it has rotted away. An X-frame 60 cm (2 ft) high, is standing a short distance from the box. A few wooden sheets, probably plywood and conceivably the remains of a table top, can be seen here as well. Forward, the bulkhead is bent and twisted, and partially blown out to aft, showing the devastating force of the big shock wave.

Forward of the box and to the left, a recess can be recognized. A large, glaring-white sink is mounted on the bulkhead. Deep at the dark forward side, to the left of the sink, a table remains standing, tilted to aft. Several bottles can be found on the table top which is covered by a few inches of sediment. Messkits, porcelain objects (probably broken plates), bowls and cups and a lot of wood pieces are dispersed among the bones here. Long, thin, red-brown stalactites hang from the deckhead at many places. To the left, a passageway and a companionway are recognizable. They are impassable because the clearing to the sediment is only about 30 cm (1 ft). A complete skeleton lies here. The darkness is complete and oppressive. The bones become fewer while advancing athwart, but a metal frame and wood can be seen. Another corner is reached, and the following cabin is a mirror image of the one on the other side. Bones are scattered in the sediment, among the remnants of bunks and blankets.

A small window allows a little light to filter in, but it is totally impossible to exit here. After a few more yards, yet another corner must be followed, and immediately another large grave site comes into view.

Many soldiers perished here aft, just as many as forward. Two tiers of bunks are mounted on the bulkhead. Because of their location, deep inside the ship, they are a little better preserved than those observed earlier. The remains of the upper bunk has sagged onto the lower one on one side. The exit may be located by going around another corner, following a companionway a short distance, ascending one deck, and following a passageway aft (forward is obstructed by torn bulkheads). Then passing a few heads and Japanese baths on both sides, finally the main deck is reached. The heavy bulkhead steel door has been ripped out and flung several feet aft by the explosion.

As can be gathered from the description, the grave sites are deep inside the Aikoku Maru, penetration is strongly discouraged, firstly because the graves should not be disturbed and secondly, its is totally dark, with one exit only and many dead ends and traps. The mortal remains of the fallen soldiers of the Aikoku Maru should not be disturbed. Piety and dignity simply forbid touching or moving any of them. The ship is a grave site with beautiful soft corals, like flowers, growing at the entrances, and it is only fitting to observe respect for the dead.

The author discovered the tween deck accommodations and the remains of the Japanese soldiers on August 2, 1979, and made deep penetrations to record the mortal remains during that year, and on 14 separate dives in 1980, 1981, 1982 and 1984. During the documentation of the grave site, we never touched any of the bones, but we always placed flowers there and observed a one minute silence, to honor the fallen soldiers, despite the premium of time at these depths. As it is the custom, and of great spiritual importance for the Japanese to recover the mortal remains of their dead, to afford them a ceremonial burial, Al Giddings was able to persuade the Japanese officials, after they had been officially notified through Dr. Yamada and the author, to recover the bones, and to make a commercial film about the recovery and the cremation, in 1984-1985. However, not all bones were recovered and those in the adjoining rooms remain there, as the soldiers died.

From inside the tween deck accommodation, two doorways lead forward on starboard and port farther into the ship. The bulkheads, particularly on port, are badly mangled and the deckheads are lowered, so that the doorway is only about 3 to 4 feet high, where it used to be six and a half feet. The cabin on port contains a complete set of bones to the right of the doorway, and there are a large number of bales, probably blankets and linen, littering the deck. A break in the deck allows a glimpse onto the next lower deck. This area is part of the midship superstructure, and there are further decks dividing the ship. It is doubtful that this room has been checked by the recovery team. Another smaller cabin is to the right, toward midship.

On the other side of the ship access can be gained to further accommodations and deck levels, while in the middle there used to be a companionway, and evidently a head, there is a white ceramic sink. The area is in shambles, but as there are more accommodations forward, it is certain that there are more human remains here, as well as in the engine room.

The second hold aft is built conventionally with tween decks on the sides. There are shelves mounted on the forward bulkheads of which only traces remain now. Two sculls may be seen in the forward part of the port tween deck. Two femurs are resting nearby, one is broken, evidence of a violent death. The other bones are buried in the sediment.

There is a Japanese toilet bowl resting on its side, near the middle of the tween deck where it had been flung. At one end of the open hold, two cylinders can be seen. They look very much like wire fencing rolled up into a coil. Next to them, close to the hatch coaming of the tween deck, two urinals are lying on their mounting side. A large shovel blade lies next to a few layers of plywood, or a layered object resembling it, and a semi-crumbled, torpedo shaped cargo net. Between the cylinders and the net, a complete skeleton came to rest. Aft of the net, shards of porcelain, another coil, a bale of fabric and several other items lie close together. All these items may now be disturbed and the bones recovered 1984.

The bottom of this hold appears to be empty. It is, however, too deep to penetrate to the bottom of the hold and the lower tween decks. This area is beyond the reach of sport diving. The Exceptional Exposure Tables must be used, and they carry a heavy penalty of decompression, and a high risk. Even a strong underwater light can not penetrate the thick layer of colloidal suspended matter in that area, which shows up as thick fog in the beam of an underwater light.

The third and aftermost hold is small by comparison to the previous two. The hull carries a deck house aft. The aft deck house is built around the rear part of the hatchway, in the shape of a horse-shoe. A covered passageway was formed by extending the deck head on both sides and supporting it with vertical extensions of the bulwark. There are two ladders which lead from shelter deck to the upper level of the deck house. The one on port is bent.

The deck of the large aft superstructure extends over the width of the ship and forms wide, covered passageways on both sides of the stern. A gun platform has been built on top of its second deck. The platform is about 10 ft (3 m) wide and reaches almost to the stern. A big gun is placed on it, and can be seen from quite a distance. Evidently, it is a 8 cm High Angle Gun Type 88, design year 1928. This type of gun was frequently fitted on auxiliaries. This not particularly modern artillery piece has a an effective calibre of 7,62 cm/L 40, and could fire a shell of 5,67 kg or 12 and a half pound 10.800 m or 11800 yards or about 7.200 m (23.600 ft) high into the air at an elevation of 75 degrees. The gun is trained over port beam with an elevation of about 60 degrees, indicating that it was firing at aircraft at the time of the attack. The gun is the dominating feature on the stern. It does not have a shield. Barrel and lock are overgrown with sessile forms of marine life.

The magnificent hydroids and many coral sponges provide shelter to many small fish, which swim rather unconcerned around this weapon. Only the click of a camera shutter and the flash seem to signal danger to them, and then they dart back to their hiding places among the corals of the gun. This is one of the two high-trajectory guns with which the ship was fitted. The second was mounted on the forecastle and has disappeared in the explosion. This armament, and the machine weapons on sun deck, reflect the changed defense objectives for the Japanese forces at that time: Defense against enemy aircraft.

On the aft deck house, a narrow tapering catwalk is built at the stern of the ship. Rail guards lead around it. It was originally planked with wood. The Aikoku Maru has a cruiser stern and large twin propellers. They are buried up to their hub in sand. The ship itself lies in a depression of the sea bed. On both sides the sea floor rises slightly, dips forward, but it is beyond the normal swimming range of a diver. Only on days with extremely good underwater visibility can this underwater panorama be seen and appreciated. It is very probable that a crater was carved out by the tremendous explosion. Sand and sediments slowly fill the depression, and reach already about eight feet up the hull.

It is quite interesting to dive inside the passageway of the aft superstructure. There are fairleads built into the bulwark, with mooring bits mounted behind them. A capstan and a winch are fastened to the bulkhead of the deck house. Several doorways are tightly closed, except for one, which leads inside the totally dark deck house. There is a lot of suspended matter in the water here, and even the beam of an underwater light does not penetrate far. A companionway leads below deck and disappears in the haze.

There have been shadows spotted on the sea bed astern of the ship. At one time we were convinced that one of the two landing crafts had been located. It was tied to the stern at the time of the explosion, and nothing has been seen of it ever since. This landing craft can also clearly be seen in an attack photo as a small shadow at the stern. The other craft was reportedly on its way back from the ship to Dublon pier, with soldiers on board. It was said that all but the two men inside the bridge of this small vessel were killed in the explosion and that the survivors received eye injuries from the flash. The craft, being almost halfway between the ship and the island, went more or less out of control but the men just managed to run it up the beach on Dublon.

During the searches in July 1980 and January 1981 it was discovered that the two shadows are parts of one of the forward goalposts. The two masts were torn out and hurled past the aftship. The bigger piece looks like a large, inverted umbrella. The post held just a few fractions of a second longer than the rest of the deck to which it was fastened. The sturdy deck reinforcements remained attached to the mast. In the few fractions of a second, when the deck plating was bent up by the pressure and tore off, the mast followed then and broke off as well, and was sent flying with the bent-up deck plates and supports still attached. This mast is really one part of the goal post and is bent at the top, but some of its original horizontal member is still attached. Nearby, the other half rests on the sand. There are a few other shadows, which we discovered, but they all turned out to be large pieces of unidentifiable debris, mostly shell plating, from the foreship. The landing craft has not been found.

During the searches for the Momokawa Maru in 1982, a fairly large fragment was found nearly 800 m north of the Aikoku. It turned out to be a 15 m by 10 m corner of a hatch coaming with attached shell and deck plating. It is amazing that such a big piece could be catapulted through the air for such a long distance.

Because of the great depth, descents on the Aikoku Maru should be done only with very experienced divers. The decompression problems involved require knowledge and peak physical condition. It is quite common to experience significant nitrogen narcosis, and as there are many traps in the superstructure, this ship is generally considered beyond sport diving limits.

Aikoku Maru, together with her two sisterships, Gokoku Maru and Hokoku Maru, were the finest cargo-passenger liners the Japanese built just prior to the war. They had excellent stability, were powered by large diesel engines, which transmitted their power on to two propellers. The ships reached over 20 knots at maximum speed. This was quite a considerable speed for their time. Even when cruising at 17 knots they could outrun almost all merchant ships then.

Originally, these ships were intended for the Japan-Africa liner service, but probably only the Hokoku Maru, which was finished first, made a trip on that service. The Hokoku Maru, Gokoku Maru, and

Hailstorm - *The Wrecks*

later Aikoku Maru were then used exclusively in Japanese dominated waters. Gokoku Maru and Hokoku Maru sailed between Japan and Manchuria.

All three of these excellent ships were lost in the war. As the Aikoku Maru was completed only at

inally, they were able to shoot a projectile of 100 lbs (45.4kg) 22,970 yds (21.000 m) at a 45 degree elevation.

Two twin barreled 13 mm machine weapons were placed on both sides of the bridge and abaft the funnel on the boat deck, but it is not certain when these

Aikoku Maru 1942, in the dual role as merchand raider and subtender, in Penang, probably 1942. The ship [IWM] carries dazzle paint, and sorties into the Indian Ocean. The gun can be identified as an old cruiser-type 14 cm breech loader. Another gun can be seen on the welldeck, another farther aft on shelterdeck, pointing aft.

the end of August 1941, she did not enter civilian service at all. The accommodations for 48 First Class passengers were luxuriously and spaciously furnished, better than, of course, those for the 48 "Special" Third Class and 304 "Regular" Third Class. However, fitting out for the First Class passengers was never completed, because it was clear that the ship would be taken over by the Japanese Navy.

When the three sisterships were laid down they were built with special deck reinforcements. They were designed to bear the load of guns to be mounted on the decks of the foreship. Heavy derricks were fitted to handle float planes at the aft kingposts. Indeed, shortly before the outbreak of the war, the Aikoku Maru was taken in hand by the Navy and converted to an armed merchant raider.

Immediately, the ships were armed very heavily, albeit with ancient guns. There was a gun each placed on platforms on the forecastle and the poop. One pair was on both sides athwart hold 2 on main deck, a second pair port and starboard hold 3 on shelter deck, and most likely the third pair just aft of the superstructure athwart hold 4 on shelter deck. The records indicate that the main armament originally was 8 - 15 cm guns, old cruiser guns of Sino-Japan War vintage, built by Vickers, England or copied under the name Type 41st Year Gun, design year 1908. Nom-

weapons where installed first. Evidence suggests that there were two twin torpedo launchers mounted on main deck aft of the superstructure athwart hold 5. A wartime photograph shows two float planes on the ship, carried on the hatch of hold 4, and on hold 5.

The original base of the Aikoku Maru as fleet auxiliary was Kure. She was part of Special Cruiser Squadron 24, (24 Sentai) under the direct command of the Commander Combined Fleet, Admiral Yamamoto. This squadron consisted of Aikoku Maru, Hokoku Maru and Kiyozumi Maru. The first sorties of the Aikoku Maru, in tandem with the Hokoku Maru, were reasonably successful. She destroyed two American ships. During the late hours of 12 December 1941, the 6120 ts United States Lines ship, SS Vincent was sighted, a long distance northeast from Pitcairn Island. The ship managed to radio her position before two warning shots were fired by the Hokoku Maru. The crew abandoned the Vincent, were taken aboard the raiders and the ship sunk.

On 31 December 1941, a float plane from the raiders sighted the Malama. This ship carried a cargo of trucks, trailers and a lot of aircraft spares. The plane disappeared completely and was lost, but not before it had broadcasted the position of the Malama. On New Year's Day 1942 a second plane appeared from the raiders with the intention to bomb the ship but insisted

Hailstorm - *The Wrecks*

that the crew abandon her. They did so in the face of warning machine gun fire from the plane, but opened the sea cocks and scuttled her. The area was south of Tahiti. Aikoku and Hokoku Maru then retired to Japan via Truk. After their arrival the "24 Sentai" were decommissioned and the ships re-rated as "attached" ships to the Combined Fleet. They were now: submarine tenders and merchant raiders.

During a refit at the Kure Naval Yard the old

resting place is about a mile south of the Aikoku Maru.

At a later raid - the two ships were operating in tandem again - they approached a sizeable merchant ship on 11 November 1942. It was the Dutch tanker Ondina. A small minesweeper of the Royal Indian Navy, the Bengal, a vessel of only 733 ts, armed with a single 7,5 cm gun, fought valiantly in the ensuing battle with the total armament 16 - 14 cm guns against 1 - 7.6 cm gun, and scored a hit on the Hokoku Maru.

After the fall of Singapore, the Aikoku Maru was temporarily based there. She is seen here in Seletar on 29 July 1942.

guns were replaced with more modern 14 cm, cal 50 guns. These were Third Year Type (1914) breach loaders, and handed down also probably from secondary armament of battleships. However, they were used to arm the Sendai-Class light cruisers. The guns had a maximum range of up to 21,600 yards (19.750 m) at 35 degrees elevation. The slightly smaller range compared to the previous armament was insignificant. It is doubtful that the guns would be shooting accurately and the fire control system was certainly not as well developed as on a warship. At the same time, Rufe float planes were taken on board, instead of the antiquated Type 94 aircraft. The ship's base was shifted to Singapore, which had fallen quickly under the skillful attack of the Japanese army under General Yamashita on 15 February 1942. Her anchorage was at Seletar, in the North of Singapore, in waters which separate Malaya and Singapore. Since Malaya had fallen as well, and Penang was secured, it was decided to have an advanced base there. Penang offered advantageous access to the Indian Ocean, which was to become the next hunting ground.

In their dual role Aikoku and Hokoku Maru serviced submarines in the southern part of the Indian Ocean. During their sorties they captured the 7986 ts Dutch motor tanker Genota on 09 May 1942, sank the Elysia off Durban, South Africa on 05 June 1942, and captured another ship with the name of Hauraki. The Genota, built in Germany in 1935, was taken over by the Japanese Navy as a fleet oiler, and commissioned on 20 07 42, renamed Ose Maru. The ship sank in Palau during an US carrier raid, code-named Desecrate 1, on 30 March 1944. The Hauraki was taken a prize while on a voyage from Fremantle to Colombo, on 12 July 1942. This ship was used as general transport for the Navy, under the name Hoki Maru. Her final

Immediately, the sins of converting a thin skinned merchant vessel to a combat ship were exposed: In a dramatic explosion the Hokoku Maru blew up, and the Aikoku Maru withdrew at high speed.

The idea to use armed merchant raiders became increasingly unpopular. Despite camouflage techniques (like adding a second - dummy - funnel and changing the silhouette), radio signals of the ships pursued were used to bring in either enemy surface reinforcements or planes to turn the table on the attacker. Supply ships were concentrated in convoys, and given anti-submarine and fighting capabilities. Additionally, the toll taken by American submarines on freighters began to create transport problems. As a consequence, the concept of raiders was abandoned. The Aikoku Maru was re-rated transport and used to run troops and equipment supplies. On a voyage to Truk she was damaged on 16 July 1943 by a submarine torpedo. In October 1943, the Aikoku Maru was re-rated as transport. All low-trajectory guns were removed without leaving a trace on the decks and the platform fore and aft were armed with 8 cm high angle guns of the type 88. This gun had a bore of 3 inch (7.62 cm). Lack of adequate fire control diminished the accuracy and effectiveness against highly mobile, small targets like carrier aircraft.

Her last voyage was typical for the changed fortunes of the war. In the Guadalcanal and New Guinea area, the American forces made progress, and the Marshalls had fallen. As it was unlikely that Russia would enter the war, it was decided to relocate troops from Manchuria and Korea to the Marianas and other garrisons in the Mandated Islands. The troops were taken by the former Nippon Yusen Kaisha liner Yasukuni Maru and the Aikoku Maru in a convoy, covered by three destroyers, on 25 January

Hailstorm - *The Wrecks*

1944, from Yokosuka and Tateyama to Truk.

En-route, the Yasukuni Maru, a beautiful passenger liner, converted to a sub-tender, then re-rated as a transport, even larger than the Aikoku, was torpedoed by the US submarine Trigger on 31 January 1944, right at the doorsteps of Truk. The Aikoku reached Truk the next day, but departed almost immediately to Wake to bring reinforcements to that garrison. There was too much American air activity in the area, which foiled this attempt.

The Aikoku was then directed to Ponape, where she put in on 14 February. With cargo and troops partially discharged, she steamed back to Truk the next day, and was only about half a day ahead of the approaching ships of the three American Task Groups. After a journey of one day, she entered Truk Lagoon and anchored within the Fourth Fleet Anchorage during the late hours of the 16 February 1944, Truk date. The attack photo taken on the following day by an American aircraft shows the ship heavily laden and deep in the water, with a landing craft tied to her stern. The carrier raid unfolded at dawn with a fighter sweep, and waves of combat aircraft descended on the anchored ships. The Fourth Fleet Anchorage was the target designated for the planes of Task Group 58.2, at Strike 2 B. The planes were loaded with bombs. In their reports Avenger pilots from the Essex state, for the second strike of the first day:

"Ammunition ship of 10-12 000 ts sunk. Ship looked very much like an ocean liner with a large superstructure and one single stack in the superstructure. It was anchored approx. 2 miles East of the eastern point of Dublon. Two hits were obtained. It was seen to explode with terrific force and as a result sunk. No other planes were seen to attack between time hit and explosion. " (Aircraft Action Report, Torpedo Squadron 9, Strike 2 B Dog-minus-one-Day, 17 February 1944, 0815 h, Truk date and time).

The attack photo, taken a few minutes after the explosion shows a giant pillar of smoke rising over the site of the Aikoku Maru. However, it looks, from the shape of the cloud, as if two successive explosions had taken place. The Japanese sources also speak of one subsequent explosion. Probably, there was one blast immediately following the crash of the plane and a sympathetic reaction afterwards, further forward. Previous to the attack, some cargo, such as coastal defense and high-trajectory (anti aircraft) guns, communications equipment and other material had been transferred to the Nippo Maru. When the Akitsushima returned to Truk after a supply voyage on 15 February 1944, she also was loaded with cargo from the Aikoku Maru. It was related, that some soldiers had been disembarked from the Aikoku, and went to Dublon. A number of them returned to the ship at dusk on the 16 February 1944, to stay overnight. The exact number of crew and embarked soldiers which found their grave on the Aikoku Maru could not be established.

The ship was attacked by the sub Tinosa on 15 July 1943, but according to Patrol Report issued, the torpedo missed.

The Aikoku Maru was discovered by Sam Redford in 1972. Because of its great depth the wreck is not often visited. The location of the remaining grave site deeper inside the ship is not commonly known, and for obvious reasons is not visited.

Time was up for merchant raiders. The crew of the Aikoku Maru resorted to putting up a dummy stack as disguise. Apart from the bow and stern gun, two seaplanes can be seen on top of hold four and five.

Technical Data:

Aikoku Maru, combined freighter passenger liner. Ship No: 48 519.

Gross tonnage :	10 438 ts	
Length :	150,0m	(492.0 ft)
Breadth :	20,2 m	(66.3 ft)
Depth :	12,4 m	(40.7 ft)
Draught :	8,84 m	(29.0 ft)
Speed, max.	20.9 knots,	
service	17,0 knots	
Horsepower, max.:	15 833 hp	
Engine:	2 X Mitsubishi - B&W Diesel	
Launching :	25 April 1940	
Service :	31 August 1941	
Builder :	Tama Shipbuilding, Tama.	
Owner:	Osaka Merchant Marine (OSK).	

Hailstorm - *The Wrecks*

AMAGISAN MARU

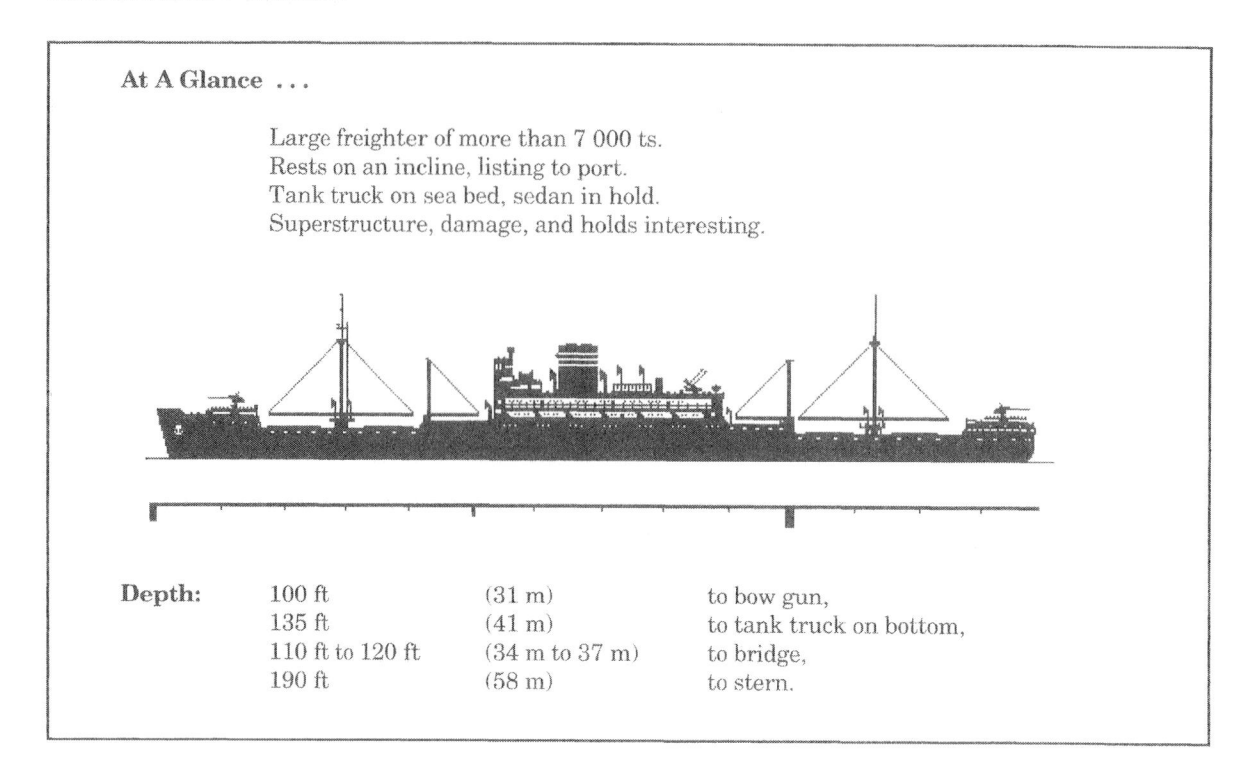

At A Glance ...

Large freighter of more than 7 000 ts.
Rests on an incline, listing to port.
Tank truck on sea bed, sedan in hold.
Superstructure, damage, and holds interesting.

Depth:
100 ft	(31 m)	to bow gun,
135 ft	(41 m)	to tank truck on bottom,
110 ft to 120 ft	(34 m to 37 m)	to bridge,
190 ft	(58 m)	to stern.

The name of the ship is given variedly as Amajisan or Amagisan Maru.

The Amagisan Maru is a large ship. She rests on a sloping ground; the stern is considerably deeper than the bow. There is no problem getting to the foreship and the bridge; even the tank truck on the lagoon bottom may be reached. But as the wreck lies on an incline, the stern is too deep and would require an Exceptional Exposure Dive. If a depth of 140 ft (43 m) is carefully maintained, the stern presents itself in a bird's perspective. The ship has a heavy list of about 45 degrees to port.

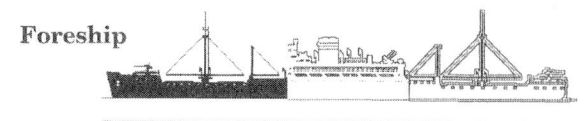

Foreship

The bow is raked. The scuppers on the bulwark form two distinct lines on both sides of the bow. The starboard anchor is not completely retracted. It hangs cock-a-bill a few feet down on the chain and rests against the stem. On the other side, the port anchor is out; the chain leads straight down and continues in a northeasterly direction on the sea bottom. Slightly above the hawse hole a few strands of wire can be seen. They lead all the way continuously around the hull. These are degaussing coils to demagnetize the ship.

The forecastle used to be enclosed with rail guards. Most of the stanchions and stays are still in evidence. There are two large windlasses, from which the anchor chains lead into the hawse holes forward and the spurling pipes aft. Slight damage appears to be on the bulwark on starboard. It probably stems from the nearby explosion of a bomb.

Right aft of the windlasses a gun platform rises about 4 feet above the forecastle deck on a single support post. The platform consists of a square central part from which radiating spokes lead to the circular rim, which is fitted with railings. The gun itself is mounted on a conical shaped gun support. It is a nice looking piece of artillery of 3.7 inch (9,4 cm) calibre. It points straight forward with no elevation. The breech, training mechanism and the recoil springs are heavily overgrown by many shells, corals and sponges. The barrel is encrusted with a particularly fine looking orange sponge.

Hold 1 is almost empty and contains only a few drums. The hold is followed by a goal post. The big winches are located on top of the winch house. The cargo derricks have fallen over to port. Following them outboard as they point to the sea bed, a tank truck and other assorted materials, mainly steel lines, can be seen on the bottom. A derrick lies on top of the tank truck. It is 135 ft deep here. When the vehicle is approached from the side, as is the case when following the derrick, it is not immediately apparent that the big tank container is half knocked off the chassis. The radiator stands upright in front; it is one of the old fashioned, high ones. On the right side of the truck - it rests roughly parallel to the axis of the ship, facing aft - the fender remained in place. It is topped by a headlight, which is a little deformed. On the other side, the mudguard is corroded away, but remnants of the second headlight can be discerned. The hood is also gone. The thin sheet metal has long since corroded away. The view into the engine compartment is unobscured. It was only a small 4 cylinder engine which drove the vehicle. The driver's seat and the windshield frame remained in their place. Looking at the truck from the front now, it can be clearly seen that the tank is halfway off the frame. The vehicle rests on his tires, which all remained mounted on their axles.

The second hold contains more drums, and aircraft wings. A lot of dunnage material and wood can be seen here as well. It is scattered now on port side. This hold is either particularly large or it is partitioned off to form a third hold. Further aft, a very sizeable passenger car, a sedan, fell to the lowest part of the ship. Its size suggests that it was intended for a flag officer. The car body jumped the frame and is now draped almost at right angles over the forward part of the chassis, facing to the right. There is a large dent on the roof, as if a drum fell on it, and a big hole shows in the middle. This damage looks a bit as if the car was subjected to intense heat, weakening the metal. Also the trunk shows a hole. The drive shaft is broken, and at the break, probably the U-joint, it rests against the body of the car. Near to it, a whole side panel of the same kind of car leans against some pieces of wood. It suggests, that a second car was carried as cargo. Between these cars, a lot of wood planking can be found. This is remarkable, because the Amagisan Maru was burning very severely before she sunk. Evidently, the fire did not spread to other holds, as the torpedo hit spelled the fairly rapid demise of this ship. Another fact which is surprising is that there is wood at all remaining at the ship. Evidently, tropical hardwood has been used.

A kingpost is located between the second and the elevated third hold. It is a bit smaller than the others forward, and there are a few drums stored inside. The rest of the cargo probably burned up, because it looks as if a fire was raging in this area. Leaving this hold and getting back on deck, a power vane can be seen lying on port, resting with its horizontal fins on the hatch coaming. The triangular holding frame faces the companionway leading into the bridge. This torpedo shaped body is about 12 feet long and was used for minesweeping.

Midship

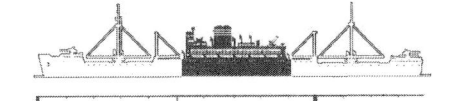

The midship superstructure rises three decks above the third hold. On the third deck, an open passageway leads around the forward part of the bridge. The recessed bulkhead bears portholes. The navigation bridge is located above it, with its bridge wings extending to both sides. Midships, a ladder leads up to the passageway. The top of the flying bridge was constructed out of wood, which is gone now. Steel reinforcing supports is all which remains of the bridge deck house. It is therefore possible to look down on to the navigation deck through gaps in the deck beams and identify the compass, the engine telegraph and the ship's helm. Underneath the bridge house, on port,

inside the superstructure, two large radio sets are located. The meters can be seen clearly, as well as some switches and tuning knobs. One deck lower is the mess, where plates and saucers still can be found. The tableware bears the Mitsui - emblem. This is positive proof, that the ship is the Amagisan Maru, because she was owned by the Mitsui-Line. Other Japanese characters are still legible on the back of the plates.

Aft of the bridge, forward of the funnel, a deck house with a rectangular opening facing forward can be seen. It has a platform is mounted on top of it. This was the location of the anti-aircraft gun. It toppled down and rests on the sea bed. Behind the deck house the boat deck continues to the funnel. In front of it, four ventilators are installed. The stack is stout, not particularly high, and is best described as motor ship-type. A second pair of ventilators is mounted next to it. Aft of the funnel another deck house and the engine room skylights can be found. Paired boat davits are mounted on the boat deck. Aft of them, the superstructure drops down to hold number 4. It is elevated by one deck over shelter deck.

Aftship

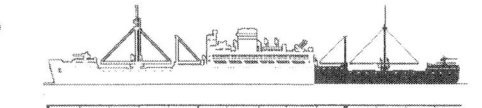

The aftship is a mirror image of the foreship. The elevated fourth hold is followed by a kingpost, then follows the long fifth hold, the goal post with the mast top, and the sixth hold. The ship has a poop and a deckhouse aft. A gun, of the same type as seen forward, is mounted on the platform aft on top of the aft deck house. However, port quarter shows very severe damage, caused either by a bomb hit or a second torpedo. The deck has collapsed here and there is a lot of twisted steel. Right across at the starboard side the pressure of the explosion blew out part of the shell plating. The plating detached itself from the deck by about one foot. This damage can be seen on the forward part of the poop. The Amagisan was attacked by Helldivers and Avengers of Bunker Hill, Strike 3 D, at about 1300 h. Both squadrons claimed hits on the ship.

The destruction at port quarter is not the only damage the ship sustained. Right abeam of the forward elevated hold, hold three, a large hole is evident in the hull. It is triangular in shape and about 15 ft wide at the base. The aft plates are bashed in and the forward plates are badly mangled. The torpedo hit the bilge keel, or very near to it. Fragments of this strong reinforcing structure point into the hole on both sides, but the middle is blown away. There is a lot of twisted steel, but the damage is probably not as extensive as seen on other ships. The bilge keel may have deflected some of the pressure. It did not save the vessel, though. Water incursion was so massive, that, with the damage at the stern, she sank fairly rapidly. Before the hull slipped under water, the fire forward produced a huge smoke plume.

An attack photo shows the Amagisan Maru at the moment the torpedo exploded. It is exactly the spot, where the damage can be seen today on the wreck. The resulting explosion threw up a water and

Hailstorm - The Wrecks

Amagisan Maru

smoke plume more than double the height of the midship superstructure. It is evident from the photo, that the ship had not been hit or damaged substantially before the torpedo hit. The wake of the torpedo can be followed clearly on the picture. Even the point, when it hit the water, dolphined and began to run true can be identified. Careful observation confirms the existence of a second torpedo by the wake it left. It is aimed at the stern. At first glance it appears as if it will miss the ship, but this may be because of the perspective distortion of the long telephoto lens the picture was taken by. It is not clear, whether a bomb or this torpedo hit the Amagisan Maru at the stern. If the torpedo hit low at the counter it may have caused the damage, i. e. the blown out shell plating.

Another attack photo taken a bit later from very long distance shows the ship sinking, but burning real heavily at the second hold. A huge pall of smoke is drifting to the southwest. The Amagisan carried aviation fuel and diesel oil in drums, of which a few remain in the holds. Once in a while, even today, small droplets of gasoline rise from the wreck. This happens most often after divers have been inside the wreck. The exhalation bubbles displace some of the gasoline, which has leaked out of the corroded drums and accumulated underneath the deck head. The gasoline droplets are almost as clear as air bubbles, but they rise much slower, and do not increase in volume. They maintain the same shape on their ascent. Upon reaching the surface, they immediately spread, give off a typical smell of gasoline, and disappear.

The ship was attacked off Davoa on 14 Februaru 1942, by the submerged Swordfish, during daylight hours, and sustained medium damages.

The Amagisan Maru was serving the Japan - New York line as a cargo-cum-passenger liner. From 28 September 1941 onwards, she was used by the Japanese Navy as special transport. The ship was one of the largest freighters sunk in Truk. It was discovered 1973 by Sam Redford.

Technical Data:

Tonnage :	7 621 ts
Length :	137,16 m
	450.0 ft
Width :	18,26 m
	69.0 ft
Depth :	11,27 m
	37.0 ft
Draught :	8,40 m
	27.6 ft
Speed max :	18,83 knots
Speed ser.:	15,00 knots
Engine :	1 x Mitsubishi - B&W Diesel
Horsepower:	8 407 hp
Launch :	06 November 1933
Service :	26 December 1933

THE BETTY BOMBER

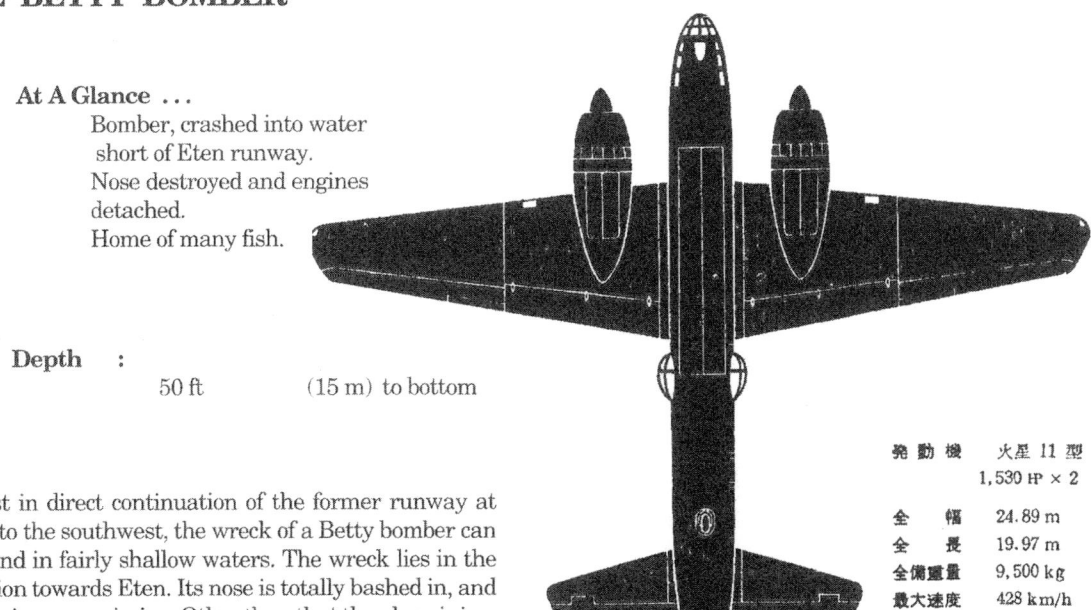

At A Glance ...
Bomber, crashed into water short of Eten runway.
Nose destroyed and engines detached.
Home of many fish.

Depth :
50 ft   (15 m) to bottom

発動機　火星 11 型
1,530 HP × 2
全　幅　24.89 m
全　長　19.97 m
全備重量　9,500 kg
最大速度　428 km/h
Hashimoto

Almost in direct continuation of the former runway at Eten, to the southwest, the wreck of a Betty bomber can be found in fairly shallow waters. The wreck lies in the direction towards Eten. Its nose is totally bashed in, and the engines are missing. Other than that the plane is in a very good state of preservation.

The Betty is the code designation for the Mitsubishi G4M bomber. It was a very successful plane early in the Second World War for the Japanese, but was later dubbed "Flying Cigar". This was on account of its shape, and because her fuel tanks were unprotected, most Bettys went up in flames when hit. The long range of action of these planes revolutionized operational concepts early in the Pacific war. It was a plane designed for the Navy - there was no independent Air Force in Japan at the time - in 1937 to 1939. The first prototype took to the air in 1939, and mass production was begun in 1940. The plane was of excellent design, and easily surpassed all performance specification laid down for it. A few modifications including armour for the crew were made in later models; the plane was produced until the end of the war. The Betty was a twin engined tactical bomber which could be used for torpedo attacks as well.

The position of the wreck suggests that it was either shot down or developed troubles shortly before touch-down at Eten. Its approach was from the southwest, against the wind. The altitude must have been low, because the plane did not crash and disintegrate upon impact with the water. The engines were running, because they continued to be carried further in the direction of the flight. It is also not clear, that the Betty was shot down during the hostilities, and it is more likely that she crashed some other time.

It is quite a sight to see this almost completely intact bomber laid out on the bottom. The rather narrow and trapezoid wings stretch to the edge of the visibility - on a medium nice day. Immediately, the descending diver's attention will be drawn to the nose. There is hardly anything left of it but a mess of window frames, bent to one side. The destruction extends to close to the wing roots. The Betty had a glassed-in nose, and a large cockpit slightly aft. It is the remnant of the cockpit which can be seen today. The actual nose is destroyed.

Two gaping holes and a lot of twisted steel and aluminum can be seen on both sides of the forward part of the wings. It used to be the location were the two engines were mounted. They are torn out. The rest of the wing is almost undamaged. At the aft end of the cockpit is the rear gunner's position. The rear visor is open and clearly visible.

Almost everyone likes to go into the bomber. The easiest way is probably through the gunner's bay, located on both sides of the aircraft, directly behind the aft edge of the wing. The forward facing part of the bay is made out of metal, while the aft part used to be glass, which is gone. Very popular is a snapshot taken from one of the bays on one side, while the buddy squeezes in on the other side. Once inside, a lot of interesting objects can be found. There is a machine gun, a radio set, several boxes and various other smaller items, such as a fire extinguisher. Frequently, interesting fish, such as zebra, lion or turkey fish can be seen inside. The aft section is dark and rarely visited, because everybody immediately faces forward to the cockpit. The tail was glassed in and housed another gunner's position.

The enterprising diver may find both radial engines about 100 m or so among the coral heads, almost in a direct line from the bomber to the old runway, but just slightly to the North. As opposed to the clean airplane - marine growth does not seem to like to settle on bare aluminum - the engines are heavily overgrown with corals and sponges. Somebody put the pilot's seat on the bottom nearby.

The Betty bomber is a very interesting second, repetitive dive. While swimming in and around the wreck, care should be exercised not to get cut by the very sharp edges of the aluminum skin.

DAIKICHI MARU OR X 10

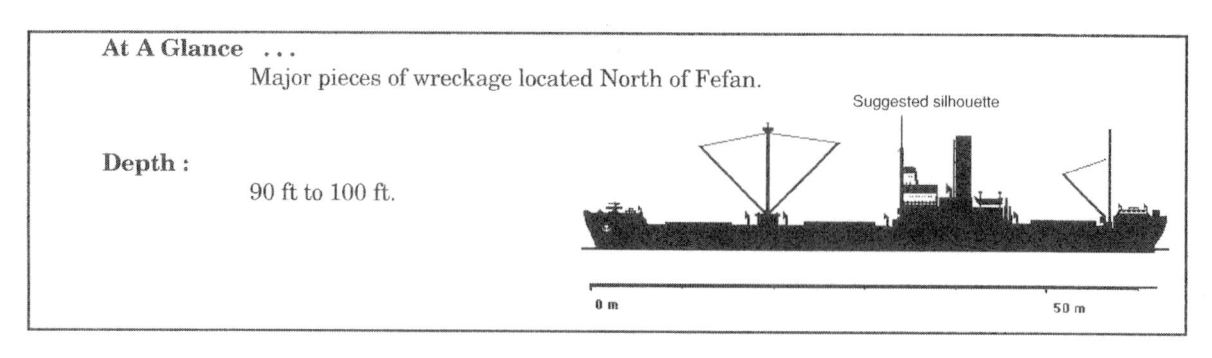

At A Glance ...
Major pieces of wreckage located North of Fefan.

Depth:
90 ft to 100 ft.

Suggested silhouette

The sea bottom north of, and quite a distance away from, Fefan the sea bottom undulates, and forms rolling hills and valleys. It is a beautiful underwater scenery. Swimming, almost gliding effortless from one hill to the next and passing over valleys it feels as being in a fairy tale landscape. Only the absence of trees imparts an eerie impression. However, in a valley, several pieces of large wreckage have been seen. They are about the size of a one-family house. Three individual chunks have been made out. The one most readily identifiable piece is particularly large. It is the whole midship section, mainly the engine room and probably the aft section of the midship superstructure. The hull remained intact between the breaks forward and aft. The breaks in the hull are fairly clean, considering the force which tore this ship apart.

Amazingly, the stack is still attached to the superstructure. It does not appear to have been damaged. It is a fairly tall, tubular funnel, and suggests that the ship burned coal. Four ventilators have broken off from the boat deck. They were originally placed on all four corners of the engine room skylights, and are now resting on the bottom very close by the wreck. Shell and deck plating at the fore and aft ends of this middle section are deformed, severely buckled, twisted and torn. The wreck lies not quite on the side - which one it is could not be ascertained beyond doubt - but has a 75 degrees list.

Another piece of wreckage was found about a hundred feet away. It resembles a piece of the bow, with attached forecastle and shell plating. The third piece was smaller and could have been part of the mast and winch house. Exact identification could not be made. Other smaller pieces of debris are scattered around in the immediate vicinity.

Without doubt this area has been the site of a major explosion. The ship must have carried either a cargo of ordnances, gasoline or both, which were triggered off by a hit, resulting in a sympathetic explosion. As both fore and aft ship had been severed and the bridge destroyed, it may be that there were two successive and very large explosions which occurred almost simultaneously.

From the pieces found, it may be deduced that the ship was a medium sized freighter or oiler of about 1500 to 2500 ts, burning coal, and being propelled by a turbine or a steam engine. The pieces found do not allow to make a conclusive assessment how exactly the ship looked. Most likely, it was a cargo ship with three islands and four holds, such as a Standard 1 D cargo, which were measured at around 2000 ts. The size of the wreckage would support this assumption. The pieces of wreckage could be the ship which was reported by pilots of Bunker Hill to be an oiler, but thought to be a freighter by Enterprise aviators. The estimated tonnage was 5,500 tons, but given the usual exaggeration, it was probably only between 1500 and 3000 tons.

Bunker Hill planes attacked this ship at about 1430 h, Strike 3E-1, and placed a large bomb squarely midships. They reported a very large explosion and a fire. Pilots from Enterprise were a little more descriptive and wrote that the ship exploded violently with big force. The vessel disintegrated completely. The only ship known to have sunk in Truk at the first carrier raid which has never been found, and for which the whereabouts are a complete mystery is the Daikichi Maru, a ship of 1999 tons. This size suggests a Standard 1 D ship.

A few attack photos exists of the Combined Fleet Anchorage. In one a ship can be seen anchored west, and slightly to the north of the Heian Maru. This picture was taken rather early in the day, probably at the first or second strike. At this time the Heian Maru was not burning, but the Tonan Maru 3 was blazing at the forward superstructure, the Akashi appears to be undamaged, the Kansho Maru looks as if she is going slowly down by the stern, Kiyozumi Maru is undamaged, but the Hoyo Maru is already mortally wounded and her stern is submerged.

At another picture only parts of Dublon, the Heian Maru and this particular ship can be seen. The photo was taken much later. Heian Maru burns fiercely, but the Daikichi Maru is almost equally engulfed in flames and smoke. From both photos it appears as if the Daikichi Maru was painted white or a light shade of grey, and that she had a engine at three quarter deck profile.

In fact, when we were looking for a ship at the Combined Fleet Anchorage in June/July 1980 we were followed up on the hint received from an old man living in Dublon, long deceased, that a ship was burning there. An exact description of the location was not given. After we had searched in the vicinity of Yanagi unsuccessfully we decided to return to the Kiyozumi Maru for the last dive of the day and discovered the Kansho Maru.

THE DUMPING GROUND

> **At A Glance ...**
> Very interesting underwater junk yard.
> Redundant war material scattered on the bottom.
> Vehicles, machinery and torpedo bodies among them.
>
> **Depth:**
> Fairly uniform 85 ft (26 m).

This is the second of the three attractions in the channel between Dublon and Fefan. It seems hard to believe, that every time the dive boat passes through the channel between the islands of Dublon and Fefan, it practically rides over this very interesting dive site.

It is said, that the Japanese troops began to discard vehicles, spare parts with no anticipated future use, and other material supplies shortly before the surrender of Japan. Apparently, the dumping was continued after the surrender, before and after the American forces signed the official surrender papers on USS Portland.

In common with the ill-fated destroyer Susuki - Patrol Boat 34 - and the equally ill-starred fleet and the harbor tug, this area is also subject to heavy silting. It is the rain run-off from both islands which carries the silt down. There is, as a consequence, very little coral growth on the bottom. Corals do not thrive in waters with a high silt load. They get smothered. Only a few coral heads, few and far between, can be seen. There is no real pattern to the dumping. A mooring buoy used to be anchored in the area. It was sunk later, and can now be seen on the bottom. Whenever a barge load was full, the material was just thrown over board at the vicinity of the buoy. Some of it is piled up in a heap, and at another place it is just scattered. It is difficult to say how far this junk yard extends in length and width. A few highlights may give an introduction of what is all there:

There is a sedan type car. It is similar, if not the same model, as the car on the Amagisan Maru and rests on its wheels. The hood is completely gone, but the body work is holding up. The front wheels are sticking up to their axle in mud. The engine can be seen, but the radiator must have fallen down. The doors and the rear roof are heavily overgrown with orange sponges and corals. The roof is corroded away, as well, and allows a cut-away view from above. The steering wheel is located on the right. No seats can be discerned inside anymore. It has been said, that it had been Vice Admiral Hara's official car, because it has been seen when it was loaded onto a barge at the end of the war. A medium-sized, four bladed ship's propeller is buried more than half into the bottom. Two blades stick out. Not far away is a half-tracked vehicle, half on its side. The tracks are still attached. It could have been a work or salvage vehicle, because a big winch is mounted on the rear. The steel wire is still wound tightly around the winch drum. Another half-track is resting near it on its chassis. This one may have been a personnel carrier. Amidst the heap of debris, a cone shaped yellow subject is pointing upward. It looks like a propeller hub, properly called a spinner, particularly as a circular hole can be seen, where one of the blades was attached. Other pieces look like aircraft parts. For example, the tail wing of a Val dive bomber is resting among assorted bits of piping and other hardware. Also, complete wings may be found here as well. One or two tank trucks are resting on their wheels. The body work is corroded and gone, but the tank and the engine can be seen. One particular truck looks strange, because its front wheel is overgrown by a sponge, which lights up bright orange in the beam of an underwater light or flash. Torpedo bodies are scattered around. High pressure vessels are lying among them.

These are just a few things to see. Most interesting are the half dozen or so tracked vehicles in their various state of disrepair. They have been used originally for a variety of purposes. Some of them look outright mean, even today. The pieces of machinery, generators and engines are just too numberable to describe. A hard hat diving helmet has been brought up, restored and picked clean of all marine growth.

Large remnants of a torpedo net are located in the vicinity. The torpedo net consisted of heavy linked steel rings of 5 inch diameter. It was kept on the surface by pontoon-like foats. Those were sunk and the net now lies on the bottom, resembling a huge snake. It terminates on one underwater hill betweem Dublon and Fefan. Following it, the cockpit of a Kaiten suicide torpedo will be reached. It is a fairly narrow contraption, with a hollow side on the bottom to fit the round 24 inch diameter torpedo body. On the upper side, only about 75 cm or so high, a cockpit can be seen, with the remains of a half steering wheel, and some wire attachment. The lower half, with attachment bolts, is lying in the sand nearby. Next follows the torpedo body, evidently based on the Long Lance torpedo. The body is also well preserved. Several hundred feet away, the tracked carriage can be located.

Hailstorm - *The Wrecks*

THE EMILY FLYING BOAT

At A Glance ...
Upside down wreck of very large plane,
Broken in three, but not scattered.
Very interesting flying boat.
Engines on wreck, but dropped from mounts.

Depth :
50 ft (15 m) to bottom

There is a very interesting story attached to the sinking of this huge flying boat. The Commanding Officer of of the Fourth Fleet, Truk, probably Vice Admiral Hara, his Chief-of-Staff, and a number of high ranking officers were taking the Emily for a flight to Palau, to attend a military conference. The trip toward their destination proved uneventful. On the way back to Truk, the Emily and the high ranking passengers were ambushed by US fighters. The Emily put up fierce resistance, and tried to escape by flying above her maximum ceiling of almost 30 000 ft, but in altitude and speed the Emily was no match for the fighter planes. Burst after cannon burst exploded in the plane, and the pilot performed all kinds of acrobatics to shake the pursuers. Finally, he managed to escape into a large cloud, and stayed within its tossing turbulences for just long enough to loose the hostile planes. There was sheer carnage inside the plane. The co-pilot lay spread dead over the controls, and several of the officers in the passenger compartment of the plane were killed. It was a small wonder that the Vice Admiral and his Chief of Staff were not injured.

The pilot did manage, with a great deal of coaxing, to fly his severely damaged plane into Truk. With much diminished power he came in low between the islands of Uman and Fefan, to his designated area, the Dublon seaplane base. Sheltered waters would make his water landing easier. The plane had become so unwieldy because of its extensive damage that the touchdown was heavy. It broke the frame of the sturdy plane. Water immediately rushed into the many big holes ripped out of the fuselage during combat, and the Emily immediately began to tilt forward. Passengers and crew scrambled into the open, jumped into the water and were picked up by rescue boats standing by. Shortly afterwards the plane nose dived down and sank. The pilot was decorated.

The unofficial name of the Emily was "the Flying Porcupine". It was heavily armed with defensive weapons, and carried no less than 5 - 20 mm cannons and 4 machine guns. The Emily was an outstanding plane in many regards. Its range of action was longer than those of the famous Superfortress, in fact, it was just a little smaller than this American mammoth. As probably one of the first Japanese planes, it

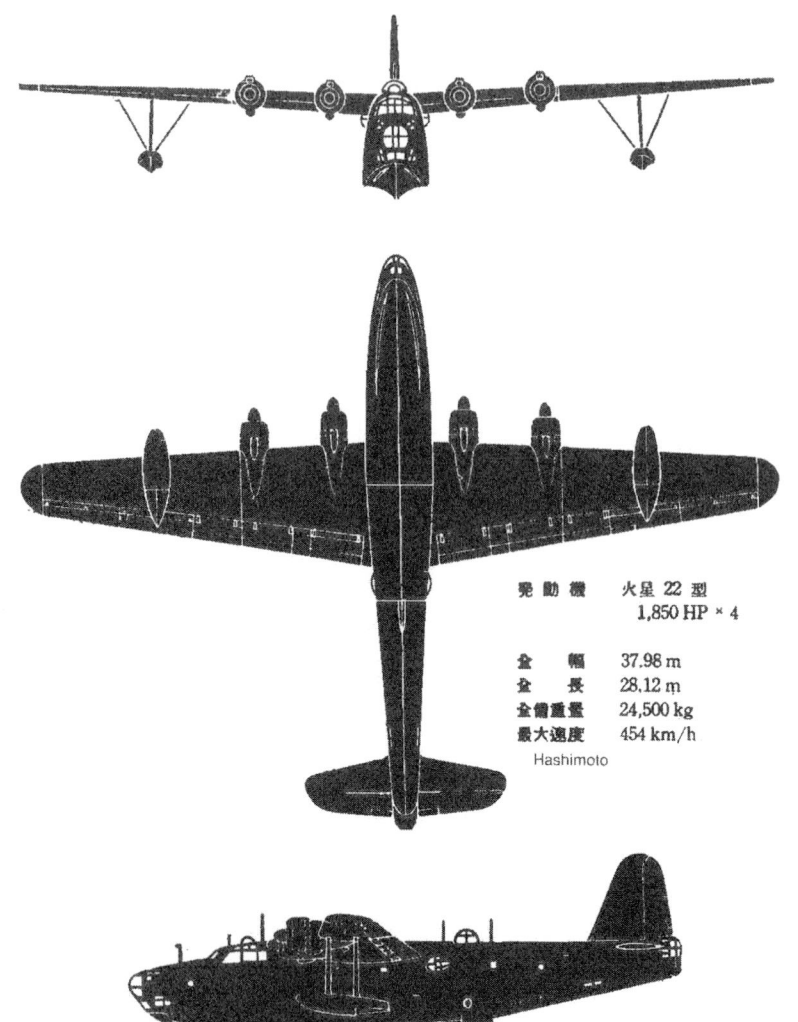

発動機　火星 22 型
　　　　1,850 HP × 4

全 幅　　37.98 m
全 長　　28.12 m
全備重量　24,500 kg
最大速度　454 km/h

Hashimoto

had self-sealing fuel tanks in the wings and in the fuselage. It carried a fire extinguisher system, and was able to withstand an unusual amount of punishment.

It is interesting to note that the American forces relied on large, heavy bomber strips on land, while the doctrine of the Japanese said that some of their fighters and heavy bombers should be able to start from the water. The Rufes, seaplane versions of the Zero fighter, were stationed on almost all Mandated Islands, and did not require extensive airfields. Two Emilys made a bombing run from the Marshalls to Oahu on 04-05 March 1942. Although it was only a nuisance raid, it proved the feasibility of long range bombings with the Emily.

The Emily is broken into three major pieces, and lies upside down among an undulating underwater reef. For many descending divers, the huge plane appears to convey the impression of an upturned railroad wagon. The aft part of the fuselage is broken off about 3 m forward of the aft wings. The fuselage can be entered, but there is nothing special to see other than the inside bulkheads and the support frames. The hull is designed with relatively sharp edges, and therefore contrasts with the round configuration of other planes. To the right of this aft section a lot of crumbled metal can be seen. It is the tail rudder.

The break occurred forward of the gun or observer's position. There is a radio with dials, an electric-motor with a small compressor and other assorted pieces of gear located to the right of the fuselage, near the break.

The main part of the hull looks very strange, because of the inverted gull-shaped bottom, which was hydrodynamically designed to give greatest stability in the water during take-off and landing. In fact, a lot of engineering had to be done, and the lower part of the plane had to be redesigned, as the original solution proved to be unstable. The shape resembles the cathedral hull form, commonly found in Boston Whalers. A stabilizing fin can be seen on the bottom. The sides of the plane are straight, and the edges form sharp angles.

All four engines remained attached to their nacelles, except that their mounting gave way over the years and they tilted forward, until they came to rest on the sea bottom. The propellers are attached, and partly overgrown by encrustating orange sponges. The wing tips are rounded. All aluminum plates have been riveted. The scoops and spinners can be readily identified. The wing float on the right wing (actually, it is the left wing, as the plane is upside down) is intact, but the struts are shorn off. They are witness of a dramatic landing. The left wing fared worse. Here, the float is badly mangled and twisted. There is a recessed landing light with a large reflector built into the left wing.

The cockpit of the plane is badly destroyed. Only the bottom windows, now on top, remain intact. The portion of the plane forward of the wing root is broken. It lies at an angle to the hull. It is possible to enter the fuselage. A few feet off the nose, a cockpit instrument panel and a large gear can be seen on the bottom. Not all damages may have resulted from the crash.

The Emily is a very impressive wreck of an airplane. Its size and design is fascinating, and after mentally reassembling the wreck, one is impressed with the lines of this once outstanding aircraft.

THE FLEET TUG

At A Glance ...
Large, oceangoing tug.
Resting on a steep incline.
Interesting bridge and hold.

Depth:
50 ft to 90 ft   (15 m to 28 m)

As far as tugs are concerned, this is a big one. It certainly was used in the open seas for major towing jobs. It is called Fleet Tug to differentiate it from those smaller harbor tugs, which were towing the barges in the lagoon. The Fleet Tug is the third of the three attractions in the area between Dublon and Fefan. The others are the destroyer and the Dumping Ground. All of them have in common that there is a lot of fine silt deposited on everything. The fact that the two sites, the destroyer excluded, are hardly ever visited, accounts also for the undisturbed sediment. The Fujikawa Maru looks polished by these standards.

The shallow stern, it is about 50 ft deep there, hides the fact that it is 90 ft to the bow. This sloping wreck makes dive planning difficult. For a second or other repetitive dive the forward section is a bit deep. There is not enough to see to justify spending prime bottom time of a first dive, however.

The description leads from stern to bow.

Descending at the stern, the rudder, slightly turned to starboard, is one of the first things to be seen. It becomes apparent now that the tug has a 45 degrees list to port. Two relative small, medium pitched propellers can be seen on both sides of the rudder, slightly forward of the rudder post. They are three bladed. Despite the mud which appeared to have settled on them marine growth, some sponges, can be seen.

The stern is well rounded, relatively flat, and has the slightly inboard curving bulwark of tugs. A hatch is located aft, close to the tow bar. It is quite roomy in this hold, but very dark. An underwater light will reveal that there are a few coils of hoses. A massive instrument with gauges could have been a pump. A second set is located to the right. It may be that these are salvage pumps, used to assist a ship, which is taking in a great deal of water. Next to the port bulkhead are two instruments resting on the deck. They are half hidden behind a pipe bridge. Although water has gotten into one of them, it is only half filled. The upper part of the dial can still be read. Close to it a brass flow meter is located, with its cover resting against a coiled hose. An insulated pipe above at the deck head, the asbestos cloth hanging from it like a torn curtain, leads from forward to aft. An electrical distribution box for the overhead lighting has fallen down and rests amid the debris on the bottom of the hold. On one side of the hold two large racks are constructed, which are stacked with 20 ft (5 m) long hose sections. Their diameter is about four inches (10 cm). Almost all of them are orderly placed. Interestingly, the upper two most layers look very clean and there is little growth and sediment on them. The black rubber withstood the ravages of time remarkable well. The couplings on both sides are made out of brass. Closer to the hull, and further down at the stack, hoses with couplings of a smaller diameter can be seen. The ladder leading into this room has fallen over them.

Ascending out of the hold, swimming forward, and passing the tow hook, the outside of the engine room will be reached. Access to it is denied, as the doorways are not open, and the doors would not budge in their hinges. The passageways on port and starboard are dead ends. It is extremely messy to enter them as a lot of mud is stirred up, and one has to back out in a cloud of silt. The more interesting part of the tug is the bridge. It is a bit of a tight squeeze to get through the windows, but the visit is quite worth it. Inside the navigation bridge two engine telegraphs are flanking the helm. The telegraph on port is in the position Full Ahead, but it could be that the pointer has been moved at one time by divers. The helm's wheel is gone, but its mount can be seen facing aft. A compass is mounted on the helm, and the cover rests at the helm base to starboard. A round rim is located on the port bulkhead close by the telegraph, together with a number of pipe sections. If it is what is left of the helm's wheel, it certainly has peculiar handle spokes.

The starboard telegraph pointer is in the same position as the one on port. The glass is still in place, as opposed to its counterpart on port, but it is heavily overgrown by an orange encrustating sponge, commonly found on the wrecks. A voice tube can be seen forward. Inside the tube a coral makes its home. Soon, the stirred up silt and the debris raining down from the deck head forces the visitor to leave, and the forward hatch may be entered. One of the interesting pieces located here is a very large coil of hemp rope. It is interesting to note that it is still in excellent condition, because it could have been expected to have disintegrated after so long immersion.

There are cabins forward and on the sides of the hold. A wide open porthole suggests that the crew had their accommodations here. There are also some storage facilities in the same general area. A doorway leads further forward, but penetration becomes a bit risky as it is a tight squeeze and quite deep.

The bow has a slight rake. The sea bed descends farther. There is no apparent damage, and the reason for the sinking remains a mystery. It has been suggested, that the tug was scuttled at the end of the war.

FUJIKAWA MARU

At A Glance ...
This is *t h e* wreck in Truk.
It is most exciting, easy to dive on and has interesting cargo.
Large, 6-hold freighter, resting on even keel.
Bow and stern guns, cargo of fighter planes.
Superstructure wide open.
Excellent for multiple first and second dives.
Superb photographic possibilities.

Depth:

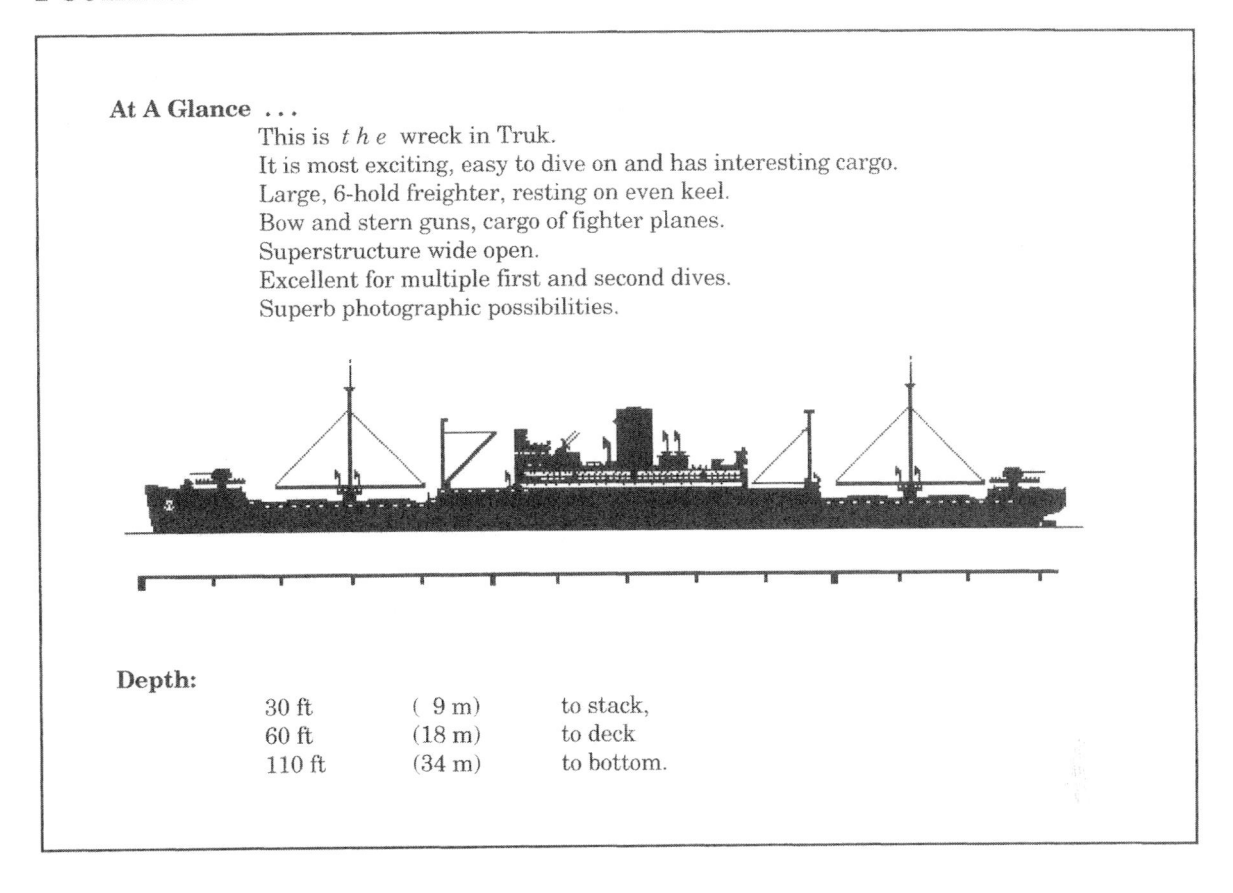

30 ft	(9 m)	to stack,
60 ft	(18 m)	to deck
110 ft	(34 m)	to bottom.

The Fujikawa Maru was built 1938 by Mitsubishi. The ship was just a little shy of 450 ft in over-all length when completed, and 58 1/2 ft wide (137 m by 17,8 m). Originally, she was used by the ship's owners, Toyo Kaiun, for liner service to North American ports on the Eastern Seaboard. It appears, however, that only a few month after the Fujikawa began this service, she was chartered to Mitsui Busan. In her new role, she went mainly to South America and India, and apart from passengers, for which she had comfortable accommodations, she carried raw silk as cargo. At later voyages this somewhat exclusive cargo was supplemented by other fibres. Records indicate that cotton, jute and flax were shipped to Japan on this ship.

If her peacetime career was just a bit unusual, the war saw her in an entirely different, yet equally exclusive role. Taken over by the Imperial Japanese Navy on 09 December 1940, which, one will remember, was about one year before Pearl Harbor Day, she was converted to an aircraft ferry. There are some sources, which refer to the Fujikawa Maru as an aircraft carrier. That kind of a ship she was not. The term aircraft ferry or aircraft transport would be more precise, as she could not launch or recover airplanes.

After the conversion in 1940, she was fitted out with 6" bow and stern guns. These guns were of old design and cannibalized from decommissioned cruisers of the Russian-Japanese War. A bronze tag at the bow gun attests that the guns were built in 1899. Later, she was fitted out additionally with anti-aircraft automatics on boat deck, close to the bridge wings.

As a form of passive protection, a degaussing coil was laid around the ship to render it "invisible" to any magnetic detonators. She was under the command

Identification on the forward gun of the Fujikawa Maru.

of the 11th Air Fleet, originally stationed with the 22nd Air Fleet in Indo-China. It appears that several of the aircraft transports were used after the Malaya campaign to ferry aircraft to the Mandated Islands in the Pacific. There are several trips on record for the Fujikawa Maru, between the Marshalls (Kwajalein), the Gilberts (Tarawa) and the Caroline Islands.

On 12 September 1943, she was steaming from Kwajalein to Truk, when she was hit by a torpedo fired from an US submarine, USS Permit, at 0230 h on the 12th (at N 8:53, E 165:12). Despite extensive damage she was able to reach Truk on 15 September 1943.

The inquisitive diver will find some peculiarities on the hull of the ship. For instance, there is a bulge fitted at the original waterline on port. It is about 100 ft long, 10 inches wide, and 12 inches deep (30,5 m by 0,25 m by 0,30 m) and extends to about the length of the midships superstructure. A counterpart on starboard is missing. Instead, there are a few large 1 to 1 1/4 inch (2,5 to 3 cm) thick steel plates welded onto the shell plating. They can be found about midships abeam of the funnel. These modifications to the hull are certainly the traces of a major repair job. The ship was back in service in January 1944, but was re-rated from an aircraft transport to general transport.

Apart from general cargo, she continued to carry aircraft. She was back in Truk, shortly before the air raid, and got caught. The report of a Japanese officer after the war speaks of the Fujikawa Maru having discharged 30 Jill torpedo bombers (Kawasaki B5N2), successor to the hopelessly outmoded Val. These Jills were piled up on Eten airfield and contributed to the concentration of aircraft on the apron and the runway. The planes were not operational, being shipped semi-assembled. They became defenceless prey for the American planes which strafed and bombed Eten repeatedly.

The Fujikawa Maru sank by a single torpedo hit starboard midships, just aft of the superstructure. The planes were launched as Strike 3E-1, from the carriers Bunker Hill and Monterey, at 1324 h and hit the ship at 1430 h. Of the two torpedoes dropped, one did not run true, missed the ship, and crashed into the reef surrounding Eten, without exploding. The wake of the second ceased to show. The pilot cursed, but the momentum carried the weapon to the ship, resulting in an explosion slightly aft of the midship superstructure, and a fire. A photo taken some time later shows the Fujikawa sinking slowly by the stern while at anchor. It took her some time to sink, and she landed most orderly, almost perfectly on even keel. A little off the stern the remains of a small vessel are located.

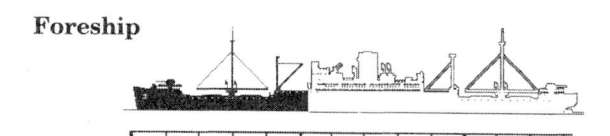

Foreship

The forecastle is large with a big windlass. However, it is dominated by the large gun, located on top of a circular platform. This massive piece of artillery is an old fashioned cruiser gun of 6" (15,2 cm) calibre. The lock is enclosed in the armored shield, which has a trapezoid shape. Its wider part is opening to the rear, for loading and training of the gun. The roof of the shield slopes down forward. The barrel is slightly elevated and trained forward over to starboard, approximately 45 degrees. It suggests, that it was in action, although it is hard to believe that a single purpose, flat trajectory gun would have been very useful against airborne targets. There are a few boxes of ready ammunition standing on the platform to the rear of the gun. The bronze plate with the inscription of the manufacturer, the date and calibre can be seen bolted to the breech. Probably early 1980 or late 1979, the aft part of the gun platform sagged by a few feet, and now some of the boxes of ammunition perch precariously over hold one. The gun itself does not appear to have shifted.

The first forward hold is not too inviting at first glance, because all hatch cover beams on both levels are still in place. Divers have to maneuver around them to get below into the hold proper. It is, however, well worth the effort. A variety of different cargo can be seen here. On the bottom of this hold, several drums are scattered around, and between them spare propeller blades, three heavy machine guns, and aircraft wings can be seen. A few flap covers have corroded away on the wings, and the holmes are exposed. There are also a number of large six inch shell casings lying around. They are expended casings from the bow gun, and are evidence that the gun was fired.

A little forward in this hold 40 to 50 shells can be seen. They are neatly arranged in rows. Only the tips protrude above the deep layer of brown sediment. Their orderly arrangement in the sediment suggests, that they have been packaged in boxes. It is probably ammunition for the bow gun which is stored here. A lot of small arms ammunition in clips and cartridges, some of them still packaged in boxes and others scattered around, and a dented drum completes this still life. An outboard boat engine lies on the bottom of this hold. Farther forward, drums are orderly stowed underneath the tween deck.

Continuing the examination of this hold, one should ascend to the tween deck. A lot of material was stowed here which later fell to the bottom. A great number of propeller blades, engine cowlings, various aircraft fuselage parts, a tank assembly and other materials point to the fact, that the ship was bringing in major supplies for the airplane base. There is a torpedo body with a ruptured high pressure vessel inside, tires, coils of communication wires, ammunition shells, porcelain insulators, welding tanks and yet more fuselage parts.

The two decks of hatch cover beams look interesting from below. Ascending out of the hold and upon returning to the deck, the large winch house can be seen. It is shaped like a square - edged mushroom. The view up the mast, which has a crosstree ten feet below the surface, was breathtakingly beautiful. The cargo derricks remained in their resting places. There is no trace of the jumbo derrick, and the only indication that the ship was fitted with such a boom is that there is a strong clamp way up above the crosstree.

Most dive boats used to tie up on the mast, which, together with the mainmast aft broke the surface and gave the position of the ship away. However, in September 1983, the forward mast, with much rumbling, broke off and fell over to starboard, breaking the bulwark. Fortunately, it happened when no boat was tied up, and nobody actually witnessed the disappearance of the mast. But as the material becomes weaker and weaker by corrosion, it is inevitable that exposed structure collapse. Eventually, this fate will befall all ships in Truk: They will become so weak and the metal so thin that they will collapse.

Many divers consider hold two to be the most fascinating attraction. It is a safe bet that everybody goes down to the bottom first. Several fighter aircraft are jumbled here. The odd assortment of cockpits, fuselage parts, wings and tail assemblies are confusing at first sight. The part which attracts attention immediately, however, is the cockpit of a Mitsubishi A6M Risen, the Zero fighter plane. As the engine is not fitted, the fuselage is open forward. Slightly further aft, the windshield is mounted. The frame is intact and hardly dented, except a little on the top. Frames for the panorama windows enclose the front piece. The glass was probably not inserted during transport. Two holes, in front of the windshield, at the fuselage, show where the plane's board weapons were positioned. The cockpit itself contains a very elaborately designed instrument panel. Although there are no gauges and switches fitted, their position can be seen from their holes in the panel. On the right side are flanges mounted, for taking up hoses, probably designed for the oxygen supply of the pilot. The shell of the seat and the stick are prominent in the cockpit. A second set of radio dials and other gauges are located low on the instrument panel. This cockpit is certainly the show piece of this hold, but there is plenty more to see.

For example, the aft part of a fuselage with its tail assembly points up at an awkward angle. End cap and rudder are missing, holes in the shell indicate where they are supposed to be fitted. It is difficult to ascertain which wing belongs to which fuselage. There are certainly more than three aircraft in this hold. Identification is made difficult, because there is also more than one type of plane. Additional wings and other spares contribute to this fascinating, yet slightly confusing picture. Shell casings, propeller blades and a single hatch cover beam are strewn in between. In the beam of a light, an interesting view of the inside of an aft part of a fuselage is offered.

The tween decks show most of the parts missing from the airplanes on the bottom of the hold, such as radial engines, and stacked engine cowlings. There are also a few drums. Some are still stacked, while others have broken loose. The bulkheads between the two holds are rusted through in many places.

The third hold is elevated and the deck is raised by one deck. Entry at main deck level is difficult and can only be accomplished by diving through the manholes, which are spared out in the hatch cover. The only light getting into this hold is from this manhole, consequently, it is very dim inside. The cargo consists of drums. Exploration is tedious and not particularly rewarding. As there are so many other things to see, this hold may justly be left alone; it is not worth the bottom time. An interesting aspect is the presence of wood here. It has withstood the attack of marine organisms, probably because of the darkness, or because of some unknown substance in the hold, which is incompatible with life.

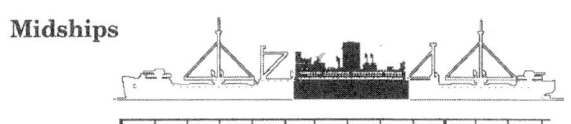

Midships

The bridge is a literal treasure chest, apart from the fact that there are no treasures to be found. However, there are a great number of interesting things to explore. The wide open passageways invite the diver to swim through. However, electrical circuits, originally laid on the deck head, have dropped and are dangling down. Care must be exercised not to get hung up with the equipment. As the cables are mostly overgrown by hard, calcareous algae or other sea life, and their insulation has become hard and broken, they scrape the skin easily. These scrapes have a tendency to get infected in sea water, so avoid the cables.

Most of the bridge area is exposed. The wood planking either burned or has rotted away. Only the steel support structure remains, allowing the outside light to filter through to the lower decks. Despite the ambient light it is recommended, however, to take a light along. It will make exploration of recesses and rooms, which are not open to day light easier. Approaching from forward it is interesting to swim through the starboard shelter deck passageway. The exit aft of the passageway can be seen, indicating that there are no obstructions.

The underwater light will ensure safe passage and avoidance of the hanging cables. Buried in the silt of the starboard passageway many small medicine bottles can be found. Close by, beer and liquor bottles have been seen. A gin bottle, its tin cap still in place, albeit corroded, and the cork dissolved in the liquid has been sighted here as well, but somebody has dislocated it. The exit is at hold four. Ascending one deck, at the aft part of the midship superstructure, the next passageway may be used to swim back to forward. After entering it on starboard, however, the first doorway to the left, facing in-board, reveals the ship's very remarkable galley.

Centerpiece of the galley is the very large stove, which almost extends over the width of the room. It has burned coal. Somebody put a large pan and a spatula on top of one of the hot plates. It is an interesting picture to photograph. A number of other kitchen utensils are lying around, but they come and go, courtesy of those, who have never seen these things before and have the irresistible urge to pick them up, and to put them at some other place. Fortunately, the stove is a bit too massive to lug around, and the galley is certainly worth a visit. Swimming out, after having traversed it, through the door on port, a doorway can be seen on the out-board side of the port passageway. It is appropriately dark in this room: it is the head or bathroom. Three toilet bowls are located here. Those, who are not familiar with Japanese customs and bathroom fittings, may be a bit puzzled at first. Any doubt is removed, when turning to the left, that is aft, in this room. A row of several urinals is fastened to the bulkhead. Partitions, dividing this head, have long disintegrated. They can be found, in part, as the high level of brown sediment. Swimming into this room reduces the visibility quickly to the particular appreciation of the following underwater photographer. It

Fujikawa Maru

takes a while before the sediment settles again.

Continuing forward in this port passageway an open doorway leading in-board will be reached next. It is almost completely dark inside the room. The only light appears to be coming from the heavily overgrown skylight above, and from a few other doorways on other levels. This is the engine room. A good light is a must if an exploration is desired. There appears to be a strong haze in the water, created by finest suspended particles. It is the equivalent of smoke or fog on land, except that the particle density in the water is layered.

The first thing to be seen are the catwalks leading around the engine room at various levels. A chain pulley is draped over one railing. Bolted to the bulkhead is a cylinder liner and a spare piston. They are a common sight in diesel driven ships and are intended for on-board maintenance and repair.

Various other pieces of machinery are found on different levels in this very large room. On the bottom are two times three cylinder heads of the main engine. They are all connected with each other by a common high pressure air pipe, used to get air into the cylinders for starting up. Various instruments are attached to pipes, to monitor the engine's performance. The cylinder heads were tied down with remarkable fist-sized bolts.

A door leads into the deeper insides of the ship, but it is narrow and completely dark there. Swimming back out into the passageway, a few valves can be seen recessed into the in-board bulkhead. To the left - when facing forward - another doorway is evident. This cabin contains sinks, all still very white, and a tiled Japanese bath, with an upper and a lower tub.

After swimming out of this passageway, the next higher deck can be reached best by swimming out of the superstructure and re-entering forward. This is the location of the officer's accommodation or first class passenger cabins. The non-structural partitions are gone, and what used to be a number of individual cabins today appears as a single, spacious room.

Electrical cables are hanging from the deck head. On the deck, however, is still a lot of material which is difficult to identify. One part of this space used to be the mess. A few pieces of china, including a little mortar and plates can be found here. They do not bear the ship's name, and this is probably the reason why they have not yet been bagged and taken away. A grat deal of electrical equipment hangs suspended from the deckhead, and what appears to be the remains of one or two radio sets are located in the sediment. Also porcelain insulators can be found and readily identified. The structure still standing appears to be the helm. The radio components located at this deck may have come actually from the deck above. They may have fallen to the lower deck when the floorboards gave way. Inside the bridge house the helm, the engine telegraph and more radio sets are located. Outside, at the bridge wing, the anti-aircraft guns can be seen. They are not overgrown very much. Right underneath the starboard gun, a small heap of spent cartridges can be located. Unfortunately, its size has diminished, because treasure hunting divers picked "just one" up as a souvenir. Hardly anything grows around this heap, because the slowly corroding copper is a poison for marine life.

The funnel is stout and large. All engine room skylights are closed and almost blind due to marine growth. A deck house is built abaft of the funnel.

Aftship

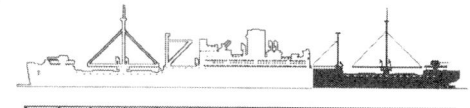

The first hold aft of the midship superstructure, hold four, is the counterpart to the one forward, hold three. It is also smaller than the others and elevated over main deck level. There is no cargo in this hold. A solitary aircraft tire rests forward on the tween deck. A large triangular hole, its base formed by the sea bottom, shows underneath the point where the bulwark curves down from the elevated deck, promenade deck, to shelter deck. The shell plating parted at its seam and curved inward. Frames and other structural elements are bent into the hold. All fragments point away from the center of the explosion. Although the hole appears to be only four to five feet high, it is large enough to swim through it comfortably.

The damage to the bottom of the ship can not be ascertained as sand has covered this area and filled in part of the hole at the base. Here the torpedo hit and exploded, ripping the hull open. The damage extends up to the bulkhead of hold five. The water incursion was massive, and the hold flooded quickly. Evidently, the explosion opened up other bulkheads as well, so that the flooding could not be confined to hold four. Possibly, there is damage to the propeller shaft as well. It is possible to swim inside the hull past the damaged area from hold four to hold five. Both holds flooded simultaneously. Ascending out of hold five, the exact counterpart of the forward winch house and the mast will be passed. The last hold may be reached now.

A lot of galley equipment is located on the first tween deck. A bowl rests next to a tea kettle, next to which another bowl or sauce pan can be seen. Two messkits are to the right and left; their handles are still attached. There are a lot of sticks, arranged in parallel, suggest kitchen utensils, chopsticks or something similar, packaged originally in a box, and showing in the mud. A little further, a number of scattered plates, some rice bowls, a sauce platter, more messkitts, bottles, and, of all things, a shoe sole can be seen. The messkitts had metal inserts, which fell out of the enclosing vessel and are now lying around in the sediment. On both sides to the area just described, a great number of bottles are littering the deck. They have been packaged in boxes, because in some places they are still placed orderly. Obviously, this area was utilized to stow kitchen supplies and eating utensils.

On the bottom of this hold lies an outboard engine, complete with propeller and shaft. There is also what appears to be a large steel box. Aft, several round pipe segments with a large wheel and a mechanism attached have been found. They have not been identified. Various fuse boxes and distributors are mounted on the deck head, together with lamp sockets and cables.

An interesting object may be found in the dark recesses of the aft tween deck: A large compressor, together with an air bank, consisting of about ten gas storage tanks. Although this arrangement certainly looks like the air bank to refill scuba tanks from, they had an entirely different purpose. The storage tanks contained carbon dioxide, and they are a giant, remote controlled fire extinguisher for the engine room. In case of fire, the valves are opened, and the gas is piped to the affected area, to smother the flames. It is totally dark in this area. An underwater light must be used.

It is interesting to note, that in the foreship almost all hatch cover beams are still in place, while they are all removed from the aftship. Evidently, discharge of cargo had been almost completed aft, whereas forward it was not touched yet.

The deck house at the stern can be entered. It is, however, very dark inside as well. A bulb dangles from the deck head from its circuitry, but it was good only about 37 years ago. Inside the deck house are a lot of ropes, some of them have blocks attached to them. They are coiled and come in various sizes. Boxes in

Hailstorm - *The Wrecks*

various stages of decay are stacked in one doorway. On top of the deck house deck a platform has been built. The stern gun is mounted on it. Being of the same design as the one forward, it also points into the same direction, starboard forward, with little elevation.

Both masts used to break the surface, but the one forward has broken off. As a rule, the dive boat ties up to a buoy. Divers have a good point to orient themselves on the way back. They are also ideal for the usual safety decompression stop. From the photographic point, this may be particularly rewarding, as the cross tree thrive with an abundance of marine life. One can find almost everything here, a small moray eel, cock's comb oyster, soft and hard corals and plenty of fish. Other subjects to photograph may include the dive buddy, the boat and diverse combination with and without mast or flash. Generally, the many possibilities this part of the wreck offers are not exploited. Most divers use up their film on the wreck. There are, however, some very exciting photographic motifs on the wreck as well as on the mast.

Since the wreck is so interesting, the opportunities to take good pictures so varied, the diver certainly would like to take home pictures which reflect the exciting dive on the Fujikawa Maru. A few suggestions are offered about picture compositions which may not have occurred to the spell-bound underwater photographer. It is of great importance to avoid to stir up the sediment. Clouds of silt will spoil the best photographic effort, not only for the particular diver, but for everyone following him in the dive party.

Shooting up from the foremast, against the surface. It can be done best with wide angle lenses. Possibilities are silhouettes with or without the boat or divers. A strobe may be used to light up the mast close to the photographer, to add color to the picture. Shooting from the shield of the gun, with a diver swimming at the muzzle may give the picture a lot of depth and dimension. The other direction, with the diver at the shield, and the muzzle in the foreground, may yield pictures with a dramatic statement. The planes are very difficult to photograph. Individual cockpits are great subjects. Hold two is best suited for two-strobe flash technique.

The bridge area has a few subjects, which are in totally dark rooms. If the flash does not have a build-in modelling light or an underwater light has not been converted to this purpose, the dive buddy should be persuaded to illuminate the subject to be taken, to enable the photographer to frame it. The galley, the bathrooms and the Japanese bath are subjects which may be taken advantageously from outside the room. If other divers are cooperative and hold off the exploration of these areas until after the flashes have been fired, the backscatter may be a little less. The bridge deck shows some interesting available light subjects. Pictures taken from an upward angle from the tween decks, with the hatch cover beams in place, may yield interesting pictures, particularly, if the mast is incorporated into the composition.

The ship was attacked by the US sub Permit on 12 September 1943. During a night surface attack, the sub fired three torpedoes, which all hit the ship. Miraculously, the Fujikawa made it from a spot south

Hailstorm - *The Wrecks*

of the Caroline Island back to Japan, where extensive repairs were undertaken. Traces of this work are very evident. The most conspicuous part, already described, is a large hull bulge fitted from the funnel to the end of hold 5, at the waterline on port. The deck abeam hold 4 is visibly reinforced and built up. On both sides of the ship, a diagonal beam reinforces the area where the shelter deck descends to maindeck, aft of hold 4, and two other beams are placed below it, slightly offset against each other. There is a significant and large deformation of the hull on port at hold 5. The plating is pushed in by about 1 to 2 feet, and the ribs of the ship are deformed but holding.

The present state of the wreck gives reasons for concern. The pilothouse on the bridge has deteriorated and has vanished. So have the guns on the bridge nook, including the heap of cartridges. The steel plates of the midship superstructure have become extremely thin, and are rusting at a fast rate, being unprotected by a layer of marine growth or a layer of ferric hydroxide. Many of these plates are detached at their welding lines and hang free, ready to crumble. The funnel top has broken off and hangs askew from the uptakes. All neatly packed ammo for the forward gun has been cracked open and the powder removed. The forward mast broke off some time ago, and the aft main mast is in a very poor state of repair. It may fall soon. The hull itself, being not touched by divers or bubbles on the outside, seems reasonably strong.

The remains of a wooden vessel can be found at 30 degrees to the left off the stern, and consist of two large diesel cylinders, a fuel tank, two high pressure air bottles for starting the engine, a shaft with a three bladed propeller, and forward of it a long keel beam with small ribs sticking out of the sand.

Technical Data:
The Fujikawa Maru was a cargo ship with passenger accommodations.

Tonnage :	6 938 ts	
Length :	132,60 m	435 ft waterline
Width :	17,83 m	58.5 ft
Depth :	10,00 m	32.8 ft
Speed max. :	16 knots	
Speed serv. :	14 knots	
Engine :	1 x Mitsubishi-Sulzer Diesel	
Launch :	15 April 1938	Builder : Mitsubishi Heavy Industry
Service :	01 July 1938	Owner : Toyo Kaiun

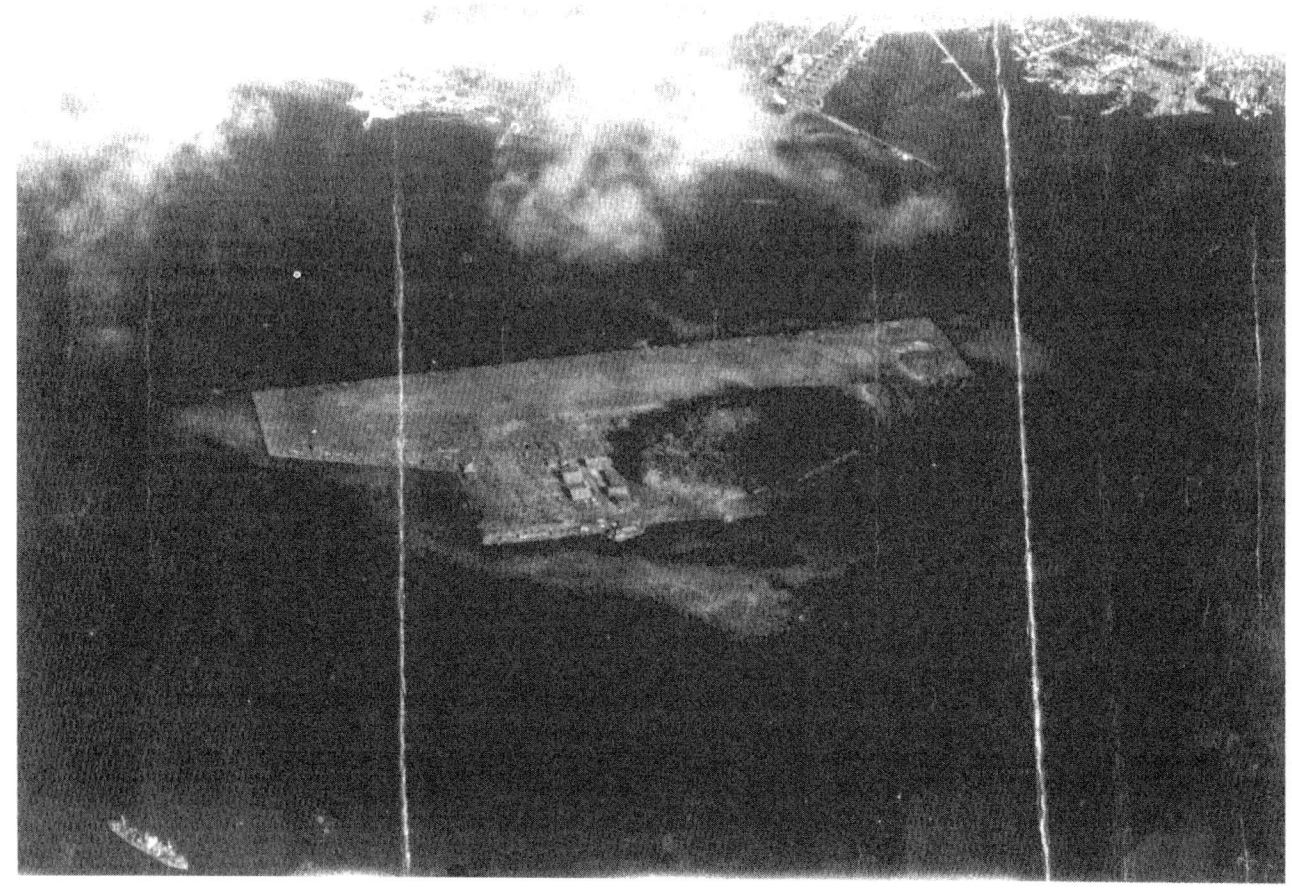

Fujikawa Maru (bottom left), Eten and part of the bunker facilities in Dublon have been subjected to repeated attacks. The runway of Eten is cratered, and the Fujikawa Maru appears to be sinking stern first.

FUJISAN MARU

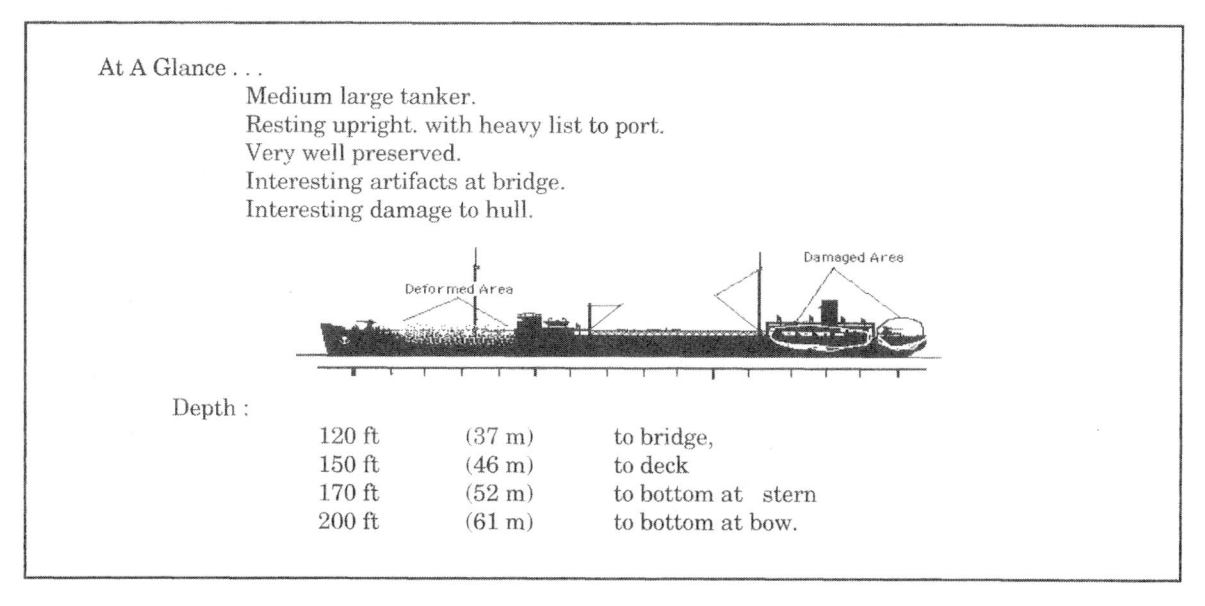

At A Glance . . .
Medium large tanker.
Resting upright. with heavy list to port.
Very well preserved.
Interesting artifacts at bridge.
Interesting damage to hull.

Depth :

120 ft	(37 m)	to bridge,
150 ft	(46 m)	to deck
170 ft	(52 m)	to bottom at stern
200 ft	(61 m)	to bottom at bow.

The Fujisan Maru was a fairly large oil tanker of about 9500 tons, a length of about 490 ft at the waterline, and a beam of 61 ft. The ship was heading in a northeasterly direction when it sank. The Fujisan Maru was one of the few ships, which were running and trying to escape when she was hit.

Her whereabouts during the first day of the attack are a matter of conjecture. To begin with, all tankers sunk in Truk may be found at the Combined Fleet or the Repair Anchorage. However, in one of the first attack photos taken a large empty tanker at the oil jetty off south Dublon can be clearly made out. The ship is riding very high, and is probably trimmed to aft, to allow to give the prop a proper 'bite'. Obviously, her forward cargo tanks were empty. The area of the former oil jetty is fairly close to the new fisheries dock, and the semi-molten, huge oil storage tanks are only a few hundred feet inland. It would be safe to assume that the Fujisan had just pumped her cargo of heavy oil into the shore tanks.

The attacking photographic planes made a series of pictures of this location, of which two survived in the Archives. Both show an oblique view across the waters between Moen and Dublon, from the southeast and the other one from the north, over the mountains. In common, they both show the Fujisan tied to the jetty, and a string of smaller freighters at anchor close inshore along the southern line of Dublon. Anti-aircraft fire was intense in that area, and the attacking planes chose other targets during their first strikes.

There are two conflicting theories about the location of the Fujisan during the first day of the attack, but there is no doubt about the second day.

One suggests that the ship was safest at the oil jetty, because she was protected by the concentration of anti-aircraft batteries at Moen and Eten, and should she have been hit, she would would have sunk in fairly shallow waters and thus fascillitate salvage afterwards. Actually, none of the freighters strung out alongside the southern shore of Dublon was sunk, as searches have confirmed. However, certain evidence from the Aircraft Action Reports suggests that the Japanese decided on another course of action.

The other theory says that with the priority given to the American pilots to destroy oilers, this ship would have been a sitting duck and may have been reduced to a flaming wreck had it not cast off very quickly from the jetty and sailed away. Later in the day there are definite reports and photographs which show that a large tanker being underway was attacked by planes from Bunker Hill on Strike 3B-1, just as the ship was clearing the North Pass. The pilots observed hits. It was about at 0830 h, on the first day. Although the American pilots reported a "550 ft long, 13,000 tons oiler", identification is not certain. There is no Japanese account of a tanker sunk or damaged in that area. On the other hand, both Akagi and Zuikai Maru, which were attacked in that area, and sunk, were freighters with an entirely different profile. The pilots erred a few times, as with the Hanakawa Maru.

Enterprise pilots reported a tanker to head north at about 1000 h, while pilots from the same carrier reported an oiler to head south, located west of Moen, at 1400 h. (Strike 1C and 1E, resp.) These reports refer, almost certainly, to the Fujisan Maru. Originally trying to escape through the North Pass, she was subjected to heavy aerial bombing without taking a hit or suffering damage. The huge smoke columns, rumbling sound of bombs been dropped some distance away and the thundering gun fire of the American battleships and cruisers, would have been a clear indication for trouble ahead. So she was turned around, and dashed back into the Lagoon. Subsequently, she may have anchored during the night at the Combined Fleet Anchorage. It was probably intended to sail her through the North Pass, as she was taking the common route from the Combined Fleet Anchorage to that pass, with the first light of the next day. Early on the second day she was running through the channel between Moen and Dublon. She had just cleared Yanagi reef by a few minutes, on

Hailstorm - *The Wrecks*

starboard, when she was subjected to a bombing attack from planes of the Enterprise. It was the first strike of the second day. Several 1000 lbs armor piercing bombs with a 0.1 second delay fuse were released. One was a near miss on starboard quarter, the second was seen to have hit the ship at the stern (but was a very close miss at port quarter) and the third one was a near miss off port quarter slightly forward of the previous bomb.

The ship was rocked wildly from the three heavy explosions. The stern was lifted out of the water, then the ship fell back and submerged the bow, and rocked a few times before she came to rest. In the process the guns were shorn off their mount. The port anchor broke free from the bow stopper and took almost all the anchor chain with it to the bottom. All

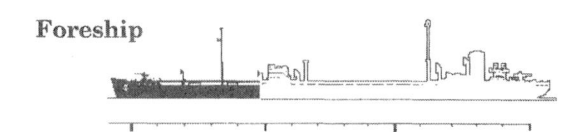

Foreship

The bridge is intact, and there is no damage. Inside the superstructure, underneath the bridge house, particularly nice china, large, nicely decorated platters, used to be located. One or two of these are now at the Fisheries Department awaiting transfer to the museum. The rest has, unfortunately, disappeared.

The starboard side shows significant and interesting damage. There is a deep, large, V-shaped indentation in the hull between the bridge and the forecastle. The shell plating is not opened or torn, just deformed over about 60 ft (18 m). This notch extends

The Fujisan Maru seen here tied to the oil jetty on Dublon. Insert shows a bird's view of the ship. She is empty, trimmed bow up, but undamaged. Below, the tanker has been hit at the engine room, burns and sinks stern first. The large oil slick from her bunker fuel can be seen on the water.

USNA/USNOA (all)

forward motion was stopped after she ran over the anchor chain.

Her bunker fuel at the fuel tanks aft had been ignited by the close miss. The fuel started to burn with a large black plume of smoke. The stern quickly submerged, and extinguished the blaze; the smoke changing from black to white, from the steam when the water hit the red glowing hull plates. The fuel oil was now bubbling up and formed a large oil slick. When the water had displaced all air at the damaged area the ship lost all buoyancy aft. The aftship was heavy enough to eventually drag the foreship under as well. The bow had pointed almost straight to the sky for close to an hour. The ship hit bottom at the stern, the bow pivoted slightly so that the anchor cable crossed the bows, and then the Fjisan Maru sank.

The description leads from the bridge on starboard, around the forecastle, back to the bridge on port, and finally to the stern.

from close to the shear strake to the bilge keel and forms a nose right underneath the deck. Immediately forward of the notch the hull is undamaged. The second deformation in the hull is approximately 20 ft (6 m) farther forward. It is an equally deep depression or dent, but it is much longer, about 80 to 100 ft (27 to 33 m). It so happens, that the lower part of the depression, in combination with the list of the ship, forms a ledge where the hull resumes its normal shape. Sediment has even collected on it.

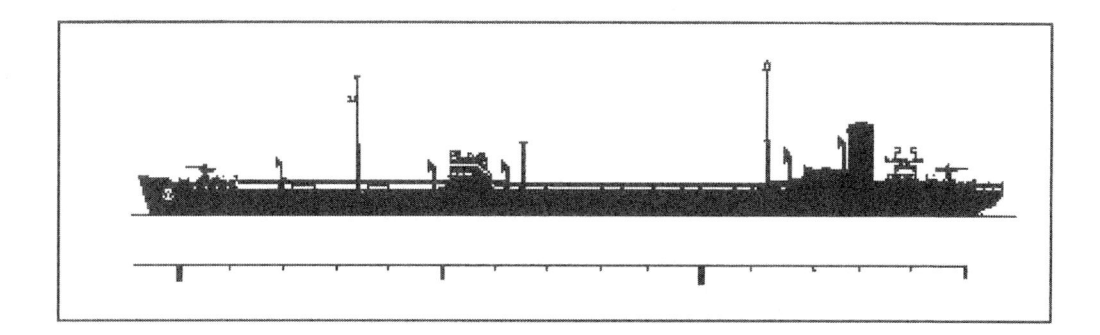

When looking over the deck to port, it can be seen that the deck has caved in. These large areas of deformed plating suggest a slow force, unrelated to the violent damage expected from the bombs. When the visibility is very good at the Fujisan, it can be seen, that these two distinct deformations follow a certain outline at the hull. This outline indicates the location of the two forward cargo tanks. The deck maintained its normal position at the boundary between them, but bulges inward considerably, a few feet further forward and aft of the separation. Both tanks were empty and closed. When the Fujisan was dragged under by the heavy stern, the hull was not strong enough to withstand the increasingly higher ambient water pressure as she settled on the bottom. She was "squeezed" by the ambient pressure of about 4 atmospheres.

The forecastle bears the usual windlasses and an empty gun platform. There is a gun mount, but the gun has disappeared. The starboard anchor is a-cockbill, i.e. it hangs down about 10 ft below the hawse pipe. It is not fully retracted and not secured. The port anchor is run out. The anchor chain is draped across the bottom of the ship, and curves back until it disappears underneath it. The ship drifted with the bow down wind. The slightly raked bow is bent to port underneath the former water line.

The pipe bridge can be seen when the forecastle is rounded and the bridge is faced. It is built clearly off the centerline of the ship to port, and is a catwalk, accommodating pipes and control valves. A tall mast stands between the forecastle and the bridge. Two power vanes are bolted to the deck between the mast and the bridge. They are used for mine sweeping. It is somewhat surprising to find minesweeping equipment on a large ship like the Fujisan Maru, but it has been seen on other ships as well.

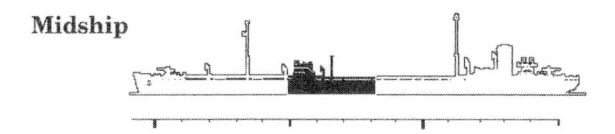

Midship

The bridge has some interesting features. There is a bridge house. Inside is a working compass, partially overgrown by a mauve colored sponge. Underneath the glass the compass card still moves. Also, there is an engine telegraph. Its pointer clearly indicates, to this day, FULL AHEAD. This is evidence that the Fujisan Maru tried to escape by running away. She was caught in full flight. In the event, nobody bothered to put the engine telegraph back to FULL STOP. There was probably nobody alive anymore. There was also no need for that. The ship was mortally wounded by the hit, and the engine stopped immediately by itself.

A case of machine gun ammunition and some loose clips are located on port off the deck house on the midship superstructure. The position of the anti-aircraft weapon can only be surmised from the location of the ready ammunition; it appears to have been positioned on top of the tall deck house. A galley and a triple stove are located on the second deck aft at the superstructure.

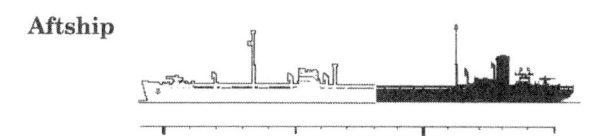

Aftship

The catwalk running from the bridge to the aft superstructure definitely is not in the exact middle of the ship, but moved clearly to starboard. The aft structure rises first by one deck, and than by another, just a little farther aft. The funnel, which is tall, stands undamaged. The area abeam port of the funnel is a very good example of the terrible force of a large bomb explosion in the immediate vicinity. It is also evidence that the bomb did not hit the ship directly.

The steel of the boatdeck is bent upward at a right angle to its former position over a distance of 60 ft (18 m). Aft it is destroyed and crumbled towards inboard. The shell plating is missing over about 75 ft (25 m). The edges are jagged. All structural elements are blown upward. The poop deck is largely destroyed. There are only a few parts remaining of the gun platform. Damage is so severe and the destruction so intensive, that there was no chance of survival for the ship. The burning fuel oil developed tremendous heat. The bent stanchion of the rail guard at a distance from the bomb damage bear silent witness to it.

A late attack photo, taken by a plane from Yorktown on the second day, shows the Fujisan Maru as the bow points skyward, and the stern is submerged. Fire is still evident from the large amount of smoke, but since the color is whitish, water was

Hailstorm - *The Wrecks*

Yamada

already extinguishing the blaze. A large oil slick formed to the sides and aft of the ship, drifting downwind.

The ship was discovered by two Air Micronesia pilots, Keith Jaeger and Ed O'Quinn, who were avid divers. At the time when the airline pilots still circled the islands routinely, they discovered an oil slick on one particularly calm day, and got a tentative fix on the location. After their return to Honolulu they obtained a depth finder, specifically for finding the wreck, had themselves taken to the location and promptly found the ship. It was probably around 1976.

The Fujisan Maru was owned by Iino-Kaiun, and the diesel driven oiler was an unusual fast ship. The service speed, i.e. the speed fully laden, was 16 knots, while the she could make almost 19 knots as maximum speed when empty. For stability reasons, the cargo tanks were subdivided into three segments, not two, as was most commonly done at the time. The double bottom was specifically reinforced.

Before the war, she hauled crude oil between the US and Japan. Late in 1941, she was taken in hand by the Navy. From 1942 onwards, the ship was used to supply the Navy with bunker oil. She was taking part in the attack on the Aleutian islands, which was a diversionary attack, simultaneously to the Battle at Midway. Later, her fast speed was used in a desperate attempt to reinforce positions in New Guinea. With a "deck cargo" of 1900 troops, according to records, she was probably one of the participants of the "Tokyo Express". A bomb hit by a land based B-17 bomber put her out of commission in December 1943. She was back in service early in 1944. Troops had to be carried, probably most miserably on deck, on later voyages, literally on top of her cargo of oil supplies.

Technical Data:

Tonnage	:	9 524 ts gross; 12 501 tdw	
Length over all	:	156,06 m	512 ft
water line		149,35 m	490 ft
Width	:	19,81 m	61 ft
Depth	:	11,28 m	37 ft
Draught	:	8,26 m	27 ft
Speed, max.	:	18.79 knots	
service	:	16.00 knots	
Horsepower	:	7 200	
Engine	:	1 x MAN-Diesel	
Launch	:	31 May 1931	
Service	:	29 August 1931	
Builder	:	Harima Dockyard	
Owner	:	Iino Kaiun	

Hailstorm - *The Wrecks*

IJN Destroyer FUMIZUKI

At A Glance ...
- Medium sized destroyer of old design.
- Resting on even keel, with 15 deg list to port.
- Interesting wreck in fairly good condition.
- Gun on whaleback forecastle,
- Shielded triple torpedo launchers forward well deck
- Crack in hull aft of second funnel/ aftship.
- Large propellers.

Area of Hull Damages

Depth:
125 ft (38 m) to bottom
100 ft (30 m) to superstructure.

The 1923 Fleet Program called for building of 12 destroyers units, to be slightly bigger and faster than those authorized by the 1921-1922 program. These group of new destroyers were all of the Mutsuki-class, named after the type-ship.

The Fumizuki was built 1925 and launched 16 February 1926. She was almost to the day 18 years old, but already, at the time of sinking, considered obsolete as a fleet destroyer. The builder was Fujinagata Zosen, Osaka. Originally, this Mutsuki-class destroyer was numbered, as were all in her class, and she was carrying the number "29". Incidentally, the number on the bow is the tactical number of the Destroyer Squadron, not the ship's number. In 1928 the ships were given names, and from then on she was known as Fumizuki.

This class of destroyers was an improvement of the Kamikaze-class, of which the Hayate, the last of the series, was launched only in March 1925, just a year earlier then the Fumizuki. Originally, the Mutsuki-class of destroyers was also equipped to perform minesweeping and minelaying duties.

Although the design speed of these ships was 37 knots, quite fast for their times, they only reached 33.5 knots in the full load condition. Only when lighted were they able to achieve 37.25 knots. They reached this speed with 4 Kampon boilers and two geared turbines, generating almost forty thousand horsepowers. The aftship clearly conveys the message of high speed. Because of the sleek form of the ship below the waterline, the propeller shafts emerge from the hull just slightly behind of the aftermost engine room. They are fixed to the underwater hull with heavy A-brackets. Each one of the two turbines drove one shaft. The propellers are 3-bladed with a high pitch. Although the stern is differently shaped compared with the Susuki - Patrol Boat 34 -, the destroyer wreck off the west shore of Dublon, the propellers and the rudder of the Susuki and the Fumizuki are very similar.

Two interesting innovations set the Mutsuki-class apart from the previous class of destroyers and set marks for the subsequent Japanese destroyer development. First, there was the characteristic double curvature bow, which, modified, became a standard feature on many Japanese warships. The second was the introduction of 24 inch torpedo tubes, which could launch the "Long Lance" torpedoes. These weapons were propelled by combusting gasoline and oxygen and had a much longer range, higher speed and more punch in form of a heavier warhead. The triple torpedo launchers were located aft of the forecastle, in a well deck forward of the bridge and aft of the second funnel.

The forecastle carried originally a solitary 4.7 inch (12 cm) flat trajectory gun, later to be replaced by a quicker firing dual purpose weapon of the same calibre. The well deck aft of the slightly whale-backed forecastle and the location of the torpedo tubes, was a feature copied from the torpedo boat destroyer design of the German Imperial Navy before World War I. At the time the Fumizuki was launched, navies of other nations had long abandoned this particular construction of a well deck with torpedo tubes forward. It was considered to be wet in heavy seas and a structural weak spot in the design.

The conning tower, the lower part of the bridge, was quite narrow at the main deck level and had two prominent portholes just below the sideway extension. The pilot house, one deck higher than the conning tower, was widened and extended forward and athwart. At the main deck there were passageways on both sides of the conning tower. The upper part of the bridge was glassed in, above it two optical range finders were located. At the aft edge of the bridge, a pole mast rose, with a stay fitted and possibly some antennas added during the war.

The two funnels were slightly raked, and of about the same size. Originally fitted with spark

Hailstorm - *The Wrecks*

arresters, they were later topped by raked funnel caps. This was done during their first refit 1935/1936. At the same time their hulls were strengthened and shields were added to the torpedo launchers.

Between the two funnels was the second gun position. Aft of the second funnel on a platform, large searchlights were located. In some units they were replaced with anti-aircraft automatic weapons but in others not. Immediately aft, a pair of life boats were suspended from the davits. The second triple torpedo launchers followed. Aft a deckhouse was built onto the aft ship, and one gun each was located on their respective circular gun platforms, one facing forward, the other aft. Some time later 21" launchers were replaced by 24" triple torpedo tubes.

The configuration of the aftship was changed during the 1941/1942 refit. The remaining destroyer units were converted to fast escorts. The aft facing aft gun was removed, and anti-aircraft guns installed in its place. Minesweeping and laying equipment was completely removed and in its stead the anti aircraft defenses further beefed up with 10 to 20 barrels of 25 mm machine weapons. In some destroyers, 13.2 mm anti aircraft machine guns were placed for some of the 25 mm guns. Aft torpedo launchers were evidently removed on some units, including the Fumizuki. 36 depth charges carried normally could be launched by 4 throwers. Consequently, the tonnage increased from 1315 ts displacement light and 1772 normal to 1590 ts resp. 1913 ts standard, with a resultant drop in speed to 34 knots max. light.

The Fumizuki belonged to the Destroyer Flotilla 5, being part of the Third Blockade and Transport Fleet, based in Formosa/Taiwan. All units saw extensive combat during the fierce struggle for the Solomons in 1942 and 1943, and the majority were lost there on various occasions. Fumizuki formed part of the famous Tokyo Express, the relief attempts for the Japanese forces in Guadalcanal. Eventually, no ship of its class survived the hostilities.

Up to October 1943:

The Fumizuki was stationed in Rabaul as an escort and transport.

30 March 1943:

While en-route from Finschhafen to Kavieng, she was damaged by an air attack.

03 April 1943 (night 01 to 02 April 1943):

Fumizuki was caught in an air attack on a convoy to Kavieng while doing escort duties and again damaged. One of he boiler rooms was flooded by damages to the shell plating due to a near miss of a bomber counterstrike by General Kenney's bombers. At the same attack, heavy cruiser IJN Aoba took a hit on the stern which crippled her and took her out for the rest of the war and the Florida Maru was sunk out of this convoy.

05/06 October 1943:

Fumizuki was part of the evacuation force, Destroyer Transport Group under Capt. Yuzo Kanaoka, together with Mazukaze and Yunagi. The group pulled out of an engagement with US destroyers at the Slot, whereas the escorting group slugged it out and lost.

09 October 1943:

While on a transport trip from Buka to Rabaul/Kavieng she was attacked by planes and damaged.

04 January 1944:

While passing the Stephen Strait she was attacked and damaged by Rear Admiral F. C. Sherman's aviators from the new fleet carrier Bunker Hill and the light carrier Monterey.

31 January 1944:

She received serious damage during an air attack by land based B-24 bombers on Rabaul on this date. From Rabaul she proceeded to Truk for much needed repairs and refit. The Fumizuki, pretty badly damaged, formed part of the escorting forces for a convoy, which arrived in Truk on 06 February 1944. Many of these ships from this convoy shared the same fate to sink in the Truk Lagoon.

Temporary repairs were to be carried out in Truk. The fleet repair ship Akashi was available in Truk Lagoon, as was a floating dry dock. Evidently, the repair party had taken her well apart. Not all guns were serviceable and both engines and the boilers were disassembled. As the repair commenced, most of the ammunition was taken off the ship. Instead of being fixed to be a fighting ship, the Fumizuki sank in Truk.

Mr. Heigo Matsumoto was the Chief Gunnery Officer of the Fumizuki, and the executive officer on board during the raid. He reported that the Fumizuki entered Truk Lagoon on 06 February 1944, in the evening. Despite being significantly damaged herself, she had been escorting a convoy from Rabaul, which laboriously made its way from the south to Truk at 5 knots. The destroyer temporarily anchored at night at the Combined Fleet Anchorage, but because of her poor condition and damages sustained previously, she was assigned a berth near the fleet repair ship Akashi. Consequently, she moved over to the Fleet Repair Anchorage off Dublon in the morning of 07 February 1944.

The Akashi was moored approximately equidistant between the north-west point of Dublon and the north-east point of Fefan. Next to the Fumizuki, there were the Kansho Maru, Hoyo Maru, Kiyozumi Maru and the Tonan Maru 3, all being worked on because of torpedo or bomb damages sustained on the open seas while supplying war material.

The Fumizuki was still anchored in the morning at the Repair Anchorage, and an early attack photo shows her fairly deep in the recess between the islands of Dublon and Fefan. Repairs to the hull structure and machinery were commenced immediately with the aid of personnel and material from the Akashi.

When the raid on Truk began, the Fumizuki was anchored rather helplessly at that spot, with both turbines and boilers in a state of disassembly.

The ship's engineers and the repair crew worked frantically to put together the machinery and succeeded during the lull between the first and the second attack wave, however, only one of the two turbines could be returned to duty. The ship made up steam and began evasive maneuvers in the open water west of Dublon, driven by one propeller only.

At 1030 h, on the 17 February 1944, the

Hailstorm - *The Wrecks*

Fumizuki was subject to a bombing attack. All bombs missed, and only one was a close miss to port. The bomb had a short delay fuse and exploded underwater

maintained that their wing position and tail lights were on as well. However, when the senior officers looked back at the Fumizuki they saw her sinking. Her

The Fumizuki or one of her sisters, before rebuilding.

IWM

at slightly abaft midships, port of the aft engine room. The explosion of this 500 lbs bomb was powerful and close enough to damage the hull significantly. It put the one working engine out of commission.

The ship's crew endeavored to patch up the hole in the shell plating and build a cofferdam with all sorts of dunnage material, but to no avail. The destroyer began to develop a list and settled in the water. The first day's raid ended and the Fumizuki was still afloat.

With the only engine out of commission and the engine room hopelessly flooded, the captain ordered the starboard anchor dropped to prevent the destroyer from drifting onto the coral reefs or beaching.

After the status of the engines was verified, the skipper called a tug for assistance, the intention being to tow the destroyer to the Naval Station in Dublon. The tug strained to pull the destroyer to the island.

The idea had to be abandoned at about midnight of the 17 February. Why the tug did not succeed is rather obvious, as the anchor cable had not been cut and the anchor held the ship firmly. No tug would be able to pull an anchored ship.

While this was going on the crew observed the hospital ship Tenno Maru, also called Hikawa Maru 2, taking evasive actions to prevent being hit by bombs, although American sources specifically mentioned that "a hospital ship in the northern part of the lagoon" was not attacked. The Tenno Maru was the captured Dutch KPM passenger ship SS op ten Noort, converted and commissioned for the IJN.

The skipper was forced to order "Abandon Ship", because the situation became untenable. The Fumizuki's complement were taken over by the tug. Finally, also the three senior officers, skipper, chief gunnery officer and chief engineer, after retrieving flag, the Emperor's portrait and other important items, went into a boat and were towed by the tug towards Dublon, leaving Fumizuki to her fate.

While the tug was making its way to the island, the night radar raid from Enterprise unfolded. The tug was bombed, but the bomb missed without causing casualties or bad damages. The men could clearly see the exhaust flames from the single engined planes and

bow rose high against the night skies which became tinged with the early morning rays. Then the stern settled. She slid under water at about 0530 h on the 18 February, in the first light of dawn.

The wounded were taken to the hospital ship, Tenno Maru, now anchored near Fefan.

The searches for the Fumizuki proved unsuccessful, because we had taken her last documented position into account and searched intensively at the Repair Anchorage, specifically at the southern part. The details of the sinking of IJN destroyer Fumizuki were not revealed to me before Mr. Masaharu Yamamoto's letter of 10 April 1987. Mr. Yamamoto is attached to the Historical Research Institute in Japan. It had been my intention to look for her at the location which Mr. Heigo Matsumoto had indicated as the location of the sinking. It was ironical that just at the same time the ship was found independently. Its location far out west of Moen and close 30 degrees from a marked sandspit, suggests that the destroyer did a lot of running and evasive action before it was bombed.

The destroyer rests with 15 degrees list to port. Only the starboard anchor is out; there is no chain or anchor on port. The heavy chain leads to a large windlass on the slightly convex "whale back" forecastle deck, which does not carry any guardrail anymore. A narrow empty deck space follows. The broken off part of the port anchor cable lies here. A wavebreaker is located in front of the 12 cm gun. The long barrel of this weapon is very much overgrown with hard and soft corals and hydroids, which alter its form grotesquely. The gun shield is a boxy structure with slanting halfs, the widest part being in the middle of the shield. It suggests that a change to a dual-purpose weapon has not been effected: This gun is part of the original armament and is not useable against aircraft. It is also well overgrown. Ammunition boxes are placed forward of the gun. A few empty cartridges can be seen next to them. The forecastle deck is slightly extended aft, so that it partially shelters the very large triple torpedo launchers, which are mounted on maindeck, the deck below the forecastle deck. The three large tubes are topped by a shield, which is just about at the same height as the forecastle deck. These are modern

Hailstorm - *The Wrecks*

weapons for "Long Lance" torpedoes. They are covered way forward with a box-like structure. The launcher tubes have rusted through in places allowing a peek inside. The extension of the gun mount can be seen slightly forward of this cover forward. Aft of the launchers a set of two twin anti-aircraft guns were placed on platforms fitted retroactively. It appears that the guns are missing. Only their mounts and shields remain, which are luxuriously overgrown by corals. The guns may have been taken off during repairs.

The bridge used to be compared with a Japanese tea garden. Everything was very petit and beautiful inside. There is no chance to see this anymore because in 1988, the bridge fell over to port and now lies upside-down on the sea bottom, next to the hull. At the break on the deck, the picture is very confusing, as there is an array of bent pipes, plates and steel beams. Somebody had collected plates from the mess and displayed in this area, which distracts a little from the desolate picture of the amputated bridge. Arguments how it happened have been voiced with various degrees of acrimony, but the possibility that this top heavy piece of the ship just bent over and finally separated appears to be inviting the theory that this was a constructive weak point of the design. The narrow conning tower was followed by a substantial horizontal extension of the flying bridge. The two forward facing portholes can still be well seen immediately above the extension, which rests on the white sand bottom. Also the first funnel has fallen apart. It can be seen how the uptake was bisected, serving two boilers. Some steam pipes can be seen leading into it. There are long cylindrical structures built on deck, with rounded upper corners, extending from the first funnel past the second. These structures housed the reload torpedoes. Forward and slightly inboard, the storage bins for the torpedo warheads can be seen. The second stack, slightly flared at the base, carries a conspicuous funnel cap. Between the two stacks, a platform carried the second 12 cm gun. However, this piece was removed and two machine weapons took its place. Some of the ammo boxes on the platform were retained. The exposed parts of this ship are well overgrown, making identification difficult at times. Immediately aft of the second funnel, a searchlight platform was installed. A long empty deck space continued aft of the funnel. It is surprising to see such a large area without deck structures. The torpedo launchers, originally located here, were removed, but not the elaborate railroad tracks, for the carriages, to carry the reload torpedoes. Boat davits built on the sheerstrake of the ship, point outward. Aft of the empty space, the aft gun platform can be seen. Originally it carried one gun facing forward and the other facing aft. Latter has been removed. The forward gun and this are of the same make, but it was difficult to verify this because of the growth. The gun shield covers only about one meter of the sides and the breech of the weapon is exposed. It is not quite clear whether the main deck assumed a whaleback designed aft or whether this originated from the bomb damages, which now come into view. Going down at the hull here, the in and outlets of the large condensers have been partially ripped out of the hull. Only a short distance farther aft, the hull is severely buckled on port. The hull is actually badly bent upward, and the deck shows damages. On port, a depth charge can be seen, and several other box-like structures, throwers perhaps. The stern appears to be squared off, but this may be an optical illusion. The well rounded and hydrodynamic hull is severely bent and buckled. The propeller on port is buried up to the lower half of its upper blade in the sand. The heavy A-bracket holds the shaft, which is below the sand. The rudder is trapezoid, but with very much rounded corners. The starboard propeller clears the bottom by several feet, and bears a large hub. It is particularly on port where the ship was damaged very badly. The strands of the degaussing coils have snapped in some places; in others they were significantly dislocated. The plates of the stern and the starboard aftship are crumbled, crushed and warped for about 20 m forward. At one area the one meter long, 15 cm wide tear in the hull can be seen, which was the bad leak, resulting in the ultimate abandoning of the ship. One triangular shaped hull plate of the stern had been blown out. The whole of the aftship is warped badly. It is surprising that the ship was able to sail at all. The shafts must have vibrated badly.

The bottom is at 121 ft (36.9 m). It is 115 ft (35m) to the top of the deck on starboard and 105 ft (32 m) to the deck on port midships.

The superstructure, although not damaged, shows its age and is weakened by corrosion. The weight of the superstructure is high, accounting for a high center of gravity and making the ships of this class roll badly in the Pacific swells.

Sources and Appreciation:

Boueicho Bouei Kenshujo Senshi Shitsu (Shohon Shinbunsha) for details of the Fumizuki's fleet operation.
Mr. Masaharu Yamamoto, special thanks for communication with the senior surviving officer, Mr. Higo Matsumoto, and his continued efforts to set the record straight.
Rod and Kathy Canham, who have been on the wreck as first Americans and who contributed details about the present state of the wreck. John Varty contributed to my understanding of the wreck.

169

Hailstorm - *The Wrecks*

Technical Data:

Launched: 16 February 1926   Commissioned: 03 July 1926

First Rebuilding 1935-1936:
Hull strengthened, raked funnel caps and shields for the TT fitted.
Second Rebuilding 1941-1942:
Conversion to DD/ASW-Transport/DDE

Displacement light:	1315 ts	after conversion:	1590 ts
Displacement stdrd:	1772 ts	after conversion:	1913 ts
Length waterline:	338 ' 9"	Length metric:	103.25 m
Length perpendic:	30 ' 0"	Beam metric:	9.15 m
Draught:	9 ' 8"	Draught metric:	2.95 m

Machinery: 4 Kampon boilers, 2 Parsons geared turbines, 2 shafts
Shaft horsepowers: 38,500
Fuel: 420 ts oil
Speed max, light: 37.5 knots   Radius: 4000 ms at 15 knots

Armament:
<u>as built:</u>   <u>after conversion:</u>

4 x 4.7" (12 cm), 45 cal, low angle   2 x 4.7" (12 cm), 50 cal, dual purpose
2 x 7.7 mm mg   10 X 25 mm AA
6 x 24" torpedo launchers   6 x 24" torpedo launchers,
10 torpedoes   same
16 mines   mine gear removed
18 depth charges   36 depth charges, 4 throwers,
Complement: 150   transport facilities (track and winch)

These sketches show the official appearance of the Fumizuki in 1926 (top two sketches) and her modification and re-armament after 1942. The handwritten notes indicate the positions of triple 25 mm anti-aircraft automatics. When converted to Patrol Boats, these destroyers showed increased anti-aircraft armament, but the remaining aft gun was removed together with the aft torpedo tubes. The appearance of the Fumizuki differs in some details from the sketch on the bottom. The gun midships has been removed. In its stead, anti-aircraft machine guns were installed port and starboard. From the ammunition located in this area it appears that they were single 13.2 mm guns, but it looks as if the gun itself was removed, leaving the mounts and the shields. All structures aft of the radio mast, just aft of the second funnel, have been removed. The forward pointing aft gun remains standing, but aft of it all structures are in a state of disrepair. The boat davits aft of the second funnel remained, and the life boats were retained. Instead of the indicated triple barrelled 25 mm anti-aircraft guns, it appears that twin weapons were fitted. The ship probably retained its original 12 cm low trajectory guns.

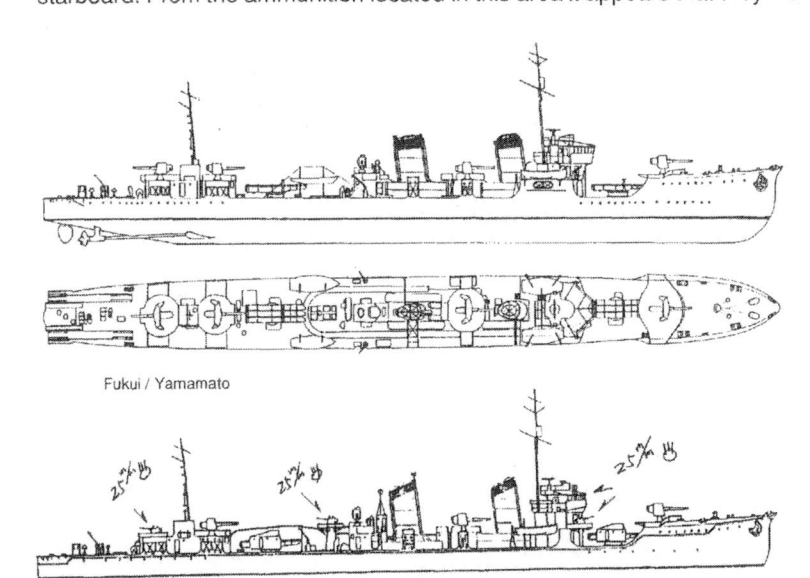

Fukui / Yamamato

GOSEI MARU

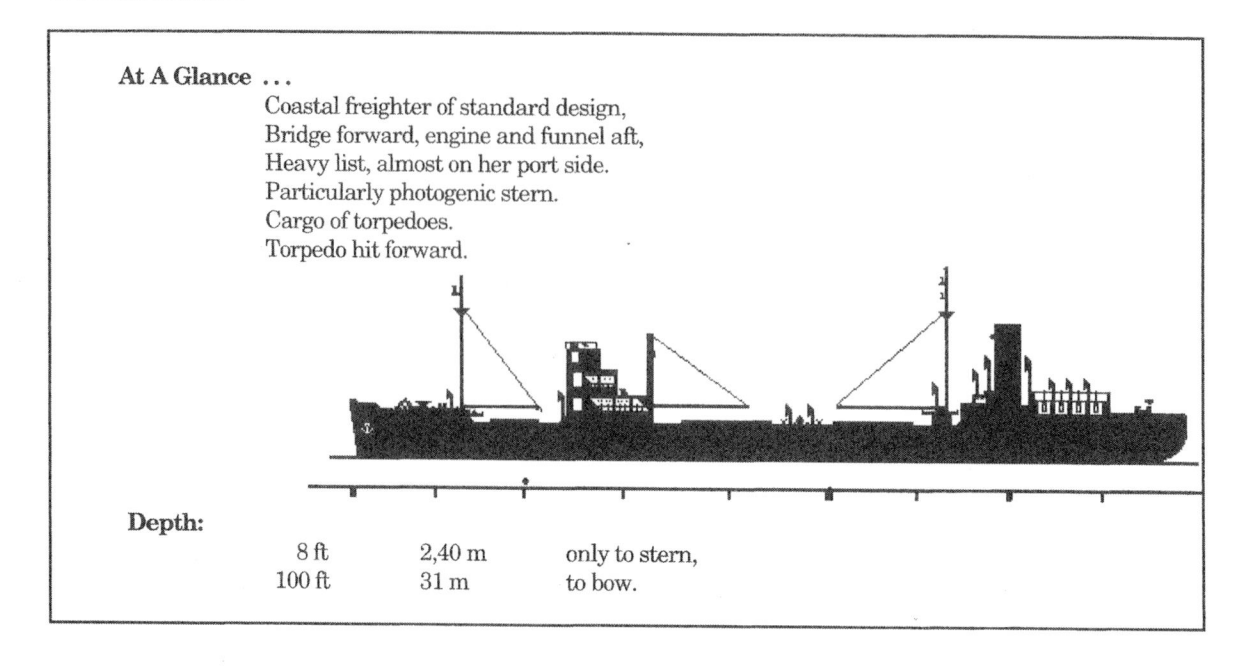

At A Glance ...
Coastal freighter of standard design,
Bridge forward, engine and funnel aft,
Heavy list, almost on her port side.
Particularly photogenic stern.
Cargo of torpedoes.
Torpedo hit forward.

Depth:
| 8 ft | 2,40 m | only to stern, |
| 100 ft | 31 m | to bow. |

The Gosei Maru was a supply ship for the Sixth Fleet (submarines). She carried torpedoeas and depth charges. Latter were removed after the war. The lines of the Gosei Maru are unconventional, and she looks different than the other ships sunk in Truk. However, she was one of the ships built in large numbers . The design was adapted for the Standard D freighters during the war. The bow has a small rake. The foremast is located directly after the large forecastle. It has broken off. The forecastle is followed by a hold, and the bridge follows more forward than midships. It is fairly square in shape and two decks high. Right aft of the bridge a kingpost is located, which carried two cargo derricks. There are two holds between the bridge and the after superstructure. They appear to be long. The second mast aft of the hold is immediately followed by the long superstructure at three quarter deck. A deck house and the funnel are built on top of it. There used to be ventilators in this area. The stack is an open, tall, narrow tube, indicative of a ship burning coal. The flag of the Rising Sun was flying from a flagpole at the stern. The ship carried a pair of life boats abaft the funnel.

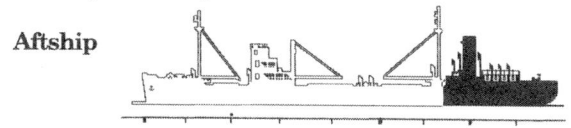

Aftship

Normally, the Gosei Maru can be located easily on the east shore of Uman. Her stern is so shallow that it is visible from the dive boat. A shallow dive begins here, and the visit is indeed worth it. The large, four bladed propeller with the beautifully shaped counter of the ship is a great photographic subject. It is called a clipper stern, reminiscent of the tea-clippers of by-gone days. The tall, single plate rudder is moved slightly to port. The broken off part of the after mast can be seen in the sand nearby. On the deck at the very stern of the Gosei Maru stands the bent flag pole. The wreck almost lies on its port side.

The poop rises one deck. Rail guards, now partially disintegrated, used to enclose this area. The doorways are open. It is, however, a bit confusing to swim inside the aft superstructure. Inevitably, the diver tends to align himself with the bulkheads of the ship, and assumes the same heavy tilt to the left. Since gravity tries to upright him, almost everybody gets slightly annoyed with this problem and adjusts the weights on the belt.

Inside the superstructure bulkheads seem to be in the way all the time. The head, the galley, the crew accommodations, and lastly, the engine room are interesting to visit. It is easy to weave in and out of the various compartments, and swim back to the deck. Generally, there is plenty of light inside the wreck. Since it is so shallow, the feeling of being confined does not creep up, as it may do during the visit on other wrecks. Even the most timid divers enjoy a harmless little tour through the superstructure of the Gosei Maru. Access may be gained through the boat deck. Originally, it was covered with wooden planking. Since this has gone a long time ago, it is possible to dive through the rectangular openings. There is a big shell casing in the lower deck. Nearly everybody diving in this area places it somewhere else, so it is not useful to give a detailed description where it was seen last. The steel structures on deck are overgrown with various species of coral, particularly the shallow, exposed parts.

The funnel is not quite as tall as it used to be. The top plates have corroded away over the years, and the stack looks slightly tattered at the open end. It had been built on a long, narrow elevation on the deck. Next to the funnel are the engine room skylights. They are mounted on the sides of a broad based triangular structure. The planking on the other part of the boats deck is gone as well, of course. Now the steel support beams form slit-like openings. The boats davits are pointing inward at starboard. They may have have swung back, because the crew certainly had enough time to abandon the ship. Most ventilators have disappeared. Only the shafts indicate their former position.

Hailstorm - *The Wrecks*

Midship

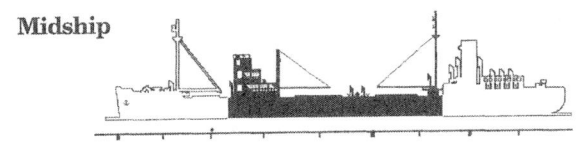

At first sight, the hold midships appears to be empty. This is because the majority of the remaining cargo has shifted to port and forward. The hold does contain, however, several rather large tubes of about 21" diameter. They may be 10 to 15 feet (3 m to 5 m) long. Most of them seem to have exploded somewhere in the middle. The force of the explosion was far less than that expected of a war head. The explanation is simple. These tube shaped objects are torpedo bodies without warheads. They contained one or more high pressure vessels for storage of air or oxygen. Either one of these gases, depending on the model of the torpedo, was used to burn kerosine or alcohol in a combustion chamber into which water was injected. The steam generated drove a steam engine, which transmitted the power, via a reduction gear, to a double shaft and counter rotating propellers. During the years, these high pressure gas tanks inside the torpedoes have continued to corrode from the outside and from within. They were almost certainly filled when the Gosei sank.

The time was finally reached, when the internal pressure ruptured the tanks. As there were a great number of torpedo bodies inside the holds of the ship, they went off at unpredictable intervals. This was considered dangerous for sport diving. The decision was made in 1976 to detonate the vessels from the outside, by an explosive charge. Most air tanks were destroyed this way and the wreck is again considered save to dive on. On the inside of one particular torpedo, the combustion chamber and the engine housing can be recognized. The war heads have been stored in the lower parts of the ship. They generally can not be seen, except for one, which is still beautifully packaged, its nose facing upwards.

Bottles and other general cargo can be found in the holds as well. The torpedoes and their warheads were destined for the 7th Flotilla of the Sixth Submarine Fleet. This fleet was headquartered in Truk. The final resting place of the Gosei Maru is the anchorage of the Sixth Fleet.

A bridge follows this hold. It is accessible and the visit here is quite interesting. Underneath the bridge deck, accommodations for the ship's officers can be inspected. The hold forward of the bridge appears to be empty. The forecastle bears the large windlass. The port anchor is out. The anchor chain leads to the bottom.

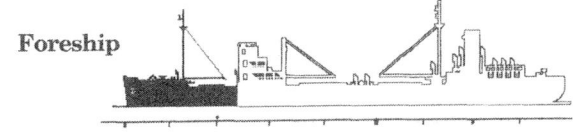

Foreship

When swimming forward from the bridge on starboard, the extensive damage to the hull can clearly be seen. A torpedo hit destroyed the starboard side of the ship. The hole extends almost from the ship's bottom to the sheerstrake. The shell plating is torn wide open and the jagged edges point inward. All frames and structural members of the hull are either destroyed or considerably bent. The hull shows a compression mark. The plates are dented in a gentle S-shaped wave form. The bow is considerably bent to starboard underneath the former waterline. There is a second compression mark at the 17th of the 24 freeing ports in the bulwark, i.e. about midships.

The ship lies on sloping ground. The ease with which the stern and the aft ship can be reached, should not distract from the fact that it is about 100 ft deep at the bow. The Gosei Maru, although attacked by bombers on the first day, was sunk by a torpedo on the second strike of the second day, by planes from the light carrier Monterey. The pilot and the crew of the Avenger reported that the wake of the torpedo stopped, but nevertheless, it exploded shortly afterwards. The ship burned, listed and sank.

Technical Data:

The Gosei Maru was a medium sized coastal freighter.

Tonnage	:	1 931 ts
Length	:	82,3 m 270.0 ft
Width	:	12,2 m 40.0 ft
Depth	:	6,2 m 20.3 ft
Speed, max	:	12,7 knots
serv	:	10,0 knots
Engine	:	1 x reciprocal steam engine, coal
Launch	:	August 1937
Builder	:	Tsuromi Iron Works Dockyard
Owner	:	Koun Kisen

Gosei Maru

HANAKAWA MARU

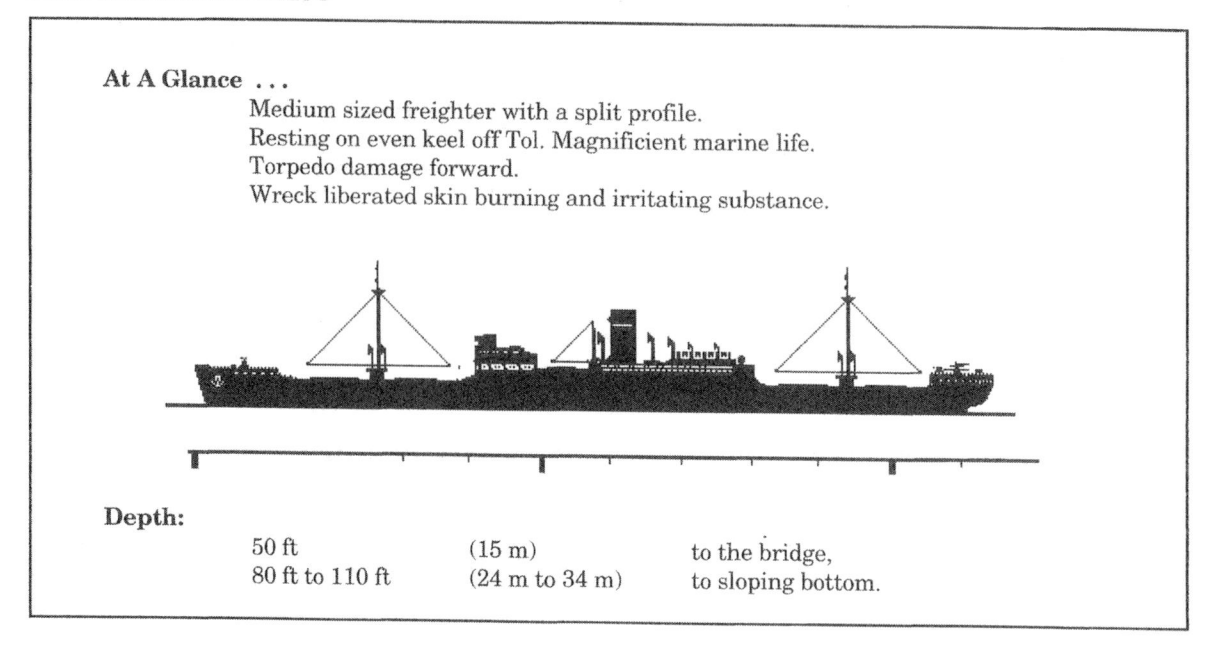

At A Glance ...
Medium sized freighter with a split profile.
Resting on even keel off Tol. Magnificient marine life.
Torpedo damage forward.
Wreck liberated skin burning and irritating substance.

Depth:
50 ft   (15 m)   to the bridge,
80 ft to 110 ft (24 m to 34 m)   to sloping bottom.

The Hanakawa Maru would be a very attractive wreck to dive on, if it were not for the skin burning substance found at the ship. The vessel rests almost perfectly straight on the bottom and is magnificently overgrown by all forms of corals and sponges. Even black coral grows here in abundance. However, an unknown substance oozes out of certain parts of the ship and burns the skin. These burns are painful and they leave temporary scars. The exact nature of the substance has not been established, although the opinion is favored in Truk that it is gasoline. Also, the exact area of the ship where the substance has been encountered, has not been pinpointed. Reports are conflicting. Although this wreck represents an interesting dive, it is not popular. The tour guides in Truk have prudently decided for many years to declare the Hanakawa Maru out of bounds. However, over the long years, the high-octane aviation gasoline, probably responsible for these problems, has slowly dissepated, and the wreck may probably be safe now. Apart from that, it is probably the wreck farthest away from Moen, although the distance to Tol looks deceptively close. It will take a solid hour by speed boat, and that is longer than to all other wrecks.

The description begins at the bow and leads via the the midship structure to the stern.

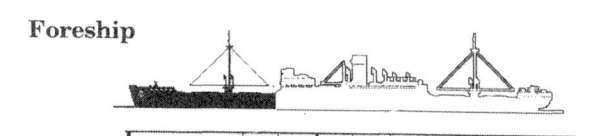

Foreship

The bow is almost straight; it hardly has a rake. The anchor chain runs in a shallow angle from the hawse hole to the seabed, meeting it more than a hundred feet away. It still remains under tension and indicates that the ship sank slowly by the bow, which clears the sloping bottom by a few feet.

The forecastle is quite big and high. There is no gun. Looking aft on the port side, many drums, objects resembling depth charges, a cargo derrick and several hatch cover beams are strewn all over the sea bed. They have been flung here by a large explosion. The forecastle is enclosed with rails, which, although mostly intact, are heavily overgrown by corals. There are many cylindrical objects in hold 1. These are gasoline drums. Hatch cover beams and derricks have all disappeared. No penetration into the tween decks of this hold has been attempted, because of the danger of getting burned.

The mast stands tall and bears a large cross tree. There are ventilator shafts fore and aft of it, as well as cargo winches. When continuing the exploration towards aft, the tremendous damage that a single torpedo can cause can be seen on starboard abeam of hold 2. There is a huge, gaping hole in the side of the ship. It extends from the bottom to near the sheerstrake. The jagged pieces of plating point inward. The hole is so large, that two divers can easily swim through it side by side. Two large broken frames point like fingers into the break. It is easy to look into the hold from the outside, and to recognize the tween decks on port, where little damage is apparent.

A great number of cylindrical objects still remain scattered on the bottom of the hold. Parallel and just a little off to the side of the hull, the long jumbo derrick came to rest on starboard. On the other side on port, a steel splinter penetrated the deck and left a hole and a break in the plate.

Midship

The midship superstructure is raised behind hold 2. The first deck can be entered through the open doors, which are located close to the fashion plate. The fashion plate is the reinforcing piece of steel, which forms the transition between the bulwark and the superstructure. Two ventilators are standing upright, inboard of the doorways. The second deck of the superstructure is recessed, and a passageway is formed on both sides of the ship, which is enclosed with rail guards. The next higher deck, the navigation bridge, is again as wide as the ship, and fairly long. Guard rails are in evidence here as well. Above this deck, a flying bridge must have been located originally. As was common at the time, it was of wooden construction and is totally gone now. The Hanakawa Maru burned like an inferno before she sank. The flying bridge certainly fell victim to the fire.

The superstructure drops aft of the bridge, and the midship hold follows. It is elevated by one deck above shelter deck. This hold is considerably smaller than the two forward and aft of it. Right aft, the superstructure again rises by one deck, into which a narrow, rectangular coal hatch with a coaming has been built. A quadruple combination of kingpost and ventilators follow. They are connected at the top with a cross bar, and standing on a narrow, about 2 ft high base, which extends all the way to the aft end of the superstructure. On both sides on this deck, the passageways are secured with rail guards.

The once high and tubular smoke stack used to stand right behind this quadruple combination. The base of the funnel is very much destroyed, and its upper part assumed an almost elliptical shape, probably due to the impact, when it fell backwards and to port. The tremendous heat of the conflagration may have caused the funnel to sag or the shock wave of the explosion blew it over. Slightly inboard, at the upper end of the funnel, next to a fallen beam, a large running light can be made out. There are two engine room skylights on both sides of the skylight house. The boiler feed vessel, a cylindrical vessel, rests athwart on the deck aft of the skylights. A pipe curves from the top and leads into the engine room. Boats davits are located on both sides. They point inboard. The crew never had a chance to use the life boats.

There is no problem to enter the aft end of the superstructure. The crew of the Hanakawa Maru was killed in the tremendous explosion and the pyre. Mortal remains of many sailors are still evident inside the aft part of the superstructure. The galley was located on port. There is a large stove, plates and bottles can be found as well. Even a large earthen crock can be heaved out of the coal and ashes. Slightly forward of the galley, a number of 2 feet (0,6m) long stainless steel high pressure vessels have been seen buried in the thick sediment. Remnants of a partition separate this area from a rest room, in which four urinals and three or four Japanese toilet bowls can be seen. Interestingly, the partition, of which some segments remained, was made out of plywood. This is evidence, that the fire raged outside, and that the ship probably went down fast. In the same room, the engine room casing extends from the deck to the deck head.

An open doorway allows penetration into the engine room. Catwalks and grating lead to lower levels. Part of the machinery can be seen below; it is about 90 ft down there. An open doorway, outside the engine room, next to the head, leads directly on to the midship hold.

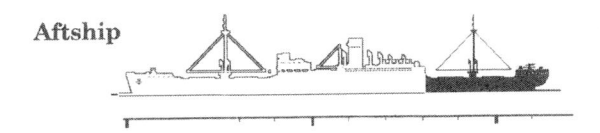

Aftship

Turning around and swimming aft in the cabin just explored, away from the hold towards aft, the exit will be reached. The midship superstructure drops back to shelter deck level. The fashion plates, ventilators and other open doorways can be seen. The derricks of hold 4 are lying across the hatch, over to port. More drums can be located inside the hold. Two winches are bolted onto the deck in front of the mast. The derricks are goose-necked onto posts on both sides of the mast, which stands upright. A solitary hatch cover beam remained in its place on hold 5. The derricks are displaced to port as well on this hold. Several drums were flung onto the deck.

There is a very large platform built on to the poop deck. A strange looking piece of artillery is mounted on it. This is clearly the 12 cm Navy Short Gun of calibre 12. The short, stout barrel points upward at an angle of 45 degrees. The stern has a clipper shape, i.e. it has a counter stern. The four bladed propeller and the rudder are undamaged.

The Hanakawa Maru was reported by the pilots of Bunker Hill to be a tanker. There may have been a certain resemblance to an oiler from above, particularly if the hatches were closed. Since the hatch cover beams are scattered on port on the sea floor, it may be assumed that they were in their places and were flung there by the explosion. The ship was not attacked the first day of the strike. However, on the second day Avengers from Bunker Hill and Cowpens descended on her, at about 0630 h, Strike 3A-2. An Avenger from Bunker Hill, launching a torpedo, is credited with the destruction of the ship.

When his torpedo hit, the Hanakawa Maru was immediately engulfed in huge flames. Behind the black smoke and the rapidly spreading flames, the ship completely disappeared from sight. Also, the observing planes - and when the torpedo hit, quite a number of pilots had, as the Aircraft Action Report said, "ring side seats" - fell for the optical illusion of thinking that the ship had totally disintegrated. That had not been the case, but certainly a lot of debris and cargo was flying high through the air. In fact, the burning liquid spread the flames, which were driven by the wind toward the mangroves studding the shore line of Tol. They started to burn as well. The Japanese had their hands full fighting the fire on shore, shooting at the attacking planes and pulling injured soldiers out of the fire. The Americans had suspected that there were fuel storage facilities at that particular area of Tol.

It is a pity, that the violent end of the wreck still

Hanakawa Maru

reverberates and claims skin irritations for unsuspecting divers. The Hanakawa Maru would make a fine dive, but safety is paramount to pleasure. On the other hand, the risk is much smaller than it used to be. Use of a body suit or the usual thermal protection, but also the use of sun cream and vaseline, lower the risk. As a consequence, the wreck may be visited and dived these days. And, after all, the skin irritations are not lasting.

Technical Data:
The Hanakawa Maru was used by the Navy as special transport from 25 December 1943 onwards. The ship is a Standard B (a) freighter.

Tonnage	:	4 793 ts	
Length	:	112,0 m	367.5 ft
Width	:	15,8 m	52.0 ft
Depth	:	9,1 m	30.0 ft
Speed max.	:	15 knots	
serv.	:	10 knots	
Engine	:	1 x turbine, coal	
Horsepower	:	2 000 hp	
Builder	:	Kawasaki Dockyard	
Owner	:	Kawasaki Kisen	
Launch	:	31 August 1943	
Service	:	25 October 1943	

THE HARBOR TUG

At A Glance:
Small harbor tug at 30 ft (9 m)

Why the little tug boat sunk we do not know. At Dublon, at the mouth of a small river, it found its final resting place. There are no signs of injury to the hull. The tug was used to pull the barges and other non propelled vessels from the cargo ships inside the lagoon to Dublon, and aided in the redistribution of material to the other islands. It must have been quite an enterprise to get the small boat to Truk over the open seas. After it had found its new base there, it did not leave ever.

The first two objects which can be seen upon descent on the aft deck are the big tow hook, and the bow shaped reflector beam aft of it. Both are in good condition, although the beam shows some signs of wear.

The engine room may be entered quite easily through the open engine room skylights. It is recommended to leave the fins outside, and secure them. Otherwise, the fine sediment, which covers everything, is too easily stirred up. The engine room looks spacious, despite the small size of the tug. Twin big diesel engines are mounted here, with all their instruments still attached. They provided the power to pull the load. Aft of the diesel engines are the large gear boxes, the shaft can be seen leading further aft. There is a door in the forward bulkhead.

The thick layer of mud inside the room feels none too comfortable when one treads on it. The foot sinks in, and it feels soft and mushy, but it is harmless. However, one should move slowly and deliberately. It is possible to swim through the doorway forward into the next compartment. This is clearly the area, where the crew quarters were located. Remnants of bunk beds can be located. Also, a washroom can be seen here, with sink and faucet still in place.

It is best to go back and exit through the engine room skylight, where the fins may be recovered.

The bridge should be entered through the doorway at deck level. The door is open. Forcing the entry through the window will result only in a diver getting stuck. The interior of the bridge is worth a visit. Fairly well in the middle of it is the engine telegraph and the voice tubes. They are nicely illuminated by the light falling through the windows. The frames are heavily overgrown. The telegraph almost looks like a precious instrument, with a ruby colored piece set in the center. The scale is clearly visible, and the pointer seems to be at Full Stop, if the Japanese characters are interpreted correctly. They stand out on white ceramic, on which no marine growth has settled.

Finally, the low pitched prop may be inspected.

Visibility is hardly good, and the 20 ft average found here, at the river mouth, is a disappointment, for Truk standards.

HEIAN MARU

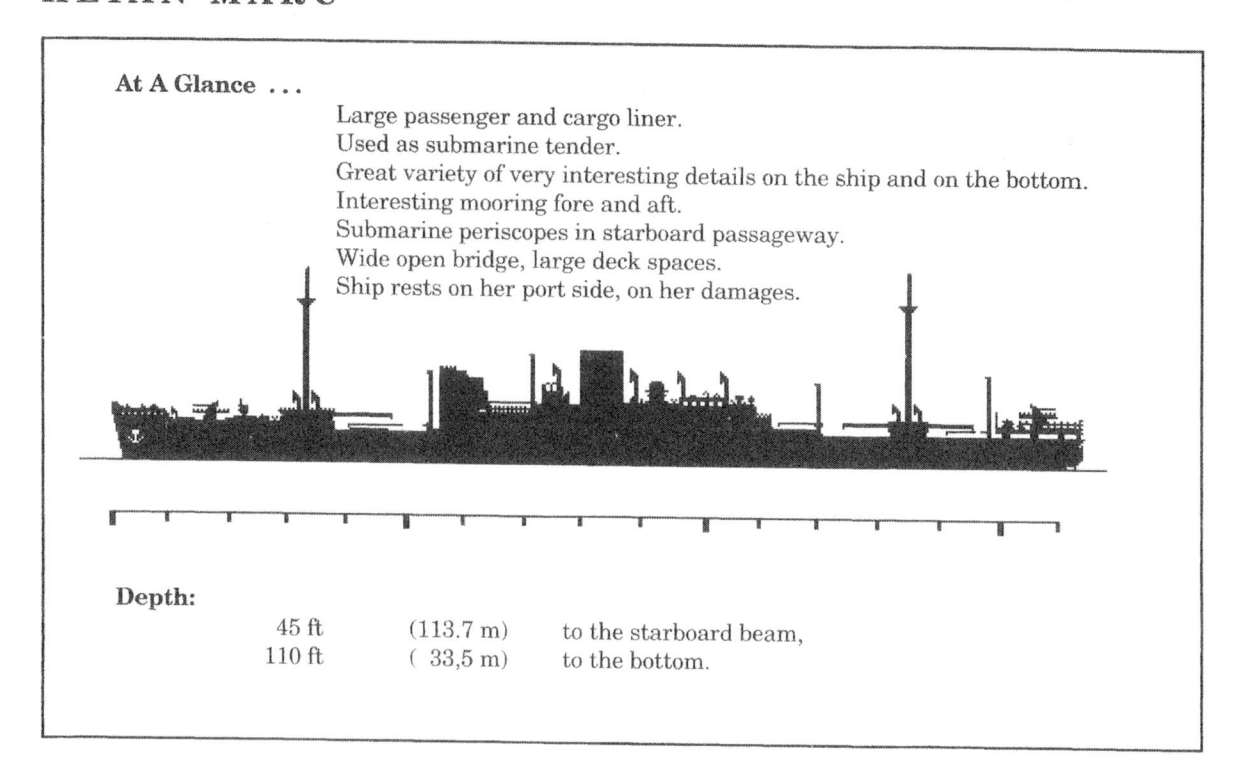

At A Glance ...

Large passenger and cargo liner.
Used as submarine tender.
Great variety of very interesting details on the ship and on the bottom.
Interesting mooring fore and aft.
Submarine periscopes in starboard passageway.
Wide open bridge, large deck spaces.
Ship rests on her port side, on her damages.

Depth:

45 ft	(113.7 m)	to the starboard beam,
110 ft	(33,5 m)	to the bottom.

The Heian Maru was a large combined passenger-cargo liner of 11 616 tons gross and is the largest ship in the lagoon. Before the war she was converted to a submarine depot ship, and remained in that role until sunk on the second day of the attack by a torpedo. The damage to the hull can not be seen. There is only a large compression mark in the hull; the shell plating is buckled midships on starboard. There is, however, widespread destruction on the port side of the hull and on this side the engine room is badly damaged.

Japanese sources indicate that the ship received a bomb hit at hold 6. There is no damage apparent in this area, which would be at the quarter deck. The time given by these sources is unreliable, as 0455 h was indicated. Given a one hour time difference to Tokyo time it would still be too early for the first strike. It is unlikely, and not according to American reports, that the planes of the Initial Fighter Sweep attacked ships. The Heian Maru was strafed by fighter planes of the Enterprise on Strike 1 C, the third strike on the first day, at about 1010 h. The Hellcats were over the target area at 1000 h. Their board ammunition consisted, in alternating sequence, of amour piercing, incendiary and tracer rounds. It is known, that the ship started to burn, after the strafing, in the later part of the morning of the first day of the attack. The fire spread rapidly, and continued to consume the ship.

The crew had been ordered to abandon the ship very early in the morning. There was fear that the submarine torpedoes in the hold and the workshops would explode. A skeleton crew remained a little longer. They tried to pump fuel oil from the aft tanks to the forward storage, to get it out of the area endangered by the fire. The attempt was futile. The fire raged out of control. The Heian Maru was given up and the blaze continued to consume the once glamorous ship. Evidently, the ship was subjected to many more attacks, but no direct hit was scored. Eventually, Avenger torpedo planes from Bunker Hill scored a torpedo hit midships at the engine room. This final hit was obtained on the last effective strike of Bunker Hill on the second day, Strike 3 B. The Heian Maru had listed before this coup de grace, and sank quickly thereafter, although the departing planes did not witness the sinking.

The Heian Maru is greatly underrated in popularity by most divers. This is because most make their second dive on it. The sheer size of the ship makes it difficult to obtain a perspective. The fact that at the starboard side is only at 40 to 50 feet to the surface disguises the fact that the water depth is 110 feet to the bottom at the stern. To dive that deep would be difficult for a repetitive dive and has to planned well. A dive computer will certainly help. On the other hand, there are so many interesting things to be found there, which have been shed when the ship heeled over, that just swimming through the upper passageways doesn't do the wreck justice.

For one reason or the other visibility at this wreck site is never as good as at some of the other wrecks. Perhaps it has something to do that the Heian Maru is visited in the afternoon, when visibility always appears poorer compared to the morning.

The description leads from the bow to the stern.

Hailstorm - *The Wrecks*

Foreship

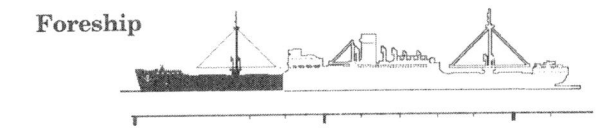

The huge starboard anchor is housed in its rest position on the bow, while the port anchor is out. The anchor chain leads straight down from the hawse hole. Right next to it a big cylindrical mooring buoy can be seen on the bottom with the chain still attached to it. A very large, old fashioned stock anchor is resting on the sea floor, next to the buoy. Anchor and buoy are not part of the ship, but her mooring system. As the mooring used three anchors, it is not surprising to find two more of the same kind of stock anchors near the ship. One is located at the aft end of hold two, the other at hold four, about 20 ft off the hull. Incidentally, the same kind of mooring anchor can be seen in the front yard of the Police Headquarters in Moen. A second and third anchor are resting on top of the reef next to the destroyer-patrol boat Susuki, off the west shore of Dublon. They are certainly large, and one would not believe that it is only the stock and ball of one of them which shows above water at that wreck site.

Two heavy chains run parallel to each other from this buoy towards east, and are clearly visible on the bottom. They can be followed for a distance of about 500 ft (150 m), when they climb up a coral ledge, cross it, merge, and terminate in a coral head. This coral head may have been a large block of concrete originally, and used as a mooring weight. An electric cable runs parallel to the chains, but about 20 ft (6 m) north of them. It is still under tension and hangs suspended over the valley, continuing further in an easterly direction. In the other direction it follows towards the hull of the Heian Maru, turns after about 100 ft to the north, and continues to the west. This is no doubt part of the communication, power and detection network laid on the bottom of the lagoon by the Japanese.

The ship's bow is not quite plumb, but slightly raked back, only to curve aft at the bottom. The starboard anchor can hardly be recognized as it is overgrown by coral. The prominent letters of the ship's name are the most striking feature. Frequent cleaning have kept them free from marine growth. This sight offers indeed so many interesting possibilities with a camera in regard to composition that it is perhaps the single most photographed place on any wreck. More than one foot high Japanese as well as the Roman characters have been welded onto the hull, can easily be read and hardly be overlooked. The bow carries a spirket plate, behind which an engine telegraph was located. It has fallen to the side, and the head of the instrument hangs from the internal chain. The forecastle deck was planked with wood. It was probably teak as it still can be seen at the lower, port part. Up on starboard it is evident that it burned away.

A few large size shell casings can be seen underneath the bow, close to the stock anchor. They are ship's spent ammunition. The forecastle carries a gun platform but no gun. It is very large, exactly 33 ft (10 m) in diameter. The gun presents a small mystery. It may have broken off when the Heian Maru was rocked severely from the close bomb misses and when the fatal torpedo hit, but it is not at the bow. There is a gun mount and two barrels at the aft end of the superstructure, which will be described presently. How they got there is a riddle.

The two very large windlasses are mounted on the deck underneath the gun platform. A relatively small hold is located in the long forecastle. More ammunition can be found inside. There are six 14 cm or 12 cm rounds resting on a metal box, of which the upper side is buckled. Interestingly, the more than 3 ft (1m) long cartridges are looking pristine, but the shell, which is located on top, is heavily rusted and looks expanded. More shells and other interesting debris is located in the lower reaches of this hold.

Farther aft follows the mast house, which is large, extends over the width of the ship, and has passageways on both sides. Rail guards, stanchions, and stays remain mounted on the winch house deck. The mast is particularly thick and tall, bearing a large crosstree. Mast and crosstree clear the sea bed by about 20 ft (6m). They are overgrown, but still carry a lot of steel lines, one of which leads to the bow. Ventilators are mounted on the mast house.

The second hold, which follows aft, is plated over at main deck. Only a fairly narrow slit of about 3 feet width and 15 ft length is left open. The original hold was very wide, and the plating work can be seen quite clearly as it contrasts with the hatch coaming. It is possible to get into the opening, but the hold is very dark. It is necessary to pass the first tween deck as well to reach the interesting cargo of torpedoes. The first one is leaning against the bulkhead, and there are no propeller fitted. The aft end of the fairing has corroded away. Several others follow deeper inside the hold. They are standing mostly on their nose. A warhead does not seem to have been fitted. Several of the bodies show damages at the aft part, such as a partially crumbled skin. The question is whether they have been subjected to the raging fire. In many of the torpedo bodies, the twin propellers can be seen on the tail end, together with the horizontal and vertical rudders. Quite a large number of torpedoes are located here. They are all submarine torpedoes with a diameter of 21 inches. The deck, now horizontal, appears to have been a workshop area. At the same general area, at least one torpedo war head could be made out. Interestingly, there are several high pressure vessels, high pressure tubing and armatures, suggesting an air fill station for the torpedo motors, which were using compressed air. The hold is very wide, and there are many things to explore. As it is very dark, it is suggested to have two lights and to buddy up with an experienced dive guide. Generally, orientation is not very difficult when realizing the way the ship was constructed and bearing in mind that it is now lying on the port side.

A kingpost and a wide deck house are positioned immediately in front of the forward bridge bulkhead. A torpedo war head and a much shorter practice head are resting against the forward bulkhead of the bridge at maindeck. The second of the mooring anchors is located at the aft end of this hold on the bottom

Hailstorm - *The Wrecks*

Heian Maru, prior to World War II

Hikawa Maru, sistership of the Heian Maru, was a hospital ship during the war, but survived the hostilities. After the war she was used on repratriation duties, and finally retired as a floating museum and Youth Hostel. A third ship of the same class, the Hie Maru, was fitted out similar to the Heian Maru - as a submarine tender - and was also lost during the war.

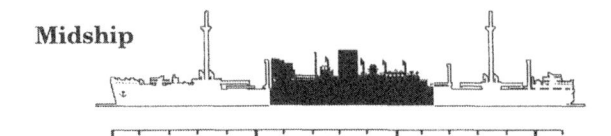

Midship

The midship superstructure is three decks high. The pattern of the windows facing forward can be clearly seen. The windows on the lower deck were subdivided and glassed in originally, whereas the two upper decks show portholes in the bulkhead behind.

The bridge used to be topped by a wooden bridge house, which has disappeared. The bridge wing extends slightly over the side of the ship and carries an engine telegraph as well as the remains of the running light. On the bridge deck, the platform for a small calibre anti-aircraft machine weapon can be recognized. The gun itself has disappeared.

Aft of the bridge, the superstructure drops to promenade deck level. An interesting observation can be made regarding the forward windows of the promenade deck passageway. The first six windows used to be glassed in. They afforded protection for the passengers carried before the war. These forward windows alternate in shape between being rectangular and square. The glass in the windows was divided horizontally into the larger bottom part, at about 2/3 of the height, and a smaller part on top. They were parted by a metal frame. To increase stability, the square windows were again divided once vertically, whereas the rectangular windows were subdivided twice. The frames all remain in their place, and the shape of the windows can clearly be recognized today. After the six forward windows, the shape changes. The windows were not glassed in but open. This distinct pattern tallies exactly with the pre-war photographs. The promenade deck is very long and extends to the quarter deck.

The passageway on this deck can either be entered through the divided windows just described, from forward through the bridge, or, more comfortably, through the open ones aft. It is very interesting to swim through the passageway from forward to aft.

At its forward part, four tubular shaped objects will be seen, resting against the bulkhead. They are approximately 6 m to 10 m (20 to 30 ft) long and their diameter is about 10 inches, 25 centimeters. On one end some of them have folding handles, while the other end tapers to an asparagus-shaped head. These tubes are spare periscopes for submarines. As one progresses towards aft, a single, another single, then two and finally another single periscope can be seen. Close observation will show that the heads of these periscopes are of two distinctly different design. Periscopes are sensitive instruments. Due to their size and their delicate optical system they were kept out of the general cargo area, and stored in the glassed-in passageway for protection. The periscopes face forward. One of them is also much smaller than the others.

There are several doorways and a break in the bulkhead which allow entry into the next lower passageway - originally the one farther inboard. This inboard passageway is very dark, but not obstructed. Assumed that the direction is reversed and the diver faces forward again, the exit can be seen in the distance at the bridge. Light shines in from there, but an underwater light should also be used.

It appears to be a bit of a long swim to reach the bridge. About half way, a 60 cm (2 feet) wide hole in the top can be seen. This bulwark was facing outward to port, when the ship was floating. All torn fragments of the edges point inward. There is no further damage, nor are there other signs of another explosion. The projectile which caused the hole has not been found. The hole is too small for a bomb explosion, and there is no trace of an impact on the opposite side. The long passageway leads into a large opening, which had been the bridge and the forward part of the superstructure. All deck planking is gone. The few steel support beams reinforce the impression of spaciousness. The area presents an unique sight, because of the lighting effect thus created. It is easy to swim around and exit at any one of the many openings. A short sortie into the totally dark engine room can be made, but is more frightening than enchanting after the magnificent view of the bridge.

It is also possible to follow the bottom to reach the midships superstructure. Entrance into the superstructure may be easily obtained by swimming into the passageway below the bridge deck. At first the progress is quick and unobstructed, and the spacious passageways are fairly well lit. When approaching midships, evidence of the damage becomes much more obvious. There is not a single bulkhead which is not bent, torn and twisted. The decks are all bent outward, the bulkheads are buckled upward. When uprighting the wreck mentally, it is apparent that a tremendous blast originated from the lower port side of the hull. That confirms the reports that one or two torpedoes struck the ship. (Bunker Hill VT 17, Strike 3B-2.)

Weaving in and around the the torn and grotesquely deformed metal, several large passageways and cabins are reached inboard. One of the cabins was a head. Several of the urinals mounted on the bulkhead were shattered. A sink, now suspended by its pipes only and filled to the brim with brown sediment, is located in the same area.

The engine room may be reached by turning inside the ship. The large diesel engines seemed to have remained fastened to their mountings, but there are so many twisted pipes, gratings and bulkheads that any attempt to identify the objects in this area will be in vain. It is very dark and dangerous as the many steel fragments may easily trap the diver. This is in contrast to the upper regions of the ship which have many doorways and windows, allowing the light to shine in and the diver to exit.

The boat davits outside on the superstructure are of the cradle type, typical of passenger liners at the time. Hold 4, fairly small and also plated over at the uppermost deck is located between the bridge and the funnel. Aft of the bridge and passing the midship hold, the funnel will be reached. It is big, rather stout, but very badly dented close to the base on starboard and forward. It appears to tilt forward. The plates of the funnel have not separated. The deck plating around the funnel and the area of the engine room skylights is bulging upward. This evidence may be interpreted in two ways. One is, that a bomb exploded nearby and the pressure wave bashed in the funnel plating. This kind of damage has been seen on other ships, for example, the Kansho Maru. The other explanation may be, that the force of the torpedo explosion in the engine room vented upward, and dented stack and deck plating.

Looking over the side of the ship in this area, the remnants of the gangplank can be seen, as they are still attached to the hull. The bulwark is open. It is here, that the hull displays the S-shaped compression ripple mark, indicative of a major explosion nearby, severe structural damage to the hull, and frequently associated with the destructive force of a torpedo.

The boat deck shows the somewhat confusing picture of engine room skylights, ventilators, air ducts and fan housings, deck houses and an anti-aircraft gun platforms. All of them are a little difficult to place, because there are many structures built on that deck. Another platform, most likely the range finder platform is built at the extreme aft edge of the superstructure. The anti-aircraft gun appears to have fallen off and is now be located a little off midships, on the sea floor. A lot of debris can be made out in this area. Much of it is military equipment added on later at the time of conversion to an auxiliary and was mounted on the boatsdeck. At times it is hard to identify individual items. For example, there is a round brass rim of about two feet in diameter which holds a very thick (5 inch or 13 cm) piece of glass. The glass has cracked many times and has a striking resemblance to a solid piece of ice. The piece is half buried in the sediment. It is so heavy that it is impossible to move it. Another, yet larger circular steel rim rests on the bottom just a little farther aft. A closed iris diaphragm identifies it as a former searchlight. These are only two of the many diverse things which can be found here.

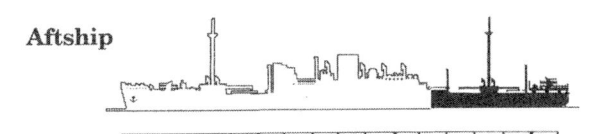

Aftship

Aft of the very long superstructure follows a kingpost. Also this hold, which is located between kingpost and the built-up, large mast house, is plated over, identically to the one at the foreship. A huge stock anchor rests on the anchor head, on the sea bed, between the masthouse and the kingpost. The stock points upward. This is really a massive anchor. It is a little difficult to see that a big gun barrel leans against the anchor's shank. Only a part of the barrel is visible, the rest is buried in the sand. Its muzzle points upward, and the breech disappears in the sand.

The calibre was measured to be 5 inches (12,7 cm) or very close to it, such as 12 cm. This is the kind of gun used on the old Japanese battleships as secondary batteries. When these ships were decommissioned the artillery was kept in the arsenals, to be resurrected as coastal defense guns or to arm fleet auxiliaries, during the war. Similar gun barrels and turrets may be found in a hold of the Rio de Janeiro Maru.

Evidently then, it is a barrel from the Heian's main artillery. The gun barrel leans against the anchor shaft. Next to it the gun mount can be seen, with several hand wheels attached. Even the brass elevation/distance scale could be made out. The question is, how did the gun and the mount get to this position? This enigma is even more puzzling if one swims back to the hull, a distance of perhaps 25 feet. The eyes have adapted to the shadow side of the hull, so things can be seen clearer. There is a second gun barrel located on the deck. It is of the same size as the former. The breech rests between the two bits of a mooring cleat and the bulkhead, and the muzzle lies on deck, pointing upward - forward. It has been said that the Heian Maru also carried guns on deck, but this is very doubtful, considering the huge platforms built for the bow and stern guns. There is no equivalent or any other indication for a gun mount anywhere else on the ship. The present position of the two barrels remains unexplained for the time being.

The masthouse extends over the width of the ship and forms passageways on both sides. The mast is as large as the foremast, and this mainmast also clears the bottom by several feet. The poop shows a nice passageway, and is of an appealing design. The poop deck, which is fenced in by rail guards, carries a deckhouse, on top of which the huge stern gun platform has been built. The gun itself has broken off together with its mount.

There is a bit of ammunition at the area off the stern as well. A strange structure is located roughly 50 feet off the poop. It is a cylinder of no less than 30 ft (9m) diameter, and probably 6 ft (1.8 m) in length. After this cylindrical part the object tapers almost to a point. The steel plates forming the side of the tapering portion are staved in. It resembles a closed container which has collapsed under the ambient water pressure. The sides of the cylindrical part carry two rims, spaced one foot apart. Vertical bars are connecting these rims every 5 inches. In the middle of this piece of equipment is a hollow pipe, which runs through the length of the object. There is no direct evidence regarding the purpose of this structure. In all likelihood, it was a large mooring buoy. Its design is somewhat similar to the mooring buoy of the Yamato, which is washed up on the Yanagi Reef. It could be that the Heian dragged it under water when she sank, and thus caused the staved-in plates.

The two large propellers are eye-catching when diving around the stern. The starboard, upper propeller retained its hub, while the one on port fell off. The rudder is half balanced. This can be seen from the shape of the blade, which partly extends forward of the rudder shaft. The shape of the underwater aft ship is very interesting. The flat ship's bottom becomes increasingly contoured until the twin shaft tunnels emerge, which end at the two propellers.

The Heian Maru had two sisterships Hiye, (or Hie) Maru and Hikawa Maru. The two other sisters had a bit of a checkered war time career. Hiye Maru was fitted out similarly to the Heian Maru, and also served as a submarine tender and depot ship. She would frequently service her submarines in the open sea. Whenever she put into Truk, the Hiye Maru, as well as the Rio de Janeiro Maru, would take Heian's berth at the Sixth Fleet Anchorage, while the Heian would move to the mooring off the north side of Dublon. This was the spot where she sank. Hiye Maru was reclassified as transport in October 1943, but was sunk already on 17 November 1943, by the US submarine Drum, about 200 miles (320 km) south of Truk.

Hikawa Maru was converted to a hospital ship at the beginning of the war, survived the hostilities, and was surrendered. At the time of the February 1944 air raid against Truk, Hikawa Maru was not in the lagoon as previously assumed, but plying the waters between Kobe and Yokohama, according to new Japanese sources.

Prior to building these three ships, Heian, Hikawa and Hiye Maru, Japanese naval architects were sent to England, France and Denmark to study the latest design, propulsion units, and features of ships of this type. When they were finally laid down with seven decks, and built to the highest standards of naval architecture then developed, the furnishings the ships afforded where enjoyed by even the most spoiled passengers. A model of the Heian Maru was shown on the Osaka World Exhibition.

The maiden voyage of the Heian Maru was from Hong Kong to Seattle. The ships were put into service at the time of the Great Depression, and of course, it put severe strains on the financial resources of the owners. From 1935 onwards, the three ships were servicing the route Kobe-Seattle in two week turns.

The Heian Maru was abruptly recalled from Seattle in August 1941, to go to Yokohama, where conversion to a submarine tender was begun. From October 1941 onward she was commissioned as a sub tender for twelve submarines, and formed part of the Sixth Submarine Fleet, based in Kwajalein, together with the flagship, Katori, and the submarines I 15 to I 26.

The boats serviced by the Heian were credited with the sinking of one large US carrier, Wasp, one light cruiser, Juneau, two destroyers, one submarine, and torpedoing a battleship and a carrier. By the end of 1943 only two submarines remained operative.

Technical Data:

Tonnage	:	11 616 ts	
Length	:	155,44 m	510.0 ft
Width	:	20,11 m	66.0 ft
Depth	:	12,49 m	41.0 ft
Draught	:	9,14 m	30.0 ft
Engine	:	2 x B & W diesel.	
Horsepower	:	13 404 hp	
Speed max	:	18,38 knots	
service	:	15,00 knots	
Launch	:	16 April 1930	
Service	:	24 November 1930	
Builder	:	Osaka Iron Works	
Owner	:	Nihon Yusen Kaisha (NYK).	

Hikawa Maru No. 2 (Tenno Maru)

Japanese records and statements made by officers after the surrender in Truk show that there was a hospital ship in Truk during the raid. If the available attack pictures are scanned very carefully, the ship can be seen as the most northern vessel off the Repair Anchorage. Size and its bright white color leave little doubt about the identity. Her location tallies with the account given by the American pilots.

The name given by the Japanese was hospital ship Hikawa Maru 2, and for a long time it was thought that the sister ship of the Heian Maru was in Truk at the time of the first raid. But this was not so.

There was, however, another hospital ship stationed in Truk at that time. It was the Tenno Maru. This name was changed again by the Japanese to Hikawa Maru No. 2. This is how the confusion about the two sister ships being in Truk started.

The Hikawa Maru No. 2 was originally the Dutch passenger ship "op ten Noort" owned by the KPM, Batavia, Dutch East Indies (now Jakarta, Indonesia). She was converted by the Dutch just as World War II began, and re-named "Hospital Ship 14", in February 1942. Records by the Dutch indicate that the ship was dispatched as a hospital ship to rescue sailors from the sea after the continued Battle of the Java Sea, during which the English heavy cruiser Exeter and the destroyers Encounter and Pope were sunk by superior Japanese forces on 01 March 1942, the same day, but at a different location when the USS Houston and HMAS Perth sank near the Sunda Straits.

14" was later allowed to pick up some of the rescued men from an island in the Java Sea, Pulau Bawean, and directed to sail to Makassar, Celebes (Ujung Pandang, Sulawesi). Evidently, she was used as a floating hospital ship for the POW camp there. Subsequently, the op ten Noort - Hospital Ship 14- was transferred to the Imperial Japanese Navy, classified as transport, renamed Ten No Maru, later on 01 April 1943, reclassified as hospital ship, now named Hikawa Maru 2. After various journeys, where she returned the gravely ill troops from the outer island bastions of the Japanese and probably returned with rather healthy individuals, the ship came to Truk and was present in the lagoon during the raid.

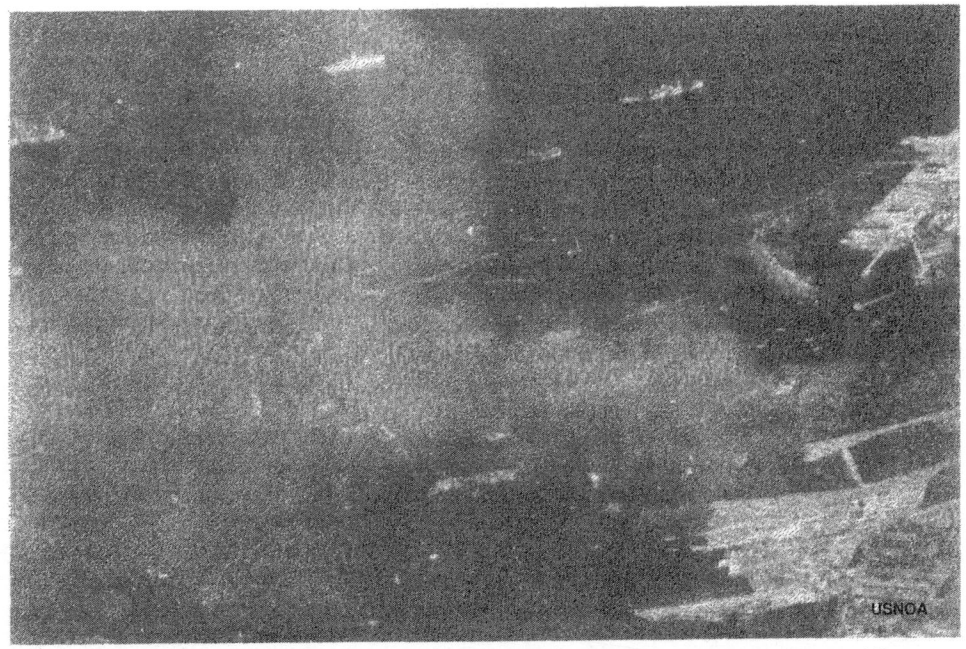

The white ship is the Hikawa Maru 2. Strictly from left to right: Burning Tonan Maru 3, Hikawa Maru 2, Momokawa (relocated later), Heian Maru. Floating dock, deceptively similar looking to a carrier, is near bottom of picture.

The ship displayed all insignia specified by the International Red Cross as a hospital ship. As so often during the war and specifically dealing with the Japanese, the permission to enact the Samaritan role was denied by some junior Japanese officer of a destroyer, the Amatsukaze, and in gross violation the ship was later seized after several confrontations between the Dutch captain and Japanese naval officers. The "Hospital Ship

She was clearly marked with Red Crosses, and was not attacked. To forestall any erroneous assault during the night raid of planes from the Enterprise, all her lights were switched on as soon as the Avengers crossed the outer reef. At this particular time she was located inside the atoll, near the North Pass. She was seen leaving the North Pass, when the planes departed on the second day.

The ship was lost in or about October 1944, south of Japan, to unknown causes, with no survivors. Nobody claimed responsibility.

HINO MARU 2

At A Glance...
Small armed freighter.
Totally destroyed by bombs.
Bow gun shallow and prime subject for pictures.

Depth:
3 ft (0,9 m) to gun barrel
30 ft to 70 ft (9 m to 21 m) at the bottom.

This wreck lies on a sloping reef. The bow is only at 25 ft to 30 ft (8 m to 9 m) of water, while the hull follows the incline. It is considerably deeper in the area of the stern. The Hino Maru 2 was destroyed during the second carrier based air raid against Truk. Japanese sources indicate the date of sinking to be 01 May 1944. The ship shows severe signs of bomb damage. Even this statement is not quite adequate to describe the state of the ship. It is so thoroughly demolished, that only twisted parts of the hull exist, apart from the bow, which remained reasonably intact.

The Hino Maru 2 is also known as the Dai Ni Hino Maru, Dai Na Hino Maru - which is incorrect - or One-Gun Boat.

The reason for the descriptive phrase One-Gun-Boat is obvious. There is a solitary gun on the bow, standing on a cone shaped mount. Nothing else is left than the long, horizontal gun barrel, the breech and the mount. Some growth can be found on the underside of the barrel and on the lock, but the rest of the gun is clean. It is one of the most famous sights in Truk, being popularized by posters, advertisements and T-shirts. There are of course many ways to capture this image on film. On a sunny day the available light will overpower all but the most powerful strobes because the water is so shallow. If the water is clear, the flash still can be used to advantage as fill-in, to add a touch of light to the shadows, or to enhance the foreground, such as the anchor winches.

The shallow depth of the gun affords interesting possibilities in photography. Although difficult, composing the picture to avoid the showing the surface camouflages the shallow position. On the other hand, using the total reflection of the surface, a bright mirror-like effect can be achieved where the waves show. The exposed part of the gun offers a wide variety in composition.

The gun points straight ahead over the windlass. The winch is a bit overgrown, but still well recognizable, as well as, the chain leading into the hawse pipe. The deck has rusted almost completely away, which may be indicative of a fire here. An enterprising snorkeler can easily drop through the holes thus created and swim in and out of the forecastle. This is an interesting snorkel dive experience. The port anchor used to be out, but the chain is broken at the hawse hole.

Underneath shelter deck, the remaining decks are held up by a series of posts, which resemble an alley way. It is only about 20 ft (6 m) deep here, and the distances to be covered under water are not too long. There are many ways to exit through the forecastle decks or through the hold. Care should be taken not to scrape against the metal or to make contact with stinging hydroids.

Hold one is still recognizable. The mast has fallen over to starboard. Its crosstree is half buried in a coral head. A big diesel engine is located next to it. This is the ship's main engine, with a portion of the 10" stainless steel propeller shaft still sticking out. The only thing remaining of the second hold is a part of the hatch coaming. The same goes for the third hold. The midships superstructure used to be located between the holds. The port side of the ship is partially very well staved in by a bomb close miss, and in another area flared out and almost lies flat on the bottom. Some of the poop remains. The rudder is broken off and lies on the bottom. The propeller is still attached to the shaft.

The bombs really devastated the ship. A bomb must have hit the superstructure. The boats davit is almost positioned horizontally. Other pieces of machinery, pipes and assorted other parts of the ship lie scattered around.

There is hardly more to see at this wreck, unless the diver is prepared to go over it with a fine tooth comb. This is the reason why it is generally chosen for a relaxing snorkel run between dives.

Technical Data:

Tonnage	:	999 ts	
Length	:	61,0 m	200.0 ft
Width	:	,5,2 m	17.1 ft
Draught	:	4,8 m	15.7 ft
Speed max	:	12,5 knots	
serv	:	10,0 knots	
Engine	:	1 x Diesel	
Launch	:	16 September 1935	
Service	:	14 December 1935	
Builder	:	Mitsubishi Heavy Industries	
Owner	:	Nihon Shokuen.	

HOKI MARU

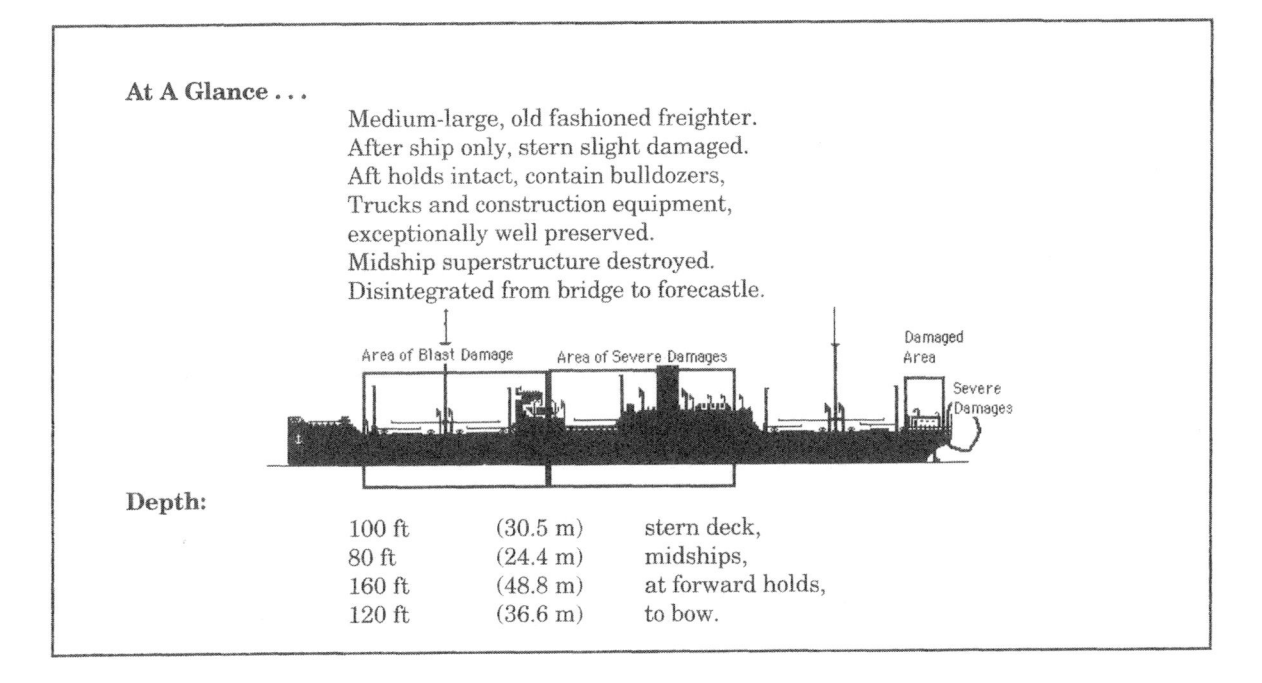

At A Glance...

Medium-large, old fashioned freighter.
After ship only, stern slight damaged.
Aft holds intact, contain bulldozers,
Trucks and construction equipment,
exceptionally well preserved.
Midship superstructure destroyed.
Disintegrated from bridge to forecastle.

Depth:

100 ft	(30.5 m)	stern deck,
80 ft	(24.4 m)	midships,
160 ft	(48.8 m)	at forward holds,
120 ft	(36.6 m)	to bow.

The Hoki Maru is an old fashioned, medium-large freighter, built around 1920. She is not a Japanese ship, but was captured and utilized by the Japanese Navy during the war. The wreck is known in Truk as the Bulldozer Wreck or X-6.

The Hoki is rarely visited by sport divers. Firstly, the wreck is far out in the Fourth Fleet Anchorage, therefore the site is mostly exposed to waves during the regular Trade winds. Secondly, just the aft ship and the forecastle remain intact. An explosion thoroughly destroyed the part of the ship between the forecastle and the bridge. The midship superstructure is badly damaged, particularly on port. From this description it may appear as if the Hoki Maru is not an attractive wreck at all. But the two holds in the rear certainly make up for it: They contain items unique in Truk. The main cargo is road building equipment, and trucks. Whereas the body work has been completely obliterated by corrosion on the vehicles of the Sankisan and San Francisco Maru, the Hoki Maru displays them almost entirely intact.

There has never been an investigation made before the 1984 expedition. An attempt had been carried out about 10 years earlier. It was abandoned because a stinging substance painfully burned the skin of the divers. It forced them to turn around without accomplishing what they set out to do. The burning substance is gasoline. The holds contain drums with aviation gasoline. During the years, to this day, it seeps out through small holes where the corrosive salt water ate through the metal of the drums. The escaping gasoline does not mix with the water, but ascends. Part of it is trapped underneath the deckheads of tween and main deck. When diving into this invisible layer the skin will come in contact with the gasoline. The exhalation bubbles displace some of the trapped gasoline, which may rise reach the next diver. Areas where the equipment straps chafe against the skin are particularly sensitive to an intense, but short-lived burning sensation, particularly after leaving the water. Applying vaseline or sun screen lotion to the skin before the dive will prevent this unpleasant experience, or generally takes care of the problem quickly after the dive, without any consequences.

The description of the Hoki Maru leads from the stern to the bow.

Aftship

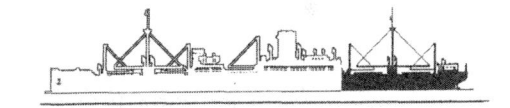

The beautifully shaped clipper stern has a considerable overhang. The ship was constructed with two propellers. Their blades are almost elliptical, have a low pitch and are located exactly at the aft end of the keel. Both shafts are integrated into the hull with shell plating.

The lines of the aftship are very much simpler than the impressive looking shaft tunnels of the Heian Maru or Rio de Janeiro Maru, which have twin propellers as well. Also, the rudder of the Hoki Maru is of an entirely different design. It resembles the rudder blade of a sailing ship. The Hoki possesses the classical lines of a counter stern.

Evidence from the wreck suggests a very close bomb miss near the stern. A large piece of the stern is missing. It looks as if some giant creature has taken a bite out of the overhang. A stretch of the sheerstrake, the deck, as well as part of the shell plating in this area

Hailstorm - *The Wrecks*

is missing or blown up. The damage bars the view into the decks and compartments below. The steering room is located here as well.

The last hold, it is hold 5, does not appear to be damaged. The hatch coaming is about one foot high, and the hatch cover beams on main deck stayed in

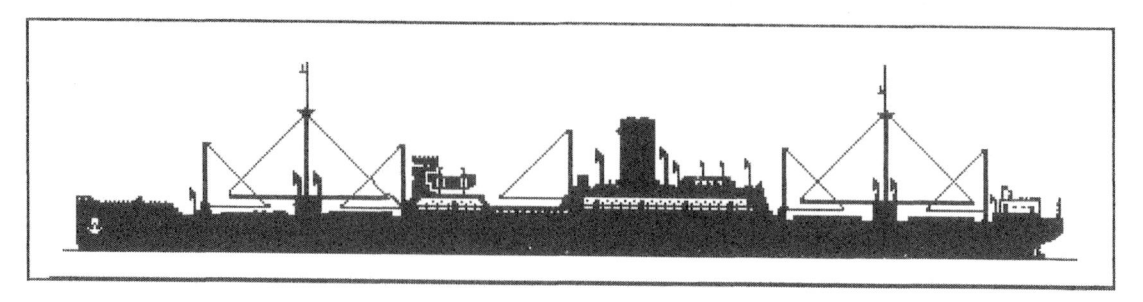

After the wreck had been rediscovered and its position plotted, the existing American attack photos were scanned to see whether they provided any clue to this damage. One of the photographs does in fact show the Hoki Maru just about a minute after the close bomb miss. Slightly more aft then starboard at the stern, the ring of foaming white water can be seen, and the cloud of the explosion has drifted downwind. The ship is smouldering at the bridge and at the aft deck house. This picture does not show the actual destruction of the Hoki Maru, which will be described below.

A flagpole at the very stern remains standing, but curves graciously forward. It bears silent witness to the explosive force of the bomb. The Hoki Maru has no poop as she was a flushdecker. However, a deck house was built onto the deck aft. Evidence of a severe blast from port aft can be seen very clearly. The deck house, a sturdy construction, is partially crushed and bent forward and leans towards starboard. Inside this structure the steel partitions and bulkheads are all twisted and torn, which can be seen when peering in from one of the portholes or the open doorway. The ventilator shafts, their cowls gone, are bent as well. They are located on the forward part of the one deck high deck house aft.

Two interesting objects can be found between the deck house and the hatch coaming of hold 5. A large cargo handling hook can be seen next to the port winch, close to the hatch coaming. It looks like a small anchor without flukes, and was used to hook into the sturdy cargo nets, with which cargo is handled. The other are two spare blades of the ship's propeller, lashed securely to the deck. They are quite large, elliptical in shape and with a flange showing the holes for the mounting bolts.

The main deck is enclosed with a guard rail, which remained partially intact. The stanchions are almost all in place at the aftership. The Hoki Maru was not fitted with a bulwark, between the midship superstructure and the fore and aft ship which is another indication of her old design. A pair of tall kingposts are located forward of the deck house. They served also as ventilators for the lower decks. It appears that mushroom cowls were mounted on top, which have corroded away. The posts were not connected with a cross bar. Normally there should be a pair of derricks, but all traces of them are gone from the ship. It appears that they have been blown over board.

place. They are partially overgrown with white-grey wavy algae, some hard corals, and a few other forms of sessile marine growth. It does not look particularly appealing to dive into the hold, as the hatch cover beams are closely spaced and overgrown, despite the fact that the casual observer will see a bulldozer resting on the hatch cover beams of the first tween deck. The long whitish hood of the machine is eye catching. Nevertheless, it is here where the ship has a big surprise in stock.

All told, there are five pieces of machinery resting on the hatch cover beams of the first tween deck. All of them except one face forward. The first caterpillar is located close to the aft edge on port. A truck rests at the port edge, slightly aft but touching the tracks of the caterpillar.

This truck is the least well preserved of all vehicles on this ship. It appears as if it has half dropped through the hatch cover beams and only is held back by resting on the fenders. The hood is narrow; the radiator slightly rounded with a vertical dividing bar in the middle and horizontal air slits. A few of the air slits on the left have broken out, and most of them on the right are missing. The fenders are still intact. A large table coral grows on the one on the left. Both headlights remained mounted and the bumper is in place as well.

A strong blast wave evidently reached the hold from the rear as the cabin of the truck is clearly blown forward and folded over the hood. The loading platform was made of wood, which, except for a few remnants, has disintegrated.

A second caterpillar rests on the hatch cover beams towards forward, in line with another truck but just a little forward. It is half hidden in the tween deck. Both trucks are partially intact. Their bodywork is still recognizable, but the loading platform, made from wood, is gone. The fourth piece of equipment is a bulldozer. Its shovel and long hood are facing to starboard. The tracks remain mounted on the running and suspension wheels. The lifting mechanism for the shovel, and the hydraulic cylinders can be made out clearly. Control levers and the driver's seat can be seen in the cabin of the vehicle, but now it looks as if there no instruments were fitted in the dashboard. The battery compartment is on the left, while the large air intake filter is on the right and in front of the driver's seat. The heavy bodywork of the bulldozer has very well withstood the ravages of time and the corrosion by sea water. The hydraulic pumps, controls and winches are assembled underneath the trunk, behind the driver.

Finally, there is the fifth piece of machinery a vertical deck support post. They show the radiator grill on one side, which has 9 vertical pipes supporting the radiator loops in the front and the attachments for the hoses in the rear. They rest on wheels.

Union Steamship Corp.

The Hauraki during her maiden voyage. The ship was captured during World War II, by the raider Aikoku Maru, and commissioned into the Japanese merchant marine as Hoki Maru.

parked on the hatch cover beams opposite of the second truck. It is another bulldozer, its bodywork is intact as well. As explained, all the vehicles can be seen, at close inspection, resting on the hatch cover beams on the first tween deck. And so far nobody bothered to look beyond this level. These vehicles are great photographic subjects, in particular for wide-angle shots, using the rows of hatch cover beams above as artificial sky.

Next, the insides of the first tween deck should be examined. It appears to be fairly empty, except for the spaces way forward. On port two single cylinder diesel engines with a large fly wheel each are located. A set of generators nearby certainly were coupled to them and detached for transport. A heap of organic matter has not been investigated further, but from size and consistency it resembles coal. At the far end to starboard a very large heavy object is located. It resembles a giant kitchen grater, and conceivably was used for stone crushing or sorting. It is perforated on one side, and about 20 ft long. Slightly to the left of this piece a doorway is open and allows a little light to come in from hold 4, but otherwise it is pitch dark in these deep recesses of the tween deck. When turning to the left and swimming inside the tween deck towards aft a few other pieces of machinery show in the the beam of the underwater light.

First there are a few steel objects of unknown purpose and then a high pressure vessel, resembling a small chemical reactor. It is about 5 ft in length, is cylindrical in shape with a diameter of about 3 feet. Two mobile compressors like those used on construction sites can be seen close to the tween deck coaming, near

The sediment on the tween deck becomes quite high when continuing to swim in the same direction and reaching the aft part. It suggests that organic material was loaded here. There are a few 10 gallon glass acid containers resting on top of the sediment. One jar is standing up and others are laying on the side. Fragments of several more can be recognized. The very sharp edges of the glass sticking out of the sediment necessitates to keep a safe distance.

When turning to the other side, a large, 5 feet belt transmission wheel comes in sight. Another air compressor rests at the hull side of the tween deck. The fly wheel-diesel generator set mentioned previously appear out of the dark, signaling that the tour around the first tween deck has come full circle.

The most fascinating cargo of the ship is located in the second tween deck. Who would suspect that there are six almost completely intact trucks and a tractor resting partly on the hatch cover beams and the tween deck? They are stowed more or less parallel to each other, and are probably of the same model. They are probably not vehicles of Japanese design. Their hood and cabin point to an English or American manufacturer, although the name can not be made out without special effort. The side windows of the cabin are slightly trapezoid, the hood is slightly tapering towards the front, and access to the engine was gained by lifting the sides of the hood rather than the top. The sides have air slits. There is a bar running from the cabin towards the front on the middle of the hood, bending over to the front and originally bearing the company symbol. Unfortunately, it has disappeared.

At any rate, these trucks are very typical models

of the late 1930/early 1940s. Mudguards, headlights, bumpers, tires and even the base for the number plate are still intact. The spare tire is mounted on the rear of the driver's cabin. The vehicles had twin rear tires. All of these tires seemed to have been in very good condition, no marine growth has settled on them, and although the maker could not been made out due to lack of time, the raised letters "TRUCK TYRE" were recognized. The cabin are spacious. Seat, dashboard, instruments and gear lever can be recognized. On most trucks the steering wheel is gone. The non-metal parts of the loading platform are gone, as well.

A tracked bulldozer is located in the tween deck resembling a tank. Right next to it, resting at an angle to the tracks, a very large steam-roller can be seen. The massive front roller is turned slightly to the right. The body is rather angular, and there is little clearance between the body and the deck. Not far away a tractor's huge rear wheels are eye-catching. All these vehicles are spaced very close together, but because of the divers' ability to move in three dimensions it is possible to swim around them and from one to the other.

The third level is filled from deckhead to bottom with drums. They contain aviation gasoline. Almost all drums are stacked very orderly. Only on port forward there is disorder. The reason is immediately apparent: A large piece of the shell plating has been ripped away. Daylight comes in and is a welcome change to the darkness of the tween decks. It is prefer-able to exit here instead of going back and weaving in and out of the cargo in the other decks. Many rolls of fencing mash wire are located near this hole in the hull.

There has been speculation where these bulldozers came from, because the Japanese evidently did not manufacture this kind of earth moving equipment at that time. It has been suggested that the captured ship loaded the bulldozers and the other construction equipment in either Singapore, the Philippines or Wake, and took it to Truk.

The description of the Hoki Maru continues at the forward edge of the last hold. The deck plates separated near the hatch coaming on port. The part facing outboard is blown upward by a few inches. A mast and two winches are placed forward of the last hold. A large number of railroad track segments can be seen on port between the two aft holds on deck. The derricks serving the hold forward, hold 4, are resting over the port side of that hold and partially obscure three radial aircraft engines. These engines are particularly large.

The tween decks contain a lot of small items, which have partially corroded and can not be identified. There are, however, some small diesel engines, a field of beer bottles, drums, and three large blades for the ship's propeller, mounted on the bulkhead. It is really a surprise to see yet another set of propeller blades. They are two lashed onto the deck aft of hold 5.

Most of the port shell plating has been blown out, and the tween decks tilt towards port. The hatch cover beams have all been blown over board and can be seen on the bottom on both sides of the ship. A very large crumbled piece of sheet steel lies across the hold, flung there from forward by the explosion. Since there is no sign of a direct hit or an explosion in this area it may be assumed that the ship was damaged and severely rocked by the explosion forward.

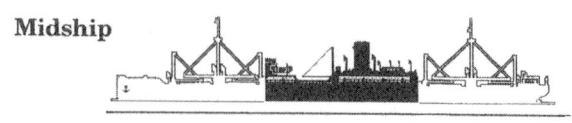

Midship

Two derrick posts are located forward of hold 4. The one on port broke and has fallen over. Forward of the hold and the posts follows the midship superstructure. It is very heavily damaged and presents a mass of twisted steel. On port the destruction is so widespread that no original shapes can be identified. However, as the damage is slightly less severe on starboard, it can be seen that the superstructure was only one deck high. The bulkheads are bent over to aft and starboard. Boats davits indicate the location of the boats deck and the original position of the life boats. The starboard main deck passageway is partly passable. Total chaos reigns on bridge deck, however. The stack, the engine room skylights and all other structures seem to be totally obliterated at first sight. Only close inspection reveals that the stack lies over to starboard and faces almost towards aft. The outer shell is badly corroded and shows holes, the two large exhaust pipes inside the funnel, positioned side-by-side, can be identified. No markings can be seen on the stack.

The deck tilts down at an angle to port. This side of the ship is half collapsed, and the passageway is buried. This is because the side of the ship was blown out by the explosion of the cargo and the decks sagged due to lack of support. A little forward a substantial bridge house can be made out, but it is futile to look for the helm or the engine telegraph. The bridge house is bent backwards. A single kingpost seems to have arrested its further collapse, but it is also bent back and to starboard. Its counter part on port is missing. These posts carried the cargo handling and derricks gear for the midship hold.

The hatch coaming of hold 3, the midships hold, remained partially intact, although the hold is unrecognizable. There is no identifiable tween deck and cargo. Only a ventilator cowl came to rest there. Just aft of the hold, the totally torn and twisted remains of the boat deck with a few askew skylight bases is all what can be recognized. The gutted engine room shows only a set of the ship's generators, but the two large diesels have not been seen. They appear to be buried in the debris of torn and twisted platings. The superstructure appears to be rather long. This area is very confusing and poses problems in orientation as the decks are heavily tilted to port.

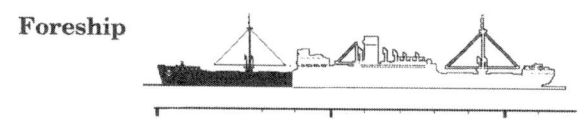

Foreship

Forward of the bridge the ship conveys the picture of total destruction. On days with very good underwater visibility it can be seen that the hull was subjected to a big explosion from within the forward hold. The port side of the vessel bulges and heavily tilts outward. The upper third of the ship's side curves out like a rolled-up sardine can top, baring the vertical supports. Nothing at all remains of the decks. The starboard side fared slightly better. It is also bulging outward over the length of the foreship, and curves out at its upper part, but not quite as much as starboard. The tween deck, bent outwards - now displaced by more than a right angle - clearly shows the individual deck reinforcements.

The ship makes a much more orderly impression here. Also, the shell plating of this side are still attached midships, whereas they have been blown out on port. The ship's bottom withstood the explosion. It connects the midship area with the forecastle, but is partially covered with sand and sediment. There is a lot of debris in this area. Over a length of maybe 150 ft (about 40 m) twisted hatch cover beams, a great number of drums, a thick layer of coal and unidentifiable pieces of machinery can be seen.

The damage from the explosion extends up to the first hold. The forward part of the hatch coaming of this hold remained in place, but it is bent forward, and tilted to the left. Fragments of the broken off aft part dangle into the open spaces where the deck used to be. King posts, winches and all other gear are blown over board and are missing. It is easy to continue to swim farther forward, but great care must be exercised not to exceed the depth limit of the dive when going over the deep part alongside the keel to the forward hold. It is between 160 and 170 feet here. Eventually, the forecastle will be reached.

Two large windlasses dominate the forecastle deck. The port anchor is out. The anchor chain forms a small heap on the bottom and leads away from there at a slight angle. This is a significant clue to the very last moments of the ship. It appears that she began to smoke fairly early during the attack, but evidently the fire did not spread to the critical forward holds. Only after the torpedo hit later in the day did the gasoline cargo blow up, and caused the quick sinking by the bow. The ship went down fast, and the anchor chain accumulated in a heap. The starboard anchor is retracted. The foremast lies about 100 yards in front of the bow on the bottom, at right angles to the axis of the ship. The stem of the Hoki Maru is vertical and does not have a rake. It is slightly bent to one side.

Subjected to several bombing attacks it was a torpedo from an Avenger from Bunker Hill which eventually sank the ship. The weapon was seen to explode on port beam forward, and the ship was immediately engulfed in large flames. The hit was recorded on the fourth strike of the first day (Strike 3D-1, time over target 1245 h). The ship sent a high smoke column into the air.

The Hoki Maru had carried drums with fuel oil, aviation gasoline and diesel oil. A hit on her port beam ignited the cargo, and the gasoline exploded. As drum after drum blew up, the forward part of the ship became an inferno. The center of the fire and explosion was located in the second hold at port. This scenario would account for the considerably higher degree of destruction on this side, as the pressure wave was stronger there. The exploding gasoline created a 'soft' pressure wave, that is the velocity of the pressure was comparatively slow. It was thus able to deform the steel, instead of ripping it to shreds. If ammunition would have been involved there would have been nothing left of the sides and the forward part of the ship, as can be seen in the case of the Sankisan, Aikoku or Kikukawa Maru.

The blast wave traveled to the opposite side of the ship, was trapped underneath the tween decks, and forced them up and outward. The pressure continued aft, blew through the open spaces between hold 2 and the midship hold, and the shell plating, which was not designed to withstand a pressure from within the ship was blown out over a long stretch. As the hull plating and the supports blew out, the decks sagged. Some of the pressure vented through the midship hold and, by folding back the engine casing, through the skylights of the engine room. When reaching this part of the ship, the main force was spent, but still, it was enough to continue the peeling of the shell plating up to the next to last hold.

The fire continued to burn for a while, fueled by many flaming drums floating in the sea. It is very interesting to note that even today, more then 40 years afterwards, the wreck still releases clear, colorless droplets of gasoline. They ascend slower than air bubbles, and disseminate a very strong odor of fuel oil on the surface.

The Hoki Maru was certainly discovered before but subsequently lost. The wreck was rediscovered in 1980, and explored at that time and in greater detail in 1981 and 1984. It lies on the slopes of an underwater hill. At starboard quarter the sea floor is inclined and forms a beautiful valley, at about 220 ft depth, which broadens, and rises slightly at the stern and port quarter. Forward of the bow it appears that the bottom rises. The bottom on port is fairly flat and even, except at the stern. Drums and debris can be seen a long way off the wreck, i.e. several hundred feet away.

The Hoki Maru was formerly the British-New Zealand ship M/V Hauraki. The Hauraki was a cargo ship of contemporary design, which had accommodations for 12 passengers. There were problems installing the two large diesels, which delayed her getting into service for several months, and her machinery was a frequent source of irritation. Her lines were considered very advanced for the times. The plumb bow, straight mast, low bridge, split profile and her aftship were all common during the era. Yet, the Hauraki was quite an achievement then. The shipyard set a milestone in contemporary design, and the "Denny-Look" was famous for ships of her class. The Hauraki was one of the first ships of this famous style.

The Hauraki was owned by the Union Steamship Corporation of New Zealand, before her capture. While on a voyage from Fremantle to Colombo she was sighted, pursued and finally seized by none else than the auxiliary cruisers Aikoku Maru and Hokoku Maru on 12 July 1942.

The Chief Engineer, Mr. W.C. Falconer, writes, in his report after his release from Japanese captivity:

"The vessel left Fremantle on 04 07 42, bound for Colombo, and the voyage was uneventful until the night of 12 07 42. At approximately 2150 h, I was writing in my room when the alarm sounded. On looking out on deck, saw that the bridge and the gun platform aft were flood-lit from four search lights, two on each quarter - I should say at a rough guess, about half a mile distant."

After an initial moment of confusion two gun shots rang out, and shortly afterwards a Japanese prize crew swarmed all over the ship. "Japanese guards were placed everywhere, armed with swords and automatics - some in places of advantage, with hand grenades". The ship was put to Singapore, where the first genuine trouble started. The engineering personnel had conveniently thrown overboard all special tools and pumped more than 100 tons fuel over board, hoping to attract friendly rescuers with the oil slick.

To aggravate problems the Chief ordered all maintenance work to cease, and consequently, the auxiliary engines started to give troubles, and the air valves froze up. The ship could not be maneuvered and had to be put into port by tugs.

On 31 December 1942 she was renamed Hoki Maru and rated as a 'special transport'. The captain, Mr. A.W. Crease, the chief and 22 of the crew survived the grueling experience of the Ofuna Camp, hard labour, incessant beatings, malnutrition, hard labour in the Mitsubishi Shipyard, and tunneling up north. When the Hoki Maru was brought to Japanese shores, several modifications were made, such as adding a deck to the bridge, and repairs were effected. The speed was slow. Normally it was 8 knots, and could not be much improved. Also the steering gave trouble. The ship reacted sluggishly to the rudder, and had a large turning radius.

In Summer 1943 the ship made a trial run in the home waters of Japan, but in spite of efforts made for improvements no increase of rudder space could be made and the new operators decided to use the ship as it was. Early December Hoki Maru left Yokohama for Hokkaido, returned to Yokohama in the middle of December, and loaded with a full cargo of coal. Then "carrying a full cargo of various commodities to be supplied for (the) Truk area, coal, defense materials and some personnel, the boat left Yokohama in early January 1944. The ship arrived at Truk late January 1944, where it was bombed and sunk." (Report to the Owners by the Prime Minster's Office in 1946).

Technical Data:
The Hauraki was contracted on 19 06 1919. In fact, the diesel engines were ordered before the hull was laid down on a berth just released by the Admiralty, after World War I. It was the first ship designed by Denny from keel up as a large diesel driven vessel.

Tonnage :	7 112 ts gross	
	16 160 ts displacement	
	10 810 ts dead weight	
	4 425 ts net	
Length :	137,25 m	450 ft
Breadth :	17,75 m	58 ft
Draught :	9,57 m	31.4 ft
		(34'/42' + 28.5')
Hull :	7 watertight bulkheads,	
	5 hatches, 18 derricks, 2 masts,	
	4 lifeboats 28 ft	
	1 service dinghy 18 ft	
Engine :	2 x Diesel,	
	North British Diesel Company, Glasgow.	
	8-cylinder, 4 stroke,	
	26.5" diameter, stroke 47",	
	rpm 96.	
Horsepower:	3550 hp max.	
	3010 hp service	
Speed, max:	12,6 knots	
Speed, service:	10,0 knots	
Bunkers :	730 tons	
Builder :	Wm. Denny & Bros.,	
	Dumbarton, Scotland	
Launch :	28 11 1921,	
	then to Glasgow for engine fitting	
Service :	13 03 1922	

HOKUYO MARU

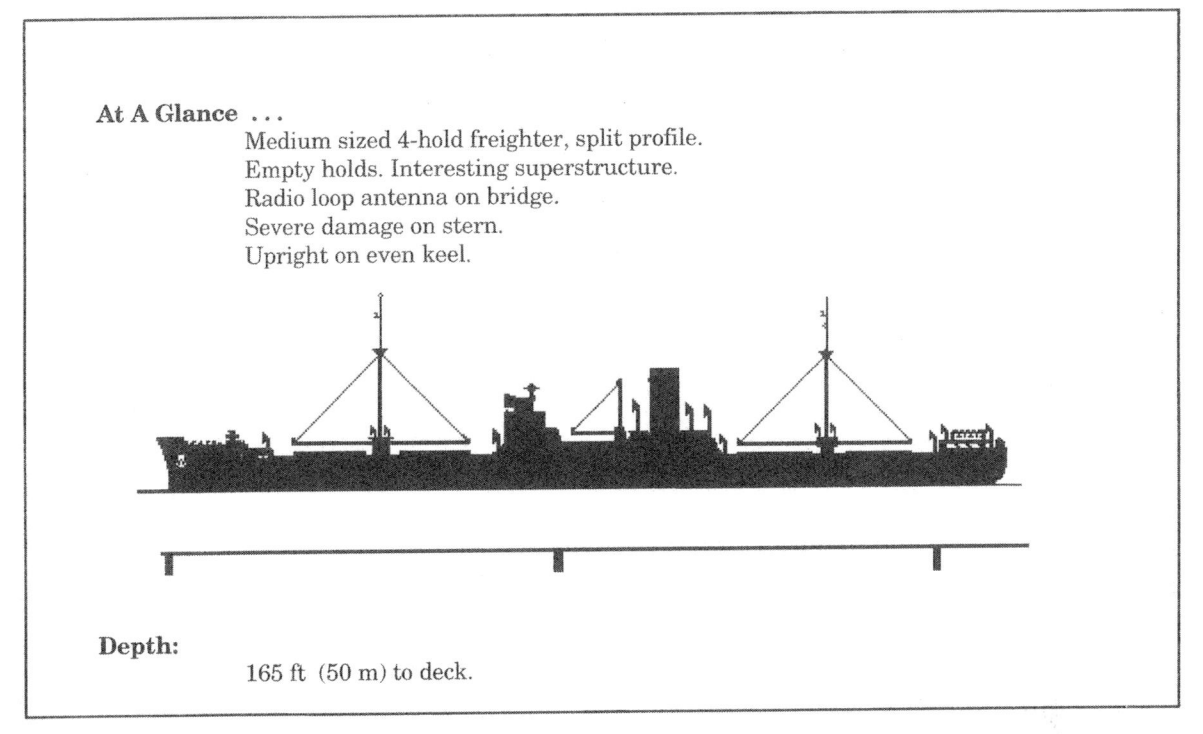

At A Glance ...
Medium sized 4-hold freighter, split profile.
Empty holds. Interesting superstructure.
Radio loop antenna on bridge.
Severe damage on stern.
Upright on even keel.

Depth:
165 ft (50 m) to deck.

The Hokuyo Maru is a very nice, but deep wreck. Except for the stern, which is severely damaged, the wreck is in a very good state of preservation. Sessile marine growth is mostly absent due to the deep resting place.

The description leads from the forecastle via the bridge to the stern.

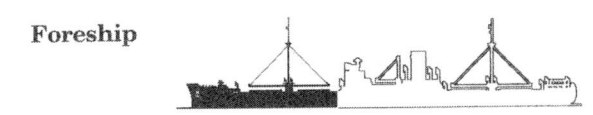

Foreship

Rail guards enclose the forecastle. All stanchions are still in place. There are two winches, or one winch and a cable drum, on the aft part of the centerline. Two mooring bits are located forward of the winches, with fairways abeam.

The double windlass is large. The anchor chains are leading - over chokes - into the hawsepipes. The port anchor is out, the starboard anchor is in its rest position at the bow. A coil of steel line rests starboard on the deck, next to the anchor winch. Slightly forward, above the hawsepipe the bulwark is damaged and dented inward over a length of a few feet.

In hold 1 the hatch cover beams, as well as the derricks, are in their normal position. A very long derrick and a smaller boom rest on supports between a mooring bit and the bulwark on starboard, next to the ladder leading from shelter deck to forecastle deck.

A large, spare anchor is bolted to the bulkhead of the forecastle. Hold 1 follows aft. On the bottom, many cement bags can be seen, which remain orderly stacked.

The mast stands between holds 1 and 2. It carries a large cross tree and is flanked by ventilators. The cargo winches are situated close to the hatch coaming and about five feet off the winch house, in which two doorways are open to aft. Most of the hatch cover beams remain in their place on hold two, on shelter deck as well as on the lower deck. Hold two is very close to the bridge. On port a tire is draped around a mooring bit. The cargo derricks rest on supports welded to the forward bulkhead of the midship superstructure.

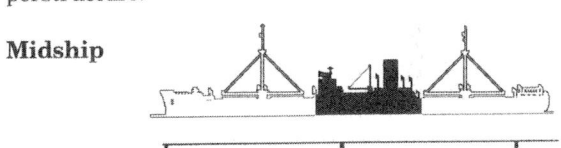

Midship

When approaching the superstructure the large fashion plate and its triangular bracket are eye catching. Next to it a ladder leads to the boat deck, but the doorways are closed. A ventilator shaft follows; the cowl is gone. Further inboard the doorway to the shelter deck can be seen. This door is wide open and appears to be secured to the ventilator. Captain's bridge deck is forming an open passageway athwart the bridge, with portholes located in the recessed bulkhead. From the steel supports it is evident that a flying bridge of wooden construction was built on top of the navigation bridge deck.

It is interesting to look through the windows of the bridge aft to the spacious area at the boat deck. This deck looks skeleton like, because only the steel reinforcements remain and the deck had been planked with wood, which is gone.

An almost square shaped bridge house remains standing aft of the bridge. Its size appears somewhat exaggerated as the flying bridge used to obscure its lower part. A circular loop antenna is located on the side of the deck house. It has a diameter of about 2 ft (0,6 m). Behind the deck house the midships hold will be found. It is considerably smaller than the holds on main deck. Some of the hatch cover beams are in place. The port derrick lies almost diagonally across this hold, while the one on starboard rests over the bulwark. Two cowls have fallen to starboard on the deck close to the coaming. They used to top the shafts near the stack.

A small rectangular coal chute is built aft of the middle hold forward of the elevated forward extension of the boat deck. This hatch is about 50 cm (about 2 ft) wide and 2 m (6 1/2 ft) long. The rear coaming is bent forward in a curve over its entire width. On both sides of the boat deck extension a kingpost stands upright, flanked inboard by two ventilators. These four posts are joined on top by a cross beam. The ventilator cowls have fallen down. The forward bulkhead of a small deck house in front of the funnel is bent outward. The deck head is curved upward here. The plates have separated by perhaps 15 cm (1/2 ft) at their welding line.

The funnel stands straight and upright, right aft of this quadruple combination, in the middle of the boat deck extension. It is narrow and tall. Ladders, companionways, lead up on both sides from the lower deck to boat deck. There is a rectangular, fairly large opening each on both sides. Inside, on port, a companionway can be seen on the inboard hatch coaming, leading down. On starboard the arrangement is identical, but a very large piece of sheet steel stands on its edge and obscures the view. The hatch coaming is bent, the deck is not perfectly flat, but appears to be bulging up.

The bent coaming of the small hatch, the damage on the extension forward of the funnel, and the blown-in bulkhead of the starboard hatch abeam of the funnel all suggest an internal pressure wave. The reason for this damage becomes immediately apparent when diving over the starboard side of the ship. A jagged hole halfway down the hull can be seen, the torn shell plates all point outward. The dimensions of this hole are roughly 2 m (6 1/2 ft) high and 10 m (33 ft) long, tapering towards forward. There is no doubt that it was caused by a boiler explosion. But this is not the only damage. A little forward and at the bottom of the ship, underneath the bridge, a much larger hole can be seen. Its appearance is somewhat cleaner than the other one and is most likely caused by a torpedo. The shell plating is missing over an area of about 18 m (60 ft) in length and 6 m (22 ft) height. This massive damage certainly spelled the end for the ship. No damage can be seen on the port side.

Just forward of the funnel, the boat deck extends to the width of the ship, forming a passageway on both sides. Open doorways lead to the lower deck across the hatches. The engine room skylights are located aft of the funnel. The four lights are all open on starboard, while two on port remain closed. The covers bear three round lights; the glass remains intact. There are four ventilators located on each corner of the skylight housing. Only one of them retained its cowl. A pair of boat davits stand on either side of the boats deck, which used to be enclosed by a guard rail. Some of the stays remain standing.

The aft part of the superstructure shows an open passageway athwart the ship. The bulwark rises and forms a fashion plate. It is supported by the same kind of triangular bracket seen forward. A ladder leads up from shelter deck to promenade deck. Next to it is the ventilator shaft and an open doorway. Further inboard a cargo derrick rests on its bulkhead support. Its counterpart on starboard leans against the bulwark. Some hatch cover beams remain in their place in hold four.

Aftship

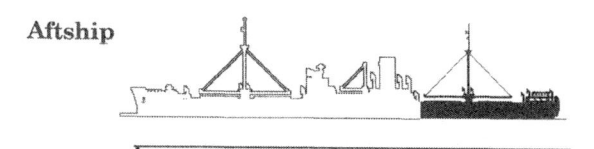

The deck abeam hold four, aft of the port winch, is severely buckled and descends about one foot. The hatch coaming is twisted. The shell plating is detached

Hailstorm - *The Wrecks*

from the deck gaping outward. The upper hatch cover beams are all gone, a few of the lower deck remain. The poop deck on port is severely damaged and blown upward. Shell platings between shelter deck and the lower decks at the stern are blown out. On port all supports, bulkheads and platings are destroyed.

The ship received a hit evidently on port between the last hold and the poop, destroying that area and part of the stern.

On starboard, at the aft part of the hold, the shell plating also detached itself from the deck, which is buckled. The rest of the deck is clean. A beam has been thrown on to the starboard winch and the derrick is off its support, pointing outboard. Looking over the stern, the rudder can be see in the amidships position. The propeller is buried up to the shaft in sediment.

The Hokuyo Maru was discovered on 19 June 1980, given the interim designation X 7, and identified by measurements and comparison to pre-war pictures. It is possible that the wreck had been found before by Sam Radford, but became lost in the intervening years. The Hokuyo Maru was designed to serve between North Korea, Hokkaido, and the other Japanese Islands. Ice floes on these waters in Winter necessitated special strengthening of the bow and the hull. The shell plating was welded. The cargo carrying capacity was unusually large. As the ship could be coaled up at the mines at her port o' call during her service, coal firing and steam as propulsion was used instead of the more modern diesel engines.

The Hokuyo Maru was a modern ship at her time. The Japanese government intervened when she and her sister ship, Hokusho Maru, were designed, demanding improvements. When finished, she was considered a considerable achievement for her class. Three passengers could be carried in the first class.

Pilots from the Essex described her position as being "the second ship from the east side of Eten". This corresponds to her resting place, which is between the Seiko and San Francisco Maru. On the second strike of the first day, at about 0800 h, two bombs were released on the ship. One hit the stern, causing a fire and subsequent sinking. An attack photo taken early on the next day only shows empty water between the other two ships.

Another view of the Hokuyo Maru, during her maiden voyage.

Technical Data :

Tonnage :	4,217 ts	
Length :	108 m	354 ft
Breadth :	15 m	50 ft
Depth :	9 m	29 ft
Draught :	7 m	24 ft
Speed max :	15.85 knots	
serv :	12,5 knots	
Horsepower :	3150 hp max;	
service;	3000 hp	
Engine :	Low pressure turbine, coal	
Laid down :	November 1935	
Launch :	03 November 1936	
Service :	15 June 1937	
Builder : No. 396	Urega Dockyard Senryu,	
Owner :	Kita Nikon Kisen.	

HOYO MARU

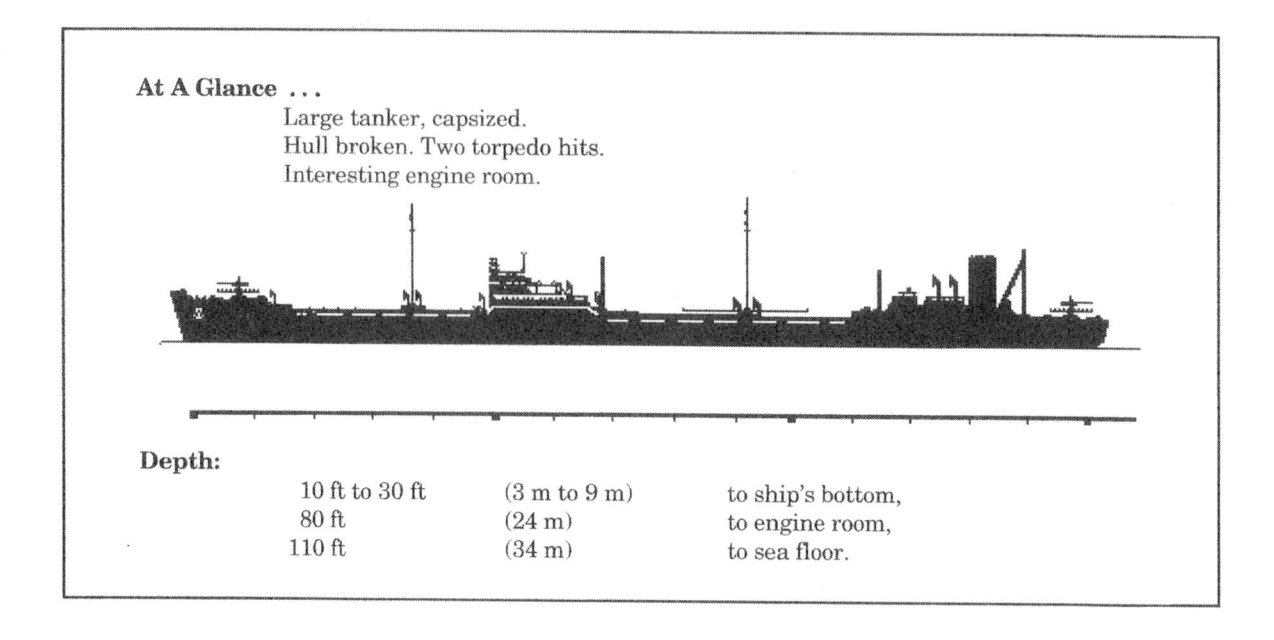

At A Glance ...
Large tanker, capsized.
Hull broken. Two torpedo hits.
Interesting engine room.

Depth:

10 ft to 30 ft	(3 m to 9 m)	to ship's bottom,
80 ft	(24 m)	to engine room,
110 ft	(34 m)	to sea floor.

The Hoyo Maru was a tanker built 1936 by Mitsubishi in Yokohama. Evidence suggests that she received several bomb hits and most likely one or two torpedo hits. The first major damage, without doubt caused by a short delay, large bomb, can be seen slightly aft of the midship structure on starboard. The blast was so big that it did extensive structural damages to the ship. It blew part of her side out and the hull plates are flared out over a large area. The second large bomb hit - may be the bombs were released in salvo - damaged the ship just forward of the aft superstructure on starboard. It totally mangled this area and caused also major damage to the ship. Each one of these bomb hits would have been enough to spell the end for the tanker.

But there was another severe damage which also would have been fatal for the ship. This one was either, and most probably, a close miss to the port side, at the engine room or a torpedo hit.

Finally, the fourth damage appears to have been caused some time earlier and may have been the result of a torpedo hit. This torpedo hit disabled the tanker and she was towed into Truk. The Hoyo Maru was undergoing repairs with the aid of the fleet repair ship Akashi, at the Repair Anchorage, together with other ships, such as the Tonan Maru, Kansho Maru, Kiyozumi Maru and others when the raid unfolded.

Due to the extensive damages, the Hoyo Maru capsized and broke into two parts, which are still partially connected to each other. The breaking up of the hull continues still today. In 1978, the difference in the height between the fore and aft section was only between a half to one foot. One year later, the two sections were off-set by several feet; the aft section is higher than the forward part. The clearance between the decks and the sea bottom has decreased correspondingly. It is therefore not possible in all locations to dive underneath the ship and look for other tell-tale damage, but in some areas the clearance is sufficient to make an excursion underneath of the 8000 ts of towering and slightly unstable steel of the Hoyo Maru. Records about her sinking are scarce, and none of the American Aircraft Action Reports make a specific reference to the sinking of the ship. Oilers were very high in priority of target assignments. It would be reasonable to expect that the Hoyo Maru was attacked and sunk early during the first day of the operation.

The description leads from the crack in the hull to the stern and from there to the bow, outside the ship. Then the hull is entered at the damage forward and the dive continued underneath the ship.

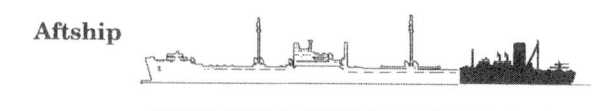

Aftship

The hull of the Hoyo Maru resembles a shallow coral reef. Many different forms of coral have settled on the ship's flat bottom. Only at a few places does the shell plating remain bare. When looking closely at the bare spaces, it can be seen that the hull is penetrated by shrapnel. Obviously the water flowing through these holes is detrimental to coral growth. The sides of the wreck resemble reef drop-offs and, since the visibility frequently is poor in this area, the sea bed can not always be seen. The wreck lies on an incline, the midships superstructure rests on an underwater mountain. Towards the stern, the bottom dips on the right side (looking forward). The long dive alongside the shadowy side of the hull, to reach the stern from midships, is very much like swimming along a deep underwater ledge, being tedious, and a bit unnerving at the same time.

The single, four bladed propeller is very large. A second diver peering around the blades while posing for a picture gives an indication of its size. The hole ripped open by the torpedo is soon reached by rounding the stern and moving forward on the port side. There is a gigantic gap in the side of the hull, extending all the way from the sea floor to the ship's bottom. The shell plating is buckled and torn, sharp fragments point up and down. The hole is so large that several divers could enter the inside of the ship swimming abreast.

The wreck is located close to the north shore of Fefan. Silt is a common problem in this part of the lagoon. The very fine, brown sediment is washed down from the mountains of the surrounding islands. Much of the silt also has found its way into the ship. Great care should be exercised when moving around, as clouds of it are stirred up. The thick brown-grey haze will make orientation difficult, and photography impossible. Although the hull can be entered and exited easily because of the enormous size of the hole, deeper penetration will involve dodging pipes, pieces of machinery and cables. It is important to have an ample air supply, a reliable underwater light and a buddy, who does not stray away too far.

The damage in the shell plating is just at the engine room. The main engine of the Hoyo Maru was ripped off from its mounting and has fallen to the bottom. This makes orientation difficult. As the ship capsized, everything is upside down, and it is very difficult to orient oneself. Nevertheless, once the diver is acquainted with these impediments there are plenty of interesting things to see. Some of the catwalks can be identified. Next to one landing a round object can be seen. Turning it upside-down mentally it becomes apparent, that this is a generator. There are a few pipes, a ladder and a drum for lubricating oil, located deep in the recess aft in the engine room.. A fire extinguisher can be seen in the mud. There is one piece of machinery, which appears to be impossible to identify at first sight. It has four gauges for high pressure pipes, a pressure gauge, and an instrument, which resembles a long thermometer, mounted on the side of a tall cylinder. There are valves for the outgoing pipes and a water separator. Maybe this is the fuel injection pump for the large diesel engine. Another object next to it is similar in appearance. A set of three high pressure cylinders with separate valves has tumbled down and the original support has been ripped out. They have been part of the fire extinguisher system he engine room. There are plenty of gauges grouped together and several pipe connections.

The central fuse panel and switch gear can be seen a bit forward and inboard in the same room. The panel is about ten feet long and two feet wide, containing a great number of white ceramic fuse holders, circuit breakers and a few instruments. The objects just described are just a few which are located in the engine room, but even when greatest care is exercised, visibility becomes poor after a few minutes, and a prudent diver will not remain longer inside. Upon exiting, one is again impressed by the tremendous damage this single bomb close miss has done.

The Hoyo Maru does not lie flush with the bottom. The clearance between decks and sea bottom seemed to have decreased over the years. The stress on the hull, which is supported by the bridge midships and the aft superstructure only, is too much, and subsequently the original crack continues to widen. It is possible to swim underneath the wreck. Most divers don't like too much the idea of swimming underneath several thousand tons of steel, which are in the process of breaking up. There are, however, a few bottles and some refuelling hoses scattered around.

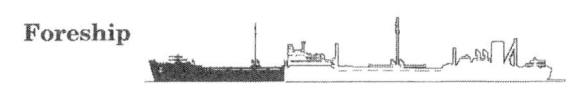

Foreship

Ascending to the level of the ship's bottom and swimming forward, a break in the continuity of the hull can be seen. From the distance it looks as if a large chunk of the hull has been taken out, measuring about 20 ft by 25 ft (6 m by 7 m). This appears to be damage caused by a torpedo hit, probably prior to the bomb damage. A lot of shell plating is hanging down. Swimming into the damaged area does not allow further access into the wreck. It looks as if the tank bulkheads have held, but that is of course an illusion.

At any rate, turning around and looking out of the hole gives a good perspective of what the damage looks like. About 10 m (30 ft) aft of the bow, the lower part of the hull and the bottom slightly beyond the keel are ripped away. Inside this hole a large number of coils and steel lines are scattered, among badly twisted bulkheads. Among the debris there appears to be a tail fin from an unexploded bomb, but identification has not been made for obvious reasons. Dodging a few plates, a manhole or companionway can be seen. Passing down through it, the forecastle will be reached. There are several large cabins located here with ship's lines and other supplies. Portholes in the side of the hull allow a small amount of light to filter in, but an underwater light is of course mandatory. It is not unusual to find fine specimens of lobster hiding behind deckhead reinforcements which are now on the bottom. Even a few fish make this area their home. A doorway in the forecastle bulkhead leads out onto the deck near the pipe bridge which is located off center to starboard.

Several valves and pipes are located on the upturned deck. It clears the sea bottom by about 5 m . There is no problem at all in swimming aft towards the midship structure. The dive can be terminated anytime by swimming out either to starboard or port.

Midship

Entry into the midship superstructure may be accomplished via the passageways which are unobstructed. The starboard side of the ship continues to clear the bottom, while the seabed on port ascends and forms a hill. The doorways in the superstructure are all open and also can be entered. When exiting aft, it can be seen that the bottom descends quite steeply, and while the depth to the deck up to this point was between 50 and 70 ft, following the deck and pipe bridge aft it soon becomes 100 ft deep. It is also possible to enter the passageways inboard the aft superstructure, but they turn out to be dead ends. Damaged

Hailstorm - *The Wrecks*

Hoyo Maru on her maiden voyage.   Yamada

bulkheads and twisted steel make further penetration difficult and hazardous. Further inboard, the engine casing prohibits further progress.

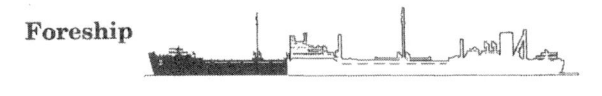

Foreship

The bow is fairly rounded on the bottom, but otherwise has only a small rake. The anchor is out. Between the bow and the torpedo hole a gun platform can be seen on the forecastle deck. The barrel of the gun is twisted totally out of shape. Returning to the break in the hull midships, some time can be spent observing fish life, crabs, coral shrimp and and a multitude of other life now making the Hoyo Maru their habitat. The depth chosen for observation can be 10 ft, which is just great for a decompression stop.

Generally, the Hoyo is seldom visited, and underrated as a dive. True, there is a bit of ugly sediment, stirring up very easily. It is great for the first diver, but less pleasant for the ones following. Also, the idea of swimming underneath such a large ship is somewhat intimidating for the average diver, but there is a very large clearance between the ship and the bottom so it can hardly be called claustrophobic. On the other hand, the advantage is that regardless of the weather, it is always calm underneath the Hoyo. Although an underwater light is recommended, as mentioned before, most of the time it can be switched off; there is enough light to see reaching the underside of the ship.

The Hoyo Maru was taken over in 1940 by the Navy and stationed in Truk from 1941 onwards. Fuel was taken to islands in the Marshalls and other places. The ship was armed with two 8 cm guns, one each on the bow and on the stern. The ship was credited with the sinking of an American submarine about 20 miles Northwest of Rabaul with gunfire, on 31 March 1942 at 1725 h. The Japanese sources about the sinking of the US submarine are not collaborated by American records. There was no submarine lost at the specific time, although the USS Halder was lost in the general vicinity, but that was after the attack on Truk. Afterwards, in early 1943, the Hoyo Maru was attacked and damaged by a bombing attack. She managed to return to Japan, where she was repaired by Hitachi Zosen. The repairs were completed in July 1943. She continued to supply bases in Micronesia afterwards. Early February 1944 she had embarked on a voyage from Singapore, loaded with supplies and fuel, when she was hit by a submarine torpedo and severely damaged just outside the lagoon. Her cargo did not ignite, but her engines were put out of commission. She was towed into Truk, where her cargo was discharged and repairs were begun at the Repair or Work Anchorage.

Other sources indicate that the submarine USS Scorpion intercepted the Hoyo Maru on 06 November 1943, launched torpedoes and obtained at least one hit, which severely damaged the tanker. Towed into Truk the ship was still undergoing repairs at the time of the raid. Again, another source credits USS Haddock with the hits, but agrees on the dates and location.

In the Repair Anchorage, she was in the company of the Kansho Maru, Tonan Maru 3, and the Kiyozumi Maru, which were all damaged and undergoing repairs. With her repairs not completed, she was a priority target for the attacking planes. It seems difficult to pinpoint the exact time of the attack, but the damage seems to indicate that she was bombarded by a salvo of 4 bombs. Two of them were hits, one a close miss and the fourth missed all together. The plane responsible for the bombs certainly flew in over Fefan into NNE direction. The hits caused such severe damage that she capsized and sunk.

Technical Data:

Tonnage :	8 629 tons	
Length :	143,3 m	470 ft
Width :	18,6 m	61 ft
Depth :	11,4 m	37.5 ft
Draught :	9,1 m	29.7 ft
Speed max :	16,1 knots	
serv :	14,0 knots	
Engine :	1 x MAN diesel	
Horsepower :	5 555 hp	
Launch :	29 August 1936	
Service :	5 November 1936	
Builder :	Mitsubishi Heavy Industry	
Owner :	Nippon Shosen (Nippon Tanker).	

Hailstorm - *The Wrecks*

I - 169 (SHINOHARA) SUBMARINE

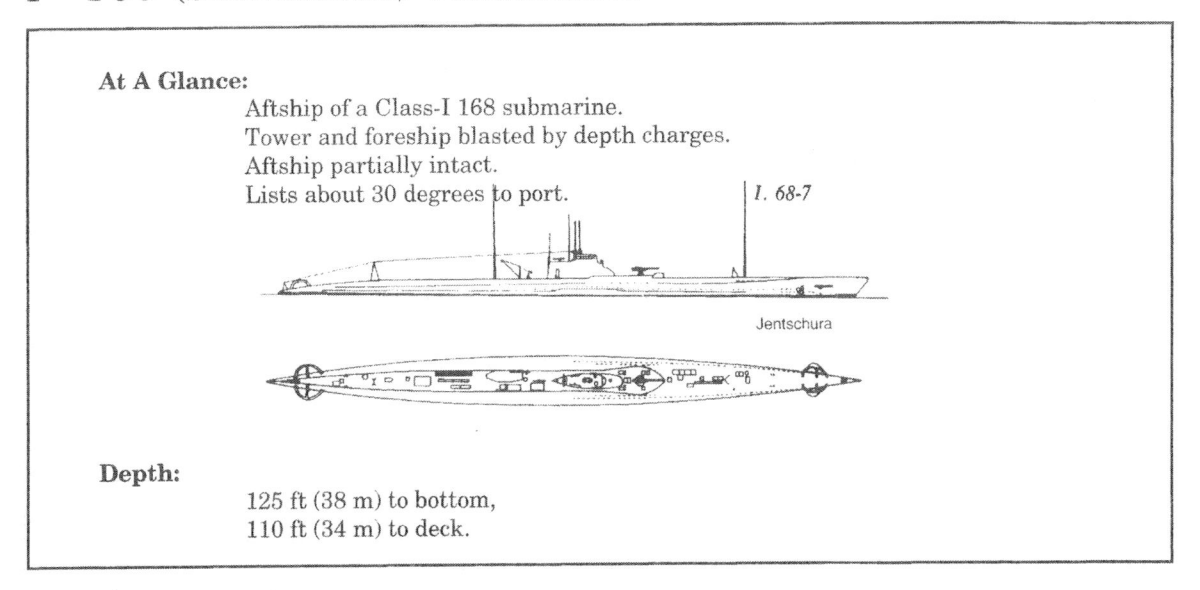

At A Glance:
Aftship of a Class-I 168 submarine.
Tower and foreship blasted by depth charges.
Aftship partially intact.
Lists about 30 degrees to port.

I. 68-7

Jentschura

Depth:
125 ft (38 m) to bottom,
110 ft (34 m) to deck.

The submarine sank due to accidental flooding. The main induction valve had not been closed when orders were given to take her down during the April 1944 bomber raid. The tower as well as the forward compartments flooded, and the boat hit the bottom like a rock. At a later time during the war, the Japanese depth charged the forward parts of the submarine.

After a very short boat ride from Moen to the submarine wreck, almost all divers descend on the completely tangled mass of the conning tower. The totally destroyed parts of the submarine convey a very confusing picture. Around the main bulk of the wreck pieces of steel lie scattered on the bottom. They are so twisted and torn that a proper identification is not possible. The conning tower, for instance, can only be recognized with a great deal of imagination. Most of the shell plating lies over to port. Many cables, pipes and valves lie on the bottom. The pressure hull is badly torn, but recognizable. Jagged pieces of steel are partly overgrown by solitary corals, orange and white, stringy sponges. Visibility is rarely good in this area. It seldom exceeds 50 ft.

Progressing farther aft from the remains of the conning tower, the boat assumes more the shape of a submarine. Some twisted steel plates can now be identified as belonging to the pressure hull. After another mount of convoluted pipes is passed, the aft ship is reached. The round and convex coaming of an escape hatch lies on the bottom.

The actual pressure hull of the submarine has a slightly elliptical shape. A deck is welded on top of it, and is about 3 ft (1 m) high. It extends from the area of destruction, the former conning tower, towards the stern. At its aft section it is raked down and meets the pressure hull about 45 ft (15m) at the stern.

Very close to the break at the conning tower, a round cylindrical vessel can be seen underneath the deckworks. It is several yards, or meters, long, and about 1 ft (0,30 m) in diameter. The plating, which covered it originally, has corroded or carried away by the depth charging, so that the cylinder is now exposed to the view. It appears to lead directly to the forward hatch, which rises above the deck. This escape hatch is round and the hatch cover slightly conical in shape. It bears a prominent hand reel on top. The cover of the hatch is not welded shut, and moves on its hinges. The deck continues aft. Most of its upper thin steel sheeting has fallen victim to corrosion by the sea water, so that the supporting beams can be seen now. A great number of whip corals grow here.

Continuing to dive past the hatch towards aft, two large mufflers can be located near the centerline of the boat. The one on starboard is exposed, while the deckplanking obscures the one on port. The exhaust pipe curves slightly to the outside of the superstructure and terminates at the stern. The next feature on deck is the aft hatch. It is of exactly the same design as the one forward. It opens forward as well, and the hinges are still working to allow it to be closed. It should remain in that position as a precaution against the temptation to enter the submarine. At the shaft of the hatch another cover in the same configuration is mounted at right angles to it below deck, allowing access to the area between deck and pressure hull.

A tripod mast is located just next to the hatch. It supported the antenna and the flagpole. Behind the tripod the deck rakes down to the pressure hull, but the area here is damaged. The stern itself appears to be heavily destroyed and a large portion of the counter is missing. Two tubes terminate at the break. They are the exhaust pipes for the twin diesel engines. This class of submarines did not carry torpedo tubes aft. The starboard propeller is attached to the shaft. The uppermost blade of the propeller is missing. The shaft and the prop on port are missing as well.

The I 169 was one of the submarines of the KD 6 A (I 168) Class, built in 1933 and commissioned in

Hailstorm - *The Wrecks*

1934. It was a fairly large submarine, ordered by the Imperial Japanese Navy under the First Replenishment Law 1931. She could travel for 45 days and cover a distance of 14 000 miles. The design depth was 245 ft (75 m). The conning tower was completely enclosed, which was a new feature at the time. The submarine participated in the attack on Pearl Harbor, where her sistership I 170 was lost. The design of the boat was outdated by the rapid progress made in the construction of submarines, and therefore I 169 was modified as an underwater transport. Most of her torpedo armament was removed. In this role as an underwater freighter she and a few other submarines carried supplies to Truk. After the fall of Saipan this was the only way Truk could be supplied. Even a scout float plane, equipped with radar, was brought in to Truk.

The boat was lost with all hands, except for the skipper, who was not on board, when she was diving to evade an American airborne attack. The official date of sinking is given as 04 April 1944. However, this is the date when salvage attempts had been given up, and when it was established that none of the crew had survived. The submarine actually went on her last dive on 01 April 1944. The boat was an indirect victim of the second carrier raid on Truk. Submarine pens were not available in the lagoon, and the submarines were supposed to dive inside the atoll to wait out an attack. As the depth does not exceed the design depth capabilities this proved to be an effective measure. At the time of the second carrier raid of 31 March to 01 April 1944, several submarines happened to be in Truk. None was damaged by bombs. The I 169 was lost due to a human error by the crew. When the boat did not surface after the attack, she was located on the bottom, and salvage attempts were begun immediately. A 35 tons floating crane was brought into position. Hard hat divers pulled heavy steel chains underneath the boat. When the lifting operation was begun, the steel line fastened to these chains broke. The flooding proved too extensive, the boat was too heavy. An attempt was made to pump air into the dry compartments, but the crew either did not understand the signals or were already incapable of action due to bad air. At any rate, all salvage attempts were unsuccessful. Since the forward compartments were flooded, Japanese divers were able to recover the bodies of the crew drowned there. Depth charges were dropped only on that portion of the sub. The Japanese hard hat divers could not enter the aft engine room section, and out of piety, did not destroy that part.

In 1973, Al Giddings and a group of prominent scuba divers successfully located the submarine, produced a film about the efforts to find her and documented the findings inside the aftship. Subsequently, the Japanese government arranged, in cooperation with the American team, the recovery of of the mortal remains of the crew from the engine room compartment. They were cremated in a traditional Japanese ceremony and the ashes brought back to the Motherland.

I-173, sistership of I-169

IWM

Technical Data:
I 169 (Shinohara), ex I 69, Type I 168 - KD 4 A

Builder	:	Mitsubishi, Kobe
Launch	:	15 February 1934
Lost	:	01/04 April 1944
Displacement	:	1 785 ts normal, 2 440 ts submerged
Engine	:	2 x diesel 9 000 hp each,
		2 x electric motors, 1 800 hp each
Length	:	104,5 m 343.5 ft
Width	:	8,2 m 27.0 ft
Draught	:	4,6 m 15.0 ft
Armament	:	6 x 21" torpedo tubes forward,
		14 torpedoes carried.
		1 x 10,0 cm gun
		1 x machine gun
Complement	:	70

THE INTER-ISLAND SUPPLY VESSEL

At A Glance:
    Small coastal oiler of about 300 ts.
    Resting upright.
    Interesting pumphouse.
    Magnificent marine life.

Depth:
    60 ft (18 m) to deck,
    80 ft (34 m) to bottom.

This small, self propelled service tanker was used at one time to supply the fuel for the fleet units anchored at Truk. It may be about 120 ft long and is of simple design. There is no damage apparent on this ship.

The description leads from the bow to the stern.

At the forecastle the ship bears a davit, a crane like structure. It was designed to hold the refuelling hoses. The stem has a small rake. The hull was enclosed with a guard rail. Most of the stays remain standing. A structure resembling a cage can be found on the foreship. It tumbled down from the midship structure and was the steel support for the wooden bridgehouse. The narrow forward part of the superstructure is about 1/2 m (about 2 ft) lower than the pump house, which follows aft. Two structures remain upright forward of the pump house. They are the ship's helm and the engine telegraph. There is an entrance on starboard. The door has fallen from its hinges and its inside faces out. It rests against the bulkhead. At the forward edge of the pump house, also on starboard, a nice looking running light is leaning against the bulkhead. Three particularly large specimen of leather coral grow next to it.

The pump house is large and takes up a substantial part of the midship area. The doorway is open; the door is secured to the bulkhead. Looking inside the structure, a multitude of pipes and valves is revealed. The pumps are mounted on deck. Although the picture presented appears confusing at first sight, the general outline of the pumphouse can soon be recognized. All four fuel lines and their valves and pumps are laid out orderly. Penetration into the pump house is tricky because of the crammed space.

A structure of about 30 cm (1 ft) height is located aft of the pumphouse. A close inspection shows some interesting details. Four pipe terminals, each about 40 cm (18") in diameter are covered with plates. Next to these covers small stainless steel plates can be seen, after they are wiped clean of the marine growth. The embossed Japanese characters, the numbers 1 to 4, can be made out on them.

The space between the midships and after structure shows a small elevation on the deck for the tanks, which are located below. The aft structure is only about 50 cm (2 ft) high. In the middle stands the smoke stack. It is about 1,5 m (5 ft) wide and was probably 3 m (10 ft) high. Its upper part is slightly corroded. Many kinds of coral and sponges grow on it. A four bladed propeller is resting between the funnel and the deck house on the superstructure. This propeller is very heavy. Strangely enough, it is not bolted onto the deck and can be moved, with some effort. It is identical to the propeller of the ship and was carried as a spare. One edge of the blade bears a particularly impressive growth of an orange sponge, and creates a strange contrast to the grayish propeller.

The engine room is located underneath the funnel. There is no problem to enter it, and the diesel engine and a few tools can be seen inside. Normally, a school of small fish makes it their home. The sediment stirs up quickly. The skylights are closed and partly overgrown. Aft of the funnel the deck house rises and towards the stern a bulwark encloses the quarters of the ship. The stern is rounded. Particularly fine specimen of soft coral grow here.

The wreck is very well worth a second dive. It offers phantastic photographic possibilities. The variety of marine growth is unparalleled on such a small place. As a rule the wreck is not visited very often. Therefore, sometimes lion and zebra fish may be encountered here. The wreck was discovered, quite accidentally, by snorkel divers.

KANSHO MARU

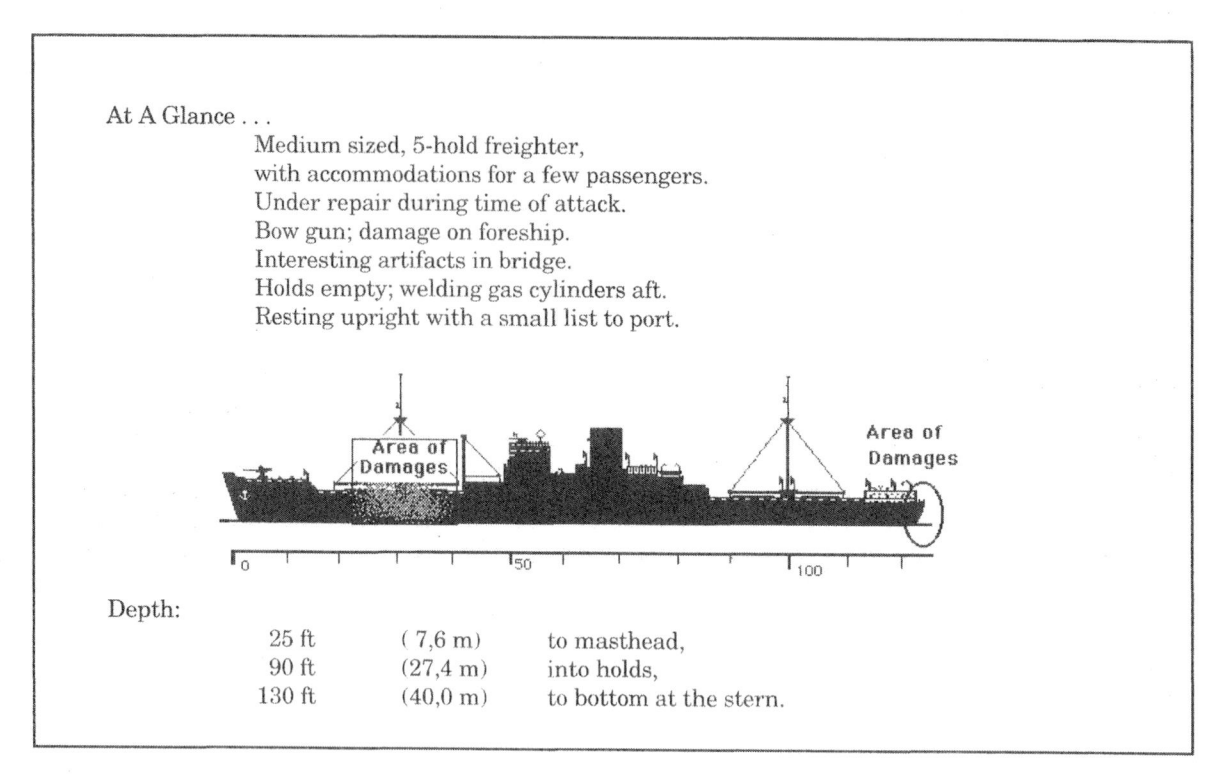

At A Glance...
    Medium sized, 5-hold freighter,
    with accommodations for a few passengers.
    Under repair during time of attack.
    Bow gun; damage on foreship.
    Interesting artifacts in bridge.
    Holds empty; welding gas cylinders aft.
    Resting upright with a small list to port.

Depth:
    25 ft   (7,6 m)   to masthead,
    90 ft   (27,4 m)   into holds,
    130 ft   (40,0 m)   to bottom at the stern.

After the totally unproductive search of 24 June 1980, the day was to be concluded with a dive on the Kiyozumi Maru. On the way to this wreck the Kansho Maru was found, more accidentally than by design. We had targeted this area for a later search.

This ship proved to be an exciting discovery, where artifacts were found on the bridge which have long disappeared from the other wrecks. At long last, the freighter had been found which was tied up alongside the fleet repair ship Akashi. This had been reported by pilots from the carrier Essex, early in the morning of the first day of the attack. The Akashi and the Kansho Maru were bombed. Although they received only close misses, the Akashi made up steam and began to move slowly towards the South Pass, eventually to escape, while the Kansho Maru was left riding her anchor. There is no doubt that repair work was carried out on her; the many gas welding cylinders aft are the evidence. In the end, it was evidently one torpedo launched by an Avenger from Bunker Hill on the second strike which caused her sinking, at about 0900 h, on the second day. The torpedo exploded at hold 1, probably broke the keel, and caused the ship to buckle.

The Kansho Maru rests very close to a frequently traversed boat traffic lane off the island of Fefan. It is a relatively shallow wreck. There are plentiful calcareous algae and coral growth on all outside structures. Due to the location, run-off rainwater from Dublon and Fefan covered the ship, over the years, with a layer of fine grey-brown sediment. It stirs up easily. Although being one of the finest wrecks in Truk it is also one of the "dirtiest". The Kansho Maru rests on almost even keel, and has only a small list to port.

There is peculiar damage on the foreship, the vessel almost broke apart at the aft edge of the superstructure where a bomb passed through the decks, and at the stern, where a sizeable portion has been destroyed.

The Kansho Maru was chartered by the Mitsui and the Kawasaki Line before the war, but taken in hand by the Japanese Navy immediately after the outbreak of the war. The ship shuttled between the Homeland and the Marshalls to bring war supplies, live stock and food for the garrisons. At some time later, probably after Midway, a gun was placed on the forecastle, and part of the chain locker modified for ammunition storage. Five navy personnel were accommodated to handle the gun. Not too long after the ship was thus armed, she was put into dry dock for a refit. The main modification was the rebuilding of hold 3. The wooden hatch cover beams were replaced with steel and the tween deck plated over. Then the enclosed space was equipped as sick bay for navy patients, and a X-ray room added. In addition to the crew and the gun staff, up to ten doctors and 20 orderly were taken on board to care for the sick and injured.

Subsequent to this yard stay, the Kansho transported arms and other war material to the islands and to take the infirm back to Japan. According to a surviving member of the crew, the Kansho Maru was bombed in Kwajalein during the carrier raid, on 04 December 1943, while discharging supplies. The engine room was hit and two sailors died. The ship could not go under way, as the engines required a major repair, and therefore the Kansho Maru had to be towed into Truk by the Momokawa Maru five days after the attack. Both ships arrived in Truk on or about 05 January 1944. It was intended to effect temporary repairs in Truk, but the ship would have to return to a shipyard in Japan for final repairs because of the severity of the damages to engine, gears and probably also the shaft. Momokawa and Kansho both anchored originally at the Repair Anchorage respectively. The fleet repair ship Akashi was moored near the Kansho Maru, in company with the Fumizuki, Tonan Maru 3, Kiyozumi Maru and Hoyo Maru. All these ships were under repair.

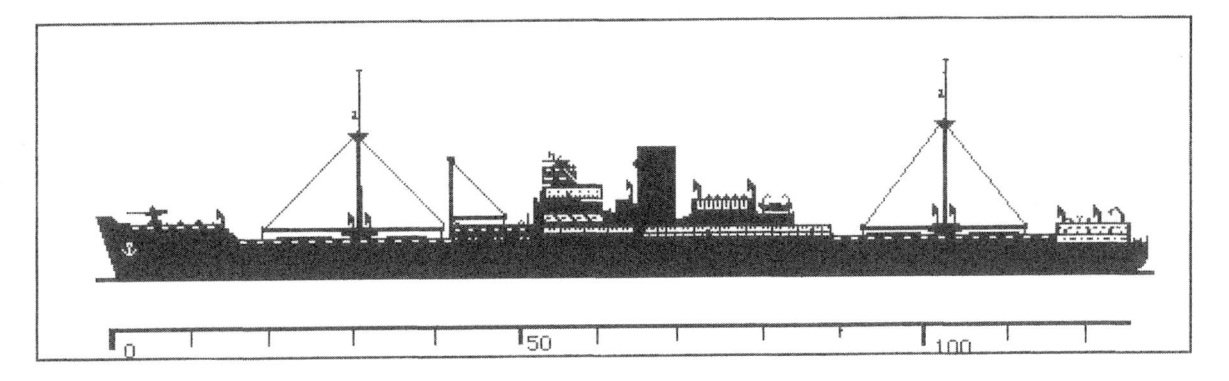

Not being able to defend themselves or to run the ship out of danger, rather than being sitting ducks for the American strafing, bombing and torpedo attacks during the two days, the ship's company took to the life boats and made it to the Naval Station in Dublon. From there they witnessed the destruction of the Kansho Maru, which evidently took at least two hits, of which one was most certainly a torpedo.

The description leads from the bow via the midships superstructure to the stern.

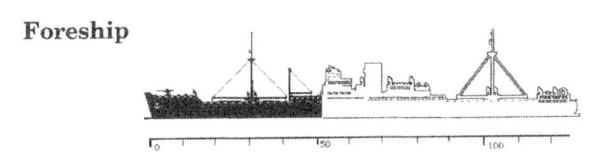

Foreship

The bow has a rake, evidence of a ship of modern design. The starboard anchor is out. The chain leads around the bow and continues forward over the port bow. This could mean that the ship went down by the stern, and the foreship drifted a bit towards south while sinking.

The forecastle is of conventional size but it is dominated by a large platform. A gun is mounted on it. This large piece of artillery points over to starboard with little elevation. The gun barrel and lock are very much overgrown with green algae, which when viewed from the distance, looks like combat camouflage. They seem to increase the size of the gun even more. The planking of the platform is gone, but algae grow on the steel structures in bushes.

The double anchor winch, bolted amidships at the center of the forecastle, is large and impressive. A cable drum can be seen aft of it. The depth here is 75 ft (23 m). A pair of ventilator shafts can be located at the aft edge of the forecastle. Their cowls have disappeared. The forecastle is enclosed by rail guards. Most of them remain in place. The doorways, permitting entry from shelter deck into the forecastle are tightly shut; they would not move in their hinges. A companionway leads from the lower deck to the forecastle deck.

A confusing picture is presented port on shelter deck, just aft of the forecastle. Debris seems to be scattered around here. At closer examination an anchor can be made out. The shaft almost touches the bulwark, while the flukes are inboard. Many steel cables and other objects are strewn around. Part of the heavy anchor chain seems to have been hauled hurriedly inboard, but the majority appears to hang overboard. The cargo derrick rests very close to the anchor. All this arrangement very much looks as if it was used to heave the anchor up. Whatever happened here, certainly this is a strange place to place an anchor.

Hold 1 follows aft of the forecastle. The hatch cover beams are all in place on the well deck. They are also present in the next deck lower, but some have been displaced and rest at an angle. The hold itself is empty. On the aft part of the hold on port, the supports are bent inward. This is the area where major damage can be seen. It looks as if the ship has been gently squeezed on both beams, at hold 1, close to the mast house. The deck buckled downwards and forms a depression several feet deep. It appears that the deck actually caved in here, right between the forward edge of the mast house and the aft part of the hatch coaming. At the exact location where the actual kink occurs in the hull, the deck plating gave way and ripped apart. This tear in the steel is about 20 cm (8") wide. Those hatch cover beams which remained in place, are bent upward. The shell plating looks intact on first sight. Even when descending on the outside of the hull to the bottom, no holes are visible in the ship, although some plates are slightly buckled and the sheerstrake is bent inward.

There are a few large objects scattered on the sea bed. It is not clear what caused the damage to the Kansho Maru. Its nature suggests that tremendous forces broke the keel of the ship, but it is puzzling that there is no evidence of a bomb or torpedo hit. The cargo derricks hang over to port beam.

The mast house is large. The entrance from aft is open. This room was used as storage for lines and cables. On the sides of the mast house its deck forms a small overhang, while forward and aft it is bent upward to afford protection. Four cargo winches are mounted on it, fore and aft of the large goal post, which

Hailstorm - *The Wrecks*

carries a mast top. On days with good underwater visibility this mast can be seen from the surface. A spare anchor is bolted to the starboard bulkhead of the mast house. Aft of this structure follows hold 2. It appears to be as empty as hold 1. The cargo derricks are lying over to port here as well.

Aft of hold 2 the deck rises, to form an elevated third hold. A kingpost and a set of winches are located forward of it. Hold 3 is slightly smaller than the other two. No cargo is evident.

can be seen. It looks as of there are wires attached to it. It nests in a gap between two support beams, created when the wooden deck planking rotted away. There is an engine telegraph mounted forward on the flying bridge amidships. It stands upright, but many corals, sponges and other sessile organisms have settled on it. The indicator handles remain in the Full Stop position. A loop antenna was originally erected on the aft part of the enclosure on the deck house deck. The pole to which it had been attached is not visible. The

Kansho Maru   Yamada

Midship

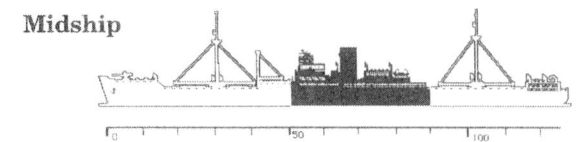

The midships superstructure is two decks high, and fairly long. Its design is typical of a freighter carrying a small number of passengers. The bridge is four decks high. On the second deck the bulkhead is recessed and forms a passageway athwart the ship, with portholes facing forward. The next deck is the boat deck. On this deck a partly covered passageway shows athwart. The highest deck is the navigation deck. Large windows afforded a good view forward. The bridge is followed by a large deck house, which included the radio shack and the chart room. On both sides companionways can be seen to lead from the deck to the boat deck.

Some interesting objects can be found on the continuous decks of the bridge and the deck house. Part of the area aft is enclosed by guard rails, with an opening to starboard aft. A companionway leads down to the boat deck. Within the enclosure, on port, a large spherical body of about 4 to 5 ft (1,40 m) in diameter

thick loop, which has a diameter of about 3 ft, now rests askew on deck.

Close to the companionway, three ceramic insulators are fasted to the starboard bulkhead of the deck house. The thick copper wires can be seen leading up towards the loop antenna. Underneath the insulators they carry insulation and pass through a fitting into the inside, where, not far from where they emerge, a 2 ft brass rim may have been a part of the turning and tuning mechanism. A rarity on the ships in Truk may be found close to the insulators: A few large pieces of broken window glass rest against the bulkhead.

The bridge may be entered from forward through the windows, which is an unpleasant squeeze, or from the sides. When swimming into the port doorway a head-sized, almost spherical metal sphere can be seen. This curious looking item was the cover for the binnacle, i.e. the compass cover. Originally mounted amidships, this piece must have fallen off before the deck planking rotted away, because otherwise it would have fallen a deck or two lower when it rolled to port, due to the list of the ship. The turning rim on the bottom can be clearly recognized. Also, the viewing glass is still intact, albeit blind and overgrown by marine organisms. Even a cock's comb oyster found a suitable attachment here. Amidships, and further inside the bridge, the helm stands upright, bolted firmly to the steel structure. No traces are left of the wheel, not even the rim. It must have been made entirely out of wood. The hub points aft and either the rudder indicator or the compass was mounted on top of it. This massive post is totally overgrown with orange encrustating sponges, which brilliantly light up when illuminated by the beam of an underwater light.

This area of the bridge is rather dark. The window frames are adorned with many types of coral and algae, obstructing, to a great extent, the path of light. However, another object can be readily identified. It is the inboard engine telegraph. It fell down and lies on the steel deck, its head close to the bulkhead. The pointers are also on the Stop position. Wires or a chain can be seen on the bottom, and a piece of bent pipe rests next to it.

The deck house continues aft, immediately adjacent to the bridge. The first cabin had been the chart room. Entering from the port doorway and looking to the right, aft, a pair of high powered binoculars can be seen. This large instrument was built with a straight optical path; it is not a prism-type. The long focal length required a big housing. The front lenses, still intact, appear as if they were coated; they look blue in the beam of a light. The oculars are connected with a rubber protector, which remained in place.

The delicate frame of a sextant, clean and devoid of any growth, rests next to it. There are certainly more nautical instruments buried in the debris on the bottom of this room. The charts have been placed on shelves, but charts and shelves have totally decayed. Careful inspection of the bulkhead reveals the original mountings of the shelves on the bulkhead. A second pair of binoculars can be found on the other side of the cabin. They are much smaller, and are lying in what looks like a metal drawer.

When going back into the bridge, the large rectangular openings in the deck may be used to dive down into the lower level. A bulb is suspended in mid water from its circuit. Open doorways on both sides allow some light to get into this deck, but it is even darker than the bridge deck. Two large sized radios are eye-catching. They are as big as small refrigerators. One of the sets has fallen forward, on to its face, while the other remained standing. Cables lead away from them both. Large size resistors, capacitors and coiled drums can be seen inside the cabinet. The face of the radio set standing upright shows a variety of dials and tuning knobs. A third set hangs suspended from wires between two steel supports, between this and the next lower deck. On the edges of the opening a few remains of the wood planking can be seen. The lower level has been the location of the mess. Several bottles and a few plates are buried in the mud. The front of a plate retrieved shows an anchor insignia with the inscription "Noshico" or "Nishico". A hot water boiler hangs from its pipes. The water level indicator can be seen. Moving aft a doorway comes in sight. It is almost completely dark in this room. The wooden door is gone. This room was the head. There is a sink with a faucet attached to the bulkhead. Further inside is a toilet bowl and an urinal, which has broken off and fallen down. There used to be a large number of staterooms on this deck and the decks below. A multitude of artifacts can be found when carefully sifting through the muck. The porthole covers have swung open, thus admitting a little light. Most of the sediment has accumulated on the port side, where it piles up close to the portholes.

After leaving the bridge and diving back on boat deck, the stout funnel dominates the view. There are ventilator shafts between the deck house and the funnel, their cowls have disappeared. On both sides of the stack closed companionways and closed engine skylights are located. The main engine room skylights, three in a row, are built into the deck aft. They are open and secured. The engine room is also very dark. Two sets of three large cylinders each are situated on the bottom. They form the main diesel engine. A spare piston is mounted on the bulkhead. Other pieces of machinery and control panels can be seen if the light is guided around. Frequently, large groupers make this area their lair.

Boats davits indicate that the ship was equipped with two life boats on each side abaft the stack. Way aft, the boat deck drops down to promenade deck, which is extended by about 15 ft (4,5 m). The galley is located here. A large stove with a few hot plates, a box of bottles, buried up to their neck in the sediment, the protective grill of a fan and a few other utensils can be found in the vicinity. The passageways on both sides of the ship are narrow. A workbench with a sizeable vise is bolted onto the deck next to the bulkhead of the superstructure.

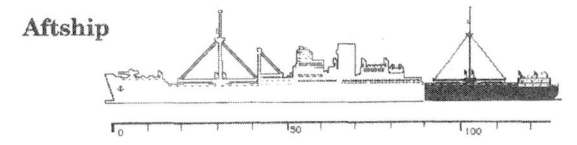

Aftship

Hold 4 follows immediately aft of the superstructure. A compressor is standing on the tween deck on port. On the starboard tween deck, a number of books can be found. The pages are completely waterlogged and swollen. A mast house, of the same construction as the one forward, is located between the two aftermost holds. The goalpost does not carry a mast top anymore. It broke off and can be seen on the sea bed off port beam. A gas welding cylinder is lying on the deck, near the hatch coaming. Almost all hatch cover beams of this hold and the one aft, are gone from their rest position. A few are lying on the deck, and one was flung overboard and is now resting on the bottom. This is a clear sign that the ship rocked very heavily, probably from bombs dropped nearby and at the stern. The cargo derricks are lying over to port.

The last hold contains an assortment of wrecked equipment. There are quite a number of welding gas cylinders. Some of them are placed orderly, others are scattered around. A large heap of bicycles can be seen. Only the frames and the rims of the wheels remain.

Hailstorm - *The Wrecks*

This area is so untidy, that at first even the bicycles appear only as a tangled mess. A large coil of a strong hose, various large pipe segments, their ends very much corroded, valve segments and other pieces of unidentifiable material can be seen in this hold as well.

The poop rises one deck. A door leading into it hangs askew from its mounting. There is no gun on the stern. The lines of the fantail are well designed, the ship has a clipper stern. However, a sizeable part of the stern has been ripped away by a bomb near miss. Both doorways are open at the forward bulkhead. The one on port is obstructed by a steel door which has swung open, blocking the passageway. The starboard door leads to a line storage area. Penetration can be continued to aft, which opens to a spacious cabin. This is the steering compartment. To the left, in the center of the room, a sizeable electric-motor is coupled to gears which are connected to the large steering mechanism. The circle segments and the gear train are part of it. A jagged hole appears at the very stern. Shell and deck plating are destroyed. The damage allows a diver to exit here comfortably. Alternatively, the skylight in the middle of the compartment can be utilized. The propeller has four blades, and the rudder has a bulge in extension of the line shaft tunnel-propeller hub.

Before the wreck could be identified it was coded X 11, but it was then better known in Truk as the "Mary D. Maru", after M.D. Lindemann, who spotted the echoes of the ship first. The Kansho Maru was used from 15 September 1940 onwards by the Japanese Navy as transport for special cargo. Other records indicate the arrival in Truk on 18 January 1944, with an escorted convoy, which contradicts the statements of the former crew member.

The name of the vessel is also given as Kensho Maru.

Technical Data:

Tonnage	:	4 861 ts	
Length	:	116,0 m	380 ft
Width	:	16,0 m	52.5 ft
Depth	:	9,25m	30.3 ft
Draught	:	7,6 m	25 ft
Speed, max.	:	16,8 knots	
serv.	:	15,0 knots	
Horsepower, max:		3 450 hp	
Engine	:	1 X B&W Diesel	
Launch	:	30 June 1938	
Service	:	30 August 1938	
Builder	:	Mitsui Dockyard	
Owner	:	Inui Kisen	

KIKUKAWA MARU

At A Glance ...

Foreship of a medium sized freighter.
Rests on the starboard side.
Three holds forward with cargo.
Mid and aft ship disintegrated.

Depth:

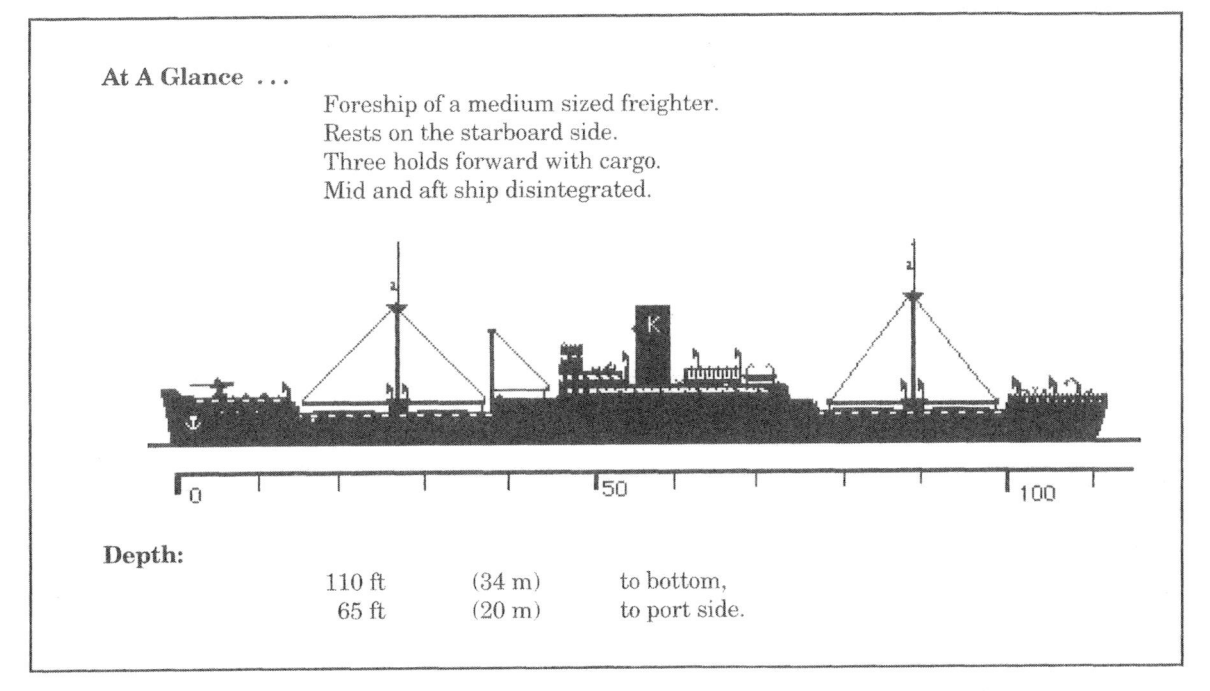

110 ft	(34 m)	to bottom,
65 ft	(20 m)	to port side.

The Kikukawa Maru was very similar in appearance and dimensions to the Nippo Maru and the Momokawa Maru. In fact, positive identification could only be made by the letters of the ship's name. They are welded onto the bow. The Japanese characters appear above their Roman equivalents.

The ship did not sink during any enemy action. While anchored at the Fourth Fleet Anchorage, and loading supplies for an outlying garrison in the Marshalls, she caught fire in the aft hold on the morning of 07 October 1943. This fire was particular dangerous because of the ordnances, loaded in the after holds.

The ship's own fire fighting capabilities were augmented in the morning by a specially equipped 800 ts tug. Pumps were put on two landing crafts, and two rescue ships of 300 ts and 150 ts, respectively. These vessels were also dispatched to extinguish the blaze, but all efforts were to no avail. In the evening of the same day, at around 1830 h, the Kikukawa Maru exploded violently. The tremendous explosion defoliated trees in Eten and Dublon and shattered many windows. The aft ship and the midship superstructure were completely torn up and disintegrated. Only small pieces of debris remained. In comparison to the explosion, which followed the hit on the Aikoku Maru, the explosive force was much bigger on the Kikukawa Maru, and the damage was much more extensive. The tug and the rescue boats were lost together with all hands on all vessels.

Foreship

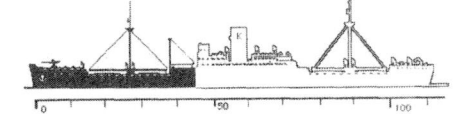

The foreship of the Kikukawa Maru appears to be particularly large. The description leads from the bow along the port side of the ship, then a turn is made were the hull broke apart. A pass close to the lagoon bottom, alongside the starboard side of the ship ends the dive.

The bow is raked. Both anchors are out. The chains cross on the bottom, but they are buried quite deeply into the sediment. The sides of the ship are straight, the shell plating is riveted. A bilge keel can be seen where the sides meet the ship's bottom. When approaching the break in the hull, a deep compression mark can be seen, which is followed by four more S-shaped ripples in the steel. They follow each other in decreasing distances. Behind them the steel plates are badly torn, forming huge jagged edges.

The vessel broke in two forward of the bridge. There are only a few pieces of steel plating remaining aft of the break. No substantial parts of the ship could be found on the bottom despite intensive and repeated searches in this area. Only a part of the aft bulkhead of the elevated third hold can be recognized.

When swimming around and through the break the twisted and torn plates are passed, but an underwater light must be used to avoid the sharp fragments.

Most of the cargo of hold 3 tumbled out and lies in the tween decks or close to the ship on the sea bed. There are a great number of spare parts, such as aircraft propeller hubs, spinners, cables, spare wheels, radial aircraft engines and so on. A diesel engine is located close by, and more aircraft engines can be found further down in this hold. A piece of machinery on tires was crushed by a derrick. Parts of the fuselage of Japanese fighter planes, a complete nose assembly and many spare propeller blades can be seen here as well.

In the hold forward, bottles and general cargo is in evidence. There is, for instance, a pump on wheels,

Hailstorm - *The Wrecks*

Kikukawa Maru

together with a compressor on tires. It is difficult to identify exactly the pieces of machinery. Much more remains to be studied and interpreted regarding the cargo. On the sea bed two pointed, conical objects are located, which are not resembling anything found in the Truk wrecks; they are not ammunition. Drums are the dominant cargo in the forward holds. They have spilled out of the hold and form a heap on the side of the ship. If the search is continued towards the stern, but slightly more to the left, a few shadows can be spotted on the seabed. Approximately 500 ft (170 m) from the foreship, a large cylindical object can be seen. It is of heavy, riveted construction. A firedoor is located on one side, and the ripped out smoke uptakes are on the opposite side. This is the boiler. Several pieces of machinery can be seen close to it. It is difficult to identify them. The path of debris continues, but the pieces become smaller and thin out. This is the deepest part in the seabed, and this depression looks like the center of the explosion. Here and there, a piece of deck and shell plating can be seen, crumbled and beyond recognition. Close inspection of the bottom will reveal a large number of steel fragments of fist-size. It can be seen that the foreship rests on an underwater mountain, but this may just be an optical illusion. The foreship rests on the rim of the crater, which the explosion carved out. Also all other ships which exploded violently, such as the Aikoku Maru, Sankisan Maru or Hoki Maru, rest on the edge of a cratered sea bed.

The Kikukawa Maru was discovered on 16 June 1980.

Technical Data:

Tonnage	:	3 833 ts	
Length	:	108,1 m	354.7 ft
Width	:	15,2 m	50.0 ft
Depth	:	8,4 m	27.5 ft
Engine	:	1 x turbine, coal	
Horsepower	:	2 000 hp	
Speed max	:	14,9 knots	
serv	:	12,0 knots	
Launch	:	December 1938	
Service	:	February 1939	
Builder	:	Kawasaki Heavy Industries	

KIYOZUMI MARU

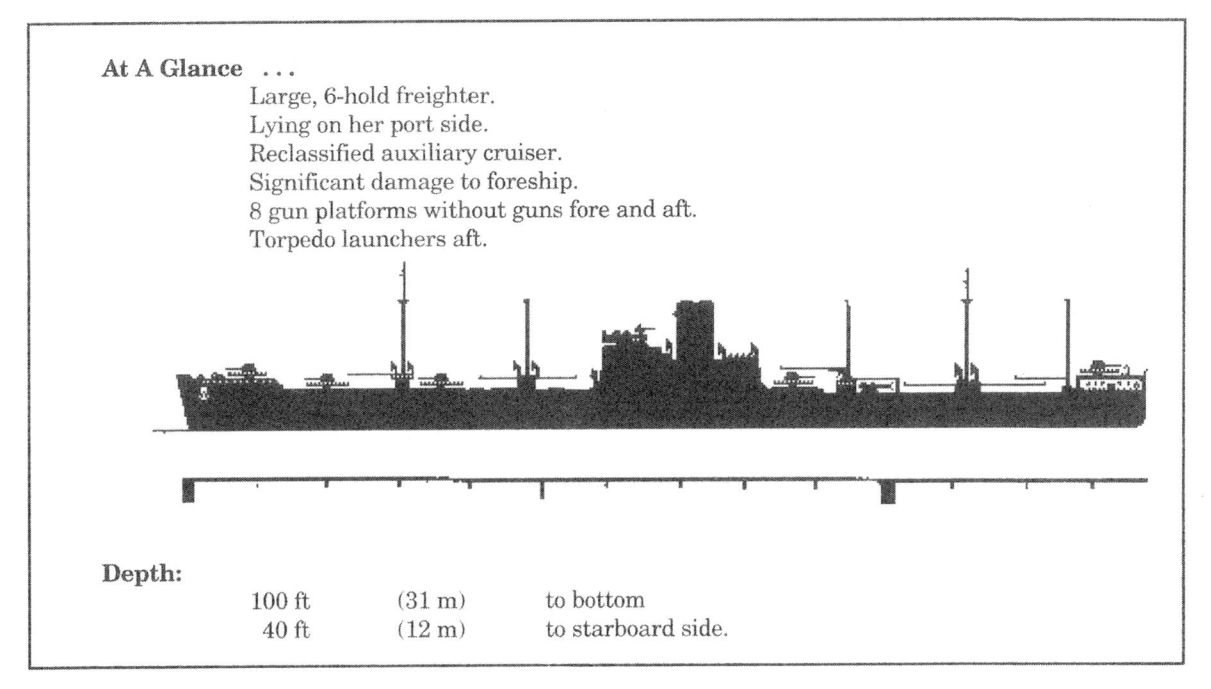

At A Glance ...
Large, 6-hold freighter.
Lying on her port side.
Reclassified auxiliary cruiser.
Significant damage to foreship.
8 gun platforms without guns fore and aft.
Torpedo launchers aft.

Depth:
100 ft	(31 m)	to bottom
40 ft	(12 m)	to starboard side.

The correct spelling of the ship's name is Kiyozumi Maru, but variations, such as Keyusumi or Keyosumi, are frequently encountered. The ship is a bit underrated as a dive. Mostly, second dives of the day are made on it, and the depth limit imposed prevents diving and exploring at a depth where the most interesting objects can be found. As her starboard beam is shallow, an unusual amount of marine growth has settled on hull and superstructure. In particular, the wavy, grey-white algae makes the ship appear ugly. Nevertheless, the history of the Kiyozumi Maru warrants a close inspection of the wreck.

The vessel was converted to an armed merchant raider and fitted out with eight 14 or 15 cm guns, which were weapons cannibalized from old cruisers. In addition, she carried 2 twin torpedo launchers and anti-aircraft machine weapons.

Her career in this adapted role was not particularly successful or eventful. Therefore, in October 1943, she was reclassified as transport, together with the Aikoku Maru, and a number of other ships converted to merchant raiders. It could be that some of the guns were removed at that time, but her anti-aircraft armament, torpedo tubes and fire control equipment were left untouched. The ship was undergoing repairs; she was still damaged from a submarine attack.

The Kiyozumi Maru was bombed repeatedly, and hit twice in the foreship, which made her sink fast. Another bomb exploded on the midship superstructure, causing extensive damage, and ignited a fire. Today, she releases diesel oil into the water. If the West wind prevails, and the current is right, some of the oil is pushed out. She had been leaking fuel for many years, and was known, and referred to, as the "Oilslick Wreck". These days, diesel oil bubbles, which ascend to the surface, spread and smell characteristically, are still common, but not as frequent as in former years. The basic problem on this wreck is that it is difficult to identify objects and shapes. The marine growth has altered forms grotesquely.

The description leads from the bow, via the midships superstructure, to the stern.

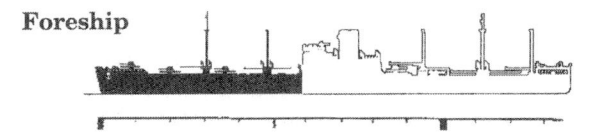

Foreship

One of the anchors is out, and the chain is still under a bit of tension. This means that she went down by the bow, while her aft ship was still floating. The bow has a slight rake. Everything located on the forecastle seems to be underneath the large umbrella of a gun platform. Four more identical platforms are built on the deck of the foreship, abeam of hold 1 and hold 2. The ones on the starboard deck are buried almost half in the sand. All guns are removed, and not a single one remained on the ship.

A substantial winch house can be seen between hold 1 and hold 2. The cargo winches on the winch house deck are big. The mast bears a large cross tree, and many cables are descending to the bottom.

The first hold is plated over on main deck. Only manholes lead further inside. Much unidentifiable debris lies in the tween decks. The bulkheads between the forward holds are destroyed. It is possible to dive from hold 1 into hold 2. Either a close bomb miss or a torpedo destroyed the starboard side. Since this side of the ship now points to the surface, the jagged hole shows overhead. The structural members are either totally blown away or bent downward. Hold 2 is empty. In the next hold aft, a torpedo or a bomb must have exploded underneath the ship near the keel, and ripped an even larger hole into the bottom plating. The

Hailstorm - *The Wrecks*

bulkheads in hold 3 show remains of cork insulation, and a few cooling coils can be seen. It suggests, that is was a refrigerated cargo storage.

together with most of the spokes, but some stringy marine growth add an unreal touch to them. An empty gun platform is located on both sides of hold 5. Heavy rubberized refuelling hoses with metal couplings are

Kiyozumi Maru   Yamada

Midship

The bridge is largely destroyed, particularly the upper deck. It bears witness of a bomb hit. A large range finder can be found at the forward section of the bridge. This instrument is about 6 feet (1,8 m) long. It was part of the fire control system for the artillery mounted at one time. It has two forward facing lenses at the end, and an ocular in the middle, facing back. The instrument resembles a tube in shape. An anti-aircraft gun mount is located on the bridge as well.

It is possible to swim through the midships superstructure, but an underwater light is necessary to avoid entanglements with the many cables. Frequently, the superstructure is entered aft, because the entrance forward does not look too inviting. After passing the tiled deck of a head, light can be seen in the passageway coming from forward, indicating the point of exit.

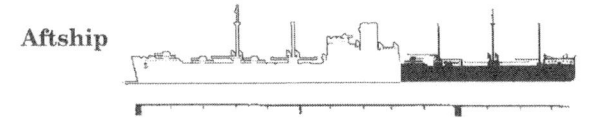

Aftship

The aftship is similar constructed as the foreship. The first hold aft of the superstructure is somewhat smaller than the others. Two larger holds follow aft of it. In one of them, bicycles can be seen, hanging from the bulkhead. Their rear wheels point down. The saddles have deteriorated and are gone,

visible starboard off the aft hold.

A flat structure raised over part of the aft hold. It was the shelter for the twin torpedo launchers. The starboard launcher has fallen off its mounting, but the pair on port remained in place, and can be recognized. Torpedo tubes are complicated weapons. Many big hoses run down and alongside the launchers. A command stand with the seat for the fire control officer can be seen. A variety of valves and gauges are attached to it.

The eighth empty gun platform is erected on the deck house aft.

By a quirk of coincidence the large, four bladed propeller is aligned with the rudder. One of the blades points exactly upward. The other one, which is heavily overgrown, points down, and the other two are parallel to the rudder.

When the Kiyozumi Maru was laid down, her construction was aided by money from the First Ship Improvement Plan, which enabled ship owners to build new vessels with government subsidies. Subsequently, new designs and building techniques were employed. Reports of the ship speak of a particularly designed cargo area aft, and the use of special bulwarks, which must have been novel for ships of this class built at the shipyard. A gyro compass was fitted, which also was a noteworthy improvement. Although the ship was principally a freighter, passenger accommodations were available as well, and evidently stylishly furnished. While the dining area was decorated in contemporary Japanese style, the smoke saloon was appropriately designed in Jacobean style, named after James I of England, Maria Stuart's son.

Hailstorm - *The Wrecks*

The Kiyozumi Maru was taken in hand by the Navy as early as 01 November 1941 and converted to an auxiliary cruiser. One of the ship's missions was the participation in the Midway campaign, which ended in disaster for the Japanese. She was used as a heavily armed troop transport. The soldiers embarked in Saipan, but after the Midway engagement was lost for the Japanese, the Kiyozumi steamed back to Guam, where she arrived on 13 June 1943.

On 30 December 1943 she sailed from Rabaul to Truk, but was sighted by an American submarine, the USS Balao, on 01 January 1944. The submarine commenced an radar controlled, submerged attack and fired a spread of six torpedoes at 2300h. Three of the weapons hit, putting her engine out of action, and flooding the forward hold. Although the ship did not sink, she lay dead in the water and had to be towed into Truk by a tug. The damage at holds 2 and 3 forward probably stems from that submarine torpedo, and others. Repairs were commenced, and it is possible, that the guns were removed at this time to lighten the ship. She was still undergoing repairs, when the carrier attack of 17 and 18 February unfolded. Unable to move, and anchored at the Repair Anchorage at Fefan, she became easy prey for the aircraft.

The damages the Kiyozumi Maru received were severe. Records of the exact nature of the damages from the sub torpedoes are not available. Also, the extend of the repairs effected are not known. The damages at the midship superstructure are no doubt caused by a bomb. It is also likely that the damage at hold 2, where the hole appears overhead, i.e. at the side of the hull, may have originated from a bomb which exploded close to the hull. The ripped up bottom of the ship suggests a torpedo hit.

Technical Data:

Tonnage	:	6 983 ts	
Length	:	137,16 m	450 ft
Breadth	:	18,59 m	61 ft
Depth	:	12,19 m	40 ft
Draught	:	8,3 m	27 ft
Speed max	:	18,73 knots	
serv	:	15,00 knots	
Engine	:	1 x Sulzer Diesel	
Horsepower	:	8 375 hp	
Launch	:	30 June 1934	
Service	:	05 October 1934	
Builder	:	Kawasaki Dockyard	

MOMOKAWA MARU

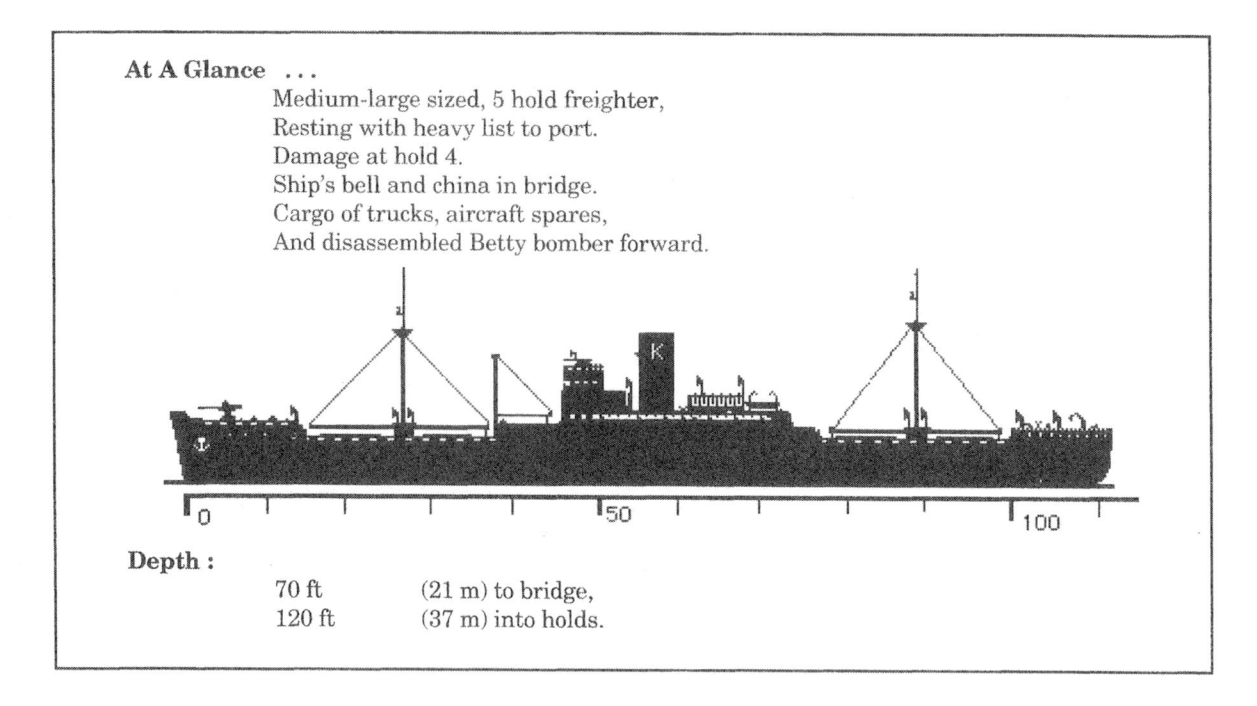

At A Glance ...
Medium-large sized, 5 hold freighter,
Resting with heavy list to port.
Damage at hold 4.
Ship's bell and china in bridge.
Cargo of trucks, aircraft spares,
And disassembled Betty bomber forward.

Depth :
70 ft   (21 m) to bridge,
120 ft   (37 m) into holds.

The Momokawa Maru, in appearance very similar to the Kikukawa Maru and Nippo Maru, was launched in 1940, as a timber transport. It was intended to use her in the northern waters, and she was to bring wood from Siberia to the Japanese mainland. As for most of the year, ice floes were encountered in those areas, provisions were made to strengthen her hull. The bow and the midship section were substantially reinforced. In line with her service, she was fitted with special heavy cargo handling gear. A 40 t jumbo derrick was installed at the foremast. The hatches of the holds were enlarged to be able to accommodate the long tree trunks. Three holds could be found forward. The smaller third hold was elevated over shelter deck. A kingpost was located at its forward edge. The forward part of the midships superstructure was three decks above the third hold; the bridge carried an open flying bridge. The funnel was high, as was commonly found in ships burning coal. Passenger accommodations took up the promenade deck. The aftship continued with two holds. At the stern a deck house was mounted.

The Momokawa Maru was a ship full of surprises. In previous expeditions, the area of the Fourth Fleet Anchorage had been thoroughly investigated, with interesting results. Ships like Reiyo, Hokuyo, Shotan, Nagano and Kikukawa had been discovered, others which had been found previously, but lost again, were rediscovered. Only the Momokawa Maru eluded our search. The Aircraft Action Report of Bunker Hill reported that the planes had hit a sizeable freighter just a quarter of a mile off the southeast point of Dublon. The ship exploded violently and had disappeared when the planes departed. For one, we had never come so close to shore in our searches, and from the reports, only pieces of wreckage were expected.

The bearing and distance given in the official Japanese account proved unreliable, and the American report was not much more accurate. Both reports were in basic agreement however, that the ship was not far off shore. In the first series of searches, basically northeast from Dublon Marker #6, many small pieces of wreckage showed up on the graph paper of the recording instrument, but none, with the exception of one, was large enough to warrant any dive to investigate. The one spread was considerably larger and an exploratory dive was made on it. It turned out to be a 10 m (33 ft) by 8 m (30 ft) large piece of a hatch coaming with attached shell and deck plating, about 5 m (15 ft) high. Sweeps around it did not show any coherent wreckage. When the search was extended south, the Aikoku Maru appeared on the instrument. Incredible as it seems, this large piece was part of the Aikoku, flung not less than 800 m to the north by the gigantic explosion. The search for the Momokawa continued.

An attack photo shows a ship listing north of the Seiko Maru. Using this wreck site as a starting point, the search commenced in a northerly direction and within 15 minutes the graph showed a wreck's echo nested at the foot of a steeply ascending underwater mountain. From the recording, it appeared that this wreck may rest on its side, the size seemed to be unusually small for a big ship, and we were tempted to credit to the Bunker Hill report. However, the Momokawa Maru had another surprise in store: she was fully intact, resting with a heavy list to port in a valley. Close to the port side, the underwater mountain rose conspicuously.

Hailstorm - *The Wrecks*

Aftship

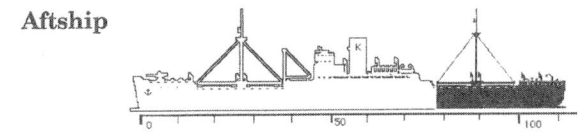

This description leads from the stern to the bow. The poop is wide, but the stern tapers to a fairly sharp cruiser stern. At first sight it appeared to be the bow, but when looking down, the hull recessed and the large single propeller could be seen, complete with hub and 4 blades almost oriented alongside and at right angles to the rudder. The rudder blade is very slightly turned to starboard. It appears to be of modern design. On its leading (forward) edge, almost in continuation of the propeller axis, a colony of white tubular sponges can be seen.

The poop deck used to be enclosed with railguards. Most of the posts and stays are still in place, but overgrown. A field artillery piece is mounted on the starboard side, well aft and to the side. It points almost straight aft. The gun barrel is slightly elevated. The support legs are slightly spread and are guided on a semi-circular rail welded onto the deck. It extends from the railguard to beyond the centerline of the ship. The gun is mounted on a steel support with struts, an arrangement similar to the ones found on the Nippo Maru. The protective shield is rectangular.

Although the field gun was originally fitted with wheels, they have been taken off. The weapon pivoted on the gun mount. It is difficult to identify this artillery piece; it may be a 10.5 cm army howitzer. At any rate, it is larger than the gun on the Nippo Maru. On the Momokawa, the starboard gun is overgrown with a thick layer of all possible forms of sessile sea life. The dominant color is red-orange from encrustating sponges. Corals and oysters are also present, and obscure the training mechanism and the lock, and enlarge the diameter of the barrel grotesquely. At the circle segment, a few whip corals point upwards; inboard a mooring bit is bolted to the deck, next to the support leg.

There used to be a counterpart of this gun on port, as evidenced by a gun mount, but the gun is gone. Also, the circular rail is absent. Three boxes of ready ammunition slid down and hung up by the edge of the stern. Eight circular holes in the cover of the boxes show how the rounds were packed. Underneath the hull, on the sea floor, several objects can be seen. They appear to be the missing gun and other debris.

A skylight is built into the poop deck. The glass is gone. Underneath it, one deck lower, the rudder engine can be found. A little forward of the skylight, a second mooring bit can be seen across the other, inside the rail. The forward port part of the poop, the deck between poop and hold on the aft part of the hatch coaming are destroyed. The steel plates are torn and partly ripped away. Slightly to midships, a spare anchor is mounted on the poop bulkhead.

Damage to the port side of the hull is not evident; shell plating and tween decks are intact. A spare blade for a ship's propeller and a coil of heavy steel wire came to rest here, among a lot of spent shell casings. Evidently, the gun was fired for a long time.

Quite impressive destruction was suffered diagonally across the hold, on the starboard forward side. The tween deck is detached from the shell plates over a long distance, and hangs twisted and torn inside the hold. The bulkhead to hold 4 has been blown out between the mast and the hull. A large tear shows in the upper portion of the hull, which bulges outward. It closely resembles a shallow bubble which burst. The deck plating is also torn and points up. It seems that a bomb hit at the port deck near the poop exploded and vented the the blast to starboard.

A possible explanation is that the ship listed to starboard at the time the bomb hit, and that the shock wave was trapped underneath the tween and the maindeck, tearing up the decks, bulkhead and shell plates, and opening the hull after deforming it. The picture which shows the ship early during the first day, long before sinking, indicates that it listed to starboard. Both aft holds are almost empty, suggesting that most of the cargo either was blown out or burned in a flash fire. Some unidentified pieces of cargo can still be seen in hold 4. Steel lines descend from the mast to this hold. It is interesting to note that the hold openings are unusually large. The large shaft tunnel can be seen in both holds, and is located halfway up the hold due to the heavy list.

Four large cargo winches are flanking an exceptionally stout mast. A substantial jumbo derrick is lashed to the mast. All derricks lie over to port.

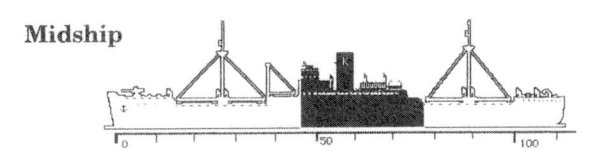

Midship

The midship superstructure is two decks high, when approaching from aft. The second deck forms a passageway with a bulwark athwart. Ladders mounted on the aft bulkhead lead to the open passageway alongside the ship, and two doorways allow access to the inside on shelter deck.

The boat deck carries railguards. Two pair of boats davits can be seen, some point out, the others inboard. The aft pair is larger and fastened to the outside of the superstructure. A pair of ventilators are located at the aft end of boat deck. Forward of them a few triangular supports have been welded onto the deck. They are followed by first a small and then a large pair of ventilators. The cowl of the large starboard ventilator fell between the two shafts. The long skylight base contained two times four covers which are in the open and secured position. The funnel used to be tall. It is now flattened and its upper part is blown over to port. Cracks show in the plating. A few of smaller structures on boat deck are forcefully displaced to port. This certainly is evidence of a bomb miss in the vicinity.

A deck house is built between the funnel and the bridge. On top of the bridge a single structure is all that remains of the flying bridge. It is so heavily overgrown that it is difficult to identify whether it was an engine telegraph or a helm.

The inside of the bridge conveys an orderly

Hailstorm - *The Wrecks*

Momokawa Maru

impression, but it is tight there. A large helm can be seen. Two instruments are mounted on its aft side, a crown gear is located in between them. The wheel hub is located below, the rim of the the wheel fell down and can be seen on the accumulated debris on port. An engine telegraph is bolted close to the forward bulkhead. Its base ends about an inch above the steel deck which is an indication that the deck was planked with wood. Both instruments are overgrown with orange encrustating sponges. The second level of the superstructure can be reached by a ladder. Up forward the bulkheads enclose the forward part of the bridge on both sides, and the entryway from the forward looks like a large "T" with its inboard horizontal part shortened. Doorways with open doors to the shelter deck level appear between the ladder and the bulwark.

Many artifacts have been found on the bridge and on the level below. Out of the sediment, several large serving platters have been resurrected. They are beautifully decorated with the contemporary blue design of Japanese landscapes on the white porcelain. There is a locker full of china at the mess and bowls, even ashtrays with the insignia of the ship owners have been found, together with a small dinner bell. The ship's bell, buried in the debris on port, has been taken and partially cleaned of hard calcerous growth. The name, in both scripts is clearly visible, even the black print inside the engraving.

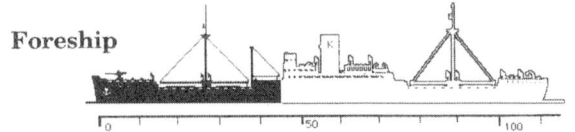

Foreship

The foreship consists of three holds, a kingpost, a mast and the poop. Again the ship conveys the impression of an extremely sturdy and stout vessel. Its lines are square and strong, little compromise has been given to good looks. The kingpost and the masts are very heavy duty, the holds have large openings and fairly narrow tween decks, and the winches are big. The exception is the third hold which looks decidedly small compared to the others. It is elevated as was common for Japanese built ships at the time. The hatch cover beams are all in place and at the bottom of this hold, many heavily dented drums can be seen. The kingpost is located at the forward edge, flanked by winches. The deck then descends and the second hold comes into view. All cargo tumbled to port and is jumbled, making identification difficult. There are several 2.2 m (8 ft) long cylindrical objects with a diameter of 50 cm (1 1/2 ft). They used to be aerodynamically shaped, but on all of them the nose and the tail are crumbled. Probably they were belly tanks for fighters. A wing of an aircraft can be seen, then follows a truck.

On the bottom, three large radial engines can be made out. Farther inside, the hold contains many dented drums and forward, three more cylindrical tanks can be seen. Two trucks came to rest in the debris, their engines facing to port and down. The driver's cabin, steering wheel, their loading platform and twin rear wheels can be recognized. They are large. Closer investigation reveals that two smaller trucks and several tires are located close by. The presence of large sized aircraft propeller blades and a few parts of a fuselage suggests that more aircraft parts are buried in the deep debris. Another indication are two tail wheel assemblies.

When diving to the forward hold the mast is passed. There is no jumbo derrick lashed to it. The most conspicuous cargo in hold 1 is two large aircraft wings and a large piece of aluminium which resembles the tail of a large sized plane. There are numerous fuselage parts scattered around and many other disassembled pieces. Their size suggests that one or two Betty Bombers were carried as cargo.

A cluster of small sized, tear shaped bombs and several large calibre gun shells are located a little forward. They are resting on top of 5 stacked pieces of molded metal sheets and several corrugated steel sheets are leaning against it. Four radial engines can be readily identified, they are at different locations in the hold. Close to one of them, several of the large propeller blades came to rest. A piece of wing with a conical shaped piece of metal can be seen in the beam of the underwater light in the deeper part of the hold. Many tires, some of the with the typical radial profile of aircraft tires, others with conventional truck profile, are positioned at the aft part of the hold. A row of welding gas cylinders are tied down at the tween deck.

The forecastle bulkhead shows a spare anchor mounted on the starboard side, next to the ladder which leads up to the forecastle deck. Here, the large windlass dominates. The port anchor is out. The chain leads away from the ship, and as it is laid out straight, it tells the story of the slow sinking.

The name Momokawa Maru can be seen on the bow. As usual, the Japanese characters are welded above the Roman letters. A patch of brain coral grows on the second "M". The Momokawa Maru was discovere by the author on 29 March 1982.

Technical Data:

The Momokawa Maru was ship No. 47 967, and requisitioned by the Navy on 18 06 1943.

Tonnage	:	3 829 ts	
Length	:	107,29 m	352 ft
Width	:	15,24 m	50 ft
Depth	:	8,38 m	27.5 ft
Draught	:	6,94 m	22.8 ft
Speed, max.	:	14,93 kn	
serv.	:	12,00 kn	
Horsepower	:	2 468 hp max.	
Engine	:	1 x Turbine, steam, coal.	
Launch	:	17 08 1940	

Hailstorm - *The Wrecks*

NAGANO MARU

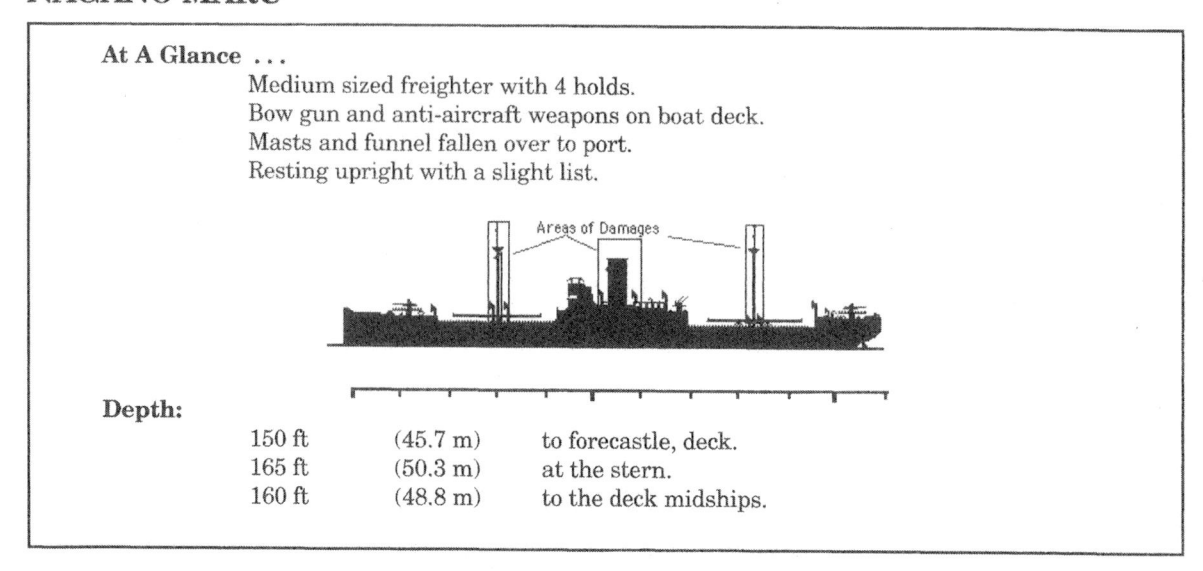

At A Glance ...
Medium sized freighter with 4 holds.
Bow gun and anti-aircraft weapons on boat deck.
Masts and funnel fallen over to port.
Resting upright with a slight list.

Depth:

150 ft	(45.7 m)	to forecastle, deck.
165 ft	(50.3 m)	at the stern.
160 ft	(48.8 m)	to the deck midships.

The description of this rather deep wreck leads from the bridge to the poop and then to the bow. The ship rests on slightly slopping ground and has a small list of about 20 degrees to port.

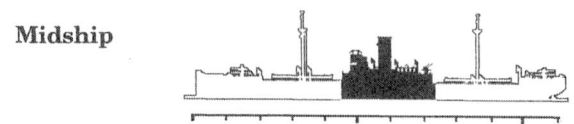

Midship

The navigation bridge is almost totally gone, only the steel supports are visible. The helm has been bolted to one of the horizontal supports. It stands upright all by itself. A platform is integrated into it. Most likely it was either the direction indicator or the compass. The helm's wheel was made of wood with a steel or brass rim. All this wood has decayed and the rim fell over the helm, sliding down and resting draped around the base. A piece of steel or electrical wire, one end much frayed, hangs over the other side of the rim.

An engine telegraph can be seen not far from the helm. It has fallen down and balances now on a support beam. Its base and head are suspended over the lower deck. Originally it was bolted to the wooden planking. As the wood rotted or burned away, it lost its support and crashed down to port. It is now precariously perched on the beam. The indicator appears to be in the position Half Forward. A second engine telegraph was mounted on the port wing of the bridge. It also fell down, and now hangs overboard, held in place only by its signal chain, quite literally by a thread.

The tall and straight stack used to be located slightly aft of the bridge. It now has a severe kink at its base can be seen. The funnel yielded here and sagged over to port. Its lower part looks very much mangled, and the rest is no better shape. In fact it is so corroded that the owner's markings can not be recognized.

It is a common sight to see the tall stacks of coal burners in bad shape. They consisted only of a hollow tube, and this metal was probably weakened by the hot flue gases. Considering that the masts and the funnel all fell over to port it certainly is evidence of the blast wave of a bomb explosion nearby. With this kind of damage apparent on the superstructure it is only reasonable to expect damage to the hull plating, and possibly a fire above on the decks. This deductions were confirmed by correspondence with the ship owners a few years after the discovery.

Extensive use of wood was made on the upper decks of the ship. As it disintegrated over the years of immersion in salt water, bridge and boat deck assumed a skeleton-like appearance by the bared steel supports. This way easy access is gained to the lower decks. Two anti-aircraft machine weapons are bolted to the boat deck on both sides abaft of the funnel. Two rows of skylights of which one is in the open position, are located amidships. Some particularly fine specimen of black coral grow on the bridge wing on port.

Three cylindrical objects are resting on starboard deck, close to the railing and the aft edge of the superstructure. It is a bit surprising to see these objects, which look like large rice bowls or cauldrons, mounted on a base which in turn is welded onto the deck plating. Their purpose is not immediately apparent, but they could be field kitchen, as there appears to be a fire door set in the base facing inboard. Her military role suggests that she carried troops. It would be sensible to assume that these vessels were in fact used to prepare food for the most miserably accommodated troops during transport.

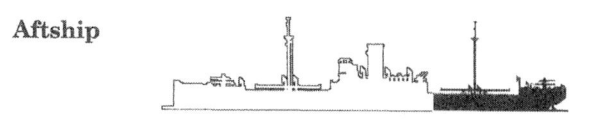

Aftship

Hold 3, which follows aft of the superstructure is either empty or was gutted by fire. The ship's antenna fell down and can be seen on the starboard side of the hold. The mast was flanked by two pairs of ventilators. One pair is located on deck, between hatch coaming and railing. This position is unique for a ship in Truk. The large winches are mounted on deck - the ship does not have a mast house - close to the hatch coaming. The aftermost hatch cover beam on maindeck and a few on the lower deck remained at their places.

There is cargo in hold 4. At the aft part, underneath a single hatch cover beam many drums have tumbled out of the tween deck and can be seen as they form a heap on top of a fallen hatch cover beam. Unidentified long cylindrical objects are located on the tween decks on port. Several drums are scattered on the sea bed. About two or three drums are wedged between the aft hatch coaming and the poop bulkhead.

The poop was enclosed by a railing. The stanchions and the lower stays remain, but are overgrown. A spare anchor is mounted on the forward edge in the middle of the poop bulkhead. Above it a 5 ft diameter platform is built on the poop deck. A tall helm with a large wheel of about 4 feet diameter dominates the deck. The stand and the brass rim, which rests over the wheel hub. They are overgrown by orange sponges. The actual wheel was made of wood and has decayed.

A steam engine is located, together with a large gear box, aft of the stand. A very heavy chain emerges from here and runs right and left to the sides of the ship on chain guards. They are guided around to continue aft, on port and starboard of the poop, until they reach two very large circle segments. This machinery is the old fashioned rudder machine, similar to those found on the Unkai and Yubae Maru.

The flagpole is standing but is bent forward. The ship has a very large 4-bladed propeller, which happens to be aligned perfectly with the rudder post. The rudder itself is turned all the way towards port and faces forward. The stern has a large overhang.

Swimming from the stern on starboard alongside the hull, forward, and passing the midship superstructure, no obvious sign of damage to the hull can be seen. On the way back it is possible to enter the superstructure through one of the two open doorways on port. The inboard door leads into a large room which contains a lot of bales, probably uniforms or blankets.

The outer door in the bulkhead can be reached by going around a ventilator. Also this cabin is quite spacious. It was probably subdivided with plywood partitions, which are gone. There are many cases of beer bottles, rows of large sized soy sauce bottles, and a lot of china, such as plates and dishes. The exit is towards inboard, where it meets the passageway from the other doorway.

A lot of unidentified debris can be seen on the deck. Portholes allow a little light to enter. A little forward a small hatch or companionway comes into view. Very close to it a steam pipe emerges from the engine casing and leads down diagonally through the hull to the outside. The exit is a small distance forward, just aft of where the funnel was located.

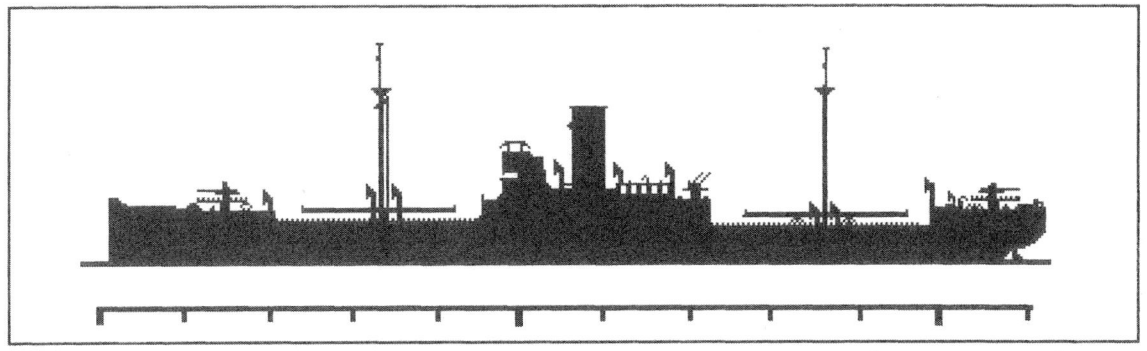

Foreship

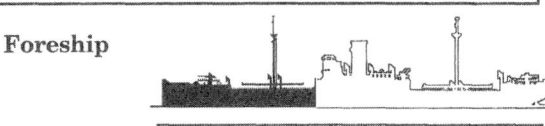

Forward of the bridge, abeam of hold 2, two large coils are resting on starboard deck. Apparently, they were power cables wound on wooden cores. These reel drums have disintegrated, and the wire coils are resting, half collapsed, on their sides. These cables were carried as deck cargo.

The second hold appears to be empty. The mast is broken and together with the jumbo derrick has fallen over to port. Hold 1 follows forward of the mast and is empty as well. Hatch cover beams are still in place in both forward holds. A few drums are stacked against the forward bulkhead of the first hold.

There is another spare anchor bolted to the forecastle bulkhead on starboard. Inside the port doorway of the forecastle are a number of kerosene lanterns, the type used for ship's lights in emergencies. They are located inside the boatswain's locker. A bow gun is mounted forward of the two large anchor winches. The gun is overgrown with corals and encrustating sponges, which makes identification difficult. Shield and breech are also covered with sessile marine life. The barrel points slightly to starboard with no elevation. This flat trajectory gun could not be used against aircraft.

The bow itself looks very round on the forecastle deck. The starboard anchor is out. The chain leads directly to small heap of chain; an indication that the ship - probably after burning - settled quickly. A curious looking object is lying over the rail guards above the anchor on the forecastle. It is 200 to 210 ft to the bottom.

The reason why this ship sank is not clear because the hull below the waterline could not be examined. It is too deep. The nature of the damages, such as fallen mast and funnel, is clear evidence of bomb near misses. The ship must have sprung a leak and sank fairly quickly. The Nagano Maru was discovered by the author in the morning of 13 June 1980 and is known in Truk also as X1, as it was the first discovery during the deliberate search in 1980, of a ship not immediately identified.

A plate of chinaware, found inside the bridge bears the following marking:

Hailstorm - *The Wrecks*

NIPPON YUSEN KAISHA,
with an emblem containing an anchor, on the front,
and
THE IRONSTONE CHINA: MATSUMURA & CO.: MADE IN JAPAN,
on the back.

The Nagano Maru was positively identified by the plates and the lines of the ship. She was freighter.

The Nagano Maru served mainly domestic Japanese lines, was taken over the Japanese Army on 12 September 1937, and used as transport during the China war. She was returned to the owners on 12 December 1937 and reverted to her civilian role. The Japanese Navy requisitioned her 16 June 1941 and used her until 10 September 1941. Afterwards, the freighter's fate is unknown until 27 December 1941, but she was probably repaired or armed. From the 27 December 1942 onwards the ship was rated auxiliary transport back under the command of the Army, until she was sunk in the February carrier raid.

According to communications with the previous owners, the Nagano Maru arrived in Truk in mid-January and departed with supplies for the airfield on Morotok. She probably returned to Truk on 22 January 1944. The Initial Fighter Sweep was observed by the crew, and her anti-aircraft weapons were fired.

This drew attacks from fighters and bombers, and many hits of the board weapons were seen at the crew quarters. The ship was not attacked at the first wave, but during the second wave a division of bombers swooped down and registered four close misses. Fires were started in hold 1 and 3. The crew worked feverishly, and was able to bring the fire in hold 1 under control, but the fire at other locations raged soon out of control. The hull had sprung leaks at various places from the close bomb explosions. At 0735 h the captain died from the wounds caused by a bomb fragment. At 0900 h the remaining crew, taking along the wounded and dead, abandoned the ship, which sunk at about noon.

Pilots from Essex described her location as being in the middle of the (Fourth Fleet) anchorage, and dropped a salvo of 4 bombs across the midship section. Although none of the bombs was a direct hit, the hull suffered damage. The attack was the first of the first day, and to the pilots it appeared as if a large explosion occurred. This was certainly the bomb blast, as the ship itself did not explode. The ship sank later at about 1200 h.

Nagano Maru

Technical Data :

Gross Tonnage	:	3.810 ts	
Length	:	345	105,16 m
Breadth	:	50 ft	15,24 m
Depth	:	29 ft	8,87 m
Draught	:	23' 9"	7,25 m
Speed, max.	:	14.3 knots	
service	:	11.0 knots	
Horsepower	:	max 2920 hp	
Engine	:	1 x reciprocal steam engine	
Launch	:	25 April 1917	
Service	:	21 May 1917	
Builder	:	Mitsubishi Heavy Industries	
Owner	:	Nippon Yusen Kaisha (NYK)	

NIPPO MARU

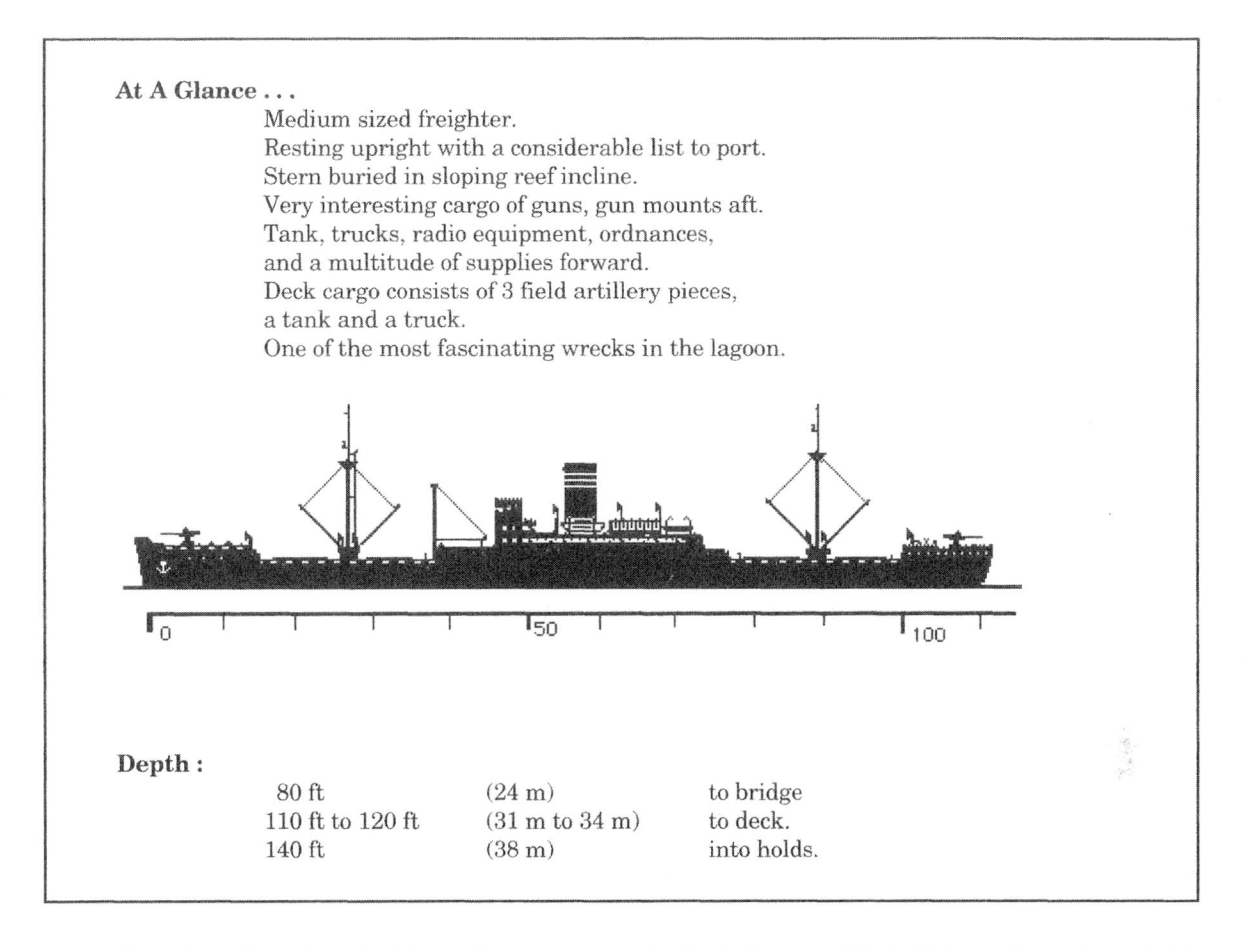

At A Glance ...
Medium sized freighter.
Resting upright with a considerable list to port.
Stern buried in sloping reef incline.
Very interesting cargo of guns, gun mounts aft.
Tank, trucks, radio equipment, ordnances,
and a multitude of supplies forward.
Deck cargo consists of 3 field artillery pieces,
a tank and a truck.
One of the most fascinating wrecks in the lagoon.

Depth :

80 ft	(24 m)	to bridge
110 ft to 120 ft	(31 m to 34 m)	to deck.
140 ft	(38 m)	into holds.

For a long time there had been the nagging suspicion on a few islanders' mind that a wreck might be located off the long reef due east of the two peninsulas, jutting out from the east side of Dublon. There was no firm evidence, however, a local fisherman, Akao, repeatedly had his lines fouled at a particular spot. Every so often oil could be smelled in the wind, without leaving a distinct mark. One of the things which puzzled Kimiuo Aisek were two large containers which washed ashore in the very early morning hours of the first day of the attack. Remnants of the steel reinforcement edges can be seen to this day in the vicinity of the wrecked navigation light on the reef. When snorkeling on it, a small quantity of mercury was discovered. There is no trace of this ship in anyone of the attack photos.

The ship had not been seen on any of the attack photos. When Kimiuo witnessed the explosion on the Aikoku Maru, the Nippo Maru had already been sunk for an hour. Pilots from the Essex dropped a salvo of several bombs on a ship, which tallies with the location of the wreck site. This was at about 0700 h. Although the pilots did not observe the result of their attack in detail, all evidence clearly points to the assumption that the Nippo Maru sustained heavy underwater damage and sank swiftly.

The actual damage to the hull can be seen on port. Roughly between hold 4 and the midship structure, a large, yet rather inconspicuous hole shows close to the bottom at 160 ft. It looks like a torpedo hit because the damage is confined to the underwater portion of the hull. The shell plates curve inward and are absent over a diameter of about ten feet. It may be that the damage extends even further into the bottom of the ship, but is concealed, as the Nippo Maru lists to port.

Assuming that she sank early would preclude a torpedo as the weapon which caused her sinking, because torpedoes were not used during the first strike. Rather, the damage might originate from a bomb with a short delay fuse, which exploded right next to the ship. This would account for the fairly clean underwater damage. Other bombs may have been very close misses as well, contributing to the very severe rocking of the ship which is evident from the jumbled heavy cargo and the dented funnel.

The Nippo Maru is one of the most fascinating wrecks. The ship is in almost perfect condition with no major damage apparent at first sight. The superstructure is partially overgrown by various forms of sessile marine life, but decks and holds are comparatively clean. It competes with the Fujikawa and Shinkoku Maru to be the most adventurous dive. The draw-back is that the Nippo Maru is just a little bit deeper and the wreck site is frequently exposed to winds and big waves. Currents can be swift here, as well.

It is the unusual cargo which makes this ship so interesting. The fact that she was only discovered on 16 June 1980 accounts for the fact that there are still so many unusual artifacts on the ship.

The Nippo Maru was a water carrier, but apart from this rather simple cargo, there are several disassembled coastal defence guns, three pieces of field artillery on wheels, a tank, two trucks and a large amount of shells, shell casings and electrical components on deck and in the holds.

It is possible that the cargo was destined to reinforce the defences of Truk. Although there is presently no proof obtainable for the contention that the freighter carried supplies for the 52nd Division, just arrived and stationed in Truk, this may be regarded as very likely. This division had arrived a couple of weeks before the attack, practically without any supplies. Some of them were en-route, others were on the bottom of the ocean, because the ships were sunk by submarine torpedoes. The single tank and the trucks - all on port - suggests that on starboard vehicles either fell over board or were already unloaded. The ship has five holds. The description leads from the stern via the midship structure to the bow.

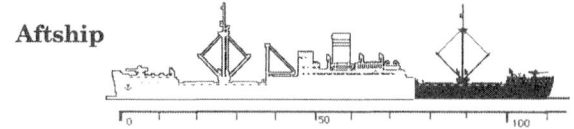

Aftship

The stern seems to be damaged close to port quarter. However, this is an optical illusion. The ship rests on the bottom with a list to port. It impacted on the sloping reef stern first. Over the years coral sand has continuously moved downwards from the upper regions of the reef. On port it has built up so high, that it crept up on the stern, spilled over on the poop deck and encroached several feet forward. The reef will continue to encroach upon the wreck and eventually cover the aft ship. There is no evidence of war damage in this area. The sheerstrake of the poop continues straight and unbroken, up to the point where sand covers it.

The poop deck was enclosed with sturdy railguards. Most of the stays remained standing and are overgrown by many different forms of sessile marine life. The poop deck itself looks rather clean and uncluttered. There is a gun platform set fairly well aft. Near it is a square opening in the deck, probably originally a skylight. A very large double winch, resembling a windlass, is mounted forward of the gun platform, which shows a conical gun mount in the middle and stays around its perimeter. All other mechanical parts of the gun have tracelessly vanished. The gun mount stump looks as if barrel and other parts have sheared off.

A cable drum can be located at the forward most edge of the poop deck. Two ladders are descending to the well deck near the bulwark to passageways. Both of them are open. The doorway on starboard is half obstructed by a ventilator and its cowl, which fell down, and now rests between the hatch coaming of the last hold and the poop. On the other side, the port doorway is half hidden by a large spare anchor, which is firmly fastened to the poop bulkhead. Heavy, massive rods, in appearance very much alike to a shaft of an anchor, rest on the deck near the upright, bolted anchor. Literally hundreds of concrete steel reinforcement rods are laid out on port between the bulwark and the hatch coaming.

Despite the obstructions to both doorways, they can be entered without particular difficulty, and although the cabins look uninviting at first, they open up and become spacious further aft. The visit to the aftermost part of the ship is very informative. Assuming the doorway on starboard is entered first, the first cabin is built athwart the ship and light can be seen coming from the other side. However, it is fairly narrow and not particularly inviting. The passageway continues and opens into a large room in the middle of the poop, which is lit by the open skylight. The large rudder machine, the steering mechanism, takes up the majority of the space. Two large quadrants, a powerful electric motor and a gearbox are the major components of the ship's steering. To the left, a doorway opens to a long cabin running parallel to the outside of the ship. A little light is admitted through the portholes about 1 m (3 ft) above the deck. There are a few objects scattered here in the brown sediment. One item looks like a helmet, and farther forward a number of wheels may be seen with the light of a torch. There is no problem in swimming either around or above the steering machine and to exit at the port door into the open, although the opening is not very wide.

There are two gun barrels tied down parallel to each other, but end-to-end, to the deck plates next to the hatch coaming on starboard, at the last hold. They are about 5 m (15 ft) long, have a slightly thickened muzzle and were designed with a screw type breech.

Hold 5 contains very unusual cargo. The open space in the middle of this hold contains an untidy array of gun stands, mounts and bases. The gun stand is a slightly conical piece of steel which is riveted on its wider bottom end to a strong steel plate. On top the gun mount can be seen consisting of the circular hole where the gun barrel is to be fitted with three recoil tubes, two on the bottom and to the side, the other one on top. There is one prominent hand wheel attached to some gears and mechanical devices, on the right side of the mount. Most of them are resting on their left. These gears are part of the training mechanism.

There are 7 gun stands scattered around. Actually counting them is not as easy as it appears, because they are resting one on top of each other, presenting a very confusing picture. They tumbled out of their original storage area at both sides of the tween deck and fell down into the middle of the hold. The tween decks are fairly empty - an excursion through them to make inventory follow shortly - which suggest that they broke lose when the ship rocked severely due to bomb close misses.

The gun barrels for the gun mounts are placed orderly athwart on the bottom of the hold. Their location at the first tween deck level indicates that they are resting on top of the water containers. These big tanks, in shape and size similar to a modern 20 ft cargo container, are located on the bottom of this and all the other holds. The gun barrels in the hold are of the same type as the two which are tied down on shelter deck.

While gun mounts came to rest at the forward part of the hold, most of their bases can be found a little aft of them. They are large cylinders, roughly 2 m (6 1/2 ft) high and a diameter of 1 1/2 m (5 ft), of special configuration, which would be imbedded into steel reinforced concrete. There are seven of these pieces in the hold, matching the number of open mounts. Only one tween deck can be seen in this aft hold.

Starboard aft, moving to port, steel plates with handles can be seen. They are followed by packs of 3 by 6 cylinders, longer and thicker than today's beer cans, and obviously the powder charge for the shells found forward in the ship. A few of the cases are missing, obviously victim of corrosion. Quite a number of tightly wound wire coils are scattered in the vicinity, closer to port. They are probably barbed wire. A cart, manufactured with a tubular frame follows; there are many bottles resting underneath it. 12 more coils are found next to it on its other side.

The tween deck on port is almost empty and only a few pieces of steel grating can be found. Three large cylinders and bottles are strewn among them, together with 4 containers. The forward part of the tween deck is reached, where two large cable drums can be seen three quarters buried in the accumulated sediment. The high-voltage cables still tightly wound around the core. Two smaller coils of telephone wire are resting nearby.

The foot of the mast is bent. Evidently a heavy object crashed against it. More communication wire follows towards starboard, and also there are round, brass rimmed glasses of about 20 cm (8") diameter, resembling an engine telegraph. A lot of rotten wood is piled up in the corner. The starboard tween deck has not much more to offer than a lot of hardened cement bags, and five sets of double walled cylinders.

When ascending from the hold and passing the mast, flanked by ventilators which are connected with a beam and winches, a lot of steel cables can be seen on deck. The cowls of the ventilators are gone. One of them rests close to the starboard cargo winch. The aft derricks lie over to port.

Two slightly conical, ribbed objects which carry a ring of about 20 cm diameter on top are located slightly forward of the mast on the deck. They appear to be supports for a cylindrical object, such as a single gun barrel. One of these objects is clearly visible, while the other is half buried in the sediment on deck. Three 4.7 cm anti-tank guns of the type M-1 (1941) are located on shelter deck abeam the starboard hatch coaming of hold 4. The guns, being able to penetrate up to 5 cm armor, appear to be pointing right to the sky. They are characterized by their trapezoid gun shield.

Although this field artillery appears to be deck cargo at first glance, this may not be entirely true. Close inspection of the deck reveals not only three, but four provisional gun mounts, welded in equal distance to each other onto the deck. They are not exactly in one line, however and are about one foot high cylinders, with four supporting struts. The guns were lifted onto them so that their wheels cleared the deck. Of the three guns, only the one forward closest to the bridge remained halfway on a mount. This may not be its original mounting, because all guns jumped their mounts and the first gun just happens to to rest on this particular one. Subsequently, the guns appear to be jumbled and untidily parked on deck, yet more evidence of the violent rocking of the ship.

The last of the three guns points over starboard beam with maximum elevation. It rests against the hatch coaming. Two white tube sponges grow close to the muzzle. This is the only gun which looks ready to fire, despite its small tilt and being displaced several feet aft and inboard from its mount. The second gun points aft and slightly to port with no elevation. A piece of tree coral grows out of the barrel. The right wheel is suspended over the hold and the gun rests on the hatch coaming. It is interesting to note that a large portion of the protective shield on the right side has broken off and disappeared. This is another piece of evidence for the violence of the last moments of the ship. Its mount is located forward of the present position of the weapon, so the piece must have moved back and rotated to port when it jumped the mount. The first gun makes the most orderly impression, but this is only because it faces right over to starboard, with no elevation. It is askew on the mount, being half on, half off. There is some growth on the breech. Slightly forward, a very much dented drum can be seen on the deck.

When swimming diagonally across the hold, the inventory may be commenced at the aft port side moving forward. Immediately it is apparent that many kinds of communication sets have been carried here. There are several half open boxes visible in the sediment, which consist of the mounting plate, front piece with many dials, turning buttons and switches and the internal components of old fashioned radios, such as large capacitors, resistors, and vacuum tubes.

Moving forward in the tween deck, small ceramic or glass objects can be seen in the sediment. They may have been insulators. Various kinds of bottles and galvanic cells are located close to them. A number of small glass dishes of about 10 cm (4") diameter and an edge 2.5 cm (1") high, which appear to be stacked together in pairs, are hard to separate and are resting partly on top and partly inside the sediment. Quite a large area is taken up by small flat bottles, similar to pint-sized liquor containers.

By far the largest part of the hold is taken up by what literally looks like a field of bottles. They are scattered from the very deep recesses of the hold to the middle. When going way forward on port, light can be seen coming from below and the side. The hull is opened here and this is the damaged area. It appears incredible that a big explosion which destroyed the plating did not break all glass and bottles, but almost all of them appear to be intact. Several sizes can be differentiated, and farther away, large 3 liter bottles can be seen, while those closer to the hatch coaming resemble beer bottles.

The reason why there are so many bottles accumulated at port may be seen when going in the tween deck forward from port to starboard. Most of the cargo shifted to the lower part of the ship. The forward part of the starboard tween deck is fairly empty, but further aft, several remnants of lead-acid batteries and a large number of zinc-carbon batteries can be found. When looking very closely, one or the other radio vacuum tube can be seen protruding slightly out of the sediment. When pulled out of the brown-grey material, the glass is clean and the intricate internal design can be seen.

The aft part of the tween deck, underneath the third gun on the well deck, contains cans, larger than today's beer cans. They are packaged a dozen per set and are probably gun powder cases. A set of about 6 or so bed frames, resembling hospital beds with tubular head and a foot rest, are stacked. Way aft a small collapsible cart can be identified, also made of tubular steel with bicycle type wheels and tires. The spokes are gone. The forward part of the tween deck, from starboard to port, shows two very large bowls with a diameter of about 4 ft. A second tubular framed hand cart takes up the remaining space.

After the tour of the interesting cargo of hold 4, curiosity may be aroused about the opening in the hull seen at the forward part on port. The damage can be seen when passing over the side of the ship where superstructure and well deck meet. There is a large, irregular jagged hole of 3-4 m (10-13 ft) length and about 2 m (6 1/2 ft) height underneath the former waterline. The shell plates are partly bashed in and partly separated. Massive water incursion into the engine room and the hold must have followed. The ship certainly sank very quickly.

The damage is typical of a bomb very close miss. The detonator was certainly triggered by a medium-short fuse. When looking at the sea bed it appears that a bomb crater can still be seen close to the ship. The bottom generally shows some small coral growths, but an almost circular patch of 30 m (100 ft) diameter next to the hull is devoid of any life forms and the bottom is bare. A hatch cover beam was flung about 30 m (100 ft) onto the sand. Blast damage on the stack may stem from this bomb, but it also could have been caused by other close misses. The hull is buckled on port. A boarding ladder was hung outside the opened section of the bulwark. The only pieces remaining are those which were fastened to the steel lines which suspended the ladder from the ship. The rest was blown away by the bomb explosion.

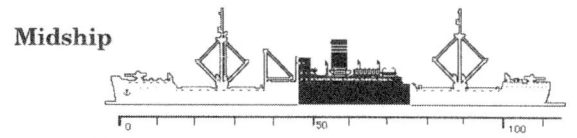

Midship

The superstructure is two decks high. When approaching the midship superstructure from aft, it can be seen that the two doorways leading into the main deck level are wide open. Ladders ascend from the maindeck to the passageways on both sides, one deck higher. Between the port ladder and the bulkhead, several welding gas cylinders have been stacked on their sides. The valves, pointing inboard, can be clearly recognized.

A large steel workbench has been bolted to the main deck and the bulkhead of the superstructure. A sizeable vise, mounted at the edge of the bench, still holds firmly in its jaws the nose handle of one of the bomb-like objects. It seems as if the mechanic was working on it just before the attack. This however, is not quite true and just one of the little optical illusions so commonly found in the depth. The jaws of the vise are slightly ajar, the bomb rests on its nose on the workbench between the vise and the bulkhead. It seems to have fallen down from the passageway above.

Overhead, the superstructure forms a promenade on shelter deck level, which has a bulwark and railguards. A number of the same bomb like objects are littering the passageway athwart the ship. One of them slid down to the railguard on the port side, due to the list of the ship. They are all identical in shape. Their bodies are about 1 m (3 ft) long, drop shaped with a blunt nose and a tapering body. A fin is curving over the nose, continuing on both sides and ending in an eighth of a turn at the tail. Two stabilizing fins are located at the tail as well. The nose carries a hook as support for handling.

If these objects are indeed bombs, they occupy a most peculiar storage area because the galley is located right behind them. However, these bodies are used for minesweeping. They are designed to be towed and to ensnarl the anchor rope of a mine, and causing the mine to detonate. This gear seemed to have been mounted with a swivel and rotated when pulled through the water, to set off mines with other triggers.

The ship's kitchen can be reached from the open passageway on the second deck by entering the doorway and turning right at the first door. This narrow, but long room is dominated by a very large stove which has several hot plates. It was originally heated with coal. At the base, the fire doors are all open. When the ship was found a large cooking pot was still resting on a hot plate. Evidently there was forced ventilation over the stove, as an air duct is mounted on the deckhead. A lot of kitchen utensils and different sized pots can be seen hanging at the aft bulkhead of the galley. This room can be easily traversed and offers interesting photographic possibilities.

The cabins forward can be explored without much problem, although they are considerably narrower as are the ones below. Still, a lot of artifacts can be found in them. Of course, all doorways are unobstructed. The doors were made out of wood. A complete lock with doorknobs on both sides can be seen resting on top of the sediment at the starboard passageway at the door sill of one of the cabins.

Entering through the starboard doorway one deck below, on the main deck of the superstructure, the diver should pause a moment to allow the eyes to get adjusted to the dim light prevailing in the cabin. It can then be seen that quite a bit of light comes in from the evenly spaced portholes at the outside bulkhead. Nevertheless, a light is recommended for closer investigation and to avoid the cables hanging from the deckhead. A large distribution box has fallen down and hangs suspended from the circuits.

The first room inside the superstructure is quite spacious and extends over the width of the ship. Way forward, two very wide passageways are located on both sides of the engine room casing. Although the one on starboard is a dead alley, and is fairly dark because the bulkhead door forward fell shut as a result of the list of the ship, exploration is very interesting. Each of the portholes was the window for an individual cabin. The traces of the rotten wooden partitions can be observed on the bottom. There is very little sediment here. Most of it actually went to the other side. As each of these former cabins was the home of the ships officers, many artifacts can be seen at close examination. In fact, almost everything which could withstand the exposure of seawater for 38 years may be found here. Little personal effects from buttons to ink pots, a single shoe, brass lamps and hundreds of small objects are revealed when carefully sifting through the mud. Even phonographic records and two pair of deer antlers have been found. However, it is best to leave them at their original place so that the following divers may see them as well. Tempting as they may be, they are not to be brought up as souvenirs. Their presence and discovery has been an adventure and a joy when the ship was found. It would be sad if they would disappear, robbing others of the excitement to see.

There is a thick and a thin pipe running near the outer bulkhead, close to the deck. Way forward, the thicker pipe connects with the smaller with a U-joint. This has been the steam or hot water heating for the cabins, necessary for colder climates. Since there is no exit forward, the diver has to make an a about-face and go back to the mess near the entrance. It pays to have been careful and not to stir up too much silt. The narrow passage between the engine room casing and the forward bridge bulkhead is definitely not recommended to be used in getting to the other side. A great deal of debris and sediment has piled up, almost to the height of the portholes. It would make the traverse hazardous.

The only advantage is that the doorway forward is wide open and allows light to come through. When swimming into this direction a door to the right in the engine casing can be seen, and entrance into the engine room is possible. This is a narrow door, but does not present a major obstacle. When entering, one gets to a catwalk landing, but immediately to the left at the door frame, a light switch can be seen. It is always somewhat reassuring to find something so trivial as a light switch at the proper place. There are a number of catwalks and gratings leading up and down in the engine room, which is illuminated by light coming in from another open door, one deck up, and the two rows of four skylights, which are secured in the half open position. The engine room of this ship is considerably smaller than those on the Kansho or Fujikawa Maru. This is not a function of the size of the ship, but its propulsion unit. As opposed to the mentioned diesel driven vessels, the Nippo had a turbine, which takes up considerably less space. In fact, the largest piece of machinery is the large boiler, close to the bottom of the ship. Therefore, the many catwalks present a slightly confusing picture. When looking down, a little light can be seen coming from the outside, near the bottom of the ship. A few shell plates have been ripped away by the explosion, causing a leak into the engine room. Pipes, tools and pieces of machinery are fastened to the bulkhead of the engine room.

After exiting through the same door and turning forward, two rooms can be seen to the left. They have been heads, and the white ceramic bowls are still in evidence. The doorway forward is reached and entrance to the coal bunker gained, which are really a rearward extension of the main tween deck of the third elevated hold. Companionways lead up and down. Ascending one deck, the open starboard passageway is reached, which can be used to swim aft to the end of the superstructure where finally, the cluttered promenade with the galley is reached again, but now on the left at boats deck level.

An overview reveals a cylindrical object, the boiler water feed vessel aft, the boats davits on both sides of the deck, a few triangular structures like pipe vices, ventilators, and the funnel, on a base with skylights aft and abeam. If the underwater visibility is good, the bridge house and bridge deck can be seen.

Entrance to the engine room should not be attempted from the top because the engine room skylights are partly closed. Those which are open are secured with a rod to keep them in that position. It would be hazardous to negotiate an entry.

Two pair of ventilators are located forward, and aft of the stack, respectively. The funnel is big and fairly tall. It is considerably dented on its base on starboard. The plates even parted and show a crack but the stack remained standing. Continuing to swim from the funnel forward over the midships superstructure, a circular railing can be seen in the middle of the bridge deck. The rail guards lead to a passage with a ladder descending to boat deck on starboard. Inside the railed-in enclosure, two tubes are protruding from the deck, one which is bent about one meter (3 ft) off the deck and quite overgrown, as is the railing itself. Forward of it the navigation bridge was located. As it was essentially a wooden structure with a few steel supports, it has disintegrated. An engine telegraph and the helm, with the rim of its wheel draped over the base, can been seen forward on bridge deck.

Two anti aircraft twin weapons used to be located on the upper deck probably at the bridge wing. Both have broken lose. The one on starboard fell onto

Hailstorm - *The Wrecks*

the elevated deck next to hold 3 whereas the port gun fell over board and can be seen on the sea bottom. Both are resting with their base facing upwards.

The bridge is certainly one of the most impressive sights of all wrecks, particularly when approached from forward. The former windows are overgrown with particularly colorful and varied species of coral, hydroids, sponges and oysters. It is a beautiful view. Inside, the bridge is spacious and well lit. In the middle, the helm and compass is overgrown completely with orange encrusting sponges, which brightly reflect the light of an underwater lamp. The wheel is gone, but its rim hangs from the hub. Because of the list, the rim hangs over to port. Above the hub, three instruments are mounted. Two face aft and the other upwards. On top, a compass has been mounted.

Two strands of wire are descending from the deckhead, just aft of the helm. An engine telegraph stands close to it, its double handle in the 2 o'clock position. There is another set, close to the forward bulkhead. Several articles rest on the deck. They appear to be a cover each for the engine telegraph and the compass housing. The bridge house extends over the width of the ship. At boat deck, a passageway is formed inboard cabins on either side. On port, the door is a quarter open, but would not open any further. Just aft on both sides, a companionway leads down deck, the sides secured with railguards which have remained standing. Even further aft, at the funnel base, just abeam of the stack, a large rectangular skylight is in the wide open, secured position. The opening is secured by a grating.

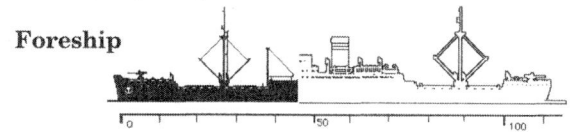

Foreship

Hold 3 is elevated by one deck over the foreship. On first sight it appears to be empty. It is very likely that the two water containers washed up on the reef after the ship sank, broke loose from this hold and floated up. There is cargo evident in the tween decks. A twin barrelled machine weapon lies next to the bulkhead of the midship structure, upside down, and presents its 4 ft diameter wide and conical base. Boxes of ready ammunition are resting next to it. The rounds are a bit corroded.

When descending into the hold, it is easy to swim into the tween deck, and to continue to go aft, where, below and aft of the bridge, the coal bunkers can be reached. It is fairly spacious there. No obstructions are encountered and light shines in from the portholes and from above the coal chute. These coal bunkers are arranged symmetrically on both sides of the ship. The clearance in the middle, deep in the recess of the tween deck, is reduced by coal, and it almost is a squeeze to get from one side to the other.

A large jumbo derrick rests athwart the deck and a few 10 cm shell casings can be seen in this location as well. In the aft part of the first tween deck in the hold, the sediment reaches up to the hatch coaming. Buried inside are hundreds of bottles, some of the necks protruding from the silt. Forward, in the tween deck, there are about 3 or 4 cylindrical objects 2 m (6 1/2 ft) long and 15 cm (6") wide. From all appearances they resemble range-finders, and may be part of the equipment for the guns carried aft. Going aft on starboard, a urinal lies in the middle of the deck, which is otherwise fairly empty. A hatch cover beam has been placed here and evidently steel lines were hung up on hooks from the deck head. The rest of the tween deck is taken up by bottles, and there is not too much other cargo evident.

On the lower level, forward, are a very large number of bottles, many canteens and messkits, and a heap of other kitchen supplies. To port, 14 boxes of 4 x 3 cylindrical cans of gun powder charge can be seen, and a large area is covered with soles, remnants of army boots. Since there is no dividing bulkhead it is easy to swim underneath the kingpost from this hold to the one forward. This area is covered with large numbers of bottles and messkits. In between them rests a long tubular object, resembling an optical range finder. Close to it stands a kind of a boiler, which is about 1.20 m high.

Hold 2 has only one tween deck because the large water containers take up the bottom of the hold. These tanks have shifted and look jumbled about. Most of the corners are bashed in and bent. One of the containers is missing, the others have shifted forcefully. They were probably only partially filled. They caved in and shifted when the ship rocked. The missing one from this hold, floated up and beached on the reef, slightly south of the reef marker east of Dublon.

Swimming from starboard aft to forward, ropes and hatch cover beams indicate that unloading of cargo was in progress in this hold. Way forward, there is a large area, about 5 m (18 ft) long by 2 m (6 1/2 ft) deep, where 10 cm shells are stacked 75 cm (2 1/2 ft) high. Most of these shells are still orderly stowed and have not shifted, except for a few on the top and sides which point their sharp top upward. Some sediment has settled on them and they are encrusted with hard calcareous growth. At first glance they resemble beer bottles, but they are infinitely more dangerous. It is very likely that they have been the ammunition for the guns carried in the aft holds, or destined for the heavy anti-aircraft guns. The war heads had been packed in boxes and were strapped together, which accounts for their relatively undisturbed appearance.

On port, some assorted gear and materials can be seen in the sediment, and at the aft part, the deck shows was subdivided with wooden partitions. Six compartments can be recognized. They are empty.

Two sets of machinery, either pump or generator, coupled to a motor, mounted on a steel frame, and are resting on the top of the water container, leaning against the tween deck hatch coaming.

An armored car, a tank, is parked on port maindeck. Its rear faces the bulkhead where hold 3 raises. This vehicle appears to be in good condition. It is, evidently, a light tank of the Type 95, described in the chapter of the San Francisco Maru. There is no gun barrel in the turret. The metal tracks run on two twin suspension wheels. The upperwork appears to have lifted about 10 cm (4 inches) from the chassis, on the

Hailstorm - *The Wrecks*

Nippo Maru

Yamada

rear part of the vehicle, but this is an optical illusion. The suspension of the rear guide wheel has broken down, and the track angles down a bit. The body of the tank is undamaged. It looks as if the tank is resting on something, like a mooring bit.

A tire lies between the tank and the bulkhead. The mast is located between hold 1 and 2. It was flanked by ventilators; their cowls are gone now. It is possible to swim between the mast and the ventilator shafts. Three water transfer pipes can be seen leading from one hold to the other. They are overgrown with marine life. Cargo winches are mounted on both sides of the mast forward and aft.

The first hold seems to be just as large as large as the second, but because the hull tapers to form the bow, the tween decks are narrower. At first sight there seems to be a lot of material scattered all over. In the open part of the hold, registering from aft to forward, boxes of ammunition for 2 cm and 3.7 cm anti-aircraft guns, many messkits and field kitchen supplies, a heap of detonator caps, a single hatch cover beam and a large number of "anti-boat" mines, Type 38, can be found. They are the same kind as those found in the San Francisco Maru.

The inventory in the tween decks shows a variety of different cargo. When swimming into the tween deck on starboard, beginning from aft and working towards forward, the first items to be noted are a large number of gas masks, corrugated rubber hoses still attached. They are manufactured from white-grey rubber which is remarkably well preserved. In many instances the glass eye pieces remain in place. Several high pressure armatures and fittings are resting in the sediment of the deck. Their intended use is unknown.

No doubt exists about the next items. They are rubber soles. On some of them, fragments of the top leather is still attached. Many cartridges for guns of 12 cm calibre follow, which thin out towards forward. A large number of mines over a distance of several feet can then be seen. Way forward, these mines appear to be resting on top of drums, most of which are severely dented. Both, drums and mines continue to be the cargo in the forward section of the tween deck. Looking upward against the deckhead, a few grotesquely deformed steel drums can be seen lodged firmly on the ceiling. Evidently they were empty so the ambient water pressure caused their partial collapse. There was still enough air in them to make them float up. Some of them hung up underneath the deckhead. Those we can see today, but a large number floated out of the hold and washed up on the reef to the east of Dublon.

When going on port from forward to aft inside the hold, the first things observed are the brown, 5 gallon glass acid containers. Although they are all jumbled around, almost all of them remained in one piece. As was common at the time, the battery acid jars were wrapped with a thick jacket of straw. This has long rotted away, together with the stopper, so there is seawater in all of them. They are prominent in the first half of the cargo area and are followed by a few mines, several crated 5x2 cans, gun powder charges, then many more gas masks and a substantial number of their activated charcoal cannisters.

Somewhat inconspicuous are a few boxes of small arms ammunition, close to the aft port corner of the hold. Moving from port to starboard, many more of the 12 cm cartridges can be seen. One of them opened at the top and about 50 to 100 thin long sticks fell out of the round brass cartridge. This was how the gun powder was put into it. It is a gun powder compound, whose principal contents was picric acid. Deep inside the tween deck, several 2 and 4 cm rounds and gas masks with cannisters can be found. A pile of wood, timber about 60 cm (2 ft) long and 10-25 cm (4-6") in diameter, are orderly stacked against the aft bulkhead. Finally, an oil or water transfer hose can be seen when maneuvering back into the open part of the hold.

Hailstorm - *The Wrecks*

A large truck came to rest on port beam across hold 1, hanging half over the bulwark. The twin rear tires and the majority of the chassis are still inboard but the engine and the front wheels hang overboard. The truck frame seems to have broken where it rests on the bulwark, because the front wheels are not parallel to each other and the engine is at a slight angle to the axis of the truck. The vehicle points forward over the port side. On the sea bed underneath, a second truck can be seen. It is angled toward the ship, the engine facing forward and against the hull. All that remains of these two trucks are their wheels, their chassis and the engine. The bodywork has completely disappeared, as if it was ever fitted.

A spare anchor is bolted to the bulkhead of the forecastle. A doorway into the forecastle is open, but access to the cabin forward is hardly possible because a large drum has firmly lodged against the deckhead, obscuring the entrance. It is less of a problem to stick the head into the gap and shine a light inside. The first objects seen inside seem to be the remnants of a foot locker which has disintegrated and left the contents on the deck. A bottle, a single shoe and several other artifacts and personal belongings are lying around close together. A little to the right, closer to the bulkhead, lies some cargo. A huge pile of tabies (Japanese light shoes with separate big toe) seem to have defied decay to an extent, being made from rubber. They are heaped one on top of the other. There seems to be a number of blankets or bales in this cabin as well.

The forecastle deck, with its big anchor winches, bears a platform. Except for the conical gun mount, the gun itself is not there. It is identical to the picture presented on the poop. It is strange that both guns have disappeared.

The port anchor is out. The bow, which has a slight rake, clears the bottom by a few feet. The slope of the reef is steeper than the incline of the ship, and it rests on a small underwater knob.

The wreck is without doubt one of the most exciting in the lagoon. The deck cargo is quite unique and the ship is in very good condition. There is very little growth on it except on the elevated structures. It is open to speculation whether the slowly oozing out of acid stored in the jars contributed to the lack of abundant growth, or whether there is poisonous mercury in the ship. This metal has been found, as mentioned before, at the remnants of the fourth container washed up on the reef, and coral growth in that area is considerably retarded.

The ship was discovered by the author on 16 June 1980. The Nippo Maru is ship no. 42071. She was used as a fruit transporter hauling bananas from Taiwan to Japan. From 24 August 1941 onwards she was utilized as a water transport ship for the Japanese Navy. In that capacity she was a frequent visitor to Truk, where she would load water. The island water was mainly ferried to her from Dublon by a water barge, and she would haul the water to the garrisons on small coral islands, which did not have enough of their own supply.

Technical Data :

Tonnage	:	3.763 ts, gross	
Length	:	107.3 m	(352 ft)
Breadth	:	15.24 m	(50 ft)
Depth	:	8.38 m	(27.5 ft)
Draught	:	7.23 m	(23.7 ft)
Speed, max.	:	16.34 knots	
serv.	:	13.00 knots	
Engine	:	1 x Turbine, coal	
Horsepower	:	3.600 hp, max.	
Builder	:	Kawasaki Dockyard	
Launched	:	16 September 1936	
Service	:	09 November 1936	
Owner	:	Mitsubishi, previously Okazaki Kisen.	

THE FIGHTER AND THE JUNK YARD AT PARAM

At A Glance ...
Three major pieces of a Zero fighter, shot down during take off.

Jettisoned fragments of fighters and bombers off the West side of Param.

Depth :
50 ft (15.2 m) at the bottom of the fighter, surface and very shallow for the plane parts.

While snorkeling about 500 yards off the West of Param, parts of a Zero fighter were discovered, in 1981. It was shot down by Hellcats of the carrier Enterprise during the pre-dawn fighter sweep, at about 0630 h, on the first day of the attack in February 1944.

The pilots of the Hellcats of the Initial Fighter Sweep were surprised that they were not met with much more vigorous opposition in the air. Particularly the main fighterstrip Eten was everything else but busy. A few planes taxied up and took off. The runway and the facilities in Param did not seem to have been completed. Only a few planes were seen on the apron. However, the approaching American fighters saw a Zero taxi up and begin a scramble. The pilots of the Hellcats maneuvered themselves into position, and came from the clouds in the west, descending on the plane the moment it became airborne. The automatics hammered at the small fragile Japanese plane, and the tracers beat a fiery staggered path to the target and disappeared in fuselage and wingroots.

The Zero burst into flames and cartwheeled into the water, breaking up in the process. Today, the pieces rest exactly at the western extension of the former Param air strip, in clear, nice waters. The bottom is sandy, only a few large coral heads break the monotony. It was near such a huge coral that the Zero was found.

The cockpit, parts of the forward fuselage, and a piece aft of the seat are resting close to the coral head, together with the left wing. The front glass of the visor remained in its place. The engine has ripped out, and can be found about 50 m north-west of the coral. A long strip of the fuselage, together with the tail assembly can be seen near-by. The right wing is probably detached and buried in the sand. A long, narrow section of the center fuselage lies on the other side of the coral.

The Param junk yard consists of a stone wall, which encloses a stretch of water off the south-west side of Param where the old air strip ended. After the attack in February 1944, the Japanese took all pieces of planes which were damaged beyond repair by bombs and strafing, and dumped them into the water. There is plenty of twisted, torn and holed pieces of fuselage, tail sections and other plane parts to see. All this lies in very shallow water, which is very turbid. Great care must be taken not to get cut by the razor sharp edges

OITE

The destroyer Oite was a ship of the Minekaze-Class. These destroyers were the first to have steel reenforcements at the bridge. This resulted in a high center of gravity, and in order to increase stability in the open seas, the beam was made slightly wider. Their speed was reported to be 37.5 knots. However, this could only be achieved by running the ship lightened, and without all of its armament during the trials. Even then, the specified speed was reached just barely and could not be sustained over a longer period. Most units of this class were rearmed during a 1941/1942 refit. Dual purpose guns were installed instead of the original low trajectory guns. One set of torpedo tubes was removed in most units. Others were further modified to carry a large number of troops over short distances. The ships of this class, removed from front line and fleet duties, became escorts and fast transports. The Oite is an older half-sister of the Fumizuki. Both destroyers are deceptively similar, but Oite originates from a slightly older series.

The Oite left Truk Lagoon on 16 February 1944, escorting the light cruiser Agano to Japan. Both ships were scheduled for a refit. The Agano was a lightly armed light cruiser, used as flagship of a destroyer squadron. The ships were joined by Subchaser 28.

This convoy was about 360 km (200 miles) north-northeast of Truk, when the US submarine Skate, after a periscope approach in twilight, fired a spread of four torpedoes from a submerged position into the Agano. The time was 1800h. It was reported that all torpedoes hit, and two exploded close to the boiler room. The ship began to list. The hits had knocked out the power supply, and the damage control was severely impaired. The skipper of the Agano ordered the crew to abandon ship, and stayed with a skeleton crew for further damage control. This proved fruitless, and the Agano went down at 1205h (Tokyo Time), on 17 February 1944.

At this time the raid on Truk had unfolded. Both escorting vessels took the survivors on board. Most of the cruisers crew of approximately 450 men went on board the Oite. The rest went aboard Subchaser 28. Considering the size and the space of both ships, all inboard compartments must have been filled like sardines and there were people wall-to-wall, with no place to stand or to sit or to lie down. The Commanding Officer of the Agano went on board the Oite. It was reported that 128 men went on the Subchaser, while more than 400 were cramped into the Oite. Both ships commenced retirement to Guam.

At 1600h on 17 February, radio operators on both ships intercepted a message ordering them immediately to shape course for Truk, to engage possible enemy units. When the skipper of the Oite followed this order, he had no idea that he would sacrifice his life together with all others, crew and survivors, and his ship for absolutely nothing.

The Oite had been made almost defenseless as all of her shells for her main batteries had been unloaded in Truk, in preparation of refitting in Japan. Only a few rounds of machine gun ammunition remained on board.

Both ships sailed for Truk. The Oite was very considerably faster than the Subchaser, and immediately drew away. Subchaser 28 stayed out of harm's way, and was not attacked.

Planes from Bunker Hill reported that the Oite was approaching the North Pass, at 0655, on the second day of the attack. But at this time she was not attacked.

The Oite cleared the North Pass shortly after 0700h, and continued with high speed to Dublon. She was sighted by Hellcats from Bunker Hill at that time. The pilots began a continuous strafing attack. The shells of their machine guns hammered at the bridge and the midship section, causing severe losses of personnel. The most casualties seemed to have ocurred in the bridge. The skipper of the Oite, Lt. Cdr. Uono was killed very early in this engagement, and the gunnery officer of the Agano took over the command of the Oite. He was quickly killed by the stream of bullets hitting the bridge. The Commanding Officer of the Agano then assumed command.

In the meantime, the pilots of the Hellcats had radioed for assistance. One division of five Avengers began to circle the Oite. The ship continued on a straight course. In the meantime, a fire and damages at the second stack were observed. It did not seem to slow the ship down, however it appeared to trail oil.

The Avengers formed a circle and began their torpedo attack from the stern. The Oite's rudder was put hard to starboard. This had been expected by the pilots of the torpedo planes. They fanned out and aimed at the swerving bow. One of the torpedoes hit aft of the bridge with devastating results The destroyer immediately broke in two after the explosion and sank immediately. Only a very few survivors were picked up later.

The wreck of the Oite has been found, however the two parts of the destroyer, lying on their sides, are resting in deep water of 200 ft. There are still many bones on the wreck and sharks seem not to able to forget the feast they once had - the area remains shark infested.

Hailstorm - *The Wrecks*

USNA

The destroyer Oite is seen here already well inside the Truk Lagoon and under attack.
Above:
The Oite commences a tight turn with full speed to starboard to avoid torpedoes launched at her. At this time she does not seem to be damaged yet, although the presence of a Hellcat indicates that the strafing has already begun. It looks as if there was a torpedo launched and dolphined, i.e. broke the water just starboard abeam of the ship. Drop marks of other torpedoes seem to be located to the right and ahead of the ship.
Below:
The destroyer continues its hard starboard turn. Two torpedo tracks. one of them curving, are off the bow. Splashes to the left of the torpedo tracks are probably machine gun fire.

USNA

226
Hailstorm - *The Wrecks*

The sequence of these pictures is evidence that a ship has almost no chance against a well coordinated aerial torpedo attack, regardless whether it is a battleship (such as The Prince of Wales, Repulse) or a lowly old escort destroyer, such as the Oite. The Oite appears to be damaged from strafing attacks, and is trailing an oil slick.

1 - The Oite has almost completed the 30-knot starboard turn, almost a complete circle. This is the standard anti-torpedo maneuver of the Japanese Navy. Just a very few moments ago, the rudder was turned sharply around for a desperate turn to port. The bubble track forward of the bow does not leave any doubt about the deadly accuracy of the weapon. This is probably a torpedo which dolphined, i.e. splashed, ran deep, came up and broke the surface then began its proper run. The turn by the Oite, designed to "comb" the torpedoes, comes too late.

2 - The Oite is hit and erupts in a huge explosion. Presence of black and white smoke is an indication that her boilers are exploding. An Avenger follows the oil track left by the ship.

3 - The End. Part of the bow is showing out of the water, very close to the oil slick, and the aftship is partly hidden at the border of white and black smoke. The two halfs of the ship are plunging to the seabed, 60 m (200 feet) down, taking with them 420 crew and survivors of the Agano.

REIYO MARU

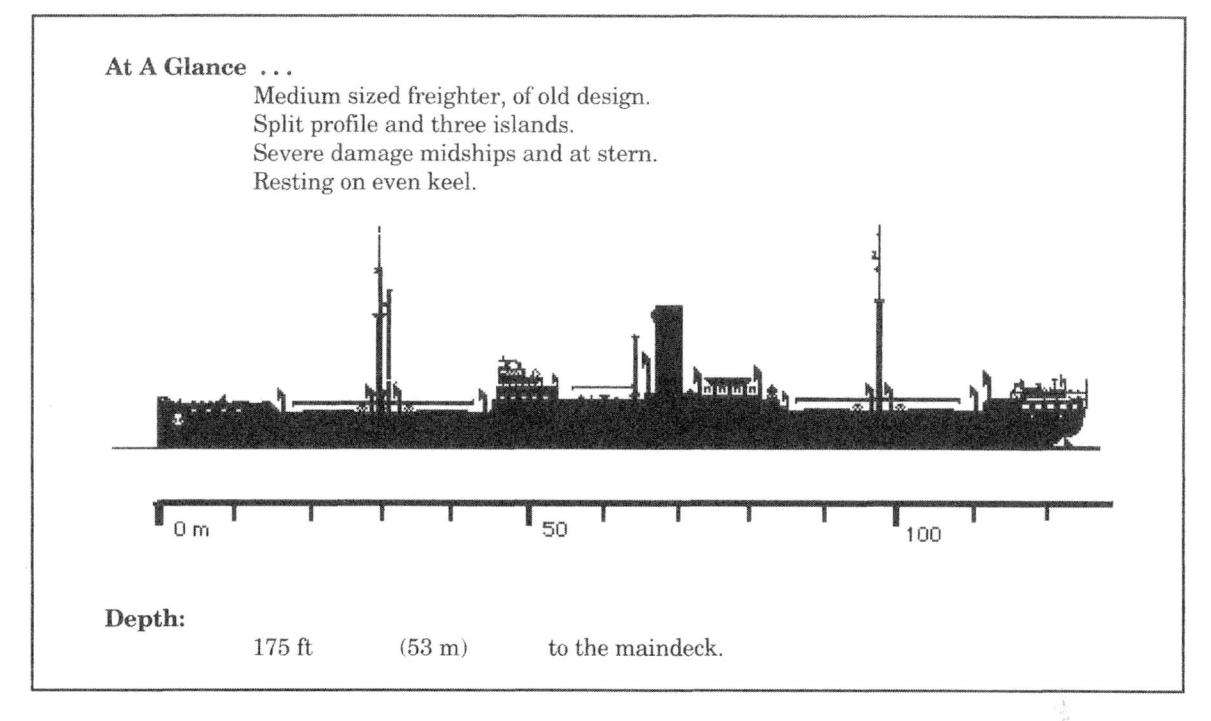

At A Glance ...
  Medium sized freighter, of old design.
  Split profile and three islands.
  Severe damage midships and at stern.
  Resting on even keel.

Depth:
  175 ft   (53 m)   to the maindeck.

The Reiyo Maru is one of the deep wrecks. Comparatively little growth settled on the wreck, because of the deminishd light intensity, and the wreck appears very clean. The wreck is well preserved. In general, visibility in this area is excellent. Resting on even keel, it would be one of the most popular wrecks if it were not for the depth. Dives on the Reiyo Maru have to be planned carefully, and the use of dive computers is recommended.

The description of the wreck leads from the bow via the bridge to the stern.

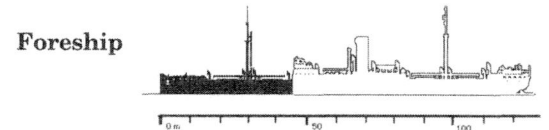

Foreship

The forecastle is fairly well rounded. The bow is straight without a rake and suggests the design of an older ship. Both anchors are out, and the anchor chain leads away from the ship. They cross right under the bow, and a small part of the chain lies underneath the ship. The bow points to east-northeast.

The ship does not carry a gun on the forecastle, which is dominated by a large twin windlass. It is eye catching how the anchor chain leads into the hawse hole, because there is very little sediment and growth on this ship. It is 160 ft deep to the forecastle deck.

The first hold is almost empty, except for a few drums. The hatch coaming is bent. The mast behind the hold is broken and has fallen to port. Actually, the masts of this wreck aided significantly in identifying the ship. It is the only known wreck in Truk, which has a conspicuous triangular cross tree mounted on the upper third of the tall pole mast. Characteristically, the apex of the triangle is above its base. More modern crosstrees are built the other way around.

When the forward mast broke off, the top mast crashed into the bridge and broke off right above the apex of the cross tree. The main part of the mast came to rest on the deck, port of hold 2. It lies on top of a derrick and assorted other poles. A ladder is welded to the mast. Also, the ventilators on both sides are broken. The substantial cargo winches fore and aft, starboard and port, are set well apart from the mast-ventilator combination.

The view into the second hold is obscured by more than 50 rail road track segments. Originally, they were orderly laid upon the hatch cover beams on main deck, but the force of the explosions and the impact of the ship on the sea bottom dislocated them. Many of these segments are scattered over to starboard, and point over the railing.

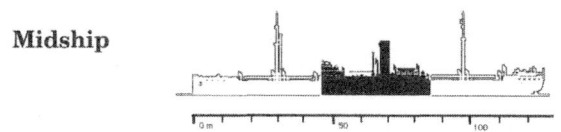

Midship

The bridge is damaged on port where the mast hit it. The steel structure is bent forward and outward. There is evidence of a severe blast wave from aft. A third hold is located aft of the bridge. It is smaller than those forward and aft. It seems to be undamaged. Looking inside, however, it can be seen that the aft bulkhead is bent forward in a gracious curve.

There is a crack in the hull on starboard. A kingpost is located behind the midships hold. The starboard member is bent. A pair of ventilators follow. The cowls are attached on both of them. The ventilator on port is bent and leans against the funnel, which is very tall and straight. It is a round tube; the ship

Hailstorm - *The Wrecks*

burned coal. It is surprising that the stack still stands upright, because on port, abeam of the stack, the ship

Reiyo Maru

suffered tremendous damage. A large gaping hole shows almost from the boat deck to the ship's bottom. The surrounding steel plates are twisted and torn. All support structures are completely destroyed.

This damage is evidence of a very close bomb miss. The bomb must have hit the water very close to the ship and detonated with an instantaneous or a short delay fuse. The force of the explosion was so large, that the shell plating, mainly underneath the waterline, was destroyed. Just inboard of the damage the coal bunker of the ship was located. Although the coal stocks absorbed some of the shock wave, the force was still strong enough to bend internal bulkheads out of shape. The coal spilled out of the hole and accumulated in a large heap on the sea bed. The heavy pole masts could not withstand the heavy rocking of the ship and they broke off.

The engine room skylights are located behind the funnel. All hatches are in the wide open position and secured. There are three windows on both sides. A deck house has been built behind the skylights. None retained their glass. The boats davits, which are situated abeam the skylights, point outward. Behind them, the midship superstructure drops down to shelter deck level.

Aftship

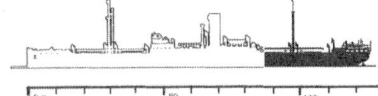

The fourth hold, which follows the superstructure, remained intact. Right aft of the hold, behind the winches to port, a hole can be seen. It has been caused by a bomb fragment, and measures about 1 ft to 1 1/2 ft (about half a meter).

The aft mast has fallen as well, and lies to port, crashing into the bulwark below the cross tree. The mast bent but did not break where it lies over board. The fifth hold, which follows, is very badly damaged. The hatch coaming and bulkheads are a mess of twisted steel. They are totally bent out of shape. The damage continues up to the stern. There is complete destruction on port at the poop, which has all but disappeared. A gun at the stern could not be found.

The damage to the ship evidently stems from one or two bomb hits and one close miss. The bombs were probably dropped in a salvo. The major destruction at the after ship would have certainly be enough to make the vessel sink, but also the midship near miss was fatal.

The ship was rather old at the time, and was driven by a reciprocal steam engine with coal boilers. It was built in 1920. The Reiyo Maru was taken over by the Japanese Army on 10 October 1941, and used as transport until 27 April 1942. Her whereabouts were unknown until 17 November 1943, when she was taken over by the Navy.

The Reiyo Maru was found on 14 June 1980, by the author. The wreck was also known in Truk as X 3.

Technical Data:

Tonnage :	5 445 ts	
Length :	121,92 m	400 ft
Width :	16,15 m	53 ft
Depth :	9,75 m	32 ft
Draught :	8,05	27 ft
Speed max :	14 knots	
serv :	10 knots	
Engine :	1 x reciprocal steam engine, coal	
Horsepower :	2 800 hp	
Launch :	November 1920	
Service :	27 December 1920	
Builder :	Asano Dockyard	

RIO DE JANEIRO MARU

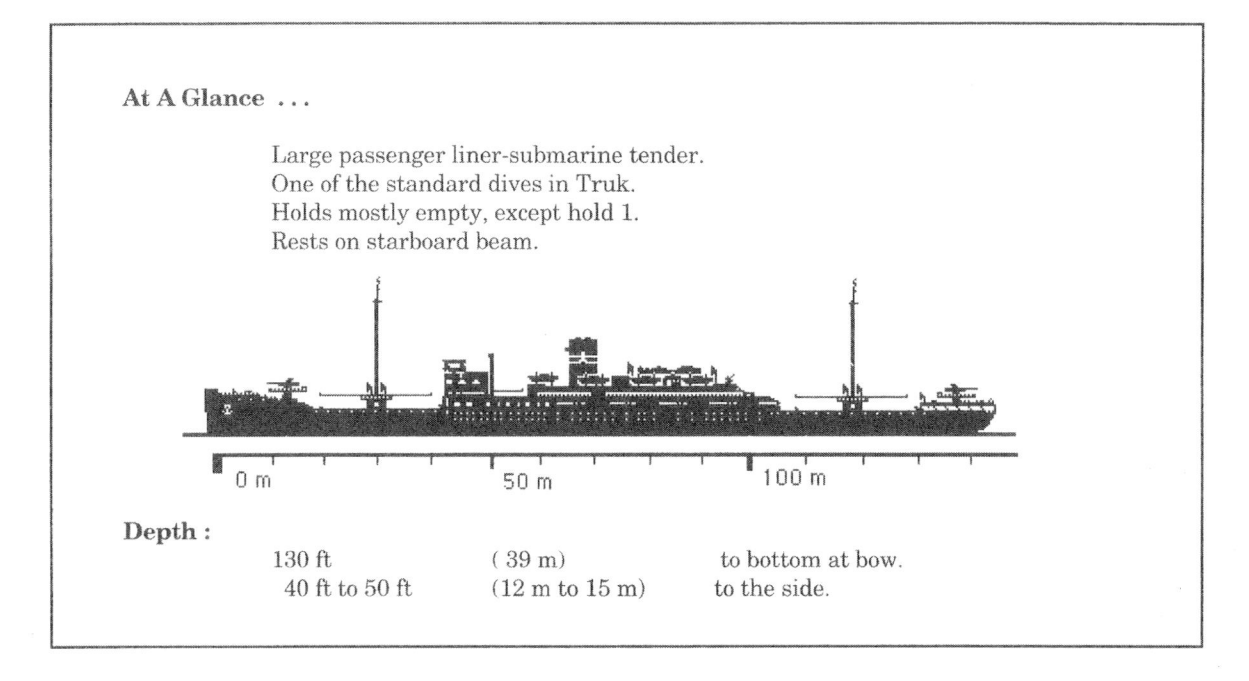

At A Glance ...

Large passenger liner-submarine tender.
One of the standard dives in Truk.
Holds mostly empty, except hold 1.
Rests on starboard beam.

Depth :

130 ft	(39 m)	to bottom at bow.
40 ft to 50 ft	(12 m to 15 m)	to the side.

When descending on the Rio, the wide beam of the ship comes into view first. It is best to start the dive at the bow.

Foreship

The forecastle carries a big gun. It points straight down over the starboard side into the sand. This is a big, but not a particularly modern gun. Descending from the hawse hole at the bow, the starboard anchor chain runs straight to the bottom. The anchor is located about 150 ft (45 m) forward of the ship. Its position suggests that the Rio sank slowly. Also, the port anchor is out. The chain leads over the bow and descends straight to the bottom.

The bow shows damages. The uppermost row of shell plates is blown away on starboard, except for one plate, which points forward and makes it look as if the ship had a bow sprite. Diving underneath the bow is interesting. Evidently the shadowy underside of the ship is the ideal place for whip corals to grow. They grow like some ghostly, crooked, long whitish fingers pointing downwards. The name of the ship is welded in Japanese and Roman characters on the bow. One has to look very closely to recognize the letters.

At the side of the hull, a few feet aft of where the poop deck meets shelter deck, a hole in the shell plating can be seen. It is about 60 cm (2 ft) across, but easily overlooked, because several pieces of coral camouflage it effectively. The torn pieces of the plating point upward, indicating that the penetrating objects came from either inside or the other side of the ship.

This curious damage will certainly prompt the inquisitive diver to look closer at the hull plates in this area. A second hole, only about fist size, can be located close by, and the plates in this area are deformed considerably. There are many dents and lumps visible. They all point outward. The degaussing wires have snapped several feet aft of the large hole. They hang down the hull at the fastener, which held the rest of the strands alongside the hull.

The dents, buckles and holes are a clear indication of an explosion, or a series of explosions, inside the ship. These explosions, bad as they may have been, were certainly less extensive than those seen on other ships, as Sankisan or Aikoku Maru. On the other hand, the damage suggests that ammunition was involved, probably a limited quantity. After these deductions it is imperative to have a closer look at the area of the forecastle, to determine whether those assumptions are correct.

The large bow gun points straight down, over the starboard side. The barrel is in the rest position, it is not elevated and was not used during the attack. This flat-trajectory gun would not be suitable to shoot against aircraft. Aft of the gun, the forecastle deck sagged several feet and the bulkhead is torn and twisted out of shape. A large piece of plating near the gun was forcefully peeled off and hangs down.

The reason for all this damage can be clearly identified when swimming into the ship at the forward part of the first hold. Increasingly torn decks and bulkheads are passed. Underneath the aft edge of the forecastle, at "A"-deck (the third deck below the exposed shelter deck), an explosion took place. There is little doubt that the magazines for the ammunition of the bow gun was stowed here, and the explosion centered right there: Something triggered the rounds and the magazines blew up. The fragments of steel all point away from this area. The flash of the explosion and the subsequent fire was observed by the planes of Bunker Hill, on Strike 3A-1, and duly reported.

Hailstorm - The Wrecks

The Rio de Janeiro Maru is anchored of the east coast of Uman, and burns severely. Clearly, two different sources of the smoke can be identified. The first is from the bow, where ammunition "cooks off", i.e. is exploding in the heat of a fire. The second source is at the starboard aft part of the midship superstructure. It probably is the result of the bomb hit, which damaged the superstructure significantly.

When penetrating the forward part of the Rio, just a little bit towards the stern, the culprits of the damage can still be seen. There are many large sized cartridges scattered around. They are bent and torn. Many of them show lateral tears, others are opened like flowers. They have all exploded, except for a single one, which still carries the shell itself and appears undamaged. The others seemed to have been hurled around. Of course it is necessary to use an underwater light to see properly. When looking at the lower side of the hull, the starboard side, large holes can be seen. The damage caused by the explosion is much more extensive in that area.

An interesting observation can also be made when looking closely at the shell plates at the bow. They show a different sign of rusting. The steel here corrodes with the typical color of the burned out metal. This severe corrosion may be contributed to two factors. The fire, and the gun powder. It can be seen that the gun powder contained picric acid. When this material dissolved in water, it becomes very coorosive. The steel assumes a bright brown color.

Aft of the empty hold 1 follows the large mast house and the sturdy mast. Winches and steel lines can be seen. Passageways lead past the mast house on both sides. The deck of the mast house carries a railguard. This superstructure is unusually large and bears the distinct design of a once fashionable passenger liner. There is no problem swimming through these passageways.

When entering the second hold, the maindeck comes into view first. It was once covered with wood which is gone now. Below the maindeck a large cylinder with a diameter of about 3 m (10 ft), rests on its side. A solitary gun barrel sticks straight up a little forward of it. The barrel shows some hard calcareous growth. The calibre is 15 cm and the rifling can be clearly seen. It is easy to overlook the barrel as it is located in a very dark forward part of the hold.

The entrance to the hold itself is almost obscured by another cylindrical object, the insides of which are geared. A gun lock, recoil springs, trigger and the training mechanism can be seen lying across the cylinder on top. A large quantity of coal inside the hold forms an acute angle. The cylinder originally was placed on cement bags on top of the coal. The cement hardened to rocks. A second gun barrel rests in the aft part of the hold. There is no doubt that these objects are single-barreled 15 cm guns in a turning turret, and they are probably old type ship's artillery.

There were a great number of these guns available to the Japanese when they modernized their fleet and decommissioned old cruisers built around the turn of the century. Since the armament had not seen very much action, and was in good condition, it was removed from the ships, which were broken up, and put into storage. At the time, when the Army and the Navy had stopped their advances and consolidated their wide-flung possessions, the guns were resurrected from the Navy arsenals and used for secondary purposes, i.e. as coastal defence artillery. It is therefore reasonable to assume, that the Rio, together with the Aikoku Maru, was bringing reinforcements to the Mandated Islands, and possibly provisions and arms for the 52nd Division, which had just been shipped to Truk. A very interesting part lies on the bottom of the tween deck. It is the trigger pistol for the gun and resembles a signal pistol. It is quite corroded now.

The derricks are in their secured position on deck. Turning around and looking out of the hold, they form a very large "V" over the hatch opening. The mast is also in place. It is so tall, that the cross tree is just at the edge of the visibility, when looking from the deck.

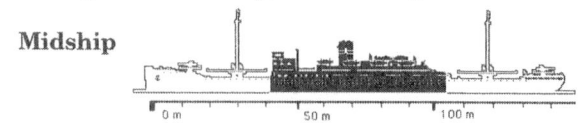

Midship

The bridge has straight lines, and carries a bridge house. Several steel plates have fallen off the bridge and are now scattered on the sea bed. They could have been reinforcements for the bridge and the midship superstructure. The port running light is clearly visible on the bridge wing, which slightly protrudes above the side of the ship. It is also carried an anti-aircraft machine weapon, which fell down. Its platform is almost broken off and tilted to aft.

The bridge deck, which was covered with wood, is buckled. An engine telegraph and steering wheel were located here as well. A paravane can be seen just after the bridge. Its lower part points down. Right below, a gang plank and landing can clearly be seen at the hull. One of the doors in the bulwark is open. The degaussing coil is visible here as well. Rubbing the exposed broken ends will reveal shiny copper metal.

Aft of the bridge the superstructure drops down half a deck, then rises again forward of the funnel to bridge height. There is a hold between the bridge house and the the stack. It is considerably smaller

Hailstorm - *The Wrecks*

than the two in the foreship. A large piece of the port bulkhead detached itself and hangs down precariously, almost blocking access into the hold. The clearance between its lower edge and the sediment is only about 1 m (3 1/2 ft). It is possible to dive underneath it, but the hold is almost empty except for a few decorated ceramic sake bottles and a few other vessels.

A large mushroom-type ventilator next to the stack is half torn off, it now points downward. The stack is worth examining. It is round and tall. A ladder is welded to the forward port side. Mounted on the stack forward is a trumpet-muzzled, big whistle. Directly underneath a running light can be recognized. It is well covered with marine growth. A very large Japanese character is welded on both sides of the funnel on its upper half. It is the character for "dai", meaning "great", and represents the symbol of the owners of the Rio. Part of this symbol has rusted away, particularly the edges, but it remains clearly recognizable. The interesting design of the rain deflection plates inside the stack are worth a quick glance. In front of the funnel a large cylindrical vessel is located. The engine room skylights and a big deck house are built on boat deck aft of the stack.

The aft part of the superstructure is damaged. Aft of the funnel, at hold 4, the ship received a full bomb hit on starboard. The destruction in this area is considerable, but it can hardly be recognized when swimming over the port side of the hull. There does not appear to be damage, except for a few plates on the promenade deck, which are bent inward. Amidships and on starboard the superstructure is a mass of twisted steel. The side of the ship on which it rests now, is blown out. Damage was so severe that it caused listing and later sinking.

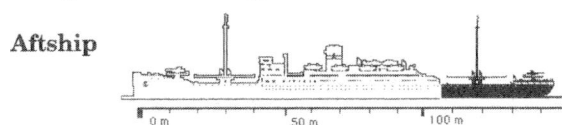

Aftship

Coal forms the principal cargo in hold 4. A third of the large disassembled guns can be seen, but the barrel and lock seem to be buried by the coal which shifted. The gear originally located inside the hatch, is half detached and draped over the hatch coaming.

The large aft mast house follows, aft of which the last hold is located. There the cargo consisted of a very large number of bottles. They are now scattered all over, and may have contained beer judging from their shape and size. Forward in the hold a lot of wood can be seen, probably remainders of bottle crates.

The poop is designed with the graceful lines of a fashionable passenger liner, but this impression is marred by the stern gun. It is located on a platform and points to stern with medium elevation. There are several large shells in this area, some of them presenting their warhead to the visitor. An engine telegraph is located on the poop deck. It fell from its mount and is hanging down. An inspection of the stern and the exposed underwater part of the hull of the Rio does not reveal any damage.

The name of the ship is clearly legible on the stern. As usual, the Japanese characters are above their Roman name. The rudder, semi-balanced and quite similar to the one on the Heian Maru, is very large and slightly turned to starboard. The underwater aftship is very impressive, the bottom becomes increasingly contoured, The twin shafts emerge, and the keel separates them. Both propellers remain on the ship.

The Rio de Janeiro Maru was a combined

Rio de Janeiro Maru   Yamada

passenger-cargo liner. She was built 1929 by Mitsubishi in Nagasaki. After World War I, the owners Osaka Shozen Kaisha (OSK) found themselves in a predicament: They had too many ships. To remedy this situation the decision was taken to sell several of the ships, modernize some others, and build modern units.

In order to remain competitive, modern vessels had to be designed, and the Mitsubishi Shipyard in Nagasaki was given the order for combined passenger-cargo ships, which could also serve the routes of the Japanese immigrants. The new generation of ships should meet the high technical requirements of Lloyds in London, who were to classify them. The naval architect Watsuji Haruki had a high reputation in Japan as a designer, and was therefore given responsibility for planning the ships. It was intended by the owners to accommodate 60 First Class passengers, out of which 33 were supposed to have cabins at the bridge deck. The furnishings for passengers of this class were designed after the classic Japanese Fujiwara-period. Accommodations for 1076 Third Class passengers were available.

The cabins for the Third Class passengers, and for the immigrants were located at the A-deck and main deck level. They were furnished with bunks, but nevertheless, considered quite spacious. One cabin was generally designed to accommodate eight to twelve passengers. The lower bunk beds were intended to sleep mothers and their infants, and were a bit wider

Hailstorm - *The Wrecks*

than those on top. Also for the immigrants, a smoke saloon and medical facilities were available. Eight washrooms and five Japanese baths were at their disposal.

The installation of electrical ventilators, which forced fresh air through all cabins was quite unusual and a modern feature for these ships. For journeys of long duration, three sick bays and two quarantine cabins for infectious diseases were furnished additionally. When the ships began their return voyage, fewer passengers were on board. Subsequently, the beds, made in Germany by Fritz Kaspari, were folded up, removed, and the space made available for dry cargo.

The Rio de Janeiro Maru had five holds and seven watertight bulkheads, and was furnished by an autopilot with gyro compass by Spyro-Anschuetz. In case of emergency, 22 life boats were available for passengers and crew. The ship was powered by Mitsubishi-Sulzer diesel engines, giving the ship a maximum speed of 17.6 knots. Between 1925 and 1929 four sisterships of the Rio were built. They were the Buenos Aires Maru, Santos Maru, La Plata Maru and Montevideo Maru. These liners served the route Japan, Hongkong, Singapore, South Africa and South America. The trip lasted an average of 61 days, but was shortened to 46 days with these ships. The return voyage went via the Panama Canal, the West Coast of the US, to Yokohama.

The Rio de Janeiro Maru was taken in hand by the Navy on 08 October 1940, and put into the navy yard of Sasebo for conversion to a submarine tender and depot ship. For active self defence she was armed with two 5.7 or 6 inch (14,5 cm or 15,2 cm) guns and anti-aircraft machine weapons. Her passive protection consisted of degaussing coils and internal strengthening of bulkheads. Originally attached to the Combined Fleet, she had to service 6 submarines, by replenishing ammunition, fuel, do minor repair work and exchange crews.

Part of her career was spent in Penang, Malaya, when she was attached to the 30th Submarine Squadron, which intended to intercept the Allied ship traffic in the Indian Ocean. From 15 April 1943 onwards, after Japan had lost the majority of her fleet submarines and the tactics proved to be ineffective, the Rio was re-classified as a transport and based in Truk.

The ship was hit on the first day of the attack, most likely by a bomb dropped by a plane from the Essex on Strike 2 B-1 or by planes from the Yorktown, Strike A-1. The hit was observed by pilots from Bunker Hill, who confirmed a hit, an explosion and a fire on the ship. On the last strike of the second day, the Rio de Janeiro Maru was reported to burn still, and going down slowly by the stern. However, this assessment is not without some doubt. An attack photo, which was not identified when exactly it was taken, shows the Rio sunk with a narrow streak of oil drifting to the beach of Uman, driven there by the wind. The same photo shows the Gosei, Unkai and Fujikawa Maru evidently still undamaged. This would suggest that the Rio de Janeiro sunk earlier then previously assumed.

Technical Data:

Tonnage	:	9 627 tons gross	
		8 227 tons dead weight	
Length	:	140,5 m	450 ft
Width	:	18,9 m	62 ft
Depth	:	16,0 m	41 ft
Draught	:	7,9 m	26 ft
Engine	:	2 x Mitsubishi Sulzer diesel	
Horsepower	:	7 515 hp max, each	
		6 000 hp service	
Speed	:	17,6 knots max	
		14,0 knots service	
Builder	:	Mitsubishi Zosensho, Nagasaki	
Owner	:	Osaka Soshen Kaisha (OSK).	

SAN FRANCISCO MARU

At A Glance ...

Medium-large, old 5-hold freighter, with split profile.
Deck cargo of 3 tanks. Forward hold full of mines.
Half tracked vehicles in cargo area.
Interesting objects in the last holds.
Boatdeck and stern damaged.

Depth:

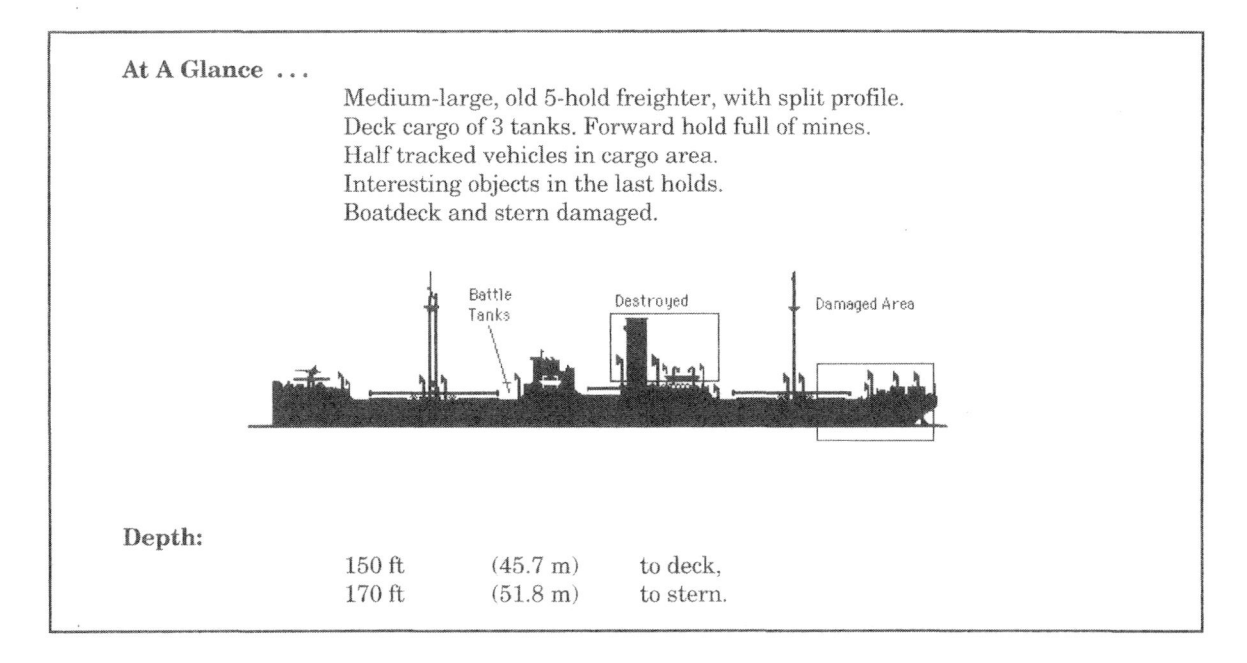

150 ft	(45.7 m)	to deck,
170 ft	(51.8 m)	to stern.

The San Francisco Maru was a medium-large sized freighter of almost 6000 tons. Her lines were old fashioned, as evidenced by the straight bow, the low bridge and the midships hold. The ship was built in 1919, and probably nearing the end of her useful life as newer and modern freighter had come into service. She was taken from semi-retirement, as a stock boat, and fitted out to serve the southern routes again.

The description leads from the bridge forward to the bow, back to the bridge, and finally to the stern.

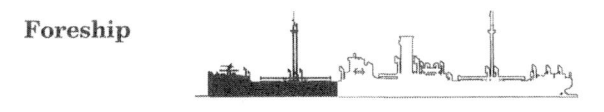

Foreship

Descending at the bridge towards shelter deck, three objects compete for the attention of the diver. First, the tall pole mast with its rigging comes into view, then the open hatches and the battle tanks on the maindeck can be seen.

The diver has certainly been primed to expect the unusual picture of battle tanks as deck cargo on this wreck, and they are quite a sight. When descending on the midships superstructure it is worthwhile to stop for a brief overview at the forward part of the bridge.

The foreship indeed presents a fascinating and unique sight. There are three battle tanks, one is on port and two are on starboard, forward of the bridge, parked on the maindeck. They are pointing forward, and are in some state of disarray. All three of them are Type 95 Ha-Go or Ke-Go, built by Mitsubishi. Their armored bodies are partly riveted and partly welded. Originally armed with a 3,7 cm gun in the turret and a machine gun in front, weighing about 7,5 tons each, they were powered by a diesel engine of 120 horsepower, and manned by a crew of three. This type of tank was used frequently, certainly not to best advantage, in the static defenses of the Pacific Islands.

The single tank on port came to rest at an angle of about 30 degrees to the left off the centerline. It evidently rests on the sheerstrake as it has a slight tilt to the right. The turret is small, and carries a short barrel in the depressed position. The muzzle does not even quite reach the front of the body. The turret is somewhat oblong towards the barrel and oddly shaped, extending with a circular segment over the side of the chassis. In fact, the turret is mounted clearly off the centerline of the tank to the left, while the gun barrel itself is located at the center. This strange arrangement results in a characteristically asymmetrical look. The turret escape hatch can be identified clearly on top. The mudguards on the sides are still intact, and are corroded only in the front. Ventilator slits can be seen just behind the turret. The engine of the tank is located in the rear half. The forward left drive wheel is resting against a mooring bit, probably preventing any further dislocation or even sliding off the deck when the ship went down. A metal ring came to rest on the tank body aft of the turret. It is all which remained of a ventilator cowl. This relic of a tank on deck is worth a couple of pictures. It poses a challenge to the photographer but framing is very difficult. At the distance required to back off the object to frame it, backscatter may ruin the best intended photographic efforts.

The fact that the San Francisco Maru had rail guards and not bulwarks may be taken as a sign of her advanced age. Aft of the tank this guard railing remains intact, but forward it has disappeared, and fell down to the sea bed. Undesirable trimming of the ship for a voyage would have resulted if the tanks were positioned as they remain today. It suggests that more deck cargo was tied down forward of the tank on port.

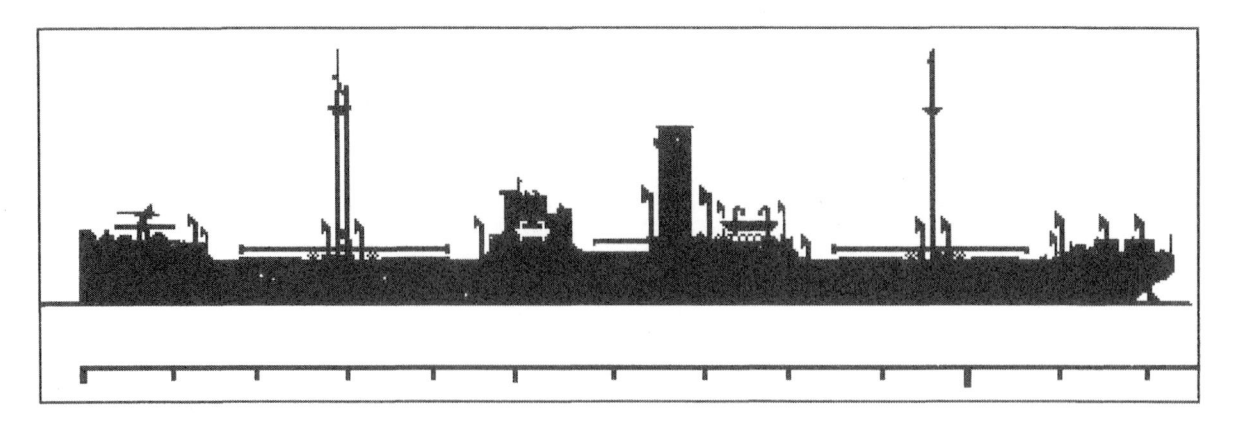

The question whether there was a second tank on port is answered when swimming about 100 ft (30 m) off the port side of the ship aft of the bridge. A large steam roller rests now on its side in 240 ft of water, but can be well recognized by its wide single front and the tall double aft rollers, and the typical long steering column. When it fell over board it took a length of railguard with it. So, it was not another tank but a heavy steamroller which was carried as deck cargo.

The other two battle tanks are located directly across the first one, on starboard but are parked perpendicular to the ship's axis. The tank located aft made a valiant attempt, it seems, to save itself by trying to jump over the guard rail. It only got half of the way and now mounts the one in front of it resting with most of its weight bearing down on the forward tank. Not surprisingly, the suspension of that vehicle broke down. The large sprocket drive wheel is the first of the track wheels forward. Two sets of twin road wheels are mounted in tandem, and share a common hydraulic suspension. The large hydraulic cylinder is fastened to the tank body between the street wheels and the guide rollers between the up and down portion of the track. The sizeable take-up wheel is positioned aft.

A steel line is draped around the second tank. It looks as if the vehicle was to be unloaded. In order to gain a good perspective, and to be able to do some interesting photographic work it is worthwhile to swim a little off to the side of the ship. Care must be taken not to descend inadvertently, and to stay within the depth and time limitations of the dive plan. A large truck is parked on deck, perpendicular to the two tanks, next to the hatch coaming of hold 2. It is a large chassis with some corroded remains of the bodywork, an intact engine compartment and twin tires in the rear. A steel line is wrapped over the fender of the vehicle on one side; it chafed and took a headlight off.

It is a safe bet to assume that a similar arrangement of deck cargo existed on port. As the steam roller has been identified to have taken the place of the second tank on port, there also was a large truck, the twin to the one on starboard, carried inboard of the tank and steam roller. Indeed, there rests a large truck on the sea bed on port near hold 4, aft of the superstructure. From all appearances this truck would not have fit underneath the hatch cover beams of the holds, except hold 5. But as the damage in this area would suggest it would have been flung to the other side. So, all evidence points to the fact that the deck cargo was arranged in the orderly way a sailor would have it.

The second hold is located between the tanks. The hatch cover beams are still in place here. Therefore, one has to look carefully underneath to see the two large tank trucks, which are resting on the hatch cover beams, parked side-by-side on the second tween deck level. The tank containers mounted on both vehicles were empty and closed. When the ship sank the ambient water pressure was so high that the tank containers caved in.

A walkway and stowage for the transfer hoses are located on the left side on both tank trucks. The hood of one of them has disappeared, while it is reasonable intact on the other. The radiators are high and have vertical bars. A close look at the headlights is quite interesting. Corrosion has taken off most of the cover, and the internal design with the reflector can be seen in a cut-away view. As the cabin on one of the tank trucks has disappeared, the steering wheel and instrument panel can be easily made out from above. The windshield frame is in place on both. The vehicles are surrounded by many stacked drums inside the tween deck.

The remains of a peculiar vehicle rests between and slightly forward of the tank trucks, also on the hatch cover beams, while its forward wheels appear to rest on the tween deck. The left has collapsed, the right is turned slightly to the left. It is difficult to identify the purpose of this vehicle, particularly as all bodywork is completely gone. The size suggests a limousine.

There are a large number of single wheels with a holding assembly located at the aft port side of the hold, below where the engine telegraph fell from the bridge and rests on the hatch coaming. Their pneumatic tires are small and carry the radial threads typical for aircraft tires. The wheel mechanism and the tires mounted resemble the tail wheel assembly of light aircraft. They are difficult to get into perspective as they are all jumbled. The next level of the tween deck comes in view below and between the front tires of the two tank trucks. The sediment is very high in this area, but a large radial aircraft engine can be seen sticking out of the yellow-brown muck. The exhaust manifolds are mounted on the engine block while no manifold has been fitted at the intakes.

A large number of 50 lbs aerial bombs are

Hailstorm - *The Wrecks*

The San Francisco Maru in peacetime, transitting the Panama Canal.

located forward of the aircraft engine. They are standing on their tip with part of the body and the tail fins exposed. More ammunition, mostly boxes of three inch shells, is located on this tween deck. Clearance between deck head and tween deck is very low, because of the cargo still resting there.

Penetration into this tween deck is next to impossible and depth depth here is about 170 ft. Two pieces of machinery on rubber wheels rest a little forward in the hold, on the hatch cover beams. Between them lies a steel wheel with a hard rubber rim, behind which a drum is located. There is a lot more cargo stowed in the tween decks of the second level underneath the tank trucks.

The pole mast is very high and flanked by posts, to which the derricks had been attached with goosenecks. From the cross tree above, several lines descend to the deck. On some of them colonies of sea life have settled, which look like bird's nests. The mast itself is overgrown by many colorful forms of sedentary marine life. The ring which held the jumbo derrick can be seen above the cross tree. The derricks are all gone. They were made out of wood and disintegrated during the long years of submersion. At their end the derricks were reinforced with long tubular steel gloves with tips and a sturdy ring for the cargo lines. One of these tips can be seen on maindeck, resting at an angle between the hatch coaming of hold 2 and the single tank on port. Inside the hollow part, a few traces of wood remain.

Passing the mast, which is flanked by four large winches mounted on the deck, on the way forward, the first hold is reached. Hatch cover beams are also in place in this hold. The first impression is that of a minefield. This is literally true, because the cargo area is filled to the brim with "anti-boat" mines, Type 38. These are semi-spherical bodies of about 60 cm diameter and a flat bottom. Two handles are welded on the sides of the spherical half. The detonator device would be fitted into the round raised segment on the top but is absent on all mines.

A closer look reveals a few gaps in the otherwise neatly arranged rows. Here, mines have been taken by native divers. Their explosives has been used for dynamite fishing. Today, this wreck is frequently patrolled by the Police, to prevent further pilferage. When anchoring at this wreck the dive guides lower their anchor slowly, with some deliberation and good reason, before the wreck was buoyed.

Towards starboard and the aft part of the hold, several coils of wire can be seen between the mines. There are also many can-shaped objects and a very large number of detonator caps forward. The view into the next lower tween deck is totally obstructed, as the mines, detonator caps and wire coils are loaded on top of the hatch cover beams.

The forecastle rises one deck. A spare stock anchor is mounted on its aft bulkhead. A second anchor is bolted to the forecastle deck port and aft of the gun. A gun platform has been built on the forecastle, carrying an exceptionally well preserved gun. The individual parts of the gun, the barrel, lock and the mount, are coated with the bright red-orange colored sponge, which is commonly found on exposed parts of deep wrecks. There is very little disfiguring growth on them, and the gun is considered to be another of the prime photographic subjects on this wreck. The gun appears to be very large, and the typical conical gun mount resembles the ones found in the fourth hold of the Nippo Maru, and on land on Moen and Guam. It is a flat trajectory gun of approximately 12 cm caliber.

When arriving at the bow it is suggested to look down on the port side, because the anchor chain tells convincingly the story of the last moments of the ship: The port anchor is out. The chain leads straight to the bottom and forms a small heap underneath the hawsepipe. From this heap the chain runs back a little distance, slightly turns towards the ship, then in a sweep away, runs towards forward by coming closer to the ship, and finally straightens out and disappears in a line away from the ship off the port bow towards north-east. This neatly laid out figure on the sea bed resembles a slightly bulbous, irregularly U - shape. How does it relate to the sinking of the ship?

It can be explained if the San Francisco Maru was riding the anchor, was damaged and sank quickly by the stern. The stern touched bottom while the foreship was still above water. The ship thus formed a steep angle in the water. The anchor line was taut. The north-east wind pushed the foreship to starboard. That is when the line made the sweep, and as the sinking bow approached the bottom it naturally did so in an arc, like a pendulum, subsequently laying the chain out orderly as it went down.

The pattern of the anchor chain may very easily duplicated experimentally with only a pencil and a string or a small chain tied to one end, and re-enacting the movement of the sinking ship. The position of the tanks on starboard collaborates the story, and the location of the steam roller and the truck farther aft provides additional evidence. Therefore, the description is continued to midships, with the dive leading along the port side of the hull, which is overgrown with whip corals and sponges.

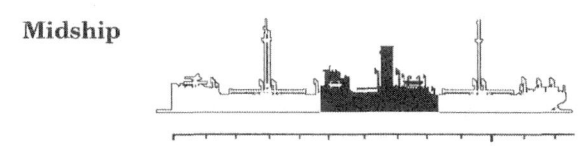

Midship

The ship had a split profile. The upperworks of the bridge, made of wood, was followed by a small midship hold. Aft of this the quadruple ventilators-kingpost was mounted. The funnel came next, and then the crew quarters, with the life boats. The skeleton-like bridge provides a dramatic backdrop to the tanks when viewed from forward. The bridge does not appear to be damaged, there are only small kinks in the framework, however, wood was used extensively. It has rotted away during the long years of submersion or was consumed in a fire. The ship has a two deck high bridge. On top of the steel structure was the third level, a flying bridge.

The lower deck is made of steel but the second level consists of steel supports, girders and frames. Of course, an engine telegraph was built on the upper level. It tumbled down and can be seen at the aft edge of the hatch coaming of hold 2. The five feet high base of the instrument lies on the deck while the telegraph itself is suspended over the hold.

Many dishes have been collected into a box, and placed into a sink on shelter deck level. Unfortunately, the ship's bell, which was located nearby, was stolen between 1978 and 1979. It was a wonderful, solid piece of which only photographs exist today. As already pointed out, it is against the law to take anything from the wrecks, and it is ironic that the bell now graces the Hawaiian home of a former law enforcement officer. Certainly, it belongs back on the ship. Originally hanging from the deckhead of the bridge deck, it crashed down two decks where it was found and displayed on the upper deck, only to be taken later. In various parts of the superstructure a lot of unsorted debris, such as electrical appliances, can be found. The superstructure looks a bit confusing.

The ship carried a tall, fairly narrow stack, typical of coal burners. This is a landmark on a wreck. However, here the stack is missing. It was blown forward by a tremendous force, crushed the two ventilators right forward of the stack, and finally was completely flattened itself. The root of the funnel can be seen, and the hole where the stack was mounted. It seems rather corroded, and the edges where the break occurred are ragged.

When descending at the hull slightly aft of this area, on port, a hole in the shell plating about 10 ft (3 m) underneath the sheerstrake can be seen. It is about 3 ft in diameter, and the jagged steel fragments all point outward. The shell plates remained in place, but are bent outward. There is little doubt that it was caused by a boiler explosion. The superstructure aft does not show discernible damage.

A large sized truck can be seen on the bottom slightly aft of the superstructure, about 150 ft (45 m) to port. The chassis, engine, forward and twin rear wheels are all which remains of it. Its position relative to the wreck suggests it was flung here when the ship rocked severely. It can therefore be assumed that the ship carried one tank, one steamroller and a truck on port as deck cargo, and two tanks and a truck on starboard.

Further aft, below the boat deck, a very fine Japanese bath is located. It has two tubs, as was common on the ships. A porthole originally allowed light and ventilation. The plumbing and faucets can be seen. As the deckhead was wood, it has gone, so the cabin may be entered easily from the top. A tall pair of ventilators are to be seen nearly at the aft end of the superstructure, just past the double row of engine room skylights. There is evidence of a severe fire at the aft part of the midship superstructure.

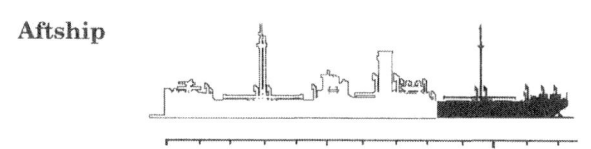

Aftship

Considering the many attractions of the foreship it is only natural that very few people dive on the aft ship. Time is very much at a premium at that depth. There are, nevertheless, many very interesting objects located at this part of the ship.

Hold 4, the first hold aft of the superstructure, does not appear to be very appealing, but really has a surprise in store. There are no hatch cover beams left on maindeck, except for the last one aft. The beams are all in place on the next lower deck, however, and two large steel frames can be discerned resting on them side-by-side. Actually, these steel frames are the remains of two large sized trucks. Their radiators are facing aft.

Two hatch cover beams from the maindeck have fallen down. One knocked the engine clear out from its mounting of one of the trucks, and crushed the cabin of the other. The truck with the knocked out engine shows further damage. The rear axle with the twin tires fell down. This is the vehicle located on the left. The radiator of the other truck can be still recognized, but the metal of the body is corroded away completely.

When looking into the tween deck the cargo can be seen. The cargo space is filled from deck to deckhead with ammunition boxes. They are very tidily and tightly stacked, no space is wasted. The shells are of 3 and 4 inch caliber, crated in boxes of 12 pieces. Towards port the rocking of the ship after the bomb hit loosened the stowed material. A few boxes tumbled down. Shells and boxes are scattered on the hatch cover beams. The other cargo spaces on starboard and forward remained orderly stacked with the same kind of boxes, containing artillery rounds. It is surprising to see such an abundance of ammo, and that they did not explode when the ship was hit. This is an unique sight in Truk, and well worth a visit.

The mast and the 4 winches are located between hold 4 and 5.

The last hold is damaged. The hatch coaming on port is bent inward by about 5 feet. The deck is blown up by several feet where it meets the poop. The poop bulkhead at the aft end of the hold is folded over almost diagonally and ripped on port. All hatch cover beams have been dislodged. Many of them can be seen in the hold.

A large number of torpedo bodies are scattered all over the cargo space. They are not fitted with warheads. It appears as if the torpedoes are assembled from three parts. The warhead may be forward, the high pressure air and the propellant vessels in the middle part and the engine and double propellers with the rudder as the aft part. These aft parts have been packed differently than the others. They still carry a wooden transport frame on both ends. On one side the propellers and the steering can be seen. The other torpedo parts seem to consist of vessels mounted inside the body, with a few tubes inside. There are a few torpedo bodies resting on the deck, between the railguard and the hatch coaming. One of them shows the typical signs of an internal explosion.

The internal air or oxygen cylinder had exploded after it had been weakened by corrosion. A similar fate befell the torpedoes carried on the Gosei Maru. But in this particular case, the recoil of the explosion sent the body up on to the deck. The war head, which can be clearly identified, was not set off.

Ammunition would not explode from even a sharp jolt. A picric acid compound was the explosive most commonly used by the Japanese. This material is very insensitive to impact. This is why short of a direct hit, a very close explosion or a fire, ammunition would normally not be involved in a secondary explosion.

Drums can be seen on the starboard tween deck. They are orderly stacked, whereas those on port have all been dislocated. One section of the tween deck is filled with depth charges. Although they look like chemical drums, there is a difference, and they can be easily told apart from the former.

The San Fransisco Maru sustained very heavy damage from a close bomb miss on port just between hold 5 and the poop. The shell plating is ripped open over a length of well over 15 ft (5 m), and the break extends almost from the bottom to the sheerstrake. The deck plating is ripped and the adjoining plates are severely buckled. The damage extends to the starboard side. A few of the steel plates just across the large damage on port are missing and some are crumbled. Significantly, on starboard all fragments point outward, indicating that they were blown out from the pressure wave originating from port. The pressure was trapped behind the bulkheads aft and destroyed them in the process.

The poop is unusual. Its deck appears to be not particularly high, and it was enclosed by rail guards. There are three deck houses mounted, one each on the side and one aft. The have a doorways, which are open, and a ventilator on top.

The San Francisco Maru sank quickly by the stern from this damage. Several attack photos show the ship burning severely at the midship superstructure. Evidence shows that a fire raged through the aft part of midships and the upper decks of the bridge. The presence of quite a number of fragile glass artifacts and unbroken tableware in the lower decks can only mean that the fire did not consume all of the forward area.

The ship was built according to plans drawn up to facilitate standardized ship building during World War I, when German subs were taking a heavy toll on cargo ships. A fairly simple, but very sturdy design evolved, and the ships were called collectively, "Hog Islander", for the place where the shipyard was located and their prominent three "islands" or castles profile, i.e. forecastle, midship structure and the poop.

These standard ships, between 5 and 6 thousand tons net, were the predecessors of the 'Liberty-Ships' of World War II-fame. The San Francisco Maru was such a standard ship at the time of World War I.

She ranked as the Norm-type, as opposed to many variations, and although there were many more built during and shortly after the war, still about 500 remained in active service. Most of them were British owned. The ship was relegated to a stock boat of the Kawasaki Dockyard, but pressed back into cargo service because of the scarcity of shipping space.

The San Francisco Maru was found in 1972 by Sam Redford.

Technical Data:

Tonnage	:	5 864	tons gross
Length	:	385 ft	117,34 m
Width	:	51 ft	15,54 m
Depth	:	36 ft	10,97 m
Draught	:	27 ft	8,16 m
Engine	:	1 x reciprocal steam, coal.	
Horsepower	:	3 946 hp	
Speed	:	14,27 knots max.	
		10,00 knots service	
Launch	:	01 March 1919	
Service	:	14 March 1919	
Builder	:	Kawasaki Dockyard	
Owner	:	Yamashita Kisen.	

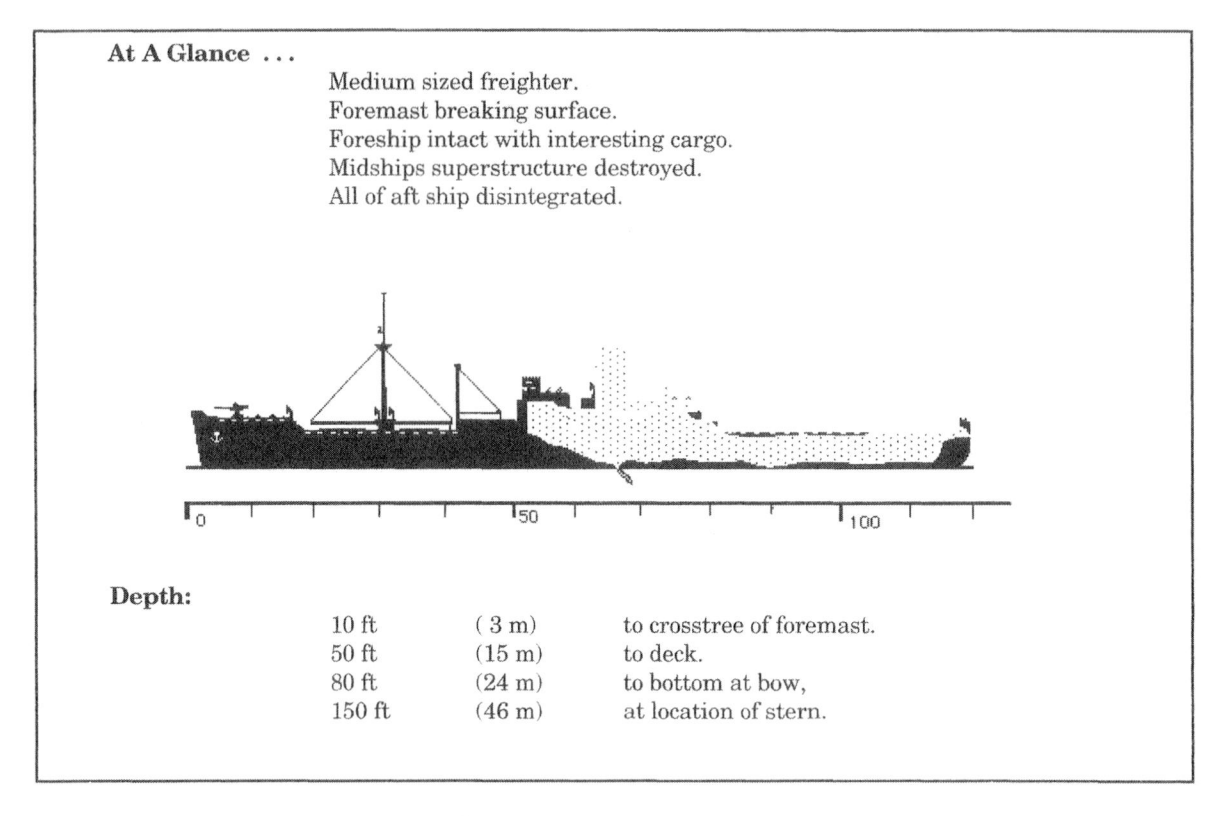

SANKISAN MARU

At A Glance ...
Medium sized freighter.
Foremast breaking surface.
Foreship intact with interesting cargo.
Midships superstructure destroyed.
All of aft ship disintegrated.

Depth:

10 ft	(3 m)	to crosstree of foremast.
50 ft	(15 m)	to deck.
80 ft	(24 m)	to bottom at bow,
150 ft	(46 m)	at location of stern.

Somewhat enigmatic are the details surrounding the tremendous explosion, which tore this ship apart. The attack photo showing the Amagisan Maru burning fiercely and going down by the bow also shows the Sankisan Maru. At that time she was riding her anchor, but smoke came out of her funnel. One has to realize that the coal burning steam ship took a long time to make up steam. This picture was taken on Strike 3 E, at about 1400 h. Bunker Hill planes bombed a freighter at Strike 3 A, at 0600 h, on the second day. The location given corresponds with the resting place of the Sankisan Maru. A hit slightly aft of midships was recorded, and a large fire ignited. There is no record of an explosion, however.

No doubt, the Sankisan received a hit into the aft hold, which detonated its cargo of ordnances, and blew the after ship apart, devastating the midship superstructure in the process. The major force of the explosion centered on the starboard fifth hold. Therefore, starboard is even more thoroughly destroyed than port. During my researches of the files and in the correspondence, I have never come across a reference that the Sankisan Maru exploded, which would tally with the location of the wreck. True, the American pilots reported explosions of bombs and torpedoes, which were throwing huge water columns up in the air. The disintegration of the Aikoku Maru was well recorded, but no specific mention of the Hoki Maru was made either. The explosion, leading to the disintegration of these two ships, must have been spectacular, but they were not recorded. It is possible that they happened after the plane had retired from their raid, after the fire had reached the ordnances, or during the night.

The Sankisan Maru is a very remarkable wreck, because the foreship is very well preserved, and contains interesting cargo in the holds, as well as on deck. This contrasts sharply with the totally destroyed midships superstructure and the disintegrated aftship.

The description begins at the bow, continues with the deck cargo, and gives an inventory of the three forward holds. The excursion then leads through hold 3 into the midship structure, out of it, and follows the sloping ground at the area of the stern.

Foreship

The dive boat generally ties off at the mast. From here and swimming forward, the bow of the wreck will be reached. The stem is slightly raked, the starboard anchor is out. After so many years, the last link of the hanging portion of the anchor chain has rubbed through, and the chain hangs free now. Underneath, a heap accumulated on the sea floor.

The way the anchor chain is positioned frequently tells a story, and is indicative of the last moments of a vessel. A heap of an anchor chain accumulated on the bottom, with the upper portion leading directly into the hawse pipe, provides evidence that the ship sank fast. The Sankisan Maru is a good example. She immediately went down after more than half of the hull had been blown away in an explosion.

There was no time for the foreship to drift in the wind. However, if a ship drifts in the wind stern up, the anchor chain generally is still under tension, and leads away from the bow, spanning over the bottom, in direct continuation of the ship's axis, like on the Hanakawa Maru. If the ship sank by the stern and came to rest on the bottom aft, while the forward section continued to float, the bow may sway broadside to the wind. In this case, the anchor chain will lead away from the bow at an angle. If both anchors have been out, the chains may even cross.

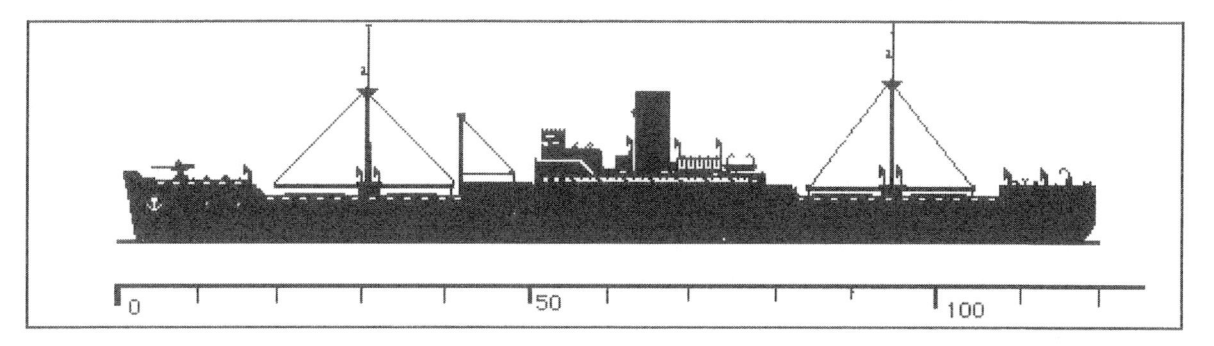

The bow bears the large windlass on a base plate, which has lifted at the back, so that the winches are tilting slightly forward. A pair of ventilators are located at the aft end of the forecastle. Their cowls are gone. The botsun's locker inside the forecastle contains emergency kerosene running lights.

The description of the decks begins at the aft end of the forecastle on port, facing aft.

A hatch cover beam leans over the forecastle. Abeam of the hatch coaming is truck 1, lying on its right side. The double wheels are facing forward, the engine, radiator and front tires to aft. As all of the trucks on the Sankisan Maru, it is only consisting of a chassis, wheels with tires, engine, radiator and drive train. The bodywork is completely gone, only a few small remnants remain at the corners.

Truck 2 is parked on deck, so that its radiator faces the radiator of the first vehicle. It is a skeleton of a truck, but it is interesting to see the spare tire, located roughly in the middle of the chassis to the right, and the battery.

Turning to the left, the two winches for the cargo handling gear are mounted on the deck. The mast house carried four ventilators, but their cowls are gone, so that only the shafts remain. One of the cowls rests forward against the mast house bulkhead. A jumbo derrick is lashed to the mast in the upright position.

Truck 3 is resting on starboard deck. The steering wheel has parted from the steering column and is frequently placed on the dashboard. Divers just love to sit in this truck, shift gears and steer, only to find, that wheel and gear stick fall out when touched. The high and old fashioned radiator shows a mark where the manufacturer embedded his emblem. The trucks were made by Toyota and Isuzu. A hatch cover beam came to rest between forecastle bulkhead and the forward hatch coaming.

Hold 1 contains small arms ammunition in heaps, boxes and clips. It is amazing, how many cartridges are in the hold and in the tween decks. Some of the boxes contain detonator caps. All this ammunition may be looked at, and photographed, of course, but it should not be touched. Particularly, individual cartridges may find their resting place in the pocket of a buoyancy compensator or other deep recesses of a diver's attire. Even with the many cartridges available it it predictable that they will thin out eventually. Detonators are outright dangerous to handle. It is interesting to see, that many wooden boxes withstood the immersion in seawater. Undoubtedly, sea life cannot settle on and in it due to the poisonous character of the copper ions, which are slowly liberated in the water.

The second pair of winches are passed when getting out of hold 1 and swimming to hold 2, aft of the mast. There is no deck cargo abeam of hold 2. A very large jagged fragment of shell plating, about as long as the hatch opening, lies on the starboard hatch coaming. It was flung here from the aftership by the force of the explosion. At starboard rests truck 4 on the bottom of this hold.

The description of the cargo in the first tween deck of hold 2 begins at the forward corner, facing port.

At the extreme forward corner, a stack of half collapsed and corroded airplane engine cowlings for Zero fighters is located. Some semi-round objects close by are radial engine exhaust manifolds. Further towards midships, the tween deck is littered with fragments of hemp rope. It suggests, that originally a large coil or several coils of rope was stowed here. A small open, rectangular hatch is located port forward in the corner, and was used to reach the next lower tween deck level.

When turning left and aft, the port side is faced in the first tween deck. Immediately, truck 5 can be seen. The front wheels face forward, the dashboard is quite well preserved with a triangular shaped group of instruments. One gauge is on top, and two are on the bottom of the panel. This truck carried a spare tire as well. Truck 6 is parked back-to-back to the former. Both vehicles are parked well near the outside, i.e. near the hull, and are therefore located deep in the dark recesses of the hold. A compressor stands on the tween deck, at the rear wheels of truck 5, towards the hatch, the inboard opening of the hold.

Turning left again, starboard is faced at the end of the tween deck. Truck 7 stands in the midst of a lot of debris, deep inside the tween deck. Part of the mudguard is still in place. In fact, it is the only vehicle with any bodywork at all. The forward part of hood, which is half gone, suggests an austere military style. One headlight remained in its proper place, but the other has fallen down. The other part of the tween deck is littered with remnants of cans, which resemble opened and badly corroded corned beef containers.

Sankisan, a War Standard 1B-Ship.

The last turn completes the tour of the first tween deck of hold 2. Starboard, facing aft the last truck is located. This is the eighth vehicle on board. At its rear tire, towards inboard, two large radial aircraft engines are resting on the deck. They are arranged like show pieces on a shelf. The ribbed cylinders, valve lifters, even the ignition cables, can be seen clearly. The engines were certainly spares for the service facility of the airfield in Eten. The deck contains several more cowlings and other parts of the fuselage, scattered in the general debris forward of the engines.

Part of the second tween deck is accessible, underneath the the deck just described. However, the clearance between deck head and the deep sediment is much narrower, and there is much less space to maneuver. It is not a popular spot for the normal diver to visit; the quarters are a bit cramped. A lot of provisions must have been stowed here, because the first object to be seen, is a pile of hundreds and hundreds of plum pits. When touched they immediately disintegrate.

Continuing forward, way back in the narrow, deep and dark recess of the second tween deck, curious looking, cigar- or torpedo-shaped objects are located. Their diameter is about 3 feet (0,90 m) or slightly less, and their length may be about 12 ft (3,50 m) but this measure is based on an assumption only, as only very few of these objects remained completely intact. Those are located farthest away, and they have not been measured. From about 4 ft (1,20 m) of the blunt shaped nose they are open at the top. They strongly resemble the fuselage of gliders. A metal block with a joy stick is built into the area which could be the cockpit. Strong round metal fittings have been attached to both side of the body, slightly behind the metal block. The bodies were of very light wooden construction, and in some cases, only the wooden structural ribs remain. They were painted with heavy coats of white or grey paint. Even after only gentle poking, the finger goes through, because it is only the paint which seems to retain the original shape of the structure. It also could have been, that the objects were covered with painted canvas.

Only the nose was constructed more solidly. It is amazing to see that there were at least 30 of these objects loaded. Most of them are still orderly carried.

Extreme care should be exercised when diving into this area, as these objects are very fragile and break apart quickly when touched. Also, the visibility will rapidly deteriorate, and the dark, tight quarters require somewhat steady nerves. Since the purpose of the objects is not known, it may be assumed that they were not destined for the next friendly gliding club.

Penetration into the third hold can be made from the top or from the second hold. There are no dividing bulkheads between them. The kingpost stands on the elevated deck forward of hold 3, which appears to be smaller than the two forward. However, this was the site of removal of numerous depth charges in Summer 1973. Not all of them were recovered, as they were buried too deep in the mud.

Midship

Swimming into the first tween deck, the lower decks are obstructed by debris. A big heap of coal can be seen on port. On starboard, the heap is not quite as high, and it is possible to continue to swim aft. Again, the clearance becomes a bit narrow, but it is not dangerous. Light can be seen to come from forward and behind. The dividing bulkheads between hold 3 and the midships superstructure have been cleanly blown out to forward, due to the pressure wave of the explosion rolling forward in the passageway.

It is not difficult to navigate around the vertical support posts and to enter the midships superstructure at this area. There is plenty of light. The inboard area conveys a picture of utter destruction. Bulkhead, pipes, deckheads, partitions and structural elements are totally torn and twisted out of shape. Although they are in total disorder, it is still fairly spacious in this part of the ship.

Midships, the engine room casing can be seen. It is cracked. The view into the engine room is obstructed by the large boiler, and the root of the smoke stack, which stands askew near the crack. At port is less destruction, but also less light, indicating that there is no apparent exit. Penetration is therefore discouraged.

These devastated rooms seemed to have been crew accommodations. Portholes remained intact in the hull plating. It is no problem at all to exit this area forward, without the need to go all the way back. The gaps torn into the superstructure are wide enough to allow a diver to swim through, without any problem. There is ample natural light to find the way.

An examination of the superstructure reveals major destruction on starboard, while part of boats deck and the boats davits can be recognized on port, despite being bent considerably. Also, the starboard plating on the aft part of the superstructure is ripped out, while the one on port is only bent outward, but remained attached. The propeller shaft tunnel can be recognized when going farther aft. It is bent to port, broken in many places and completely disappears farther aft, baring the shaft itself. This propeller shaft is a piece of steel of probably 10 inches (25 cm) diameter, bent like a match stick, mainly in the direction downward and to port, and finally cracked in several places. The rear most part and the propeller are missing. The hull is blown apart in this area, about 45 ft (15 m) aft of the end of the superstructure.

Aftship

On no wreck can the consequences of a major explosion be better observed than on the Sankisan Maru. The hull fans out, but soon there is little debris visible on starboard. The sea floor dips from the original 90 feet, and a huge U- shaped depression is caved out. Swimming into this depression conveys the impression to be on stage of an amphitheater. On both sides, the terraced sides, overgrown with corals, rise, while the middle is white and sandy and continues to lead deeper. The white crater bottom may be about 200 to 300 feet across, and the total area with its sloping sides is perhaps 500 feet wide. On the right when swimming away from the midship section of the ship towards aft, large, sometimes very large chunks of the hull can be seen. They only thin out when the sloping coral ground meets the totally barren sandy area. It is 155 feet deep here, and a shadow can be seen in the middle of the sandy bottom. It is a total surprise to see the stern of the ship resting upright in the bottom. The stern frame, the four bladed large propeller and about 30 ft of the aftermost hull are located here. A massive rod with a gear attached to it, sticks about 3 ft out of the top. It is the rudder shaft. It means that the maindeck is razed completely and that even the massive steering engine was ripped out of the stern by the explosion. The rudder, apparently undamaged apart from the caved in plates, appears otherwise undaged and is turned at right angles to port.

The foremast and its cross tree, and the kingpost top, are forming the base for the most magnificent miniature coral reef. Hard and soft corals, oysters, fire corals, hydroids, sea squirts, sponges, feather dusters and anemones are just a few of the many sessile and semi-sessile marine life forms, which have settled here. Clown fish, a great variety of small reef fish, which form a halo around the mast, and an occasional predator will be found here as well. Mounted on the mast, but hard to see, because it is so much overgrown, is the forward running light of the ship. The many forms of life are worth an extra roll of film, particularly, if one is inclined to play with the different aspects of illumination.

The Sankisan Maru is one of the most interesting wrecks. Its location to the west of Uman means that it is sheltered when other wrecks receive the full brunt of the choppy seas during the trade wind.

The ship enjoyed only a short operational career as civilian and military transport. She was requisitioned by the Navy for special cargo on 07 October 1943.

Technical Data:

Tonnage	:	4 776 ts	
Length	:	112,0 m	367.5 ft
Width	:	15,8 m	51.8 ft
Depth	:	9,0 m	29.5 ft
Speed max	:	15,8 knots	
serv	:	12,0 knots	
Horsepower	:	2 846 hp	
Engine	:	1 x Turbine, coal	
Builder	:	Harima Dockyard	
Owner	:	Kaburagi Kisen	
Launch	:	29 January 1942	
Service	:	20 March 1942.	

Hailstorm - The Wrecks

SEIKO MARU

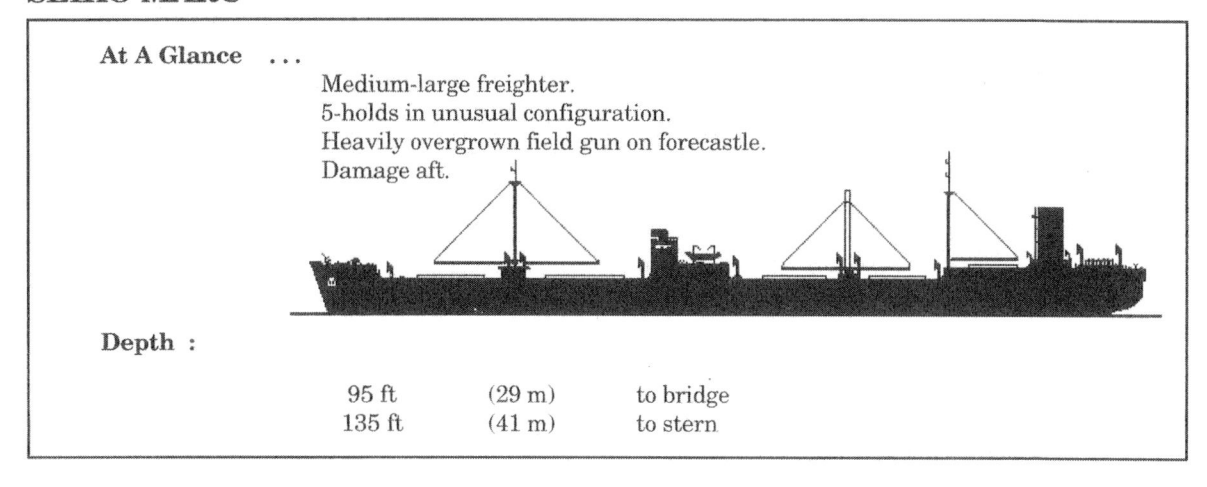

At A Glance ...
Medium-large freighter.
5-holds in unusual configuration.
Heavily overgrown field gun on forecastle.
Damage aft.

Depth :

95 ft	(29 m)	to bridge
135 ft	(41 m)	to stern

This almost 6000 ts freighter looks different from most other cargo ships built at that time. In fact, were it not for the distinct cargo holds and cargo handling gear her silhouette would closely resembles a tanker. She has been incorrectly identified in a few strikes as an oiler by the crew of the attacking planes. Aft of the raised forecastle are two holds, followed by a mast and a bridge. Two more holds follow aft on main deck level, there is a kingpost between them. The fifth hold is raised to shelter deck level and followed by the aft mast. The stack is fairly tall and narrow. Aft of that is a deck house; the stern follows.

The Seiko Maru received a single hit on port beam between hold 5 and the engine room. This explosion ruptured the fuel tanks and ignited the bunker oil. The aft superstructure on port was engulfed in flames, and the oil spilled on the water burned as well, drifting astern. She sank fairly rapidly by the stern. The first idea about the fatal hit will be gained by looking at the deck plating of the raised aft hold. It is very much warped abeam of the hold. The damage extends to the superstructure which is elevated by one deck.

Between the funnel and the mast, a pair of ventilators is located. Aft of the stack, built on a small podest, two more pairs of ventilators follow. The engine room skylights are located in the middle.

The boat deck extends to the sides of the ship, beginning forward abeam of the stack and ending about 20 feet or so forward of the counter. Underneath the boat deck is a passageway with railguards extending from the stern to aft of Hold 5. A companionway with a coaming is located abeam of the stack. On port the ladder to boat deck aft has fallen down. The one forward is still in place.

The rails forward of the boat deck passageway have fallen completely inboard and are crumbled. Also the forward port ventilator is bent inboard and leans against the stack. The deck on port and the bulkhead, where the superstructure begins after hold 5, is badly damaged and looks as if some pieces have been cut out. This damage is caused by the very close large bomb explosion and the fuel oil fire in this area here. Stanchions and ventilators have been bent and sagged in the intense heat.

A different kind of damage is apparent on the deck, the sheer strake and the shell plating at hold 5. There is a tremendous hole through the side of the hull. It is quite irregular, but so big as to allow a diver to pass through, although he would have to navigate around all the jagged pieces of torn up plating.

While swimming ahead it appears as if the Seiko Maru lists slightly to starboard. The cargo booms of the mast are over to that side. Those serving hold 4 from the kingpost are in their rest position. Forward of the kingpost is hold 3 which is followed by the 2 decks high bridge.

The inside of the bridge is spacious and well light, because the planking is gone. The crew's accommodation can be made out. There is a passageway on the lower deck and a partially open deck above. However, in the middle is a 15 ft long raised structure on both sides, which may be additional crew quarters. A doorway on port is open.

On the forward hold most hatch cover beams are still in place. The mast forward is flanked by a pair of ventilators. The booms are in place. The mast carries a cross tree, and lines descend from it.

The forecastle rises one deck and is enclosed by a railguard. A cable drum is located port aft. Forward of it but more amidships, is a mooring bit and the twin windlass follows. Both anchor chains lead, of course, into the hawsepipe. Everything in this area is heavily overgrown with coral.

Way up at the bow is an old fashioned artillery piece. It was mounted on wooden wheels. All spokes are gone, but one on which the guns rests. This gun is worth quite a picture, but nevertheless it is very difficult to make out details as so many different animals grow on it. Particularly the wheel is totally overgrown with a large orange sponge. Large leather corals further disguise this gun.

The undamaged ship's bell has been salvaged and is on display. The inscription reads "SEIKO MARU - 1940 -"
The wreck was found by Sam Redford..

Technical Data :

Gross Tonnage :	5.386 ts	
Length :	120.4 m	(395 ft)
Breadth :	16.16m	(53 ft)
Depth :	9.14m	(30 ft)
Speed, max :	16.14 knots	
Service :	14.00 knots	
Horsepower, max :	3927 hp	
Engine :	1 x turbine	
Launch :	14 May 1940	
Service :	17 July 1940	
Builder :	Harima Dockyard	
Owner :	Darien Kisen	

SHINKOKU MARU

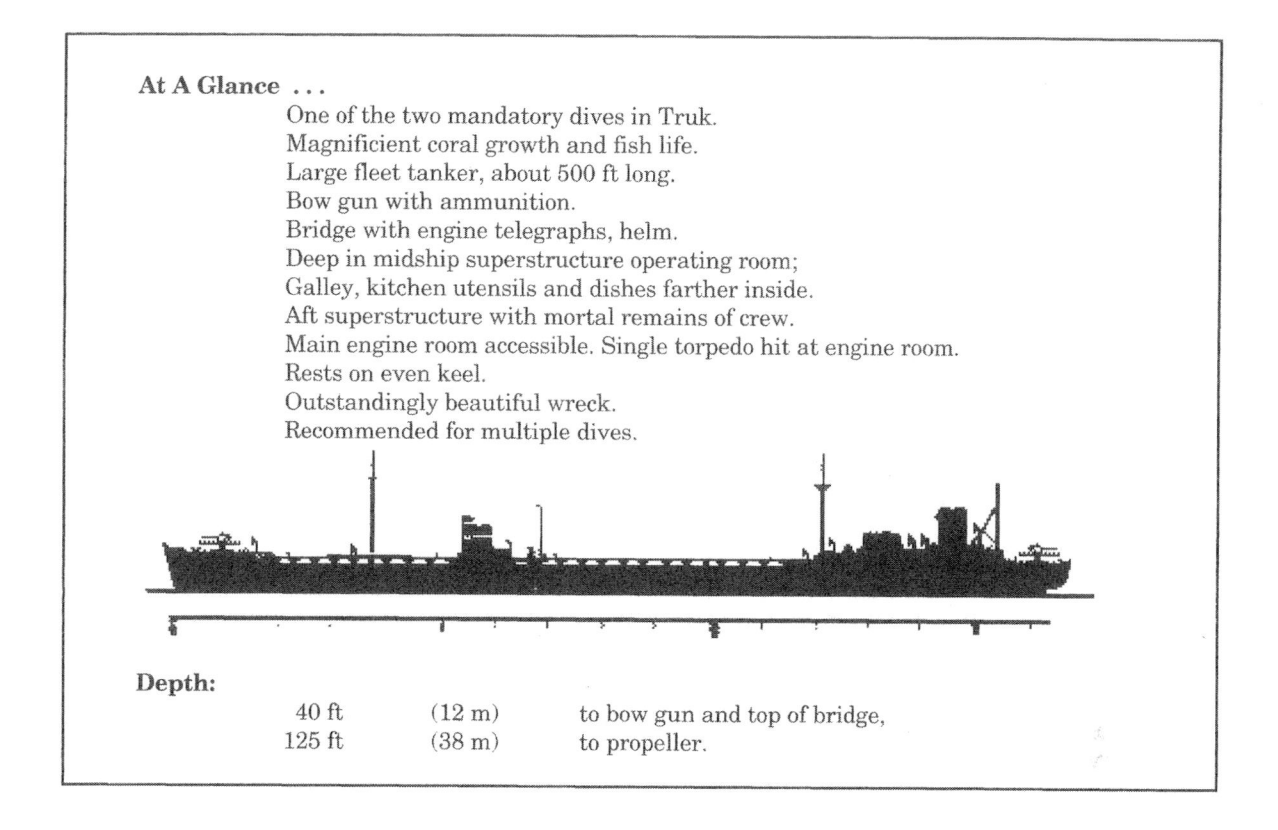

At A Glance ...
One of the two mandatory dives in Truk.
Magnificent coral growth and fish life.
Large fleet tanker, about 500 ft long.
Bow gun with ammunition.
Bridge with engine telegraphs, helm.
Deep in midship superstructure operating room;
Galley, kitchen utensils and dishes farther inside.
Aft superstructure with mortal remains of crew.
Main engine room accessible. Single torpedo hit at engine room.
Rests on even keel.
Outstandingly beautiful wreck.
Recommended for multiple dives.

Depth:
40 ft	(12 m)	to bow gun and top of bridge,
125 ft	(38 m)	to propeller.

General

Certainly, the Shinkoku Maru competes with the Fujikawa to be the most popular wreck in Truk. There are so many interesting things to see on this ship that multiple dives are recommended. The depth is ideal for a more shallow repetitive descent, and different areas of exploration may be chosen. It is best to begin at the stern, as it is deeper, and reserve the bridge and foreship for the subsequent dive.

Like the Fujikawa, the Shinkoku rests on even keel. Other beautiful ships, such as the Heian and Rio de Janeiro Maru, loose their appeal because they lie on their sides. The Shinkoku Maru is also in a good state of preservation, and disfiguring damage is not apparent. The diver, directing the beam of the underwater light on the bulwark and masts, which are luxuriously overgrow with magnificent forms of red-orange-yellow soft corals, and surrounded by a thick halo of juvenile fish, will hardly ever forget this image.

At night, the upper structures of the ship are transformed into a world of phantasy, a symphony of colors and forms, unequalled anywhere in Truk.

The Shinkoku Maru is a big ship. She was a tanker. Her attraction as a dive site today somewhat disguises the fact that she was a heavily armed fleet oiler during the war. A short overview of her operational career will allow a small glimpse into Imperial Japan's strategic thinking at the time.

The need for transport facilities to bring the urgently required crude oil to Japan was clearly recognized. In consequence, the civilian tanker fleet was steadily built up before the war, and even before the outbreak of hostilities the government influenced design and construction of these vessels. In 1939, when the Shinkoku was laid down she was not only subsidized by the Japanese Government, but also the Navy took a keen interest in the strategic role tankers were to play in an armed conflict: After all, Japan had been at war with China for two years.

The Shinkoku Maru was launched by the Kawasaki Dockyard for the Kobe Sanbashi KK on 13 December 1939. On her first few voyages she carried crude oil from the USA - a net exporter of oil at that time - to Japan. With a gross tonnage of 10.020 ts she was exactly 500 ft long at the waterline, and attained almost 20 knots as maximum speed on her sea trials.

Already 4 months before Pearl Harbor Day (7 December 1941) the Shinkoku Maru was taken in hand by the Navy and fitted out as a fleet oiler: One heavy gun was mounted on the forecastle and the stern each. Some structural reinforcements were made, and a strong tripod mast added aft of the smoke stack. This tripod served to support the heavy fuel lines used during refuelling operations of naval vessels in the open sea.

In fact, the ship was one of the 8 fleet oilers which refuelled the Striking Force under Admiral Nagumo on December 3, 1941, which proceeded to attack Pearl Harbor, opening hostilities between the US and Japan.

Her operational career continued with participation as fleet oiler for the Japanese carrier thrust into the Indian Ocean and the carrier raid on Ceylon (Sri Lanka). Later, the Shinkoku served to supply the Mandated Islands with bunker and diesel oil for ship stores. On one of these voyages, on 17 August 1942, she was torpedoes by an American submarine.

Despite considerable damage she was able to limp back to Truk. Repairs were commenced and finished on 17 October 1942. Her subsequents trips lead her mainly between the refineries in Japan and the fleet bases of Truk and Palau.

She was lying at anchor on the day of the raid. Several Avenger torpedo bombers attacked this price bounty. A single torpedo hit the Shinkoku abaft of the funnel, at the engine room. It ripped a large hole into the ship's bottom and tore several shell platings on port beam off. Water flooded the engine room and the ship was pulled under from the weight of the aft ship. There are indications of an explosion and a flash fire. Several crew members perished in the flames.

The Shinkoku Maru, which was described by the pilots as being a large tanker, larger than the American fleet fleet oilers of the Cimarron-Class, which had refuelled the Task Groups just a few days earlier, was attacked by planes from USS Bunker Hill and Monterey. The planes skirted the western part of the reef in a southerly direction, from the North Pass, until they were well south of Tol. In a giant S, they delivered the attack from the north very early in the morning of the second day of the raid. Several planes launched torpedoes, but only the first from a plane from Bunker Hill was credited with the hit, as the resultant explosion obscured the ship.

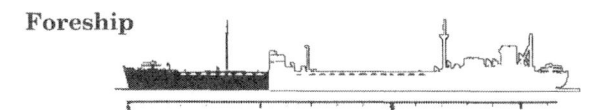

Foreship

The forecastle is rather big. There used to be rail guards enclosing it, but many stanchions and rails are gone. While the deck itself is fairly clean of coral growth, everything built on it, particularly the gun, and the stumps of the stanchions, are heavily overgrown by stony and soft corals, sponges and various forms of oysters.

The bow gun of the Shinkoku points forward with hardly any elevation of the barrel. The protective shield has an opening on the left side for the gun trainer. Cock's comb oysters are growing on the side of the breech, soften the hard, straight lines of this fairly modern, medium sized piece of artillery. The gun is probably of 7.5 cm or 10 cm calibre. It is mounted on a comparatively small platform. Many clumps of star coral grown on it.

The platform seems to be extended further aft of the breech. Four boxes are resting here. The cover of the third box from port is removed and reveals its contents of 16 shells for the gun. They are untouched. The bottom plates with the clearly discernable detonator caps are facing upward. The shells are "live" and therefore dangerous. They should not be touched or manipulated. The other closed boxes are of the same shape as the one which is open, and contain the same ready ammunition for the gun. It is about 40 ft deep in this area.

The bow is raked and of modern design. Both anchors are out; the chains lead away from the ship in northeasterly direction. The windlasses are big.

It is easy to penetrate the forecastle as the doorway on port is wide open. Several very large kerosine position lights used to be stored in the botsun's locker in the forecastle. On one of them the Fresnel lens was red. These spare lights have, regrettably, been removed, and were displayed in the Fisheries Department in Moen, pending their transfer to the museum. The exposure to air without measures to preserve the metal bodies is leading to slow decay.

Several paint cans and other objects for example, hurricane lights, with their glass gone, are located right at the entrance. Further penetration necessitates the use of an underwater light. A number of items typical for the botsun's locker can be found in the sediment covering the deck, such as many different lines and ropes. A hose drum stands on its base; the hose is tightly rapped around the revolving core.

Way forward, close to the bow, are the two hawsepipes. The one on starboard is half rusted away and is held in place by the chain only leading trough it. Entrance into the forecastle deck may also be gained on starboard.

The enormous size of this tanker is the first impression when swimming aft. The pipe bridge is about a deck high. It leads from the forecastle past the kingpost to the bridge, which is located slightly forward of midships. The pipe bridge is not located exactly amidships, i.e. not at the ship's center line.

There are a few open hatches on deck. Below the first, a large storage area was used for the cargo transfer pipes. A rack with about 20 or so pipe segments, stacked on top of each other, is welded onto the bulkhead, close to a companionway. The hoses are about 20 feet long and those on top have disintegrated. Only fragments remain.

The next hatch, aft of the former, is open as well. The visibility in this hold is extremely poor and even a light will not penetrate for more than 2 feet, subsequently, nothing can be seen here. It is a nightmare to penetrate.

There are a few pipes leading off the pipe bridge, at about 3 feet height. Their flanges point outward and they were used for loading and unloading the liquid cargo. A valve is mounted close to the flange, its hand wheel overgrown and hardly recognizable. Instruments, such as gauges and flow meters, can be seen at and in the deck house, which served as a pump control station.

The kingpost has two cross bars on top, between which two beams are crossing diagonally.

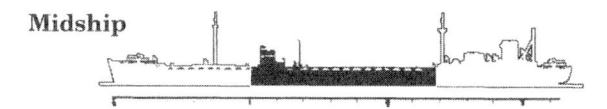

Midship

The bridge and the decks below are, no doubt, the most interesting parts of the Shinkoku Maru. It is only about 60 feet to the upper deck. This allows for relatively long dives, alas, with heavy nitrogen absorbtion. There are so many things to be seen here that hardly all of the attractions can be taken in at a single dive.

The inside of the navigation bridge looks confusing at first sight because of the many electrical cables hanging around. The wood planking from the upper deckheads has decayed, and the rectangular holes formed by the support structure allow light to illuminate this spacious room. Partitions subdivided the room into cabins, but all of the dividers have disintegrated now, as well.

The helm is bolted onto the deck of the navigation bridge, close to the forward bulkhead, in the middle of the cabin. The wheel is gone. The only thing remaining of the mechanism is a sprocket wheel which transmitted the helm's wheel movement via a chain to the steering mechanism. Base and sprocket wheel are partially overgrown with orange and mauve colored sponges. A direction indicator is incorporated into the helm in front, and a voice tube is located to the right of it.

A compass is attached to the frame of a window facing forward. The glass is damaged, and a big tube worm (spirrobranchus) grows out of it. Next to it, green penny algae can be found. Electrical cables lead to the compass. All surfaces in this area, the window frames in particular, are heavily overgrown. Also, the compass base is covered with sponges.

There are two engine telegraphs flanking the helm. They are located slightly closer to the forward bulkhead. On one of them, the glass is gone, but the twin indicator handle is in the "Dead Astern" position. This is not necessarily the position in which it was when the Shinkoku Maru sank. Some divers have an irresistible reflex to play with engine telegraphs. It looks now as if the instrument is tilted slightly to aft, so it may not be anchored properly to the deck anymore. In front of it is a voice tube, but it is considerably overgrown and hardly recognizable. Cables are hanging down next to it.

The second engine telegraph is standing up straight. The majority of the glass seemed to have remained in place; it is overgrown from edge to edge. In the beam of the underlight, the sides and the top are presenting themselves in a deep purple color of sponges growing on it. The handle of this telegraph is gone.

Incidentally, there is a third telegraph on top of the bridge, standing in free water. A flying bridge of wooden construction was located there. The telegraph's handle is in the Full Ahead position. A bunch of shells grow on top of it. A helm cannot be found.

Farther aft the mess and galley are located. It is dark but spacious there. However, low hanging electrical cables, the remains of circuits, are frequently in the way. The dividing, non structural partitions have gone. The stove is located not far from the doorway. A hot water boiler lies on the other side of the entrance way inside the room on deck. The galley stove is the center piece of the room. There are many objects resting on the hot plates. When approaching the stove, a lot of dishes and table ware can be seen. Instead of having the dishes, plates, canteens, flasks, ask trays, bottles, tea kettles and cups scattered around in the silt, some orderly soul has piled them all up on the stove. The cupboard which contained them has long since disintegrated, and subsequently they spilled onto the deck. The plates bear a flower design.

There are two doorways further aft. One leads into the bathroom, called the head on ships. Inside, along the aft bulkhead, is a two-tub Japanese bath. The smaller upper tub is followed by a slightly lower and larger second one. A faucet can be seen, the pipe being bolted on to the bulkhead. A sink, mounted originally on the outside bulkhead, has fallen on its side. This was the officer's bath. There is a porthole facing starboard beam.

The room next to it has been another head. There are two Japanese toilet bowls on the bottom next to the aft bulkhead, and two urinals. The plumbing is still intact, even the valves on the water pipe on top of the ceramic urinals can be clearly made out. They were separated, as were the bowls, by plywood dividers. A sink is in its original position. It is interesting to note that the sediment is close to 10 inches high. All the vessels, including the sink, are filled to the brim with it. A porthole is situated at the outside bulkhead.

An medical operation room is located in the deeper recesses of the superstructure. It is dark in this room. The porthole is overgrown and allows only very little light to filter through. The operation table is a give-away for the purpose of the cabin. It was the sick bay. The cover of the operating table shows a hole now, but other than that it is quite well preserved; it can be clearly identified and recognized. A light fixture hangs from the ceiling. The instrument table, its glass top broken, stands at the head of the op-table. Slightly forward is a sterilizing cooker and the instrument-box. A sink is located next to it.

Another bulb is hanging from the ceiling a little to the left. Water has gotten into it and it looks blue-grey. Turning further, a post comes into view, next to which hospital instruments are lying on the bottom. A heater and a bulb are hanging from cables next to the post.

Farther to the left, one can see a beam. A storage locker must have been attached to it, which was filled with blankets.

Although the locker has disintegrated over the years, the blankets are not totally gone now, but hang from the beam, so that they look as if they hang from a line. Bales of tightly rapped blankets are scattered on the deck. Remnants of bunks can be seen on the deck. Further traces of wood on vertical support posts and the bulkhead indicate where the bunks have been attached to originally. A network of cables and a fuse or distribution box are hanging from the deckhead.

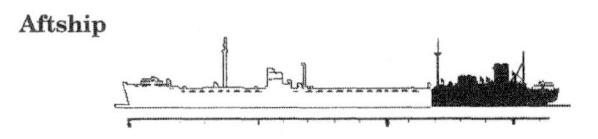

Aftship

The distance from the bridge to the aft structure is long, longer than from the forecastle to midships. The pipe bridge leads all the way aft to the 2 decks high superstructure. The stout funnel is built on top of it,

Hailstorm - *The Wrecks*

halfway to the stern. Between the two superstructures a kingpost, identical to the one forward, can be found.

Almost all divers turn to the starboard doorway on shelter deck when approaching the aft superstructure. The door is wide open and secured to the bulkhead, and the passage can be entered easily. However, it is almost completely dark inside, there are no portholes because it is inboard, and the door on the other end is closed.

A doorway can be seen about 6 ft inside the passageway, leading to starboard. It is either right at this door inside the passageway or just around the corner, where the two skulls have been placed last. The favorite activity of about every visitor is, regrettably, to pick these skulls up for a closer look. It may be much more tactful to leave them alone and refrain from touching.

Inside the room two parallel structures are bolted to the deck. There are also remnants of bolts sticking out from the mud. It used to be the crew's mess and the wooden remnants is all what is left of a table.

The room off the left of the passageway is a stateroom, probably for the ship's engineer. It is even darker than the passageway. The light will reveal other human remains. There are femurs and other bones, half buried in the sediment. Another doorway is revealed when looking farther inside towards the outside of the ship. This room may be entered with due caution to prevent stirring up silt. In this cabin or rest room, a few things have escaped decay, for example, a sink and a white ceramic object. There were more bones and unidentifiable objects scattered on the deck.

Going back into the passageway, and dodging the low hanging electrical cables, another doorway off the same side will be reached farther aft. This room is much larger and it appears to have been used as crew accommodations. A flask, a plate and a bowl were scattered in the sediment here, but it could be that they have been removed since. A number of bales look like tightly folded blankets. Because of the absolute darkness, the fast decreasing visibility and the hanging cables, further penetration into this passageway is not advised. A sink is mounted on the inboard bulkhead of the passageway.

While the cabins and passageway described are located on starboard, the corresponding doorway on port is half hidden behind the ladder leading up to the second deck. The door is wide open, as well. This passageway is a mirror image of the one on starboard,

Shinkoku Maru, during the war.

with the exception, that the first room, to the right, contains a lot of assorted material. This was the botsun's locker. The second, larger room certainly was used as crew quarters as well. On the outer bulkhead the wooden remnants of a 2 tier bunk can be made out. Off the passageway is a companionway leading inboard.

After getting out of this passageway by swimming its length towards aft, free water will be reached. The second level on port is the boats deck. This passageway here looks inviting, because at its end an open door allows light to enter and halfway in the middle is a door through which more light is admitted. To the left is another officer's cabin. A second stateroom can be seen connected to it.

After entering the passageway, the open doorway from which light shines in, will be passed. It is located to the left of the diver facing aft. Investigation of it will be done after a brief check of the cabins aft of it. First there is a head complete with toilet bowl at the very rear, an urinal, which has fallen down and lies half buried in the silt, and a sink, complete with faucet.

The following room is the bathroom, containing a tiled Japanese bath. Its upper part contains two small tubs and is followed by the larger single, lower tub. There are three faucets, one for each tub. All of them are in very nice condition, but old fashioned in design. From there on, the dive leads back.

The open doorway previously passed by may be entered now. Immediately, the impression of a wide open space inside a large building comes to mind. It is fairly well light up here, and getting onto the grated catwalk conveys the impression to be in a balcony seat of a theater. The light comes mainly from above. The spaciousness is a relief after swimming through so many tight cabins and passageways.

This is the engine room. Catwalks on two levels can be seen; they are connected with a ladder. On the bottom the huge diesel cylinder heads of the main propulsion engine can be made out immediately. Large square pieces of sheet metal, some of which have a circular hole in the middle, have fallen down to the bottom of the engine room. Where they came from is not clear.

Catwalks are built around on both sides of the cylinder heads. One is higher than the other. A high pressure start-up air pipe connects the heads. A smaller line curves uniformly over the side of all heads and was the fuel line. Each head is torqued down to the cylinder with twelve, fist sized nuts. There are also wires leading away from the heads. These were used to monitor performance and conditions of the engine. There seem to be 8 cylinders in the main engine.

Located next to a walkway on the lower level, and a ladder leading up, is a large instrument, with three windows and 10 pipes leading out of it. They are curving back in a U-shape. The two on the side are slightly smaller than the inner 8. Attached to it, on one side, is a smaller unit with 8 pipes coming out of the top. This is probably the fuel injection pump.

Mounted on a bulkhead is a measuring instrument of sorts, with one pipe leading to it and another U-shaped leading away. It resembles a flow meter. Underneath it, a partially torn grating can be seen. Many other pieces of equipment, such as a water separator, lines, valves and an auxiliary engine can be found here as well.

Low on the port side of the engine room, the torpedo hit shows as a big jagged hole. It is no problem to swim out here into open water. The damage to the hull is extensive. It is quite uncanny with what accuracy the lethal torpedo found its mark. All three tankers sank in Truk, the Shinkoku Maru, Fujisan Maru and Hoyo Maru, received hits into the engine room. Torpedo damage to other parts of tankers may not sink them as they have many airtight inboard tanks. However, there is little remedy against a flooded engine room compartment.

Inside the superstructure aft of the engine room are some interesting things to see, such as a carbon dioxide-type fire extinguisher and a lot of plates in a mess room. In another compartment, a cable drum and several lines may be found. An electric motor is half buried in the silt, together with other unidentified material. Finally, way aft, a single blade of a ship's propeller is bolted to the bulkhead. If this find is not an optical illusion, it certainly is a surprise.

Ship's propellers at this time were cast in one piece. Therefore it could not be intended for the actual propeller of the Shinkoku Maru. A few oil drums, stacked in two tiers, can be seen in a storage room.

Swimming up the smoke stack - outside, of course - one is impressed by its size. Right aft of it is a large tripod mast. It was certainly fitted during the Shinkoku Maru's conversion to a fleet tanker. Its purpose is to support fuel pipes through which navy vessels were refuelled in the open sea, thus extending their range of action. There is a pair of ventilators just aft of the tripod mast and then the boats deck drops one level to the sizeable poop. There is a gun mounted on the stern platform. It is the same model as the one on the bow.

A few smaller deck houses and companionways can be found on boat deck. Most of the companionways are so narrow that it is not possible to go further down than one deck. One of them leads to a very narrow control room with many gauges and valves. Care must be taken not to get stuck, it is so tight that the diver has to slide in and out, with hardly any room to maneuver. It is in this vicinity that a samurai sword and scubbard is carefully hidden by a dive guide, who shows it only to very few visitors. Aft, in the hatch, a few depth charges can be seen.

The Shinkoku Maru was a tanker, converted to a navy fleet oiler. Some sources list her as Kamikuni Maru, which is the wrong transposition of the Japanese characters.

Technical Data:

Tonnage	:	10.020 ts	
Length	:	152,40 m	500 ft
Breadth	:	19,81 m	65 ft
Depth	:	11,28 m	37 ft
Draught	:	8,98 m	29,5 ft
Engine	:	1 x MAN Diesel	
Horsepower	:	11 565 hp	
Speed max	:	19,8 knots	
serv	:	15,0 knots	
Launch	:	13 December 1939	
Service	:	28 February 1940	
Builder	:	Kawasaki Dockyard	
Owner	:	Kobe Sanbashi K.K.	

SHOTAN MARU

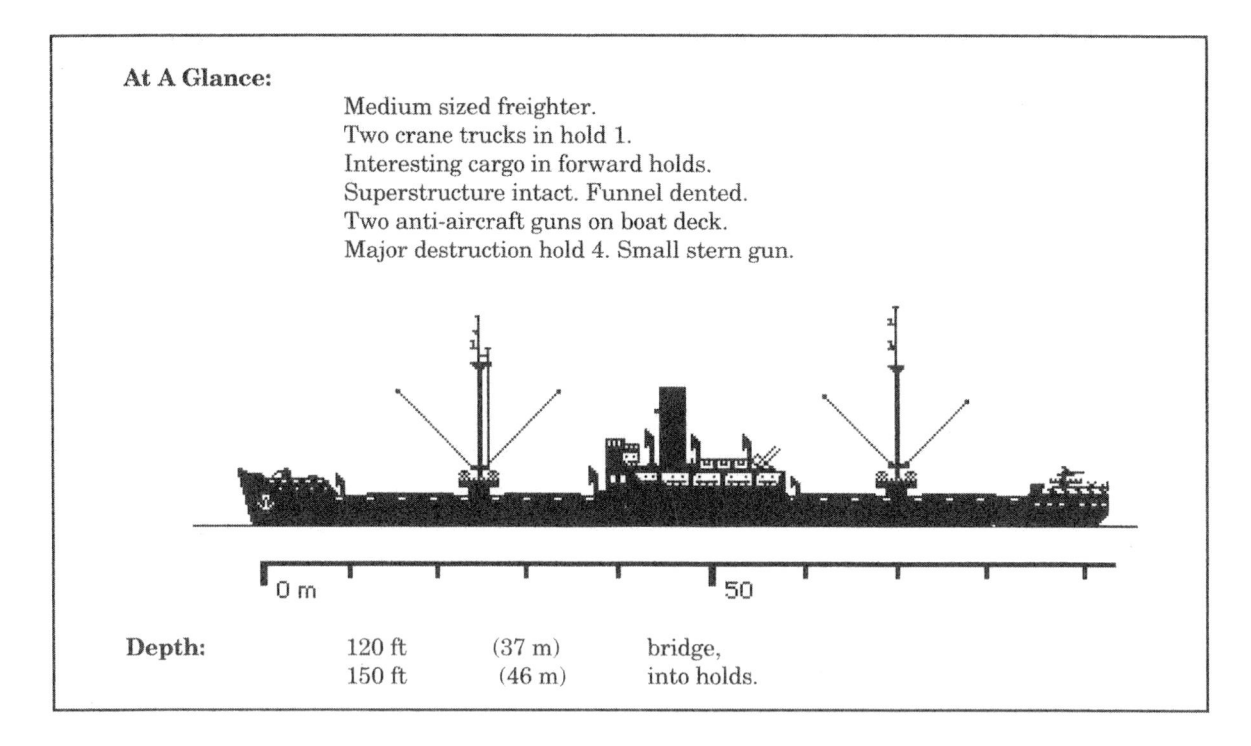

At A Glance:
Medium sized freighter.
Two crane trucks in hold 1.
Interesting cargo in forward holds.
Superstructure intact. Funnel dented.
Two anti-aircraft guns on boat deck.
Major destruction hold 4. Small stern gun.

Depth: 120 ft (37 m) bridge,
150 ft (46 m) into holds.

This medium sized freighter rests on even keel at the flank of an underwater mountain. The upperworks are overgrown with marine life, but the lower parts of the ship look clean.

The description leads from the stern to the bow.

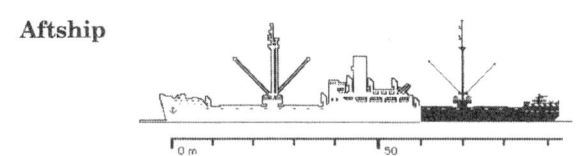

Aftship

The poop conveys an orderly impression. The deck bears a few pieces of machinery, such as winches. A platform raises in the middle, a gun is mounted on top of it. It points straight astern with no elevation of the gun barrel, and does not appear to have been fired during the attack. The deck of the platform is partly carpeted with green penny algae. Patches of coral show between them. The platform is enclosed with a guard rail, which remained mostly intact. The base of the gun is overgrown as well. The gun itself, the mount, breech, training mechanism and barrel are all covered by encrustating sponges, which seem to glow under the beam of a strong underwater light. This piece of artillery is of medium calibre, about 3 inches, 7,6 cm. It is an excellent photographic subject. A helm is located close to the gun platform on the poop. The wheel had a metal rim, which fell over the base of the mount when the wooden spokes rotted away. A large, disk shaped object rests next to it. There appears to be a ventilator cowl resting on deck as well. The poop has rail guards leading around it, and the stays are overgrown with bright red forms of sea life.

There are a few interesting things bolted to the bulkhead of the poop. Roughly midships was mounted a large, old fashioned stock anchor.

Hold 4 is located forward of the poop. It is an area strongly contrasting with the aft superstructure because of the obvious destruction. There is no doubt, that the ship received a full bomb hit between the bulwark and the hatch coaming, destroying major parts of the shell and deck plating at the aft and under section of the hold. The coaming on starboard held, did not break, but is bent in a large U-shape right into the hold. The ship rests on starboard against the flank of a steeply ascending slope. It looks as if almost all shell plating in that area is blown out. The damage extends to port. Hatch coaming, posts, girders, and other structural elements are twisted and torn. The winch house and the deck sagged by abut 10 ft on starboard, and the deck is severely buckled on the other side. The hull cracked in this location.

The mast broke off a few feet above its base on the winch house, and fell to starboard where it rests on the bulwark and the slope of the mountain. Also, the top mast broke off a few feet above the crosstree. The lower part of the mast is separated from its stump by about a foot. To port, however, fell the port derrick. It rolled down the rather steep incline, and can be seen on the bottom of the valley, about 100 ft (30 m) down.

Hold 3 remained largely intact, although the hatch cover beams and the derricks are missing. The derrick resting post is located on the fashion plate aft of the superstructure. There is some cargo evident on the bottom of the hold. It looks like drums.

Midships

Foreship

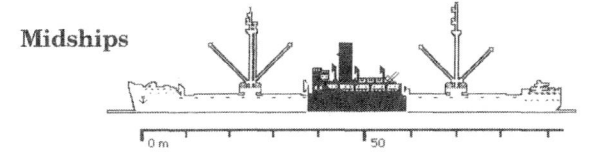

The midship superstructure remained in good shape. It is two decks high aft. Both passageways on the different levels show intact rail guards. The boat decks extends to slightly forward of the funnel. A deck house is constructed at the aft end of the superstructure. A cylindrical object, resting on its side athwart of the ship, with a pipe connection on top, follows slightly forward. It appears to be a boiler water feed vessel. The engine room skylights are built into a triangular base forward of it. The lights are closed. Ventilators have been built on all four corners of the engine room skylight base. The forward pair retained their cowls,

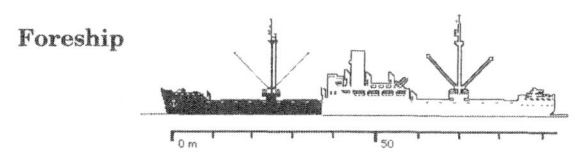

A large number of cement bags are stowed on the bottom of hold 2, which is located forward of the midships superstructure. In the tween deck, two pieces of machinery can be seen. The bigger of the two is a mobile compressor of considerable size, and resembles those used in heavy construction work. The motor and compressor are coupled with two sets of 5 V-belts each. The ission wheels can be clearly recognized. The machine is mounted on four flat rimmed steel wheels with spokes. The other piece is a heavy diesel engine. Farther forward a large number of messkitts, a long spouted oil can and a few drums are strewn among

Shotan Maru, a War Standard D(b) Ship.

whereas the aft two have fallen of.

Two 2 cm anti-aircraft machine weapons are located abeam and slightly aft of the engine room skylights on both sides of the boat deck. The one on port fell forward, and the twin barrels face down. They had been bolted to the wooden planking and to the steel reinforcement beam, but the bolts corroded, allowing the top heavy weapon to fall forward. The gun is still loaded and one large box of ready ammunition rests on deck. The weapon on starboard remained in its last firing position, and faces forward over the side. It appears to be of different design than the one on port, having only a single barrel.

There are two small skylights abeam of the funnel, next to which a rectangular opening can be seen in the deck. These are companionways, leading down to the next lower deck. Two pairs of boats davits remain standing on both sides, on boat deck. The forward pair is smaller than the one aft.

The funnel is tall and narrow. Its tube-like construction is evidence that the ship burned coal. The stack is dented considerably on both sides. A ladder is welded onto it. A pair of ventilators is located in front of the funnel, where a small, long and narrow coal chute can be found as well. The boat deck ends here and recesses inboard by about 6 ft (2 m). The bridge house follows, which extends forward to the flying bridge, the aft part of which is enclosed by rail guards. The bridge is 3 decks high, and portholes have been built into the forward bulkhead.

other objects. Another multi-spoked wheel, drums, lines and shell casings make up the remainder of the contents of the tween deck. It is possible to swim through from hold 2 to hold 1, underneath the mast house. The area is covered with a huge number of shell casings. They were packaged in groups of 4, and many of them are still arranged that way. The casings litter the tween deck way up to forward in hold 1. In between, a few drums and a strongly ribbed object can be seen. The cargo derricks are in their rest position.

It is fairly dark in the forward hold. The reason becomes obvious when looking up. There are two trucks resting on the hatch cover beams on main deck. The tires, engine, drive shaft, axles and their flat beds can be seen from below. It is possible to ascend between the hatch coaming and the engine of the forward truck, and by doing so, shelter deck is reached. Most of the bodywork of the trucks has rusted away, but the steering wheel, instruments, gear shift stick and driver's seat are all in good condition. The hood is gone, exposing the radiator, engine, alternator and steering column. The steering is located on the right side, indicative of left hand traffic. The radiator is high. Green algae grow on it, as well as on part of the cranes. The cranes of these identical trucks are installed between the driver's cabin and the flatbed. The loading platform remained almost completely intact, but in some places the rust has eaten holes into it. Twin tires are mounted on the rear wheels. The trucks face to port. A third truck has fallen over board and rests

Hailstorm - *The Wrecks*

upside-down on the sea bed, leaning against the hull.

The mast house is fairly small. On its sides, the doors are open, the one on port hanging askew from one hinge. Steel lines are visible inside this superstructure. A strange pedestal, very similar to the gun mounts found on other ships, can be seen in front of the mast, welded to the deck. It is debatable whether a gun was mounted here. it would have a rather narrow field of fire. Some of the objects, looking very much like a barrel and lock in appearance, are located next to it. It may have been that this was the rest for the jumbo derrick, but identification is not certain. In the same area a large ship's compass has been sighted, complete with its box and suspended from gimbals.

The forecastle bears two doors which are wide open and can be entered easily. At the port entrance six stacked shovels can be seen. Their handles have rotted away, with only traces remaining of where they were stuck into the mount. Many dented paint cans appear in the otherwise empty cabin, dimly lit by portholes. The forward structure does not carry a gun and the two large windlasses dominate the forecastle. Both anchors are in their rest position at the bow. The Shotan Maru is one of the very few ships, which did not sink while at anchor. The final resting place close to the island of Fanamu suggests that the crew intended to beach her. However, the Helldivers were faster and sank her before shallow waters could be reached. The ship's axis points to east-northeast. It means, that the Shotan Maru went down very quickly, as it did not have time to heave broadside to the wind, which was blowing at about 17 knots from northeast, 70 degrees.

The tentative designation X 2 had been retained for a long time, as the identity could not be verified beyond doubt. The large amount of tableware inspected provided no clue as to the original owners, as the insignia had disappeared. The wreck was found by the author on 13 June 1980. Eventually, the identity was established by computer analysis, and confirmed by measurements taken under water, together with a comparison of the present appearance with existing photos of the ship afloat.

In some references there is a mention of Matsutan(i) Maru for this ship. The ship was built during the war and records are scarce.

The name of this freighter, Shotan Maru, has been taken from the original Japanese list of ships sunk in Truk. It is identical to the name shown in the list of ships lost in Truk, compiled b the Japanese in Truk after the war, including in the Joint Army-Navy Assessment Committee report. There are references to the ship in other literature, notably Jentschura et. al. (Warships of the Imperial Japanese Navy 1869 to 1945) stating the name to be either Matsutan Maru or Matsutani Maru. At any rate, there is no doubt that the reference is to the same Standard 1 D ship.

Technical Data:

Tonnage :	1 999 ts	
Length o.a. :	87.0 m	285' 8"
Width :	12.8 m	43 ft
Draught	7 m	20 ft
Machine:	1 x Vertical Triple Expansion Steam Engine	
Fuel:	Coal	
Horsepower:	1110 ihp	
Speed, max.	12.5 knots	
Speed, cruising:	10 knots	
Radius:	3,800 miles	
Owner:	Matsuoka Kisen	
Builder:	Unknown	

SPECIAL SUBCHASER NO. 38

At A Glance ...
Small capsized vessel of about 300 ts,
Two structures on ship's bottom.

Depth:

10 ft to 30 ft	(3 m to 9 m)	to keel,
40 ft to 50 ft	(12 m to 15 m)	to bottom.

The identity of this ship is not confirmed. It could have been a small merchant vessel converted to anti-submarine warfare, or a small submarine chaser. The ship turned turtle, i.e. it capsized when it sank. The highest part is the starboard bilge keel. It was said in Truk that the ship was sunk at the same date as the Hino Maru 2, during the March-April bombing raid, which would fit perfectly with official records.

A curious looking instrument is mounted about midships on the keel. It is a disk 10" (25 cm) thick and about 1 ft (30 cm) in diameter. The mounting keeps it about 10" off the ship's bottom. The forward facing part has a square shaped plate insert, which is subdivided into two separate rectangular plates. Looking from the inside of the vessel, a tube with a diameter of 10" can be seen welded to the keel. Its telescopic configuration suggests that it could be possibly lowered, raised and turned, with the instrument attached on the outside of the hull. It is a bit overgrown, which makes identification difficult, but cables can be seen on the inside to emanate from it. The purpose of this apparatus is not entirely clear, but it is possible, that it was either a hydrophone or a sonar. Submarine chasers were generally fitted with this kind of detection gear.

A few feet of the device described, another protuberance can be seen on the vessel's bottom. This one is a bit larger, streamlined, and hugs the keel. Although larger, it is not as high as the previous one, and on port very much overgrown by coral. Inside the hull, a simple S-shaped pipe leads up to the superstructure, close to the mast. As most of the area on deck is destroyed, its purpose could not be ascertained. It may be associated with the main diesel engine.

It is easy to enter the ship about midships at the engine room. Metal supports at the deck look like ribs, and have to be passed to get to the interior. The engine room is spacious, but dark. This is because the ship is upside-down, and the clearance between the bulwark and the bottom is only a few feet. An underwater light should be taken along. A lot of black oil sloshes around at the highest part of the hull inside. Care must be taken to avoid contact with it. Getting out of the hull midships does not present a problem. With a certain amount of effort, the other parts of the wreck may be visited, but the quarters are crammed, and there is no special incentive to get inside.

The ship is located about half a mile (800 m) east of the Hino Maru 2. It is very probable, that she was in motion at the time of sinking. Evidence to this effect can be found when examining the propeller. All blades are bent very much at the top. Even the propeller shaft is pulled out by one foot. This damage is typical for a ship in motion striking an object with the propeller and rudder hanging up on the obstacle. The rudder of the ship has been torn off.

PATROL BOAT 34 ex Susuki

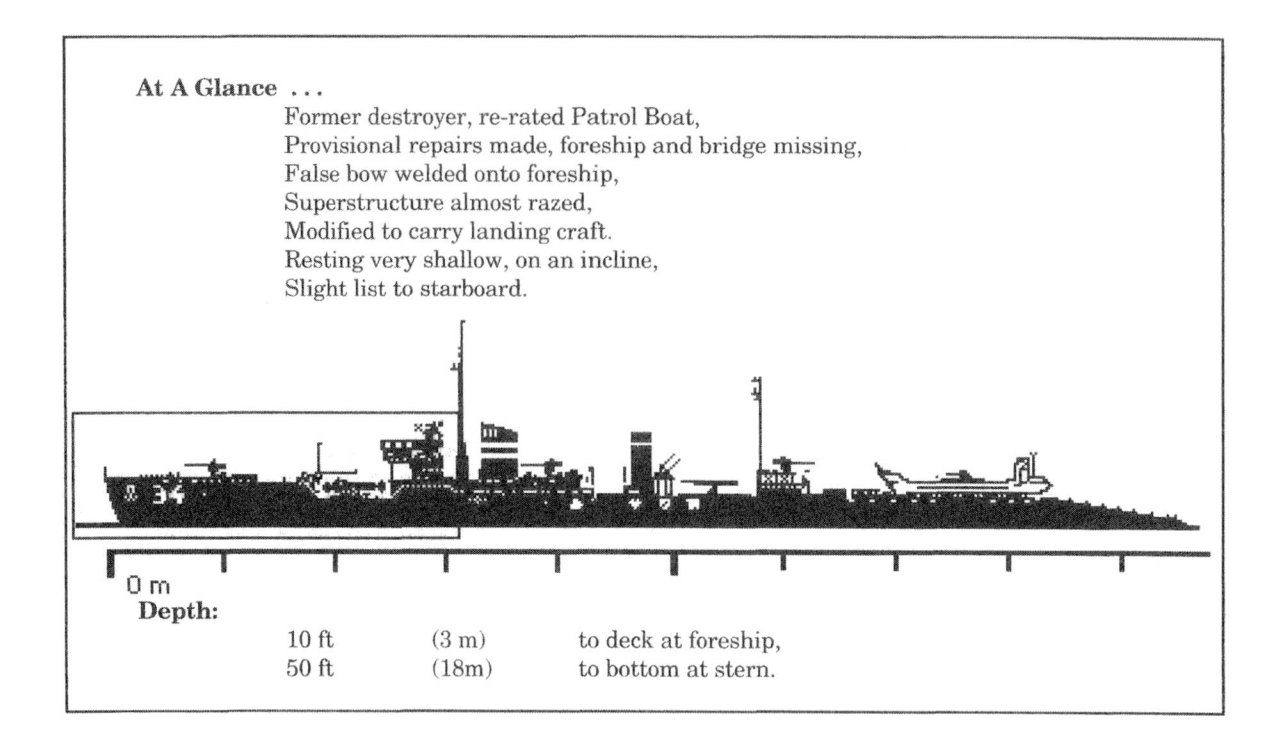

At A Glance ...
Former destroyer, re-rated Patrol Boat,
Provisional repairs made, foreship and bridge missing,
False bow welded onto foreship,
Superstructure almost razed,
Modified to carry landing craft.
Resting very shallow, on an incline,
Slight list to starboard.

Depth:

10 ft	(3 m)	to deck at foreship,
50 ft	(18m)	to bottom at stern.

The area of the former Repair Anchorage is the site of a very peculiar wreck. The ship resting here on an incline used to be a destroyer. At the time this Momi-class destroyer was built, in the 1920's, these ships were hailed as one of the fastest in the world. The heavy guns and torpedo launchers were built on a weapon platform that was able to move with better than 35 knots through the water. Double turbines transmitted their power to large twin propellers with a very high pitch. Alas, the propaganda value was higher than their actual combatant status accorded to them by the Navy. They were considered second class destroyers, something the Germans used to call torpedo boats. The builders had to go to some length and manipulations to attain the design speed. When the time for the acceptance runs came, some of the guns were conveniently taken off and the ship lighted as much as possible to reach the speed and to surpass it by a few decimals ... .

The ships were a bit top heavy, and outdated by the time the war broke out. A few vessels of this class were taken in hand and converted to carry Daihatsu landing craft on the stern. The Japanese Navy had an urgent need for fast transports to bring troop reinforcements to their embattled garrisons and to reinforce the position at Guadalcanal. Conventional cargo ships had proven to be too slow and vulnerable, and the second-line destroyers were rebuilt. Their armament was reduced. The torpedo launchers were removed. The stern was pared down to the waterline and extended by about 10 m. Two sets of rails were welded onto the deck aft and heavy electric winches and handling gear installed near the aft gun platform. Two landing craft were put on each side and carried piggy-back to their destination. The troops carried were accommodated at the aft compartments. At their target zone they would climb into the landing crafts, which then were lowered into the water. Afterwards the crafts would be pulled back up the stern.

The destroyer, now re-rated Patrol Boat, was very heavily damaged and either towed or limped back under its own power into Truk. What exactly happened is not confirmed. The foreship was severed or very heavily damaged, probably destroyed up to, and including the bridge.

Reports about the cause are scarce. A target ship, Yakaze, a converted destroyer and sistership of the ill-fated Tachikaze, was known to have collided with Patrol Boat 34, and cut the foreship off. The date was 6 March 1943, and it happened south of Kavieng. Somehow, the amputated mid and aftship made it to Truk. The guns were taken off to lighten it, and it was put into the floating dry dock for repairs. Truk did not possess a machine shop to bent the shell plates to a new bow. Instead, raw plates were welded together and fitted. The false bow resembles a "V". It looks very makeshift to this very day. Crude would be another way of putting it.

The watertight integrity restored, the ship was taken out of the dry dock and tied to a mooring. There were no anchors. It was intended to refit the guns. There are no records of the ship being damaged during the first carrier raid, but it was demolished on 3 Juy 1944. A fire consumed the ship, the superstructure was literally blown over board, and the ship sank. Today, the ship appears totally stripped with only the integrated parts of the superstructure still standing.

The wreck is located at the west shore of Dublon.

It is only about 100 m north of the large mooring anchors. The shank of one with its ball-like tip can still be seen above water. The vessel faces south, and rests on sloping ground. While the deck forward is at 3 m the aft deck is in 8 m water depth. The false bow is very interesting to look at. The discontinuity to the streamline rest of the hull is eye-catching. Holes at the sides afford a view into the interior. It appears that the ship begins right at the forward edge of the first boiler. As the bridge was part of the foreship which is missing, a small square deck house was welded onto the deck.

The twin funnels are reduced to mere stumps, and are hardly recognizable. Boat davits or cranes can be seen slightly abaft the funnel. The two gun platforms have been retained. One is located between the funnels and one aft of it. The aft ship is particularly long. It contrasts with the shortened foreship. When looking closely at the side of the vessel, the stern extension can be seen were it meets the original hull. The stern rails have largely corroded and are gone, but traces remain on the deck. Heavy steel lines and a heavy electrical motor can be seen at the port side of the aft gun platform. They are missing on starboard.

There are four parts of the ship which warrant closer inspection. However, very few people dive on this wreck with scuba. Mostly it is visited between dives to snorkel. However, a little dive excursion in and around the wreck is very fascinating.

Firstly, the internal design can be studied by looking onto the large holes which have been formed by corrosion of the hull plating. They are located at the port bow and the many other places on the shell plating.

Secondly, an excursion into the engine room is very interesting. Entry is gained through the engine room skylights. It is a bit narrow, but not dangerous. The visitor is confronted with many gauges and instruments. The huge boiler can be seen and many asbestos cloth wrapped steam pipes. A generator and various other pieces of machinery can be located at various places and levels inside the engine room. A listening room or command stand the size of a broom closet can be seen to one side. It is best to take the fins off and move cautiously through the interior to avoid stirring up the fine sediment.

Thirdly, the aft compartments can be entered, but not before the interior of the ship is left, as the passageway aft is barred by a heavy mesh screen door. The man hole can be found at the vicinity of the aft gun platform, on port. There are two spacious compartment, which are empty, except for a steel cabinet housing a few dry cells, a gas mask and a little debris in the forward room. There is plenty of light coming in from the many holes in the hull.

Fourthly, the lower stern with its remarkable twin propellers and almost square rudder is certainly worth a visit. The propeller shafts emerge way forward from the hull and are fastened with a heavy A-bracket to the shell plating. There is no doubt that this was a very high speed vessel when looking at the high pitched props. Finally, when diving alongside port beam, a lot of debris can be seen on the bottom. They are part of the razed superstructure. Even the remnants of one of the funnels can be made out clearly.

It was the old Susuki, a destroyer of the Momi-class. This ship was stricken from the destroyer list and renamed Patrol Boat 34, after the modification at her stern was completed. Measurements taken at the wreck conform basically with the published data. This is the only genuine warship in Truk accessible up to 1985, when the Fumizuki was found.

Susuki's sister can be seen in Palau. It also was converted to a Patrol Boat, but lacks the pared down stern. Its present site is described in "Desecrate 1".

TAIHO MARU

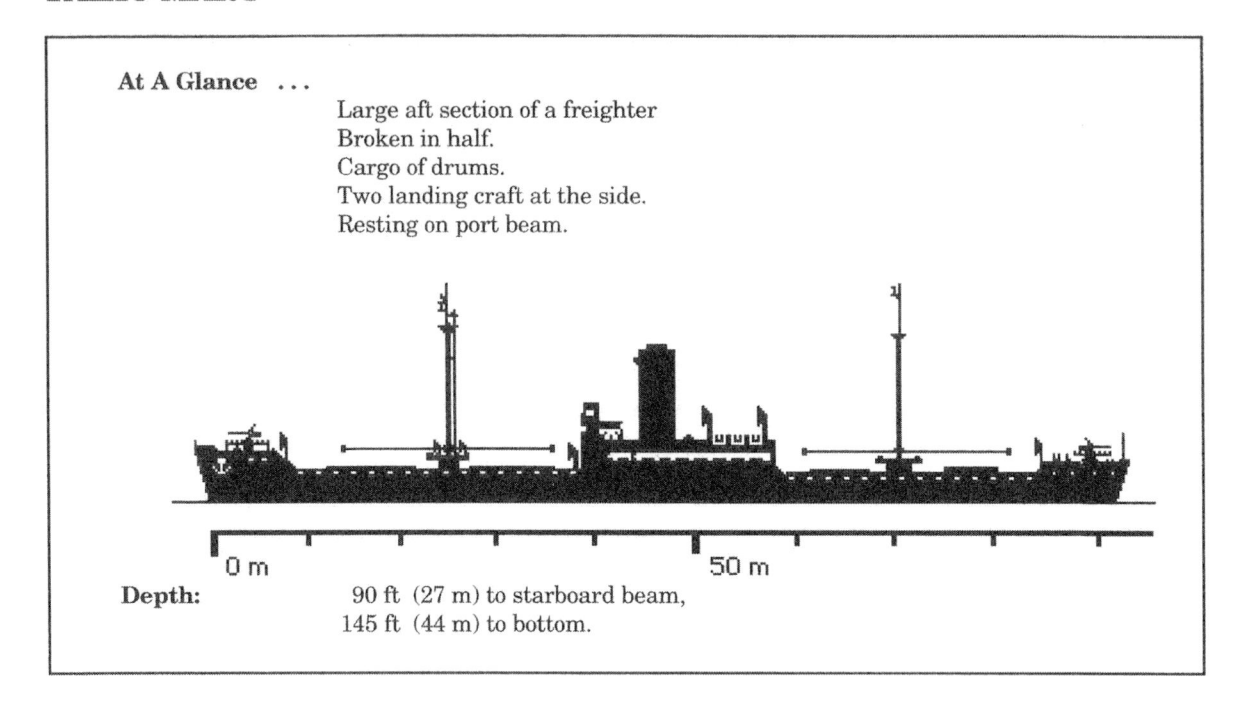

At A Glance ...
Large aft section of a freighter
Broken in half.
Cargo of drums.
Two landing craft at the side.
Resting on port beam.

Depth: 90 ft (27 m) to starboard beam,
145 ft (44 m) to bottom.

Although this wreck is quite interesting hardly anybody dives there. The cargo and the the way it sank after being hit make a dive worthwhile.

The ship broke in half after an explosion. The break occurred right aft of the funnel at the midship superstructure. Two or three landing craft were tied to port beam. The rudder was put to port, probably swinging the stern slightly into the wind creating somewhat smoother water conditions on her port. This made the handling of cargo easier. The forward section of the ship disintegrated in a violent explosion where she anchored. The torn off aft ship did not sink right away but floated, aided by the landing crafts, which were still tied to it. For a little while, all of them drifted before the wind but then the part of the ship sunk. It pulled down the other, smaller vessels as well. Lacking stability on the inclined sea bed, the aft ship rolled over and came to rest on the port side.

Aftship

Orientation is difficult when descending at the area where the break occurred. The wreck looks just like a mountain of twisted, torn and buckled steel. A close look shows that the force of the explosion vented into the engine room, and blew out the skylights and boat deck. It is also possible that the steam boiler exploded.

A little forward of the hull, a shadow appears on the bottom. It looks like a crane on first sight, however, turns out to be only a large piece of shell or deck plating with a frame attached to it. The frame stands upright but bent on the plating, which lies flat on the bottom.

Numerous large sized steel fragments can be found on the sea bed in continuation of the line wreckplating. They are part of the foreship. The debris thins out after about 300 ft. Drums can be seen scattered on the bottom. The remains of the foreship have not been found, despite repeated intensive searches in the area north to east of the location of the wreck.

A steep underwater mountain reflects the ultrasonic waves and creates the allusion of a piece of wreck. As the Taiho Maru lies in the navigational pass between Uman and Fefan - a route frequently traversed to reach the South Pass - it may be assumed that the original anchorage was further northeast and inshore of Uman.

The aft section of the ship lies in a beautiful valley. Facing the deck of the wreck, an almost barren flank of a white underwater mountain ascends steeply at an incline of almost 45 degrees. A coral reef rises less steeply on the side of the ship's bottom. It is really a magnificent underwater scenery. The position of the wreck can be best described as lying just on the base of the one underwater mountain, the coral reef, but not quite down in the valley.

Close to where the ship broke apart, two landing crafts are located. Their flat deck and the bridge, which have portholes, can be seen, resting at an angle to the hull of the freighter. Certainly they were used to transport cargo to Dublon.

The crafts look somewhat broken up now, although their original shape can be identified. They may have been about 50 ft long.

The hold following the break, hold number 3, contains a lot of drums. Some of them have fallen out and accumulated close to the deck on the bottom.

The mast is standing, but all derricks have fallen over to port. The mast carries a big cross tree. Four winches are located on either side and fore and aft of it.

The following hold, hold 4, must have been

Hailstorm - *The Wrecks*

Taiho Maru — Yamada

filled to the brim with drums. They have tumbled out of it, and form a really imposing heap on the bottom, reaching all the way up to the hatch coaming. Most of the drums are dented, and the number of them is staggering. Evidently, some of the cargo has already be discharged from hold 4, or spilled out, or even floated up, when the ship was sinking, because there are considerably fewer in the forward hold compared to the one aft of it.

The poop raises one deck. On top of the aft part is a gun mounted on a platform. This platform looks like a huge wagon wheel with spokes radiating from the hub. However, in the center is an about 4 foot square steel reinforcement. The platform appears large and high, but the gun is squat with a fairly small barrel. This is the same type of gun found on the Hanakawa Maru. It is the Navy 12 cm Short Gun, a short barreled gun of simplified design. About 550 guns were made and they were intended for ships under 5000 ts. Their maximum range was 5300m, and they were intended to fight off submarines on the surface. A huge yellow sponge grows on the lock, and on the gun itself, corals have settled. There are several whip coral growing on the platform.

The stern has an unusual shape. Contrary to all other wrecks which have rounded, conventional lines, it is straight and looks cut-off. This form resembles the lines of large modern vessels. Of course these cut-off sterns are much easier and faster to build than cruiser or clipper sterns. The design of the Taiho suggest that she was built during the war, when speed of construction was at a premium, and short-cuts are made. The shell plates are welded.

In fact, the ship belongs to the numerous Standard 1-C freighters. The Japanese saw the urgent need for standardized ships to speed up replenishment of the many which were lost in the war. Several standard designs evolved. The C-Class was a medium-small steam freighter. Some ships in this class were built with a counter stern.

The rudder blade is turned to port. The propeller has four blades. On starboard beam, close to the very stern the sheer strake was damaged. It is broken over a length of a foot or so and bent outward. Also the deck in this area is broken. It suggests that the aft section was hit here by a fragment hurled up by the explosion, impacting in this area.

The Taiho Maru was discovered in 1972 by Sam Redford and, although being dived on subsequently, has been lost or all practical purposes. Hardly anybody dives on it anymore.

The Taiho Maru was a freighter. Identification is made on account of the angular stern.

The ship was a war time Standard C - freighter and used from 15 October 1943 onwards as a transport for the Navy.

Technical Data:

Tonnage	:	2.829 ts	
Length	:	93,0 m	305 ft
Width	:	13,7 m	45 ft
Depth	:	7,6 m	25 ft
Speed max	:	13,7 knots	
serv	:	10,0 knots	
Horsepower max:		1.800 hp	
Engine	:	1 x reciprocal steam engine	
Launching	:	May 1943	
In Service	:	5 July 1943	
Builder	:	Hitachi Dockyard	

TONAN MARU 3

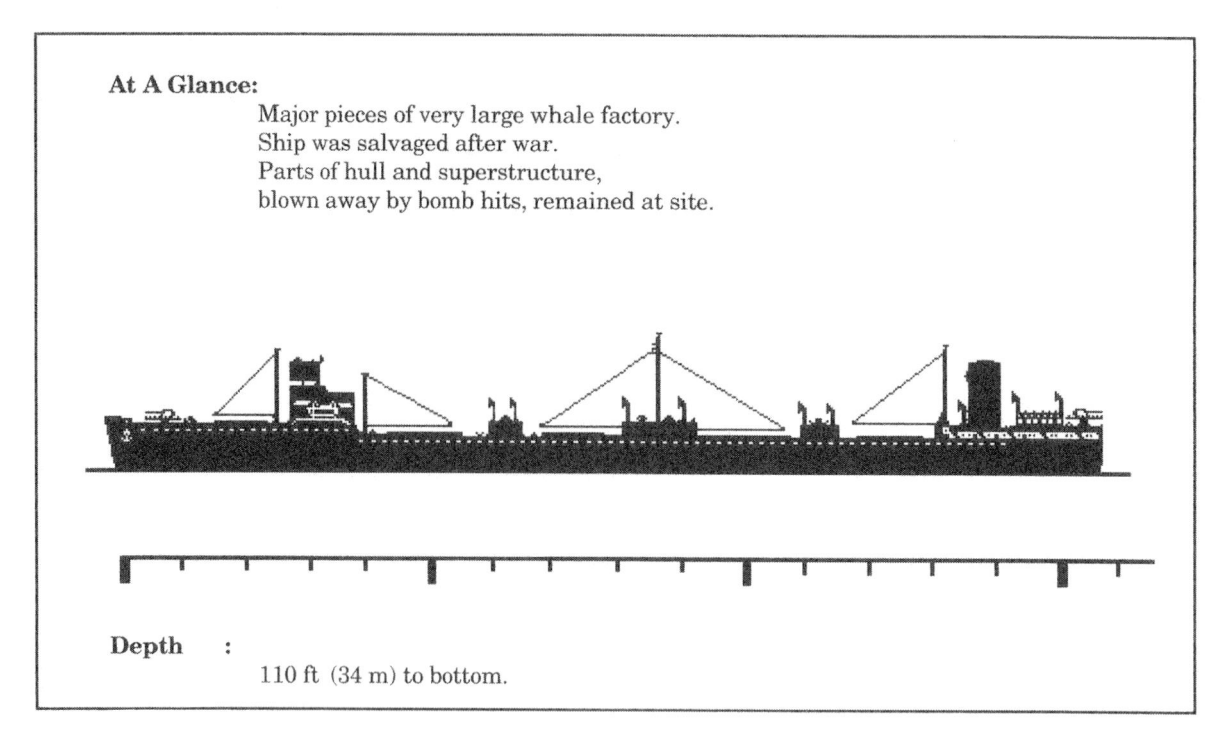

At A Glance:
Major pieces of very large whale factory.
Ship was salvaged after war.
Parts of hull and superstructure,
blown away by bomb hits, remained at site.

Depth : 110 ft (34 m) to bottom.

The Tonan Maru 3 used to be the largest wreck in Truk. Indeed, it was a very large ship for the standards of her time, and very modern. Built in 1938 as a swimming whale factory, she was used to convert whale blubber into oil, and process whale meat. For packing the meat, she carried even a can factory. Most of her inboard spaces, however, were taken up by oil tanks. She was designed to operate in the Antarctic Ocean. Even before the war erupted, from 08 November 1941 onwards, the ship was used by the Japanese Navy to supplement the precious tanker tonnage. Oilers, being of prime importance for Japan's war efforts, were preferred targets for US submarines. The Tonan Maru 3, together with her sistership Tonan Maru 2, was the largest tanker Japan had available.

It was therefore with a great deal of excitement that the skipper of the US submarine Tinosa, led by Lt. Cdr. L.R. Dan Daspit sighted the huge ship ploughing through the waters west of Truk. No escorts and anti submarine patrols were in the vicinity. The day was Thursday, 24 June 1943. After a short chase to get into a firing position, the skipper of the Tinosa fired a spread of 4 torpedoes from an acute angle astern. As the range could not be closed by the submarine, the spread of 4 torpedoes was fired from 4000 yards. Out of these, two torpedoes exploded with devastating results. The Tonan Maru veered off, and heaved almost broadside to the submarine. From this more advantageous position, two more torpedoes were quickly fired, and both exploded resoundingly. The ship belched a huge column of smoke and steam, and settling by the stern, lay dead in the water.

This was a situation almost too good to be true for the submarine skipper. He had all the time to deliver the coup de grace. Only the big guns forward and at the stern of the whaler prevented the skipper of the sub to surface and to use the deck gun. The sub closed to 875 yards directly off the ship's beam and fired a single torpedo. The sound station inside the Tinosa could follow the running torpedo. It was a perfect run, which ended in a metallic clank - but no explosion followed. Lt. Cdr. Daspit fired an eighth torpedo with exactly the same result. He dove away and had all torpedoes thoroughly checked. They seemed to be in perfect order. He maneuvered the Tinosa again directly abeam of the big ship and fired all others, except one, 7 in all. All were duds. Totally frustrated he left the scene and Tonan Maru to its fate. Upon returning to Hawaii, he reported and submitted the last torpedo as evidence. By doing so he triggered off the total rearming of all torpedo detonators with a different model.

The Tonan Maru remained afloat, and was finally towed into Truk. She was anchored at the Repair Anchorage between the islands of Dublon and Fefan. The damages sustained were so extensive, that she was still under repair, together with Hoyo Maru, Kiyozumi Maru and Kansho Maru, when Operation Hailstone began at dawn on 17 February 1944.

Very early in the morning of the first day, planes from USS Enterprise attacked a very large tanker West of Dublon on Strike 1 B, the second strike of the first day. The planes were over the target at about 0815 h. Two bomb hits destroyed port quarter. The Aircraft Action Report reads: "Two bomb hits on stern, blew sides out. Debris was flying high. Ship settled."

In common with the other empty tanker at the Repair Anchorage, Hoyo Maru, she capsized and sank. The water was partly shallow, and at low tide some of the ship's bottom could be seen. Reports from other carriers never mentioned her again.

However, the ship and its equipment was considered so valuable that the Japanese obtained special permission to salvage her after the war. On 03 March 1951 she was up-righted and refloated, with the aid of many lifting buoys. After towing her to Japan for refit, she was rebuilt and recommissioned on 08 October 1951, and renamed Tonan Maru, without the number 3. She continued her service as a whaler, and was finally scrapped in April 1971.

Not all parts of the ship were salvaged. Part of the aft structure, and the funnel, which had been blown out, was left on the site of the wreckage. They were found on 05 January 1981, at a depth of 110 ft.

A huge, broken off ventilator shaft led to the boat deck, which is about 20 m long. Railguards and portholes can be recognized. Other major pieces of wreckage are scattered in the vicinity. One of her twin funnels is draped over the remains of the superstructure. It is badly dented and bent, and broken off very near the base. It bears the owner's insignia, which were welded onto the upper part. They show a large, full circle, and a cross connects it to a wide outer rim. It is the circle-and-ring emblem of Nihon Suisan. The four spokes were reinforcements for the two circles.

Assuming that the twin funnels carried the insignia only on the outside, it was thought originally that this was the port funnel. Unfortunately, this assumption proved incorrect when more pictorial material was available. In fact, the insignia were placed on both sides of each funnel. Consequently, it can not be determined on which side of the ship the funnel was originally located. The size is roughly 6 m in height and 1,5 m to 2 m in width. A lot of steel lines, part of a kingpost, and other large pieces of debris are scattered around over a large area. Abandoned salvage gear abounds.

Technical Data:

Tonnage	:	19 209 ts	
Length	:	163,07 m	535.00 ft
Width	:	22,56 m	74.00 ft
Depth	:	17,32 m	56.8 ft
Draught	:	11,05 m	36.25 ft
Speed max.	:	14.12 knots	
serv.	:	12.00 knots	
Engine	:	2 x reciprocal steam	
Launch	:	01 May 1938	
Service	:	23 September 1938	
Builder	:	Osaka Iron Works	
Owner	:	Nihon Suisan K.K.	

Above: The whaler - canning factory Tonan Maru 3 during the war and below, salvaged, repaired and returned to service after the war, during her sea trials.

TONY, VAL AND ZERO

At A Glance ...
Pieces of wreckage of Japanese aircraft.
In very shallow water, for snorkeling.

East of Eten, on the shallow sandbar, pieces of former Japanese fighter planes can be found. The shallow bar extends quite a stretch further to the East and terminates in a reef. Although it is said that the plane parts have been dumped here after the attack, it looks more of planes which have been shot down after take-off. When the runway was cleared, the irreparable aircraft were just dumped into the water.

Most of the wreckage is so mauled that identification is difficult. The depth of the water is only between 6 and 10 feet. Therefore this site is very popular and many people spend time snorkeling between tank dives. The water is not particularly clear but because it is so shallow it does not really matter.

The first thing to see is a small object sticking out of the water. The dive boat generally anchors here. This object is a propeller, complete with spinner, attached to a radial engine. The parts are partly overgrown but the major components can clearly be identified. The Y-shaped exhaust manifolds, and the cylinders can be made out, together with push rods and other parts of the engine.

A solitary stick is standing up from the sand not far away. This is part of the landing gear. A big piece of the wing is still attached to it It lies flat upside-down on the bottom.

There are a number of smaller parts scattered in the area, for example, part of the cockpit cover, an instrument panel and a whole tail assembly. An entirely different plane rests with its propeller hub against a coral head. The propeller shaft seems to have been broken. It is attached to the engine, and the cowling is still intact. The shape of this part differs significantly from other planes. It covered an in-line engine.

In the Pacific air war, high performance fighters - and bombers - used almost exclusively radial engines. They were air cooled. However, the liquid cooled in-line engines were tried, but an entirely new plane had to be designed around it. The Japanese developed the Kawasaki Ki 61. This plane used a license-built Daimler Benz type 601 A inverted V 12 engine. The plane was an excellent performer, but the Japanese never quite came to terms with the high performance engine. Therefore, the plane was not entirely successful, as it was not considered reliable, and modifications to the engine resulted in even more frequent breakdowns. The machine guns troughs can be seen on top of the fuselage, on both sides. The high-performance German 20mm Mauser cannon, a formidable weapon, had to be substituted by a slower firing Japanese gun, because the Mauser were not available in sufficient quantities and the ammunition was scarce.

The major piece of fuselage, which can be seen close-by does not necessarily belong to the forward section described before. It has a magic attraction for divers to sit in the cockpit, and for their buddies to take pictures of them. Further on wings and parts of a fuselage are located in the water.

Quite a stretch away, in considerably deeper waters, is another plane wreck. Major parts of the fuselage, the engine, and the wings are fairly well intact. It is about 25 ft to the bottom.

The in-line engine of the Tony (Kawasaki Ki-61-I Hien) necessitated an entirely differently designed aircraft - much sleeker than those using the radial engines so common in the Pacific theater. In fact, although the Japanese maintained that they developed the Tony from scratch, it is known that the Germans provided the Japanese with blueprints for the Messerschmidt Bf 109-D. The Tony bears a strong resemblance to that plane. The engine was a licence-built Daimler-Benz DB 601A, with 12 cylinder in V arrangement. Heavy protection, excellent maneuverability and performance proved to be a formidable adversary to the Hellcats, but the lack of adequate training of the Japanese pilots and constant problems with the powerplant never led the Tony reach its potential. This airplane crashed off Eten and broke in half. The engine and the spinner with prop came to rest - quite hard as it appears - against a stony coral.

UNKAI MARU NO. 6

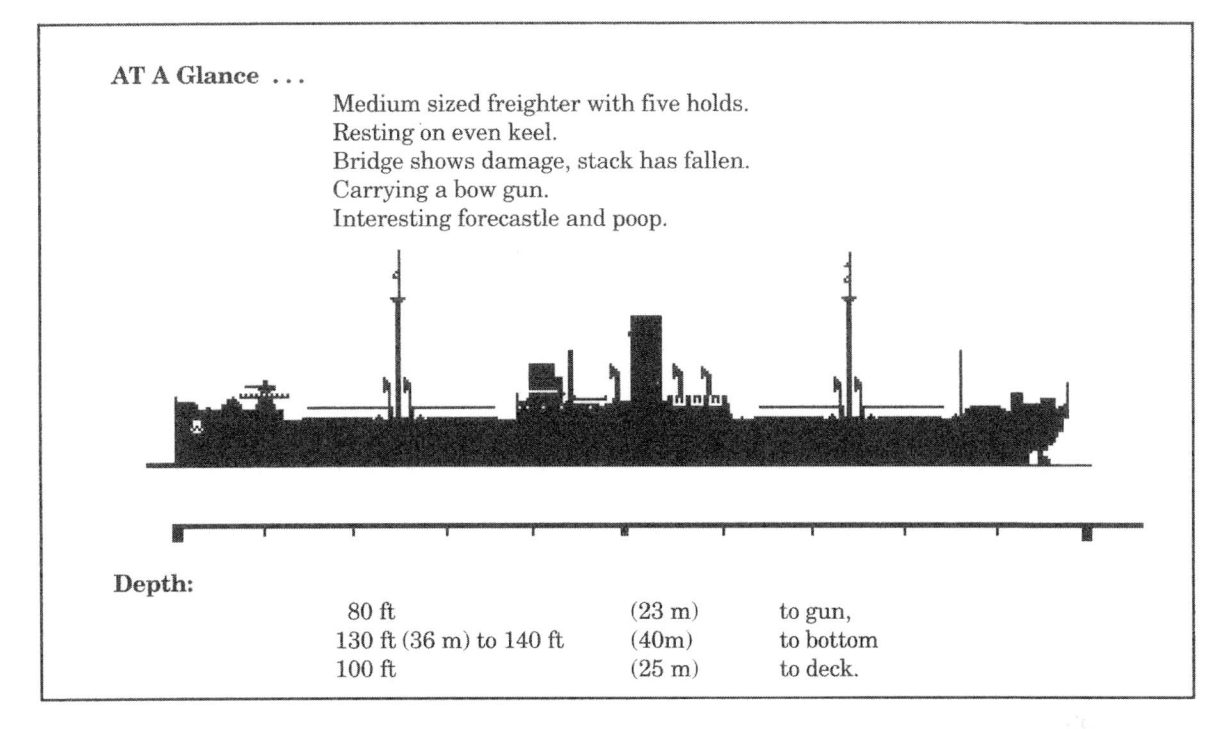

AT A Glance ...
Medium sized freighter with five holds.
Resting on even keel.
Bridge shows damage, stack has fallen.
Carrying a bow gun.
Interesting forecastle and poop.

Depth:
80 ft (23 m) to gun,
130 ft (36 m) to 140 ft (40m) to bottom
100 ft (25 m) to deck.

This wreck is an antiquated, medium sized, coal burning freighter of very old vintage. According to the Aircraft Action Report of Bunker Hill, Strike 3D, a ship was was torpedoed at about 1200 h. A single torpedo was observed to hit the ship, located northeast of Uman. The explosion was followed by a large fire, "sending black smoke up to 4 to 5000 ft". The ship was attacked again at the following strike but the torpedo missed and two bombs were close misses. One of these detonated near the bridge, and intensified the fire. Planes from Yorktown also attacked the Unkai Maru No. 6. An attack photo shows the freighter burning fiercely from either one of the forward holds or the bridge, possibly both.

There is significant coral growth on most exposed parts of the ship due to its shallow location. The description leads from the forecastle, via the bridge superstructure to the poop.

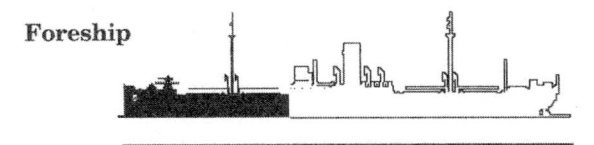

Foreship

The forecastle carries a very picturesque gun. It is probably a three inch artillery piece. There is no protective shield for the gunners. The gun itself is now overgrown and the various forms of sea life give it a fancy, colorful look, particularly if a light is trained on it. The barrel points straight forward with no elevation. The gun was not used during the attack. It is mounted on a large base with four supports.

A few cases of ready ammunition, equally luxuriously overgrown by colorful forms of marine life and showing one or two large pearl oysters, can be seen at the rear of the gun on the platform. The corals on all these structures afford shelter to numerous small blue baitfish and wrasses. They swim around, forming a halo, and with the slightest disturbance make an about-face and head back to their protective shelter.

Rail guards enclose the forecastle, and are still in place and intact. Their thin stays are partly overgrown, giving the impression they are very thick. Both anchor chains lead to the spurling pipes. Just slightly behind of where the chains run into the hawse pipes a manhole with a coaming is located amidships on this deck. The cover is off and rests toward the aft part of the coaming. It looks as if somebody has just climbed out and thrown the cover off. More likely is the explanation that the escaping air displaced it when the ship went down. A round glass insert in the middle is almost free from marine growth, but a spiderweb crack can be seen at the lower end of it.

Steel lines are located in this area as well, adding to the somewhat cluttered look of the forecastle deck. This impression is enhanced by the fact that most of the deck plating has just corroded away. The diver is now afforded a bird's eye perspective into the compartments in the forecastle. A cable drum hangs askew between two deck support beams which remained standing.

The forecastle is also accessible through the door at the aft end. Next to the door, the boatswain's locker is located. The interesting thing in this rather narrow and confined cabin is the accumulation of different running, anchor and position kerosene lights. These were spares, kept orderly on shelves, which gave way so that the lanterns crashed down on top each other. A second cable drum fell all the way from the forecastle to the maindeck, in the next compartment forward. After these small cabins, the diver can enter the spacious midship room, which is literally a treasure chest.

The deck is littered with small personal objects, like an ink pot, brass buttons, a teapot, a soldering lamp and many other things indicating the crew's preoccupation. The sediment is a few inches deep here, so that only the upper half of the smaller objects protrude above it. Frequently, the part above the sediment is overgrown, or a coat of calcareous sediment has settled on it. If the object is lifted out, the buried half comes out sparkling clean.

The two hawse pipes run from the deckhead to the outside, way forward at the bow. Turning to aft, a hatch opening can be seen, and although it is fairly dark below in the chain locker, some objects can be made out on the bottom in a few shafts of light, coming in from holes in the lower part of the bow on starboard.

The forecastle may be exited by either one of the two doors to aft or alternatively between the support beams of the deckhead which are gone now. It can be seen that the forecastle forms a recess in the middle, right aft of the gun. Resting posts for the derricks can be found at the forecastle deck. A spare anchor is bolted to the bulkhead, a second one to the deck.

The hatch cover beams are in place on hold 1. A few square bottles have been seen close to one bulkhead. Otherwise it is empty. The second hold appears to be empty as well. Fire damage is not readily apparent.

Looking at the mast closely, something very odd can be noticed immediately. There are two very heavy structures - one has a square configuration, while the other is round. In fact, the Unkai Maru is a curiosity - her masts are not round at all, but square, and built into a rather small mast house. The round object is a jumbo derrick, lashed securely to the mast, of which the mast top is gone; it toppled down. Heavy steel wires can be seen on both sides of the mast. The mast was supported by heavy shrouds and stays, the standing rigging of the ship. It is probable that the masts were raked and the rigging was quite elaboarate, as was common for ships built around the turn of the century. The four winches are grouped around the mast.

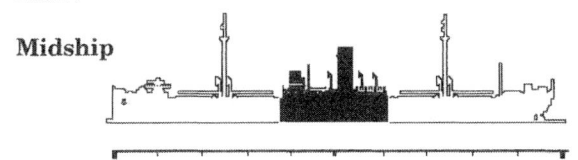

Midship

Another interesting feature is the construction of the superstructure. Amidships, the hull rises one deck and forms a distinct island. The superstructure is erected 3 feet behind the forward bulkhead, thus creating a passageway athwart. Railguards were built on its forward edge for safety. Today, the railing has partially collapsed and is draped over the hatch. The second deck shows two rectangular doorways, slightly inboard of two ladders ascending to them. They are decorated with an abundant amount of green, calcareous algae.

Above the boat deck, the bridge used to be located. It must have been of wooden construction with steel supports, as only these supports are now visible. The boat deck forward is buckled. The steel framework of the bridge is twisted and has sagged forward on port. Damages to light steel structures are clear evidence of great heat, which softened the steel, causing it to sag under its own weight. The cargo in the forward holds burned and lighter structures were destroyed. There is no evidence of violent damage.

Entering the doorway on shelter deck level through doors which are securely battened down in the open position to the bulkhead, the inside of the superstructure appears to be dark on first sight. Soon however, when the eyes adapt to the dark, the outline of the inside gains form and structure.

When going aft inside the superstructure, one passes first through a passageway with cabins arranged to the outside. Then it becomes very light and a large opening, a shaft like structure, comes into view. This is the midships hold, which allows much light to enter. Looking around, the barrenness of the ship is harrowing. There is not a single artifact to be seen, not anything to betray human occupation, just steel bulkheads, a few portholes and the two companionways, their stairs completely obliterated together with the large coamings of the hold. An eerie combination of light shafts and darkness, the depressing mood of a ghost town and an oppressive silence is accentuated by the exhalation sound of the diver. No other wreck conveys these impressions like the high and stark rooms inside the Unkai's superstructure. The area is completely burned out, only the bulkheads remain.

The midships hold is empty. At maindeck, the coaming seems to have come undone and dangles free. It is no problem to ascend up one deck, through the hold, to arrive at the boat deck. The ship's bell can be found here. It was probably located in the wooden bridge house originally. It is so overgrown, that its inscription could not be made out. A pair of boats davits are located between bridge and funnel, and a kingpost was built on boat deck forward of the hold where the superstructure drops to shelter deck level.

A large, perfectly round hollow cylinder, perhaps about four feet in diameter, rests on port boat deck. It is quite long. This is the stack, which yielded at a welding line, parted from its base and tumbled down. It is not otherwise dented or mutilated and the break is fairly clean. Inasmuch as it invites the diver to swim through it, this is made impossible by the inside supports. The open circular shape confirms that the ship burned coal originally. The stack is held inboard by the davits, which prevent it from rolling off. The ventilators in front of the fallen stack remained standing and the superstructure raises to boat deck level.

The skylights of the engine room are open. It is no problem to take a close look at the main propulsion unit, a steam engine. Beams run inside the room and carry block and tackle. An auxiliary machine, apparently a small sized steam engine with hand valves, enclosed in protective rails, can be made out. An electric motor is located close to it, coupled to other pieces of machinery, possible two pumps.

Hailstorm - *The Wrecks*

Aftship

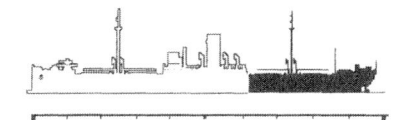

A ladder can be found aft of the superstructure. Hold 4 follows, and appears to be empty. A derrick has fallen on the winch. On deck, off hold 4 on port, an accumulation of steel lines, probably stemming from the cargo handling gear, can be seen. The next cargo area, hold 5, appears to be empty, as well. A long, half cylindrical object on the bottom of the ship leads from the ship's superstructure, via holds 4 and 5 amidships to the stern. This is the tunnel for the propeller shaft. In it the big shaft turned and transmitted the power from the steam engine to the propeller. It is large enough to allow a man - albeit small - to enter and service the bearings inside.

The aft mast is also square in shape, but the jumbo derrick is missing, if it ever was fitted. The steel lines of the mast rigging can be inspected, they remained intact here. This mast top is gone also. A large sized running light crashed from the height of the aft mast onto the deck, close to the hatch coaming, on port of hold 5. At the aft end of the hold, the poop rises on deck. A sampson post is built at its forward edge.

The poop is dominated by a very old fashioned rudder mechanism. While in later years the steering machine had been built inside the ship, it was exposed on the poop of the Unkai Maru. Two large and massive circle segments are located on top of the poop deck. The centerpoint of the quadrants is the ruddershaft. A big chain leads to the rudder drive. This design went out of fashion about 1910 to 1920. It is another proof for the age of this wreck. In fact, it seems to be the oldest ship sunk in Truk during the raid. It is amazing to find yet another hold in the poop, which is empty as well. It is, of course, considerable smaller than the two forward. No major damage has been observed on the hull itself. When swimming alongside the hull the many whip coral growing on the sides of the hull are impressive.

The Unkai Maru 6 was built in England by the W. Grey Shipyard, and launched as S/S Venus, in 1905. The ship was sold 1911 to Japan for 32,500 Pound Sterling, and used from there on by the Japanese Navy as general cargo freighter.

The Unkai Maru 6, also known in Truk as X 13 was found on 4 July 1980, by the author. The circumstances of her finding were unusual. Whereas normally we would cruise and criss-cross the lagoon systematically in search for wrecks, I memorized the position of the blazing wreck from one of the attack photos, taking the Gosei Maru as reference, which also showed in the picture. We briefly anchored at the Gosei Maru, and I took aim at the landmarks at Dublon and Fefan. Then the boathandler was asked to go to a specific direction which I indicated by pointing my hand. When we had gone a certain distance, I dropped a buoy. Around this buoy we run search circles with the depthfinder and within 10 minutes I had found a new wreck, the Unkai Maru 6. The identity of the ship was first assumed, but confirmed when we found the large ship's bell..

Technical Data:

Tonnage	:	3,188 t gross	
Length	:	92.96 m	305 ft
Breadth	:	13.37 m	44 ft
Depth	:	8.3 m	27 ft
Speed max	:	12 knots	
serv	:	10 knots	
Engine	:	1 reciprocal steam engine - coal	
Builder	:	W. Grey Dockyard	
Owner	:	Nakamura Kisen/ Imperial Japanese Navy.	

Hailstorm - *The Wrecks*

OJIMA, LANDING CRAFT AND OTHER WRECKAGE

X 8 A,B,C	Ojima, foreship
X 12	(possibly larger vessel or a few smaller ones)
X 15	(landing craft)

At A Glance ...
Several large pieces of wreckage, and a complete landing craft.
On and around an underwater mountain.
About 1/2 mile North-east of Kikukawa Maru.

Depth:

80 ft	(24 m)	to Ojima
130 ft	(40 m)	to landing craft

When fire broke out on the ammunitions carrier Kikukawa Maru several vessels were despatched to fight the blaze. The Ojima was a salvage and repair ship of 750 tons, equipped with powerful pumps and heavy lifting gear. Evidently, she was anchored close to the burning freighter, together with 3 landing crafts, which had pumps mounted on their flat decks, and a small tug boat. The fire fighting was to no avail. In the late afternoon of 07 October 1943 the ammunition in the aft holds of the Kikukawa Maru blew up with tremendous force. It completely obliterated the mid and aft section of this freighter, shattered the Ojima and all other vessels, and none of the crew survived the blast.

The first piece of wreckage to be seen on descent is the foreship of the Ojima, resting a few hundred feet northeast of the remnants of the Kikukawa Maru. The bow is pointing East. The starboard anchor is out, the port anchor remained in the retracted position. The wreck lies on starboard beam.

The stem is raked. There is a single hold forward and aft of the mast. Aft of the second hold, the bulwark ascends one deck. It resembles Hino Maru 2 regarding its basic design. The hull and everything from the hold aft is very badly destroyed and the hull has broken off at about bridge level.

This part of the hull lies on top of an underwater mountain at about 120 ft depth.

Farther southeast, by about 200 ft, the rest of the ship lies in waters of 140 ft to 150 ft (43 m to 46 m) depth. This wreckage consists of part of the midship superstructure and the stern. The sea floor is sloping considerably and drops fairly steeply to about 200 ft and deeper (61 m). The aft ship lies on this incline.

Almost halfway between bow and stern section, a little to the North, rests a smaller piece of this ship and a few remnants, like ventilator cowls, derricks and steel plating can be seen scattered around.

On a day with good underwater visibility a shadow can be made out to the north of the halfway mark, between the two major parts of the ship. It is a landing craft, resting in 130 ft of water on the top of the underwater plateau which gently dips to the northwest. This 60 ft Daihatsu landing craft appears undamaged; at least there is no visible damage to the hull.

The craft faces roughly in a southerly direction. It rests perfectly straight on the bottom and appears to be in mint condition, with very little disfiguring growth on it. The bow ramp is up. There is no stack and the small aft bridge appears to be bent over to one side.

In the same general location lies the midship section of a medium sized freighter, which does not appear to be part of the wreckage described before. It is a midship section with some railing identifiable, including portholes, ventilator stumps, engine room skylights etc. Not far, in the visibility range, is yet another piece of wreckage, which is so torn up that it could not be identified. Its size was about that of a one-family-house. Smaller fragments have been found around it, but not identified.

Finally, some distance away, there seems to be a large piece of a ship as yet unidentified. From the records it cannot be excluded that these are the remains of the Kikukawa Maru.

Various passes have been made over the general area in June and December 1980. At that time, and in January 1981, several exploratory descents were made as well.

Technical Data:
Ojima, salvage and repair vessel.

Displacement	:	750 tons
Machinery	:	2 shaft reciproc. steam engines
Built	:	1940
Builder	:	Maizuru Navy Yard
Owner	:	Imperial Japanese Navy

YAMAGIRI MARU

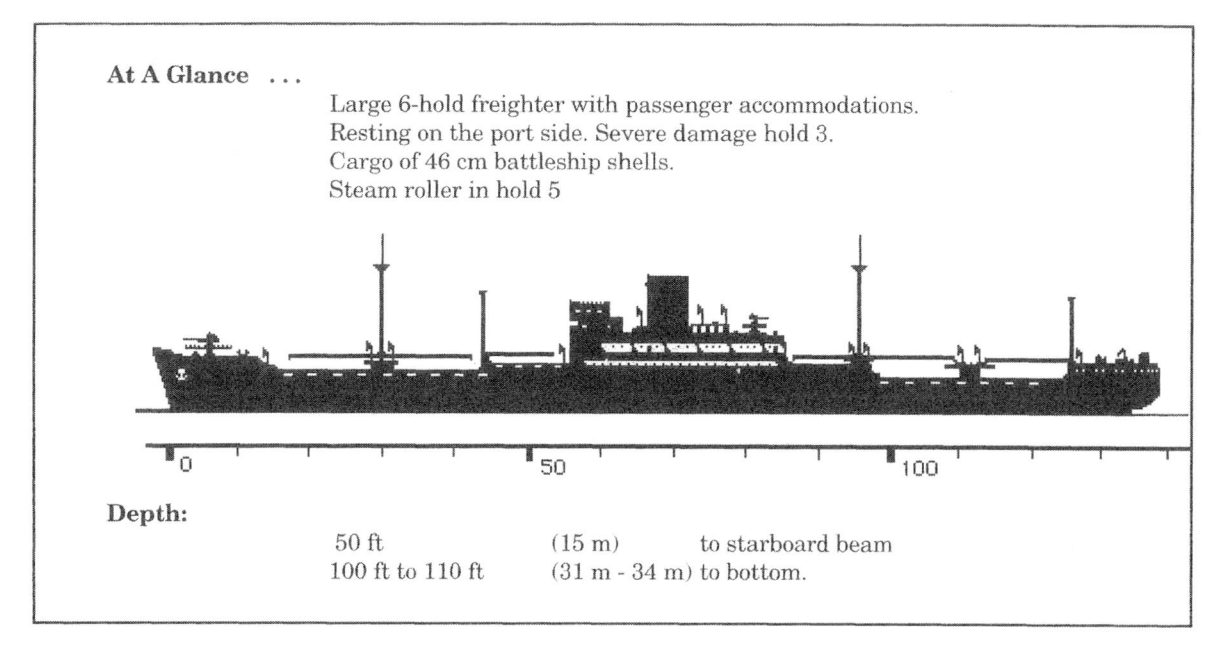

At A Glance ...
Large 6-hold freighter with passenger accommodations.
Resting on the port side. Severe damage hold 3.
Cargo of 46 cm battleship shells.
Steam roller in hold 5

Depth:
50 ft   (15 m)   to starboard beam
100 ft to 110 ft   (31 m - 34 m) to bottom.

The greatest attraction of this armed freighter is its cargo of giant artillery shells destined for the 46 cm (18.1 inch) guns of the battleships Yamato and Musashi. Both ships, being part of the Combined Fleet, repeatedly anchored at Truk before the carrier attack. The 9-46 cm guns of these ships, mounted in triple turrets, were the largest artillery ever put on board on any ship. For example, the caliber of the biggest American guns was 40.6 cm (16 inches), the English and Germans used 15 inch (38 cm) guns as main artillery of their battleships. Indeed, the Japanese arms - the battleships and the guns - were the last and the biggest of their kind and proved to be obsolete at the time they began their operational carrier. They were never used in a major surface battle.

The Yamagiri Maru was severely damaged in a night torpedo attack, on 28 August 1943, by the US submarine Drum. The sub fired a spred of four torpedoes, of which two hit. The ship was on a voyage between the Salomons and the Carolines. The damages on the ship were in the same area of the ship where she received the fatal blow. The attentive diver will see a large reinforcement in form of a bulge on port, extending from hold 2 to aft at the midship superstructure. In addition, three more heavy reinforcements are located on the freeboard at the forward part of the midship superstructure. Finally, there are three heavy metal beams welded onto the hull at hold 2. These reinforcements were placed there to increase the stability of the hull, after its integrity was shattered by the torpedo explosions. Similar repairwork can be found on the Fujikawa Maru in Truk and the Gozan Maru in Palau.

The Yamagiri Maru is a large ship. Its main attraction is the cargo in hold 5, the engine room, and the spacious bridge and superstructure.

The description of the Yamagiri Maru leads from the bow to the stern.

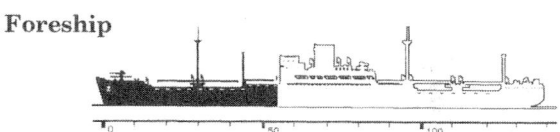

Foreship

The starboard anchor is out, while the one on port is retracted at the bow. The anchor chain is heavily overgrown up to a few feet above the ground. It leads away from the ship, indicative of a slow sinking. The anchor itself can be found about 150 ft forward on the bottom.

A gun is mounted on a platform on the forecastle. It is of smaller calibre compared to the guns of the Fujikawa, and points straights ahead. Evidently, it was not used against the attacking aircraft.

The forecastle is followed by a hold, which is empty, except for a few very large steel beams or girders. The mast and a winch house are located aft of the hold. Shafts of ventilators can be found here, as well as, cargo winches.

Hold 2 is also empty. It shows some strange damage. There is a hole in the double bottom of the ship, but the hole on the outer shell plating is offset against the inner bottom plates. Inside the hold is a very large piece of sheet steel which is twisted considerably. It is not quite clear where this large plate came from or what purpose it served.

The deck raises, and apparently there used to be deck cabins for third class passengers built all the way here to the end of hold four, aft of the superstructure. A kingpost follows hold 2, aft of which hold 3 is located. As with the previous two holds forward, the third is also empty. It presents a very confusing picture, however, as most of the bottom and starboard plates are blown inward and the hull shows a gigantic hole. To describe it as barn door - sized would be an understatement. All steel frames and beams in the damaged area are twisted and torn. This damage is

Hailstorm - *The Wrecks*

evidence of the devastating explosive force of a heavy bomb. One hit had been enough to spell the death warrant for the ship.

Yamagiri Maru

The engine room can be entered aft of the superstructure or through the open skylights. The entrance is located at the aft end of the boat deck. A light is necessary to see the row of 2 times 3 cylinders. The fuel pipe and the injection pump, positioned nearby, appear to be on the bottom of the ship, and can be easily identified, as well as, the ring of fist sized bolts with which the cylinder heads are tied down.

Aft on the superstructure is a toilet. The urinal has broken off from the wall and lies face down in the silt.

Midship

Aftship

The superstructure is quite large and contained accommodations for passengers. The bridge is four decks elevated over the third hold. There is evidence of a small flying bridge on top. Aft of the bridge a deck house is located.

From hold 3, the dive can be continued through the superstructure and the bridge decks. It is sometimes necessary to bend around a few support beams, but yet, it is not really tight. Portholes can be seen in the forward facing bulkheads at different deck levels. Just a little light manages to shine in, past the marine growth which has settled on the glass. After weaving in and out of the different decks, anyone of the many exits somewhere on the bridge may be taken. The bridge remained well intact. As all wooden deck planking has gone, this area conveys the impression of generous spaciousness. An engine telegraph is located on the navigation deck.

The funnel is typical of a diesel driven motor vessel. A large letter "Y" inside a circle is welded on the plates of the stack on both sides. The ship was owned by the Yamashita-Line, and these insignia are their markings. The rain deflection plates can be seen inside the funnel.

There are a pair of ventilators abaft of the funnel, and probably two pair of boats davits on both sides. They point outward, suggesting that the crew had time to lower the lifeboats, saving themselves from the slowly sinking and probably burning ship. As boat deck is reached, the next lower deck forms a small promenade athwart.

Armor-piercing 46 cm shell, destined for Musashi.

Hold 4 is, in shape and position, smaller than the others and elevated, being a mirror image of the hold 3. However, it is covered at main deck, and access is only possible through two man holes. It could be that it was refrigerated, and appears to be empty. A mast, a double combination of ventilators and deck winches follow aft. The deck then drops back to shelter deck level and is followed by the regularly sized hold 5.

The large shells for the Japanese super battleships Yamato and Musashi are located in this hold. The shells are about one meter (three feet) long and weigh 1460 kg (3219 lbs) a piece. These projectiles were hurled out of the gun at 780 m/se, equivalent to

2559 ft/sec, and the guns had a maximum reach of 42 km (46000 yds). These shells were armor piercing and were shipped without detonators, as the kind of detonator to be used in the battle was determined ad hoc by the gunnery officer. The hole on the tip of the shell is the place were it would be fitted. Copper or brass rings indicate where the shells embedded themselves into the rifle of the gun barrel. The rings can be wiped clean of sediment, no marine growth has settled on them, and they are very well preserved.

Some shells are lying on the bottom, inside the hold, at a depth of 97 ft, but there are also more than 20 located on a shelf far inside the hold. This shelf is actually the propeller shaft tunnel. Here, they are orderly placed as they have been packaged in boxes, of which a few are still in evidence. There were four shells to a strong metal box. Interestingly enough, these boxes appear to have been put in a narrow gauge railroad car, similar to those which are used for mining. Possibly, this is how the shells were transported and handled. A number of spade blades are visible close to a set of shells. They are stacked, used to be laid down, but rest upright now because of the position of the ship on the bottom. The blades do not have handles attached to them.

A steamroller can be found a little forward of the shells in the same hold. The front roller can be made out clearly, and identified readily, whereas the back part of the machine is broken up. As a matter of fact, there are a number of very heavy duty pieces of machinery, resembling heavy road building equipment, located in this hold. Even a small, 2 ft diameter propeller can be seen among all this material. A further suprise are boilers loaded in this hold. A number of hatch cover beams came to rest on the sea floor.

A small deck house with ventilator shafts separate this hold from hold 6. The original cargo of drums tumbled out of it. They are now all scattered on the bottom. Two ventilators can also be found on the sea bed. They have broken off from the poop.

The poop is one deck high. It was enclosed by a guard rail. The majority of the stanchions remain in place. Several winches are mounted on the deck. Coils of line can be seen inside the poop in the beam of the underwater light. At the far end, a single blade of a propeller is tied to the bulkhead. This obviously is a spare part for another ship because the Yamagiri Maru does not have a propeller with detachable blades. Besides, the shape of the blade is different than those on the propeller of the ship. It is probable that the blade was destined for a major warship. The silt is so deep here that the lower part of the blade is buried. At another part of the poop a lot of electrical equipment can be seen. Copper coils of a large sized transformer, big resistors, and other copper wound reels can be recognized.

It is a little unusual to see that the aft kingpost is right in front of the poop. On most of the ships in Truk it is located forward of the main mast.

The single propeller forms an almost perfect "X", when viewed against the straight rudder.

When the Yamagiri Maru sank is a matter of conjecture, as the ship was attacked repeatedly. Pilots from Bunker Hill scored a hit and a near miss about at 0800 h, on the second day. The ship was described to be of about 13.000 ts, and located west of Fefan. The exaggerated size is consistent with overestimations of other ships. The hit caused an explosion and a fire, but as this strike was the last of the second day, the planes departed without actually witnessing the sinking. There is no doubt that the ship mentioned was the Yamagiri, because there was no other freighter of large size located in this area.

Pilots from Yorktown reported to have placed a bomb each on the bow and the stern at about 1300 h of the first day, Strike 1 E. At the same time planes from the Enterprise attacked and reported 2 bombs to explode at starboard stern and aft of midships. No clear evidence of damage to the hull can be detected, although it was reported that the ship listed.

The Yamagiri Maru was a freighter with passenger accommodations. She was taken over by the Imperial Japanese Navy on 15 September 1941 for special cargo transport.

Technical Data:

Tonnage	:	6.439 ts	
Length	:	133 m	436.4 ft
Width	:	17,76m	58.3 ft
Depth	:	9,75m	32 ft
Draught	:	7,84m	25.7 ft
Speed max	:	17,0 knots	
serv	:	15,0 knots	
Horsepower max:		4 976 hp	
Engine	:	1 x MAN Diesel	
Launch	:	03 May 1939	
Service	:	30 June 1939	
Builder	:	Mitsubishi Heavy Industries	
Owner	:	Yamashita Kisen.	

Hailstorm - *The Wrecks*

YUBAE MARU

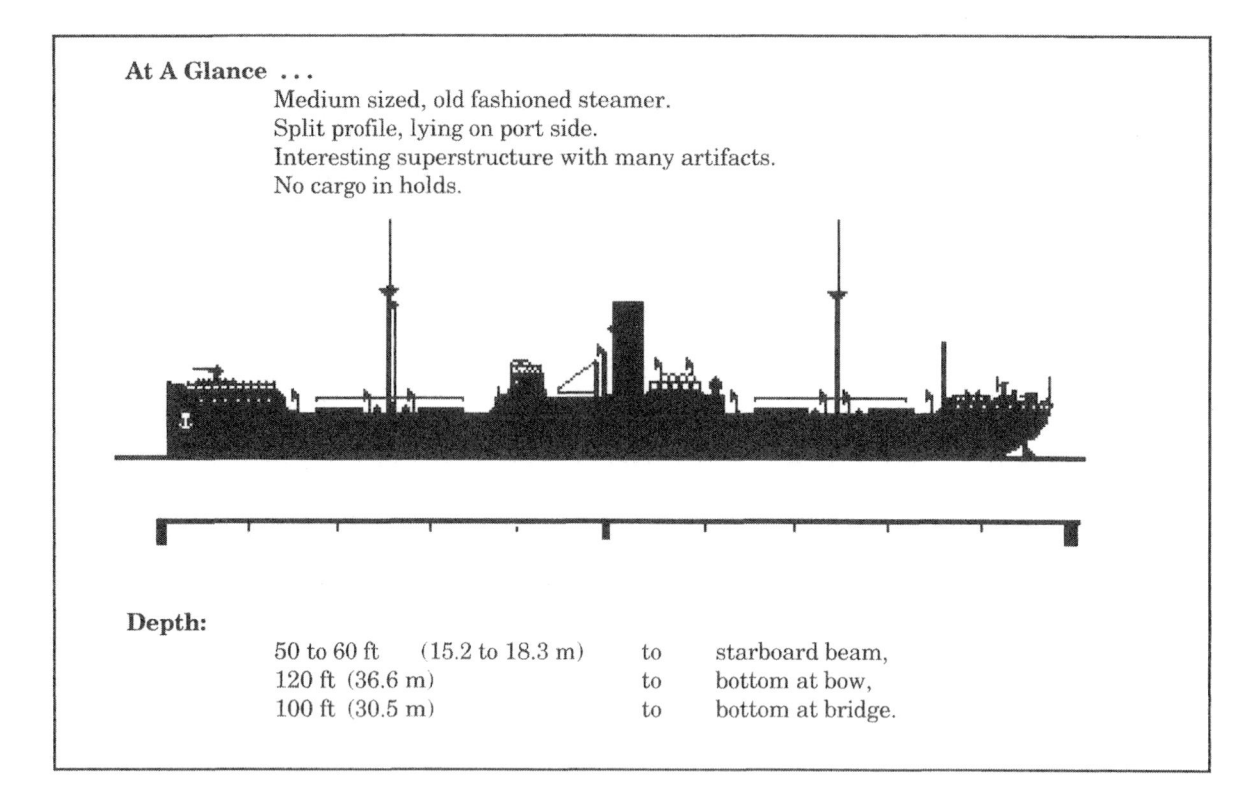

At A Glance ...
Medium sized, old fashioned steamer.
Split profile, lying on port side.
Interesting superstructure with many artifacts.
No cargo in holds.

Depth:
50 to 60 ft (15.2 to 18.3 m)	to	starboard beam,
120 ft (36.6 m)	to	bottom at bow,
100 ft (30.5 m)	to	bottom at bridge.

From available pictures, the Yubae Maru was expected to be an old fashioned, coal burning steamer, with a narrow funnel, and high pole masts, a split profile, and generally of old design. This appearance was assumed to be very similar to the Nagano Maru, and it proved to be correct. Even closer is the resemblance to the Unkai Maru No. 6. All these ships were similar in size and of roughly the same vintage. Before the age of specialization there appeared to be far less variations in the basic ship design.

The Yubae Maru is very well preserved. There is very little disfiguring growth on it, and only little damage is apparent on the hull. The sea bed undulates and forms shallow hills and valleys near the wreck. Due to its sheltered location near Uman it can be dived on even during stormy days.

The description leads from the bow to the stern.

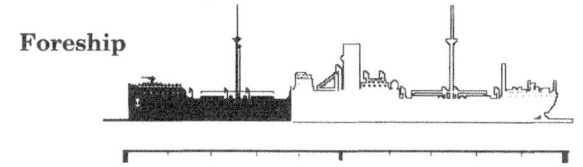

Foreship

The ship lies on her port beam. The bow is perfectly straight, only at the ship's bottom, at the keel, it curves slightly back. The massive stem bar can be well recognized. This shape of a bow is called a plump bow. The water is 120 ft deep here.

The forecastle is high. It is enclosed by rail guards. Some stays have fallen off, but the stanchions are all in place. Many of them are overgrown by oysters, corals and sponges. A very large windlass dominates the deck. The winch itself is located in the middle, and the two take-up drums can be seen on both sides. The anchor chains are blocked with bow stoppers (the maritime term for a choke) just before they disappear into the hawse pipe.

A couple of ventilators are built on the forecastle deck. Behind the windlass is an empty space. Here a gun platform and a gun were located, but both tumbled down. The platform now lies on the bottom among a lot of debris, very close to the hull. Heavy steel beams were used for its construction. The gun itself appears to be buried in the sand, but close inspection reveals the gun mount, the breach and the aiming devices. Both are partly overgrown by marine organisms. The gun shield is half exposed, as well as, part of the gun barrel. A few shells, roughly 18 inches (45 cm) long, can be seen very close-by.

The starboard anchor is out. There is no heaping accumulation of the chain underneath the bow. Its absence indicates that the ship turned over and sank slowly. The chain disappears in the sand, emerges several feet off the bow and runs straight to the southeast. The port chain dangles down from the hawsepipe, but there is no anchor attached. Indeed, a large, stockless anchor lies on the bottom, not very far away from the bow. It is located very close to the hull, a little aft of the forecastle, near a mooring bit.

The anchor ring does not carry either shackle or chain. The shank may be about 5 feet long, and the large anchor head with its flukes is heavy and massive. This type is mainly used as ships' main anchors, as the stockless shank can slip easily into the hawsepipe. It is certain that this is the missing port anchor. Evidently, the shackle just broke when the Yubae Maru was

Hailstorm - *The Wrecks*

rocked by the bomb explosion, sometime before she sank and touched the bottom. This would explain the present location of the anchor.

The forecastle extends by about 10 ft (3 m) on both sides, is recessed amidships, and forms a slight horseshoe shape. There is a doorway located on the side facing inboard, on both sides of the extension. The forecastle can be accessed though them. These doors swing outward and the one on port, closer to the bottom, is now secured to the fastener overhead.

It is a question how secure this particular fastener remains after 40 years immersion in salt water, and whether the door will not crash down one day just when one has entered the dark cabin behind. If it is desired to enter the forecastle, it is advised to take the door on port. It is necessary to ascend to the starboard, the upper side. Here the door is opened but fastened below, so there is no risk.

The forecastle is very spacious, and appears to be a single room. Up forward, where the space becomes narrow because of the tapering bow, a pair of hawsepipes can be seen. Frequently, a number of unusual large soldier fish, about two feet long, have selected this place as their day lair, and get irritable and confused by the beam of the underwater light. Some debris can be seen on the bottom. Outside, a shoe sole and other unidentifiable pieces are lying on the forecastle extension. The chain locker is located between the forecastle and hold 1. A large heap of chain can be seen in it.

The first hold is empty, except for a few sections of wood and several segments of bamboo. The sediment in the single tween deck is several feet high, and probably stems from old dunnage material. No regular cargo remains here. On the bottom of the hold the construction of the ship's double bottom can be inspected, and the reinforcing rips be seen. The hold conveys the impression of a huge, cavernous space. The bulkhead dividing the two forward holds has rusted through in many places.

The ship does not have a mast house. The winches are mounted on deck at both sides of the mast. The mast is supported with a double combination ventilator/derrick posts, which are two sturdy, about 6 feet high posts, set about three feet from each side of the mast, and joined with a cross tie on top.

Just above the vertical cross bar the mast bent about 45 degrees to port, and now the cross tree touches the bottom. The very tall top mast has broken off. A jumbo derrick is still attached to the lower part of the mast. Its lower part is secured to the deck with a heavy universal join, called a goose-neck. The boom was able to accommodate the bent at its heavy joint.

The second hold appears to be empty, as well, but a few pieces of large, cut timber can be seen on the bottom. It is possible to swim through the tween deck, underneath the bridge, into the third, small midships hold, which has two tween decks. It is also empty.

Midship

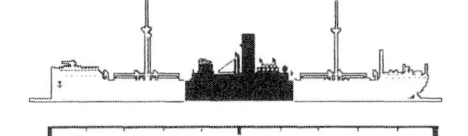

The bridge is two decks high. The first bridge deck has six portholes facing forward. Two are mounted on the far side, and a group of four are located in the middle. The next deck up shows a passageway running athwart. Above it was a flying bridge of wooden construction. It is gone now, with only the steel supports showing. The recessed steel core remains amidships, and it looks like a deck house. Actually, it was the center of the bridge. Passageways lead aft, on both sides and levels. The port passageways are, of course flush with the bottom now. In this area a lot of interesting pieces tumbled down from the bridge.

There are, most conspicuous, a lot of plates, rice bowls, cups, saucers and other pieces of china. Some of them are unmarked, but most bowls show a simple blue leaf design without further markings. Interestingly, a few plates carry the inscription "The Sarawak SS Co Ltd., Kuching, Sarawak", on the face, and "Apsley Pellatte Co. Ltd., 10, Northumberland Ave, Charing Cross, W.C." on the back.

How did get fine plates, made in London, owned by an English ship company, to Truk? Sarawak is the name of the former colony British Borneo, and today is a state within the Federated States of Malaysia. It is one of the two Malaysian states on the isle of Borneo; its capital is Kuching.

The Sarawak Steamship Co. is a subsidiary of the Straits Steamship Co., Singapore. It exists to this very day and is based in Kuching. The Sarawak Steamship Co. then owned a few small ships, mainly coasters, under 1000 ts gross, and Vyner Brooke, of 1600 ts. With these ships they serviced the ports of Sabah, Sarawak, Malaya and Singapore.

None of these vessels conform to the description of this wreck, and their dates and places of sinking does not bring them into any connection with Truk. The oil fields of Borneo, at Miri (Sarawak) and Seria (Sultanate Brunei), as well as the refinery at Lutong were of great strategic importance to the Japanese. Against little resistance, they were taken by a Japanese assault beginning on 16 December 1941, even before the fall of Singapore in February 1942. At this time they captured all vessels of the Sarawak Steamship Co. It is very probable that the crew of the Yubae Maru, possibly involved in transporting Army material, and thus being present in that part, helped themselves to some nice china from those ships by the "fast procurement plan".

Many of the individual plates have firmly fused, and can't be separated without breaking them. They are a bit fragile. Thin brown spider web crack lines appear on the glazed finish, suggesting very careful handling to prevent breakage.

There are many other items buried in the debris on the bottom of the passageways, including part of the nautical equipment carried on the bridge. For instance, there is the base of the compass, lying on the bottom, covered with brown encrusting sponges, with four bolts sticking up. The upper part of a voice tube can be seen on the deck. It looks like an old fashioned hearing aid. The very old and heavy engine telegraph and the binnacle can be seen in the sand.

On the lower, port passageway a few curious

Hailstorm - *The Wrecks*

items came to rest and are worth mentioning. There is a white, almost opaque, pear shaped light cover and a 4 inch shell casing. The projectile had fallen off some time earlier, but the powder was still inside the casing, which is a very rare occurrence. The gunpowder was not a powder at all, but literally hundreds of very thin, half inch wide and almost 12 inches long stripes jammed tightly inside the shell casing. While inadvertently tilting it many of them fell out, but a lot remained inside.

The starboard passageways are much more overgrown with sessile marine life. They present a very colorful picture. Large oysters, as well as, many forms of hard and soft corals, have attached themselves to stays and posts. Even a number of green penny algae can be seen, and carpet exposed parts of the hull.

Aft of the midships hold a low deck house has been build on the boat deck. The shafts of a pair of ventilators are the only things standing on it. Their cowls have toppled to the bottom. The ventilator shafts are flanked by a pair of kingposts. The funnel used to be located right abaft this quadruple combination, but it has broken off about one foot above the deck.

The break is fairly clean, except for a few jagged edges where reinforcements were positioned. The stack was rather narrow and very tall. It lies on the bottom, very much crumbled, twisted and corroded. Forward of the base of the funnel a ventilator grill, and aft of it the skylights are located. They are partly open and allow easy access. A more convenient way to enter the engine room is to enter hold 4 and swim forward.

The boiler room, when approached in this way, will be immediately recognized. A huge cylindrical steam boiler of at least 12 ft (3.5m) diameter is located in the center. The fire door and some instruments can be seen. The smoke ducts lead away from the sides to join in the middle and enter the root of the funnel. A few breaks on the side of the funnel and the open engine room skylights allow a little light to come in.

There is a confusing array of steam pipes and valves, and at the very right of the diver, towards the ship's bottom, 3 different sized cylinders are recognizable: The heart of the ship's steam engine. There are many gratings, ladders and companionways which allowed easy access for the crew to the various levels of the engine room. One particularly large hand wheel for a valve is located on the bottom of the ship.

Back at the boat deck, the life boat's davits have been mounted onto the outside of the hull. Those on starboard point inward. The deck was covered with wood, which has completely rotted away, except a few small pieces on the edges. Therefore, the cabins below the boat deck can be examined without the need to squeeze through the fairly narrow passageways.

There is the tiled bathroom, and a head, located a little further aft, where the crew quarters used to be. The ship's antenna lies across this part of the deck. If the passageways are entered, it will be observed that not only are they narrow, but also partly obscured by marine growth and hanging electrical cables. Nevertheless, swimming through them is possible, and the adjoining staterooms may be examined at leisure.

An interesting sight is the complete life boat which rests on even keel, just a few feet away from the port davits. It was of steel construction, and sank with the ship. The benches can be recognized as they run athwart the boat. The hull shows severe signs of corrosion. It is rusted through in many places.

A passageway runs athwart at the aft edge of the midship superstructure. It is enclosed with rail guards.

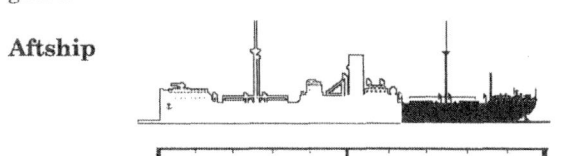

Aftship

Hold 4 is empty, except for some dunnage material. The steel beam supporting the deck against the massive shaft tunnel is bent out of alignment. The ship has twisted a noticeable amount over to port. Further evidence is gained by looking at the steel braces between main and tween deck at the forward and aft end of hold 4.

The damage leading to the sinking of the ship is on port quarter, near the aft edge of the hold. It is conceivable that the impact and explosion deformed the ship towards starboard at the stern. As the ship is of an essentially rigid construction, it accommodated the torque of this one-sided impact by twisting the upperworks in a lever action slightly to the other side and forward. The aft mast is bent to port at the deck, and its two flanking supports follow the kink. The aft hold (No. 5) is empty but shows bent and destroyed shell plates.

Close examination of the damage reveals that the deck plates on starboard, the up side, have been blown upward. They have detached from their supports, which are deformed in a Z-shape. The hull shows a outward bulge. All this is evidence of an explosion originating from the port side of the ship. Also, an inspection of the bulkhead dividing holds 4 and 5 shows that it has been blown out to forward.

Curiously, there is very little damage apparent on first sight, on port where it is supposed to be. The deck plating is blown away here as well over a stretch of more than 30 ft, and the heavy hatch coaming is bent inward. From the inside very little further damage can be seen. The tapering reinforcements of the stern seem to be all in place and undisturbed. The ship, however, lies on it damages, and debris and sand has settled on it, effectively camouflaging it.

The poop raises one deck. On its forward edge a large steam engine used to move the heavy chain, which continued in guides to both sides of the poop, turns and runs towards aft to a huge forged circle segment, and around its radius. The center of this circle section is the rudder stock. Movement of the chain thus pulled the rudder in the desired direction.

Normally, the steam engine was doing this while the ship was underway, but the rudder could also be manually operated. A pair of very large wheels of about 5 feet (1.5 m) were mounted onto a tall helm just forward of the rudder stock. From the position of the two brass rings, which are the only remains of the ship's wheels, and which are now hanging from the hub of the stand it can be seen that the original wheels were positioned fore and aft of the stand. It certainly took a handful of able-bodied seamen to turn the rudder manually, unassisted by the steam engine.

There is a small hold in the poop. It contains a lot of steel lines and cargo handling gear.

The stern is well proportioned, and the large, 4-bladed prop is aligned in a V-shape against the propeller post. There is some growth on the blades. The underside of the ship's hull shows a lot of whip corals, which looks like giant hairs growing on the dark side of the ship.

The Aircraft Action Report for Strike 3D-1 by Torpedo Squadron VT 17, based on board Bunker Hill reads:

"Four planes attacked a large transport anchored off the southeast point of Fefan. One and possibly two torpedo hits were secured. Photographs show the decks awash and the pilots of subsequent strikes report the ship was gone."

Taking this basic information, several intensive searches were made during the 1980, 1981 and 1982 expeditions. They were not successful. The searches had been close to Fefan, but rarely quite as far inshore to Uman where the wreck rests today. With the benefit of hindsight it appears inexplicable that the clue from an attack picture had not been utilized; this attack photo has been well known. It clearly shows the Yubae Maru as the ship on the right, obviously riding high with cargo discharged.

Well, firstly the ship was not recognized to be the Yubae Maru, and secondly these two ships showing in the background were assumed to have gotten away. Thirdly, as a result of the distortion of the perspective, they were thought to be small coasters. The other ship appears to have gotten away.

In another attack photo taken hardly half an hour later, the Amagisan Maru can be seen burning fiercely and going down by the bow. Also in this picture the Sankisan Maru and the Taiho Maru can be identified, and a second ship not too far from the Taiho. This ship, taking into account the known resting place of the Taiho Maru, was assumed to be Yubae Maru. The area to be searched was close to Fefan. This was definitely incorrect. This unknown vessel did get away. The area at the wreck symbol showing on the chart had been investigated at the time, as well, and we must have missed the wreck just by a few yards. On a clear and particularly calm day in the second half of 1983 Gradvin Aisek, Kimiuo's son, returned from a dive on the Hino Maru 2. His boat run over a slight discoloration on the sea bottom. He noted the location, came back one day and had found the wreck quite accidently. It was left alone, and no divers had been on it before the thorough investigations in February 1984.

Technical Data:

The Yubae Maru was a coal burning freighter. It was used by the Japanese Army from September 22, 1941 onwards as a transport for Army supplies.

The spelling of the ship's name is also given as Yubai or Yuhai Maru.

Tonnage:	3 200 ts net; 3 217 ts gross; 4 930 ts deadweight
Length:	305 ft 93.0 m
Breadth:	44 ft 13.4 m
Depth:	27 ft 8.2 m
Draught:	23 ft 7.0 m
Engine:	1 x triple reciprocal steam engine; coal
Horsepower:	1500 hp
Max. Speed:	12.3 knots
Service:	10.0 knots
Builder:	Ishikawajima Dockyard
Launch:	May 1919
Service:	End 1919

APPENDIX

PARTICIPATING SHIPS

It was a mighty armada the US Navy mobilized and included into the Battle Order for Operation Hailstone. Unfortunately, it would explode the frame of this text if justice would be done to each and every participating ship of Task Force 58, and the campaigns and achievements listed individually. As most of the action centered around the fleet carriers, only their history have been mentioned briefly.

Armament, complement, dimensions and many other details are slightly different with ships of the same class. In particular during refits, sometimes substantial changes were effected. Therefore, the discriminating reader may find differences, but in this context, the chapter provided here is designed for general orientation.

AIRCRAFT CARRIERS

a - Fleet Aircraft Carriers

Enterprise CV 6

Standard Displacement (as built)	ton	19 875	
Length (perpendicular) / o.a.	ft/inch - m	770 / 827'4"	234.7 / 252.2
Beam at waterline/ o.a	ft/inch - m	83'3"/ 114'	25.4 / 34.7
Draft	ft/inch - m	28'6"	8.7
Main Armament		8 - 5"-12.7cm a/a	
Belt	inch - mm	4"	102mm
Decks	inch - mm		
Speed	knots	32.5	
Shaft HorsePower	(bhp)	120 000	
Fuel Oil tons Endurance	naut.miles	12 000 @ 15 kts	
Aircraft Handling Capacity		72	
Launch / Commissioned:	03 Oct 1936	12 May 1938	
Builder:	Newport News		
Complement		2919	

While the heavy cruiser Wichita may lay claim to one of the most complex participations in all theaters of World War II, gallant Enterprise' exploits are certainly adequately expressed in having received the Presidential Unit Citation, the Navy Unit Commendation and no less than twenty Battle Stars. Describing her action would be writing the history of the war in the Pacific. As this is beyond the scope of this text, some highlights must suffice and the interested reader is kindly referred to the Bibliography for some detailed accounts.

Seven of her 18 SBD's launched during the time of the Japanese attack on Pearl Harbor were shot down by friendly fire when they arrived over Hickam to land, but the rest accounted for at least two confirmed downed Japanese planes, while the carrier stood out to sea, was missed by the Japanese and in turn missed

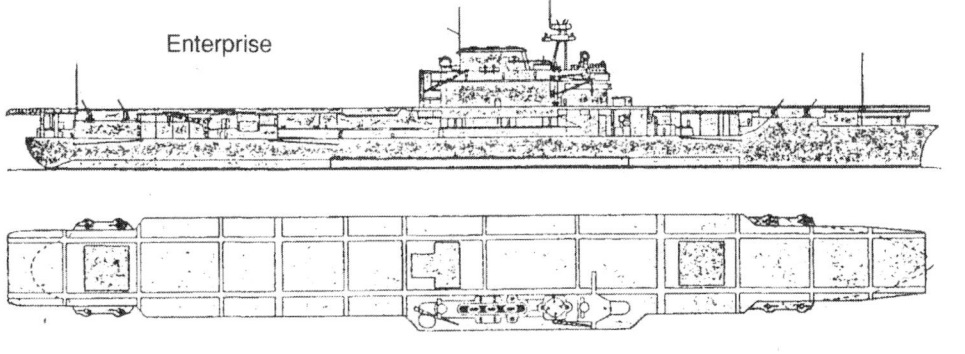

Hailstorm - *Appendix*

the Japanese forces for retaliatory attacks. No sooner had the smoke lifted when the ship entered the harbor for replenishments. Her squadrons hit Kwajalein hard and square, with only small own damages. After repair/modernization in Pearl, she sailed in company with the Hornet to deliver the famous Doolittle Raid to Tokyo. For the Battle of the Coral Sea she was too late but prepared for the upcoming Battle of Midway. Being flagship of Admiral Spruance, her squadrons wrote history in sinking Japanese carriers.

Landings in the Solomons were covered and finally she was damaged by three hits and four near misses. Repaired in Pearl within 7 weeks, and ready for the Battle of Santa Cruz Islands, she was hit twice by bombs, but continued to be in action due to the outstanding training of her damage control party. She even took on board several orphaned planes from Hornet. The ship had always been a particularly fine example of combat readiness and served as a launching pad for several flag officers.

Still under battle repair, Big E entered the Battle of Guadalcanal and accounted for more than a dozen ships sunk. Rennell Island saw fierce action and finally the carrier steamed for Pearl for some much needed R&R. On September 27, 1943 the ship was the recipient of the first Presidential Unit Citation ever granted to an aircraft carrier.

Makin and Kwajalein were the next targets. During her raid against Truk, Enterprise made history by launching the first radar night attack. She was subsequently detached from the Central Pacific Forces and went south to cover landings at Emirau. In March 1944 she rejoined Task Force 58 for Desecrate 1. After this and some rest at Majuro, landings in New Hollandia were covered and a new strike against Truk initiated. The Battle of the Philippine Sea saw Big E in action and she covered the Marianas landings. After some other actions, from 24 December 1944 onwards, she was the first night operation carrier, with a specially equipped Air Group. The carrier kept aircraft continuously in operation for 174 hours, during the Iwo Jima operation. In the subsequent campaign she did not escape two separate damages, during the operations against the Japanese Islands and the Inland Sea, and during the Okinawa operation. A final Kamikaze attack took her out of the war and she had to be repaired. She was decommissioned in 1947, and despite some efforts to preserve the ship as a museum for the national heritage, Big E was finally broken up.

ESSEX - CLASS FLEET CARRIERS

The following carriers participating in Desecrate 1 were part of the Essex-Class fleet carriers

Bunker Hill,	CV 17
Intrepid	CV 11
Yorktown,	CV 10
Essex	CV 9

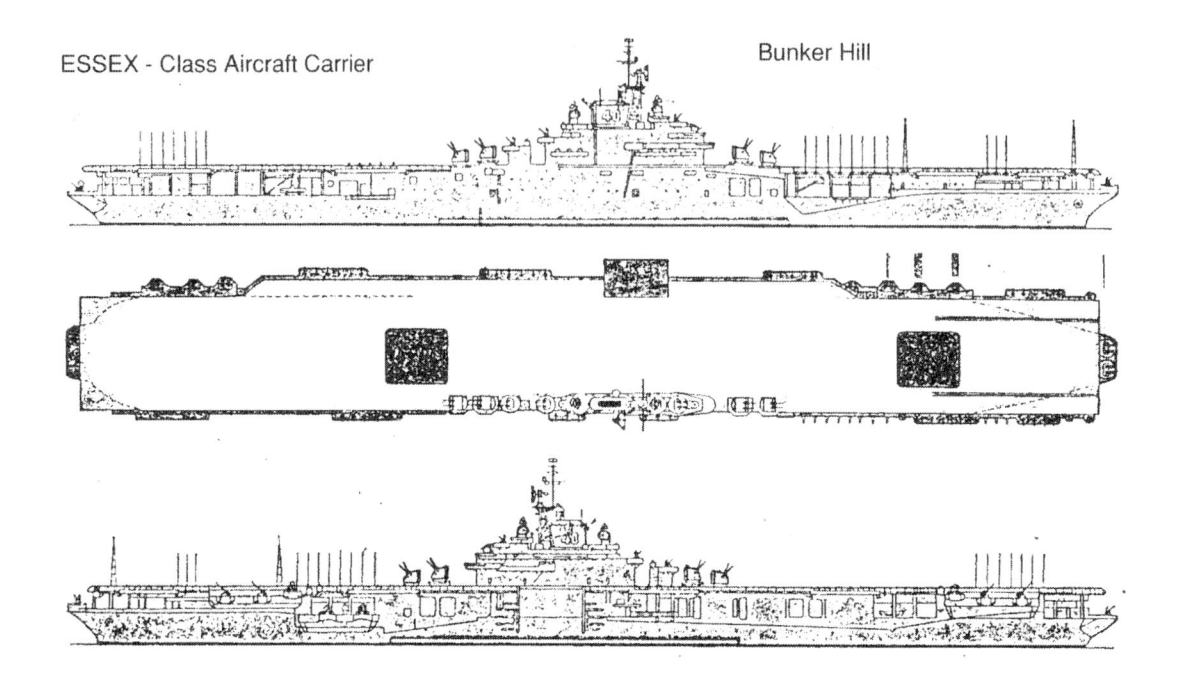

Hailstorm – *Appendix*

All these Essex carriers were of the earlier "Short Hull Group". Small variation existed between individual ships

Standard Displacement (as built) ton		27 200	
Length (perpendicular)/ o.a.	ft/inch - m	820' / 872"	250m / 265.8m
Beam at waterline / o.a.	ft/inch - m	93' / 147'	28.3m / 44.8m
Draft	ft/inch - m	21'8"	6.60m
Main Armament		8 x 12.7 $cm_{(2)}$, 4 x 12.7 $cm(_1)$ various a/a	
Belt	inch - mm	4"	102 mm
Decks	inch - mm	2.5"	64 mm
Speed	knots	33	
Shaft HorsePower	(bhp)	150 000	
Fuel Oil	tons	6160	
Endurance	naut.miles	20 000 @ 15 kts	
Aircraft Handling Capacity		90/103	
Complement		3448	

Bunker Hill

Launch / Commissioned: 07 Dec 1942; 24 May 1943
Builder: Bethlehem, Quincy

The Bunker Hill reported to the Pacific in the fall of 1943, and saw very extensive service, ranging from the daring Raid on Rabaul (11 November 1943) to the Okinawa invasion. The ship received eleven Battle Stars. During the opening phases of the Battle of the Philippine Sea, a near miss sprayed the ship with shrapnel, causing 2 fatalities and wounding 80. On 11 May 1945, during the Okinawa Invasion, Bunker Hill was hit by two Kamikaze planes. Very bad gasoline fires erupted and explosions took place. The ship became a flaming inferno. Of her complement, 346 men were killed, 43 missing and 264 wounded. The damage control party was able to douse the flames and she made it under her own steam via Hawaii to Bremerton for repairs. The Presidential Unit Citation was awarded to the ship.

The carrier was a common sight off the West Coast, when she was used as a radar target. She was not modified later but decommissioned and broken up in the mid-50ties.

Essex

Launch /Commissioned 31 July 1942 - 31 Dec 42
Builder: Newport News

Essex sailed to the Pacific in May 43, and apart from a single overhaul in the Continental US and a repair of a kamikaze attack, she participated in a string of engagements, which ended in Tokyo Bay. By the time she took part in the Truk raid, she had already attacked Marcus, Wake, the Gilberts, Tarawa, Kwajalein and the Marshalls again. After Truk she flew missions against the Marianas and then proceeded to an overhaul. Although the carrier was not back for the first strike against Palau, she participated in the landings at Peleliu. From there it was non-stop operations. Leyte Gulf was one of the most significant operations. On 25 November she was hit by a Kamikaze. Further operations involved raids against Japan.

The ship received 13 Battle Stars, and the Presidential Unit Citation. During her service in the Korean War, she received an additional four Battle Stars.

Intrepid

Launch /Commissioned 26 April 43/16 Aug 43
Builder: Newport News

Before the operation against Truk, Intrepid participated in the preparation of the Marshall Islands invasion (Kwajalein). At night after the first day of operations, the ship was torpedoed and returned to the States. On 9 June, she sailed back to Pearl Harbor and bombed Peleliu and other positions in Palau. Several raid against the southern Philippines followed, and then it was Palau again, in support of the invasion. Okinawa and Formosa were next. During the Leyte landings, planes from the carrier spotted the Yamato, but two hours later, the Musashi was attacked and finally sunk. Intrepid's involvement in the Battle of the Philippines was dramatic. During a strike on Clark airbase, on 30 October 1944, a kamikaze struck, but damage was minor. Two more kamikazes crashed into the carrier on 25 November. It was neccessary to sail back to San Francisco. In mid-February 1945, she was back on the war path. Continued operations took their toll by another kamikaze attack. That particular plane missed, but started fires. Another hit on her flight deck on 16 April 1945, this time the carrier was sailed back to the States.

Yorktown

Launch /Commissioned 21 Jan - 15 April 1943
Builder: Newport News

The second Yorktown of World War II is now a National Monument in Patriot's Point, North Carolina. She was one of the carriers participating in almost all raids and battles, and her statistics include the statement: "Days of operation lost due to enemy action:

Hailstorm - *Appendix*

Zero". The ship was called The Fightin' Lady, and a dramatic film was produced of her operations during combat conditions.

Yorktown participated in all the comparatively small but important raids after her arrival in Pearl Harbor on 10 November 1943. Makin, Tarawa, Jaluit, Mili, Wotje and many others were on the list where her squadrons drew blood and established the excellent reputation. Kwajalein in January 1944 was next, and it was a hard fierce battle, a fitting prelude to the grueling two days in Truk in mid-February, which were followed up without respite for friend and foe, with attacks on Saipan. Retreating for replenishment to Majuro Atoll, she again sailed until 08 March 1944, from where she steamed to Espiritu Sancto. She played a support role there, but then was recalled northwards and joined the fleet disposition for Operation Desecrate 1. Lesser strikes followed, but then 5 days later the ship was back in Majuro.

There was an interlude of close support for the Hollandia Operations, but during her retirement she laid a good work-over on Truk, the second raid against this Japanese naval installation, and retired to Majuro. There were only a few days rest and recreation, and a short stint in Hawaii. Then the carrier participated in the attack against Saipan and Guam, the latter being the main target. The continuation of softening up of the Marianas was a raid against Bonin Island. Yorktown's air power returned to Guam on 19 June 1944, and participated in the operations associated with the Battle of the Philippine Sea. Iwo Jima was next and Yorktown launched another series of raids. Following a short stop in Eniwetok, the carrier proceeded to strike the Marianas, Iwo Jima, and continued on 25 July with strikes against Palau, Ulithi and Yap. This was the second strike on Palau. The Marianas was the next stop, but then the carrier was recalled for overhaul in the US.

Yorktown was back in time for the Leyte Landings and returned for a longer rest to Ulithi. Preparations for the invasion of Luzon were undertaken and she participated in that operation as well. During the retirement from this strike, the Task Force 38 steamed right through the eye of a particularly vicious typhoon. Repairs to the big ship were soon made and strikes against Formosa (Taiwan) followed already in the first days of January 1945, and with no letting up, the Philippine operations were covered with significant number of ships sunk. Early February it was Iwo Jima's turn and then Yorktown moved against the Tokyo area of Honshu. Iwo Jima had an umbrella of American planes, Yorktown's among them. After that it was the Bonin again, and the Japanese Homeland.

The following operations within Japanese waters also saw an increased Japanese air activity. 18 March 1945 was particularly taxing, as two Kamikaze bore down on the Yorktown. The carrier's defences were able to knock them down from the sky, but of the 5 planes, one managed to plant a bomb into the the signal bridge. It passed through part of the ship before it exploded near the ship's hull, leaving 5 killed, 26 injured and the ship with two neatly punched out holes to plaster over. Later in the month, a Kamikaze Judy splashed only 60 ft from her portside, showering hot glowing shrapnel up and down the deck.

As Yorktown was part of the Okinawa Battle Order, she immediately was embroiled with the hectic activities to deny Yamato's mission and sink her. Yorktown planes claimed torpedo hits. The rest of the war was spent in daring raids deep into Japan proper, and she was pulled out of combat after the Japanese surrender. She was instrumental in bringing personnel home to the States and was finally decommissioned, but preserved as a floating museum.

B - Light Aircraft Carriers

Independence Class carriers were involved in Operation Hailstone:

Belleau Wood, CVL 24; Cabot, CVL 28; Cowpens, CVL 25; Princeton, CVL 23; Langley, CVL 27; Monterey, CVL 26

Standard Displacement (as built) ton		11 000	
Length (perpendicular)	ft/inch - m	622'6"	190m
Beam at waterline	ft/inch - m	109'2"	33.3m
Main Armament		18 - 40 mm a/a	
Belt	inch - cm		
Decks	inch - m		
Speed	knots	32	
Shaft HorsePower	(bhp)		
Fuel Oil tons Endurance	naut.miles		
Aircraft Handling Capacity		33	
Complement		1569	

Hailstorm – *Appendix*

Belleau Wood
Launch /Commissioned 06 Dec 1942 - 31 March 1943
Builder: New York Shipbuilding Company

Cabot
Launch /Commissioned 04 April - 24 July 1943
Builder: New York Shipbuilding Company

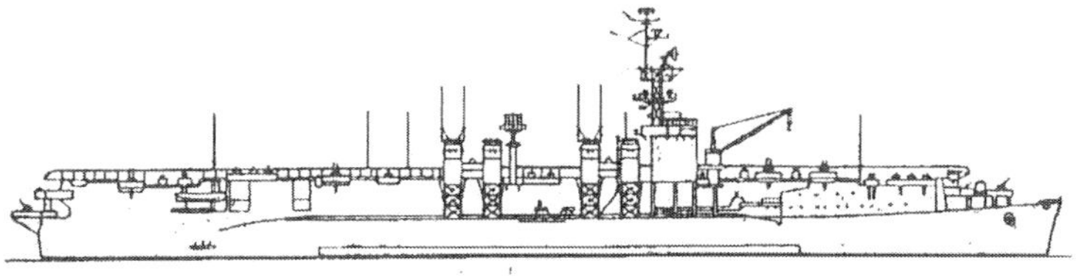

Cowpens
Launch /Commissioned 17 Jan - 28 May 1943
Builder: New York Shipbuilding Company

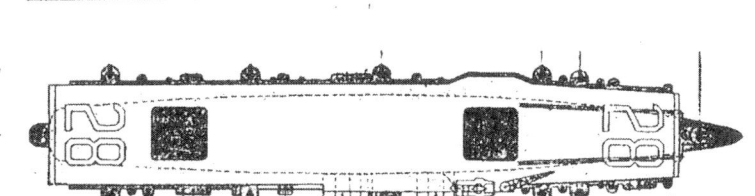

Monterey
Commissioned 28 February 1943
Builder: New York Shipbuilding Company

BATTLESHIPS

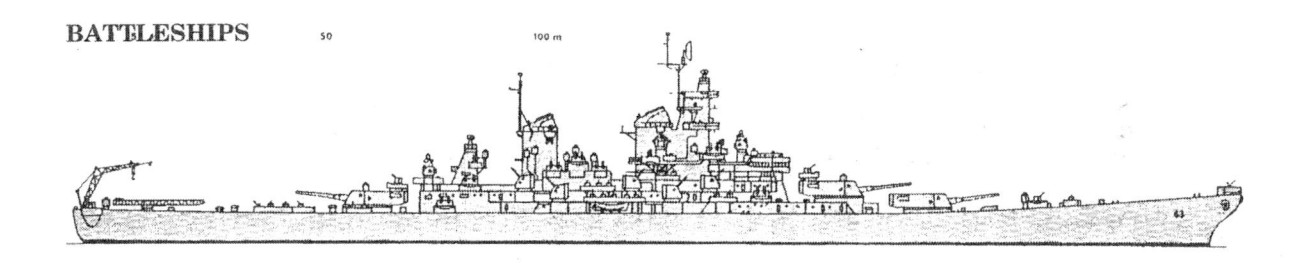

Of the four <u>**Iowa Class**</u> battleships, two were steaming with Task Group 58:

Iowa   BB 61
New Jersey   BB 62

Standard Displacement (as built)	tons	45 000	
Length (perpendicular)	ft/inch - m	887'3"	270.4m
Beam at waterline	ft/inch - m	108'1"	32.9m
Main Armament		9 - 16" 40.6 cm$_{(3)}$; 20 - 5" 12.7$_{(2)}$ a/a, various a/a	
Belt	inch - mm	19"	482mm
Deck		11"	285mm
Waterline	inch - mm		
Speed	knots	33	
Shaft HorsePower	(bhp)		
Fuel Oil tons Endurance	naut.miles		

New Jersey   **Iowa**

Launch /Commissioned 28 Aug 1942 - 23 May 1943   Launch /Commissioned 07 Dec 1942 - 22 Feb 1943
Builder: Philadelphia Shipyard   Builder: New York Navy Yard

Hailstorm - *Appendix*

Battleships of the **South Dakota Class** included in the fleet formation were

Alabama, Massachusetts, South Dakota

Standard Displacement (as built)	ton	35 000	
Length (perpendicular)	ft/inch - m	680'	207.3m
Beam at waterline	ft/inch - m	108'2"	32.9m
Main Armament		9 - 16"- 40.6 cm$_{(3)}$; 20 x 5"-12.7 cm a/a$_{(2)}$	
Belt	inch - mm	18/16"	457/406
Decks		6/4"	150/102
Artillery		18"	457
Decks	inch - m		
Speed	knots	28	
Shaft HorsePower	(bhp)		
Fuel Oil tons Endurance	naut.miles		

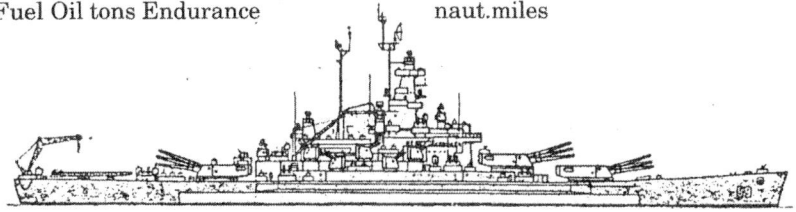

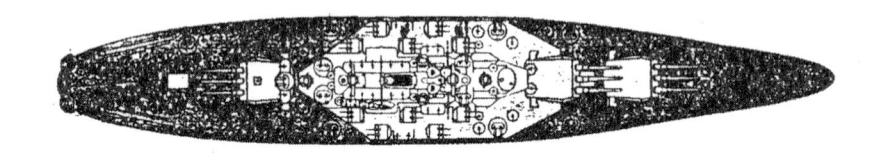

Alabama

Alabama	BB 60		
Commissioned	16 August 42	Builder:	Norfolk Navy Yard
Massachusetts	BB 59		
Commissioned	12 May 1942	Builder:	Bethlehem, Quincy
South Dakota	BB 55		
Commissioned	20 March 1942	Builder:	

The **North Carolina Class** of battleships contributed the type-ship to the line-up:

North Carolina

Standard Displacement (as built)	ton	35 000	
Length (perpendicular)	ft/inch - m	729'	222.2m
Beam at waterline	ft/inch - m	108'4"	33m
Main Armament		9 - 16" - 40.6cm$_{(3)}$; 20 - 5" - 12.7 cm$_{(2)}$ a/a	
Belt	inch - mm	16"	406
Decks	inch - mm	8.25	210
Artillery	inch - mm	18"	457
Speed	knots	28	
Shaft HorsePower	(bhp)		
Fuel Oil tons Endurance	naut.miles		
Commissioned		09 April 1941	
Builder:		New York Navy Yard	

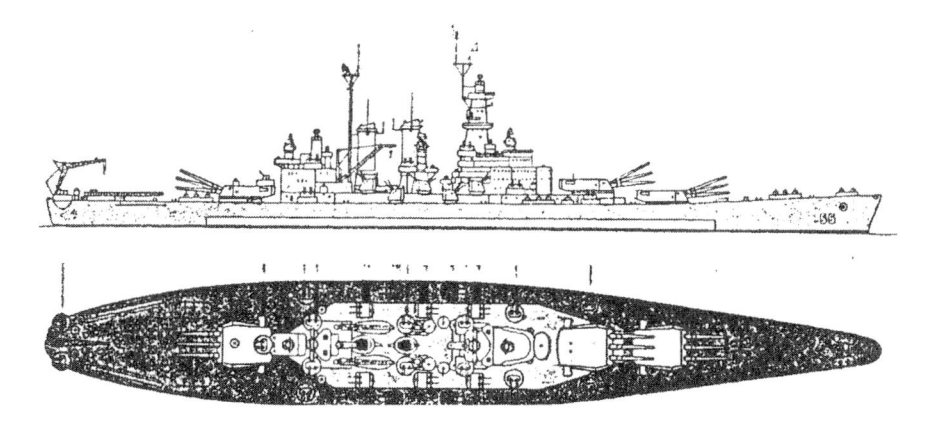

Hailstorm — *Appendix*

HEAVY CRUISERS

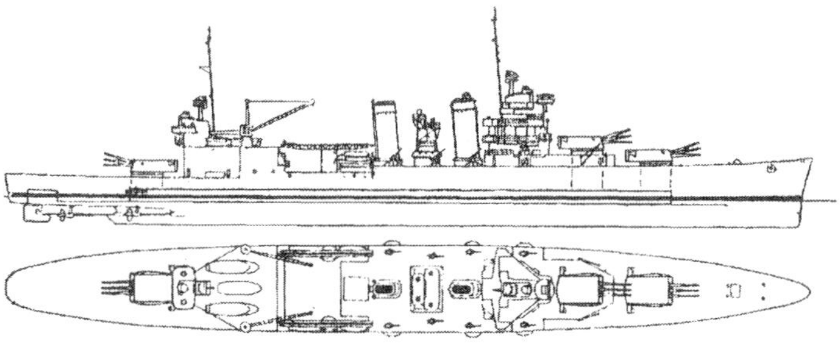

Astoria (New Orleans) Class

San Francisco,

New Orleans,

Minneapolis,

Standard Displacement (as built)	ton	9375 - 9975	
Length (perpendicular)	ft/inch - m	588'2"	179.3
Beam at waterline	ft/inch - m	61'9"	18.7
Main Armament		9 - 8" 20.3 cm $_{(3)}$; 8 - 5" 12.7 cm a/a	
Belt	inch - mm	5" - 1.5"	127/ 38
Decks	inch - mm	3" - 2"	76/51
Artillery	inch - mm	6"	152
Speed	knots	32.5	

Minneapolis
Commissioned 19 May 1934
Builder: Mare Island Navy Yard

San Francisco
Commissioned 10 February 1934
Builder: Philadelphia Navy Yard

New Orleans
Commissioned 15 February 1934
Builder: New York Navy Yard

Wichita

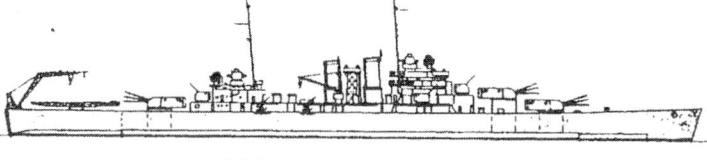

Standard Displacement (as built)	ton	10 000	
Length (perpendicular)	ft/inch - m	608'4"	185.4m
Beam at waterline	ft/inch - m	61'9"	18.7m
Main Armament		9 - 8" 20.3cm $_{(3)}$; 8 - 5" 12.7 cm a/a	
Belt	inch - mm	5" - 1.5"	127 - 38
Decks	inch - m	3/2"	76, 51
Artillery	inch - cm	6"	152
Speed	knots	32.5	
Commissioned		16 February 1939	

Builder: Philadelphia Navy Yard

Hailstorm - *Appendix*

Baltimore Class:

Baltimore,

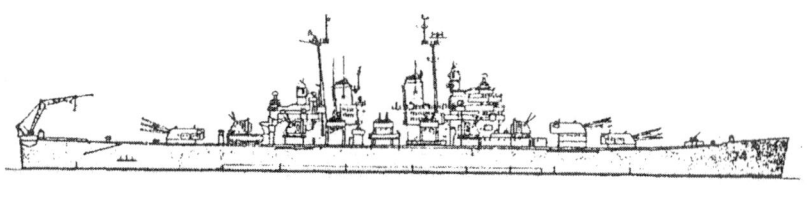

Standard Displacement (as built)	ton	13,600	
Length (perpendicular)	ft/inch - m	673'5"	205.25 m
Beam at waterline	ft/inch - m	70'10"	21.6 m
Main Armament		9 x 8" - 20.3cm; 12 x 5" - 12.7cm a/a	
Belt	inch - mm	6";	152 mm
Decks	inch - mm	3"/2"	76, 51 mm,
artill. 152			
Speed	knots	33	

Baltimore
Commissioned: 15 April 43
Builder: Bethlehem, Quincy

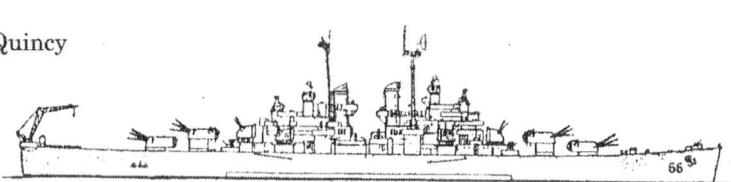

LIGHT CRUISERS
Cleveland (Vincennes) Class

Santa Fe, Mobile, Biloxi,

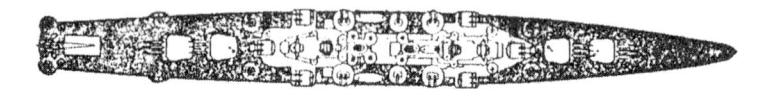

Standard Displacement (as built)	ton	10,000	
Length (perpendicular)	ft/inch - m	610'	186 m
Beam at waterline	ft/inch - m	66'3"	20.9m
Main Armament		12 x 6" (15.2cm); 12 x 5"(12.7cm)a/a	
Belt	inch - cm	5" to 1.5"	127-38 mm
Decks	inch - mm	3" to 2"	76 to 51 mm
Speed	knots	32.5	

Biloxi
Commissioned: 31 August 1943
Builder: Newport News

Mobile
Commissioned: 24 March 1943
Builder: Newport News

Santa Fe
Commissioned: 24 November 1942
Builder: New York Shbldg C

DESTROYERS

Fletcher Class and Derivates

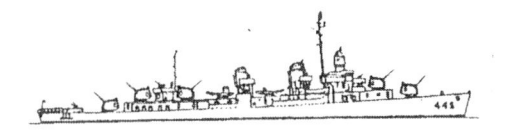

Standard Displacement (as built)	ton	2050	
Length (perpendicular)	ft/inch - m	375'10'"	114.5 m
Beam at waterline	ft/inch - m	39'4"	12.1 m
Main Armament		5 x 5" a/a; 10 x 21" t.t.	
Speed	knots	35	

Hailstorm – *Appendix*

LIGHT ANTI-AIRCRAFT CRUISERS.

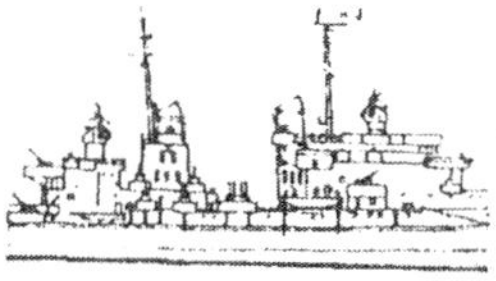

Atlanta (Oakland) Class

Oakland

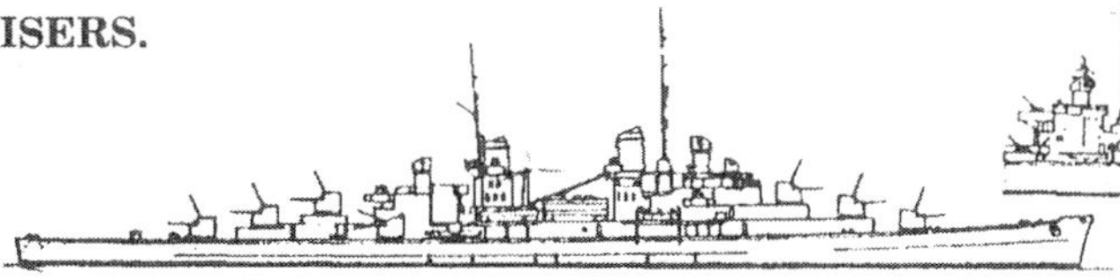

Oakland has both twin 12.7 cm a/a turrets athwart deckhouse aft removed (See side sketch)

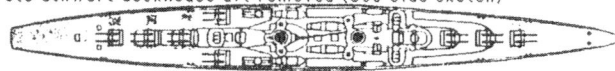

Standard Displacement (as built)	ton	6000	
Length (perpendicular)	ft/inch - m	541'6"	165 m
Beam at waterline	ft/inch - m	53'2"	16.2 m
Main Armament		12 x 5"- 12.7 cm a/a; 20 x 4 cm a/a	
		8 x 21" torpedo tubes	
Belt	inch - mm	3.5"	89 mm
Decks	inch - mm	2"	51 mm
Speed	knots	33/35	

Commissioned: 17 July 43
Builder: Bethlehem, San Francisco

San Diego Class - San Diego
specification as Oakland, except:
Main Armament: 16 x 5"(12.7cm) a/a; 20 x 4 cm
torpedo tubes removed

Commissioned: 10 January 1942
Builder: Bethlehem, Quincy.

SUPPLY SHIPS

Fleet Tankers **Cimarron Class**

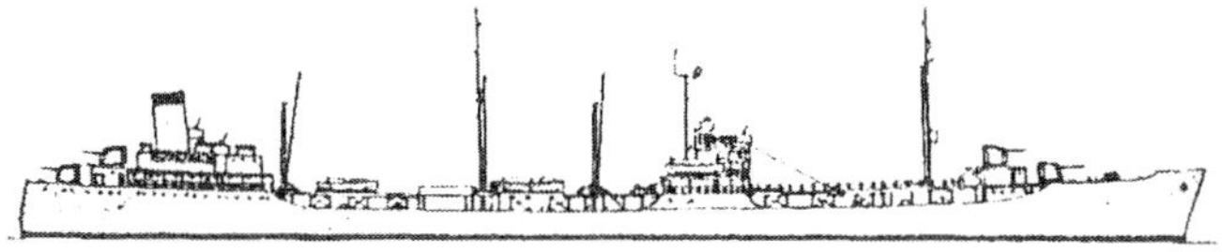

Standard Displacement (as built)	ton	7260
Length (perpendicular)	ft/inch - m	
Beam at waterline	ft/inch - m	
Main Armament		4 x 5" - 12.7cm a/a
Speed	knots	18.5

Hailstorm - *Appendix*

PARTICIPATING AMERICAN AIRCRAFT

Grumman F6F3 -5   Hellcat

Grummans of Bethpage, Long Island, New York, were popular fighters for their pilots and feared by their adversaries. It was not the fastest, not the most spectacular and not the most agile fighter the US produced, but a solid performer with good armament, excellent protection, and the ability to be used in several key combat roles, such as fighter, night fighter, fighter bomber and rocket platform. The aircraft accounted for more Japanese planes shot down than all other planes combined.

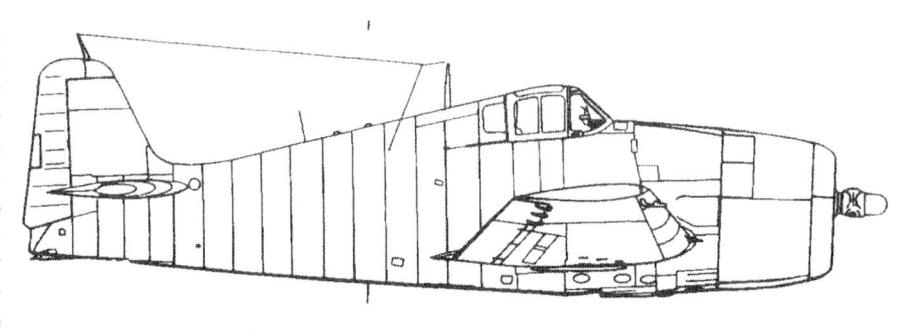

Only 14 months passed between the flight of the first prototype and the first combat engagement. A total of more than 12000 Hellcats were produced in two major variants.

The predecessor of the Hellcat was the F4F Wildcat. This plane was also a good performer, but the Zeros flew little circles around it. The Hellcat was ordered to be produced - prototypes first - on 30 June 1941, and the program had all the advantages of the first combat experiences. Consequently, many modifications were incorporated even as the planes were rolling off the assembly line. The use of the 2000 hp Pratt&Whitney radial engine proved to be a far-sighted decision and the extra power was used to improve the passive protection, such as pilot armor plate. In January 1943, the first Hellcats were assigned to the Essex, and Yorktown and Independence followed. Several hundred Hellcats were delivered to Great Britain and saw combat in Europe. Also, more than two hundred planes were modified for night fighting and some of the planes were stationed on the fleet carriers. The main variant was the F6F3, superseded by the F6F5 from April 1944 onwards.

The largest success in one operation for the fighter was the Battle of the Philippine Sea, when on 19 and 20 June 1944 the largest confrontation of carrier based aircraft ever took place. The Hellcat could - with great skill on the Japanese pilots' part - be outmaneuvered by the Zeros, but yet the Zeros did not have a chance. These planes were built to sacrifice protection for speed and endurance, and it was easy for the American pilots to shoot down the Japanese planes. The fact that the creme of the Japanese pilots had fallen already in the attrition air battles, that the pilots now going to the front were inexperienced and that the American pilots had excellent control by their own radar, helped the American victory, which became known as The Great Marianas Turkey Shoot.

Grumman F6F5
Wing Span	13.06 m
Length	10.24 m
Height	3.99
Gross Weight	6.970 kg
Engine	2000 hp Pratt & Whitney R 2800--10W
Speed	610 km/h
Ceiling	11.370 m
Max. Range	1670 km
Bomb Load	800 kg
Armament	6 machine guns .50" 12.7 mm
Number built	probably around 10.000 in all variations

Hellcats remained in the skies during the Korean War, were flown by Allied forces well after the war, and are now a much sought after by plane enthusiasts.

Curtis SB2C1, 1C, 3   Helldivers

The Curtiss SB2C Helldiver was hardly loved by the pilots, and was at best a mediocre dive bomber. It had a number of nicknames, none of them flattering. The printables were "Big Tailed Beast" which was frequently shortened to The Beast, a name that stuck. "Son-of-a-Bitch, 2nd Class" did not stick, but voiced the general sentiment.

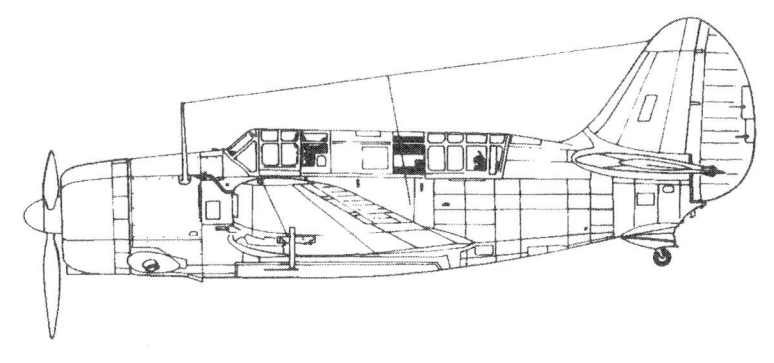

Hailstorm – *Appendix*

In the opinion of the experts it was a plane which attempted too much because of the Navy specifications. The Navy Bureau of Aeronautics wanted a plane which was built around the new 1500 hp radial engine, had an enclosed bomb bay with a capacity of holding a 1000 lbs bomb, and fitting, two at a time to the standard elevator of the Essex Class carrier. Consequently, the aircraft was wide by any standards and had to have a large tail to improve the resultant poor stability. Design, and mock-up of the plane was done hurriedly in some cattle barn on the Ohio State Fair grounds. The prototype rolled out on 13 December 1940, just about two and a half years after its predecessor, the Dauntless, went into production. Totally untested and with lingering, and well founded doubts about the plane's stability, the company received the order to manufacture 370 planes. However, the prototype was tested extensively and more and yet more idiosyncrasies had to be ironed out. About one year later, the modified prototype was taken for the final test, a 22.000ft terminal velocity dive with a high G-load pull-out. The right wing and the tail failed simultaneously . . .

Production Helldivers were supposed to have rolled out of the plant end-December 1941, with production of 85 planes scheduled for April 1942. Because of the crash of the prototype, the production start was delayed, but to add to all illogical things, the navy ordered no fewer than 3000 planes even before a single plane had rolled off the assembly line.

The first airplanes rolling out the production hangars were assigned test roles, and the start of that test program was considerably worse than expected. Many features for front line duties had to be added, among them armor, self-sealing tanks, and radio gear. Many light-weight magnesium forgings were replaced by heavier alloys during actual production. All performance data suffered accordingly.

The further development is extremely interesting and included a lot of drama; unfortunately, this is not the right place to relate it. Suffice to say that there were several variants, of which the SB2C-1C was the one used during the Operation Desecrate 1, and that it was recommended by some of the Carrier skippers to use the plane as anchors. Slowly but steadily the many flaws were ironed out and the pilots got used to the idea of flying the Beast. On the positive side, they recognized that they had an extremely rugged plane, which was able to absorb a lot of punishment and still make it home to the carrier. The forward firing armament had been changed from two twin machine guns to two 20 mm cannons, which proved their tremendous punch on strafing. The twin .50 machine guns aft were a strong defence.

The aircraft remained a mediocre performer, but it was still good enough to see service much after the war, and with other nations, which had been given these surplus aircraft, notably the French fighting their war in Indo-China. A total of 778 planes had been produced by Curtiss alone, with quite a number of others produced in Canada.

SB2C-3

Wing Span	15.16 m
Length	11.18 m
Height	4.01 m
Weight, loaded	7.537 kg
Engine	1500 hp
Speed	452 km/h
Ceiling	7650 m
Max. Bombing Range	1785 km
Bomb Load	907 kg
Armament	2 x 20 mm; 2 x 7.62 mm

Douglas SBD   Dauntless

The Slow-But-Deadley Dauntless made World history. It was the diminutive Dauntless which sank the creme of the Japanese aircraft carriers at Midway. Their advanced half sisters, the Avengers, were

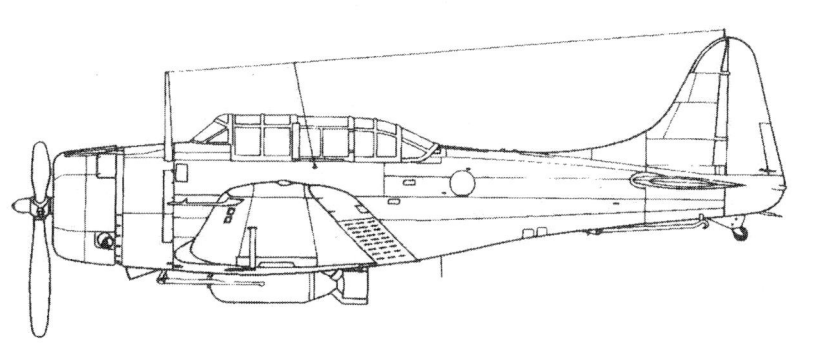

Hailstorm - *Appendix*

slaughtered and their elder half brothers, the Devastators. felled. But, almost at the end of her operational career, the Dauntless started bombing dives in the crucial moment of the battle unmolested and hit the Akagi, Kaga and Soryu. Fifty of the planes peeled off for their dives and when they pulled out and headed home, the carriers were blazing hulks. The tide of the Japanese offensive had turned. The Hiryu was a victim of a later attack by Enterprise with her Dauntless and ten which had been orphaned from the Yorktown.

John Northrop, the famous aircraft designer and entrepreneur, left Douglas Aircraft in 1932, and that, in a way was the beginning of the Dauntless. The Bureau of Aviation had issued a Request for Proposal, and Northrop responded with a modern monoplane design which was accepted against stiff competition of biplanes and other monoplanes. His chief Designer, Heinemann, had built the smallest possible airframe around the powerplant which was in 1934 the state of the art - a paltry 850 hp radial engine. In 1936, the Navy accepted the design and ordered a prototype. The first generation, called BT 1, was a flop. Fortunately for Northrop, the contract provided money for development of a second generation dive bomber, and when it was rolled out it was carefully flown to the only available wind tunnel then, and thoroughly aerodynamically tested. The hitherto semi-retracted landing gear, a landmark with huge bulges under the wing were made fully retractable without bulge and a better power plant was available. Further improvements were made, and finally, in 1939 the Navy ordered a total of 144 planes. Many improvement were made in the long production history of the SBD. The planes saw many a tragedy and a lot of glory. In Pearl Harbor, 7 of 18 Dauntlesses from Enterprise, tried to land at Hickam and were shot down one by one, because they tried to land in the midst of the Japanese attack.

The planes operating from the Enterprise in March 1944 were the latest and the last versions of Dauntless', the SBD 5. The planes had evolved into extremely popular flying machines, stable bombing platforms, well protected, well armed and with very appealing handling characteristics. Their advanced sister, the Helldiver, one will remember, was a real problem to handle at the time. So all pilots which had to change horses did so with the greatest of reluctance and the SBD 5 was the dive bomber of choice. Weight savings had been affected, the power plant had advanced to a 1200 Cyclone engine. Self-sealing tanks were standard and the dive flaps had been improved such that they slowed the plane down without sacrifice to the lift. When the SBD 5 was gradually replaced during late 1943 and 1944, the planes were assigned to shore-based squadrons, where they continued to chalk up important damages to the enemy.

Wing Span	12.5 m
Length	10.06
Height	4.14
Empty Weight	2965 kg
Gross Weight	4850 kg
Engine	1200 hp Wright R-1820-60
Speed	405 km/h
Ceiling	7400 m
Max. Bombing Range	1700 km
Bomb Load	550 kg
Armament	2 fixed .50
	2 free .30
Number built	2965 for Navy
	675 for Army Air Force

Grumman TBF Avengers

The innovative designs for fighters and dive bombers were far advanced over the torpedo bombers. The Devastator, having insufficient speed and range was without a successor, while the other types of aircraft were already in their tooling stages. The Navy's requirement included a crew of three (pilot, radioman and gunner) accommodated in a large "greenhouse", self-sealing tanks, armor protection for the crew, and a powered dorsal gun turret. It was the latter which led to a particular innovative and successful design, involving General Electric and a principle involving precision control and speed.

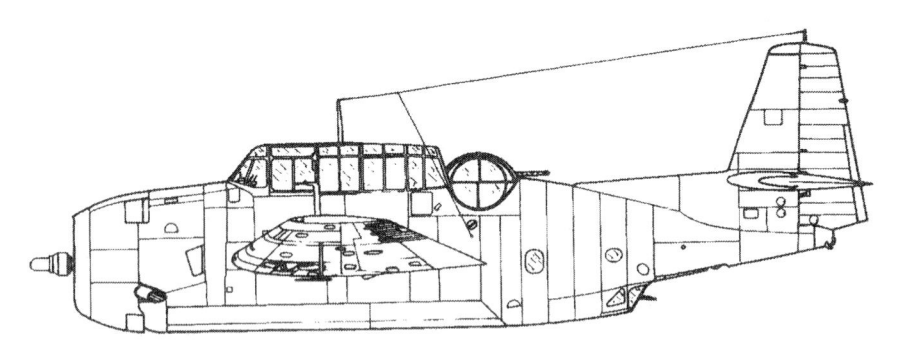

Grumman and Chance Vought submitted winning designs, leaning on the previous successes of the F4F. The Bethpage, Long Island, New York plant turned out the prototypes and in December 1940, the Navy ordered 286 aircraft. Internal equipment changes and additions increased the weight and the performance suffered. However, the landing gear retracted outward for a wide landing footprint and increased stability. The wings folding back laterally gave this design the winning edge over the competition.

The dorsal turret carried a .50 machine gun, with 400 rounds. Originally, a .30 machine gun mounted on top of the fuselage in a specially designed groove, was later changed to 2 wing mounted guns. The radioman could operate a .30 machine gun in the "stinger" position. The internal bomb bay could either hold a torpedo, two 1000 lbs bombs, depth charges, fragmentation clusters, mines or a special 270 gallon tank. For dive bombing missions, the main landing gear could be used as dive brakes and could be extended up to speeds of 380 km/h.

The first prototype was successful, unfortunately, an internal fire in the bomb bay destroyed the plane, but the second prototype was soon ready. On 23 December 1941 the Navy officially accepted the design and as the plane was ordered so closely after Pearl Harbor Day, it was christened Avenger.

The standard radar fitted to the Avengers was an air-to-surface Type B radar, and its dipoles, the Yagi Antenna, was installed on the outboard part of the wings. Radar scope and controls were installed at the radioman's station.

The baptism of fire during the Battle of Midway was devastating. Hornets and Midway's Avengers were wiped out but for one plane. Their sacrifice, they had drawn down to sea level the defending Japanese fighters, enabled the following planes to score.

The variant flown against Palau was the TBM 3. It had a more powerful engine, which required slight modifications of the fuselage. Additionally, they were equipped with launching rails for rockets. There were over 4000 planes produced before the end of the war and the planes saw extended service after the war, including Korea, and even, in a limited way, Vietnam.

Wing Span	15.90 m
Length	12.20 m
Height	5.00 m
Empty Weight	4918 kg
Gross Weight	8280 kg
Engine	1900 hp Wright R-2600-20
Speed	430 km/h
Ceiling	7130 m
Max. Bombing Range	1820 km
Bomb Load	900 kg
Armament	1 x .50; 3 x .30

Seahawk

The Curtiss SOC Seahawk was a light float plane, seeing extended service in World War II. It was also the last float plane embarked on cruisers and battleships of the US Navy. Its main purpose was reconnaissance, but during raids, planes of this type were catapulted from the surface ships to perform lifeguard duties, such as described in Strike 3C-1 Lexington.

The plane was designed in 1942 as an improvement over the Kingfisher and was in many respects superior to them. They could carry up to 340 kg bombs, and were armed with two machine guns. Interestingly, this plane was larger and more powerful than the Dauntless.

Wing Span	12.50 m
Length	11.07 m
Height	5.48 m
Gross Weight	4082 kg
Engine	1350 hp Wright R-1820-62
Speed	504 km/h
Ceiling	11400 m
Max. Bombing Range	1750 km
Bomb Load	340 kg
Armament	2 machine guns
Number built	576

Kingfisher

Production of this shipborne float plane ended in 1942, and by that time an estimated 1000 planes had been built by Vought/ United Aircraft Corporation under the designation Vought OS2U-3 Kingfisher. Frequently, the plane was referred to simply as OSU or Kingfisher.

It was a small, tough and versatile plane on board capital ships of the US Navy. Its drawback was that it was underpowered, which created problems in the assignments during various raids, of picking up downed aircrew. With a crew of two and only a 450 hp engine, the plane would just about lift off a reasonably calm surface, with little to spare. High swells and more than one rescued person would convert it into a lead duck. In fact, the planes were catapulted from the cruisers or battleships with only a limited amount of fuel on board, to decrease weight. The rescued pilot had to sit on the lap of the rear man.

Wing Span	10.94
Length	10.31 m
Height	4.59 m
Gross Weight 4000 lbs	1815 kg
Engine	450 hp Pratt & Whitney R-985-48 Wasp Junior
Speed	264 km/h
Ceiling	5950 m
Max. Range	1200 km
Armament	2 machine guns
Number built	1519

Hailstorm - *Appendix*

THE JAPANESE SHIPS
(for sketches, please see "The Official Japanese Report")

Light Cruisers

Katori

The Katori was the type ship of a class of 4 light cruisers, designed specifically for training purposes.

Three of these semi-combattant ships were actually built. The fourth was cancelled. The Katori carried out only one cruise before the outbreak of the war. The ships of this class were then modified and used as flagships. The Katori was the flagship of the Sixth Submarine Fleet. Compared to light cruisers of other navies, these ships were very much under-armed, slow and not suitable for heavy combat. Nevertheless, it speaks for the good internal design of the Katori that it absorbed such terrific punishment by bombs, torpedos, and eventually gunfire, before she succumbed. She had made good her escape through the hazardous North Pass, when she was attacked by US aircraft, which scored repeated hits. The ship lost all headway and burned heavily at the bridge. Practically defenseless and beaten to death, she finally managed to launch a torpedo spread, which missed the American ships, only because the air spotter had given advanced warning.

Technical Data:
Length overall:	129,5 m	425 ft
Width:	15,8 m	52 ft
Draught:	5,5 m	18 ft
Displacement:	5 890 ts	
Speed:	18 knots	
Horsepower:	8 000 hp on 2 shafts	
Armament:	4 x 14 cm (2 x 2) 5.5"guns	
	2 x 12,7 cm (1 x 2) a/a	
	4 x 21" TT	
	various machine a/a weapons	

Naka

The Naka was an old light cruiser, built by Mitsubishi in Yokohama, and launched on 24 March 1925. She was one cruiser of the Sendai-Class. Originally six of these ships were laid down, but because of the provisions of the Washington Naval Treaty, only three were actually built.

The appearance of these cruisers seemed to be highly unorthodox, with one tall, narrow funnel forward, and three shorter aft. The third stack was wider than the others. A catapult was built above the foreward gun mounts. In 1940 they were modernized. All ships of this class were lost during the war.

It was probably Naka, which went to the rescue of the sailors of Agano. This other light cruiser sank after a torpedo attack by the American submarine Skate in the afternoon of the day before the attack on Truk.

Technical Data:
Length overall:	162,75 m	534 ft
Width:	14,17 m	47 ft
Draught:	4,9 m	16 ft
Displacement:	5 195 ts	
Speed:	35,25 knots	
Horsepower:	90 000 hp on 4 shafts	
Armament:	7 x 14,0 cm (7 x 1) 5.5"	
	2 x 12,7cm (1 x 2) 5" a/a	
	various a/a automatics	
	8 x 24" torpedo tubes	
	1 aircraft	

Destroyers

Maikaze and Nowake

Both destroyers were of the Kagero-Class. This class was one of the best destroyers launched by the Japanese Navy, before the war. The Navy learned from the problems they had with the design of previous classes of destroyers, and these ships embodied substantial armament, high speed and good maneuverability, without sacrificing stability. The design proved to be very good, and most of the ships saw a lot of combat action. The major modification undertaken during the war was the removal of the aft turret, to be replaced by anti-aircraft guns.

The Maikaze is reported by American sources to have aided the survivors from the light cruiser Agano, but Japanese sources indicate it was the destroyer Oite which helped. The Nowake (alternative spelling: Nowaki) received repeated hits and near misses, was immobilized outside the North Pass and finally sunk by gun fire. The Nowake seemed to have been spared for inexplicable reasons. Evidently, after an attempt was made to save some of the crew of the Katori, the skipper decided to leave the scene of the sinking at the highest possible speed. It had about a half hour handicap, when the heavy 16 inch batteries of the US battleships were firing at her. At that time, she was already beyond the horizon. It was good long range shooting, above the horizon, target showing only stern-on, and moving. The aircraft detailed for spotting reported straddles but no hits. Even an increase of speed to 31 knots by the battleships, did not close the range, and the Nowake escaped.

Technical Data:
Length overall:	118,6 m	389 ft
Width:	15,8 m	35,5 ft
Draught:	5,5 m	12,5 ft
Displacement:	2 033 ts	
Speed:	35,5 knots	
Horsepower:	52 000 hp on 2 shafts	
Armament:	6 x 12,7 cm (3 x 2) 5"dual purpose guns, various a/a	
	8 x 24" torpedo tubes	

Harusame and Shigure

These two destroyers were sisterships, launched 21 September and 18 May 1935, respectivly. They were modernized 1942-1943, and were considered well designed. The log of the Shigure must have been one of the most interesting books to read, because the ship saw an unusual amount of very heavy combat action, and escaped sinking until 1945, being the last of her class. Both destroyers were at anchor in Truk during the carrier raid, but escaped through the North Pass about an hour later then the Katori. Both were subjected to bombing attacks and damaged.

Technical Data:
Length overall	:	102,25 m	335.5 ft
Width	:	9,91 m	32.5 ft
Draught	:	3,50 m	11.5 ft
Displacement	:	1580 ts	
Engine	:	2 x gear shaft turbines, 42.000 hp	
Speed	:	34 knots	
Armament	:	5 x 12,7 cm (5") dual purpose	
		4 x 25 mm anti-aircraft	
		2 x 4 torpedo tubes 24".	

Fumizuki

The Fumizuki was launched 16 February 1926, and was one of the older destroyers of the Mutsuki-Class. Their basic design evolved from the Minekaze-Class, via an intermediate step. The ship was out of commission when the raid started. Severe bomb damages had been received by land-based bombers on 31 January 1944, in the Kavieng/Rabaul area. She was escorting a convoy of merchant ships to Truk. At the time of the attack, she was repaired. During the overflight of the photo plane it was probably this ship that was tied up next to the fleet repair ship Akashi. One of her enginines was totally, the other partially disassembled. At 1400 h on the first day of the attack, a bomb hit close to the side of the ship and bashed in plates at the engine room while the Fumizuki was undergoing evasive maneuvers in the area between Tol, Dublon and Fefan.

Technical Data:
Length overall:	102,4 m	336 ft
Width:	9,1 m	30 ft
Draught:	3,0 m	10 ft
Displacement:	1 313 ts	
Max. Speed:	37 knots	
Horsepower:	38 500 hp on 2 shafts	
Armament:	4 x 12 cm, 4,7" guns, various a/a machine weapons	
	6 x 21"torpedo tubes	

Oite

The Oite was a destoyer of the Kamikaze-Class. These were the first Japanese destroyers with a protected bridge. The ships became top heavy due to this weight, and the beam was widened, compared to ships of the previous class, to increase stability. Their main battery was modernized during the war, and 12 cm dual purpose guns were fitted. One set of torpedo launchers was removed. Although these ships were considered old, they fought with distinction.

The Oite rescued several hundred sailors from the Agano, then proceeded to Guam. During the attack she was recalled to Truk to assist in combat action. She made up steam and ran into Truk. The Oite was spotted as she entered the North Pass. Consequently, she was severely strafed by Hellcats, which caused a tremendous number of casualties on the wall-to-wall survivors. Finally, after various changes in command and desperate evasive maneuvers, she was hit by a torpedo and sank in less than 90 seconds, breaking up in the process. Only a handful survived the ordeal.

Technical Data:
Length overall:	102,4 m	336 ft
Width:	9,8 m	32 ft
Draught:	3,1 m	10 ft
Displacement:	1 270 ts	
Max. Speed:	37 knots	
Horsepower:	38 500 hp n 2 shafts	
Armament:	4 x 12 cm, 4.7" dual purpose guns, various a/a	
	6 x 21" torpedo tubes	

Tachikaze

This Minekaze-Class destroyer was old, but at the time she was commissioned, outstanding in terms of

Hailstorm - *Appendix*

Tachikaze, beached on Kuop Atol, and under attack.

speed. The ships of this class were about to be relegated as escorts, and two of the class were actually disarmed. However, it was decided to modernize them after all, and they received new guns for their main battery. The mine laying and sweeping gear was removed and water bomb throwers installed instead. Four of the original six torpedo launchers were removed, as well.

The Tachikaze ran aground on the reef at the southwest corner of Kuop Atoll on 04 February 1944. The ship was grounded very firmly and could not be pulled off the reef. Work seems to have been in progress to lighten the ship. It looks as if the gun between the stacks had been removed, and possibly the forward torpedo tubes. A workboat or landing craft is tied to the port side.

The Hellcat shown in this picture silenced the accurate anti-aircraft fire from the destroyer. At this time it appears that the ship suffered already a few misses, but the delay fuzed bomb from Enterprise planes was not yet dropped, which destroyed the hull.

Technical Data:
Length overall:	102,5 m	336.5 ft
Width:	8,8 m	29 ft
Draught:	3,1 m	10 ft
Displacement:	1 215 ts	
Max. Speed:	39 knots	
Horsepower:	38 500 hp	
Armament:	4 x 12,0 cm, 4.7" dual purpose guns, various a/a - 2 x 21" torpedo tubes	

JAPANESE PLANES INVOLVED IN THE DEFENSE OF TRUK

List of Japanese Aircraft Encountered in Operation Hailstone

Only those planes are listed which have been mentioned in the text, and therefore no attempt has been made to embrace all Japanese planes in operation in the Pacific theater of war. Specifications may slightly vary in this listing, depending on the model. Drawings are courtesy of Kikuo Hashimoto.

Allied Code Name	Japanese Designation	Description
Betty	Mitsubishi G4M1/G4M3	Navy Attack Bomber
Dinah	Mitsubishi Ki-46	Command Reconnaissance
Emily	Kawanishi H8K	Flying Boat
Frances	Yokosuka P1Y Navy	Bomber Ginga
	Yokosuka P1Y-S	Navy Night Fighter, Byakko
	Yokosuka P2Y-S	Navy Night Fighter, Kyokko
Hamp/Hap	Mitsubishi A6M3	Navy Carrier Fighter
Irving	Nakajima J1N1-C & R	Navy Reconnaissance Plane
	Nakajima J1N1-S	Navy Night Fighter Gekko
Jake	Aichi E13A	Navy Reconnaissance Floatplane
Jill	Nakajima B6N	Navy Carrier Att Bomber, Tenzan
Kate	Nakajima B5N/B5M	Navy Carrier Attack Bomber
Mavis	Kawanishi H6K	Navy Flying Boat
Nate	Nakajima Ki-27	Army Fighter
Nell	Mitsubishi G3M	Navy Attack Bomber
Oscar	Nakajima Ki-43	Army Fighter Hayabusa
Pete	Mitsubishi F1M	Navy Observation Seaplane
Rufe	Nakajima A6M2-N	Navy Fighter
Sally	Mitsubishi Ki-21	Army Heavy Bomber
Tojo Shoki	Nakajima Ki-44	Army Single Seat Fighter,
Tony	Kawasaki Ki-61	Army Fighter, Hien
Val	Aichi D3A	Navy Carrier Bomber
Zeke	Mitsubishi A6M3	Navy Carrier Fighter

Betty Mitsubishi G4M1/G4M3
Navy Attack Bomber

Crew	7
Span	24.89 m
Length	19.63 m
Height	4.11 m
Wing Area	78 sq m
Weight empty/ Gross	8391/12500 kg
Horsepower	2 x 1850 hp
Speed km/h, max. at 455/5000 m	
Range km	3000
Armament	1 x 12.7 mm; 4 x 20 mm

発動機　火星 11 型
1,530 HP × 2
全　幅　24.89 m
全　長　19.97 m
全備重量　9,500 kg
最大速度　428 km/h
Hashimoto

The Betty was probably one of the best bombers at the beginning of the war. It had a range of action which revolutionized bombing doctrine. As long as the air was relatively free of enemy fighters, the G4M was a formidable weapon. As air superiority changed to the Americans, the plane acquired the nickname, "Flying Cigar" or "One Shot Lighter", on account of its shape and the fact that it burst easily into flames when hit, as the fuel tanks were unprotected.

Bettys were used in two principal roles against Task Force 58: The first was long range reconnaissance, the second was as a torpedo or level bomber. Practically all snoopers were Bettys. However, once the Hellcats sighted a a Betty, the Japanese bomber generally was

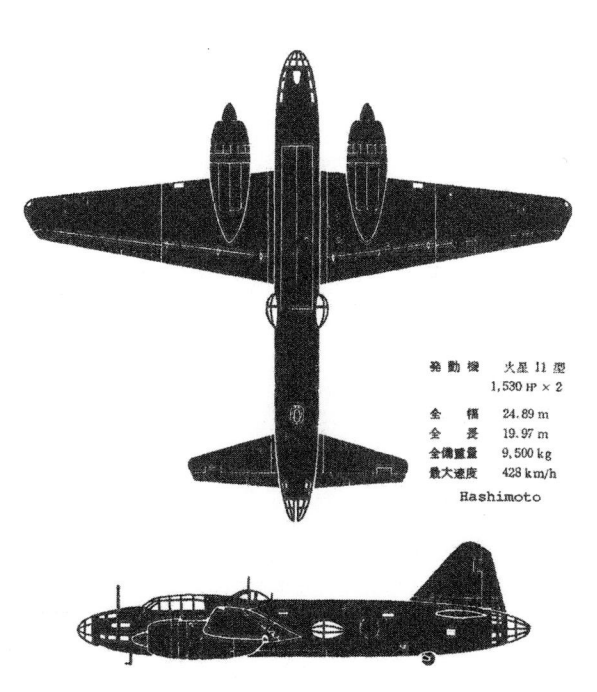

Hailstorm - *Appendix*

shot down quickly. It was surprising that despite the defensive weaponry, Bettys never seemed to have scored against the fighters.

Almost 2,500 G4M planes were built between September 1939 and the war's end. It was in two white painted Bettys, their Rising Sun symbol painted over by green crosses, that the Japanese surrender party arrived in Ie Shima. When they intended to take off, one of the planes could not fly for mechanical reasons, and the other made an emergency landing in the water, almost drowning the Japanese surrender party.

High speed and long range were the design criteria. For planes at the time, both objectives were met. Range was 5600 km, and max. speed was 430 km/h. Later models (G4M2 and 3) were armored and more powerful. Their power plants were two 14-cylinder radial engines delivering 1530 hp each (Mitsubishi MK4A-11). The plane had a wingspan of 25 m (85 ft), was 20 m (66 ft) long and 6 m (20 ft) high. It weighed almost 10 t (21 000 lbs) fully loaded and attained a speed of 438 km/h (266 mph) at 4200 m (13 780 ft). Its ceiling was 8 840 m (29 000 ft). A later version, its production started in 1942, used a methanol injection, 'Kasai 21' engine with 1850 hp. The crew of seven, piloted the plane, navigated, and manned one 20 mm cannon and four machine guns. A single 800 kg (1750 lbs) bomb could be carried.

Emily — Kawanishi H8K1 Flying Boat

Crew	16
Span	38.0 m
Length	28.13
Height	9.15
Wing Area	160 sq m
Weight empty/ Gross	15500/ 24500 kg
Horsepower	4 x 1850 hp
Speed km/h, max. at	454/5000
Range	7200
Armament	5 x 20 mm; 3 x 7.7 mm

Undoubtedly, the Emily was the zenith of Japanese flying boats. Nicknamed "The Flying Porcupine", it was one of the toughest and prickliest planes ever built. It had a reputation of being extremely difficult to shoot down, able to defend itself and take an unusual amount of punishment. This was not in small part due to the self-sealing fuel tanks and the internal fire extinguishers. Its range was a whopping 4500 miles, take-off weight was 33 tons. With a length of 28 m and a wingspan of 38 m, it was large, even by today's standards. Despite its obvious bulk, it had a speed of about 466 km/h and the ceiling was 28,740 ft (almost 9000 m). That was only 10% less than the Superfortress. Its range of 7200 km exceeded that of the B29A Superfortress by 650 km. Indeed, a remarkable plane!

Several Emilys were stationed in Palau and were probably well camouflaged, as they appear to have escaped damages. The Commander-in-Chief, Combined Fleet, Admiral Koga and his staff took two undamaged planes and flew to Davoa, on 31 March 1944. The planes and almost all passengers and crew did not make it, but this was on account of a very bad storm and had nothing to do with the attack on Palau.

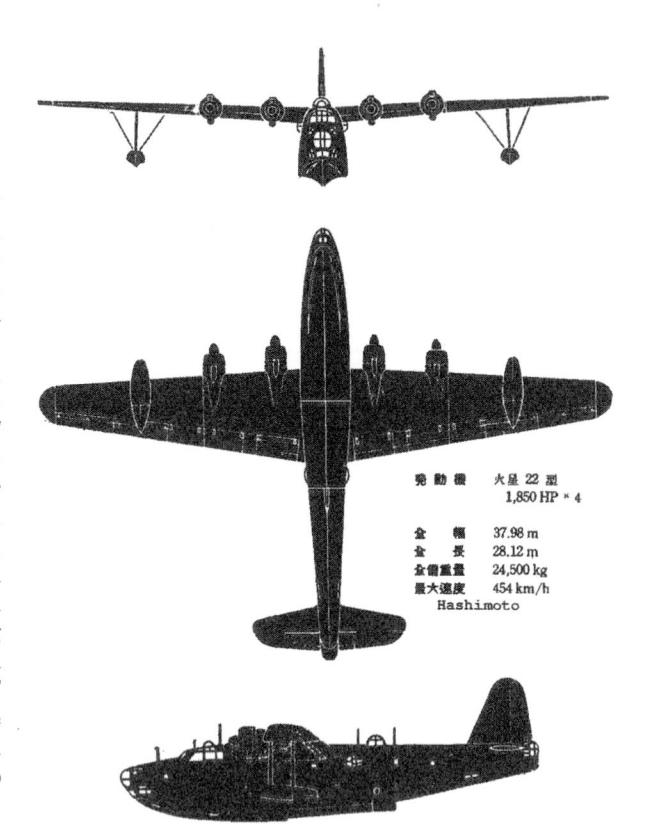

The plane, as the prototype, developed stability problems in the water, and during take-off. The entire underside had to be redesigned, but then the flying boat performed beyond expectations. The first action in the war was the bombing of Oahu, Hawaii in 1942. The 2 Emilies came from bases in the Marshalls. The moral effect was probably greater than the actual damage, but long range bombing was there to stay - on the American side, however.

Only 165 Emilies were built. Some of them were converted to accommodate passenger transfer.

Hamp/Hap/Zeke/Zero — Mitsubishi A6M3 Navy Carrier Fighter

Crew	1
Span	11.0 m
Length	9.06 m
Height	2.92 m
Wing Area	21.5 sq m
Weight empty/ Gross	1807/ 2644
Horsepower	1130
Speed km/h, max. at	541/6000
Range	2380
Armament	2 x 20 mm; 2 x 7.7 mm

Zeros saw action from the attack of Pearl Harbor to the surrender of Japan on August 15, 1945. It was probably the one most outstanding plane in the Pacific theater. Although matched, and later outclassed by US fighters, it still represented a formidable weapon. The reason it performed below par in the later years was that it had to be manned by pilots which lacked experience, training and the skill of the earlier aces, and because ground control was far inferior to US standards.

There were quite a number of improved variants being made, but after it lost its advantage in late 1942 or early 1943, it never quite caught up with the US planes. Altogether, about 11,300 planes were built - this compares with the Messerschmidt Bf 109 variants, of which about 35,000 were built in Germany.

The designer responsible for this plane was a man named Jiro Horikoshi. Work had already begun in 1937, to build a plane matching unheard-of specifications, specifically for carrier duty, laid down by the Imperial Japanese Navy. The plane performance matched, and in some respects, exceeded the design criteria. For example, the specs called for a top speed of 500 km/h. The A6M2 reached 557 km/h. This was made possible by newer, more powerful engines coming out of production. Early in the war, nothing could out-maneuver, out-turn and out-speed the Zero. Up to the Battle of Midway, the Zero dominated the skies. Yet, it was in this battle that the losses of aircraft, pilots and carriers struck the heavy blow from which the air-arm of the Japanese Navy could never recover.

Development of new models continued up to the end of the war. The final version of the Zero, the A6M8, could have been a comparable aircraft to the US planes, but production difficulties and lack of pilots prevented them playing any decisive part.

The specifications which Mitsubishi even exceeded, called for a speed of 500 km/h, endurance of 1.2 to 1.5 hours, including 30 minutes for aerial combat, and 4 guns. To lessen the take-off weight, duraluminium was used. Type A6M1 had a Mitsubishi 'suisei' 780 hp engine, but only two planes were produced. The Nakajima 'Sakae' was adapted for the airframe; this became the A6M2. It proved to be a better performer than the previous version. This plane was generally known as Zeke or Zero. By removing the foldable tips and squaring the ends of the wings, and the addition of a 2-stage supercharger to the 'Sakae' engine, the A6M3 "Hamp" was produced.

Jake - Aichi E13A1-1 Navy Floatplane

Crew	3
Span	14.5 m
Length	11.268 m
Height	4.783 m
Wing Area	39.7 sq m
Weight empty/ Gross	2642 / 3650 kg
Horsepower	1000 hp
Speed km/h, max. at	385m/ 2180 m

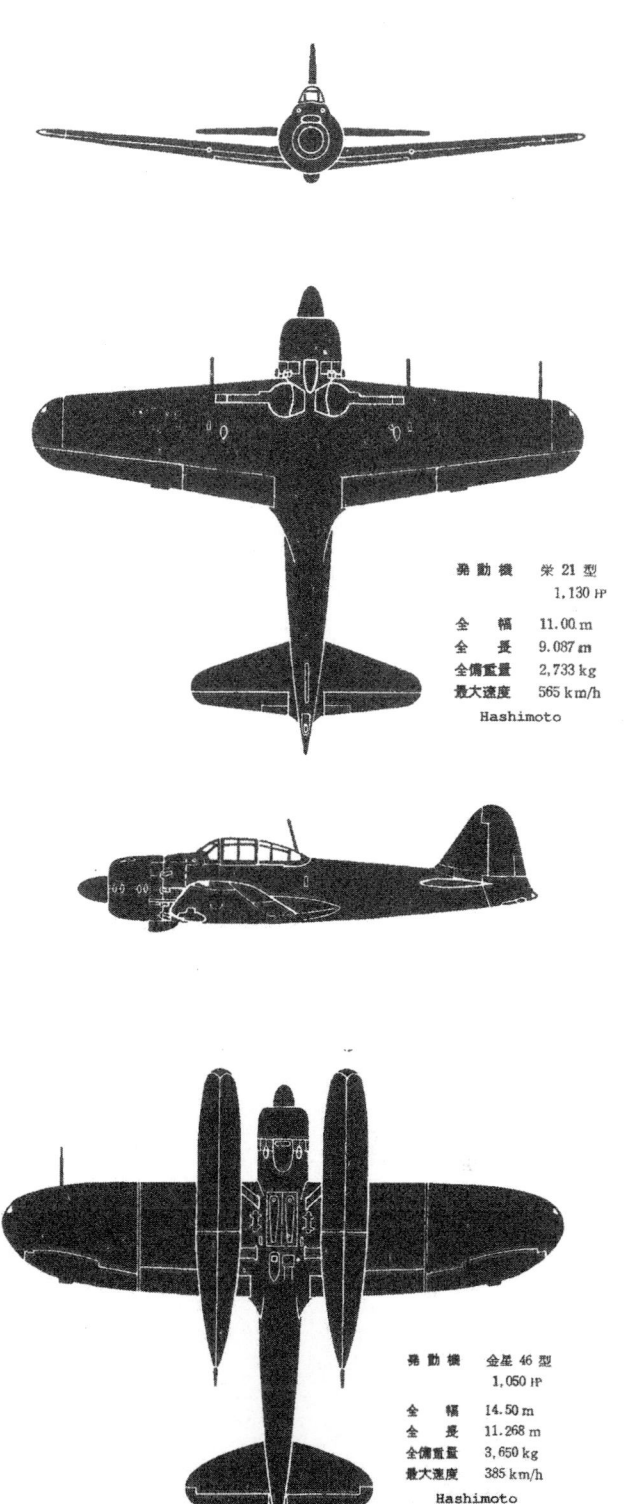

Hailstorm - *Appendix*

Range km   2000
Armament   1 x 7.9 mm

The Jake was built by Aichi from 1938 onwards, to replace the aging Type 94 and 95 float planes, but the production series did not commence until 1941. The plane had two principle roles. The first was an attack plane, carrying up to 250 kg of bombs next to its crew of three, from seaplane tenders into China, particularly against the Canton-Hanchow railroad. However, the plane was slow and vulnerable. The other role was that of a long-range reconnaisasance plane. As such it saw action at the Battles of the Coral Sea, Midway and the Solomons. Later variants carried a radar set. The Jake could be found in many lagoons where the land mass did not support an airfield, but they also operated from cruisers and battleships.

Two of these planes can be seen in very shallow waters in a cave off Babelthuap.

Judy - Aichi D4Y1, 2, 3, 4 - Carrier Based Dive Bomber

Crew	2
Span	11.5 m
Length	10.22 m
Height	3.14 m
Wing Area	23.6 sq m
Weight empty/ Gross	2501 / 3754 kg
Horsepower	1560 hp
Speed km/h, max. at	574/6050 m
Range km	3000
Armament	3 x 7.7 mm

The 'Suisei' was designed by the Yokosuka Navy arsenal and built mainly by Aichi. Its original mission was a high speed bomber, but the planes were used for reconnaissance and night interception as well. The airframe was only slightly larger than that of the Zero, but it could carry a 250 kg bomb inside the fuselage. One of the three operational types built has been reported by the Japanese to play an important role of defending Truk on the first carrier attack.

The first model was powered by a 1100 hp, 12 cylinder, inverted V-engine, the second, type 22 by a 1400 hp 'Atsuta 32' engine, with speed between 330 and 360 mph (530 to 580 km/h). The plane itself was an excellent performer, but the power plant was a consistent source of problems. Its design was well advanced. Electric controls were used throughout, but the undercarriage was operated hydraulically.

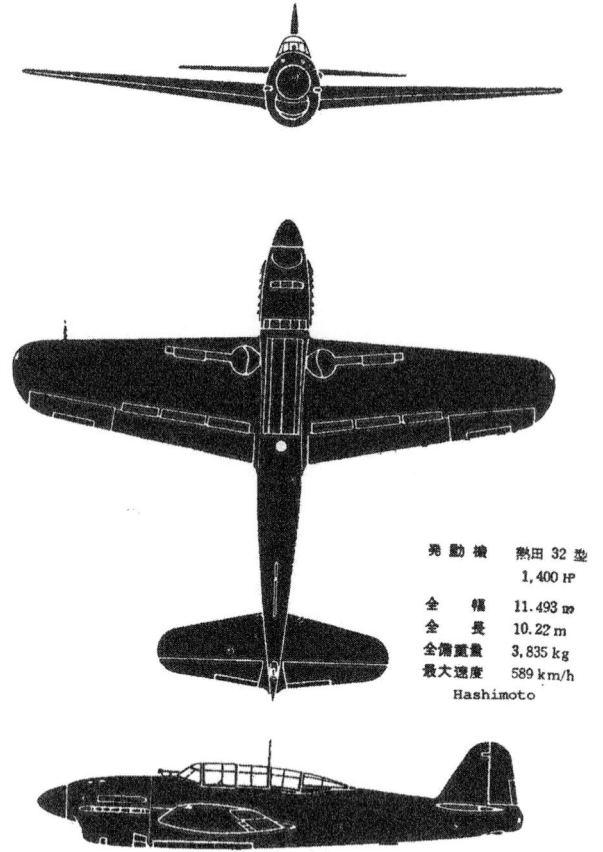

During the Operation Desecrate, a flight of nine Judys were shot down on the last day, but there were two planes which were able to outrun the Hellcats at low altitude, and escape.

発動機 熱田 32 型
       1,400 HP
全 幅   11.493 m
全 長   10.22 m
全備重量 3,835 kg
最大速度 589 km/h
Hashimoto

Nate   Nakajima Ki-27 Army Fighter

Crew	1
Span	11.3 m
Length	7.53 m
Height	2.8 m
Wing Area	18.6 sq. m
Weight empty/ Gross	1790/
Horsepower	710
Speed km/h, max. at	470/3500
Range	1710 km
Armament	2 x 7.7 mm

The Nate was a transition plane between the matured bi-planes and the fairly new monoplanes. The Nate was one of the first operational monoplane fighters of the Japanese, and had a remarkable performance. The Army selected this plane over two competing models. In doing so, they clearly set the priorities for excellent maneuvering and against just fast speed. It

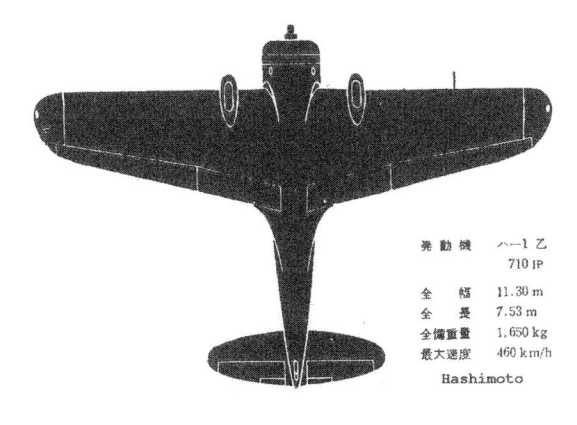

Hailstorm — *Appendix*

Range 1440 km
Armament 3 x 7.7 mm

This was a bi-plane, produced in large quantities for such an outdated design and used chiefly in its design role as a spotter plane for heavy cruisers and battleships. However, it was also used in a multitude

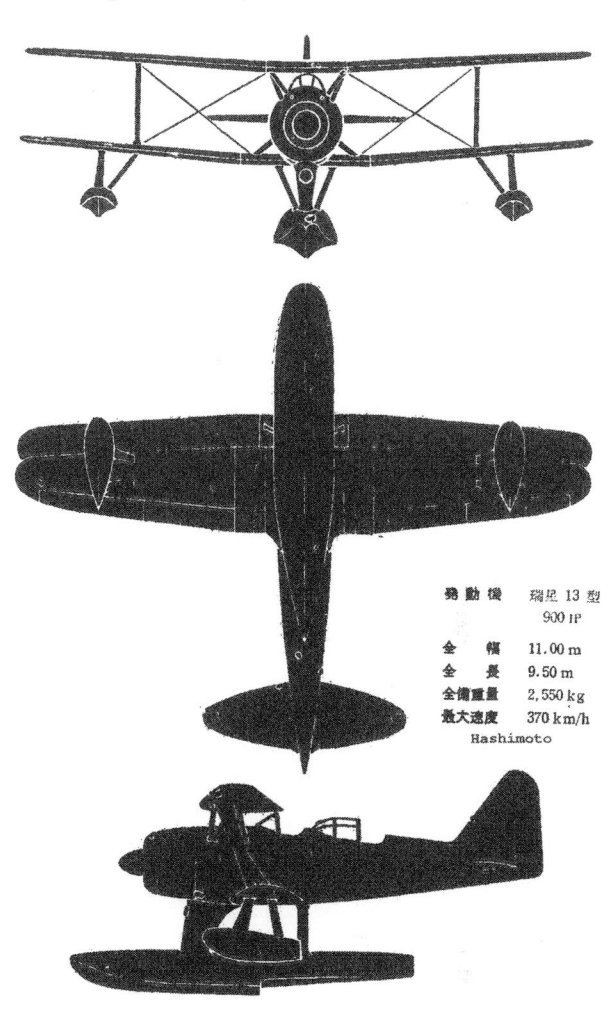

was almost impossible to stall the plane in dog-fight conditions, because of its large wing area. The two-bladed, fixed propeller, an all alluminum body and wing, fixed undercarriage and a radio mast in front of the cockpit made recognition of this aircraft easy. It was an almost identical twin to the Navy's A5M, the predecessor to the Zero.

The aircraft made its debut in the China conflict in March 1938, and proved to be a deadly weapon against the Russian bi-plane then flown, such as Polikarpov I-15 in the so-called Nomonhan Incident. It was also successful against the majority of the Allied fighters in South-East Asia in the early stages of the war. However, they were soon withdrawn to Japan as more modern planes came out to the front and most Nates were spent in Kamikaze attack in the closing period of the war. Its successor model was the Oscar.

Pete   Mitsubishi F1M2
Navy Observation Seaplane

Crew	2
Span	11.0 m
Length	9.5 m
Height	4.0 m
Wing Area	29.5 sq. m
Weight empty/ Gross	1964/2550
Horsepower	700
Speed km/h, max. at	370/3000

of other roles: coastal patrol, convoy escort, dive bombing and even interception in the early stages of the war.

Also this aircraft had a lot of severe problems when the first prototypes were flown, but Mitsubishi overcame them by almost completely redesigning the main frame and the floats. Eventually, it was a very successful plane, highly maneuverable and versatile. Its airworthiness was outstanding.

The Pete was used with preference, in the island garrisons of the Pacific, where the flat plane could maintain communications wherever landing strips were not available. The plane was slow but highly maneuverable, and the powerful Hellcats did not really have a chance to catch this little plane.

Hailstorm - *Appendix*

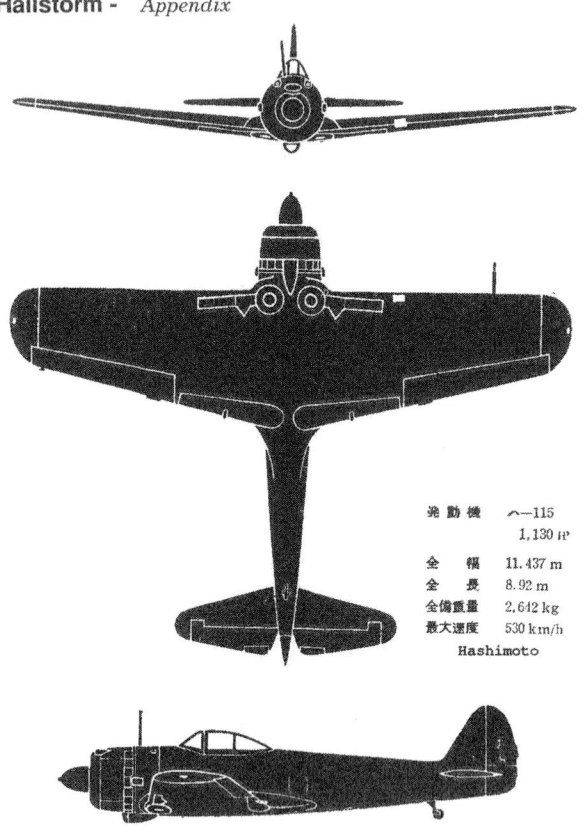

Oscar - Nakajima ki-43 Hayabusa Army Fighter

Crew	1
Span	11.437 m
Length	8.92 m
Height	3.213 m
Wing Area	21.4 sq. m
Weight empty/ Gross	1975/2642
Horsepower	1130
Speed km/h, max. at	515/6000
Range	
Armament	2 x 12.7 mm

The Oscar swept the skies clean in the Japanese campaigns of Malaya, Sumatra and Java. It proved a bitter lesson for the Allies in the beginning of the war. The majority of remaining Oscars ended up at the end of the war in desperate suicide missions to intercept American bombers during bombing raids of the Homeland.

The Oscar was an Army plane, which was designed in 1937. It was a very good plane at the time, with retractable undercarriage, and a performance, which was very advanced. Maneuverability was enhanced by the adaptation of special flaps, so-called butterflies. The plane, which the first test pilots thought was difficult to fly, was now able to make very sharp turns. Later models had an armor protection for the pilot and a rudimentary self-sealing fuel tank.

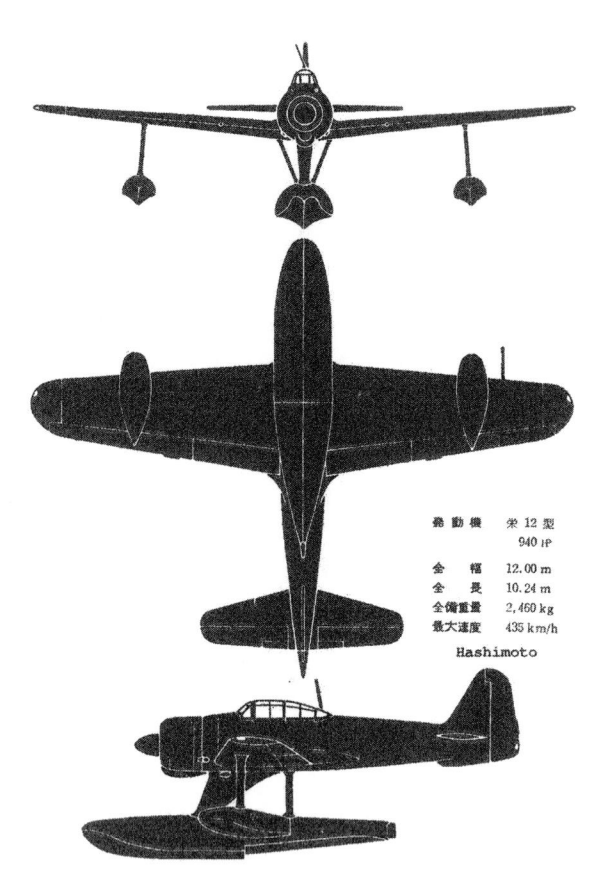

Rufe - Mitsubishi A6M2-N Navy Float Plane

The "Rufe" was a floatplane based on the Zero-fighter. Its performance was almost identical to that of the A6M2 Zero, despite the large center and two small wing floats. It was designated a fighter, but was more vulnerable and less maneuverable than the Zero.

Its operative career was interesting. The Rufe was supposed to be stationed at those Pacific Islands where it was not feasible to build an air field. This plane could safely land inside a lagoon.
The "Rufe" was built by Nakajima, and 327 planes were manufactured.

Tojo Nakajima Ki-44 Army Single Seat Fighter, Shoki

Crew	1
Span	9.448 m
Length	8.75 m
Height	3.248
Wing Area	15 sq m
Weight empty/ Gross	2106/2770
Horsepower	1500
Speed km/h, max. at	605/5200
Range km	4000
Armament	4 x 12.7 mm

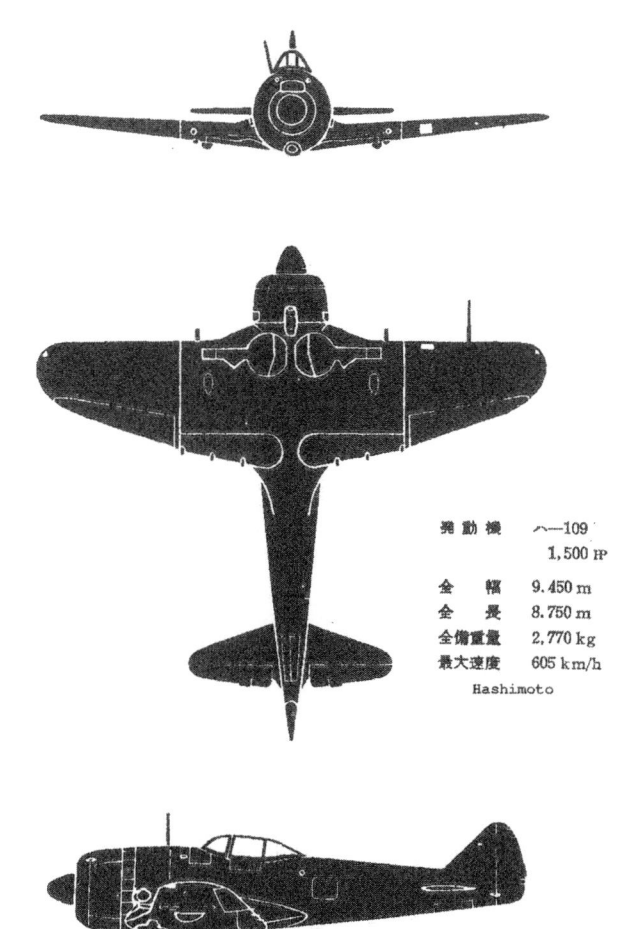

appeared over New Guinea skies in April 43. The plane proved a match, if not even superior to the US aircrafts at the time. Pilots protection, heavy armament and high speed dives were excellent. The sleek fighter in its original design had a licence series-600 Daimler-Benz inverted V in-line, liquid cooled power plant. Although the fighter strongly resembled the famous Messerschmidt Bf109 E, Japanese sources always have maintained that the design and production technique were of Japanese origin. It was probably a case that the same engine lead to very similar airframes, and after all, the Japanese had been informed about the Bf 109. In fact, in 1942, the Tony was flown in a test program with a German Bf109 E, brought to Japan, and a captured P 40. The validity of the Japanese construction was proven.

Production figures reached up to 200 per month, but yet there were severe problems. The first was with its original armament of Mauser 20 mm cannons, which were not available in sufficient quantities and had to be substituted by a Japanese gun with inferior

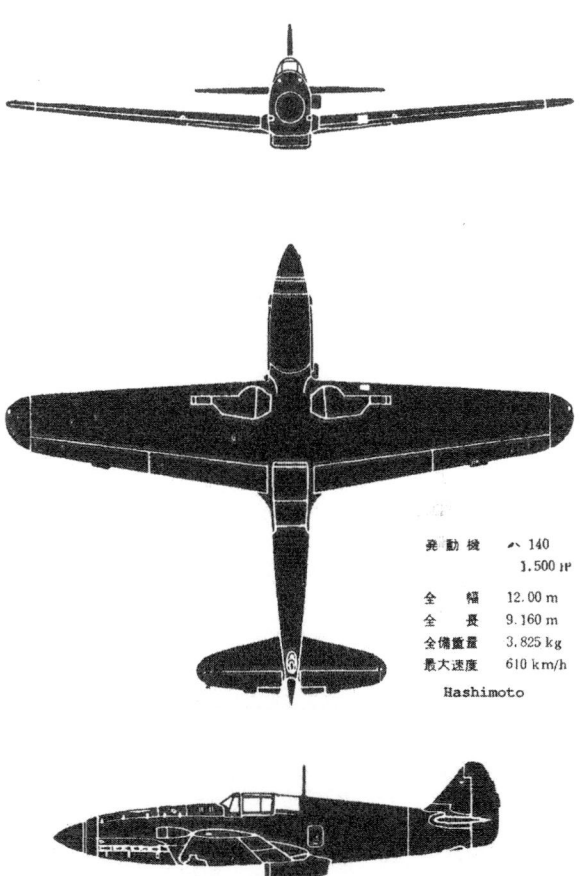

The Tojo was a fast, maneuverable aircraft which in the later stages of the war was almost exclusively used for the defenses of mainland Japan. Many of the planes were spent in ramming attacks against the high flying B29. The plane was very good in climbing and its drawback of high landing speed and high wing loads were recognized. Its performance was almost identical to the Hellcat F6F3, but while the latter had a wingspan of about 42 ft, the Tojo had only 31 ft. To handle the plane, experienced pilots were required.

Tony   **Kawasaki Ki-61**
                  Army Fighter, Hien

Crew	1
Span	12.0 m
Length	9.16 m
Height	3.7 m
Wing Area	20 sq m
Weight empty/ Gross	2855/3825
Horsepower	1450
Speed km/h, max. at	610/6000
Range	1600 km
Armament	2 x 12.7 mm; 2 x 20 mm

This aircraft startled the Americans when it

performance. The other was that the Japanese did not quite master the problems of in-line, liquid cooled engines, and there were reliability problems. Consequently, the headless airframes eventually had to be matched to a much larger diameter radial engine.

Hailstorm - *Appendix*

SHIP RECOGNITION AND TERMINOLOGY

Throughout the description of the wrecks, terms associated with merchant ships were used. The following notes on ship recognition are restricted to the ships found in Truk.

PROFILE

Hull Form

If the deck of a ship extends from stem to stern without raised "castles" or "islands", the hull is called a flush deck, and the ship is termed a flushdecker. The superstructures are built right on the deck. The Hoki Maru is a modified flushdecker. She is called modified because she has a forecastle.

Other ships have "castles" - the word is a hold-over from the old wooden sailing ships - which rise like islands above deck. These islands form an integrated part of the hull. They are called forecastle at the bow, bridge or midcastle at midships and poop (or aftercastle) at the stern. The Fujikawa Maru is a three island ship, having a forecastle, a midship castle and a poop.

The bridge deck may be extended aft and joined with the poop. In the Heian Maru and Rio de Janeiro Maru, the midship superstructure is extended but does not quite reach the poop. The place between the forecastle and the bridge is called the well or welldeck.

There may be confusion as to whether a hull has islands or not, particularly if the bulwark plating is high or the superstructure is low.

Stems (Bows) and Sterns

The forward part of a ship is the bow. In the olden days, the bow frequently was an iron bar to which the shell plating was attached. This bar was called the stem or stem stembar. The shape was almost always straight or raked straight. It was not until the shipping industry in North Ireland, in particular Harlan & Wolfe, developed the bent bar, the Belfast Bow, that the original plumb bar, offering the most resistance to cutting water, was superseded. Later, steel plates were bent in a sharp turn, and although being not as sharp as a stembar, provided the flexibility to built different forms of bows. The bows manufactured from plates are called a soft nose.

The old fashioned bow form is the straight, plumb or vertical bow. This form can be found on several of the older ships in Truk, such as on the San Francisco, Reiyo and Unkai Maru.

The more modern version is the raked bow. The lines of the bow may be either raked back straight or curved. The Fujikawa Maru, for instance, has a straight raked bow.

Other forms, like the spoon and the icebreaker bow are not found on the wrecks in Truk.

The sterns may be basically classified as a clipper or counter stern or a cruiser stern. Some ships have a deep overhanging counter, for example the Gosei Maru. The Fujikawa has a counter stern but with less overhang.

The angle of a cruiser stern may vary. The Rio de Janeiro and the Aikoku Maru have cruiser sterns.

Masts and Kingposts

A mast is any pole set along the centerline of a ship. It is the tallest structure of a ship, rising above all other uprights. The masts are called, from the bow towards aft, foremast, mainmast mizzen or after mast. They are named lower mast for the portion which rises from the deck to the platform above, which is called a cross tree. The top mast is located above the cross tree.

If a mast ends at the cross tree, and does not have a top mast, it is called a king post. If the kingpost in not set on the centerline of the ship but on both sides, it is called samson post, and if they are joined on top with a heavy bar, they are called goalposts. The goalpost may have a top mast, such as may be found on the Aikoku and Kansho Maru. (One of the topmasts of the Kansho toppled down). In the description of the wrecks in Truk, the terms kingpost and goalpost are used interchangeably, and the word kingpost is used most often.

Funnels

There are many different shapes of funnels. They were dictated originally by the kind of propulsion and fuel for the ships. In order not to become overly technical, the funnels here are described as tall, high, tubular, medium and stout. A tall funnel generally refers to a ship which burned coal as fuel. It is a hollow tube. The medium sized funnel is typical for diesel propelled freighters. The Rio de Janeiro Maru would be a good example. The stout stack, also called motor ship or motor vessel type is not quite as high as the medium sized funnel, but may be wider. Typically, the medium sized or motor ship funnel enclose one or more exhaust pipes. The border between the different types are not clearly drawn, but the differentiation in three different forms should should give an idea about the shape and the height. In the text, the words "funnel" and "stack" are used interchangeably.

Ventilators

A great variety of ventilators have been built. Except for a few of the wrecks (Kiyozumi and Aikoku Maru) almost all have cowl ventilators. The two ships mentioned have mushroom-type ventilators. In many

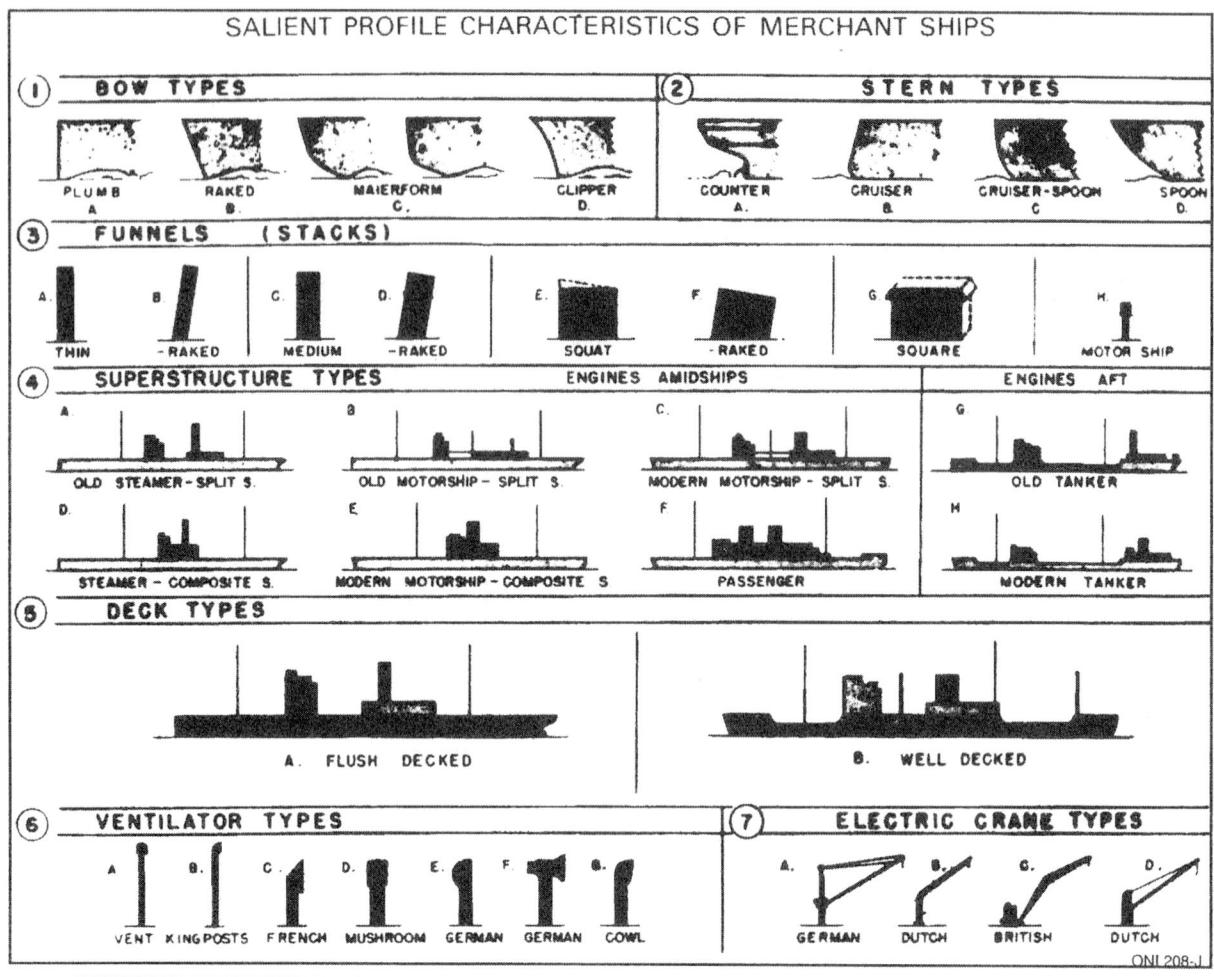

Hailstorm - *Appendix*

SALIENT PROFILE CHARACTERISTICS OF MERCHANT SHIPS

① BOW TYPES: A. PLUMB, B. RAKED, C. MAIERFORM, D. CLIPPER

② STERN TYPES: A. COUNTER, B. CRUISER, C. CRUISER-SPOON, D. SPOON

③ FUNNELS (STACKS): A. THIN, B. -RAKED, C. MEDIUM, D. -RAKED, E. SQUAT, F. -RAKED, G. SQUARE, H. MOTOR SHIP

④ SUPERSTRUCTURE TYPES

ENGINES AMIDSHIPS:
- A. OLD STEAMER - SPLIT S.
- B. OLD MOTORSHIP - SPLIT S.
- C. MODERN MOTORSHIP - SPLIT S.
- D. STEAMER - COMPOSITE S.
- E. MODERN MOTORSHIP - COMPOSITE S.
- F. PASSENGER

ENGINES AFT:
- G. OLD TANKER
- H. MODERN TANKER

⑤ DECK TYPES: A. FLUSH DECKED, B. WELL DECKED

⑥ VENTILATOR TYPES: A. VENT, B. KINGPOSTS, C. FRENCH, D. MUSHROOM, E. GERMAN, F. GERMAN, G. COWL

⑦ ELECTRIC CRANE TYPES: A. GERMAN, B. DUTCH, C. BRITISH, D. DUTCH

ONI 208-J

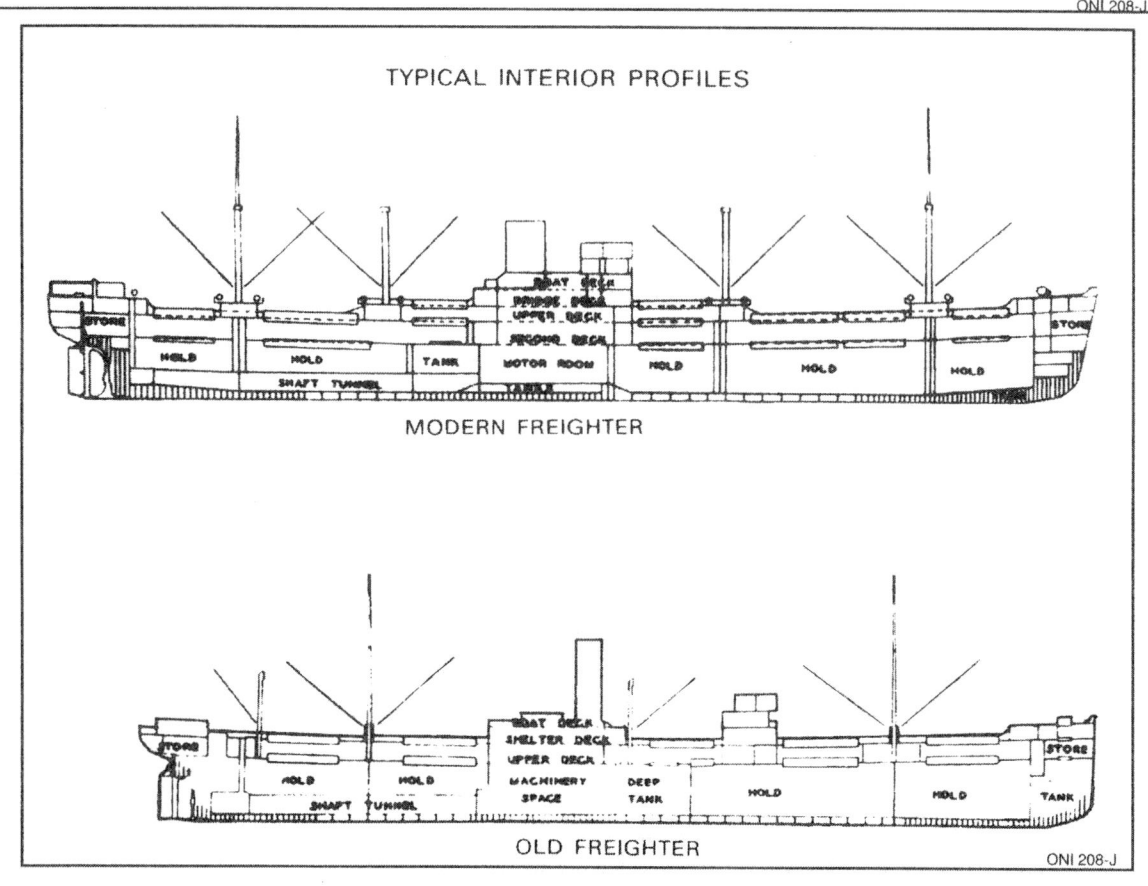

TYPICAL INTERIOR PROFILES

MODERN FREIGHTER

OLD FREIGHTER

ONI 208-J

cases, these structures have been blasted over board or their sheet metal corroded to the point where they have toppled down from their shafts.

Derricks

The derricks are long spars (or booms) attached to the foot of the mast or kingpost by a gooseneck. They generally are fitted in pairs at the base. Normally, they are secured (stowed) in a lower horizontal position while the ship is underway. The derricks are in a way cranes which handle the cargo, getting it out of the hold, swinging it overboard, and lowering it on to the dock or into barges.. They are carrying blocks and tackle for the lines, which is summarized as the running rigging.

Frequently, ships carry heavy or jumbo derricks. They are used to handle cargo heavier than the 3 to 5 tons normally handled by the derricks. As jumbo derricks are not generally used for cargo handling, they may be lashed vertically to a mast or kingpost. The clamp to secure a jumbo derrick can be seen above water on the foremast of the Fujikawa Maru, and the jumbo derrick can be seen on the Sankisan Maru.

Profile

The split profile is characterized by the separation of the bridge, i.e. the forward part of the midship superstructure and the funnel. This profile is found frequently, but not exclusively, on older ships. A typical example is the San Francisco Maru.

In the composite profile, the bridge is merged with the superstructure. This is the most common type of modern freighters. The Fujikawa Maru is a very good example.

Typical for tankers is the engine aft profile. Having the engine aft offers certain advantages and several freighters have been built like this, notably the Gosei and Seiko Maru.

TONNAGE AND SIZE

It is difficult to estimate the tonnage of a ship. Firstly the tonnage refers to the amount of enclosed space, that is the volume of the cargo spaces, or the weight of the ship or the cargo.Obviously then there may be significant differences in ships of the same dimension, not only in cargo carrying capacity but also by the weight of the displacement. The basic terms are:

Gross Tonnage

This term refers to the total volume of enclosed spaces. 100 cubic feet make one ton (2.83 cubic meters equals one ton gross). The tonnage quoted in the part Technical Data of the wrecks is based on gross tons, if not specifically mentioned differently.

Net Tonnage

This is the same as gross tonnage minus crew quarters, boilers, engine room and fuel spaces. The net tonnage is the earning capacity of a ship.

Displacement Tonnage

Tons displacement are rarely used in the merchant marine. It is the weight of the ship, and may be subdivided in terms of different states of readiness, i.e. with fuel, boilers, fully equipped and not, etc. The term is usually applied for warships.

Deadweight Tonnage

The weight of the cargo, fuel, etc, required to bring the ship up to the fully loaded condition is called the deadweight tonnage.

Length, Breadth, Depth and Draught

Length

The length of a ship may be measured at the waterline or including the overhanging parts of the stern - overall length.

Breadth

The breadth of the ship is the dimension given at the ships widest points. It may be called the beam.

Depth

The depth gives the distance between the keel and the welldeck.

Draught

The draught is measured from the keel to the waterline at the fully laden state of the ship. The difference between the Depth and the Draught is the freeboard.

GLOSSARY

The glossary is kept brief, and no attempt is made to encompass all terms other than those used in the text.

Abaft - Behind an object.
Abeam - To the side of, at right angles to an object.
A-Cockbill - Anchor hanging suspended from the hawsepipe.
Aft - To the rear, towards the stern.
Ahead - In front.
Ailerons - The control surfaces on the outside trailing edge of the wings, which control the roll of the airplane.
Airspeed Indicator - Indicator that shows the aircaft's present speed through the air, but not above ground.
Amidships - Location close to the ship's axis, at the center line of a ship.
Anchor - Implement by which a ship becomes attached to the sea bottom, and thus rendered stationary.
Anchorage - An area in which the holding ground is good and suitable for ships to anchor.
Anchor Cable, Anchor Chain - Strong wrought iron chain to which the anchor is attached via a shackle, and whose other end, the bitter end, should be attached firmly to the ship.
AP - Armor piercing, special designed ordnance to penetrate armor. In text, one type of bombs used.
Astern - Directly abaft.
Athwart - Across, at right angle to ship's axis.
Awash - Water washing over.

Balanced Rudder - Modern form of rudder in which the rudder stock is not the leading edge of the rudder.
Bank - See roll.
Battery - Ship's gun either of the same calibre or same purpose. Unmask batteries reqires the ship to maneuver to be able to bear the guns against the target, open batteries means open fire.
Beam - Transverse member between opposite ribs of a ship to support the sides against collapsing stress and to support a deck.
Beams End - Vessel lying over so much that her deck beams are nearly vertical.
Bilge - Rounded part of the ship's underwater body where the sides curve around towards the keel.
Bilge Keel - External keel placed along bilge of a ship, to stiffen, stress protection and reduce rolling in the seas.
Bogey - Unidentified aircraft.
Bombing Technique - Types of bombing are Glide Bombing, in a powered attack angle of 35 to 55 degrees without brakes or flaps; Dive Bombing, steep dive of about 60 to 70 degrees using dive brakes; Masthead Attack, shallow dive or low level attack with the variation of Skip Bombing, when the bombs skip on the water surface into the target.
Bombs - Explosive device dropped from aircraft, with fuze to explode at set interval after hitting. See also AP, GP and SAP.
Boom - Derrick (see there).
Bow - Foremost part of the ships hull, aft of the stem.

Breast Hook - Horizontal plates in fore end of a vessel, supporting and preserving the bow form.
Bridge - Navigation platform running at right angles to the center line high up on the forward part of the superstructure. In the text, frequently used to describe the forward part of the midships- superstructure.
Bridge Deck - Deck at level of the bridge.
Bulkhead - Any partition (wall) on board. Specifically, a watertight partition.
Bulwark - Vertical plating at the side of the ship to give protection against the sea and for crew safety, generally more modern form of guardrails, which it generally replaced.

Capsize - To overturn. A ship is said to have capsized when it is in a bottom-up position.
Castle - Raised part of the hull.
Catwalk - Raised gangway or passageway, mostly unprotected, narrow grating with a hand rail.
Chain Locker - Compartment where the anchor cable is stowed.
Close Miss (of a bomb) - A bomb exploding about a beam's width away from a ship. It will damage the hull, the superstructure and personnel losses.
Coaming - Raised sides of an opening on deck, such as on hatches (hatch coaming).
Collier - Vessel specially equipped to carry coal. Generally without tween decks.
Companion Ladder - Steps going from one deck to another, below or above.
Companion Way - Stairs or ladders leading to a cabin.
Condenser - Chamber into which exhaust steam is lead to outside surface of a number of pipes, through which sea water is circulated, causing the steam to condense into water, which is recirculated into the boilers.
Cowl - Wind catching, generally flared openings on ventilators.
Counter - Extreme stern of the ship, overhang, fantail.
Crosstree - Platform on top of the lower mast or kingpost to which cargo lifting gear is rigged.

Davits - Curved steel structures, to launch and receive life boats.
Decks - Horizontal division on ships, like floors.
For simplification, the upper deck of the hulls of the wrecks in Palau is generally called maindeck, although technically it could be the shelterdeck.
Decks below maindeck are generally named in alphabetical order. Above maindeck, they are generally, shelterdeck, promenade deck, boatdeck, sun deck. Boatdeck is the level where the life boats are located on the superstructure.
Deckhead - Ceiling of an enclosed space, lower side of the deck.

Degaussing - The magnetic field of the body of iron, represented by the ship, is reduced or neutralized by wrapping coils of energized wire around it. Important for passive protection against magnetic influenced detonators in mines and torpedoes.
Derrick - Long tubular or structural (lattice work) spar attached to foot of mast or kingpost, for cargo handling.
Derrick Post - Vertical post to which derricks are fixed. May also be called kingpost or sampson post and flank mast.
DesRon - Destroyer Squadron. A tactically organized number of destroyers.
Downwind - Direction the wind is blowing to.

Elevators - Control surfaces on the trailing edge of the horizontal stabilizer, which control the pitch of the plane. Elevators in the down position, force the nose of the plane down.

Fall - Hauling part of a rope, which by running through blocks, gives mechanical advantage.
Fantail - Extension of the stern by overhang of a counter stern.
Fashion Plate - Transition between bulwark and island. Usually sweeping up to avoid sharp corners and stress concentrations.
Flaps - Inboard moveable section of the trailing edge of the wings to increase lift and drag. Are generally lowered to provide both elements on landing, but also on take-off.
Flare - Upward and outward sweep of a ship's bows.
Flying bridge - Topmost command platform, frequently of light construction.
Forecastle - Raised island forward, at the bow.
Forward - Towards the front, towards the bow.
Freeboard - Exposed part of the hull between upper hull deck and the waterline.
Freeing ports - Openings in the base of the bulwark to allow water to run outboard. Part of the bulwark may swing on hinges to allow transfer of personnel while berthed or anchored. (See also scuppers)

Galley - Ship's kitchen.
General Quarters - State of alarm; getting all hands as fast as possible to their battle stations.
GP - In this text abbreviation for General Purpose Bomb.
Girder - Steel structure, functioning as a support of the ship's framework.

Hatch, Hatchways - Opening in the deck for access of cargo and personnel.
Hatch Cover - Wood or steel covering of hatches.
Hatch Cover Beams - Removable steel beams on which the hatch covers rest.
Hawse Hole - Opening at the bows through which the anchor cable runs and to which the anchor is normally retracted. The rim of the hawse hole is generally substantially reinforced to take the chafing.
Hawsepipe - Pipe through which the anchor cable (chain) passes between the forecastle deck and the hawse hole on the ship's side.

HE - High explosive.
Head - Toilet aboard a ship.
Heading - The direction into which an aircraft or ship is pointing. It may not be the direction in which the vessel is actually travelling as winds (and water currents with ships) may push it off course.
Hit - Not only a direct hit on the ship, but in the case of bombs an explosion less than a beam's width away from the ship.
Hold - Compartment for cargo stowage under deck.
Horizontal Stabilizer - Part of the horizontal "tail" or the "tail wing". A section of the plane which provides stabilization against pitch.

IFF - Identification Friend-Foe; an electronic device emitting coded signals to an engaging missile, aircraft or battery that intent is friendly, as visual discrimination is not possible.
Island - integral raised part of a hull. In aircraft carriers superstructure above flight deck, normally on starboard midships.

Kingpost - Single or double (goal) post with derricks affixed to it.

Leading Edge - Forward area of a structure which is exposed to the onrushing air.
Lightening Hole - Circular or oval opening in a structural reinforcement, to save weight with little or no sacrifice in strength.
Lower Mast - Heavy lower part of the mast, from deck to crosstree.

Mast - Vertical or raked pole. -
Midship - Section of a vessel between stem and stern.

Navigation bridge - Wheel house, chart room, high up on the forward part of the superstructure. Also called navigation bridge or frequently abbreviated to just bridge in the text.

Pitch - The ship's or plane's lateral movement, the nose pointing up or down. On propeller angle of blades.
Poop - Raised island (castle) on stern.
Port - Left side of the vessel when looking forward, showing red light.

Quarter - Section of the ship between midships and the stern.

Rails, Rail Guards, Guardrails - Fence like structure, made of stanchions and stays, connected to each other by either a tubular steel bar or steel wire, for protection against falling overboard.
Rake - Inclination of the bow, mast or funnel.
Roll - Movement about the ship's or plane's longitudinal axis. In planes specifically dipping wings one way or the other. A power induced roll may be called banking.
Rudder - In ships large submerged structure behind the screw (propeller) to turn to either side, to turn the ship around the stern and head the bow into the direction of the turn.
In planes, moveable control surface at the trailing

edge of the vertical stabilizer, governing yaw, the turns to the right or left.
Rudder Stock - Vertical part of a rudder, to which the rudder blade is attached.
SAP - Semi-Armor Piercing bomb.
Screen - Ships or planes stationed around others to protect them against attack.
Scupper - An opening in a ship's side on a level with the deck, to allow water to drain.
Sheer Strake - Upper part of the shell plating where it meets the deck.
Shell Plating - Joint steel plates, contoured at bows and stern, forming the hull.
Shrouds - Rigging supporting a mast or a funnel in the athwart ship direction.
Soft Nose - Modern construction of the stem by bent (fabricated) plates, allowing for greater design flexibility and avoiding excessive damages to other ship in case of collision.
Sortie - To depart or the act of departing. A naval force departs or sorties from their base. An aircraft or patrol vessel sorties. In the nomenclature of the time denoting an individual vessel departing its base. 146 sorties flown against Palau means that so many aircraft departed to Palau.
Spar - Round, long piece of wood or steel, generally tapered at the end, fastened to mast. Formerly to attach square sails, later to hold antenna and signaling wires.
Spirket Plates - Vertical extension of the bulwark on the bows to give additional shelter from oncoming seas.
Spurling Pipe - Tube leading from the forecastle deck into the chain locker and enclosing the anchor cable. The tube leading outboard is called hawse pipe.
Starboard - Right side of the ship, showing green light.
Stanchion - An upright bar that forms a main support.

Stay - Standing rigging to support an upright structure, such as mast or funnel, in the fore-aft direction.
Stem - The extreme forward part of the ship where she cuts the water.
Stem Bar - Solid steel bar, normally straight and plumb, to which shell plating was riveted. Old fashioned.
Stern - Extreme aft or aftermost part of the ship.
Superstructure - Deckhouses and upperworks on a hull.

Trailing Edge - Aft part of a wing or area.
Trim Tabs - Small control surfaces adjusted to give the plane neutral flight characteristics to compensate for slight variations by the manufacturer or if the plane exhibits any other small idiosyncrasies.
Tween Decks - All decks in a hold below shelter or maindeck, to compartmentalize the vessel for more efficient use of space.

Ventilators - Fittings to trap air and direct it below deck.

Vertical Stabilizer - "Tail" of the aircraft, stabilizing yaw.

Warping Drum - Concave shaped drum attached to winch axis, belayed by running rigging for cargo handling.
Well Deck - The part of a deck which has bulkheads fore and aft, which in turn support higher decks. Typically found between forecastle and midship superstructure and between this and the poop of a Three-Island- Ship.
Winch House - Structure at foot of mast or kingpost with winches either inside or on top, similar to masthouse.

Yaw - Rotational motion about the ship's or plane's

NOTES ON DAMAGES

The sinking of the ships in Truk Lagoon can be attributed to three different kinds of damages inflicted, i.e. damages from aircraft automatics, torpedo hits and bomb damages. Frequently only one of these is apparent, but almost all ships have been attacked more than once, and with different weapons.

A - Aircraft Automatics and Board Guns.

The weapons of the planes were .30 and .50 machine guns. Rockets were not used at the time of the attack. It is difficult to sink a big ship by aircraft machine gun fire. However, secondary sequences may spell the end of a vessel. Small craft have been set afire or sunk by strafing.

An example of secondary damage would be when the canon shells of the attacking plane ignite the ship's own ammunition or any combustible or explosive cargo. There are a few instances of cargo ordnance explosions. These explosions are violent and rip ships apart. Cargo of the ships in service for the Navy or Army, included ammunition, such as artillery and mortar shells of all calibres, small arms cartridges, torpedo bodies and war heads, depth charges and sea and land mines, frequently together with aviation gasoline or diesel fuel. Examples of ordnance explosions are the Sankisan Maru, Aikoku Maru and Kikukawa Maru.

Another secondary effect would be a fire on board the ship. From the records it can be seen that most of the ships burned before they sank. If not checked in time, a fire on board will consume a ship. Eventually, a burning vessel must be abandoned and will sink. The effect of the extreme heat on the steel plates is to buckle them. This results in sprung seams and leaks. The Heian Maru is the ship which burned the longest. Of all things which may happen to a ship, nothing is more feared by the crew than a fire.

Examples of tertiary sinking are the repeated strafing of the ship and the bridge area. This may suppress any command activity by the ship's officers. If the bridge and the helm positions are not reinforced, the crew's attempts to lead the ship would result only in their death. Merchant ships are built light, and their command structure is highly centralized. By destroying command capabilities, the ship would remain at anchor or adrift. With the ships, thus immobilized, the torpedo bombers and the bombers had stationary targets, which are obviously easier to hit than moving ones.

During the strafing attack on the ship-based anti-aircraft guns the planes could neutralize the ship's defensive fire. Subsequently, the attacking bombers could release bombs and torpedoes far less harassed and take more time for aiming. It is interesting to note that almost all ships sank while being at anchor. It may be explained in part that those ships driven with steam engines or turbines did not have enough pressure up in the boilers to get going. It takes a while to get coal fires stoked, so that enough steam is available.

B - Torpedoes

A torpedo is a long, cigar-shaped weapon, which carries a detonator on the tip. During the attack on Truk, the American torpedoes carried impact detonators. A safety feature prevented it from blowing up upon impact on the water. The detonator was surrounded by the actual war head, which contained high explosives. This part of the weapon took up about one fourth of the weight and the length. Behind it, the propellant storage could be found.

Different ways of propulsion had been developed for torpedoes. The silent running torpedoes with electrical motors were not used in Truk, rather than the standard aerial torpedo. This torpedo was steam driven. In general, an air/gasoline mixture was burned in a combustion chamber. Water was injected into this chamber, and the steam generated taken to a steam engine, which turned the propeller shafts with a reduction gear box. The torpedoes had twin counter-rotating propellers. The gases would be vented out of the torpedo body. When they rose to the surface a wake could clearly be seen. In fact, since it took some time before the bubbles ascended to the surface, the torpedo was a good distance ahead of its own dreaded track.

Aft of the propulsion unit, the mechanical "brain" of the weapon could be found. It consisted of a depth sensor, gyro-compass and other instruments, which aided the compass to run at a prescribed course and depth. Stabilizing and steering fins could also be found at the aft end of the weapon.

The torpedo is a complicated but very effective weapon. Many large ships have succumbed to a single hit. On the other hand, the 19,000 ts whaler Tonan Maru 3, was attacked by the submarine USS Tinosa on 24 July 1943 near Truk, sustained four hits - and an incredible 8 duds! - settled deep in the water, let off steam, and was towed into Truk the same evening. The failure of the detonators in this particular incident was decisive for the development of a new detonating device by the US Navy. The Fujikawa Maru, Kiyozumi, Hoyo and other ships are known to have survived a submarine torpedo hit.

An American aerial torpedo weighted almost a ton; only well powered planes were able to carry them. Some of the most spectacular damages have been done by torpedoes launched from aircraft, such as those sustained by the American battleships during the attack on Pearl Harbor, the sinking of HMS

Prince of Wales and HMS Repulse off Malaya, both Japanese super battleships Musashi and Yamato have succumbed to this weapon, and the pride of the Germans, the Bismarck, was hit in the rudder and became easy prey. The part this sophisticated weapon played in hands of skilled submarine skippers, was contributing greatly to the successes of battles fought far away.

Torpedo bombers had probably the toughest assignment. Since the torpedo could not be launched over long distances or from great heights, the aircraft had to go low into the target, release, and climb up in a steep turn, before the anti aircraft gunners could get a proper fix. Japanese planes preferred wave top assaults, while most Avengers made gliding drops. Once launched there was nothing to stop its running a pre-set course, except a failure in the steering. It was assumed, that the torpedo would first dive to great depth, then go back up, even break the surface and dolphin, before it assumed its course and depth.

A torpedo hit is devastating. Since the weapon explodes underneath the waterline, the damage is extensive. The ship will take water in immediately. Cargo ships have relatively thin steel hulls, which do not offer much resistance. If a torpedo strikes midships, the ship may break in two because of the different stress concentrations of the hull, and the halves will sink quickly. If the hit occurs in the cargo area, and the bulkheads remain watertight, there is a chance, that the vessel will stay afloat.

C - Bomb Damage

There is an almost infinite variety of bombs. The Helldivers and Avengers carried either 500 lbs, 1000 lbs, 1600 lbs or a single 2000 lbs bomb, but latter one only for the Avengers. They were general purpose and armour piercing types. The fuses were set with a short delay, ranging from 0,01 second to 0,8 second after impact. At the last strike of the first day, Strike F, bombs with several hours delay fuses were dropped on the airfields of Eten, Param and Moen. These bombs could not be defused. The purpose of the attack was to deny the Japanese planes the use of the airfields for launching aircraft at night. It was reported that no night air attack originated from Truk. This is an apparent contradiction to the events, which lead to the torpedoing of the carrier Intrepid. The Japanese officers, interrogated after the war, maintained that the planes originated from fields in the Marianas, such as Saipan or Guam.

A single bomb does do a great deal of damage to a merchant ship, but the ship may survive the hit, provided a secondary sequence is not initiated, or a fire does not consume the ship. Normally, the term hit is modified when talking about bomb damages. A direct hit is self-explanatory. There is generally a great deal of destruction in the area of the bomb explosion. Characteristically, the fragments of the steel plating point away from the center of the explosion. The Kiyozumi, Rio, Amagisan, Fujisan and a few of the deeper wrecks show this kind of damage. Bomb hits in the superstructure show as a crater-like destruction. This ugly sight may extend to two or three decks. Almost always the ship will begin to burn. A bomb exploding in the water will expend part of the explosive force to throw up a water column, and to send a pressure wave above and below water. In a close miss, defined to be not farther away from the ship than a beam's width, the explosive force will sweep the decks clean of any but structural elements, and kill personnel. A fire probably will be ignited due to the intense heat and the glowing shrapnel. Underwater, severe damage to the shell plating will result. Structural members and plating will be blown inward, and, depending on the size of the bomb, proximity of the explosion, and delay setting, the damage can reach from the bottom of the ship to the sheerstrake. Explosions farther away decrease the amount of damage, to the point where the shell plating spring leaks. Personnel losses, blast damages and fires may be expected from a bomb near miss.

It is difficult for pilots to judge a hit or a miss. Many times hits were recorded, but evidence from the wrecks clearly confirms that there is no damage. On the other hand it was easy to see whether a torpedo has hit. In most cases the planes carried a torpedo camera on board and took pictures as documentary proof.

Hailstorm - *Appendix*

THE POSITION OF THE WRECKS IN TRUCK

The plotting and ranging of the position of the wrecks in Truck has been given most careful attention. For the bearings of wrecks in relation to landmarks, an ENBEECO Compass Bearing Monocular, Serial No. JB 101, No. 6470, was used. This bearing compass excels in accuracy, and is far superior to hand-held, needle bearing compasses. In fact, it compares favorably with large, mounted precision bearing devices. Correct ranging may give readings up to 0,25 degrees accuracy. These fine divisions have not been utilized; the bearings are rounded, as conditions on the dive boats make decimals smaller than 0,5 degrees meaningless.

There may be, nevertheless, some minor deviations of the readings given, to the actual position of the individual wrecks. This is because the dive boat, when anchored above the wreck, has a certain amount of scope in the anchor line. These differences are negligible. Besides, the wrecks are several hundred feet long. In all cases, they have been relocated quickly, even under adverse conditions of high seas and rain.

It must be clearly stated, that the attempt to plot the ranges on a chart, even of a small scale, will present problems and meet with only limited success. The reason may be found in the magnetic abnormalities, which exist in certain areas of the lagoon. In particular, the regions around Eten, Fefan and Uman are known to throw the compass off. Cramer, an early German scientist, wrote in 1900 that there is a point in Eten, where the compass reverses direction. This phenomenon may be explained by the volcanic origin of Truk, and the possibility that large masses of subterranean iron compounds are present in the area. The abnormalities are, of course, irrelevant if bearings are taken from the actual wreck site, and are used to relocate the wreck at some other time. They were then taken under the prevailing conditions, to which the compass is subjected again.

Regarding the landmarks quoted, a few explanatory notes should be observed:
- If a small island, like Fanamu, is mentioned, the bearing refers to the middle of the palm studded island itself.
- The actual tips of mountains are used for the range.
- If the tip of a large island is indicated, such as Dublon East (E Dublon), the reference point here is either the edge of the substantial and discernible growth or the drop off of high lands, towards the horizon or the water's edge. It is assumed, that these landmarks will not change over the next years.
- Principally, the part of any island is marked as reference, which can be clearly and unmistakenly identified. This is particularly true for the two peninsulas East of Dublon. The one which can be clearly seen against the horizon and is not obscured is always chosen. References to North, East, South or West of Uman, Fefan or Dublon, etc, are to mean, that the edge of that island clearly forms a border to the sea. Intertidal flats are never used, for obvious reasons.
- All numbers given are in degrees from the wreck towards the landmark.

The positions are listed in the following sequence:

A: The bearings are established from the actual wreck site towards the landmarks, in degrees, as described above.

B: After careful plotting, the position of the wrecks has been established on the chart "North Pacific Ocean, Caroline Islands, Truk Islands, Eastern Part, No. 81327, Scale 1:50,000, 3rd Edition, May 9, 1981". This chart is issued by the Defense Mapping Agency Hydrographic/Topographic Center, Washington, D.C. It is based on Japanese material up to 1942, and the survey of USS Tanner, 1968. This reference may considered to be the authentic source, and the positions given are highly accurate. They do not, however, correspond in many cases to the wreck symbols shown in the chart.

C: The third reference is taken from the publication "Japanese Naval And Merchant Ship Losses During World War II By All Causes", issued by the Joint Army-Navy Assessment Committee, US Department of the Navy, US Government Printing Office, February 1947. The positions are unreliable, for two major reasons. Firstly, they indicate only degrees and minutes, without seconds, and are therefore not accurate enough to aid in finding the wrecks. Secondly, the coordinates given appear to correlate to the older Japanese reference charts, which were found to be different to those established later. The coordinates must be shifted on all parallels of latitude by 11.5 degrees North, and the meridians of longitude by 28.9 seconds East.

D: The Japanese source contains bearings, apparently taken from land towards the actual mooring of the ships before they sank. The degree of reliability varies significantly from wreck to wreck. They are given from a landmark in degrees, and distance from that landmark in meters. The reference to the markers is as follows:
Marker # 6 is the marker due south of the southern peninsular of east Dublon.
Marker # 8 is a structure almost due East of the north point of Eten, at the eastern end of the long reef.

Hailstorm - *Appendix*

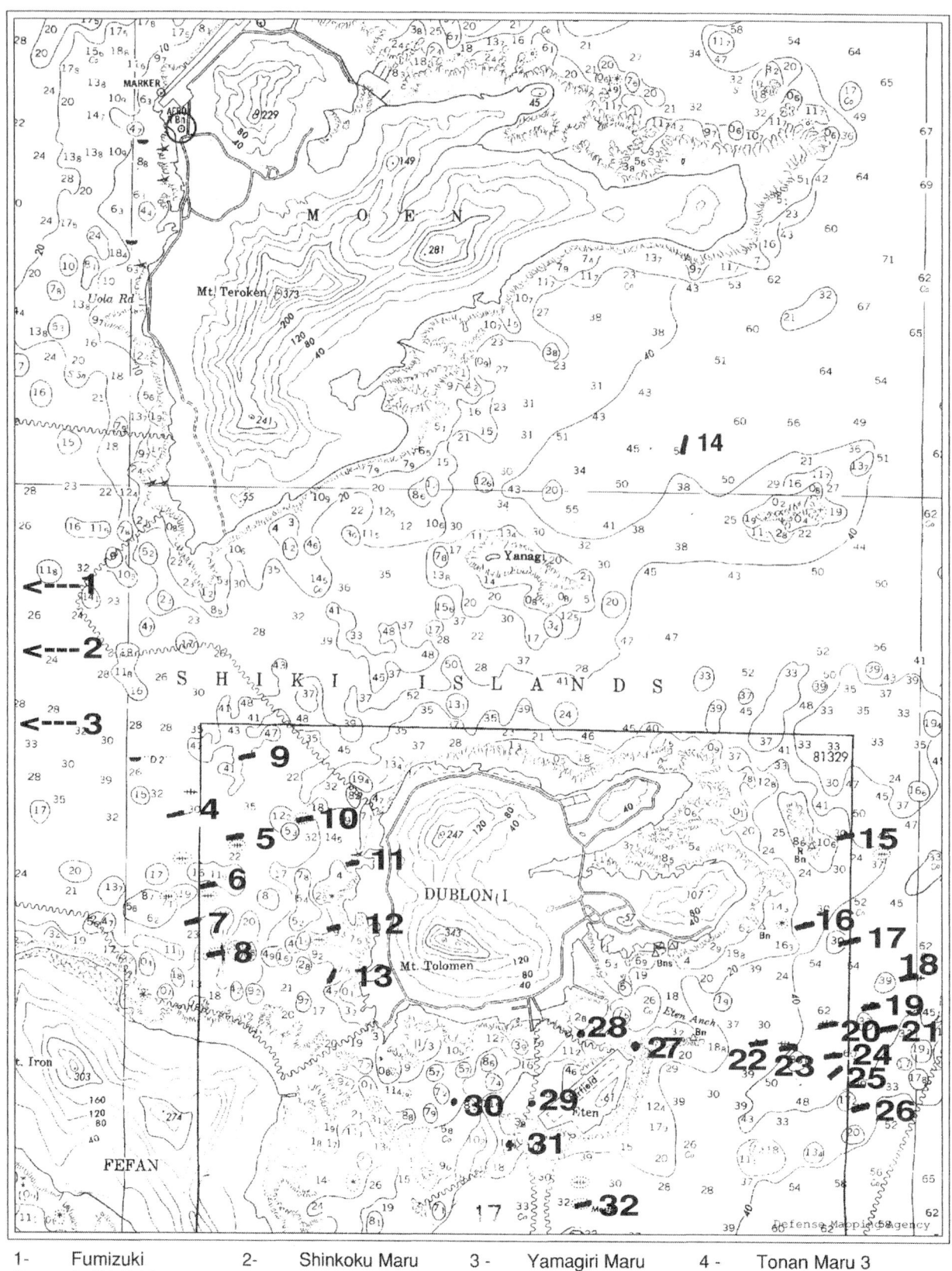

1-	Fumizuki	2-	Shinkoku Maru	3-	Yamagiri Maru	4-	Tonan Maru 3
5-	Daikichi Maru	6-	Kiyozumi Maru	7-	Kansho Maru	8-	Hoyo Maru
9-	I-169	10-	Heian Maru	11-	Harbor Tug	12-	Fleet Tug
13-	P 34 Susuki	14-	Fujisan Maru	15-	Nippo Maru	16-	Momokawa Maru
17-	Aikoku Maru	18-	Reiyo Maru	19-	Nagano Maru	20-	San Francisco M.
21-	Shotan Maru	22-	Seiko Maru	23-	Hokuyo Maru	24-	Kikukawa Maru
25-	Ojima	26-	Hoki Maru	27-	Fighter Planes	28-	Rufe Seaplane
29-	Judy Fighter	30-	Emily Flying Boat	31-	Betty Bomber	32-	Fujikawa Maru

Hailstorm - *Appendix*

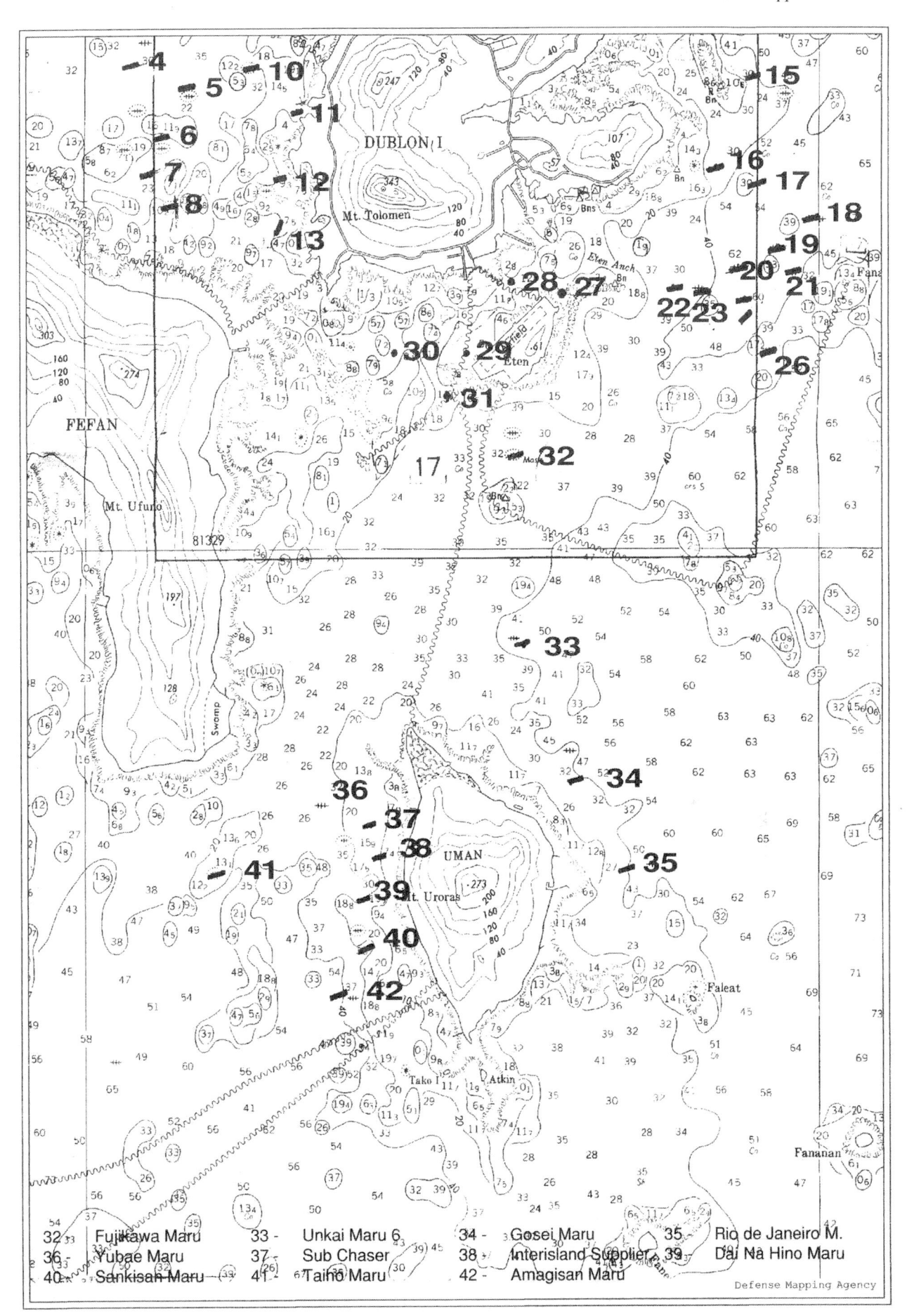

32 - Fujikawa Maru   33 - Unkai Maru 6   34 - Gosei Maru   35 - Rio de Janeiro M.
36 - Yubae Maru   37 - Sub Chaser   38 - Interisland Supplier   39 - Dai Na Hino Maru
40 - Sankisan Maru   41 - Taiho Maru   42 - Amagisan Maru

Defense Mapping Agency

Hailstorm - *Appendix*

Coordinates are shown in the sequence: North degrees:minutes:seconds; East degrees:minutes:seconds.

Degrees, magnetic

AIKOKU MARU
A :
Fanamu	129
E Dublon, Marker #6	271,5
Eten Marker	241
Dublon Reef Marker	333,5

B : N 7:22:14; E 151:54:36
C : N 7:22:—; E 151:54:—
D : Marker #6, 90 deg, 1400 m

AMAGISAN MARU
A :
Tako Island	115
N Uman	11
S Tsis	264
N Tsis	286
W Fefan	308
E Fefan	345

B : N 7:17:15; E 151:51:44
C : N 7:18:—; E 151:53:—
D : Mount Uroras, Uman, 23 deg, 1850 m.

DAIKICHI MARU, X 10
A :
This wreck is severely scattered. Three major parts are located in 90 to 120 ft deep water, roughly in line Dublon N - Fefan E;NW of Kansho Maru.
B : N 7:22:46; E 151:50:41
C : N 7:18:—; E 151:53:—
D : unknown position.

FLEET TUG
A :
not available
B : N 7:21:54; E 151:51:16
C : not listed
D : not listed.

FUJIKAWA MARU
A :
No bearings are taken, as the position of this wreck, SW of Eten, can be taken from the two mast breaking the surface.
B : N 7:20:34; E 151:52:54
C : N 7:20:—; E 151:53:—
D : Marker #8, 203 deg, 2300 m.

FUJISAN MARU
A :
Herit	96
E Dublon	167
N Dublon	217
NE Moen	9
Yanagi	237

B : N 7:25:18; E 151:53:27
C : N 7:23:—; E 151:53:—
D : Yanagi 63 deg, 2400 m.

FUMIZUKI
A and B :
not available
C : N 7:24:—; E 151:44:—
D : unknown ("coral reef Truk").

GOSEI MARU
A :
Mt Uroras	51
Mt Tolomen	347

Wreck visible from the surface.
B : N 7:18:33; E 151:53:17
C : N 7:18:—; E 151:53:—
D : Mount Uroras, Uman, 50 deg, 1600 m.

HANAKAWA MARU
A :
Wreck visited, but no bearings taken. Approximately 1.5 miles SE of jetty at Tol, at 100 ft depth.
B : not available
C : N 7:20:—; E 151:40:—
(mistakenly identified as Shinkoku Maru)
D : Tol 223 deg, 3400 m.

HEIAN MARU
A :
Mt Tolomen	129
N Dublon	59
W Dublon	165
SE Moen	339
Yanagi	36
E Mt Dublon	94

B : N 7:23:00; E 151:51:13
C : N 7:23:—; E 151:51:—
D : North summit east side Dublon 265 deg, 1850 m.

HINO MARU 2
A :
NW Uman	1
SW Uman	156
SE Fefan	336
SW Fefan	282,5

visible from surface.
B : N 7:18:07; E 151:52:03
C : N 7:22:—; E 151:45:—
D : not available.

HOKI MARU, X 6
A :
E Moen	348
E Dublon	331
Mt. Tolomen	287
S Fefan	232,5
S Tsis	228
SE Uman	196
Fanamu	62

B : N 7:21:10; E 151:54:40
C : N 7:22:—; E 151:45:—
D : unknown.

HOKUYO MARU, X 7
A :
E Moen	357
E Dublon	339
Mt Tolomen	283
Fanamu	73
S Fefan	227
S Tsis	225,5

B : N 7:21:51; E 151:54:13
C : N 7:18:—; E 151:53:—
D : Marker #8, 131 deg, 1315 m.

HOYO MARU
A :
Mt Tolomen	265
Mt Iron	50

visible from surface.
B : N 7:22:06; E 151:50:36
C : N 7:23:—; E 151:50:—
D : unknown ("close to Truk").

I - 169 (SHINOHARA) SUBMARINE
A :
Yanagi	44,5
Mt. Tolomen	125,5
W Dublon	149
N Dublon	82,5
SW Moen	339

B : N 7:23:17; E 151:50:44
C : N 7:25:—; E 151:50:—
D : not listed.

KANSHO MARU, X 11, Mary D.
A :
Mt. Tolomen	97
SE Moen	347,5
SW Dublon	126
Mt Tol	256
E Uman	144
E Fefan	153
N Dublon	54

B : N 7:22:29; E 151:50:29
C : N 7:18:—; E 151:53:—
D : unknown.

KIKUKAWA MARU, X 5
A :
E Moen	349
E Dublon	330
Mt Tolomen	285
Fanamu	62

B : N 7:21:20; E 151:54:32
C : N 7:22:—; E 151:54:—
D : not available.

KIYOZUMI MARU
A :
E Fefan	143
Mt. Iron	21
N Fefan	253
Mt. Tolomen	86,5
Yanagi	33,5
W Moen	

B : N 7:22:16; E 151:50:24
C : N 7:23:—; E 151:53:—
D : Northern summit east side Dublon 23 deg, 3150 m.

MOMOKAWA MARU, Y 1A :
not available
B : not accurately determined
C : N 7:20:—; E 151:53:—
D : Marker # 6, 60 deg, 980 m.

NAGANO MARU
A :
E Moen	346,5
E Dublon	316,5
Mt Tolomen	273
S Fefan	225
SE Uman	196
Fanamu	111

B : N 7:21:42; E 151:54:44
C : N 7:25:—, E 151:45:—
D : Marker #8, 96 deg, 2050 m.

NIPPO MARU, X 4, Akao.
A :
E Moen	347
E Dublon	289
W Tolomen	250
SE Uman	188,5
Fanamu	143,5
Dublon Reef Marker	246

B : N 7:22:53; E 151:54:32
C : N 7:18:—; E 151:53:—
D : Marker #6, 28 deg, 1500 m.

REIYO MARU, X 3
A :
E Moen	145
E Dublon	309
Mt. Tolomen	269
S Fefan	227
S Tsis	225
Fanamu	135

B : N 7:22:00; E 151:54:55
C : N 7:25:—; E 15
D : Marker #6, 100 deg, 1060 m.

RIO DE JANEIRO MARU
A :
Mt Uroras	89
Jetty Uman	85

B : N 7:18:00; E 151:53:40
C : N 7:20:—; E 151:53:—
D : Mount Uroras, Uman, 73 deg, 2500 m.

SAN FRANCISCO MARU
A :
Fanamu	94
Mt Tolomen	277
E Dublon, Marker #6	321,5
Eten Marker	259,5
E Moen	345

B : N 7:21:44; E 151:54:27

Hailstorm - *Appendix*

C : N 7:22:—; E 151:54:—
D : Marker #8, 114 deg, 1330 m.

SEIKO MARU
A :
Fanamu 83,5
Eten Marker 270,5
E Dublon, Marker #6 351
W Marker Dublon 314
B : N 7:21:52; E 151:53:58
C : N 7:22:—; E 151:45:—
D : Marker #8, 143 deg, 970 m.

SHINKOKU MARU
A :
Mt Tolomen 112
E Fefan 114,5
W Fefan 132,5
E Param 149
W Param 179
Mt Teroggen 50
B : N 7:23:55; E 151:46:30
C : N 7:25:—; E 151:45:—
(mistakenly identified as Hanakawa Maru)
D : Udot (?) 73 deg, 5900 m.

SHOTAN MARU, X 2
A :
E Moen 345
E Dublon 315
Mt. Tolomen 277
S Fefan 230
SE Uman 199
Fanamu 89
B : N 7:21:40; E 151:54:40
C : not listed
D : from Nagano Maru 131 deg, 350 m.

SPECIAL SUB CHASER 38
A :
N Uman 5
S Uman 164
S Tsis 244,5
W Fefan 276,5
E Fefan 336
B : N 7:18:17; E 151:51:55
C : N 7:22:—; E 151:45:—
D : not available.

TAIHO MARU, X 9
A :
N Uman 61
W Uman 129
W Fefan 278
E Fefan 352
Mt Tolomen 8
Fanamu 47
B : N 7:18:00; E 151:50:40
C : N 7:22:—; E 151:54:—
D : Mount Uroras, Uman, (?) 5 deg, 2700 m.

TONAN MARU 3, X 16
Note: This wreck was salvaged after the war, only the parts which were blown out by the bombs remained at this location.
A :
Mt Tolomen 107
W Dublon 130,5
W Fefan 231
N Param 232,5
Jetty Hotel Moen 356
B : N 7:22:54; E 151:50:16
C : N 7:23:—; E 151:51:—
D : unknown ("inside lagoon").

UNKAI MARU 6, X 13
A :
Marker off Fujikawa 353
N Uman 267
Faleat 139,5
W Dublon 328,5
B : N 7:19:22; E 151:52:59
C : N 7:25:—; E 151:45:—
D : Mount Uroras, Uman, 225 deg, 2500 m.

YAMAGIRI MARU
A :
Mt Tolomen 101
E Fefan 127
W Fefan 189
E Param 221
W Param 241
B : N 7:23:00; E 151:49:12
C : N 7:23:—; E 151:51:—
D : unknown ("close to Truk").

SANKISAN MARU
A :
Atkin 134
NE Uman 6
Mt Tolomen 357
E Fefan 341
W Fefan 298
S Tsis 259,5
Foremast breaks surface.
B : N 7:17:31; E 151:51:54
C : N 7:15:—; E 151:45:—
D : unknown.

YUBAE MARU, Y 2
A :
not available
B : N 7:18:25; E 151:51:36
C : N 7:18:—; E 151:53:—
D : Mount Uroras, Uman, 298 deg, 1430 m.

LANDING CRAFT; SMALL FREIGHTER, REMNANTS OF TWO SMALLER CRAFT, REMNANTS OF KIKUKAWA MARU
A :

	X 8	X 12	X 14	X 15
E Moen	347	324	347	334
E Dublon	327	-	324	327
Mt. Tolomen	280,5	282	281,5	283
S Fefan	228,5	-	230,5	230,5
S Tsis	226	222,5	227,5	-
Fanamu	64,7?	64	63,5	64,5
SE Uman	-	-	-	196,5

SUSUKI
100 m N of shank of mooring anchor on west shore of Dublon. Visible from surface.

SHIPS SUNK OUTSIDE TRUK LAGOON

AGANO
Light cruiser. Ship not sunk during Operation Hailstorm, but the afternoon before by submarine USS Skate.
C - N 10:11:—; E 151:42:—

AKAGI MARU
Converted aux. cruiser, in Convoy 4215. Outside NW North Pass, about 10 miles (16 km).
A and B - not found, depth abyssal.
C - N 7:54:—; E 151:25:—
D - outside North Pass.

GYOTEI NO. 6
Small aux. craft. Probably trawler-type, strayed into path of Task Group 50.9, and exploded violently after hits by gunfire.
A and B - not found, depth abyssal.
C and D - no detailed information available.

KATORI
Light training cruiser and flagship Sixth Submarine Fleet, in Convoy 4215. Sunk by bombs, torpedoes and gunfire, outside North Pass, NW, about 15 miles (25 km).
A and B - Not found, depth abyssal
C - N 7:45:—; E 151:20:—
D - outside North Pass.

MAIKAZE
Destroyer, in Convoy 4215, same as Katori.
A and B - not found, depth abyssal
C - N 7:45:—; E 151:20:—
D - outside North Pass.

NAKA
Light cruiser. Sunk by torpedoes Task Group 58.3, planes from Bunker Hill and Monterey.
A and B - not found, depth abyssal.
C - N 7:15:—; E 151:15:—
D - outside Piaanu Pass.

OITE
Destroyer, returning from escort Agono and subsequent life saving duties. Strafed, torpedoed in northern part of lagoon.
A and B - not available.
C - N 7:40:—; E 151:45:—
D - inside North Pass.

SHINWA MARU
Freighter, sunk by bombs from planes of Intrepid, possibly also referred to as Tatsuha Maru or Matsutami Maru.
A and B - not found, depth abyssal

C - N 7:46:—; E 150:27:—
D - 80 miles (135 km) west of Truk.

SPECIAL SUBCHASER NO 24
Aux. craft of 300 tons, strayed into path of Task Group 50.9, and was sunk by gunfire of destroyer USS Burns.
A and B - not found, depth abyssal
C - N 7:24:—; E 150:30:—
D - west of Truk.

TACHIKAZE
Destroyer, grounded firmly with bow on southwest part of Kuop Atoll, since mid-January 1944. Sunk second day of operation by bombs from Enterprise planes.
A and B - not found, beyond reach
C - N 7:04:—; E 151:55:—
D - Royalist Island (Kuop Atoll).

ZUIKAI MARU
Freighter, sunk by bombs outside North Pass.

A and B - not found, depth abyssal
C - N 7:46:—; E 150:27:—
D - outside North Pass.

OTHER VESSELS
A number of small vessels, particularly landing crafts, barges, tugs service ships, and converted sub chasers of the trawler-type, were sunk in and outside the lagoon, during Operation Hailstorm, bomber attacks and the second raid on Truk. Several large freighters were sunk outside the atoll during the submarine blockade.

SHIPS DAMAGED BUT NOT SUNK

There were a number of ships in Truk during the first carrier raid which were not damaged or only slightly damaged. Attack photos confirmed existence of a number of 600 t to 1500 t coastal freighters, service vessels and trawlers southeast and south of Eten. A large 5000 t freighter was located between Eten and Uman and two 1500 to 2000 t vessels were located each on south Fefan and west Uman.

Ro 42, Submarine
Reported as slightly damaged this submarine was attacked by Essex planes with 4 sec. delay fused bombs while diving in central part of the lagoon.

I 10, Submarine
Reported to be under bombing attack about 35 to 50 miles (50 to 80 km) north of the Northeast Pass, outside the lagoon.

Fujinami - Destroyer
Escorted convoy at Namonuito Atoll, was seen to rescue survivors, and evidently steamed into Truk.

Hailstorm - *Appendix*

Evidently strafed.

Matsukaze - Destroyer

Probably anchored originally 6th Fleet Anchorage (may be together with Namikaze; their identity may be reversed) the ship was hit and leaked oil. Evidently located at southern part of lagoon, trying to pick up downed US pilot of Essex on the second day.

Namikaze - Destroyer

Originally anchored inside lagoon, steamed burning Dublon/Moen west, was strafed, bombed and damaged inside and outside North Pass, returned into lagoon.

Shigure,
Harusame - Destroyers

Probably anchored at Combined or at 4th Fleet anchorage, followed Katori (4215) convoy about one hour later to the north. Both ships attacked in and outside lagoon. Shigure heavily, Harusame slightly damaged. Continued retirement to Palau.

Akitsushima - Seaplane tender, transport

Anchored slightly northeast of Aikoku Maru. Received bomb hit at superstructure and aft, damaging rudder. Repaired and escaped at dawn of second day probably through Northeast Pass, after being strafed by fighters.

Akashi - Repair ship

Hit at anchorage between Fefan and Dublon, Repair Anchorage, ship turned slowly towards south and was seen retiring through the South Pass later.

Shinkyo Maru - Transport

Part of convoy attacked by Intrepid planes near Namonuito Atoll (Enderby Is.). Put into Truk later.

Hakune Maru - Freighter

Ship bombed, strafed, damaged, beached and waterlogged at reef east of Dublon. Pulled off later.

Soya - Munitions ship

Bombed and beached, repaired and returned to service.

Hagoromo Maru - Trawler, weathership

Damaged, beached on reef and later pulled off.

SUMMARY WRECK DAMAGES

Aikoku Maru
Explosion, foreship disintegrated.

Amagisan Maru
Torpedo hold 3 stbd, fire;
Bomb direct hit poop/ quarter port.

Daikichi Maru, X10
unknown,
explosion,
ship torn apart.

Fujikawa Maru
Torpedo hit hold 4, stbd.

Fujisan Maru
Bomb direct hit aft engine room port, fire.

Gosei Maru
Torpedo or direct bomb hit hold 1 stbd.

Hanakawa Maru
Torpedo hit hold 1 stbd,
large fire.

Heian Maru
Torpedo(s) engine room port, severe fire.

Hino Maru 2
Direct bomb hits, ship destroyed.

Hokuyo Maru, X7
Direct bomb hit port quarter/stern.
boiler explosion.

Hoyo Maru
Torpedo or bomb hit port bow,
bomb direct hit engine room port,
bomb direct hit stern,
bomb direct hit midships stbd.

Hoki Maru, X6
Torpedo or bomb direct hit foreship,
bomb close miss stern,
fire, explosion, foreship blown out.

I 169
Accidental flooding,
later depth charged.

Kansho Maru, X11
Torpedo or bomb delay fuse hit at hold 1,
bomb delay fuse hit stern.

Kikukawa Maru, X5
Accidental explosion, aftship disintegrated.

Kiyozumi Maru
Direct bomb hit bridge,
torpedo or bomb hit keel hold 2,
bomb direct hit stbd beam hold 3,
hole keel hold 1,
fire.

Momokawa Maru, X18
Bomb direct hit aft hold 5 port,
several bomb close misses, damage superstructure midships.

Hailstorm - *Appendix*

Nagano Maru, X1
Unknown,
Funnel and foremast broken off,
bomb near misses.

Nippo Maru, X4
Bomb very close miss aft port superstructure,
several bomb close misses.

Reiyo Maru, X3
Bomb very close miss port midships,
bomb direct hit between poop and hold 5, fire.

Rio de Janeiro Maru
Direct bomb hit port aft part of superstructure,
Ammunition explosion bow gun.
Fire.

San Francisco Maru
Direct bomb hit port hold 5,
hole stbd hold 5,
direct bomb hit midship hold 3,
boiler explosion,
fire.

Seiko Maru
Direct bomb hit port quarter forward of engine room,
fire.

Shinkoku Maru
Torpedo or very close bomb hit engine room port,
flash fire.

Shotan Maru, X2
Direct bomb hit stbd beam hold 4.

Susuki
several bomb close misses,
fire.

Tonan Maru 3, X16
Direct bomb hit(s) aft superstructure.

Taiho Maru, X9
Torpedo or bomb hit,
explosion, fire,
fore and midship blown off.

Unkai Maru 6, X13
Not evident,
boiler explosion,
severe fire forward.

Sankisan Maru
Torpedo or bomb hit aft,
fire,
explosion,
aft and midship blown apart.

Yamagiri Maru
Direct bomb hit hold 2,
direct bomb hit hold 3,
fire.

Yubai Maru
Not known, probably close miss poop.

ISLAND NAMES

Moen	Haru shima -	Spring
Dublon	Natsu shima -	Summer
Fefan	Aki shima -	Autumn
Uman	Foya shima -	Winter
Eten	Take jima -	Bamboo
Param	Getsuyo to -	Monday
Ulau	Nichiyo to -	Sunday
Fala-Beguets -	Kayo to -	Tuesday
Tol	Suiyo to -	Wednesday
Pata	Mukuyo to -	Thursday
Polle	Kinyo to -	Friday
Onamu	Doyo to -	Saturday
Ulalu	Nichiyo to -	Sunday
Yanagi - ?	-	Willow
Kuop (?) -	Kunto shoto - ?	
Truk	Torakku shoto-	Truk
Kuop	Tachi bana -	Orange Is.
- Kimijima		

BIBLIOGRAPHY

Enzio Angelucci, Paolo Matricardi
World Aircraft, World War II,
Part 2, Vol.4
Sampson Low, Maidenhead, Berkshire, UK, 1978.
<c> Europa Verlag, 1977
SBN 562 00096 8Anonymous

The Japanee Air Forces in World War II
Arms and Armour Press, Lionel Leventhal Ltd,
London, UK
<c> Crown Copyright 1970 (Controller of Her Majesty's Stationary Office)

Ray Bonds, Chr. F. Foss, editors
World War II Tanks
Salamander Books, London, UK/Lansdowne Press, Sydney, 1981

Boueicho Bouei Kenshujo Senshi Shitsu, Central Pacific Ocean Regional Naval Strategy (after June 1942), Shohon Shinbunsha.

Alexander Bredt, Publisher
Flottentaschenbuch XXXVIII, 1953
J.F. Lehmanns Verlag, Muenchen, 1953

Alexander Bredt, Publisher
Kriegsflotten XXXV, 1941/1942
J.F. Lehmanns Verlag, Muenchen, 1941

David Brown
Carrier Fighters
Macdonald and Janes's
London, UK.

Vice Admiral E.P. Forrestal, USN, ret.
A Study In Command -
Admiral Raymond A. Spruance, USN
US Printing Office, Washington, D.C.

W.J. Holmes
Double Edged Secrets,
Naval Institute Press,
Annapolis, Maryland, 1979

A.J. Watts
Japanese Warships of World War II
Ian Allen, Shepperton, Surrey, UK, 1966

Ronald Lewin
The American Magic
Farrar Straus Giroux, New York, 1982

Jane's Fighting Ships 1944/5
Sampson Low Marston, Maidenhead, Berkshire, UK,

E.B. Potter/ Chester Nimitz, USN,
The Graet Sea War
E.B. Potter, editor
Prentice- Hall, Inc. Englewood Cliffs, N.J., 1980

The Staff of 'Airview', editors
General View of Japanese Military Aircraft in the Pacific War
Kanto-Sha Co.,Ltd, 1956
Tokyo, Japan

Samuel Eliot Morison
The Two Ocean War
Little, Brown and Company, Boston
<c> Samuel Eliot Morison, 1963

Samuel Eliot Morison
History of United States Naval Operations in World War II, Vol. VII
Little, Brown and Company, 1951

Edward P. Stafford, Cmdr, USN
The Big "E"
Ballantine Books, New York 1980
<c> Edward P. Stafford

The Joint Army-Navy Assessment Comittee
Japanese Naval and Merchant Ship Losses During World War II
US Government Printing Office, Washington, D.C. February 1947

Theodore Roscoe
United States Submarine Operations in World War II.
Naval Institute Press, 1972
<c> US Naval Institute 1949

Theodore Roscoe
United States Destroyer Operations In World War II
Naval Institute Press, 1972
<c> US Naval Institute 1949

Friedrich Ruge, Vizeadmiral a.D.
Entscheidung im Pazifik
Hans Dulk, Hamburg 1951

John Toland
The Rising Sun
Bantam Books, New York, 1980
<c> John Toland

Jentschura, Jung, Mickel
Warships of the Japanese Navy 1869- 1945
Arms & Armur Press, London, 1982

John D. Alden
US Submarine Attacks During WW II
Naval Institute Press, Annapolis, MD, 1989

John Campbell
Naval Weapons of WW II
Conway Maritime Press, London, 1985

Hailstorm - *Appendix*

Material, unpublished, from the US Navy Historical Center, Washington, D.C.:

a - USS Essex, Action Reports, Air Operations against Truk, 16-17 February 1944

b - USS Intrepid, dto.

c - USS Enterprise, dto.

d - USS Yorktown, dto.

e - USS Cabot, Aircraft Action Reports, Attack on Truk

f - USS Cowpens, dto.

g - USS Monterey, dto.

h - Task Group 58.3, Report of Desecrate and Hailstorm *(sic)* Operations.

i - Commander Task Group 58.1, Action Report of Operations Against Truk.

j - dto., Japanese Night Air Attacks on 16/17 February 1944.

k - Commander Task Group 58.2, Action Report of Operations Against Truk, 16/17 February 1944.

l - Commander Task Force 58, Action Report of Catchpole and Hailstorm Operations.

m - Bulletin No. 18-11, Battleship, Cruiser and Destroyer Sweep Around Truk 16/17 February 1944.

n - US Strategic Bombing Survey, Naval and Naval Air Field Team #3: A Study of the Effects of Allied Warfare against Truk (02 December 1945)

o - USS Intrepid, World War II History, War Diaries, Reports

p - USS Yorktown, World War II Action Report File

q - USS Enterprise, World War II Action Report File.

r - USS Enterprise, Ship's Log 16/17 February 1944.

s - USS Yorktown, dto.

t - USS Essex, dto.

u - USS Intrepid, dto.

v - USS Bunker Hill, dto.

w - Japanese Ship List,
Know your Enemy,
US Navy, publish.
18 December 1944

x - Japanese Ship Recognition Manual,
O.N.I. 208-J
Navy Department,
Office of the Chief of Naval Operations,
Washington D.C.,
24 August 1942

Dr. Sanae Yamada, pers. correspondence

Dr. Kunio Yamakawa, dto.

Kyuya Takenaka, dto.

Jiro Suga, dto.

Miyoji Miyazaki, dto.

Kimiuo Aisek, pers. interviews

EPILOGUE

BY SANAE YAMADA

On 8 December 1941, the Imperial Japanese Armed Forces declared war against the United States of America, the United Kingdom and Holland. Japan had forestalled other countries by winning victory after victory through the launching of surprise attacks on Pearl Harbor, the Philippines and Malaya.

On 11 January 1942, the Japanese Army conquered the Celebes Islands and on 23 January, they had taken over New Britain Island and the Rabaul Islands. Thus, within one and a half months, Japan had conquered all the Southeast Asian islands except New Guinea. The Army landed on Guadalcanal in the Solomon Islands in May, with the intention of damaging the communication network between the United States of America and Australia.

The Allied Forces finally recovered from the blows and started to launch a massive counterattack. The Battle of Midway took place on 4 June 1942. The Japanese lost four aircraft carriers. On 7 August, the Allied Forces landed in Guadalcanal to claim the islands from the Japanese. This combat was the start of a frantic struggle between the Japanese and the American forces. Simultaneously, the first, second and third naval battles of the Solomon Islands commenced. Thus, the Army, Navy and Air Force began to vie with each other desperately.

In November, 11 high-speed transportation vessels were destroyed and all organized Japanese supplies to the Guadalcanal Islands came to a halt. Moreover, in February 1943, the Japanese troops entrenched on the islands had to withdraw completely. The next step of the Allies was to drive the Japanese Army towards the north. The Japanese defense troops were retreating further and further north. This move caused the surface fleets to evacuate from the Truk Islands, an important base for the Air Force and surface troops. This event took place on 10 February 1944.

Subsequently, many Japanese transport vessels remained stationed on the Truk Island atolls. One week after the evacuation, on 17 February 1944, the American Task Force attacked the islands. The raid stretched on for two days. It ended with the sinking of 11 vessels and 31 transport vessels. With the advent of the withdrawal of a large number of naval troops, unprotected transport vessels were completely wrecked as they were unable to counterattack the enemy. Only one vessel which was half destroyed remained stranded on the islands.

During my childhood days, I possessed a keen interest in merchant vessels and kept a collection of photographs and even looked up the routes of these vessels. Since I lived near Kobe, I had the opportunity to view the liners via the Beppu Route, Dairen Route and Taiwan Route. Consequently, I became an ardent fan and even travelled on some of these vessels.

After the outbreak of the war, all these routes were shunned from further publicity. Within the four years of battle, most of these vessels were sunk and devoured by the sea. Solitary ships sailing unguarded on the wide and immense Pacific Ocean vanished into places that were almost impossible to trace.

After the war, many documents on the naval fleets were published and read with interest by the public. However, the memory of the transport vessels, with the exception of those in the spotlight, was beginning to fade. Ten years have passed since I first started my collection of old merchant fleet documents, adding to the pre-war materials acquired earlier. The documents were dispersed into several places. Fortunately, I managed to file each vessel under the headings: principal item, record, activity and concluding with the photographs. It amounted to 4800 ships and 150 of them were published in a series for the magazine *Fune No Kagaku*.

One day, the publisher contacted me and informed me that a foreigner residing in Singapore had enquired about the articles. This foreigner was K.P. Lindemann, the author of this book. That was how I came to know him. Since *Fune No Kagaku* is a special magazine, I became very curious as to how this foreigner came upon this publication in Singapore. Fortunately, my question was answered when we started corresponding with each other.

Lindemann is a German executive whose main hobby is diving. He had discovered evidence of numerous sunken ships in Truk by coincidence. He found himself eventually mesmerized by their mystifying charms. Although Japanese divers had previously explored the wrecks, they did not progress beyond the initial stages of research. Due to perhaps the inherent traits of his nationality, he began a persistent research on each ship. He tried, firstly, to figure out the name of the vessel and secondly, to trace its route and history. While searching for Japanese books on the fleets, he came across my article. I cooperated with him by sending all my acquired data and photographs. Lindemann sent me data and photographs he had acquired in his diving trips. We identified and confirmed each ship by scrutinizing the photographs and later comparing them with the model photographs and blueprints. We could then figure out the respective parts of the ship.

The photographs of the skeletons in the wrecks made me realize the significance of this research. I sent the information and photographs to the Japanese Ministry of Health. At present, despite the fact that they were informed about this, they are unable to assist us yet. We were requested to send them detailed information after they had completed the necessary preparations.

Lindemann, while asking the Japanese for the data, had meanwhile contacted the American side and had acquired data and photographs through the National Archives in Washington, D.C. I was deeply touched by his zest. I feel that the Japanese should have instigated such research.

Lindemann went to the Truk Islands several times looking for more details. His wife assisted him. Without her assistance, this project would not be such a fine and excellent book. Lindemann is not only a diver but also a specialist on ships. He possesses a greater love for the vessels than myself.

I bestow lavish and unstinted praise for his admirable achievements and am certain that this book will be appreciated. Its value will be unsurpassed for a long time to come.

7-3 Nishi-Ashiya Ashiya
JAPAN

August 1982

エピローグ

山田　早苗

　1941年12月8日、日本の陸海軍はアメリカ、イギリス、オランダに対して戦を宣した。

　真珠湾攻撃、マレー半島上陸作戦、フイリッピン上陸作戦などは、まさに機先を制した日本の奇襲作戦の大勝利であった。

　翌年1月11日にはセレベス島、1月23日には南偉4度のニューブリテン島ラバウルを占領、わずか1カ月半でニューギニアを除く、殆んどの東南アジアの島々を占領した。5月にはさらに足をのばしてソロモン群島のガダルカナル島に上陸、ここを基地としてアメリカとオーストラリアの連絡路を断たんとした。

　しかし、その頃からようやく連合国軍の態勢も立ち直り、大規模な反撃に転じてきた。

　その代表的なものは6月3日のミッドウエー海戦で、日本の聯合艦隊は一挙に空母4隻を失う大敗北をきっした。8月7日には連合国軍の日本占領地域奪回作戦のはしりとして、日本軍のたてこもるガダルカナル島に上陸、日米両軍の血みどろの戦が始まる。その間に海上では第1、第2、第3次のソロモン海戦がおこり、地上軍、水上部隊、航空部隊がしのぎを削って戦った。11月にはガダルカナル島への組織立った日本の補給はほとんど不可能となり、高速輸送船の強行突破も11隻が全滅するなど破局的な状態となり遂に翌年2月には日本軍の全面撤退となった。その後連合国軍は島づたいに次々と日本軍を北に追い上げ、日本の防衛線は徐々に北へ北へと修正され、遂には聯合艦隊司令部及水上部隊の主力根拠地であり重要な航空基地であったトラック島からも大部分の水上艦艇が引上げてしまった。時まさに、1944年2月10日のことであった。

　しかし、トラック環礁の多くの島々の泊地には日本の軍用船多数が残されたままで、1週間のちの2月17日アメリカ機動部隊のトラック島大空襲となった。空襲は17日と18日の2日にわたり、これによって沈没した艦艇は11隻、輸送船は実に31隻に及んだ。海軍の主力部隊の撤収により、この大空襲に反撃するものなく、無防備の輸送船は徹底的に打ちのめされ、わずか1隻が中破して坐礁したのみで残りの船はすべて沈没した。

　私は子供の頃から商船に興味をもち写真を集めたり行動を調べることが好きであった。住いが神戸に近いこともあって別府航路、大連航路、台湾航路の船を見る機会が多く、又実際に乗って旅行するなど熱心なファンの一人であった。

しかし、開戦後はこれらの商船の行動は一切公表されないまま4年間の戦闘で殆んどが海底の藻屑と消えてしまった。これと云った護衛もなく単独で広い太平洋を行動していた船などは沈没した場所さえ不明のままのものもある。

戦後、あらゆることが明らかになれる中で華かなりし頃の聯合艦隊の記録は、多くの書籍となって世に公表され、今日でも人々に興味をもって読まれている。

しかし、商船に関しての情報は特別話題になった船以外は、ほとんど忘れ去られようとしている。そこで私は10年程前から、私が持っている戦前の資料に加えて最近になって各地にばらばらに保存されている古い本から商船に関する記録を調査し、これを1隻毎にまとめてその数4800隻に達した、各船の詳しい要目、生いたち、活動、終末などを写真とともに集計し、これを雑誌「船の科学」に連載し、すでに150隻を越えるに至った

ある日、出版社よりシンガポール在住の外国人から私の記事に関しての問合わせがあったと云う連絡を受けた。これが本書の著者であるLindemann 氏と私の接触の始まりである。

「船の科学」と云う本は船の専門家が好んで読む本で一般の人々には一寸不向きな専門誌である。この様な本をシンガポールに居る著者がどうして見付けたかと云うことが私の頭に浮んだ第1の疑問であった。

しかし、著者と直接手紙を交換するようになって、そのなぞは解けた。

著者は海底にもぐることを趣味としているドイツの会社員である。たまたまトラック島の海底の日本の多数の沈船をまのあたりに見て驚きとともにその船にとりつかれたのである。日本のダイバーたちもトラック島の沈船を探険したことも私は知っているが、これを詳しく沈没のいきさつなどを調査するまで発展しなかった。しかしドイツ人である彼は、この船の1隻1隻について調査を始めたのである。まず船名を確かめ、それが戦前はどんな船であったかを調査するに及んで私の資料が必要となったのである。恐らく日本で発表されている船に関する本を調べて私の記事を発見したに違いない。著者の要求に応じて私はありとあらゆるその船に関する資料や写真を送って協力してきた。著者からは自分の海底での記録、写真などを次々と送ってきた。写真と、設計図、模型の写真などから、それが船のどの部分であるかを確認し会ったりした。

又写真の中には明らかに頭蓋骨が見られるものもあり、私は事の重大性をあらためて認識し、これらの写真を厚生省に送付し、事実だけを伝えておいた。厚生省も勿論その事実は知ってはいるが現在手がつ

けられな状態でいずれ時期か来れば必要な資料を提供してほしいと云ってきた。著者は、日本に対して資料を求める一方で攻撃側のアメリカの資料も集めておりアメリカ国防総省から資料や写真を入手していることは全く驚きでありその熱心さに頭の下る思いである。これは日本人の仕事ではなかったかとふと考えさせられる。

何度かトラック島におもむき、くりかえしくりかえし船の中を見てまわり奥様が船上で御主人の活動をコントロールするなど御夫妻の協力で調査が進み、その集大成がこの様な立派な本になった。著者はもはや単なるダイバーでなく立派な船の専門家であり船を愛することでは私以上の気持の持主である。

私は、著者のこの様な立派な業績にかぎりなき賛意を送るとともに、本書の価値は永遠に変ることなく年とともに評価されるものと信ずる。

1982年8月

芦屋市西芦屋町7−3

ACKNOWLEDGEMENTS, EQUIPMENT AND GENESIS

It has always been a great pleasure to be with my special friends, the boys from Blue Lagoon Dive Shop in Truk. They shared the jubilation when we found a new wreck, and the frustration of an unsuccessful day of searching. Chenney and the others helped us during pouring rain and blistering heat to accomplish our mission, and I am deeply indebted for their perseverance.

It would have been impossible to write this book without two people: Kimiuo Aisek and my wife Mary. Mary is a scuba instructor. She was watching me on every dive, and made sure depth and time limitations were not exceeded. I am sure she must have felt apprehensive when I disappeared into the inside of a wreck and nothing could be seen of me. Her caring provided me with the freedom I needed to set the hectic pace while taking pictures for documentation and illustrations. There is no more ideal dive buddy to be found than she. She would hover just slightly above me, exchange the bulky camera equipment with an underwater slate. It was ideal for us both that she got so deeply involved in Truk as well. Her contributions were many and outstanding, ranging from editing the raw version of the manuscript to flying from Singapore to the National Archives in Washington D.C. to look up reference material.

Without Mary I would not have finished the book; without Kimiuo Aisek I would have never begun it.. He set his own monument in the middle part of the book. Kimiuo has always been most supportive, generous, good humored and tremendously knowledgeable. Kimiuo's contribution can not be counted. It can only be retold. Now it can be read.

Fortunately, Dr. Sanae Yamada consented to supply the technical data on the ships and their pre-war pictures. He also answered the many questions I had. Dr. Yamada has the most comprehensive documentation of the Japanese merchant fleet, and was always willing to share the information. Details of the Hoki Maru were supplied by Mrs. J. Haviland, and the Union Steamship Co of New Zealand. I am indebted for their time and effort. Muegi and Kurt Prengemann in Singapore will probably not forget the long discussions we had about the Japanese aspect of the book. Muegi was devoting much of her time to translations which is most gratefully appreciated. Morio Toshima sat down and spent long hours, in Truk, to help me by translating Japanese material.

Many people have contributed to my understanding of the local Truk scenario. Hauoli Smith and his charming wife Lynette must be thanked, as well as Father Hezel S.J. and Clark Graham.

Diving equipment is an extremely important part of the expeditions. Our thanks go to our outfitter Tom Dehring of Tom & Jerry's Dive Shop in Michigan.

For our photographic work we used Nikonos iii and iva. Most pictures were taken with the 15 mm lens, but the 28 mm, 35 mm and 80 mm lenses were also employed. The latter lens was used for close-up work with the Nikonos Close-Up kit. For illumination the Subsea 225 strobe was used in most cases. Additionally we hooked up Oceanic 2003 and the Nikonos SB 101 flashes. Ektachrome 200 was most often used as film material, but on occasions the cameras were loaded with Ektachrome 64 and Kodachrome 64 slide films. For topside photography we used a Canon A1 and a Rollei 35. During the searches a Royal Depthfinder, manufactured by the Fuji Corporation was used. An ENBEECO Compass Bearing Monocular JB 101 provided us with an accurate aid for establishing the landmarks of the wrecks.

Such was the state of art in 1978 - 1982.

Photos and sketches in this edition are by the author, unless otherwise stated. The majority of the war pictures are courtesy of the US Navy Historical Center, Operational Archives, and are by-lined USNOA, and the United States National Archives, by-lined USNA. Dr. Sanae Yamada contributed a significant number of pictures of ships in peace time. The late Erich Gröner, doyen of the German sketchers and for decades associated with Weyer's Flottentaschenbuch, contributed a number of incomparable accurate sketches, by-lined Jentschura. A few photos have been utilized whose origin, unfortunately, are obscure. Silhouettes of Japanese aircraft originate from the General View of Japanese Aircraft, by Airview, and were made by K. Hashimoto. To all contributors, my sincere thanks.

Between 1978 and 1984, a total of 342 dives were made in Truk, during eight visits, each lasting between two and three weeks. The last visit dates April 1991. Tentative drafts of a book, in essay form, were begun in 1979. By 1980, all the great people who did my typing, went on strike. Principal objection was that they did not want to be associated with a book which never got published because of the many revisions neccessary after each visit to Truk and each letter received. A friend drew my attention to a new interesting machine, called Apple: a computer. I purchased an Apple II, and a very simple text processor program by Apple. Now I could type and edit to my heart's delight. The silhouettes were originally drawn, literally by pixel, on an Apple Tablet. In May 1982, the clean manuscript was delivered to the publisher, and the book was printed in October of the same year. New material was published in "Supplement to Hailstorm", periodically upgraded, until 1990. Due to the demands by a second project, the strike against Palau, Operation Desecrate 1, the computer hardware was upgraded to an Apple Macintosh II CI, with several peripherals. This machine was very well suited for desktop publishing. "Supplement" and "Hailstorm" were amalgamated. The manuscript, updated to 1990, was submitted to the printers as a hard disk, in May 1991, just 6 months after "Hailstorm" was out of print.

INDEX

"Catchpole" Operation, 13, 29
"Desecrate 1" Operation, 144, 253
"Flintlock" Operation, 12
"Galvanic" Operation, 11
"Hailstone" Operation, 13, 31
"Tokyo Express" Operation, 164
52nd Division 21, 27, 87, 90, 216
95 Ha-Go 233
Abemama 11
Agano, cruiser, 20, 73, 84, 126, 224
Agano Class 67
Aikoku Maru (AK) 5, 6, 31, 57, 58, 62, 114, 106, 115, 116, 132, 133, 187, 205, 208, 215, 229, 238
AIKOKU MARU 137
Air Group 5; 49
Akagi (CV) 9, 161
Akagi Maru (AK) 20, 45, 46, 51, 55, 61, 63, 67, 68, 112
Akashi 32, 67, 73, 105, 114, 126, 150, 166, 192, 198
Akitsushima 32, 43, 44, 45, 57, 62, 137
Alabama, battleship, 29, 276
Aleutian islands 164
AMAGISAN MARU 146
Amagisan Maru (AK) 10, 69, 72, 151, 238
Amatsukaze, destroyer, 181
Aoba, cruiser, 166
Asahio, destroyer, 81
Asaka Maru (AK) 21
Atago, cruiser, 84
Avenger 282
Balao (sub) 207
Baltimore, cruiser, 29, 59, 60, 117, 278
Baron Tomoshige Sameshima, Admiral, 93
Battle at Midway 164
Battle of Leyte Gulf 67
Battle of the Coral Sea 9, 14, 103
Battle of the Java Sea 181
Belleau Wood (CVL) 29, 41, 275
Bengal (MS) 144
Betty 287
BETTY BOMBER 149
Biloxi, cruiser, 29, 278
Bismarck (battleship, German) 131
Blair 59, 60
Bomber Squadron VB 10; 43
bombing run from the Marshalls to Oahu 153
Bridges 62
Briggs 138
Buenos Aires Maru (AK) 232
Bulldozer Wreck, see also Hoki Maru 183
Bunakanau 20
Bunker Hill, (CV) 29, 33, 34, 35, 47, 50, 57, 66, 75, 126, 147, 150, 156, 161, 166, 173, 176, 198, 208, 224, 229, 244, 259, 269, 272
Cabot (CVL) 29, 54, 55, 57, 58, 275
Chikuma, cruiser, 84
Chook 98

Christensen 26
Chuichi Hara, Admiral, 14, 93
Chuyo (CVL) 96
Cimarron (AO) 65
Cimarron-Class 244
Clark Graham 5
Cooper 29
Cousteau, J-Y., 5
Cowpens (CVL) 29, 33, 35, 65, 68, 74, 173, 275
Cromwell 104
Crown-of-Thorns 5
Dai Ni Hino Maru (AK) 182
Daikichi Maru (AK) 70, 150
Daimler Benz 258
Dan Daspit 256
Dauntless 281
Davao 13
Davis 29
Dew 86
Dick Emoroy 103
Dr. Sylvia Earle 5
Drum, sub, 180
DuBose, Admiral, 29
DUMPING GROUND 151
Durgun 86
Ed O'Quinn 5
Eiichi Okamoto 87
Ellis 25
Elysia, M/V, 144
EMILY 152, 288
Encounter, destroyer, 181
Enderby, island, 21, 88, 96
Eniwetok, island, 13, 29, 35, 91
Enterprise (CV) 9, 29, 41, 43, 50, 52, 54, 72, 150, 161, 176, 223, 256, 271
Espe 29
Essex (CV) 19, 29, 55, 56, 63, 84, 138, 145, 198, 214, 215, 272
Exeter, cruiser, 181
Falconer 187
Fighter Squadron 30; 74
Fighter Squadron VF 10; 43
Finschhafen 166
FLEET TUG 154
Florida Maru (AK) 166
Fubuki-Class 46
Fujikawa Maru (AK) 57, 71, 74, 94, 117, 118, 120, 125, 154, 155, 215, 243
Fujinami, destroyer, 21, 126
Fujisan Maru (AO) 5, 45, 46, 48, 68, 72, 107, 161
Fumizuki, destroyer, 126, 285
Fuso, battleship, 84
Gardner 41
Genda 89
Genota (AO), also Ose Maru, 144
German missionaries 127
Ghormley, Admiral, 10

Giddings, Al 5, 6, 141, 196
Giffen, Admiral, 29
Gilberts, islands, 10
Gokoku Maru (AK) 142
Gosei Maru 4, 71, 120, 170
Greens 25
Guadalcanal 9, 13
Guam 11, 12, 29, 88, 91, 94, 235
Haddock, sub, 194
Hakune Maru 60
Halder, sub, 194
Halsey, William, Admiral, 8
Hamp/Hap/Zeke/Zero 288
Hanakawa Maru (AK) 70, 72, 74, 124, 127, 161, 172, 255
Hanson, Admiral, 29
Hara, Admiral, 84, 86, 121, 133, 152
harbor master in Truk 25, 103
HARBOR TUG 175
Harusame, destroyer, 21, 62, 67, 126, 285
Hauraki (AK), see also Hoki Maru: 144, 187
HEIAN MARU (AK) 176
Heian Maru (AK)4, 46, 70, 106, 112, 118, 120, 124, 130, 150, 183
Heigo Matsumoto 168
Hellcat 280
Helldiver 280
Hidekichi Katari 93
Higuchi 84
Hikawa Maru (AK) 47, 48, 180
Hikawa Maru No. 2 (AH) (Tenno Maru) 167, 181
HINO MARU (AK) 2 182, 262
Hiryu (CV) 8
Hiye Maru (AK)124, 180
Hoki Maru (AK) 70, 73, 144, 183, 238
Hokoku Maru (AK) 143, 144
Hokusho Maru (AK) 191
Hokuyo Maru (AK) 4, 57, 58, 189
Hornet (CV) 8
Hiyo (CVL) 84
Hospital Ship 14, see also Hikawa Maru 2; 181
Houston, cruiser, 181
Hoyo Maru (AO) 46, 53, 104, 150, 167, 192, 256
Hustvedt, Admiral, 29
Hyuga, battleship, 124
I - 169 (SHINOHARA) SUBMARINE 195
I 169, sub, 4, 52, 120, 125
I 170, sub, 196
I 365, sub, 96
Ikata 111
Inoue, Admiral, 103
INTER-ISLAND SUPPLY VESSEL 197
Intrepid (CV) 27, 29, 50, 54, 55, 56, 57, 58, 60, 126, 138, 272
Iowa, battleship, 29, 65, 66, 76, 80, 81, 96, 275
Isuzu, cruiser, 84
Iwo Jima, island, 31, 86
Jake 289
Jennings 41
Jones 86
Judy 290
Juneau, cruiser, 180
Kaga (CV) 8, 124

Kagero-Class 46
Kaiten 85, 126
Kane, Cmdr, 43, 44
Kansho Maru (AK) 47, 53, 63, 67, 150, 167, 192, 198
Kashima, cruiser, 84, 93
Katori, cruiser, 20, 27, 43, 44, 45, 46, 51, 55, 58, 59, 61, 63, 66, 67, 68, 76, 81, 84, 96, 111, 117, 120, 124, 126, 284
Kavieng 25, 166
Keith Jaeger 4
Kenney, Jack Mr., 4, 166
Kikukawa Maru (AK) 132, 187, 203, 208, 262
King, Ernest, Admiral, 10, 12
Kingfisher 283
Kitari Kaneko 94
Kiyozumi Maru (AK) 4, 47, 52, 104, 143, 150, 167, 168, 192, 198, 205
Kobata 9
Kobayashi, Hitoshi, Admiral, 14, 18, 23, 24, 84, 93
Koga, Admiral 11, 12, 23, 31, 84, 90, 113, 121
Kumano, cruiser, 84
Kuop Atoll 21, 37, 48, 70, 75, 126
Kurita, Admiral, 90
Kwajalein, islands, 4, 10, 13, 26, 31, 52, 84, 88, 124, 156
La Plata Maru 232
Lee, Admiral, 29
Lexington (CV) 8
Leyte Gulf 11
Long Lance 165
MacArthur, Douglas, General, 9
Maikaze, destroyer, 20, 27, 44, 45, 46, 51, 58, 63, 66, 76, 81, 111, 126, 284
Majuro, island, 11, 29, 32, 54, 61, 64
Makin, island, 10
Malama, M/V, 143
Maloelab, island, 10
Marianas, islands, 31
Marriner 25
Martin 43, 47
Masaharu Yamamoto 168
Massachusetts, battleship, 29, 276
Matsumoto 166
Matsutan(i) Maru (AK), see also Shotan Maru; 250
Mauser cannon 258
McDonnell 25
Miami, cruiser, 83
Michio Sumikawa 93
Midway, island, 8, 11, 13, 103
Minekaze-Class 224
Minneapolis, cruiser, 29, 65, 76, 80, 81, 117, 277
Minton Reef 65
Mirua 121
Missouri, battleship, 59
Mitscher, Marc, Admiral, 29, 31, 32, 33, 35, 41, 65, 103
Mobile, cruiser, 29, 278
Mogami, cruiser, 84
Momi-class 252
Momokawa Maru (AK) 60, 72, 73, 130, 142, 203, 208
Monterey (CVL) 29, 33, 58, 71, 74, 156, 166, 244, 275

Hailstorm - *Appendix*

Montevideo Maru (AK) 232
Montgomery, Admiral 29
Mugikura, Admiral, 84, 85
Musashi, battleship, 26, 31, 84, 111, 113, 120, 122, 124, 125, 263
Mutsuki-class 165
Nagano Maru (AK) 45, 212, 266
Nagara, cruiser, 84
Nagato, battleship, 84
Nagumo, Admiral, 9, 243
Naka, cruiser, 20, 27, 45, 51, 69, 75, 76, 84, 126, 284
Namonuito Atoll 46
Nate 290
Nauru, island, 11
Naval Operational Archives 6
Navy 12 cm Short Gun 255
New Guinea 37
New Jersey, battleship, 29, 35, 65, 66, 76, 80, 81, 96, 275
New Orleans, cruiser, 29, 65, 76, 80, 277
Nimitz, Chester, Admiral, 8, 9, 10, 113
Nippo Maru 58, 106, 116, 134, 208, 209, 215, 230, 235
Nishimura, Admiral, 121
Nomoi, island, 31, 88, 127
North Carolina, battleship, 29, 276
Nowake, destroyer, 20, 32, 44, 45, 63, 66, 76, 81, 111, 126, 284
O'Sullivan 53
Oakland, cruiser, 29, 27
OITE, destroyer, 224
Oite, destroyer, 73, 74, 126, 285
OJIMA 262
Okinawa, island, 86
Ondina (AO) 144
op ten Noort (AH) see Hikawa Maru 2; 167, 181
Operation T 18
Oscar 292
Ose Maru (AO), see also Genota, 144
Otta (Pass) 22
Overesch 29
Owen Stanley Range 9
Ozawa, Admiral, 90
Palau, islands, 12, 13, 15, 17, 19, 67, 84, 88, 114, 144, 152, 253
PARAM 223
Patrol Boat 34 ex Susuki, 34, 151, 252
Patten 50
Penang 232
Perth 181
Pete 291
Peter Wilson 111
Philips 62, 63
Piva 26
Platte (AO) 65
Ponape, island, 31, 88, 145
Pope, destroyer, 181
Port Moresby 9
Portland, cruiser, 130, 151
Prisoners of War 95
Rabaul 9, 10, 18, 25, 26, 32, 33, 36, 37, 84, 85, 86, 90, 103, 111, 117, 166

Radar Installations 87
Redford, Sam, Mr. 5, 145, 148, 237, 242, 255
Reeves, Admiral, 29, 41
Reiyo Maru (AK) 57, 227
Resop, island, 127
Rio de Janeiro Maru (AK) 5, 57, 67, 124, 180, 183, 229
Ro 42, sub, 52
Roi-Namur, island, 14
Rufe 292
Sailfish, sub, 96
Saipan 5, 12, 13, 17, 29, 36, 37, 85, 108, 196
SAN FRANCISCO MARU 233
San Diego 29, 279
San Francisco 5, 29, 54, 277
San Francisco Maru (AK) 58, 60, 71, 106, 183
San Fransisco 29
SANKISAN MARU (AK) 238
Sankisan Maru (AK) 5, 69, 72, 125, 183, 187, 229
Santa Fe, cruiser, 29, 278
Santos Maru (AK) 232
Sarawak Steamship Co 267
Scabbardfish, sub, 96
Scorpion 194
Sculpin 95, 104
Seahawk 283
Searaven, sub, 50
Seiichi Yamamoto 88
Seiko Maru (AK) 5, 58, 71, 106, 116, 208, 242
Sherman, Admiral, 10, 29, 34, 166
Shigeju Ago 92
Shigure, destroyer, 21, 62, 67, 126, 285
Shinkoku Maru (AO) 5, 52, 72, 111, 132, 168, 215, 243
Shinwa Maru (AK) 63
Shiro Takasu 93
Shokaku (CV) 9, 84
Shotan Maru (AK) 48, 60, 248
Singapore 12, 16, 31, 84
Skate, sub, 224
Solomons 10
Soryu (CV) 9
South Dakota, battleship, 29, 65, 276
Soya (AK) 107
Special Cruiser Squadron 24 143
SPECIAL SUBCHASER NO. 38 251
Spruance, Raymond, Admiral, 9, 10, 11, 13, 30, 31, 33, 35, 65, 80, 117
Stan Beerman 5
Standard 1 D 150, 250
Standard 1-C 255
Standard B 174
Standard D 170
Sterling Island 26
Straits Steamship Co., Singapore 267
Stuart 29
Subchaser 28; 224
Submarine Chaser 24
Sukamaki, destroyer, 94
Sumikawa 86
Surabaya 15
Susuki- Patrol Boat 34, 114, 126, 165, 151
Swordfish, sub, 148

Tachikaze, destroyer, 21, 44, 48, 49, 59, 69, 70, 75, 126, 133, 285
Tagima 85
Taiho Maru (AK) 69, 254
Takao, cruiser, 84, 95
Tamura 91
Tarawa, island, 11, 26, 84, 156
Tarokina 19
Tenno Maru (AH) 167
Theodore Spawn Collection 53
Tinian, island, 13, 17, 31, 37
Tinosa, sub, 145
Tojo 12, 292
Tonan Maru 5 (AO) 15, 45, 67, 76, 104, 150, 167, 192, 256
Tony 293
TONY, VAL AND ZERO 258
Torpedo Squadron VT 10; 43
Toyoda, Admiral, 13
Trigger, sub, 145
Uchita, Admiral, 106, 115
Ulithi, island, 85, 88, 91
Unkai Maru 6; (AK) 71, 213
UNKAI MARU NO. 6; (AK) 259, 266
Unyo Maru No. 1 (AK) 96
Uono 224
US National Archives 5
Venus (S/S) 261
Vincent(S/S) 143
Vyner Brooke (S/S) 267
Wake, island, 9, 31
Wichita, cruiser, 29, 54, 277
Wiltse, Admiral, 29
Wotje, island, 11
Wyatt Brown 86
X 10; 150
Xavier High School 98
Yakaze, destroyer, 252
Yamagiri Maru (AK) 5, 73, 111, 52, 122, 263
Yamagumo, destroyer, 21, 96, 104
Yamamoto, Admiral, 9, 12, 27, 103, 143
Yamashira, battleship, 124
Yamashita, General, 144
Yamato, battleship, 84, 113, 120, 124, 125, 130, 263
Yap, island, 39, 94
Yasukuni Maru (AK) 106, 107, 144
Yawn 26
Yeowart 25
Yokosuka 18, 85
Yorktown (CV) 8, 9, 29, 41, 45, 49, 57, 60, 64, 65, 163, 259, 272
Yubae Maru (AK) 70, 213 266
Yubari-Class 55
Zuiho (CVL) 67, 84
Zuiho Maru (AK) 63
Zuikai Maru 45, 68, 161
Zuikaku (CV) 8, 84

This view of the Forth Fleet Anchorage was taken at approximately 1000h on the first day of the attack. It shows the majority of ships already damaged and burning. Conspicuously absent are the Aikoku Maru and the Nippo Maru. Both ships sank about one hour earlier, during the beginning phase of the raid. The identity of the ships is, strictly from left to right regardless of up or down:

1 - Foreship of an unknown ship, not sunk;

2 - Soya, 2224 ts Navy ammunition ship, sailing west, not sunk;

3 - Seiko Maru, evidently undamaged, half obscured by smoke; sunk later;

4 - Momokawa Maru, half obscured, may be listing, sunk later;

5 - Hokuyo Maru, evidently not damaged; sank later;

6 - San Francisco Maru (top), fire midships, stack gone; sank later;

7 - Hoki Maru, bomb damage midships, stack carried away, fire forward, bomb blast recognizable by ring of white water off starboard quarter, damages and smoke in that area; exploded forward, sank later;

8 - Nagano Maru, listing to port, sinking;

9 - Shotan Maru, points towards south-east, damaged, mast broken off, sank later;

10 - Reiyo Maru, damaged and burning, sank later;

11 - Unknown ship of approximately 2000 ts, very difficult to identify on the photo, pointing SE. probably not sank;

12 - Akitsushima, flying boat tender and used as transport, partly out of the frame, damaged aft, damaged rudder controls, escaped later through South Pass.

US National Archives

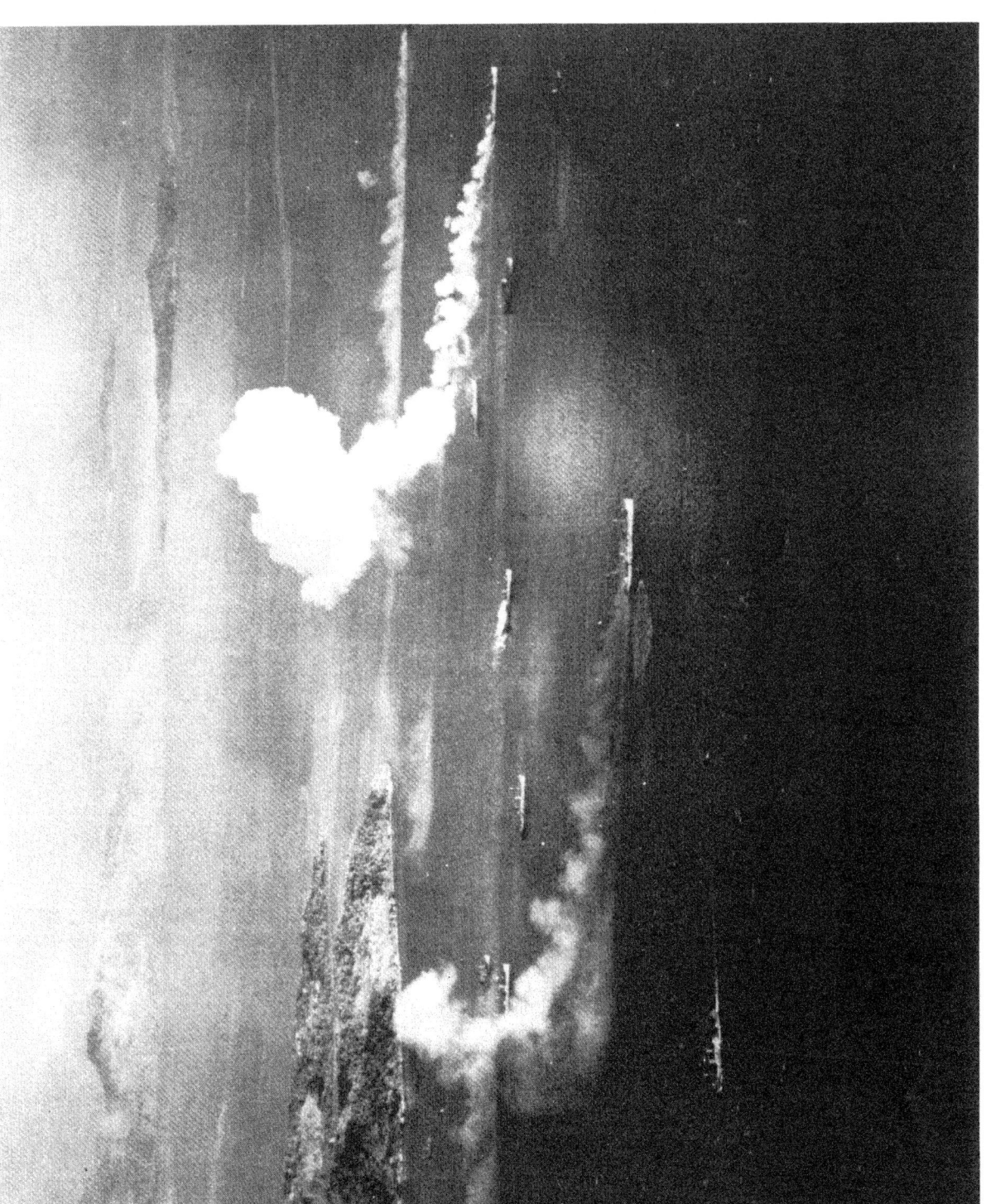

This is the same gun, a 3.7 cm anti-tank weapon, as can be seen on the Nippo Maru. This piece is located in a Museum off Honolulu, Hawaii.

▶

One of the 14 cm coastal defense guns put high up on the mountain in Moen, and overlooking the lagoon, can be visited quite easily by going up the path off the hospital. The guns were placed in caves.

Lens cap serves as size comparison.

▶

The former hospital of Truk located on Dublon remains reasonably intact, but is only a shell of a building, with an ill reputation.

◀

The tank, here located on dry land, in the Hawaii museum, is the same kind which can be found as deck cargo on the San Francisco Maru and the Nippo Maru.

◀

A flight of Dauntlesses over south Fefan.

Lt. Blair made it back in the float plane. He was sitting on the lap of the observer, who is seen here catching the hook to have the plane winched up.

Landing operations on board Enterprise during Operation Hailstone. While an Avenger torpedo bomber is located on top of the elevator - its wings are folded back - another planes taxies up while a third is on the approach for landing.

all pictures courtesy of US National Archives

A wheels up landing of a Dauntless on deck of Bunker Hill. Two men are dragging fire hoses and the others are sprinting towards the aircraft to assist the crew. Note the bent propeller and the scars on the flight deck. Men of the anti aircraft guns are looking over the deck.

◀

The Reiyo Maru is shown here prominently. She burns at the forward hold. Below the ship, Fanamu can be seen, and the Kaiten station. Three barges are tied at the shallows. A large oil slick extends in a crescent form between the island and the Reiyo Maru. Some bubbles form a white streak in the middle between the island and the ship and to the left. The ship near the bomb blast is the Momokawa Maru. She sank later. A patch of white water, almost completely obscured by the smoke, between the Momokawa and Reiyo Maru marks the site of Aikoku Maru's violent end.

◀

Shotan Maru 15 is straddled by salvoes from the 5 inch guns of the battleships. Seconds later the ship exploded violently.

◀

all pictures courtesy of US National Archives

Vice Admiral C. Hara, Commander Fourth Fleet and Fourth Base, and Lt. General Mugikura, Commander 52nd Division/ 31st Army, arrive on board USS Miami to sign the documents of surrender.

Lt. General Mugikura signs the instruments of surrender.

all pictures courtesy of US National Archives

Kaiten were suicide one-man torpedoes. They were intended to be launched against enemy ships located inside the lagoon. Several bunkers and launching points can be seen in Truk, such as on Yanagi and Fanamu. Here is a Kaiten, secured after the war. Discarded Kaitens and torpedoes may be seen near the torpedo nets between Dublon and Fefan.

◀

Part of the TG 58.3, during the Operation Hailstone, at sea. A battleship of the South Dakota Class, Monterey, the light carrier and another battleship of the same class can be seen in the background.

◀

The curtain of steel thrown against Japanese planes was almost inpenetrable. The flak or anti-aircraft fire was intense as it was dense. This Japanese plane did not get through and splashed between the Fletcher-Class (left) destroyer and the Baltimore-Class heavy cruiser on the right.

◀

all pictures courtesy of US National Archives

Two ships under attack: Seiko Maru (left) and Hokuyo Maru. Several small craft are located inshore Dublon; they escaped sinking, probably because of the concentration of anti-aircraft defenses in that area. The western slope of Mt. Tolomen partly obscures a large ship: Tonan Maru 3. Several other ships can be seen at the Repair Anchorage. The shadow extending from the lower left corner is part of the aircraft from which the photo was made. ▶

Phase I of the explosion of the Aikoku Maru. Just about seven seconds earlier, a large quantity of ammunition exploded. The developing mushroom cloud can be seen clearly. The torn fragments of the foreship have been thrown into the air and are returning as a steel rain, leaving their splash marks on the water. Ships in the vicinity were certainly peppered with debris, and casualties resulted from the explosion on other ships. The intensity of the flash is said to have blinded people. ▶

This view over the outer rim reef east of Dublon shows Phase II of the explosion of the Aikoku Maru. From the mushrom-shaped cloud it can be seen that the ship exploded with terrific force. The large explosion was followed about half a minute or so later by an equally terrific second blast. The center of the explosion may well have been just a little under water, judging from the shape of the evolving cloud.
The approaching plane is a Japanese Zero fighter, which probably makes a pass against the Dauntless from which this photo was taken. There are a number of ships, many of them already burning, located in the same anchorage. Dublon is to the right, with the smaller Eten slightly to the left, and Uman in the far background. ▶

all pictures courtesy of US National Archives

Buildings on fire after a strafing attack, east of the Naval Station, with part of the wing of a Dauntless torpedo bomber.

◀

The Rio de Janeiro (1) is still undamaged. The next ship (2) is unknown, but the sequence of the profile strongly suggests that this is the Kenshin Maru, and the Fujikawa Maru, (3) also undamaged, is located between the circular reef and Eten. The headquarters building is aflame, and probably a plane on the runway. The Fujisan Maru can still be seen at the oil/water jetty at Dublon.

◀

An unusual far view extends from the southern part of Moen, with the burning fighter strip and the seaplane base, site of the present Continental Hotel, via Fefan and Moen to Eten and the Fourth Fleet Anchorage. The ships seen here are located at the Repair Anchorage, and the Sixth Fleet Naval Station. Strictly taking the ships from right to left: The first group of six ships are all previously damaged and under repair. They are: Kiyozumi Maru, down at the bow, Hoyo Maru, down at the stern, Akashi, fleet repair ship, undamaged, Tonan Maru 3, burning significantly forward, Fumizuki, destroyer, (in the back, low shadow), undamaged, Kansho Maru, down by the stern. The white ship in the middle is the Hikawa Maru 2, ex Ten No Maru, ex Hospital Ship 14, ex op ten Noort.

Above Hikawa Maru 2 (south), the larger shadow is most probably the floating drydock. The group of two ships, one large, the other medium, off the Sixth Fleet Naval Station, is the subtender Heian Maru, before she burned, and the Momokawa Maru, which relocated to the Fourth Fleet Anchorage and sank there. The small shadow between the Momokawa Maru and the drydock is Patrol Boat 34. The group of small boats at the narrows between Dublon and Fefan are fishing boats. The Fishery Cold Storage was located to the West on the shores of Dublon.

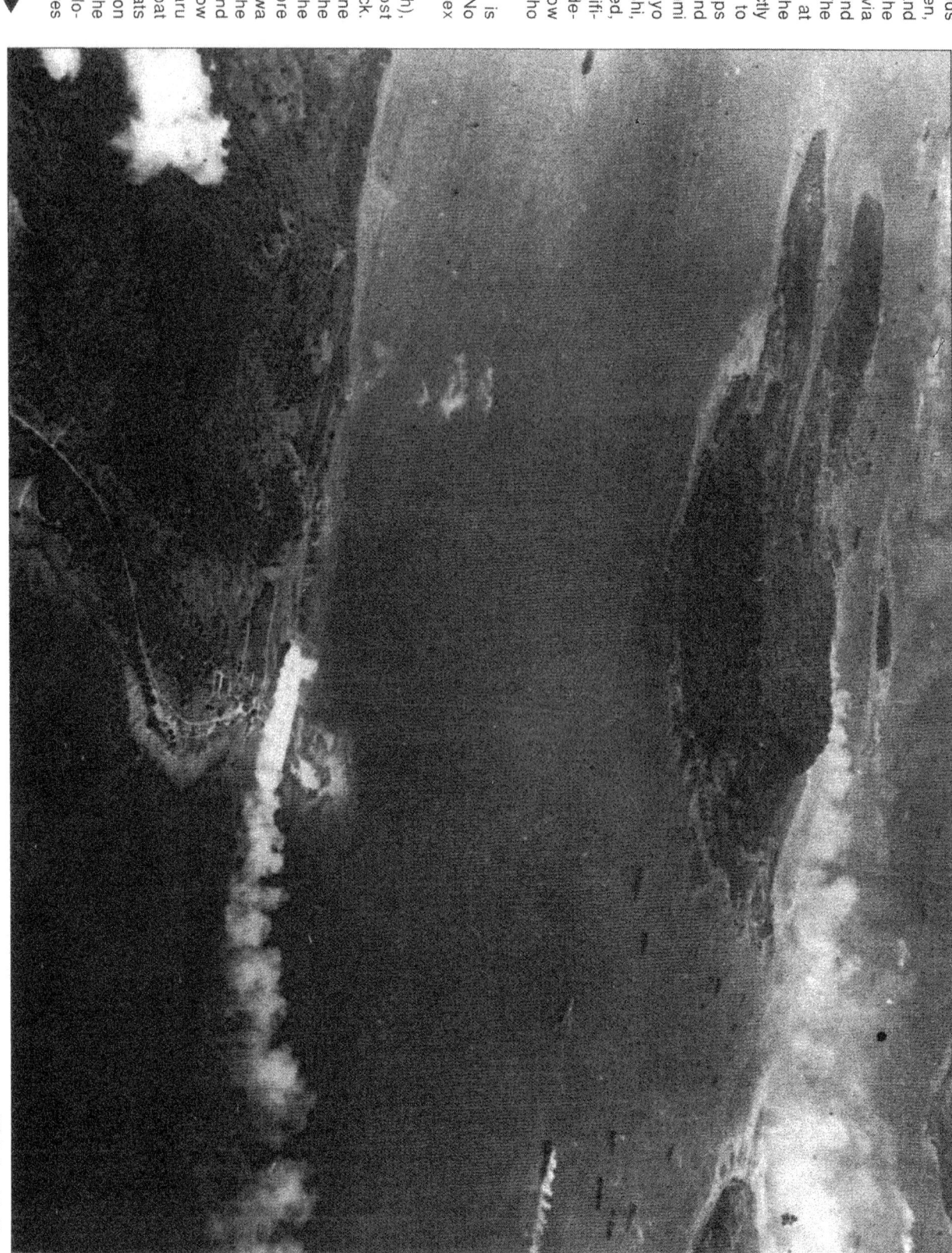

▼

US National Archives

The Aikoku Maru prominently shown in the foreground. Yorktown pilots described the ship as an ocean liner with a large superstructure and one single stack. Computer analysis shows smoke coming from the stack, the guns at sun deck, and possibly a dissipating smoke cloud off the aft gun. A landing craft is tied to the stern. Another craft is on the way towards Dublon.

The ships visible in this photograph are, from left to right: 1 - Reiyo Maru, damaged and smoking from the superstructure midships. 2 - Unidentified modern ship of approx. 2000 ts, smoking midships. 3 - Aikoku Maru. 4 - Unknown modern freighter, apparently undamaged.

5 and 6 - San Francisco Maru and Hokuyo Maru obscured by smoke. 7 - Seiko Maru evidently undamaged. 8 and 9 - Two unknown vessels. 10 - The ship facing the camera is probably the Momokawa Maru.

There is a vessel making a hard turn to port close to the Dublon Reef, which extends from the lower right. The white dot on the reef on its left upper side is the base of the reef marker, which by now has disappeared.

US National Archives

The moment the explosion of an aerial torpedo expends its full force on starboard of the Amagisan Maru. The torpedo had struck the bilge keel right between the forward side of the midship superstructure and the third hold. The explosion opened a large hole - the ship was doomed.

A torpedo plane had dropped the lethal torpedo during an approach from the northwest. The torpedo dolphined three times, i.e. it jumped out of the water. The horizontal rudder had not yet stabilized the fast running weapon. When it was dropped it went deep, and as the depth setting was only 10 ft, it power ascended to the surface. Before the rudder could force the torpedo back, it had overshot its depth setting and broke the surface. When doing the last jump, the torpedo did not quite follow its original true course, but slightly hooked over to the right. By doing so, it managed by chance to seek out the vulnerable spot of the ship and exploded. The bubble track left by the wet steam engine can still clearly be seen.

The white streak at the lower right of the picture is another torpedo. It appears to miss the ship. There are significant damages on the stern of the Amagisan, but they are associated with a bomb close miss.

Traces of the preceding bombing attack can be seen in form of the ring of white water extending from the starboard quarter to more than the ship's length to the left.

Above the bow, another ship is located. Electronic analysis points to the inter-island supply vessel. The Sankisan Maru is not visible in this picture, and may possibly be obscured by the water plume of the explosion. A streak of oil or gasoline is visible above the Amagisan Maru. Speculation that the torpedoed ship is the Sankisan Maru are groundless: The Sankisan did not have a set of goalposts aft of the superstructure and there are no corresponding damages on the foreship of the Sankisan Maru.

The other two ships look old and unkempt. The identity of the first one is unknown. It suffered a bombing attack. The bomb missed off the starboard bow. The next ship is the Yubae Maru, which also sank there.

This side of the fire on Eten, the Fujikawa Maru and the Unkai Maru 6 can be seen together with another ship of the Momokawa-configuration, which escaped sinking. It is probably the Kenshin Maru. To the upper right, several ships are burning at the Forth Fleet Anchorage.

▼

US National Archives

Printed in Great Britain
by Amazon